THE
OTHER GREEKS

THE FREE PRESS

New York   London   Toronto   Sydney   Tokyo   Singapore

THE
OTHER GREEKS

The Family Farm and the
Agrarian Roots
of Western Civilization

❦ ❦ ❦

VICTOR DAVIS HANSON

The Free Press
A Division of Simon & Schuster Inc.
1230 Avenue of the Americas, New York, N.Y. 10020

Printed in the United States of America

printing number

2 3 4 5 6 7 8 9 0

Text design by Carla Bolte

Library of Congress Cataloging-in-Publication Data

Hanson, Victor Davis.
    The other Greeks: the family farm and the agrarian roots of western civilization /
Victor Davis Hanson.
        p. cm.
    Includes bibliographical references and index.
    ISBN 0–02–913751–9
    1. Land use, Rural—Greece—History. 2. Agriculture—Economic aspects—Greece—History.
3. Family farms—Greece—History. 4. Greece—Rural conditions.. 5. Civilization, Classical.
I. Title.
HD133.H36   1995
338.1'6—dc20
                                           94–43551
                                              CIP

Other Books by Victor Davis Hanson

Warfare and Agriculture in Classical Greece

The Western Way of War:
Infantry Battle in Classical Greece

Hoplites: The Classical Greek
Battle Experience (editor)

For Cara,

and for Paulie, Billie, and Susannah

And to all the other small farmers everywhere who work

their own ground and yet walk the earth in silence

🌿 🌿 🌿

CONTENTS

PART THREE: TO LOSE A CULTURE

ACKNOWLEDGMENTS

Ten years ago this book could not have been written. But in the last decade there has been a veritable renaissance in research concerning ancient Greek agriculture and society. I owe much of the information in this study to the work of others, chief among them a gifted group of almost exclusively European scholars. Fortunately for the study of Greek history, they have devoted their considerable talents and energies to the Greek countryside.

I have gone *first* to primary sources for information about Greek agrarianism, usually through survey of Greek and Latin texts and epigraphy. But I think that I would have missed much ancient literary and archaeological evidence if I had not found it already collected and published in the work of others. Here I must point particularly to the reliable agrarian and military research of Robin Osborne (Oxford University) and especially Anthony Snodgrass (Cambridge University). I have met neither, but their articles and books I seem to have consulted at every stage of the way—as the text, notes, and bibliography attest. Many others have written extensively about ancient Greek farming and early Greek society.*

*Most notably Susan Alcock, M. C. Amouretti, V. N. Andreyev, David Asheri, Gert Audring, Paul Cartledge, J. C. Carter, Alison Burford (Cooper), Walter Donlan, Donald Engels, M. I. Finley, Hamish Forbes, Thomas Gallant, Paul Halstead, Steven Hodkinson, Singe Isager, Hans Lohmann, Josiah Ober, Jan Perírka, W. K. Pritchett, Robert Sallares, Jens Skydsgaard, and Chester Starr.

Sometimes my views have been not merely influenced, but actually formed, by their research, as numerous references in the text demonstrate. I am especially indebted to Paul Guiraud's *La Propriété foncière en Grèce jusqu'à la conquête Romaine* (Paris 1893). It is still a too often forgotten treasure house of data, and marked by good sense and sobriety throughout. I have profited as well from the wide-ranging articles on ancient agricultural labor of Michael Jameson, who kindly sent valuable publications otherwise not available to me here in Selma.

Much of the most innovative and original work on ancient agriculture now emanates largely from Great Britain—as the bibliography shows—and, to a lesser degree, from France, Germany, Italy, Scandinavia, and Russia. Yet did not Americans also once have a keen interest in, and advocacy of, agrarianism, an innate empathy with the people of agriculture? That natural interest in farming has rarely been reflected in classical scholarship of the United States, although the great majority of Greeks were employed in the countryside. This lamentable condition is also explored in the introduction to follow.

In contrast, Greek military studies, which form the other half of this book, have in the last twenty-five years been dominated largely by the research of a single, remarkable American. It is no exaggeration to say that W. K. Pritchett's six volumes on the *Greek State at War*, and eight books on Greek topography, are now the foundation of *all* further work on ancient military affairs. That those publications were largely products of Professor Pritchett's retirement—his sixties, seventies, and eighties—is, I think, a remarkable testament to the human spirit.

My three friends, professors John Heath (Santa Clara University), Bruce Thornton (California State University, Fresno), and John Lynch (University of California, Santa Cruz) read the original and much longer manuscript in its entirety, criticized it extensively, but also offered encouragement. From their own uncompromising careers I have drawn solace. They are models of academic populism at work. I owe additional gratitude to Elisabeth Sifton and John Keegan, whose encouragement gave me the confidence to keep trying. Patrick Emparan kindly checked the ancient references in the book's penultimate form.

The Center for Advanced Study in the Behavioral Sciences (Stanford, California), its director, Philip Converse, and associate director Robert Scott, in addition to a fellowship (1992–93) from the National

Endowment for the Humanities, all allowed me my first full year off from teaching. In very large part the time away from my ten-course load at Fresno provided by those institutions and individuals made the completion of *The Other Greeks* possible. I will not forget their kindness and generosity.

Professor Donald Kagan (Yale University) was also a resident fellow at CASBS during the 1992–93 year, and from this new acquaintance I learned a great deal about the fifth-century Greeks; I always appreciated in our conversations his no-nonsense pragmatism, especially when I was in error. He, too, read the manuscript and corrected many mistaken ideas. Professor Mark Edwards (Stanford University/University of California, Santa Cruz) and Kathleen Much, resident editor at CASBS, both read a final draft, and I have incorporated nearly all their advice. Adam Bellow, editorial director of The Free Press, and Charles Hanson, editor, made changes and extensive reductions; I have followed their suggestions in almost every instance. The friendship and support of John Heath, Gail Blumberg, Steven Ozment, Jody Maxim, and Susan Treggiari made tolerable an otherwise unwise visiting professorship (1991–1992) in the highly politicized, ideologically driven, and increasingly humorless Classics department at Stanford.

The five years it took me to write this book, from January 1988 to February 1993, were a time of uncertain job security, continued agricultural recession, and a bothersome chronic illness. But my wife Cara and our three children have been and are always cheerful and encouraging. Their unbounded optimism convinces me that much better times are still ahead even when I cannot often see it.

I have lived on the same ranch for all of my forty years, save seven at universities and two in Greece, a continuity and security made possible only through the heroic efforts of ancestors now nearly all deceased. All chose to forsake short-term profit and material comfort so that their progeny too could share in their own love of farming, that six generations might continue to work the same ground.

I did not know the first two generations of agrarians who built and lived in this house. They are now mere oval pictures on our staircase wall. But I do carry appreciation of them through the memory of my own grandparents, Rees (1890–1976) and Georgia Johnston Davis (1890–1983), and Frank Hanson (1889–1968). They were pioneers whose answer for every

problem that arose—be it crop failure, sickness, or death—was mostly silence, self-denial, and harder work. My mother, the late Justice Pauline
Davis Hanson (1922–1989) and father, William Frank Hanson, *parentes
cari*, were cast in that same mold. They sacrificed much—time, money,
worry, and concern—for my own education and urged us all to leave the
ranch for a time if we were to save it. Yet they were proud, I think, when
we all chose to farm, rather than to enter academic life, upon receipt of
our degrees. Almost all of what I have I owe to them.

My twin brother Alfred, brother Nels, and cousin Rees now continue
for a while longer to keep the wolf from the door: continually poor
prices, high interest rates, long-term debt, and all the urban litany of
theft, crime, and environmental problems that once seemed so distant
from our farm. Maren, my cousin, has always appeared suddenly on the
farm to help when times were darkest. Their vigilance and competence
as farmers have also helped me to continue to research and to write. A
neighbor and fellow farmer, Charles Garrigus, Jr., has offered me daily insight from his own sometimes nostalgic, sometimes bitter view of the
vanishing agrarian—and his past experience of the perils of academia.
He has quickly—and unmercifully—dispelled any nonsense I have
brought home from the campus. And so Chuck has not let me forget
that there really is always an irreconcilable divide between the farm of a
yeoman and the garden of an academic.

—V.D.H.
Hanson-Nielsen Farm
8343 East Mt. View Avenue
Selma, California
February 2, 1993

AUTHOR'S NOTE

Extensive documentation and scholarly controversy have been included in notes at the back of the book. Brief citations of quoted ancient literary and epigraphical evidence is placed conveniently by abbreviation in parentheses in the text. On occasion, longer citations and commentary which I think may still interest the general reader are placed at the bottom of the page. A list of all ancient texts and inscriptions appears at the end of the book, as well as a short appendix of ancient Greek agrarian vocabulary. The bibliography contains the secondary works in modern languages that are cited in the text and notes by last name and, where necessary, date of publication. All ancient dates are to B.C. unless otherwise noted. I have not been able to incorporate secondary work appearing after February 1993 when the manuscript was completed. Precise page numbers are noted with each citation. All translations are my own unless noted; for Homer's *Iliad* and *Odyssey* I have used those of Richmond Lattimore.

I have at no place used personal observation of modern farming alone to support *any* statement or belief about the ancient Greeks: I know well the treacherous siren song of modern analogy. Instead, *all* such comparative material from contemporary agricultural life is illustrative only of phenomena previously supported by ancient literary, archaeological, epigraphical, or iconographic evidence. It is included to help the reader assimilate the ancient sources through illustration and digression. Nor have I chosen the topics of inquiry based on personal experience alone. The chapter headings of the book reflect, I believe, the central issues of Greek agrarian history and are derived exclusively from the reading of ancient texts. Finally, I acknowledge at the outset the disturbing nature of my central thesis: agrarian pragmatism, not intellectual contemplation, farmers not philosophers, "other" Greeks, not the small cadre of refined minds who have always comprised the stuff of Classics, were responsible for the creation of Western civilization.

INTRODUCTION

*Agrarianism, Ancient and Modern: The Origin of
Western Values and the Price of Their Decline*

> It becomes ever more difficult for the professional historian to
> reach across to ordinary intelligent men and women or make his
> subject a part of human culture. The historical landscape is blurred
> by the ceaseless activity of its millions of professional ants.
>
> —A. Plumb (Andrewes 1971: xiv–xvi)

Everyone now speaks of "Western values." Both the critics and supporters of Western culture agree that these values originated with the ancient Greeks. But who exactly *are* the Greeks? And which Greeks do we
mean? Athenian democrats like Pericles or Demosthenes? Philosophers
like Socrates, Plato, or Aristotle? Men of action and great captains of
the caliber of Themistocles or Alexander? Spartans holding the pass at
Thermopylae? Or are Western values simply the stuffy ideas found in the
canon of classical Greek literature, the refined ore from Homer's *Iliad* to
Menander's late fourth-century B.C. comedies?

We can be vaguer still about the origins of the "West" and we speak
grandly of the "city-state," the culture of the *polis* that sparked the entire

1

Greek renaissance. The creation of a Greek urban entity, we are usually told, led to constitutional government, egalitarianism, rationalism, individualism, separation between religious and political authority, and civilian control of the military—the values that continue to characterize Western culture as we know it.

Most general surveys of Greek history are thus inevitably urban in origin. The Greeks appear as emerging congregations of bards, poets, and philosophers. They are seen through the rise of new centers of commerce, temple construction, and shipping, the nucleated workshops of craftsmen and artists, the clustered houses and gravestones of the living and the dead. But this traditional emphasis, while perfectly natural given the artifacts, the literature, the intellectual brilliance of the Greek city-state, is misdirected.

All these approaches to the source of Western values will lead us astray, for we owe our cultural legacy to Greeks outside the walls of the *polis*, forgotten men and women of the countryside, the "other" Greeks of this book. Classicists bump into farmers in Greek literature; archaeologists come across ancient rural habitation. But where is the countryside in general surveys of Greek history? To write almost exclusively of ancient Greek city life is to ignore the true source and life-blood of that new wealth and to forget that the new cultural attitudes and systems of social and political discourse were originally not urban, but agrarian. The *polis*, after all, was merely an epiphenomenon, the cumulative expression of a wider rural dynamism. It represented the fruits of the many whose work, uneventful as it seems to us now, created the leisure, wealth, and security for the gifted and intellectual few.

The early Greek *polis* has often been called a nexus for exchange, consumption, or acquisition, but it is better to define it as an "agro-service center." Surplus food was brought in from the countryside to be consumed or traded in a forum that concurrently advanced the material, political, social, and cultural agenda of its agrarian members. The buildings and circuit walls of a city-state were a testament to the accumulated bounty of generations, its democratic membership a formal acknowledgment of the unique triad of small landowner, infantry soldier, and voting citizen. The "other" Greeks, therefore, were not the dispossessed but the possessors of power and influence. Nor is their story a popular account of slaves, the poor, foreigners, and the numerous other "outsiders" of the ancient Greek city-state. The real Greeks are the farmers and infantrymen, the men and women outside the city, who were the insiders of Greek life and culture.

The rise of independent farmers who owned and worked without encumbrance their small plots at the end of the Greek Dark Ages was an entirely new phenomenon in history. This roughly homogeneous agrarian class was previously unseen in Greece, or anywhere else in Europe and the surrounding Mediterranean area. Their efforts to create a greater community of agrarian equals resulted, I believe, in the system of independent but interconnected Greek city-states (*poleis*) which characterized Western culture.

Scholars, ancient and modern, have never agreed on what a *polis* was, and the study of that institution has been a constant area of controversy for more than two centuries. We do not know exactly when, why, and how it appeared, or even when and why the city-state ceased to exist.[1] I cannot answer all those questions here. But I do suggest that the proper framework of the entire historical discussion of both the genesis and the decline of the Greek *polis* must lie in the realm of agriculture. The material prosperity that created the network of Greek city-states resulted from small-scale, intensive working of the soil, a complete rethinking of the way Greeks produced food and owned land, and the emergence of a new sort of person for whom work was not merely a means of subsistence or profit but an ennobling way of life, a crucible of moral excellence in which pragmatism, moderation, and a search for proportion were the fundamental values. The wider institutions of ancient Greece—military, social, political—embodied the subsequent efforts of these small farmers to protect their hard-won gains—the results of, not the catalysts for, agrarian change. And the tragic demise of Hellenic society was in large part a result of the very contradictions of the Greeks' own agrarian notions of egalitarianism, which became more and more inflexible in an increasingly complex world. Agrarian man emerges from the Dark Ages to create the *polis*; when he disappears, so too does his city-state.[2]

The original Greek *polis* is best understood as an exclusive and yet egalitarian community of farmers that was now to produce its own food, fight its own wars and make its own laws, a novel institution that was not parasitic on its countryside but instead protective of it. The history of the *polis*, then, should neither be seen primarily as linked to the rise of overseas trade and commerce, nor as a Malthusion race between population and food production, nor even as a war between the propertied and the landless, much less a saga of the intellectual brilliance of the urban few. All of that is the Greece of the university and the lecture hall, not the Greece that concerns us today. Rather, the historical background of Greece, especially its democratic background, is best understood as the result of a widespread agrarianism among the rural folk who were the dynamos from which the juice of Hellenic civilization flowed.

To understand the contributions—and limitations—of the Greeks, I seek to reconstruct the experience of the thousands of small agriculturalists who emerged out of the Dark Ages (about 1100–800 B.C.). For the next four centuries (700–300 B.C.) these farmers, or *geôrgoi*, revolutionized the economic and cultural life of their fellow Greeks, and left as their legacy the ideas that small, family-centered production on family property was the most efficient and desirable economic system; that the farmers' creed of equality could be successfully superimposed on the entire community, urban and rural; that groups of like-minded people could band together in novel, self-sufficient communities to ensure their personal liberty and equality; and that the civilian could dictate every aspect of defense preparedness, collectively deciding when and when not to make war.

Greek war ("the father of everything, the king of everything," according to Heraclitus) cannot be understood apart from agriculture, "the mother of us all" (cf. Heracl. fr. 53; Stob. *Flor.* 15.18). Nor can Greek farming be understood without knowledge of warfare. And Greek life and thought, the foundation of Western culture, cannot be studied without a grasp of both.

The Greeks envisioned themselves uniquely as farmers and freehold owners of vines, fruit-trees, and cereal land. "The largest class of men," Aristotle wrote, "live from the land and the fruits of its cultivation" (*Pol.* 1.1256a39–41). As late as 403 B.C., we can infer from a passage of Dionysius of Halicarnassus, author of a first-century treatise on oratory, that the great majority of Athenians—perhaps the most urban of all the Greek *poleis*—owned land and were engaged in farming. Thucydides, a contemporary observer of the great rural retreat of 431 B.C. inside the walls of Athens, saw that this migration was particularly difficult for the Athenians, "since most of them had always lived on their farms" (*en tois agrois*; 2.14).

Aristophanes in his comedy, *Peace*, says simply that "the farmers (*geôrgoi*) do all the work, no one else"(*Pax* 511). Euripides agrees, and in his tragedy, *Orestes*, we read that "the yeomen (*autourgoi*) alone preserve the land" (*Orest.* 920). No wonder that the Greeks simply distinguished their entire society as one that farmed in ways far different from their neighbors (e.g., Hdt. 4.17–19). Perhaps that is why the *Oeconomica*, a fourth-century treatise wrongly attributed to Aristotle, assumed that agriculture was by far the most important source of revenue for any Greek *polis*, calling it "the most honest of all occupations, inasmuch as wealth is not derived from other men," as well as a vocation that "contributes to the making of manly character"(*Oec.* 1.1343b3–5). The only economic activity discussed at length in Xenophon's earlier *Oeconomicus* is farming: "When farming goes well all other arts go well, but when the earth is forced to lie barren, the others almost cease to exist" (*Oec.* 5.17).

Twenty-four centuries ago, Theophrastus, the urban philosopher, portrayed this "other" Greek as an oaf and a clod who "will sit down with his cloak hitched above his knees, exposing his private parts. He is neither surprised nor frightened by anything he sees on the street, but let him catch sight of an ox or a donkey or a billy-goat, and he will stand and gaze at it" (*Char.* 4.8). The typical Greek farmer was a man who cared little for dress, shunned the palestra and gymnasium, was rarely portrayed on Greek pots, and never appeared in a Platonic dialogue. He owned no mounts, better to be seen soiled among pigs and goats, his mongrel hound snapping at his side. But the other Greek also has no boss, stands firm in battle "squarely upon his legs" with "no swagger in his lovelocks," a man who "does not cleanshave beneath his chin" (Archil.114), who judges the sophist in the assembly by the same yardstick he prunes vines and picks olives, and so cannot be fooled, a man who knows that his land "never plays tricks, but reveals clearly and truthfully what it can and cannot do," that it "conceals nothing from our knowledge and understanding and so becomes the best tester of good and bad men" (*Oec.* 20.13–14). Aristophanes described this other Greek "covered with dust, fond of garlic pickle, with a facial expression like sour vinegar" (Ar. *Eccl.* 289–92). He has no belly for the prancing aristocrat and even less for the mob on the dole. He idealizes his ten acres—not much more, rarely less—and he wants others like him to have about the same. He walks rarely into town, and then mostly just to vote and go home, disgusted at the noise, the squalor, and the endless race for pelf and power. And because he suffers no master, he speaks his due, fights his own battles, and leaves an imprint of self-reliance and nonconformity, a legacy of independence that is the backbone of Western society.

Even in academic life, a farmer can only remain a farmer: unsophisticated, inarticulate, irrationally independent, naively, sometimes embarrassingly suspicious of anything novel, ill-at-ease with all consensus opinion, stubborn and wary for no sensible reason, awkward, impatient with even justified subtlety and nuance. He is a searcher, pathetically and all too simplistically seeking those who would live by some consistent ethos, even if it be narrow and outdated. These are all traits crucial for survival on the land, where immediate, unambiguous action is demanded in the face of impending rain, nighttime frost, sudden bank foreclosure. Those crises are times where delay, reflection, nuance, and ambiguity are not wise and reasoned. Certainly they are not "prudent," but instead dangerous for self and family. Rambunctious, uneasy, and imprudent, a farmer in the university must naturally transfer that innate impatience to academia. He interprets, no doubt as many others would outside the campus, the quality of colleagues' research, teaching, or scholarly ethics and comportment, quite unintellectually, bluntly and without nuance or sophistication. They are seen in terms of mostly black or white. They are gauged simply as one surveys a head of irrigation water, the weld on a disk blade, the thousands of scions of a grafted orchard, by what works and what falls apart, by what appears as natural, pragmatic, accessible, or explicable and what does not—in short, by what a farmer believes will last and what will wilt, collapse, inevitably erode, and pass away with current fashion. If one looks at Greek life through that particular agrarian eye, it appears to be a very different culture from the one that is presented at the university.

Farming is the world of actuality, *never* potentiality. It is "the clear accuser of a bad soul," where reputed skill, apparent talent, assumed knowledge, predictable subservience mean little if the crop, that sole and final arbiter of human moral worth, is not brought in. By that benchmark, modern American academic life—the conference circuit, the reduced teaching load, the emphasis on theory, the depersonalization and lack of interest in human agency—is completely at odds with everything we know of the ancient Greeks.

Why then do so many scholars neglect Greek agrarianism in most surveys of Greek history, when nearly all historians, ancient and modern, agree that anywhere from sixty-five to ninety-five percent of the citizens of most city-states worked the land?[3] The idea that their Greece was mostly a community of yeomen, not an enclave of writers, artists, grammarians, and academics—not people more or less like themselves—is difficult to concede. "New" ancient historians of the last decade who seek to destroy standard orthodoxy for good in a variety of quite different contexts are to be commended for pointing out these narrow literary and philological approaches of traditional American classical scholarship. I agree with them that there is a real need for radical reappraisals of Greek culture. They are imaginative and never blinkered by traditional concerns. They and their associates in feminist, race, class, and something now called "gender" studies are correct in blaming past philology and traditional narrative history for the neglect of the ancient "nonelite." But for all their intellectual daring, even these new classical scholars are more similar than not to the entrenched academic authorities they seek to dislodge. Both are usually urban creatures. Both exist for, and are at home in, the university. Few have left the cloister of academia. Fewer have any desire—or ability— to do so.

In this sense, for a comprehensive understanding of Greek history and the origins of Western values, current scholarly revisionism delivers less than promised in the way of reform.[4] The "new" ancient world is too often the old ancient world. It is still a story of city-people written by city-people. There is little hope that the present generation of revisionist classicists in the United States will ever come to terms with Greece as an agrarian society of pedestrian hard-working yeomen. Many successful American Ph.D. candidates in Classics can still review the difficult odes of Pindar or the dry poetry even of a Callimachus. Few know when olives, vines, or grain were harvested—the critical events in the lives of the people who created Greek culture and civilization.

All ancient societies were agricultural in nature. But Greece alone, this book will argue, first created "agrarianism," an ideology in which the production of food and, above all, the actual people who own the land and do the farmwork, are held to be of supreme social importance. The recovery of this ancient ideology has enormous ramifications for our understanding of the Greeks, inasmuch as it explains both the beginning and the end of their greatest achievement, the classical city-state.

I am by birth and trade a farmer. From that angle of vision, I have developed a guarded admiration for those, both now and in the past, who have tested their wits against the vagaries of nature in an effort to feed their fellow citizens. I think I know these men and women, know how they look at the world and themselves, how they shape and affect society, and the peculiar, harsh code by which they live and judge others.[5]

This other world of American agriculture, for the most part, feeds the United States and is one of its few remaining successful industries. And although the existence of these competent and industrious persons is critical and indeed largely responsible for the comfort of modern American life, they are nevertheless, like their ancient Greek ancestors, essentially an unknown people and an endangered species.

A nation, I believe, can be judged by the way it treats those who produce its food. And herein, I discovered, lies the uniqueness of ancient Greece, a society that, despite the occasional silence of our (largely urban) sources, for nearly four centuries was an *agrotopia*, a community of, for, and by small landowners. The ancient counterparts of the contemporary (and vanishing) small agriculturalist, however great the differences in outlook and technique, were responsible, in both a material and spiritual sense, for all their community's culture—what we know now as classical Greek civilization. Their unremembered contribution deserves both recognition and respect.

Besides an empathetic acquaintance with farmers, pragmatic experience in the fertilization, cultivation, pruning, harvesting, irrigating, and propagation of fruits and vegetables, the planting—and utter destruction—of orchards and vineyards, can also add some sensitivity to the reconstruction of the fragmentary archaeological and literary record of ancient Greek agrarian history. There is value in writing carefully from personal trial and error about ancient agricultural expertise. True, this practical knowledge of agricultural tasks can also be acquired through other means. Scholars do find this knowledge in books, in any good modern treatise on viticulture, agriculture, cereal production. But the vocabulary and thinking of the modern social sciences when applied to ancient agriculture often convey little empathy or understanding of what life must have been like for the ancient Greek farmer, instead creating complicated theoretical models for the basic, instinctual knowledge any farmer knows as second nature. So by pragmatic experience I am also referring to a far vaguer "ideology" of farming that is unattainable even through the pages of a vast technical literature.

But one should not assume that the author's personal intimacy with agriculture must inevitably transform this investigation of the ancient Greeks into some romantic encomium of the glory days on the "south forty," ancient or modern. Much less is this book a tract for current political or agrarian reform, which, in any case, can do little now to save family agriculture in this country. The life of a farmer is increasingly Hobbesian—poor, nasty, and brutish, even if not always short. It has been my own experience that many who still rise to that challenge today are themselves hard-nosed, peculiar, dogmatic, and distasteful characters, better appreciated at a distance, myself perhaps included. My purposes in deviating somewhat from a 'professional' stance are threefold.

First, I wish to reach an audience outside the university, to remind them that agrarianism was once the very center of their own civilization. In the twilight of classical studies in this country, they should know that the Greeks were not distant, unapproachable grandees, the property now of a few thousand well-educated Westerners. Instead, the Hellenes were resourceful farmers who devised their own society intended to protect and to advance their brand of agriculture. Their achievement was the precursor in the West of private ownership, free economic activity, constitutional government, social notions of equality, decisive battle, and civilian control over every facet of the military—practices that affect every one of us right now. In this light, Greek agriculture is not a different approach to the traditional questions of Western civilization but a topic now vital to the existence of our own culture.

A second reason for adopting an unorthodox approach is that I do have some practical knowledge about the cultivation of trees and vines, and more important, about the ideology of those who grow these crops. For all of my life, save a near decade spent in undergraduate and graduate study, I have lived on a farm and have been considered by most a farmer of trees and vines. That angle of vision has always turned out to be disadvantageous in academic life. Pruning, irrigating, and tractor work have about the same stigma as a southern San Joaquin Valley residence. The two together form a lethal combination on most university campuses. Nevertheless, on occasion my farming experience has helped me to make some sense of ancient texts and the evidence of archaeology, epigraphy, and iconography concerning ancient Greek agriculture, and thus of Hellenic life in general.

I hope, therefore, in the manner of Herodotus, to pass that digressive method of personal autopsy and inquiry along to the reader. I also believe, as did both Thucydides and Polybius, that a historian can and should take some part in any history that he writes. Only that way can he avoid an irony that faces most modern scholars: we of comfortable circumstance and suburban physique, we free of filth, unending physical labor, disease, mayhem, and constant military service, we chronicle—and all too often pass judgment on—the brutal and ungentle world of the Greeks. The classical scholar who is concerned over this occasional infusion of personal experience in this present history should perhaps see it simply as "social anthropology," a popular interdisciplinary approach that incorporates the experiences of modern cultures into classical scholarship.

The real story, the historian's noble calling, the saga of humankind—triumph, courage, defeat, and cowardice—often gives way in scholarly studies of food production to a sterile and peopleless analysis of "carrying capacity" and the equilibrium between food output and population growth. My primary interest is precisely the opposite, to discover in human terms "what it was like" for these other Greeks who surrounded the city proper and created the *polis:* in other words, to reclaim ancient Greek agriculture and agrarianism for history from the social and natural sciences.

For example, the desire to leave an empathetic account of crop diversity among the small farmers of ancient Greece is more an accident of upbringing than formal research. In my own experience "diversification" of crops is *not* merely a strategy. It is not an element of social science investigation, but rather (in our case) a personal and desperate attempt to salvage an existence for four families after the raisin cataclysm of 1983. In that year the price of natural Thompson seedless raisins fell without warning from $1,420 a ton to $450. Entire farms in the central San Joaquin Valley, dependent solely on Thompson seedless grapes, were quietly, almost imperceptibly obliterated. Land values at year's end plummeted from $15,000 to $4,000 an acre and lower. A forty-acre vineyard no longer earned, but now lost, $40,000 for a year's work, its operator now "paying" hourly for the privilege of working his soil. The market value of his property was suddenly nonexistent. And in strictly economic terms, even $4,000 an acre was too high, as the banks' repossession apparatus soon found out.

Real disaster this was, worse even than the rain disasters of the prior decade that had rotted two entire harvests drying on the ground. The agricultural years of the 1980s created a fantasy-like world, or a nightmarish purgatory where farmers often picked their plums, peaches, and nectarines, sent them to a shipper, but then received a bill, a "red tag" demanding payment greater than the value of the crop for "handling, commission, and expenses." The wiser and less sentimental farmers sometimes let the fruit drop from the tree, or cut off all the fruit-bearing canes from their vineyards. After personally pruning, thinning, cultivating, watering, and fertilizing a three-acre Santa Rosa plum orchard all year, my brothers, cousin, and I watched its sixty tons of fruit ripen, slowly rot, ferment, and then finally decay into leathery skins. Why pay the consumer to eat your fruit?

"There is something sweet," as the comic playwright Menander saw, "in the bitterness of farming" (fr. 795 Kock). The system of family-based, small-scale, and diversified production, as the Greeks knew and as I have been forced to learn, provides much work, near constant worry—and, as its prize, veritable independence and immunity from most challenges, natural or human-induced. But that "something sweet" comes at a price. Its adherents must be willing to acknowledge the present "bitterness of farming": social and regional immobility, alienation from wealth and power, disdain from the urban professional, disregard for fashionable clothing, transportation, leisure, and entertainment—a spiritual disconnection, an isolation, in other words, from modernity itself, affinity more with an ancient past, rather than with present norms of behavior.

Third, I wish to convey some idea of contemporary American agriculture in its own right, quite apart from comparative illustrations of the agrarian Greeks. True, there are hundreds of good books on the joys of growing food. Nearly as much has been written on the science and successful technique of agricultural production. I omit the nauseating agribusiness magazines that pile up on our kitchen table. But there are fewer accounts of the daily life on an American farm in the last two decades. The record of that experience in this, the very last stage of traditional American agrarianism, needs desperately to be augmented, for time is growing short.

Much has been written about the lost life of the American farm in the era before technology, the time of the horse plow, before the appearance of advanced machinery and creeping urbanism. Yet I believe that the American farm today is unique in another way. Fortress-like it stands battered—and then slowly erodes before the relentless waves of assault from poor commodity prices and rising costs, spreading housing tracts, and ultimately the neglect of mass urban culture. But farmers of today are more similar to their ancestors at the turn of the century than they will be to their successors a mere twenty years hence. And the last adherents are now being plowed under at an alarming rate.

The greatest revolution in American agriculture—genetic and biotechnical engineering, mass application of computerized technology, uniform corporatization, urban residency, crop specialization, and near complete dependence on nonfarm sources of income and capital—is now upon us. The destruction of American agrarianism will soon eliminate in this country the entire equation of farm and farmer from the realm of food production: the man who works the ground he owns is a vanishing species. And so within twenty years the agrarian Greeks are to be even further distanced from American experience, for there will be none who understand the tenets of their rural world.

In my own locale, the San Joaquin Valley, generally recognized as the most productive expanse of irrigated farmland in the world, family farms are vanishing at an astonishing pace. Their owners are dying or, far more ignominiously, slipping silently off into urban apartments and rest homes. Irrigation, the century-old effort of agrarians to harness the waters of the Sierra, is to produce not peaches, plums, or raisins, but the private lakes of new housing developments and the grass lawns of suburban immigrants, home-equity refugees from Los Angeles and San Francisco. Their sprawling quarters now cover vineyards and fig groves, pipelines, wells, alleyways, barns, and sheds; vineyards are ripped out and replanted with gated tracts known as "The Vineyards" or "Orchard Knolls."

But even more tragic than the environmental—and visual—consequences of precipitous urbanization, whole hosts of new inhabitants now also "cover" farmers. The prior custodians of instant concrete driveways, homes, pools, and backyards have imperceptibly exited, retired, disappeared from our very midst. To grow their fruit now in California is to lose money; to continue farming in 1995 is to pay the consumer to eat your harvests; to rise in the dark morning is to preserve the comfortable livelihood, the ever-rising share of brokers, advertisers, distributors, and marketers, distant but still unpleasant men and women whom the farmer knows only by the anonymous and hurried voice over the phone.

Walk a farm each evening: a horse-shoe turned up here, over there an old half-exposed disk blade, square nails in the alleyway. All are the artifacts of a cadre of men now lost, relics in an island of farmland besieged by growing urbanization. Disturbing now, not comforting at all, are the epic memories of my own grandfather Rees Davis, his lifelong employees and friends—Manuel George and Joe Carey, his blustering neighbor Bill Hazlehoffer, and a legion of others. For a small boy of ten they were giants on the earth. But they have left a melancholy legacy, the bitter and incriminating knowledge that they have not been and will not be replaced, that we the clearly inferior successors can no longer match their struggle. Meander through vineyards and orchards of a past agrarian generation. See the residue of their work. To do so is to acknowledge our present impoverishment, to find ourselves sorely wanting, to learn that no farmers among us can match the ancestral ones, in either muscular strength, talent, or ingenuity, optimism in the face of ruin, or simplicity and independence of routine.

Doomed in very short order, of course, are the land itself and the people who would continue to work it for another decade or so, at least as I have known and understood both for my own forty years. But it is too often forgotten in our current fashionable environmentalism, our worry about fading open spaces, that we now are paving over an equally invaluable resource: men and women who can read the weather, who know the cycles and signs of plants and animals, understand the human experience of physical labor, and are about our last bulwarks against uniformity and regimentation.

These people, contrary to our romantic Jeffersonian mythology, are not 'consensus builders' at all. Most instead are plain, outspoken folk who live by their wits in a continual contest with the elements. For the majority, their judgment, word, and entire ethos of conduct were never predicated on flattery, peer-approval, career advancement, and the absence of imagination so characteristic of the modern urban workplace. There, getting along in a social, rather than a natural, environment is crucial; reinventing oneself yearly in harmony with current fad becomes a normative and inoffensive behavior that rarely draws the needed rebuke. But agrarians and their values have been mostly unchanging from the Greeks to the present day and they have therefore provided a necessary antidote to the excesses and fashions of contemporary American life. Yes, people can continue to grow food. But they may not be the farmers, who, despite their shrinking numbers, still provide us with a needed dose of social sobriety.

Farmers are, as we shall see, *real* producers. Quite chauvinistically they recognize themselves as such. They do not exchange paper. They rarely communicate through electronic gadgetry. They do not merchandise or advertise. But they do grow food and fiber for their fellow citizens, generation after generation. For all that our society now conscientiously seeks to preserve and enhance minority values, it oddly cares little for the agrarian culture that has been with us from the beginning. But agriculturalists are the one irreplaceable link in the great modern chain of acquisition and consumption. So Knut Hamsun summed up Isak, the hero of his novel, *Growth of the Soil*:

> Twas rarely he knew the day of the month—what need had he of that? He had no bills to be met on a certain date; the marks on his almanac were to show the time when each of the cows should bear. But he knew St. Olaf's Day in the autumn, that by then his hay must be in, and he knew Candlemas in spring, and that three weeks after then the bears came out of their winter quarters; all seed must be in the earth by then. He knew what was needful.
>
> A tiller of the ground, body and soul; a worker on the land without respite. A ghost risen out of the past to point the future, a man from the earliest days of cultivation, a settler in the wilds, nine hundred years old, and withal, a man of the day. (434)

A man who can produce with his own muscle, talent, and nerve enough raisins to feed a city of half a million now receives less compensation than a local insurance agent, apprentice lawyer—or a beginning Greek professor. We have completely forgotten the warning of the wise Roman agronomist Columella. "Even if the state should become destitute of its professors," he wrote, "still it would prosper just as in the past.

. . . Yet without its farmers mankind can neither subsist nor be fed" (*Rust. Praef.* 1.6).

If less than one percent of the American population are currently family farmers, it is no wonder that the present-day agriculturalist is a walking anachronism, his thought and ideology completely alien to and unsynchronized with nearly everyone he meets. Yet American agrarians are the true adherents of the Western heritage and heirs of the Greek *polis*, even though mankind is now "subsisting and being fed" without its yeomen farmers.

Our present democratic cargo must be seen in the original (rural) context of its birth, if these concepts of freedom are to retain any value for us, and not—as is now often the case—to be detached as meaningless abstractions and justifications for personal excess, materialism, brutality and mayhem, national chauvinism, and collective irresponsibility. And, again, like Hellenic concepts of pitched battle, it is all too often forgotten that nearly all Western values were ultimately agrarian in their genesis, arising out of the peculiarly rural nature of the ancient Greek city-states. Those interconnected communities of small farmers created these concepts as a means to preserve a way of life unseen elsewhere in the world at the time. I cannot here trace the subsequent and complicated post-Hellenic evolution of the agrarian yeoman, the immemorial odyssey of the independent rural person in Western history through Roman times and the Medieval and Renaissance eras into the Industrial Revolution. But I do intend to chronicle in detail when Western agrarianism first arose in Greece, how it nearly vanished, and why its fundamental creed has endured until now.

Americans today of the (endangered) middle class, who own their own houses, who feel camaraderie with those of roughly like circumstances, who have no affinity with either the idle rich or the shiftless poor, who elect their own representatives, who are not subject to oppressive taxation or religious strictures, who bear their own arms and fight their country's battles, who abhor the human and material costs of war, but are not afraid openly to face down aggression, owe that entire ideology—so often now under attack in this country—not simply to classical Athenian democracy, but indeed to a much earlier agrarian *polis*, the forgotten rural "nursery of steady citizens." To understand what has all too loosely been called the "Greek legacy," as well as to retain any useful understanding of the relationship between individual and community, we must study these Western ideas in their proper original context. Small farmers were responsible for the rise of constitutional government in the West, and so this must be a book about farming and the people who farm.

As long as there were family farmers, there were city-states. When the former lost their character, the latter disappeared. We must therefore see Greek history as an integral whole, not as mere interludes of artistic and literary expression.

Agrarianism began in the middle of the eighth century B.C. when most of the Greek-speaking world was just beginning to display visible signs of material prosperity: roads, bridges, temples, walls, theaters, and growing settled communities.* Political organization was still rudimentary. After all, since the decline of Mycenaean palace culture four hundred years earlier, the Greek countryside had become largely the domain of disconnected clans. Independent of each other and without any larger central organization of agriculture, local strongmen carved out areas of influence among the largely impoverished Greek population.

Although these regional powers probably controlled to some degree the 'economy' of the Greek countryside, they had little interest in, or knowledge of, arboriculture, viticulture, or other methods of intensive cereal production, much less the advantages of small, independent land ownership. All that was antithetical to their social and political culture, which was far removed from small farming. Wealth in early Greece was largely derived from herds of cattle, sheep, pigs, and goats, and the frequent organized raiding party—all understandable in a depopulated landscape, where the efficiency of land use was rarely explored, and the agricultural labor of the farmer-owner himself was less critical. Private property on any wide scale was nonexistent. The very notion of a busy, stubborn, and independent agrarian was itself completely unknown.

This period after the collapse of Mycenaean culture (1100–700 B.C.) is rather unimaginatively, but quite accurately, labeled the "Dark Ages" by ancient historians. That makes sense: it is a time sandwiched between

---

*Coldstream 1977: 317–66; Gallant 1982: 119–20. Farmers, ancient and modern, manifest success mostly by building things; oddly, some scholars sometimes see intricate and impressive ancient rural infrastructure as a sign that the population therefore must have been doing something else!

two better known eras of Greek history—the "Mycenean" (1600–1200 B.C.) and the "Archaic" (700–480 B.C.)—where our archaeological sources are far more plentiful, and where both pictorial art and writing are available to modern scholars. Yet by 700 B.C. at least, the progeny of these same "Dark-Age" Greeks had created well over 1,000 new, small city-states, a thriving trade and commerce, literacy among the ruling elites, Panhellenic festivals and sanctuaries, monumental temple-building—in short, a changed environment of material prosperity and civic pride surrounding the *polis*, where literature and philosophy were soon to flourish.

Nevertheless, these eighth through sixth centuries of discovery have usually been labeled the "Archaic Period." But why should we call it "Archaic"? Nearly all of Greek accomplishment—especially the rise of a new agrarianism that radically restructured the economy—had its origins at this time. No one, by comparison, would label the similar genesis of the American republic, the late eighteenth century of the United States when American institutions and culture were born, as "archaic." The reasons for the use of this rubric in the case of the ancient Greeks, I think, are twofold.

First, there is the notion of primitivism, of preparation for the better known Classical Period (480–338 B.C.) that follows. In this typical human way of triadic thinking—"bad, better, best"—the Dark Ages lead to the Archaic, which produces the Classical, all in some sort of linear progression.*

A second reason for the popularity of the traditional (but misleading) rubric "Archaic" is more significant, since it is not a question of aesthetics or taste, but rather revolves around the nature of the available source materials. Homer probably composed his epics somewhere around 700

---

*Anthony Snodgrass has aptly explained this traditional phenomenon: "On the accepted view, the Archaic period was by definition merely a prelude to the decisive achievements of classical Greece. It did not make any difference which criterion one chose to appeal to—literary, intellectual, artistic, political—there appeared to be an unanswerable case for the supremacy of the classical period as a whole, and, in Greece, of the fifth century B.C. in particular." Snodgrass: 1980: 11. This cataloguing system had its beginnings with the connoisseurship of the eighteenth-century European art-historians (cf. Whitley 14–19). They saw the crude beginnings of Greek art in the pictureless, geometric pottery and childish figurines of the Dark Ages, its adolescence among the unrealistic, stubby shapes and rigid sculptures in Archaic art, and finally the logical culmination in perfection with realistic, lifelike humans in stone and on pots during classical times.

B.C., followed a few years later by Hesiod, the lyric and elegiac poets, and the pre-Socratic philosophers. This small group comprises most archaic literature. We have little reliable information about the lives of these authors or the circumstances in which they wrote. Homer also poses questions of historicity (does he sing of Mycenean times, the Dark Ages, or a Greece *circa* 700 B.C.?). The seventh- and sixth-century Greek poets and philosophers exist in fragments, their texts more often a product of random quotation in later authors or on papyrus scraps than a result of the manuscript tradition. Finally, none of the writing of the archaic age exists in *prose* form, much less as either history or biography proper. For the Greek archaic authors the artifacts of contemporary culture, the conscious observation of historical phenomena, are usually a concern secondary to their other interests in poetry, fiction, religion, entertainment, self-expression, and natural observation.

Public documents on stone until recently were customarily considered no help either. They are simply a rarity before the fifth century. What inscribed writing does exist is more often personal in nature and extremely brief: epitaphs, taunts, braggadocio, graffiti, or personal letters left randomly on walls, monuments, bronze and lead tablets, and pots, rather than designed for formal municipal display. The Greek epigrapher usually works in classical, Hellenistic, and Roman history, eras where there is a rich record of government officials, the names of elite men and families carved on public decrees, calendars, laws, regulations, inventories, contracts, and dedications, on private gravestones, pots, curse-tablets, and votives. The sheer number of such inscriptions (totaling more than 20,000 documents in Attica alone) in large part explains the present sophisticated state of Greek military and political history of the fifth and fourth centuries.

Archaeology, the third leg of the classicist's triad, always offered the best source of archaic historical reconstruction. But private houses, government buildings, roads, ports, and other visible remains of this age were rarely found in Greece. Investigation of the archaic surface was more a matter of temple and treasury exploration, usually at Panhellenic and local sanctuaries. Below the surface, we enter the more shadowy world of burial—a practice contingent on religious, class, and demographical criteria. Those distinctions are not always well understood by even the most imaginative and speculative archaeologists, who now labor hard to discover class conflict and evidence of early *polis* strife. In comparison to either Mycenean archaeology or classical excavation, there are few spectacular archaic finds, whereas errors in interpretation and reconstruction are frequent. Until recently, although some archaeological data from the late eighth to fifth century was available to the historian, nearly all of it was shrouded in controversy and without clear reference to chronology.

Lately, however, our knowledge of the early *polis* has expanded greatly. A multitude of comprehensive accounts of the emergence of the Greek city-state appeared in the late 1970s and 1980s. Ostensibly this new interest and reexamination revolves around the literary sources and the discovery of more archaeological data. Homeric epic, for example, traditionally fraught with controversy about its precise historical context, seems more and more from recent investigation to be a valuable historical source for the late eighth and early seventh centuries. That is, much of the *Iliad*, and to an even greater extent (given our economic interests) the *Odyssey* of a half century later, can tell us about life in the embryonic stages of the *polis* in the eighth century*—even if from a bard who addressed primarily an aristocratic audience, who often deliberately sought aristocratic and reactionary themes, time-honored narratives and imagery to satisfy the canons of his conservative genre. Hence, for our purposes, as the examination of Laertes' farm in Chapter 2 attempts to demonstrate, Homer's *Odyssey* can legitimately be used as evidence for the genesis of intensive, homestead agriculture.

True, there are many elements of Mycenean culture and even more frequent references to Dark-Age custom and practice in these epic poems. But these artifacts, numerous though they are, are usually recognizable by their anachronisms. They are necessary reactionary embellishments to the underlying eighth-century fabric of the poem, which assumes growing Greek colonization, assemblies, emerging city-states, and even phalanx warfare of a sort.

Homer's near-contemporary, Hesiod, a gifted poet who could also farm, offers more important evidence about the beginning of the sev-

---

*Homer, so long our guide to either Mycenean or Dark-Age Greece, has suddenly become a veritable history of the early Greek city-state. See Morris 1986: 81–138; 1987: 45–46; Greenhalgh 156–57; Latacz 36–48; 237–44; Whitley 36–39; Sculley 1–3; 26.

enth century. In his world of the early *polis* we should expect to see a vi-brant agrarianism, and he does not disappoint us. Unfortuantely in the past Hesiod's poem about rural life in central Greece, *The Works and Days*, has been given more literary than historical analysis. Various re-cent studies, however, have looked once more at the poem from largely an agrarian aspect, in order to ascertain exactly which type of agricul-ture Hesiod's work represents. Disagreement remains over the class and status of his agricultural world. There are no longer serious doubts about the reality of his personal experience in, and observation of, early sev-enth-century farming in Boeotia.*

When one considers the additional evidence of the Greek lyric and elegiac poets, especially the poems of Archilochus, Tyrtaeus, Callinus, Theognis, and Solon, the earlier episodic flashbacks and digressions in the histories of both Thucydides and Herodotus, the corpus of pre-So-cratic philosophy, and various anecdotes about the early life of the *polis* in authors as diverse as Pausanias, Plutarch, Athenaeus, Aristotle, and Plato, one wonders why the considerable literary evidence of the era has cast doubt on the practicability of historical reconstruction before the fifth century.[6]

Archaeology in the last twenty years has not merely continued in its traditional excavation at Panhellenic sanctuaries and municipal and cult centers. It has now also developed an entirely new corollary field of "sur-vey archaeology," largely because "the traditional medium of archaeo-logical research, excavation, is in its nature ill-suited to illuminating the rural setting of the Ancient World" (Snodgrass 1990: 114). Therefore archaeologists at a number of regional sites in Greece—Messenia, Aeto-lia, the southern Argolid, Boeotia, Crete, Euboea, Laconia, Nemea, Keos, Melos, the Athenian–Boeotian border, and elsewhere—have as-sembled teams of historians, geologists, surveyors, and other profession-als to work in unison in attempts to reconstruct the total rural environment of the area under survey.

Typically, archaeological surveys in Greece record pottery sherd den-sities, architectural remnants, and other traces of ancient habitation (i.e., coins, roof tiles) over a selected rural area—landscapes all unre-

---

*See Millet 1984: 84–86; Starr 1977: 123–28; Bravo 1977: 10–14; Mele 18–28 who at least agree that Hesiod's world is a realistic portrayal of rural life in early Greece.

markable to the casual observer. Then this fragmentary information is
tallied and integrated with geophysical, hydraulic, atmospheric, climatological, and botanical data. The aim of the exploration is to present an
account of human habitation and land use within a specific space,
spread over many centuries: population density and change, settlement
patterns, agricultural strategies, resource use, and rates of urbanization.
By directing attention largely away from urban centers, by treating traditional periods of Greek history theoretically with equal attention, field
surveys can be of great value in chronicling the early development of
Greek agrarianism: they do not intrinsically favor either the classical period or the city in general.*

For the purposes of this book on Greek agrarianism, I delete the term
"Archaic."** In general, the two premises mentioned above—the notion of primitivism and the absence of evidence—are not always com-
pelling criteria. In particular, the expression "Archaic" is particularly
inappropriate for an understanding of Greek rural life, whose structures
and ideology were both created at this time. In its place, I will use the
phrase "*polis*-period," to denote the *combined* archaic and classical eras
between roughly 700 and 300 B.C.

This single term better emphasizes the "other" Greeks, the uniqueness and the influence of dynamic Greek agriculture of the times, intensive and diverse farming centered around small family-based homesteads
and supportive of novel city-states. The use here of a different label
"*polis*-period" in a book concerning Greek farming also implies that the
free city-state of the time, including both its landed and nonlanded population, was a consequence of a vigorous agrarianism, in a period when
farmers were under pressure to feed the rising population of Greece.

The chronological limits of this study, then, are four centuries
(700–300 B.C.) of continual agricultural development. That is not to say
that the ninth and tenth centuries (900–700 B.C.) did not see the beginnings of real change from past Dark-Age land use (they did), but only

---

*See Bintliff and Snodgrass 124–25; Cherry, Davis, and Mantzourani 13–21; Keller and Rupp
382–408; Alcock 24: "Synthesis and comparison of different archaeological survey results with the
goal of understanding general processes of change in both prehistoric and historic Greece are worthy ambitions, even at this relatively early stage in the technique's application . . . for its strongest
contribution is towards questions of settlement, exploitation and population."

**At least one scholar has done this for different (and nonagrarian) reasons. Cf. Sallares 46–48.

that these nascent agricultural transformations became clearer and more integrated with other social, cultural, and political developments in the ensuing century.

There is a continuum of four centuries of Greek agrarian history—socially, culturally, economically, politically, militarily, even intellectually. Within it there should *not* be an arbitrary historical subdivision based on modern subjective ideas about the changing nature of artistic or literary excellence. The unique presence of the free city-state makes these four centuries 700–300 B.C. more similar to one another than to any other hundred-year period in Greek history.* Whatever the contour of Greek sculpture, the color of ceramic painting, the meter of Greek poetry, a citizen of 650 or 375 B.C. was likely to shout in the council chamber, to thrust his spear in the phalanx, and to claim a house and ten acres in the countryside.

---

*When examining the historical pattern of property holding and the influence of agrarianism on the politics of ancient Greece, Paul Guiraud about one hundred years ago saw the singularity of the *polis*-period in Greek history: "We have also shown that in an economic context there have been three distinct periods: the first, where the dominant regime was that of large property-holding; the second, where property was largely parceled out; the third, where there is a return to the system of large property-holding. Finally, we have established that the history of property-holding has occurred in step with the history of political institutions, and that there always existed a certain concordance between the manner in which the land was owned and the manner in which men were governed" (Guiraud 635).

Part One

THE RISE OF SMALL FARMERS IN ANCIENT GREECE

🌿 🌿 🌿

The importance of agriculture was and is not merely economic. Its moral value, as a nursery of steady citizens, . . . was and still should be recognized by thoughtful men. Therefore its condition and its relative prosperity or decay deserve the attention of all historians of all periods.

—W. E. Heitland, 1923:3

Chapter 1

THE LIBERATION OF AGRICULTURE

But pattern for planting, and seedling's earliest form
were nature herself: she first created things;
for berries and acorns falling from trees
in time produced a swarm of sprouts beneath them.
At whim thereafter, men set shoots in branches
and buried fresh cuttings in earth about their fields.
They tried to grow first one thing, then another
on their loved lands, and saw wild plants turn tame
in the soil with coddling and gentle, coaxing care.
And with each day they made the woods shrink farther
up-mountain, yielding room for farms below,
for pastures, ponds and streams, grain-land, lush vineyards,
their holdings on hill and plain, for olive-groves
to run their blue-gray bands like boundary lines
flowing across the hummocks, dales, and fields,
as now you see lands everywhere picked out
with beauty, lined and adorned with apple trees;
and fruitful orchards wall them about.

> —Lucretius, *On the Nature of Things*, 5.1361–78
> (Copley translation)

Greece is not a flat territory of wide-open expanses, with regular precipitation, plentiful rivers, and ubiquitous lakes. Yet it is not a poor country either. The soil is rocky but rich, the harnessing of water possible but only through ingenuity and toil. The growing season is long, predictable, and dry, rarely humid or unsettled, accelerating more often than endangering the maturity of fruit and vegetable. Winters are cold, not harsh, and so provide critical dormancy for trees and vines rather than frosts that stunt limbs and kill canes. True, mountains and hills predominate; but slopes are more often gentle than jagged, and can shelter as well as isolate villages. Stones discourage the ploughing of broad expanses, but can be managed by the hoe and spade in more modest gardens, orchards, and vineyards. Unlike flat land, elevation encourages diverse soils and micro environments, rather than ensuring crop specialization, monotony, and vulnerability. Pasture land can be scarce for horses and cattle, but more than adequate for less impressive sheep and goats.

In agricultural terms, then, Greece offers opportunity but does not guarantee bounty. In any given year trees, vines, and grains neither uniformly fail nor inevitably flourish. Innovation and experimentation, rather than rote and timidity, overcome climate and terrain, with predictable consequences for national character and group identity. The successful harvest leads not to security, riches, and leisure, but simply the guarantee of yet one more year to come. So Greece is a poor candidate for the hydraulic dynasty, replete with vast herds, cavalry, chariotry, crop surpluses, and a complacent and ordered population. But for an insolent, self-reliant man of nerve and muscle, who welcomes the solitary challenge of the mountain terrace, the lone farmstead, the chaos of olive, grape, grain, fig, goat, and pig, the choice to fight beside his family on ancestral ground, it is an altogether hospitable place.

Before agrarianism, the Greek countryside was not extensively worked and could not facilitate population growth. But radical changes in labor, farming technique, and land tenure did more than feed more people. These brilliant adaptions to the unique terrain and geography of Greece also created a new citizen, with a completely different set of values and characteristics. When, where, how, and why he emerged from obscurity are the subjects of the next two chapters.

I. Before the *Polis*

Nearly all modern accounts of the end of the Greek Dark Ages concern burials, pottery, the myth and speculation of later Greek literature, or the identification of past migrations through the spread of Greek dialects. This emphasis is understandable. It reflects both the available evidence and the interests of art historians and archaeologists in the beginnings of the *urban* culture of the Greek *polis.*

But are not our purposes different here? The countryside, *not* the *polis* proper; farmers, *not* urban elites; changes in agricultural practice, *not* pottery designs, metals, graves, urban crafts, nor even overseas trade, are the focus. I believe the latter phenomena were only "manifestations." They were the symptoms or results of far more fundamental changes in the agricultural structure of Greek society. The appearance of these early Greek *polis* institutions was made possible only by the birth of agrarianism. It alone created the surplus and capital to allow a significant minority of the population to shift its attention from farming and to pursue commerce, trade, craftsmanship, and intellectual development. Only a settled countryside of numerous small farmers could provide the prerequisite mass for constitutional government and egalitarian solidarity.

Demographic, technological, economic, social, and cultural circumstances that prompt dramatic innovations in land use and food production, and hence the stuff of major historical changes in any preindustrial society in general, have been long studied. No monolithic "model" exists for any given historical period. Common sense, however, tells us that a variety of factors can change the way in which people produce food.

In modern communities, the development of new machinery and chemicals dramatically increases agricultural production at lower cost, often leading to a consolidation of land holdings by wealthy partnerships and corporations, which transmit their very different ideas about culture to the society at large. These complex organizations often alone possess the necessary capital to apply innovations pragmatically on a wide scale, resulting in both higher productivity and greater vulnerability. But even breakthroughs in technology do not necessarily change the size and manner of farming nearly as much as the introduction of new crop species, irrigation, government policies including taxes, subsidies, regulations, and inheritance laws, new or lost markets, growing population, and—never to be underestimated—shifting social and cultural attitudes toward manual work, agricultural life, and rural residence.

In the case of Greece in the eighth century, at the end of the so-called Dark Ages, there seems to have been a variety of just such conditions operating in the countryside. None of them was critical in itself, but when taken as a whole, these incremental changes did cause radical transformations in Greek society in general, and left Greece a rural society like none other in the eastern Mediterranean.

The original circumstance of social alteration was the sudden cataclysmic destruction of complex Mycenean society in the thirteenth and twelfth centuries and the subsequent breakdown of the political hierarchy. We are not sure whether the end of this world was due to foreign invaders, dissatisfied subjects, natural phenomena, or general systems collapse; but there is no doubt that in the aftermath came a dramatic depopulation of the Greek peninsula. With it came an erosion of government authority, at least in the centralized, highly regimented form of the past. Judging from archaeological remains and descriptions in literature, Dark-Age Greece (i.e., 1100–800 B.C.) was vastly *under*populated. Society apparently was organized loosely through groups of household units (*oikoi*). Gradually in the general detritus re-tribalization occurred. Social and political authority was predicated on the possession of large herds, landed estates, and the ability to organize gangs of raiders and warring parties.[1]

There was also a tradition among the later Greeks that at various places these early clans monopolized power formally, claiming to be descendants of mythical kings, even though actual monarchy, in any regimented, centralized sense, was probably rare after the Mycenean collapse. Thus, near the end of the Dark Ages we hear of the Neleidai at Miletus on the coast of Asia Minor, the Bacchiads of Corinth at the isthmus of Greece. Similar aristocratic cabals sprung up in Ionia, the Aegean islands, and some mainland Greek city-states. Apparently, these powerful regimes of privilege slowly wrested authority from balkanized and petty Dark-Age fiefdoms until most of the Greek countryside was controlled by an elite land-owning nobility. I say "controlled," but it is a relative term; in no instance was Greek economic life now to be anywhere as structured as under the Mycenean palaces.[2]

Despite a surprising autonomy for serfs and slaves on isolated rural estates, these Dark-Age aristocracies still had not changed traditional land use and the centuries-old emphasis on livestock and horse breeding very much. Aristotle, at any rate, claimed knowledge about some of these few early aristocratic governments. He associated them with horse rearing, not intensive agricultural practice (e.g., the *Hippobotai* [horse breeders] at Chalcis and the *Hippotrophoi* [horse rearers] at Colophon). He also believed that hereditary aristocracy followed monarchy and was supported by elite cavalry rather than landed infantry. On the Aegean island of Samos, the *Geômoroi* ("land sharers") were apparently the aristocratic successors to an earlier quasi-monarchy. By the seventh century, the *Geômoroi* controlled much of the surrounding Samian countryside, operating larger estates, concerned with overseas trade, and raising horses.[3]

The end of earlier Mycenean culture (1200–1100 B.C.) is usually portrayed negatively by social, economic, and cultural historians. It is true that the impoverished period of the Dark Ages that followed left a far less impressive cultural record in Greece.* But the sudden destruction of the mainland Mycenean fortresses, *at least in agrarian terms*, was an important first advance for Greece, not a retrogression. Specialization and the subsequent frailty of the early Greek palatial kingdoms are textbook cases in the collapse of complex societies whose imperial directive and bureaucracy strangle agriculture, limiting its range of response and adaptability, drawing off its surplus for elite activities, which bring only marginal returns for the society as a whole.

The Mycenean bureaucracies apparently practiced collectivized agriculture under central control, the age-old anathema to productive agriculture. Such a system could never have led to the free farming of the *polis* era. Much of the land in Mycenean times had been allotted to local political and religious officials. They supervised vast herds of sheep, crop selection, and agricultural technique, closely monitoring returns, reim-

---

*"One of isolation, parochialism, and perhaps of unrest" (Coldstream 52); "a period of abundant land and very few people" (Donlan 1989: 134).

bursing seed, and bringing produce back up to the palace stores. True, there was a certain efficiency to such regimentation, but it was a redistributive system of both public and private landholding that ensured little agricultural innovation. Its rigorous complexity could not have allowed much for personal initiative, and thus maximum utilization of both human and natural resources. No city-state, no community of peers could have emerged out of that environment.[4]

The system was perhaps similar to the collectivized farm in modern authoritarian communist societies. Although some private land must have been outside of palace control, we can be sure the majority of crops was always in the hands of Mycenean overlords. Wealth was not widely distributed. Food production was tightly controlled. Social life was highly regimented. Those conditions of complexity made the entire system both resistant to needed reform and extremely vulnerable to outside challenge.

From our scanty sources—archaeological remains and the Linear B records—Mycenean viticulture and arboriculture were not advanced, in the sense that the range and number of *domesticated* species of fruit trees and olives were very limited. The total acreage devoted to successful vineyards and orchards of productive varieties was relatively small. Hence the harvests of these species must have been disappointing, given the equally low intensity of labor and productivity in only a moderately populated landscape.[5]

The collapse of these centralized palace economies in the twelfth century must in some sense have been inevitable. Given the stratification, the bureaucratization, and thus the vulnerability of Mycenean agriculture, the sudden decapitation of the agricultural managerial hierarchy, whether by natural or man-made agency, left many Mycenean farmers directionless. Outside forces may have caused the end of the Myceneans, but the innate complexity and fragility of a palatial society suddenly without directors certainly ensured a disorganized and feeble recovery.*

On a more mundane level, in the ensuing Greek chaos, rural people would simply have been left without stored food of their own. The palace had traditionally usurped most individual agricultural decision making, taking most food surpluses up to the citadel for storage. Even for those

---

*Tainter (10–11; 200–204) lists the usual cargo of these centralized regimes such as religious, governmental, and military bureaucracies which inevitably leads to stasis and a failure to adapt to changing stimuli.

farmers outside the direct control of the palatial economy, the citadel often served as a central collection depot of sorts, a "food bank," which received, stored, exchanged, and lent surplus crops and seeds, both locally and overseas. The net result of bureaucratization was as always the creation of vulnerable dependence and a restriction of agricultural expertise. Without the bureaucrats and the central directive, most farm workers probably floundered and starved until new expertise was acquired.*

Paradoxically, for all the ensuing human misery, the disruption and devastation of this "banking system" at the end of the twelfth century could in time facilitate real agricultural change. If Greek farmland was eventually allowed to fall into as many private hands as possible, and *if* farmers themselves could retain their own crop surpluses, people could quickly learn new potentialities for land use, novel methods of local food storage, and the grafting and propagation of an entire range of domesticated species of vines and olives. Dissemination of agricultural knowledge and expertise was practicable if—and only if—a large number of farmers gained title to their own pieces of ground, if they became freed from outside interference from the top. In the case of Greece, the process took nearly four hundred years.

No ingredient, I believe, is so dramatically successful in agriculture as free will, the ability to implement a new idea, to develop a proven routine, to learn once, not twice, from the hard taskmaster of error, to be left *alone* from government planning to grope for a plan of survival. Self-initiative, once turned loose on the soil, can result in spectacular results for both the farmer and the surrounding community. Never have I encountered a farmer who could believe long (and many have wished to, as I can attest) in big government, centralized control, benign bureaucracy.

In the context of early Greek history, it is just this liberation from a stifling and unimaginative officialdom, and the subsequent freedom of agriculture that as much as anything ensured the rise of the Greek *polis* and the beginning of Western civilization. Individualism in early Greek poetry and philosophy was simply the manifestation of an ongoing and radically new private approach to rural life, and farming in particular.

---

*The collapse of the Mycenean clearinghouse of food storage and exchange left them ignorant and without the skill to grow, process, and store food on their own. See Halstead (1992: 116) for the results of the disintegration of a centralized food banking system in the Aegean.

The decentralized Dark Ages were for all their impoverishment an important *first* occurrence. They were "dark" only in the sense of not well recorded; in agrarian terms the earlier Mycenean period had been the true dark age. But once Mycenean palace authority was done away with, there was a second opportunity for agrarian transformation *by the sheer process of neglect and unconcern*, should other critical factors— mainly population growth—ever come into play. The Dark-Age chieftain, in an environment where efficient land use was not necessary, seems to have been indifferent to agriculture. He was more intent on raiding by land and sea, and in acquiring large herds of cattle, sheep, goats, and pigs; if anything, he was more a thug than a bureaucrat.*

As in other societies where population density is low, community life embryonic, and the natural environment characterized by mountains adjoining plains, livestock and nomadic herding naturally spread in preference to intensive agriculture. As long as the population remained static and manageable, do not necessarily envision widespread impoverishment in Dark-Age Greece, which, after all, lasted for nearly four hundred years. The material record of the Dark Ages is bleak, but small communities probably for nearly three to four centuries attained a reasonable food supply from farming cereals on flat plains and concentrating on livestock.[6]

Under the Myceneans there must have been rigid protocols concerning the operation of "farms" that removed incentives for discovering new species or for mastering optimum methods of production not officially sanctioned. But in the subsequent Dark Ages it was mostly lack of interest, not bureaucratic conservatism and micro-management, that perpetuated agricultural stagnation. There is no evidence that Dark-Age hierarchy was ever as powerfully organized as Mycenean kingship.

---

*Thucydides (1.2.2) reflected the later Greeks' general supposition that the Dark Ages had been a time of pastoralism, not intensive agriculture and agrarian *poleis*: "There was no settled population. Instead migrations were common, the majority of tribes abandoning their homes under pressure from superior numbers. Since there was no trade or freedom of intercourse by either land or sea, since they cultivated no more land than what the bare necessities called for, and since they had no capital, they did not plant their land in permanent crops (*oude gên phuteuontes*)—for they could not know whether an enemy might invade and take the produce away. And since they believed that they could supply their needs at one place as well as another, they cared little whether they changed residence. Therefore they never established great cities nor achieved any other form of greatness."

Political control was established as an informal office among noble families, who owned title to mostly flat land, and who allowed serfs and the indentured to work out crop-sharing agreements.[7]

Both Mycenean and Dark-Age Greeks were relatively ignorant of intensive farming technique for entirely different reasons. Review of the Greek mythic tradition, pollen samples, and field surveys suggests that until the eighth century B.C. in Greece, there were mostly wild olives.* These trees produced erratically a poor quality of fruit with low oil content. Similarly, even species of productive grains were few. Wild vines also predominated.** While in appearance feral plant species may seem not much different from domesticated trees and vines, and while their pollen, pits, and leaves are often hard for the modern archaeologist to distinguish, for the farmer they were quite distinct. Wild varieties of trees and vines usually produce rank growth, smaller harvests, and poorer tasting fruit. Thus before the rise of the Greek *polis*, less prolific varieties of trees, vines, and cereals probably predominated over domesticated species.[8]

This absence of crop diversity reflected the timidity of past Mycenean agronomy and the preference in the subsequent Dark Ages of aristocratic nobles for horses and livestock, as well as their own relative ignorance of sophisticated agriculture. Both the domesticated olive and vine,*** like most fruit trees, were *not* easily propagated in the wild. They usually demanded skilled human agency (grafting, cultivation, irrigation of young plants, pruning, suckering) to be farmed on any successful scale in orchards and vineyards.[9]

A few domesticated species of olives and grapes had been known for some time in Mycenean and Dark-Age Greece. But these superior varieties apparently were not formally cultivated on a wide scale until the *polis* period. In that later era the more ubiquitous wild cultivars took on less and less agricultural importance, and probably themselves became genetically more similar to domesticated varieties. Quite simply, even the plentiful carbonized remains of olive woods and stones, the excava-

---

Olea europaea subsp. *oleaster; Olea europaea* subsp. *sylvestris;* Greek: *kotinos, phulia, agrielaia*

**Vitis vinifera* subsp. *sylvestris;* Greek: *agria.*

***Domesticated olive: *Olea europaea;* Greek: *elaia;* domesticated vine: *Vitis vinifera;* Greek: *ampelos*

tion of Bronze-Age presses, and the linguistic evidence of Linear B tablets from Minoan and Mycenean Crete are not proof of widespread cultivation of domesticated species of olives and vines. More likely they reflect efforts of the palaces in collecting the fruit of wild cultivars.[10]

One should never underestimate this importance of fruit and vine propagation for the surrounding agrarian economy. Even today the entire industry of modern fruit production rests on the grafting of new and existing tree and vine species and a thorough knowledge of rootstocks. Many productive tree and vine species cannot be reproduced, at least in their most productive state, by seedlings. Those offspring are weak or revert to a wild state. They require grafting of scions onto established (and often feral) rootstocks. They need far more attention than wild varieties to produce superior harvests.*

Although nearly all modern tree and vine growers are knowledgeable about grafting—the art is not currently licensed or regulated—the wholesale conversion or propagation of an entire orchard or vineyard is usually left to a small body of expert, professional grafters. Nothing is so discouraging, so costly, so embarrassing to the farmer—as I can unfortunately also confirm—as the failed efforts of an amateur grafter: the year-long spectacle of dead scions on freshly-cut stumps in a denuded orchard or vineyard.

If the host stump survives despite its now-dead scions, in a few weeks the wild rootstock sends out rank, bushy shoots and leaves, along with small, nearly inedible fruit. This regeneration only reemphasizes the farmer's abject—and quite visible—failure at propagation. In an exaggerated sense, the wild species is all root with no fruit, the domesticated all fruit with no root. The Greeks' successful combination of the two on a wide scale marks a veritable revolution in the production of food.

This general view of a renaissance in viticulture and arboriculture rather later in Hellenic history is markedly at odds with our traditional picture that olives, vines, fruit trees, and naked wheats were *always* a substantial part of the Greek agricultural landscape. Most scholars also

---

*In a more practical sense, most small farmers in my own area feel that the successful diversified producer nearly always has about ten percent of his acreage in some type of transitional phase. Normally an orchard or vineyard each year or so is grafted over to a more productive and successful variety, or in order to replace aging and sick stock, or correct past mistakes in species selection.

suggest that there was relatively little change in either agricultural technique or crop species from the Mycenean era until Hellenistic times. But keep in mind that domesticated species require greater knowledge and care to ensure successful propagation and continued production—an esoteric art that, like writing, was perhaps known to only a few Mycenean bureaucrats. Archaeologists and anthropologists confirm the Greek literary tradition that there was a gradual increase in domesticated tree, vine, and cereal species at the end of the Greek Dark Ages. Once propagation was mastered and the expertise gained to cultivate orchards and vineyards on a wide scale, innovative farmers increased the number of domesticated tree and vine species, and began to liberate agriculture. They found specialized varieties for particular locales, thus increasing the potential for viticulture and arboriculture as a whole in Greece.[11]

New crops like domesticated trees and vines and accompanying agricultural technique did not appear suddenly and without cause. The pressure of population, as we will see, forced an end to the traditional use of land. At the end of the Dark Ages growing numbers of Greek farmers must have changed the fundamental conditions of land tenure. Thus arose the *klêros*, or the idea of a privately held plot attached not to any one person, but rather in perpetuity to a single farm-family or *oikos*.*

Renters, serfs, indentured servants, or lessees cannot invest in capital crops such as trees or vines in any efficient manner. Nor will they take the considerable risks entailed in viticulture and arboriculture without clear title to the land they farm.** Farmers, especially planters of trees and vines, will soon demand to own their own land if they are to invest labor and capital in order to enrich the surrounding community. Once they own land, and plant permanent crops there, a transformation in both values and ideology ensues. But what were the more precise underlying conditions that first prompted these changes in ancient Greek agri-

---

*Pecírka 1968: 192. Cf. Meikle 67: "Each producer produced privately and on his own account, had private property in his product and marketed it. This had not been true of palace-based cultures of the earlier period."

**So, too, in the anthropologist's experience: "The conditions under which families obtain land for cultivation is also important in the way they use it. Landless farmers who have no security of rental can only plant annual crops. . . . Low productivity of land and resistance to agricultural improvements are linked to the very high rate of tenancy" (Barlett 555).

culture and property holding? What allowed entire Dark-Age patterns of land use to erode and the agrarian revolution of the *polis* to begin?

II. The Peopling of Greece

The breakdown of the Mycenean agricultural hierarchy and the indifference to farming shown by succeeding clans in the Dark Ages created an environment that might allow for family-owned and independent small farms. However, another catalyst was needed to ensure the spread of revolutionary privately held, intensively worked farms. A critical factor was the slow but steady rise in population in Greece at the end of the Dark Ages. It began in the early eighth century B.C., when demographic increases at certain brief periods may have approached two to three percent per annum.*

This development was not always a year-by-year steady population increase, but more likely cyclical: a few years of dramatic spurts in fertility, marked by decades of retrenchment, always varying from one Greek-speaking locale to another. Nevertheless, the overall picture in Greece from (say) the ninth century to the end of the eighth is clear enough: a far more densely populated Greece, and more important, a fairly consistent pattern of varying but sustained population increase throughout the life of the later *polis*. Sometimes this peopling occurred in resettled citadels, on other occasions in new city centers, small villages, and isolated sites.

The archaeological evidence suggests that in a variety of regions throughout Greece the vast open spaces of the Dark Ages—and the culture that operated in that landscape—were gradually disappearing. A dramatic rise in recorded settlements and individual burials has occurred in many widely diverse areas of Greece such as Messenia, Melos, Laconia, Attica, and the Argolid. The emergence of various local pottery styles also reflects the spread of independent communities. And steady popula-

---

*The argument for population growth at the end of the Dark Ages is now one only of degree. See Snodgrass 1977: 10–19; 1980: 20–24; 1983: 161–71; Bintliff and Snodgrass 139–41; cf. Morris: 1987:23, 57; Donlan 1989: 134. On theoretical variations in population expansion, see Grigg 1980: 282–95; Snodgrass 1990: 131–32.

tion increase must lie behind the generalized remarks in Greek literature concerning the formation of capital and the development of rural infrastructure in the early Greek countryside. By at least the late seventh or early sixth century, coinage appeared at various *poleis* in the Aegean, Ionia, and the general Greek Mediterranean, often with agricultural and plant motifs stamped on the bronze, silver, and gold tokens.[12]

But the critical question inevitably remains *why* population in Greece increased at all at this time, even if sporadically and cyclically at first. Did greater economic opportunity afforded by improved agricultural practices lead to bigger families? Or did *preexisting* trends for greater fertility *require* agricultural transformation?

In the case of Greece, like many other nonindustrial societies, population growth may have come first: it often initiates, drives, and maintains agricultural intensification. Growing numbers of people at the end of the Dark Ages simply needed to eat, and they found existing methods of food production completely inadequate. This demographic pressure forced radical changes in the way the Greeks farmed and had previously organized themselves in the countryside. After centuries of strict agronomic control, followed by the other extreme of relative agrarian neglect, agriculture in Greece was finally becoming the property of numerous individual and autonomous families.[13]

But *why* did the number of people in Greece begin to multiply during the latter Dark Ages, nearly four centuries after the fall of the palace economies? If greater fertility first forced agricultural change, what initially forced greater fertility? Some have recently suggested that Dark Age demography must be studied in relationship to "age-class" systems, or the regulations the elite clans of the Dark Ages used to discourage early marriage and procreation: either youths were regimented into relationships that did not lead to early procreation, or women avoided marriage altogether until far beyond the age of menarche. Supposedly, the delay in childbearing and the subsequent check on the Dark-Age population ensured (even if only unconsciously) greater control over their subjects for the few Greek aristocrats in power. Before having children, men first sought to accumulate a military reputation, wealth, and prestige in nonagricultural spheres. Marriage occurred relatively late. Women delayed childbearing. Thus family size was small. Such an age-

class culture, inherently part of a warrior society, unnecessarily prolonged a dramatic rebound from the chaos and collapse of the Mycenean centers.

At the end of the Dark Ages, the gradual modification and erosion of
such an intrinsically regimented (and hence fragile) "system" may have
led to social experimentation. Greeks no longer waited for the appropriate and agreed-on moment to marry, to raise and to limit families. Instead they sought power and influence through other mechanisms (the
size of their own households, the ability to raise private raiding parties,
the chance to travel)—all activities outside the traditional purview of
local strongmen. Fertility was seen as socially advantageous, not a drawback. Military regimentation gave way to other pursuits like agriculture.
Land in Greece usually used for stock or extensive agricultural practices
was unable to support growing populations, threatening not only the system of pastoralism, but the military hierarchy that sponsored inefficient
land use.[14]

Population pressure can be handled in a variety of ways. In the absence of an improvement in food supply or the widespread use of contra-
ceptive practices, famine and disease can simply eliminate the
population surplus. People then die, usually the very old and young. Yet
surprisingly we hear of little fatal hunger on any mass scale in early
Greece. Nor was there much wholesale conquest of foreign territory or
mass importation of foodstuffs from abroad.

Thucydides and other sources remind us that another option was colonization, the mass migration of landless Greek peoples to virgin territories, usually across the Mediterranean and Aegean. Although these
large scale emigrations indicate population problems at home, not *all*
colonization was undertaken by the very poor in search of new farmland,
the destitute who chafed at existing land tenure practices. At least some
settlers were relatively prosperous traders and merchants, or social opportunists and outcasts who desired a completely new economic and political environment.[15] These more upscale individuals could be as
desirous of change as the poor, if there was little opportunity for innovation in land use at home.

Much more important, those agrarians who left mainland Greece
often did so because of shared notions of the *new* role of agriculture.

Colonists were often not critics, but supporters of agrarianism; not the poor, but members of the lower middle class who saw little chance of obtaining a hereditary plot for themselves inside Greece.*

But had foreign colonization in and of itself immediately addressed the problem of surplus population in Greece, then the economy of the Dark Ages might have continued unchallenged. Any of the early hungry or disaffected could simply have fled his local environs, abandoning hope of feeding his family by making changes in the countryside of his birth, ensuring that no transformation of any note would have occurred in his homeland, guaranteeing that pastoralism and the rule of the localized clan would have continued uninterrupted. Colonization of the eighth and seventh centuries did *not* alleviate the need for local agricultural change, but rather was a symptom that *such transformation was already occurring in Greece proper.*

Population pressure can also trigger a different and potentially more volatile sort of colonization. I do not refer to the conquest and annexation of neighboring territory in mass—as in the case of the Spartan absorption of Messenia (a tactic that was more consistent with, than antithetical to, past Dark Age practice)—but rather a more gradual *internal* colonization of land previously unwanted and underdeveloped. This incorporation of new farmland was an earlier response to demographic pressure, one far more serious to the existing social order, since changes in economic and social practice took place at home and thus were bound to have immediate local repercussions. The seeds of local Greek agrarian transformation surely *antedated* overseas colonization.

Often in the eighth century many Greeks must have also turned to alternative types of land use in response to the growing numbers of farm laborers who were ill-served by past methods of utilization. As many more Greeks sought to feed their own households, the first option would have been to look for vacant lands—either communal or unowned—in their immediate vicinity. These plots were usually on somewhat "mar-

---

*Private ownership, the sanctity of the family estate, the need for increased food production to feed a growing population, all resulted in some family members sailing overseas to *replicate* the ideal size of the family farm they themselves did not inherit. Colonization often allowed the adherents, but not the immediate beneficiaries, of early Greek agrarian life to create abroad more perfect agricultural city-states *ex nihilo* (cf. Arist. *Pol.* 2.1266b1–3; Koerner 445–48)

ginal" lands. Given the nature of the Greek terrain and low density of the Hellenic population, new farmlands were thus to be found almost everywhere.

In the old Dark-Age social and economic sense, that meant less accessibility to manorial centers, and less fertility for native grazing, less suitability for easy ploughing of cereals, but not unsuitability for crops such as vines and trees. "Marginal" land (*eschatia*) is ubiquitous in many parts of Greece, an ideal, relatively safe springboard for anyone brave enough to embark on a new sort of agricultural strategy of outright private ownership and intensive working of permanent crops.[16] Once private ownership by adventurous farmers was the rule, each Greek rural household sought its own parcel, to improve and pass on.* Previously unused and unowned land was thus developed by men on their own, marking the real beginning in the West of individual property holding on any wide scale.

But this expansive process of Greek intensive agriculture did not cease at the mere incorporation of newer farm ground and novel concepts of land tenure. It assumed other equally dynamic forms as well. The other option of internal colonization, besides the cultivation and improvement of unfarmed ground, was simply to "colonize" someone else's land, to apply new strategies of intensive agriculture to previously farmed but *underused* land. That was, in practical terms, to engage in some sort of lease agreement with a wealthier Greek landowner, who initially had neither the desire nor expertise to farm the ground productively himself, but saw advantages in drawing off surpluses from the successful work of others. Whether Greek farmers (*geôrgoi*) first sought out marginal land, and then in the wake of success turned their attention to prized baronial estates, is unknown, but it seems a likely course of progression. For those Greeks who lacked capital or were unable to find underdeveloped land, and so entered into *unfavorable* rental agreements or other forms of early repressive tenancy, agricultural success was questionable from the start and was left unresolved for generations.

Slow and sporadic, rather than uniformly gradual, rises in Greek population then created pressures on Dark-Age society and revealed the in-

---

*The *oikos* now attached itself in perpetuity to a family plot, the *klêros*; see Donlan 1989: 134–36.

efficiency of traditional land use. Because there was not a sophisticated central political organization, a majority of *geôrgoi* gradually drifted away from past protocols, becoming relatively "liberated." They could now see that pastoralism was *not* a solution to the problem of feeding additional mouths. Crops alone, not animals, could feed the greater population. Because the aristocratic landholders may have been uninterested at first in agricultural innovation, the young, disaffected elite—and perhaps later the more ambitious on the lower end of the Dark-Age social scale—were prone to deviate from the traditional social patterns and military castes. One result was encroachment on marginal ground without fear of reprisal. For many aspiring farmers this must have been a preferable alternative to moving in mass across the sea.

Population increase, however, alone did not end the Dark Ages. The neglect of farming by the old elite and the presence of unused open ground cannot entirely explain the Greek agrarian renaissance of the eighth century and later. There was no guarantee that the population might not regress into past cycles of decline, as local food production failed to match population growth. Thus one or more of the following must also have taken place: (1) a quiet revolution in agricultural technique and rural social organization in general, (2) an incorporation of new technologies and crop species, (3) an intensification of labor, or (4)—perhaps most likely—*all three* factors, which could coalesce to increase food production, and hence provide the prosperity needed to ensure that a new economic class, the independent small farmer, would be a permanent, rather than transitory, fixture on the Greek landscape.

III. The End of the Dark Ages

In characteristically Greek fashion, there was a critical adoption of foreign knowledge in a uniquely ingenious manner. Improved species of olives, grains, and cereals, along with completely novel crops, were borrowed from Asia Minor which had a rich and old tradition of intensive viticulture and arboriculture.[17] In the different environment of Greece, these species were farmed in new, more productive ways. Permanent crops and diverse types of cereals can increase production remarkably under intensive cultivation—labor, both free and increasingly slave, at this juncture must have been plentiful for the first time in Greek history—and they could be uniquely integrated to fit available soil and manpower conditions.

As we will see below, olives and vines are fertile even on rocky hillsides, where cultivation with the plough is impossible or difficult. Neither requires the moisture or fertility of bottom land to produce adequate crops; the richer ground, like the more accessible and better terraced parcels, can be reserved for barley and wheat. The triad—cereals, vines, olives—intensively farmed can provide an entire diet and produce storable crops for times of scarcity. At the beginning of the eighth century the Greeks discovered how to cultivate the domesticated olive on a wide scale, along with other trees and vines, and mastered the techniques of easy propagation such as grafting. That knowledge allowed for a lasting alternative to pastoralism.

Any farmer who plants trees and vines, unlike the pastoralist or even the grain grower, invests his labor and capital in a particular locale *for the duration of his life.* In this interdependent relationship, the cultivator's presence and commitment to a stationary residence ensure that the young orchard and vineyard will be cared for and become permanent fixtures on the landscape. People who choose this form of agriculture have confidence that they can and will stay put, that they can and will keep the countryside populated, prosperous, and peaceful. They are not just a different sort of farmer, but a different sort of person as well. The Greeks understood this. No wonder Thucydides associated the pre-*polis* Greeks' inability to settle in one place with their reluctance to plant trees and vines, all characteristic of unsettled times when there were no "large cities or any other form of greatness." No wonder later during the *polis*, Greek cultural historians themselves envisioned a clear sequence of their early Hellenic state development: primitive and random food-gathering, followed by herding, and culminating in a dynamic agriculture of "the plough, the grafting of trees, and the extension of land under cultivation."[18]

At the beginning of the *polis*-period increasing tension grew between livestock men and the less affluent (see *Chapter Three*). Sheep and goats gradually lost pasturage to cultivated land. More and more people homesteaded small plots. Intensive agriculture also meant a loss of political control and social prestige for the old Dark-Age clique and a greater dispersion of wealth among the populace. The process enriched the rural culture of Greece as a whole.*

The end of the Greek Dark Ages was a rare time in history. A period of fluidity in, and opportunity for, land ownership, it was an era where competence and work, not mere inherited wealth and birth, might now become criteria for economic success.

In a political sense, the innate conservatism that derives from the patience, worry, and waiting that cultivating the soil demands was not manifested as knee-jerk rejectionism and reactionism—at least not in the early struggle for agrarianism. After all, farmers themselves knew the value of banding together to preserve their own hard-won gains against the wealthy in a no-nonsense pragmatism that in every early timocratic agricultural city-state checked radicalism and, eventually, the excesses of both aristocracy and democracy. Here, the widespread propagation for the first time in Greek history of *permanent crops*—trees and vines— seems to me every bit as significant as the more heralded intellectual, social, and military renaissance of the Greek eighth and seventh centuries. The spread of grafting and budding, which so helped to tie the new Greek tree and vine farmer to the soil—was as important as the rediscovery of writing and the rise of philosophical speculation.

Do not arboriculture and viticulture also become diagnostic criteria of a farmer's success over an entire lifetime of work? Trees and vines are to be passed down to children and grandchildren. They force the agriculturalist to invest for the future, rather than for the current year alone. They harness him bodily to his orchard and vineyard, changing his way of thinking from mere production to stewardship of a lifetime's investment. Mistakes cannot simply be ploughed away in the fall. They cannot be replaced by a fresh animal. Bare land under annual cultivation or public grazing ground, in contrast, is in a sense mute. It is un-

---

*John Davis wrote of a similar friction between intensive agriculture and the anti-agrarian mentality of a few entrenched elites during the Ottoman occupation of Greece (1991: 199): "Control of the local economy by a minority of the population may, it could be argued, have been the most significant factor inhibiting rural settlement where agricultural goals have not necessitated increased productivity of subsistence crops."

changing, and unreflective of the generations who have staked their lives to its working.*

In a military sense, as we will soon see, there is little doubt that the superiority of Greek citizen infantry, the "planters of trees," in wars both foreign and domestic derived from the resoluteness, conservatism, independence, and physical courage prerequisite to the intensive farming of trees and vines, the need to protect and to honor the *visible* inherited vineyards and orchards of past generations. Aristotle saw a vast difference between such men and hired mercenaries: "Professional infantry turn out to be cowards whenever the danger proves too much and whenever they are at a disadvantage in their numbers and equipment. They are, then, the first to run away, while the militias of the *polis* stand their ground and die *(ta de politika menonta apothnêskei)*" (Arist. *Eth. Nic.* 3.116b19).

A variety of conditions—increasing population, lackadaisical political authority, available land and labor (both servile and free), new crops and rural strategies—were operating in Greece during the latter centuries of the Dark Ages. They were all conducive to fundamental changes in agriculture. An increase in population created pressures on land use. This peopling of Greece brought into question the wisdom of livestock raising on a wide scale. The challenged aristocratic elite who controlled the "economy" at first would have been unenthusiastic about experimenting in intensive agriculture. Wealthy barons had a long cultural tradition that stressed cattle, pigs, sheep, goats, and horses, and so they would have exhibited disdain (but also fear) for the toiler in the fields. Much land with productive potential was simply underused or even unowned in Greece, the population heretofore seeing little need or value in developing it agriculturally.

Now began the *slow* spread of improved and novel domesticated plant species that could be grown in a variety of climates, bringing in an entirely new approach to farming, whose unique properties could ensure the farmer independence and survival. Once the new agrarianism

---

*"Stable, settled populations, assured both of an economic sufficiency in return for their work and of the cultural value of their work, tend to have methods and attitudes of a much longer range. Though they have generally also farmed with field crops, established farm populations have always been *planters of trees*" (Berry 135; emphasis added).

caught on, the control of farming was gradually dispersed into too many hands ever to revert back to either the agricultural fragility of palace bureaucracies or the subsequent neglect of Dark-Age manorial clans.

In that sense, all of Greek history in the *polis* period follows from the successful creation of a new agriculture and the efforts of the many to protect a novel agrarian way of life. The rural system of the *geôrgoi* created the surplus, capital, and leisure that lay behind the entire Greek cultural renaissance. It was an agrarianism that was highly flexible and decentralized economically, socially egalitarian, and politically keen to avoid the accumulation of power by a nonagricultural elite. No surprise that the later *polis* Greeks envisioned the rise of agrarianism—which had created their city-state—primarily in moral terms.*

For the real evidence of this new class of agriculturalists, we must look in more detail to the earliest Greek literature of the late eighth and early seventh century. The story of the farmers' slow emergence from the centuries of the Dark Ages need not be a dry demographic and agronomic recital. Rather, it can provide a glimpse of how men set themselves against nature in a heroic effort to create an entirely new society in their own image.

---

*"The whole course of development seems to follow a preconceived pattern. Food gathering, pasturing, and agriculture succeed each other because each one represents a stage of development which is, in some sense, more advanced (or more degenerate) than its predecessor" (Cole 55).

Chapter 2

LAERTES' FARM

The Rise of Intensive Greek Agriculture

> The others went from the city, and presently
> came to the country place of Laertes, handsomely
> cultivated. Laertes himself had reclaimed it,
> after he spent much labor upon it. There
> was his house and all around the house
> ran a shelter, in which the slaves, who worked
> at his pleasure under compulsion, would take
> their meals, and sit, and pass the night.
> —Homer, *Odyssey* 24.205–212

I. Who Was Laertes?

To meet population pressure within Greece, cumulating at crisis levels during the eighth century, more land had to be put into agricultural production. Or existing land had to be used more productively. Or more and better agriculture were needed. That third alternative is exactly what we see in the twenty-fourth book of Homer's *Odyssey*, in a human picture of men at work in the soil.

In these few lines of the last book of the *Odyssey* a vibrant rural life comes alive, centered on an efficient household's intensive cultivation of the soil. The hero Odysseus, after his butchery of the suitors, leaves

47

his palace at Ithaca to hike out to the farm of his father, Laertes. The aged Laertes had long ago left Ithaca proper in disgust at the suitors' appropriation of his son's royal residence, and for the past two decades has been able to do little more than survive in rural exile on his own. From Homer's description it appears that Laertes' small farm—long sought out by romantic archaeologists, improperly labeled a "garden" by literary critics*—is some distance from Ithaca and located in rough terrain (24.212). Once in the countryside, Homer presents a brief but fascinating look at a world quite unlike the life in Odysseus's royal halls. There are no references to feasting, gaming, and the acquisitive arts of plundering, raiding, and thievery, which had characterized so much of the lazy suitors' life in the banquet hall while the master was away.

The different mood out on the farm is not to be attributed merely to the abrupt change of scene from the leisurely, aristocratic pace of palace life. The sharp demarcation between master and slave in the poem is also gone: Laertes works beside his servants at menial tasks. Apparently work is something to be honored, not despised. Homer terms the property "handsomely cultivated," a plot that the pioneer Laertes had created after investing "much labor" (24.205–207). His ground apparently was *not* inherited, or at least not inherited in its present state as developed farmland.

Laertes' farm and indeed Laertes himself are something entirely different from past agricultural practice. Is it not possible to see in them elements of a novel agriculture quite at odds with what many scholars have called "peasant" or "subsistence" farming, or, on the opposite end of the social scale, "manorial," "absentee," or "estate" agriculture? Even at this early date, at the beginning of the seventh century, farming scarcely resembles at all the traditional scholarly portraits of "peasant" Greek agriculture revolving around nucleated residence, underemployment, and an absence of rural infrastructure.** Because Laertes' farm reflects an agriculture crystallizing at roughly the same time as the ap-

---

*Ferriolo 86–88; numbers in parentheses in the text in this chapter refer to book number and line of Homer's *Odyssey*.

**This conventional view in large part explains why agriculture was rarely seen as the catalyst for the Greek renaissance; see Audring 1974b: 495–96; Wood 51–63; Ehrenberg 1951: 78–91; Bolkestein 19–21. Cf. Richter 12 for a discussion of labor required on Laertes' farm. "Homer's Laertes," as Gustave Glotz saw long ago (1927: 64), "was a forerunner of things to come."

pearance of the Greek city-state, the relationship between the two phenomena—farming and the subsequent culture of the *polis*—demands
close scrutiny. Odysseus's brief walk from palace out to farm is therefore
a radical passage from the Dark-Age cloister of the aristocratic hall into
the new world of the intensive *geôrgos.*

Consequently, Laertes was *not* a single, historical figure. He seems
rather a representation of an entire class of new farmers—a vivid example of those anonymous men of the last chapter who ended the Dark
Ages. Of course, historical representation in both of Homer's two surviving epics, the *Iliad* and *Odyssey,* as was discussed earlier, is difficult to
unravel and subject to constant scholarly reappraisal.* Nevertheless,
Laertes' farm provides a valuable snapshot, a brief hiatus from the epic
pageantry of the poem. It most likely reflects modes of farming contemporary with Homer's own life—that is, the era roughly around 700 B.C.
The late eighth-century environment of the *Odyssey* is especially prevalent in Book Twenty-four of the poem, since the narrative here is pragmatic and clearly deals with common, everyday things in the life of an
elderly Greek. The scene is quite devoid, in other words, of the less historical and utterly fantastic world of the epic. Gods, monsters, and feats
of superhuman heroism are for a time absent.[1]

We must remember also that the *Odyssey* is a literary document. It is
not history. Homer wrote poetry, not agronomy. The reason for this dramatic change of scene is not to portray the land, but rather its owner,
Laertes, who is first and fundamentally a *literary* character. Dramatic and
narrative necessity apparently requires in these closing lines that the
dead suitors remain unavenged, and that Laertes have an emotional
recognition scene with the son who had been lost for twenty years.
Homestead residence, the slave work force, diversified crops, the isolated location, rough terrain, and the apparent small size of Laertes' farm

---

*Mycenean (1600–1150 B.C.), Dark Age (1000–750 B.C.), and early "Archaic" (750–700 B.C.) histo-
rians at different times all draw on the poems (about 700 B.C.) for their own particular historical
needs. Material from all three different ages does reside in Homeric epic. Nevertheless, recent attempts to ground much of the *Iliad* and the *Odyssey* in the second half of the eighth century seem
reasonable, as long as one acknowledges the common presence of epic inflation, anachronism, and
distortion over some four or five centuries of oral transmission, and as long as one keeps in mind
that to an audience of epic poems, especially one composed of aristocrats, exaggeration of past elite
custom is more entertaining than the stark reality of the more pedestrian present.

are not critical to the narrative of the poem as a whole. These agricultural descriptions are valuable only to the degree that they add detail, and thus aid Homer's efforts to portray Laertes as isolated, hardworking, grim, and in the company of rustics and slaves.

In other words, the poet contrasts Laertes as much as possible with the luxury of the suitors in the palace below, the old world that, in the absence of his son, he has apparently lost. To describe this new life of hard, agricultural work requires Homer (or whoever wrote this passage) to draw on an environment completely familiar to him and to his audience as well. In all probability the poet adopted the characteristics of a class of intensive agriculturalists, a trailblazing group confined neither to Ithaca, the scene of the *Odyssey*, nor to Ionia, Homer's own purported home. The poet's artistic purposes are to make Laertes a believable "farmer"—pitied, if not scorned, by the traditional more pastoral elites who lounged in Ithaca below.[2] By design, the unenviable life of the intensive farmer would also invoke sympathy and condescension, not admiration, from Homer's own contemporary aristocratic and reactionary audience of upscale urban dwellers, listeners who themselves would have no desire to carve out new ground, to farm on their knees.

Laertes' farm reveals at least *six* peculiarities of intensive agriculture that can explain why such late eighth-century operations were becoming more productive and more successful than past farming practice at any prior time in Greek history. Laertes' plot, then, serves as a prototype by which later to distinguish intensive agriculture from other farming strategies. It is my belief that the following characteristics of Laertes' farm, like the type of agriculture described in Hesiod's *Works and Days* (Chapter 3), were all relatively unknown in the period before the eighth century, but quite common farming practices of the next four centuries of *polis* life. They were responsible for the increased capital and leisure fundamental to the culture of the Greek city-state. In sum, the emergence of the new agrarian practices described here—homestead residence, irrigation, slave labor, diversified crops, the incorporation of marginal ground, localized food processing and storage—has been largely unknown or underappreciated by ancient historians, and so the accomplishments of these farmers have never been central to, or even included in, the standard accounts of Greek history.

II. Increasing Productivity

It is striking that Laertes has built himself a permanent residence on his farm, an *oikos* that Homer calls "comfortable" and "well-furnished." A farmhouse is thus clear from the context. Homer is quite unambiguous about that. Laertes' residence is a building clearly isolated and apart from others.[3] It is a permanent residence and it is owner-occupied.

But for most of the history of classical scholarship it was axiomatic that ancient Greek farmers, both rich and poor, in *all* eras of Greek history, commuted to work from the neighboring village, there being, in this view, no permanent housing on the farm itself. Most Americans who have grown up with the image of the family farmhouse, barn, and assorted pens, fences, silos, and other outbuildings would find this image startling, if not confusing. Scholars are correct to warn us about our modern prejudices, our ignorance of the peculiar environmental, economical, and cultural predilections of the ancient Greeks. They attribute the absence of isolated farmhouses in antiquity to scarcities of water in the arid Greek countryside, to worries about theft, the organized raiding party, or the full-fledged enemy invasion, to the underemployment of nonirrigated "extensive" agricultural practice, and to the social desirability of living in communal villages.[4]

All these factors are cited to explain why a farmer would be willing to walk hours each day out to his fields. In our *first* recorded picture of a Greek farm, however, the literary evidence shows that the owner is not a commuter. Homer's Laertes is obviously living right amidst the fields he works. This passage long ago should have given rise to doubts about the traditional picture of farmer residence in town. In fact, traditional objections can be turned on their heads: it is the need to protect the rural infrastructure, the necessity for constant labor, the importance of water and small-scale irrigation projects, and the desire for a new rural identity—all characteristic of Greek agriculture after the Dark Ages—that actually argue for the notion of scattered homestead farmhouses.

Since the 1940s a number of country residences have been excavated in rural Attica surrounding Athens. John Young, for example, in brilliant research after World War II, found a complex of farm "towers" (*purgoi*) in southern Attica, most of which he convincingly associated with ancient farms. He also spotted some sixty-one similar extant structures elsewhere in the Greek countryside, suggesting that these towers illustrated rural residence—not military garrisons or mining facilities, but farmhouses whose stoutness could provide both protection and safe storage for harvested crops. A few years later, a team of British and American archaeologists excavated in Attica two substantial farmhouses on the slopes of Mt. Parnes, and later at Vari south of Athens. Since then the remains of other ancient farmhouses in Attica have turned up with increasing frequency. In the environs of Athens, the picture of a settled countryside has thus become clearer.[5]

This archaeological record of preserved farm sites makes perfect sense if one keeps in mind a literary tradition that early on the Athenians, like Laertes at Ithaca, lived "dispersed" throughout the countryside. Later there was also the tradition that the Athenians had lived scattered "all over Attica." That picture of farmstead residence may have been just what Aristotle had in mind in his *Politics* when he wrote that in "early times the city-states were not large, but rather the common people lived on their farms (*epi tôn agrôn*) busily engaged in agriculture."[6]

Other literary evidence confirms the view that people often lived on the plots they worked, and that Homer's Laertes was representative of a growing custom of homestead residence. In the Athenian orators of the fourth century, we often hear of rivalries among unruly rural neighbors over property boundaries, or disputes between descendants over the family land and house. The Greek historians also write of invasions that catch sizable numbers of farmers unawares out on their plots—families who clearly live in their country residences full-time. These are *geôrgoi*, who apparently feel that it is crucial to maintain their rural residence, despite the threat of war and the protection that the nearby village might offer.[7]

In drama there are portraits of hardworking farmers, who like Laertes live permanently in isolated residences that are clearly at a distance from town. The rural homestead farmers in Euripides' *Electra* and Menander's *Dyscolus* and *Geôrgos* both show that the phenomenon is not restricted to any one era or locale during the *polis* period, but characteristic of city-state culture in general. The Aristotelian *Oeconomica*, no doubt, is thinking of homestead residence in its advice to build a house with ample consideration for food storage, both dry and moist crops, and shelter for livestock and slaves.[8]

Throughout nearly every region in Greece including Attica, Boeotia, the Crimea, the Argolid, Ionia, the Peloponnese, southern Italy and Sicily, and the Aegean islands homestead farmhouses were a significant part of the ancient Greek landscape, as their first appearance here in Greek literature suggests. Recent survey work in Boeotia has speculated that there could have been 10,000 rural "sites," a countryside teeming with small farmers. Perhaps it is an indication too that many of the feared Boeotian hoplite infantrymen of antiquity (modern estimates independently peg their numbers at about ten to twelve thousand) resided on the land they farmed. In this instance, perhaps sixty percent of all the Boeotians lived *outside* Thebes and its small satellite villages of the Boeotian confederacy.[9]

But why and how was farm residence integral to Greek intensive agriculture and the rise of *polis* agrarianism? In short, why did Laertes, and the new farmers like him who emerged from the Dark Ages, frequently choose now to live on the land they worked?

First and foremost, one might say that a farmhouse illustrates an effort on the farmer's part to enhance and protect his property. Therefore, these residences must have been a reflection of the growth of private property and individual control over agriculture. The regular commute—in this case measured by the walk of Odysseus from the palace at Ithaca—which is a frequent agricultural phenomenon in both medieval and modern Greece, costs the new intensive farmer too much precious time.

Similarly, on the Aegean island of Melos survey archaeologists found that modern Greek farmers averaged a mean time of two hours fifty-five minutes traveling to work each day. That subsequent loss in farming productivity explains why governments have sometimes attempted to force farmers to live in homestead residences as part of a concerted effort to increase overall agricultural efficiency, and why typically sheds and barns often accompany houses. Kenneth Thompson reported that many modern Greek farmers claimed three weeks lost per year in simply walking to their disparate fields. One farmer spent almost five hours a day in commute time, sometimes simply to do a fifteen-minute operation on his distant plot. Another agrarian apparently traveled five thousand kilometers in a year to and from his farm.*

Clearly, fragmented holdings are often associated with nucleated settlement; farmsteads, in contrast, often illustrate consolidated farms. Similarly, Robert Weaver noted that he "rode a donkey from a village in the Vostizza (northern Peloponnese) for 30 or 40 minutes up steep slopes, with the grower, to a vineyard property of only one-fourth acre"—a common enough sight to anyone who has traveled through the countryside of modern Greece. It is my belief that precisely the *opposite* situation more often prevailed in many regions of Greece during the period of the *polis,* when agrarian necessity was a completely different notion from that of either Dark-Age or contemporary Greece. Commuting over some distance was not the price of social acceptance, but antithetical to the social, political, and economic environment of intensive agriculture—and the growing agrarian chauvinism of the Greek *polis* itself.[10]

This may be the moment to observe that analogies with modern Greek agricultural practice (in this case, the frequent absence of farmhouses), although certainly valuable for an understanding of ancient Greek agrarianism, are not always a reliable guide to every aspect of past farming strategies.** Hellenistic, Roman, Byzantine, Turkish, and modern Greeks *after* the *polis* period may well have farmed more extensively than their more ancient counterparts, commuted more, and had more fragmented landholdings than their modern descendants. Indeed, we will show that the eventual erosion of the *polis* period was the direct result of a decline of agrarian values and practices such as intensified labor, diversified crops, and farm residence.

With intensive farming, there is often a variety of crops. Little slack time exists to allow the farmer either to stay some days in the village, or

---

*Thompson concluded: "As long as his farm is fragmented, an individual farmer will only rarely be able to select a substantially more convenient house-site from the components of his divided holdings than the present village site offers. Regret at the inability to build a house on the family property was, it might be noted, frequently voiced" (210).

**"The rigid organization . . . of Greece today, where everyone lives in a village, in an otherwise empty countryside," Oliver Rackman (1990: 102–3) has correctly observed, "would have been unusual. More typically there would have been tracts of villages, tracts of hamlets, single farms, and occasional small towns"; see Hanson 1983: 40–42.

to invest hours each day in commuting time. Laertes and his slave workers, then, must sleep and eat amid their fields, not walk up each day from the palace at Ithaca. Residential buildings in themselves become proof of intensification. The more valuable farm plots in antiquity seem to have been either near the city-state walls, or those with homes and other buildings.

Clearly, the presence of a farmhouse reflects greater investment in the agricultural infrastructure of Laertes' farm—fruit trees, vines, vineyard stakes, pens, outbuildings, livestock, and slaves. Laertes needed close supervision to ensure against damage, theft, or vandalism from both men and animals. Capital crops such as trees and vines demanded constant attention when planted, protection against browsing animals, extra irrigation and fertilization. In addition to the construction of costly fencing, this frequently required the agriculturalist to spend the evenings, nights, and early mornings on the farm. These circumstances explain why the poor Plataeans were on their farms on the spring night in 431 B.C. when the Thebans invaded their village and countryside.[11]

Besides the demands of intensive farm work and the need for property protection, farm residence also reflects a growing ideology of "aloofness" and "quietism," of an "apartness in the fields." After all, ancient agricultural custom is not exclusively economically oriented. The homesteader, unlike the modern villagers of Melos, deliberately sacrifices the social "advantages" of communal living in favor of a new identification with agrarian life in general and his own farm in particular. Indeed, the permanent creation of houses on the land may itself explain the independent nature of the Greek city-state, which in its origin was more a forum than a home—really no more than a point of assembly where the larger community of outlying farmers could gather to exchange produce and to craft legislation or deliberate on other crucial matters. It is therefore not surprising if independent and strong-willed hoplite-farmers fashioned a separate existence beyond the confines of the city and its mores.

Significantly, Odysseus is struck by Laertes' seeming indifference to his shabby appearance—rough tunic, patched and ugly, ox-hide leggings, gloves to prevent scratching, and goatskin cap—garb that would likely draw rebuke if the old man had lived in or commuted to his farm from

Ithaca.[12] Laertes' appearance actually moves his son to tears! Odysseus emphasizes the assumed loss of social prestige that accompanies his solitary, work-filled existence.

> Old sir, there is in you no lack of expertness in tending
> your orchard; everything is well cared for and there is never
> a plant, neither fig tree nor grapevine nor olive
> nor pear tree nor leek bed uncared for in your garden
> But I will also tell you this; do not take it as cause for
> anger. You yourself are ill-cared for; together with dismal
> old age, which is yours, you are squalid and wear foul
> clothing upon you.
> —(24.244–50)

Much earlier, in Book One of the poem, Athena, disguised as the old Mentes, had said nearly the same thing.

> Laertes, who, they say no longer comes to the city
> now, but away by himself on his own land leads a hard life
> with an old woman to look after him, who serves him his victuals
> and drink, at times when weariness has befallen his body
> from making his toilsome way on the high ground of his vineyard.
> —(1.189–93)

Strikingly, though, there are few signs of disillusionment or disenchantment on Laertes' part toward his own circumstances, and little hint of a longing for city life. Laertes does recognize the problems of old age and the crisis at the palace below. While like Penelope he waits dutifully for the return of Odysseus, he does not share others' general revulsion for hard farm work and an isolated existence expressed elsewhere in the *Odyssey*.

Later in our sources—comedy especially—there is ample reference to these physical differences between the city dweller (*asteios*) and the agrarian (*agroikos*).* Most scholars suggest that this contrast is largely a product of comic distortion or exaggeration, rooted in the political gulf

---

*The country bumpkin is usually poorly groomed, smelly, and without decorum, oblivious to fashion and propriety, e.g., Alciphr. 3.29; Theophr *Char.* 4; Ar. *Pax* 1127–1210; *Nub.* 41 ff.; cf. Val. Max. 7.5.2; Sappho 57.

between rural conservatives and urban progressives at Athens during the fifth century.[13] But the contrast is too frequently drawn and too vivid to be anything but a reflection of real differences between those who live permanently out on homestead farms and those of a different stripe who reside and work in town to serve the needs of the largely agrarian population. Aristotle at any rate thought (perhaps wrongly) that the entire genre of Greek comedy arose out of an *agrarian* practice. Farmers, Aristotle believed, originally had ventured into town (*kômê*) at night to shout at and ridicule wealthier urban elites whom they felt to be oppressive and threatening. Attic comedy, in this view, was thus a ritualized version of these impromptu outbursts.[14]

Allusions to rural folk in literature go beyond puns and ridicule of dress, body odor, and the general uncouthness of rustics. From the opposite (and less often heard) agrarian point of view, there is sometimes a substantial hostility to city life and its attendant sophistication. An even sharper attitude arose in fifth-century Greece, which reemphasized the old disdain for the "social desirability" of living in town, suggesting to many farmers that urban life had moved too far beyond the original idea of the *polis* as a place to determine the economic and political agenda of surrounding property owners, and where the minority of city folk were directly involved in serving the needs of the rural majority.

This attitude is captured in Aristophanes' lost *Geôrgoi*, where a farmer—obviously no impoverished cashless peasant, nor a wealthy estate owner eager for political recognition—offers a politician a thousand drachmas if he can escape public service which would require his presence in town. During the brief invasions of the Archidamian War (431–425 B.C.), "back to the farm" becomes almost a cry of agrarian solidarity for Attic farmers cooped up in Athens. Despite agrarians' belief that those in town were shown preference, Aristotle assumed that farmers even during his own time generally did not attend the assembly unless absolutely necessary—a practice which was even more likely in the seventh through early fifth centuries.[15]

Elsewhere in Greek literature, we hear also that farmers were too busy to come into town for political gatherings. Some country dwellers rarely, if ever, had any desire to walk into the *polis*. Indeed, there was a remarkable tradition of sorts that a great many residents of Attica *never went into Athens at all*.[16] Alciphron, whose work is a vast repository of anecdotal scraps from past Greek and Roman literature, knew of a story (of un-certain date) about a young man who tried to convince his mother to venture into Athens to view its wondrous sights before she died: "Moth-er, leave the country and the rough ground for a little while, and take a look at the fine sights of the city. . . . Come, do not delay . . . may it never happen that you should leave this life without having had a taste of the city" (3.39). In another letter, the young rustic is made to say: "I don't even know what this so-called *polis* is like. So I'm eager to see this new sight—that is men living inside a wall—and to learn how a *polis* is different from country life" (Alciphr. 3.31). A near-identical tale is asso-ciated with Aesop, who supposedly began one of his allegories with the story of an old farmer who wished to see the city for the first time before he died (*Vit. Aesop* 1.140.2; 2.140.3).

Polybius, in an extreme case, claimed that the farmers at Elis had not entered town for two to three generations. More plausible was Isocrates' nostalgic account of traditional agrarian Attica, when fine country resi-dences allowed "many of the residents never to venture into Athens, even for festivals." Utopian assertions in reactionary fourth-century philosophical literature that citizens maintain residences both in town and out in the country were likewise responses to the growing split be-tween homesteaders and the urban landless.[17]

I will suggest later (Chapter 9) that the rise of rural chauvinism had critical implications for the future of the Greek city-state. For more than two centuries small farmers had fostered a stable, thriving egalitarian-ism, but in the process they also added a strong, often strident moral and ethical element to the market thinking of the *polis*. As fifth- and fourth-century Greece became more involved in the wider life of the Mediter-ranean, its indigenous "planters of trees" grew even more reactionary, more hostile to capital formation and the growth of commercial wealth in the city, which provided the incomes necessary for the expanding nonagricultural segment of the population. In short, the *geôrgoi* eventu-ally lost the *polis* which had been their own creation; and it became not a proud display of agrarian dynamism and agricultural cohesion, but a home to nonagrarian outsiders and a haunt of the elite.

By the fourth century that centuries-old symbiosis—especially at Athens—between the *polis* and the distinctive homestead farmer was, in the wake of growing urbanization and population growth, becoming more complex. At the end of the *polis* period, farm living in Greece was clearly on the decline. No wonder a kindred motif in literature is the stock complaint against the corrupting influences of the city, for often we are told that farmers must be careful not to become "hooked" on urban excitement during their brief visits. Young men were especially prone to corruption and could often come home forever ruined for farm work: they were advised to "stay out at work on the farm, for that way your hard work will result in a full grain-bin, wine-jugs overflowing with wine, and the storehouse full of all good things" (Alciphr. 3.14; 3.25, 40).

The stubbornness and self-reliance of rural residents so frequently parodied by Aristophanes is also a direct result of homestead life and a part of the distinctive agrarian character profile. "The true farmer," Plutarch says, "doesn't even wish to hear news from the city that has made its own way to the country." He adds that the "busybody" (*polypragmôn*), the scourge of Greek literature, "rarely goes out to the farmland, since he can't take the quiet and solitude of being by himself." People in town had even begun to talk differently, more effeminately than their masculine counterparts in the countryside.

From isolated residence the very independence of the Greek character itself must have originated. Perhaps the best evidence of the rural pride of these new farmers is found in the right-wing verse of Theognis, an urban poet of the mid-sixth century who complained bitterly about the "leather-wearing men who circle the city like pasturing deer" (frs. 54–57). That image of Laertes' descendants, the hide-clothed farmers with their leather hats and work capes who set themselves off from the smaller urban populace is commonplace in poetry and prose, cropping up in nearly every genre of Greek literature as men who are deeply suspicious of urban life or a commercial existence on the sea.[18]

The rise of the intensive-working *geôrgoi* did not mean a complete end to farmers' residence in nucleated settlements. Many Greeks still lived in small hamlets, villages, and in more formal small and big *poleis*. Instead, the steady growth of farmhouses marked the beginning of the end of the Dark Ages, an undeniable break with an earlier time when nearly the entire countryside was empty of homestead farmers.[19]

Some Greeks, it is true, were still completely divorced from agriculture and without title to land. There were other numerous poor of the city-state who worked extremely small plots, and an old entrenched aristocracy continued to own bottom land near the *polis* walls. All of these could reside in small nucleated clusters, rural towns, or in larger urban centers.* But for a growing group of intensive, prosperous agriculturalists, the *geôrgoi*, living on the farm itself was now becoming integral to producing food in a new and far more dynamic fashion. Farm residence, therefore, helped to forge both a new rural identity and an interest in preserving the agrarian community at large. The *polis* would have been impossible without it.

Skepticism also abounds from modern scholars concerning the frequency of artificial watering. Nevertheless, citations have been compiled from Greek literature that point to available water development outside the city-state, and often to the common practice of irrigation.** These references to water supplies must mean that residence out in the country was not merely practical, but in particular cases even necessary—given the need to maintain the developed rural infrastructure of young vineyards and orchards, as well as gardens. All cultivated trees and vines in a Mediterranean climate require irrigation at planting, and regularly thereafter, until at least their second or third year when they have developed an extensive root system. Even then good production may require some supplementary water, especially for soft-fruit harvests. Quite simply, the idea of ubiquitous irrigation on Greek farms cannot be easily dismissed.

One must not envision the vast communal projects and hydraulic dynasties of the ancient Near East—elaborate dams, ditches, level fields, and watering-lifting devices—in order to establish use of irrigation in the ancient Greek countryside. Predictably, the Greeks had no desire for the complexity of the palace. Instead, they fashioned new irrigation practices to reflect their native terrain, with its absence of enormous rivers running through flat expanses, and their own individualism. For the Greek *geôrgoi* this meant rudimentary, private efforts—small diversion of streams, wells, retaining basins, springs, dams—on modest plots devoted to gardens and the nourishment of young trees and vines in newly established orchards and vineyards. Theophrastus, for example, advised burying a pot of water next to each small vine to ensure soil moisture during the critical stage after planting.[20]

---

*For varieties of ancient rural habitation, see Hanson 1983: 41; Yoshiyuki 13.
**Gallant 1991: 56–57 sums up the traditional view: "Irrigation seems not to have been used on any scale in ancient Greek agriculture"; Osborne 1992b: 382; Isager and Skydsgaard 112. See instead the neglected work of Knapp 73–74; Guiraud 191–95; Glotz 1927: 40; cf. Cooper 1993: 116, 136, 157.

Like rural farmhouses, privately, rather than communally, developed sources of water suggest an intensification of agriculture, and therefore a sizable dispersed population of independent Greek farmers. Thus in our passage in the *Odyssey*, Laertes has a garden on his farm, which surely must have required irrigation during the hot summer months. Alkinoös, the king of Phaeacia, as Homer relates earlier in Book Seven, had developed an elaborate irrigation system.

> *On the outside of the courtyard and next to the doors is his orchard,*
> *a great one, four land measures, with a fence driven all around it,*
> *and there is the place where his fruit trees are grown tall and flourishing,*
> *pear trees and pomegranate trees and apple trees with their shining*
> *fruit, and the sweet fig trees and the flourishing olive.*
> *Never is the fruit spoiled on these, never does it give out,*
> *neither in winter time nor summer, but always the West Wind*
> *blowing on the fruits brings some to ripeness while he starts others.*
> *Pear matures on pear in that place, apple upon apple,*
> *grape cluster on grape cluster, fig upon fig. There also*
> *he has a vineyard planted that gives abundant produce,*
> *some of it a warm area on level ground where the grapes are*
> *left to dry in the sun, but elsewhere they are gathering others*
> *and trampling out yet others, and in front of these are unripe*
> *grapes that have cast off their bloom while others are darkening.*
> *And there two springs distribute water, one through all the garden*
> *space, and one on the other side jets out by the courtyard door.*
>   —(7.112–130)

Likewise in the *Iliad* Homer displays a detailed knowledge of irrigation techniques, as in this extended simile from Book Twenty-one, where the Scamander river pursues Achilles. Homer envisions Achilles:

> *as a man running a channel from a spring of dark water*
> *[who] guides the run of the water among his plants and his gardens*
> *with a mattock in his hand and knocks down the blocks in the channel; in*
> *the rush of the water all the pebbles beneath are torn loose from place, and*
> *the water that has been dripping suddenly jets on in a steep place and goes*
> *too fast even for the man who guides it.*[21]

From later Greek literature, inscriptions, and archaeological evidence, it becomes clear that farmers employed a variety of strategies to grow irrigated crops on their small farms—quite the opposite of the usual scholarly picture of extensive dry-farming by peasants. Sometimes we hear of individual wells in literature or see conduits (of 200 meters or more) running from excavated farmhouses, from which farmers must have carried buckets for individual plants. In confiscation lists there are inventories of water-lifting devices. Occasionally, even the remains of small dams and reservoirs have been spotted in the countryside.[22]

Theophrastus assumed irrigation to be crucial to certain types of Greek agriculture. Why else would he list species of figs improved by watering, or describe the combined application of manure and water, or warn that "often the water from irrigation ditches brings with it the seeds of weeds"—something any farmer knows from experience is often the price of turning to canal, rather than well water? Throughout his agronomic treatises there are special sections devoted entirely to irrigation.[23]

In addition to apparent ancient irrigation channels on the Corinthian plain, there were numerous developed natural springs in the area. Thus Corinth was described by Simonides as "well-watered." On the Aegean island of Chios large water cisterns eight meters in diameter have been uncovered amid ancient stone terraces, designed apparently for irrigation and rural residence.* The wide variety of evidence for water-use during the *polis*-period clearly makes the old view that irrigation was relatively rare simply implausible. We should imagine that anytime available water might be somehow transported downhill to relatively level fields, the Greeks piped, channeled, or carried it.

Quite simply, the establishment of arboriculture and viticulture at the end of the eighth century would *not* have been possible without constant care of young stock. That argues for rural residence and a type of rudimentary irrigation system—even if here we mean merely daily, and extremely labor-intensive, transport with clay water jugs on donkeys. These were agricultural practices still almost unknown during the Dark Ages. In a settled Greece laced with bridle paths, publicly maintained roads,

---

*On Corinth, see Salmon 1984: 8; for Chios, Lambrinoudakis 297. On Melos, too, cisterns alone can store enough rain to support households of four to five persons year-round (Renfrew and Wagstaff 100–107).

parks, and canals, we should include small farmhouses and privately constructed irrigation ditches—ditches whose presence in the Greek countryside Aristotle compared to veins carrying blood in the body.[24]

We have seen now that the new farmers built homesteads, and dug,
damned, and channeled. But as hardworking as these families were, they
could not have developed this rural infrastructure alone; their novel vision of a bustling, populated countryside required a vast cadre of
slaves—men and women more forgotten in the historical record than
the *geôrgoi* themselves.

I have farmed a single twenty-acre block of ten different species of irrigated fruit trees—apricot, pomegranate, persimmon, fig, plum, peach,
nectarine, oriental pear, guava, quince—that required more labor than an
adjoining single block of ninety acres of vines for specialized raisin production (even though viticulture itself is labor- and capital-intensive). The
several fruit-tree species demand different watering, pruning, cultivating,
fertilizing, and harvesting techniques. They are on poor, hilly ground,
compounding water, insect, and fertilization problems. All require close
supervision of labor, since pruners or thinners cannot simply be turned
loose amid the many baffling problems accompanying each species. And
more capital investment—sheds, ladders, tree props, boxes, buckets—is
needed, which demands constant maintenance and replacement.

Each small plot has different soil challenges (which can vary radically
acre by acre), and it takes constant attention (and occasional disaster)
to learn which species of tree can be grown in which particular loca-
tions—something known immediately under monoculture, but requiring a painful trial-and-error method with so many diverse crops. Lost
trees require prompt replacement with new trees that need additional
extra care—far more difficult when layering (as in the case of the established vineyard) is impossible. The diversified farmer may have to venture constantly throughout the established orchard, watering and
fertilizing individual replants, and the art of grafting becomes critical,
given the variety of trees that may perish each year.

Because we have grown these diversified crops organically and sold
them directly at farmers' markets, the fruit is picked ripe for instant consumption. Boxed, trucked, and sold within hours, it is not handled at all
through a food broker or produce exchange. As in antiquity (and indeed
as was true in this country before World War I and the advent of accessi-

ble refrigeration), there is no cushion in the timing of the harvest. Fruit cannot be picked green, put into cold storage, shipped across the country, and eaten two to four weeks later. The strategy for local fresh sale instead is to plant small plots of different species so that harvest dates do not coincide. Four full-time workers do nothing but prune, water, prop, thin, harvest, and box the sequential small harvests and aid in the selling; they move constantly from small plot to plot during *all* seasons. Any free time is devoted to ladder and bin repair, patching irrigation pipe, and driving to additional markets. On the other 140 acres, which are not farmed as intensively, and which in a strictly farming sense pose far fewer problems, there is a *single* full-time employee. Yet the small diversified plots are a headache we cannot afford to abandon, for they provide a safety net in times of natural or economic crisis. The entire success of the operation depends on the presence of a small group of skilled, permanent workers.

During the shift from Dark-Age pastoralism and cereal-based agriculture to intensive farming and the rise of the *polis*, slave labor—like homestead farmhouses and irrigation—became common in the Greek countryside. Unfree workers were known throughout the Mycenean period and no doubt during the later Dark Ages as well. Yet with the appearance of the *polis*, Greece began to import increasing numbers of servile adult male laborers. Understandably, Greek authors believed that commonplace chattel slavery was a phenomenon of recent history, one contemporaneous with the establishment of their own *polis* institutions. The preponderant agrarian nature of the Greek population, the need for extra labor under intensive farming practices, the absence of legal restraints to slave ownership, the rising social disdain among independent yeomanry for manual wage labor, the growing wealth of the Greek economy, the extension of the Greek presence overseas and to the north as well, and the absolute absence of moral stricture in owning other human beings—all explain why during the *polis* period slaves in growing numbers entered Greece. It was an area that must have had an appetite for workers quite out of proportion in the Eastern Mediterranean to its small size and scant natural resources. Sponge-like, Greece at the end of the Dark Ages began absorbing manpower for its farms from around the Mediterranean, drawing laborers apparently not in demand in their native (and often superior) agricultural environments. Plainly, the Greeks were farming in ways far different from their northern, eastern, and southern neighbors—and in ways that clearly required much more labor.[25]

Not surprisingly, Homer shows us that Laertes closely supervises his own agricultural slaves, who live in a barracks right beside his own home. An elderly Sicilian slave woman, kept free from field work, apparently cooks and presides over the indoor tasks, while the aged Dolios and the other slaves under the direct orders of Laertes himself gather stones from the fields to build a retaining or terrace wall. As they work on the farm's terraces, Odysseus approaches and discovers his father, bent down and weeding around a tree. Laertes is clearly not portrayed as an absentee or even a large landowner, a country gentleman like Ischomachos, who appears in the philosopher-historian Xenophon's fourth-century treatise, the *Oeconomicus,* and who sees his servile help more as capital to be exploited for profit than as a means to ensure income *and* a way of life. Instead, old Laertes apparently is intimate with his slaves, living and working among them at similar tasks. At the end of the *Odyssey,* Laertes fights right at their side against the families of the suitors.[26]

Dolios and his sons are not a temporary harvest gang, men needed in the crush of the season and then dismissed to avoid idling once the crops are picked. Nor do they appear as helot-like indentured serfs. At this particular place in the *Odyssey,* Laertes' servile help is *not* mentioned as engaged in harvesting, but rather in soil reclamation and food preparation, "the old man guiding them on their errand." Apparently Laertes needs slaves year-round for a variety of farm improvement and more mundane daily tasks; he can keep the men busy even outside the harvest periods. Steady employment allows the workers to obtain an expertise otherwise not possible through temporary wage labor; slave farmhands now have achieved a skill in all aspects of farm work.[27]

Interestingly enough, the slaves' labor does *not* free Laertes from work for fulfillment of social or political obligations. Nor is it designed to. Not only does there seem to be a real need for Laertes to engage in manual activity himself, but the old man apparently enjoys his hard work—despite the supposed aristocratic dislike for stoop labor—and seems to feel that it is also somehow critical in ensuring the productivity of his own workers. In other words, Laertes leads by example.

These references to servile workers are striking in light of the traditional scholarly denial of the presence of slaves in ancient Greek agriculture. Only for the Marxist historian, is it axiomatic that slaves were found at every level of Greek society: the slave mode of production offered up bodies to be exploited for their masters' pleasure, part and parcel of the brutal process of extracting the critical surplus in agricultural productivity and creating the free time that their owners' more "leisured" lifestyle required.

Others bristled at the notion that the Greeks should have had to rely on an institution so intrinsically brutish and "undemocratic" as agricultural slavery in order to find time to engage in the niceties of this new idea of "politics." Thus champions of Athenian democracy—and a great many other Greek historians—rejected the presence of farm slaves on any wide scale—at least, and especially, at Athens.[28]

Most citizens of Attica were in some way connected to farming: if it was argued that only a few farmers used slaves, Athens became a city-state of "peasants," of truly free men who did not base their democratic institutions on the backs of an exploited class. In this view, Athenians practiced a low-input type of agriculture, extensive farming that not only did not require servile help, but also allowed the farmers themselves ample free time. As evidence, critics of agricultural slavery in the Greek *polis* maintain there is a lack of clear-cut, unambiguous literary evidence for agricultural slavery. They also cite the impracticality of keeping extra mouths to feed on small "subsistence" plots whose workers were constantly underemployed. They note the exorbitant expense involved for a small farmer in purchasing slaves, and point to mechanisms other than chattel slavery to explain why Greek citizenry of the *polis* did not engage in class struggle until Hellenistic and Roman times. Yet it is evident that Laertes owns a few slaves. He himself does not seem to have much leisure. Nor is he underemployed.

In truth, the references in literature to chattel slaves who work on Greek farms in the seventh through fourth centuries throughout the Greek-speaking world are unambiguous and they have been collated by a number of ancient historians.[29] These passages occur in nearly every genre of Greek literature. Although there could in some cases be exaggeration, distortion, or confusion, the sheer diversity of authors, places, and contexts suggests that servile workers were commonplace in the Greek countryside throughout the *polis* period, essential to the success of intensive agriculture itself. The literary references further imply that not merely the wealthy few, but also the many middling farmers, like Laertes, employed slaves. They appear *not* as large gangs of unattended workers, but rather as close, intimate, fellow manual laborers.[30]

Just because Greek farms were small need not suggest underemployment or the absence of either sustenance or work for a permanent servile laborer. Most farms, like Laertes', were diversified, with harvests occurring throughout the year. Many crops were planted or grown on reclaimed land. Like Laertes' plot, they needed constant attention to both terrace and fence upkeep. Also, trees and vines can require more labor than cereals and can produce dramatically higher yields when pruned, fertilized, cultivated, planted densely, and watered methodically.[31]

The picking of olives from large trees, as anyone can attest who has attempted it, is a nightmarish task. It is the agronomic situation that the modern agricultural advisor implores the farmer to avoid: large trees, small, unevenly ripening fruit, no chance for mechanization—a process extending over not days, not weeks, but rather months on end. On Greek vases the olive harvest appears as a confused affair: pickers are simultaneously kneeling on the ground, perched on limbs of the tree, and standing beating the leaves with sticks. The introduction of vine stakes and trellises—typical in the *polis* period—although requiring far more labor and capital, could also enhance grape production and quality. Cereals, too, produce higher yields when fertilized, weeded, and cultivated.[32]

The degree of labor required on any farm, ancient or modern, depends on the level of intensification, the frequency of true fallowing, and the particular crops farmed, not merely on the size of the plot in question. Ten acres of vines and trees could easily require more labor than a thirty-acre grain field. Xenophon remarked that land "unfarmed and not planted in trees and vines" (*argos kai aphuteutos*) became "many times more valuable" once an orchard or vineyard was propagated (*Oec.* 20.23–24). The Greeks of the *polis* were aware that intensive farming often could take a toll on trees and vines, that the efforts to force maximum production sometimes led to decreased life expectancy of vineyards and orchards—a realization that must suggest Greek farmers normally invested capital and labor in their land to produce as much as possible. Intensification and diversification also invite a whole host of related tasks in addition to the cultivation of the soil: time spent marketing and exchanging produce, additional equipment and infrastructure, and renewed worries over storage.[33]

Anywhere diverse crops are grown intensively, fertilization, planting, cultivation, plowing, grafting, and harvesting allow for little slack time in the agricultural calendar. Xenophon knew well that on a diversified farm on any given day men were planting orchards and vineyards (*phuteuontes*), clearing new land (*neiopoiountes*), sowing grain (*speirontes*), or harvesting fruit (*karpon proskomizontes*). "Produce," advises the Aristotelian *Oeconomica*, "should be so used that we do not risk all our possessions at the same time." Although there are references to specialized harvest-time wage laborers who could come in handy at peak demand in the agricultural year, their employment was less common and more often confined to cereal culture during harvests. Hired free and landless agricultural workers were always despised in Greece as engaging in "brutish" work. The impression we receive from Greek literature is that the successful middling farmer usually sought to acquire one or two slaves, and then often relied on the unfortunate poorer grower or the landless to augment his permanent help during the few weeks of cereal harvesting or fruit picking.[34]

The need at the end of the eighth century to acquire permanent agricultural workers must have led to the development of skilled field laborers, since farmers, like Laertes, were able themselves to train slaves in particular tasks year-round on the farm. Thucydides much later during the Peloponnesian War refers to Attic slaves who fled their farms during the enemy invasions of 413–404 B.C. as *cheirotechnai* (skilled workers), a denotation that probably reflected their accumulated agricultural expertise. At any rate, despite occasional complaints in literature that the agricultural slave could become fat and lazy, workers of this sort seem a far cry from harvest-time gangs, who were known to be undependable and occasionally slackers.[35]

Nor is there evidence that agricultural slaves were inordinately expensive. They were not beyond the reach of most Greek farmers. If bought on the open market, servile workers in general might cost between 150 and 200 drachmas at Athens by the end of the fifth century—about the price of a pair of oxen or the small farmer's own arms and armor.[36]

There is good evidence to suggest that most agricultural slaves were *not* purchased through traditional peacetime markets, but rather were cheap byproducts of war as booty and plunder, and thus often sold sporadically in mass auctions at depressed prices. A traditional tale attested that the sudden acquisition of slaves in mass at Locris disrupted the market for free labor in general. In a more precise agricultural context, the anonymous Oxyrhynchus Historian of the early fourth century says that the Thebans bought slaves from the countryside of Athens at a "cheap" price in the closing years of the Peloponnesian War. In explanation, he adds that the Athenians themselves habitually "brought *into their own fields* whatever they took from other Greeks when fighting." This passage suggests that the slaves on the farms of Attica were themselves originally acquired cheaply by the Athenians through conquest and wartime raiding, not merely in small numbers at private sales.*

Most farmers in Greece were landed infantrymen, usually (as at Athens) drawn from the *zeugitai*, the census class usually associated exclusively until the latter fifth century with independent moderate property owners. As hoplite soldiers, Greek farmers were accompanied on campaign by a servile attendants, charged with carrying the hoplite's seventy pounds of armor and weaponry. In nearly every case, we hear that such helpers were not relatives nor hired hands, but rather slaves.[37]

If hoplite soldiers owned land, and took their own servants into war, it makes sense to conclude that in peacetime the slaves were employed on the soldiers' farms. Though this direct relationship during the latter *polis* period between middling farmer and citizen militiaman was finally modified and even ended at various locales, it remains a valid generalization for the first three centuries of the city-state: the hoplite's armor carrier proved the existence of his servile agricultural laborer. Thus Greek agrarianism itself was predicated on chattel slavery, the unknown mass of now-forgotten men like—Manes, Syra, Thratta, Sosias, Sikon,

---

*On Locris, see Timaeus FGrH 566 fr.11. On the Theban purchase of Attic slaves, see *Hell. Oxy.* 12.4–5; cf. Hanson 1992b: 217–18. Recently W. K. Pritchett assembled the *enormous* evidence of the nature and amount of ancient Greek wartime profits. His data make clear that thousands of slaves were sold off cheaply (sometimes for far less than a hundred drachmas apiece) after conquest. Servile prices must have remained low, since often booty traffickers attempted to integrate slaves in mass into the local Greek economy (Pritchett *War* 5.170–73, 223–45). Frequently in a wartime context, slaves *and* livestock are mentioned together as part of property in the countryside, making it clear that potential plunder must have been used commonly on farms as servile labor (e.g., Dem. 18.213; cf. Arist. *Pol.* 2.1267b11–12; *Rhet.* 1.1361a13; cf. *Hell. Oxy.* 12.3–5).

and countless others—who dug vines, terraced hillsides, picked fruit, cooked food, carried armor, prepared rations, and helped the battle-weary *geôrgos* trudge back to his farm. They made possible both Greek farming and fighting throughout the lifetime of the city-state.

Slaves were critical to the success of a rising breed of new agriculturalists, men whose freedom was now defined as owning land and not living or working under constraint to another. The clear distinction between those who worked under compulsion and those who managed that labor clearly went hand in hand with the farmers' own middling but chauvinistic identity as a group neither aristocrat nor serf. From this point on, the ubiquitous presence of chattel slaves on the farms of the *geôrgoi* was—like the pairing of hoplite and hoplite attendant—a constant reminder of the farmers' own freedom, of the fact they were not indentured, but rather free men who employed slaves of unambiguously inferior social status. Even modern rural sociologists tell us that nothing undermines a rural community so quickly as a large body of farm wage-laborers, with a concurrent small group of independently employed farmers. In Greece, however, only a slave or two was attached to each farm, ensuring that neither wage nor servile laborers outnumbered the *geôrgoi* themselves.

Paradoxically, the unambiguously unfree status of Greek farmer-workers attached to the plots of the *geôrgoi* ensured that there would not be a shiftless population of wage earners disrupting local agrarian communities. Nor under such a system would there be a few despots on top to siphon off the work of thousands as was typical in the East.[38]

As we will see, Laertes' wide choice of crops, his reclamation of new land, and his personal control of food processing and storage were additional pieces in the new agricultural mosaic. As with the rise of homestead residence, irrigation, and slave labor, these other revolutionary elements explain *when, why,* and *how* agrarianism and the agrarian *polis* appeared on the Greek landscape.

From Homer's description it is clear that Laertes not only possessed a farmhouse and slaves, but also had a wide variety of tree fruit in his orchard. In addition, he grew vines of differing varieties. Odysseus says to his father: "And you also named the fifty vines you would give. Each of them bore regularly, for there were grapes at every stage upon them, whenever the seasons of Zeus came down from the sky upon them, to make them heavy" (24.341–44). Besides this varied assortment of trees and vines, Laertes also produced vegetables, assorted livestock, and apparently cereals as well.[39]

At nearly every locale, and in nearly every period of the four centuries between 700 and 300 B.C., the Greeks grew a wide selection of crops on their small farms, both for their own use and that of the local community. A sign of a completely uninhabitable place for a Greek would be one "unfit for grain, vines, or trees."* That need for diversification explains why in the earliest references in Homer's *Iliad*, we hear of both cereal and orchard or vineyard cultivation. Thus the hero Meleagros was "to choose out a piece of land, an entirely good one, of fifty acres, the half of it to be vineyard and the half of it unworked ploughland of the plain to be furrowed." Bellerophontes received "a piece of land, surpassing all others, fine plough-land and orchard for him to administer." Tydeus's farm at Argos likewise had "plenty of wheat-grown acres" with "many orchards of fruit trees circled about him, and many herds were his." These plots were *not* small gardens, but real farms owned and worked by private citizens.[40]

Whether our evidence comes from land-leases or sales, oaths of the Athenian ephebes, or the advice found in agronomic handbooks, diversity of crops—grain, olives, vines, fruit trees, legumes, garden produce—was the desirable pattern on most Greek farms during the *polis* period. In an early poem attributed to Hesiod workers are portrayed ploughing the soil, reaping and threshing the grain, picking both white and black grapes, and treading the vintage. Xenophon says of his farm near Skillous, in Triphylia not far from Olympia, that "*every* fruit good to eat" was cultivated there. There were, in fact, sound agronomic reasons why diversification spread through the Greek agrarian world.[41]

First, diversity of crop species allows the farmer to select particular varieties of fresh fruits and vegetables that he knows will be profitable at precise times in nearby urban centers. In the seventh and sixth centuries, the early part of the *polis* period, trade and markets were no doubt

---

*Plut. *Mor.* 602C. Crop diversification, which soon spread throughout the Mediterranean and became the staple of agrarian culture, is what led the historian Fernand Braudel to remark: "All agricultural life, the best part of Mediterranean life, is commanded by the need for haste," where there occur "the rapid successions of harvests, reaping in June, figs in August, grapes in September, and olives in autumn" (Braudel 1. 256).

less developed. But the absence of widespread, sophisticated long-distance transport of foodstuffs by land does not mean that Greek farmers failed to supply nearby communities with a variety of produce throughout the year, freeing a substantial minority of the population from work in the fields. In the *Odyssey*, the people of Ithaca and the suitors in particular had their food brought to the village from the countryside, thus making Laertes' fresh produce highly prized by those who lived a distance from his farm.

One should imagine now small farmers themselves venturing into villages and peddling fresh fruit whenever possible. Like the farmer and his donkey laden with figs in a letter of Alciphron, or like Aristophanes' agrarian who walks into Athens to exchange his grapes, agriculturalists gradually were able to feed a nonfarm urban group, as well as to produce food surpluses for trade and the subsequent acquisition of capital.[42]

Crop diversification, along with farm residence, irrigation, and slave labor, reflects an overall attempt to maximize agricultural production in any way possible. Raising different crops on the same farm allows the farmer to minimize risks from all sources: drought, hail, frosts, unseasonable rain, gusting winds, fungal, viral, and bacterial pathogens, insect outbreaks, animal and human attack, infestations of noxious, perennial weeds, idiopathic crop failure, human error, alternate bearing of crops, and, of course, market surplus.[43] Vines, cereals, and tree fruit (not to mention different varieties within those species) all germinate, pollinate, produce fruit, and enter dormancy at different times, ensuring that a minute, an hour, a day, or a week of climatic misfortune—a March hail, an April frost, an August rain, an October spate of unusual heat or gale-force winds—will likely catch only a portion of the farmer's total produce at a stage of vulnerability.

Disheartening it is to see an entire plum orchard's bloom wiped out by five minutes of unseasonable hail, and then to look over at a neighbor's peach and nectarine grove (not yet in flower) and see it unharmed. For the farmer with a single variety of plums, now shredded, those unfortunate minutes can *end* the crop year—and for the cash-poor sometimes the farm itself. Similarly, I have seen entire acreages of plums whose blossoms did not "set," thousands of trees producing no fruit at all. Only the diversified arboriculturalist who has nectarines, peaches, pears, and apricots can survive a year like that. On the other hand, a sudden May rain causes soft fruit to rot, such as peaches and apricots. But thicker-skinned and hardier plums suffer no damage at all from unseasonsable moisture. In some years, entire varieties of delicious tree fruit—peaches, nectarines, apricots, pears, and plums—rot on the tree from want of consumers, while oddly-shaped, sour green plums are in hot demand for overseas sale to an exclusively Asian market.

It was the same in antiquity with outbreaks of disease, mildew, or bacterial fire blight; all can affect only particular crops at certain times. In themselves these challenges cannot ruin a diversified farm's entire arsenal, as there is no chance that each variety will suffer its own particular lethal disease or natural disaster in any given year. Deer may consume ripe, soft fruit on young fruit trees, but will not seriously injure olive production by occasional browsing. Thieves can steal garden produce, but have difficulty harvesting cereal crops. Enemy invasions in late May occasionally catch ripe grain—barley and to a lesser extent wheat—at its brief, vulnerable combustible state, and thus may torch entire fields, but have more trouble in uprooting or chopping down trees or vines. Although the cultivation of numerous crop varieties requires greater attention and expertise on the part of the farmer (and unfortunately assures more frequent error in agricultural practice), diversity also guarantees that few mistakes will be lethal for the farm itself. In contrast, on a monocropped cereal parcel, natural disaster, not to mention farmer error, destroys an entire agricultural year, not merely one crop of many.

The diversity of numerous crops can also on occasion result in a positive synergy all its own. Orchards can be planted as windbreaks for vineyards. Beneficial insects on one crop can feed on pests from another. I suppose that Pliny had some reason to believe that placing barberry bush branches on grain fields might disrupt grain rust. Blackberries, in my own experience, harbor a species of leaf-hopper-devouring wasp that finds easier prey on nearby vines, and will actually move into the vineyard to devour grape pests, returning only infrequently to its natural habitat in the berry vine. It is thus rare that insect damage can spread onto a variety of crops. Crop diversity tends to be a biological check against insect populations becoming, like biblical locusts, fatal to the fields of the farmer. The relative absence of monoculture during the *polis* period may thus have reduced the entire scale of plant and animal pathogens in Greece as a whole, and partly explains the remarkable growth of intensive agriculture itself at this time.[44]

The presence of livestock also can be symbiotic on the farm. Animals can feed on post-harvest grain stubble, manuring the field at the same time. Even more delicate vineyards might be "sheeped," allowing animals to prune summer grape foliage as they browsed in the vineyard. Most scholars usually assume transhumance—the annual migration of domesticated livestock from plains to mountains in the summer—and accompanying bare-fallowing of ground in ancient Greece. In actuality, there must also have been an even more direct relationship between agriculture and livestock of a rather different sort, which eventually implied integration, not antithesis, between farming and livestock. Many stall-fed animals would not have been led out to distant pasturages, but rather kept nearby in corrals and fed on increasingly plentiful agricultural residues. Animals also were crucial for grain threshing on larger farms.[45]

What transpired with the advent of *polis* agriculture was not an end to livestock raising, but a transformation of it. Farming, not pastoralism, was now the key. Large animal herds, heretofore at odds with the spread of small-scale, labor-intensive farming, gradually shrank to become the property not merely of elites, but of yeomen themselves, as the ideology of animal raising itself was appropriated and changed by a new rural class.*

Diversity, as indicated, also can alleviate the potential problems inherent in the alternate bearing tendencies of many crop species. Vines and trees both often produce heavily in alternate years, olives more than grapes. In the case of the former, an "off" year can often result in essentially no crop at all. Because of each crop species' differing response to climate, their cycles are offset. This variety ensures that a diversified

---

*"With dispersed settlement and closer plots," Paul Halstead has written of the Greek rural economy during the age of the *polis*, "herding at the household level would be more practicable, and more complex rotation schemes might be a substantial obstacle to large consolidated herds. Transhumance would then be less likely and the consequent integration of crop and livestock husbandry would in turn make manure more freely available and so reinforce the viability of intensive arable farming. Viewed in this light, discussion by ancient agricultural writers of the benefits of extensive practices like manuring and cereal/pulse rotations should perhaps be interpolated not as exploring the boundaries of contemporary agronomic theory, but rather as advocating the application to extensively farmed estates of techniques used on small farms since time immemorial" (1987: 79; but cf. Isager and Skydsgaard 99–103).

farmer is not ruined in a single year, as a result of either a complete absence of produce or a surplus of fruit that cannot possibly be all harvested, processed, stored, or sold. That is, a vineyard can develop a cycle of production quite out of synchronization with an olive grove, allowing the diversified farmer alone to have at least one adequate crop every year.[46]

The annual cycle of surplus to scarcity in tree fruit production continues to plague growers and to bewilder agronomists of the present age. Despite various strategies of fertilization, pruning, irrigation, and thinning, alternate bearing in many species appears to be an instinctual response to past cycles of production, where a year's rest protects certain varieties of trees from future stress. I myself have seen the same vineyard consistently produce about 180 tons of raisins one year and 140 tons the next, despite nearly identical farming practices and weather conditions, and despite deliberate changes in our pruning and fertilization strategy just to ward off such an anticipated cycle. Similarly, I have harvested four thousand flats off a three-acre persimmon grove, followed—despite more fertilizer, an absence of pruning or thinning, and heavier watering—by three hundred flats the next season (less than a tenth of the prior year's production!), without changes in the weather pattern. Nor is the problem confined to individual farms. Given one species' identical response to climatic stimuli, large areas usually follow light/heavy production cycles, as even newly planted orchards and vineyards eventually adjust to a more or less regional cycle of uniformity. So predictable is the expectation of short crops after heavy production (and vice versa) that contemporary price and marketing strategies are usually developed well in advance of harvest. So the move toward diversification of crops by the *geôrgoi* of the *polis* must have had enormous—and quite positive— ramifications in the agrarian economy of early Greece as a whole. The economy—itself nearly exclusively agricultural even as late as the fifth century—rarely experienced a boom or bust cycle, even when natural disaster struck. The adage that diversification "sacrifices output per crop for output reliability for all crops" is completely accurate.

A diversified agricultural scheme also allows harvests—the periods requiring the greatest labor—to be spread throughout the spring, summer, and fall. The farmer need not harvest all his acreage within a brief window of vulnerability. This plan—and we should use such a term to denote intention rather than accident—of small, successive harvests had important implications for the economical use of labor. For example, Laertes' small force of workers can move from wheat and barley reaping and threshing (late May to June), to soft-fruit picking (June, July, and August), to the vintage (August to September), finishing with olive harvesting and oil pressing (October to November), picking garden produce on occasional slack days in between. His labor force of Dolios and his sons hence remains small, skilled, and permanent (i.e. servile). Laertes has no need of supplemental workers. On the other hand, he does not lose productivity through wasteful idling—the farmer's constant, near-neurotic worry. Between harvests and during the winter, slaves can be busy with trenching, milling, fencing, weeding, pressing, curing, ploughing, staking, fencing—all the myriad tasks that the intensified farming of diversified, permanent crops requires.

Sequential harvest dates also help to eliminate the specter of wasted produce—food rotting in the field for the lack of available manpower—or the related, equally injurious need to begin a premature, low-quality harvest with a "short" work crew in order to bring in all the crop before the onset of unseasonable weather. Farmers universally tend to hedge on quality *if* that decreases the risks of crop loss, in general desiring the greatest quantity that can be harvested and become at least marketable. California state fruit regulations, like the ancient wine laws of Thasos of the late fifth century, in practice tend to concentrate more on unripe rather than overripe fruit, as a result of long experience with the farmers' eagerness to pick prematurely. To cover the entire orchard or vineyard, to market the whole crop successfully, to take advantage of good weather, to do all that, I have rarely picked a crop that was not somewhat immature on the first day or so of harvest.[47]

Even small farms—whether composed of a single contiguous parcel, or perhaps more infrequently of separate, fragmented plots—present a mosaic of soil and water challenges. The rich variety of micro-climates and their accompanying idiosyncrasies warrant lengthy treatment in Theophrastus's late fourth-century agronomic handbooks. Naturally occurring nitrogen levels, ground textures and moisture-carrying capacities, soil pH, terrain, and elevation can all deviate widely even within small acreages. With expertise and long, accumulated experience, the intensive farmer learns to adapt particular crops to the many differing individual environments of his farm. Cereals, gardens, and soft-fruit trees can be planted on bottomland where soils are richer, plowable and more water retentive. Vines, though they produce more heavily on good ground, can nevertheless thrive on hillsides where soils are thinner. Higher elevations, which reduce daytime temperatures and ensure cooling nights, can actually improve wine quality because of lower nitrogen and moisture levels. Olives, like vines, often can thrive on rich plains, but they tolerate even less moisture and nitrogen, and thus grow on barren soils where little else is viable. Some vineyards planted on rich soils are deep green, almost blue in their lushness, and look enormously productive; on examination, their impressive growth is often nothing more than canes and leaves.

In farming it is not a question of finding the ideal growing conditions for each crop variety. That concurrence is only the utopia every farmer dreams of, but none achieves. Rather it is the lengthy trial—often spanning generations—of discovering the right crop that can at least be grown on the farm under less than optimum circumstances. Rough compatibility between plant and soil ensures that nearly all of the farmer's land is cultivable. Theophrastus knew that olives, figs, and vines grew best on particular soils; nevertheless, he saw that pragmatically such permanent stock would be more likely planted "on the second best" ground, places where other crops, such as wheat, would be less practical.[48]

A similar portrait of complete agricultural utilization is, incidentally, exactly the situation glamorized in Virgil's ideal portrait of an old man of Corycus, who owned a few acres of land unsuitable for ploughing, viticulture, or grazing. Through hard work the farmer learns to grow flowers and fruit trees and to raise bees—thereby using all his acreage productively. Aelian's misanthropic Knemon, a traditional stock character in Athenian comedy and satire, apparently feels obliged to explain why a small portion of his farm near a roadside is surprisingly uncultivated: only that way can he throw rocks uninterrupted at passersby.*

So the intensive grower's goal in a Mediterranean climate is nearly

---

*Virg. *Georg.* 4.125–46; Ael. *Ep.* 14; cf. Men. *Dys.* 160–67. Excavation of the complex of farms in the Russian Chersonesos revealed a clear pattern of tree/vine/cereal diversification. One larger (about sixty acres) farm revealed fifty-one percent of the ground devoted to cereals, nineteen percent planted in vines, seventeen percent in orchards, and nearly seven percent apparently vineyard that had been recently removed. The remaining area was devoted to the farm residence and nearly two miles of terrace walls. Scarcely any ground at all was unused (Pecírka and Dufková 153).

obsessive: to find some method that allows his entire acreage on his small plot to be used. When one considers the landscape of Greece as a whole, with its diverse soils and lengthy growing season, the emergence of diverse species would have allowed more land to be brought into production in a way not possible under either pastoralism or specialized cereal production. That, of course, ultimately resulted in more food, and hence wealth, for the growing population as a whole.

Last, the diverse production of cereals, fruits, olives, vines, and livestock virtually ensures the grower self-sufficiency—*autarkeia*, the Greeks' cherished economic and social sense of independence—both for the immediate needs of the family and the wider requirements of the farm itself. Bread and gruel from barley and wheat; fresh, dried, and juiced products from deciduous fruit trees; cooking oil, soap, and cured fruit from olives; raisins, grapes, and wine from the vine; vegetables and greens out of the garden; meat, cheese, milk, hides, and wool from livestock—having all these allows Laertes to exist quite apart from the palace below. Similarly, most lubricants and lighting oil (olives), fertilizer (manure, legumes), cooking fuel, and even farming implements (local woods), are also obtainable without need for outside barter, much less purchase. Everything from grape stakes to stove wood to building materials could be fabricated from trees, reeds, mud bricks, and clays available in the countryside.[49]

As in the case of homestead residence and agricultural slavery, there is little evidence that the early Greeks of the Dark Ages were skilled in crop diversification, the cultivation of trees and vines, and the associated arts of grafting and budding, before the eighth century and the appearance of the *polis*. Wheat species, likewise, may have been relatively restricted and not so numerous.

Most important, the Greeks of the *polis* themselves believed that domesticated viticulture and arboriculture were part of their more recent history. Theopompus related that the Chians were the first to excel in grape growing. Thucydides stated flatly that the early Greeks did not plant trees and vines. A number of anecdotes associated with Solon and Peisistratus similarly reveal that special efforts were needed to encourage establishment of capital crops in sixth-century Attica, a hint that Laertes' diversified scheme, like his farmhouse and slaves, reflected the vigor of the agricultural revolution already by the end of the eighth century.[50]

The diversification of crop species, like changes in labor practice and residence, must be seen in the wider context of Greek history. Each solitary *geôrgos* who struggled to carve out an orchard next to his house, to plant a vineyard among stones, to terrace a hillside field for grain was one with a growing number of thousands. Without the aid of palaces or manors, these planters of trees were now to be self-sufficient in food production, protected from famine, eager for more land and larger families—eager soon to apply that agrarian confidence and skill to politics and warfare and thus to change the nature of Greek culture itself.

The idea of agrarianism in a spatial sense spread down from the slopes, rather than upward, just as in the terminology of class, it soon became the property of the middling agrarians, not the upper strata of society. Marginal land in a way became the source, the fountainhead if you will, from which intensive agriculture expanded in many regions of Greece. The *georgoi* went up to find economic opportunity and soon came down to spread their brand of rural life throughout the community. The men who set out onto such terrain were themselves a novel group of middling yeomen: the very rich would have no need for strenuous land reclamation; the very poor were without the means to carry it out.

Eschatia is the most common Greek word for "marginal" land. It is an apt English translation that captures well the Greeks' dual notion that such ground was on the "margin" both in location and in quality. Although Laertes' property is not explicitly termed an *eschatia*, there is good reason to believe that some portions of his farm were on marginal ground. Homer describes the land as "distant from the city," apparently ground that Laertes himself had established after "much hard work." That description suggests that it was *not* an established piece of inheritable bottom land, but rather acreage on more difficult terrain, open for any with capital and a desire for difficult labor—land also like the nasty suitor Eurymachos's "outer estate," which contained terraces, fruit trees, and plenty of hard work.

In our passage of the *Odyssey*, the slave Dolios and his sons apparently continue the reclamation of Laertes' land by clearing stones and building terraces. Earlier in the poem, Athena had said that Laertes never came to the city, but stayed on his own land making "his toilsome way on the high ground of his vineyard." This passage also emphasizes the rugged, isolated, and elevated nature of the plot, an image akin to the later farm in the *Dyscolus* of Menander, where the old man works "out on the hill" away from the plain. Plato envisioned early Greek state formation taking place after individual residents "turned to farming hillsides (*epi geôrgias tas en tais hupôreiais*), making fences of rubble and walls to find protection from wild animals and building a single large and common house." How, though, in the eighth century did this attempt of the Greeks at incorporating marginal land fit into the new strategy of intensive agriculture, one marked by farm residence, irrigation, servile labor, and diversified crops?[51]

The frequent encroachment of agriculture onto rugged terrain obviously requires greater expenditure of capital and a conviction that land relatively uninhabited and used for forestry and grazing can be in fact potentially far more productive. Initial labor must be allotted to stone removal and terrace construction, to fruit-tree and vineyard planting, and to constant care of permanent stock in the years before fertility is reached. This is all endurable, *if* it can lead to an increase in food production, *if* the farmer can survive until new plots come into production, *if* he has the prerequisite mentality to work his ground as an investment for the future. In farming, all those are big "ifs," and suggest that the original homesteaders were tough men and women, who developed the prerequisite skill and patience to farm trees and vines on hillsides.

The daily farming of such ground is beset with the constant problems that accrue from cultivating hillsides. The extra effort and difficulty are welcomed *if* they allow the less than wealthy farmer title to his own unencumbered and increasingly valuable plot of ground. By the fifth century we should imagine that in almost every area of Greece terraces and land reclamation were ongoing. This involved an enormous investment of time, capital, and effort in order to cultivate hillsides that were formerly only marginally valuable as pasture.[52] These additional, pragmatic concerns in the farming of newly incorporated land explain in part the presence of Dolios and his sons, and Laertes' own permanent residence on the farm: the old man cannot afford the hours lost in the lengthy commute into Ithaca, as long as his crop responsibilities require constant supervision and the land demands continual upkeep.

Where plains are found alongside, or in the midst of mountains, there are ubiquitous hillsides of varying slopes. All such terrain offers an array of soil and climatic challenges. These micro-environments, especially at first on lower hillsides, encourage rather than discourage agricultural experimentation and eventually a wide diversification of crops, with definite advantages to the surrounding community. In the case of the olive tree, once the art of grafting was mastered, the Greek *geôrgoi* might simply walk up into the hills, cut down wild cultivars, and then graft domesticated scions onto the stumps. In some cases virginal, unfarmed hillsides, with ample natural levels of nitrogen, could provide for the early pioneer quite bountiful initial crops without fertilization.

Be careful not to dismiss the geography of Greece simply as rugged and poor. Instead, envision its small but rich plains and unclaimed hills as the perfect laboratory for an agrarianism much different from Near Eastern practice. Agricultural theory often postulates that the incorporation of less fertile or accessible land reduces overall agricultural productivity per acre. But in the case of the ancient Greek diversified landscape, that truism may be mistaken. By the late eighth century, Greek farmers of *eschatiai* were not necessarily forced to invest much more labor and capital to achieve cereal production comparable to that found on better ground. The farming of marginal ground is more commonly to be associated with the gradual introduction of new, improved species of vines, olives, and fruit trees into Greece, and, more important, with *new* notions of intensive farming. In the *Odyssey*, the seaward slope around Ismarus in Thrace reputedly produced the best wine, an assessment borne out by the later reputation of vintages from the mountainous and often volcanic islands of the Aegean—Chios, Melos, Lesbos, Thasos, Naxos, and Ikaros—where vineyards dotted the high hillsides. Theophrastus's agronomic treatises of the fourth century reflect the Greeks' familiarity with soil types and appropriate crop species. And Xenophon confirms that belief in the potential productive capacity of marginal ground. Even in later Italy the ideal farm was always felt to be close by the mountains.[53]

If one envisions hillsides and rugged terrain as perfectly suitable for various noncereal agricultural production, then the Greek landscape in the Dark Ages was greatly underused. Plentiful land at that era was simply vacant, even though it *could* have produced quite good tree and vine crops, given the right species and the proper expertise. Once again, the planting of trees corresponds directly with the farming of land previously considered marginal through pasturage and forestry. The development of *eschatiai* lies at the heart of the agrarian synergy of homestead residence, slave labor, and diversified crops.

The late eighth-century move toward viticulture and arboriculture probably explains the creation of these new upland establishments.[54] Other unproductive swampland below the hills, and the rarer areas where problems of drainage and mountain runoff also made farming marginal, are similar cases. Under the new dynamics of intensive agriculture, this ground too could be developed through ditches and drainage canals. The picture that keeps emerging suggests a unique interdependence between farm residence, servile labor, diversified crops, and the farming of marginal lands. They all represent the efforts of a new brand of sophisticated, intensive farming. But there must have been some motive force to explain the appearance of such novel strategies on Greek farms.

The original catalyst for the change from Dark Age pastoralism and concentration on cereals was, as I have stated earlier, population pressure and the growing scarcity of good bottomland. Equally important for the agricultural development of Greece was the availability of labor and the presence of these unfarmed, vacant hillsides or, in rarer cases, unproductive marshy meadowlands. These areas were routinely in production by the fifth and fourth centuries. This intrusion onto previously distant and unfarmed ground did more than guarantee critical additional food production for an increasing population. It also ensured that the agrarian ethos of Greece was transformed. Greek farming in the past was either despised as mindless manual labor in service to another or, from the opposite perspective, prized as the exclusive privilege of the absent grandee. Soon, however, for many of these new Greek property owners the labor required to clear out privately owned plots for terraced grainland, trees, and vines—Laertes' "much hard work"—became a thing of honor, a concrete representation of independence and hours invested for one's own family. It was a reflection that hard toil was sign enough of social and even moral improvement, an endeavor that further accelerated the notion of private, family ownership of farm property.

A variety of sources imply that at the first onset of increased population, Greek farmers like Laertes were at work in some type of rugged terrain. Recall, once again, the boastful suitor Eurymachos. In Book Eighteen he had tried to goad the disguised Odysseus by challenging him to work on his outlying estate, gathering stones to make fences and terraces, and also to plant "tall" trees," on a farm probably not much different from Laertes' own. Hesiod, as we will learn, about the same time (e.g., about 700–680 B.C.), complained of the conditions on his farm at Ascra in central Greece, "bad in winter, bothersome in summer, good at no time," a site now identified as lying on the upland slopes of Mount Helicon at about fifteen hundred feet. Solon's legislation (about 600–580 B.C.) that dictated olives and figs not be planted closer than nine feet to one another (apparently to prevent shading of, and growth onto, a neighbor's property) perhaps also reflects the increasing practice of arboriculture on newly created farms. In a famous passage in Aristotle's *Constitution of Athens*, the Athenian tyrant Peisistratus (about the mid-sixth century) spotted a farmer on the slopes of Mount Hymettus who was cultivating "rocks." When asked what he was growing, the homesteader supposedly remarked dryly "aches and pains"—an understandable response if those conditions were anything like the stony environment of ancient farmhouses and terraces that excavators have found on the mountains of the Aegean island of Chios.[55]

The percentage of land farmed in Attica was greater even than that of present-day California, a state renowned for vast expanses of irrigated flatland. Nevertheless, only about thirty-four percent of the state's acreage is now used for food and fiber production. Clearly, Attica had experienced a veritable agrarian revolution in the seventh and sixth centuries. It had turned Athens' sparse countryside into a highly populated, terraced land of trees, vines, and yeomen homesteaders.[56]

By the fourth century *eschatia* was well-known in Greek literature. The references to established, long-settled agrarian communities on stony ground suggest that the development of slopes—for example in Megara and Attica—was *not* recent, but a practice that went back many generations.* When Isocrates acknowledged that the Megarians were able to build the finest houses in Greece despite the fact that they "farmed rocks," he surely was not denoting homes in the plain of Megara proper, but rather emphasizing the natural agricultural connec-

---

*"Phyle," Menander wrote in his play the *Dyscolus* (93–95), "belongs to the residents there who are able to farm rocks." Any modern hiker to the nearby cave of Pan mentioned in the play can confirm the difficult topography.

tion between hard work and material prosperity out in their more rugged countryside. The Megarians were a people with a reputation in antiquity for improving soils and preventing erosion.[57]

Finally, land is never entirely a fluid commodity. It does not always expand and contract freely and spontaneously in direct relationship to population. Humankind—unpredictable and foolish as it is—does make a difference. Its pattern of land use is no mere organism that reacts predictably to outside stimuli. Some choice holdings can be tied up by families and not made accessible to agriculture, but used instead (unwisely and uneconomically) for livestock growing by conservative wealthy mossbacks—men of privilege who initially cared more for the social, rather than economic, advantage of traditional land use. For example, a field of deep white-ash soil, table-top level, with excellent water rights, sits idle and unplanted near our own farm, its owner a widow who for nearly half a century has inexplicably refused to plant its natural crop of trees and vines. How else other than social conservatism or personal idiosyncrasy can I explain the use of horses and wagons by another neighbor in the 1950s to transport raisins to the local cooperative—a transportation anachronism costly, time-consuming, and forty years out of date?

We should not imagine, then, that all marginal estates were immediately put into production at once at the end of the eighth century, nor that all such land need be considered especially substandard. Ground deemed an *eschatia* may originally have been in some cases *gently* rolling land quite near more prized aristocratic flatland.* Later in the fifth and fourth centuries, however, "marginal" might have taken on a *different* meaning and have referred to much poorer, scarcer land, higher up the slope. Many farmers must have tried, failed, and finally succeeded in these less favorable circumstances, through a long process (the centuries between, say, 800 and 500 B.C.?) of experimentation and adaptation in incorporating new land.

The early development of some *eschatiai* (accessible to anyone and for the most part unowned) by the more ambitious who had access to some capital—if we can use such a term for the elderly Laertes—created the example, and thus the momentum for new approaches to farming. Farm residence, irrigation, servile labor, and crop variety could all work even

---

*"There are," Theophrastus reminds us, "wide variations in foothills" (CP 3.6.7).

more successfully once farmers employed these practices on productive, traditional bottomland. However, had Laertes farmed initially near to the palace at Ithaca itself on cereal ground, there would have been little reason for him to live apart from others, to employ slaves, or even to experiment with a wide diversity of trees and vines. Marginal land, in other words, worked as a sort of internal colonization in the late eighth, seventh, and sixth centuries. It introduced the Greeks at large to the advantages of new agricultural techniques learned from farming in challenging environments. Much later Plato believed that a hilly countryside (*tracheia*) was the ideal backdrop for the *polis*, ostensibly because it demanded independence and hard work among the farming population. Surely, his notion derived from the actual experience of the Greek city-state, not from some utopian fantasy.[58]

It was one of the great ironies of Greek history that the rich substantial plains of Thessaly, Macedonia, Messenia, and Crete probably fostered agricultural *stagnation*. Good land hindered rural development and the accompanying agrarian culture of the *polis*—due to the *absence* of large tracts of unwanted, unowned *eschatia*. Marginal ground was the initial springboard (in a social, economic, agronomic—and moral—sense) of opportunity for Greek farmers. In that way, it was the laboratory for all subsequent Greek history.

Control of food storage and processing in the ancient Greek world brought with it political power and social status, as the exalted position of the palatial overlords of Mycenean Greece attests. The Mediterranean triad of bread, wine, and oil shares one striking characteristic, one necessary requirement. Unlike fresh fruit, vegetables, meats, and nuts, these foods *must* be milled or pressed into flour, juice, and oil from the raw products of grains, grapes, and olives. Processing required labor, capital, and time. But it also gave *opportunity*: The ancient Greek diversified farmer could be both a food producer and processor, and a controller or broker as well.

This dual responsibility of cereal grower/flour miller, viticulturist/wine maker, and olive farmer/oil producer had important economic implications. Frequent on-the-farm processing often eliminated the "middle man"—so disliked in Greek literature, the rogue "weakest in body and useless for any other job." It allowed *geôrgoi* of the *polis* themselves, unlike Mycenean workers or Dark-Age serfs, to control their final product.

If the produce was to be sold as oil, wine, or flour, rather than as the raw yield of olives, grapes, and grains, all "expenses" involved in the cultivation, harvest, and processing were controlled (i.e., passed on) solely by the farmer himself. Although Homer does not explicitly portray Laertes and his helpers as involved in threshing and pressing, the farm seems, nevertheless, to be an exporter of refined produce to Ithaca below, rather than an importer of wine, oil, and flour. The existence of sufficient servile labor, the isolation of Laertes' estate, and permanent residence on the land all suggest that pressing and milling were done right on the farm itself.[59]

Both later literary evidence and archaeological excavation of Greek homestead farmhouses suggest on-the-farm threshing floors and presses throughout the rural community. These references and artifacts argue that the homestead farmer, not the absentee landowner, not the commuting peasant, not the urban handworker, was a regional nexus for food processing throughout the Greek countryside.[60]

Equally important for the homestead farmer would have been sufficient storage capacity. Once raw products were processed into flour, wine, oil, and dried and pickled fruits, it was critical that the farmer not only laid away his own supplies for home consumption, but also had the ability to keep his produce off the immediate post-harvest market.[61] The possession of food processing and storage infrastructure on the farm, like the other elements of intensive agriculture in the *polis* period, stands in sharp contrast to *both* the centralized bureaucracy of the Myceneans and the later rural underdevelopment of the Hellenistic age.

III. Yeoman Laertes

The Homeric poems imply that these new Greek farmers are *not* the impoverished and landless poor. They appear as hardworking men with access to capital. All the Homeric references to such early farms—be they the property of Laertes, Bellerophontes, Meleagros, or Tydeus—assume owners who are clearly not peasants, but rather men of substance. Some capital, after all, must have been necessary for slave ownership, terrace building, land reclamation, house construction, and well digging or other small-scale water projects. Capital crops, such as trees and vines, demand that the farmer have other means of support during the three to seven years before substantial crops are produced.

On the other hand, Laertes as he is portrayed in Book Twenty-four of the *Odyssey* is no aristocrat either. He works hard on his hands and knees. Horses are absent from his farm. His dress reflects pragmatism and is designed to prevent cuts and abrasions. His sorry circumstances draw rebuke from his son Odysseus. Moreover, the farm appears not to be large. In the orchard, Odysseus can at least count the number of trees, which would be impossible on a larger holding.

That knowledge of individual trees or vines on a farm—their unique size, shape, number, and productive capacity—has always seemed to me a rough, but accurate, gauge in determining the *nature* of the agricultural operation. Corporate, absentee, large-scale farmers never distinguish individual plants among expansive groves. How could they do so, when they themselves do not live by nor work within the vineyard or orchard, and thus never come to know firsthand, season after season, summer and winter, particular trees and vines? To these overseers *all* the farm's trees and vines are essentially identical and uniform, mere dots in a vast, unbroken matrix.

But to the family farmer, individual stock has its own life and identity, some strong and productive, others sickly and weak. Particular trees and vines even in large orchards and vineyards become familiar, as distinct and well known to the farmer as members of his own family—which, in some sense, of course, they are. In this regard, recall also that even Alkinoös' "estate," whose size we would expect to be much more extensive than Laertes', apparently extends only "four land measures"—about four acres (*Od.* 7.113).

Land is well developed and intensively worked in the *Odyssey*, but it is not accumulated into large tracts. There are no *latifundia*. The image from the farm of Laertes is that the Greek agrarian revolution, at least in its initial phase in the late eighth and early seventh centuries, was inaugurated by men of some substance, farmers neither poor nor yet at the very top of the social scale. The new Greek *geôrgoi* will need to work themselves, but may own slaves. They will often live out in the country. But the homestead complex will not be lavish, instead geared toward storage, processing, and utilitarian considerations. There will be numerous crops, but not large mono-cropped acreages. Agrarians will have the means to carve out marginal land, but not the accumulated capital and substance to obtain large tracts of fertile bottomland.

Some farmers were wealthier than others. Some *geôrgoi* could not afford slaves; others owned several. We should expect differences to appear once individual initiative and private ownership came into play. There were always pastoral holdovers in the Greek countryside, commuting wealthy and poorer farmers: both those upscale growers who specialized in single crops, who often employed servile overseers and lived in town, and the less fortunates who worked an acre or two and hired themselves out as day laborers.* Nevertheless, despite the existence of larger estates and tiny plots, of wealthy and very poor folk, and of differences among the middling *geôrgoi* themselves, the general lines are clear enough to identify a novel type of *polis* agriculture: a new "class" of man was appearing on the Greek landscape with quite different notions of farming—and, as we will see, radically different ideas of social, military, and political structures as well.

There was a tradition among the Greeks that the inhabitants of Chios were among the first to introduce chattel slavery. A similar legend attests to their early success in intensive agriculture, especially their skill at viticulture. The difficult terrain of the island is well known and modern archaeological work has suggested the long presence there of isolated farmhouses on marginal land. Most important, however, Chios is one of the first Greek city-states where we have direct evidence, through an inscription of the early sixth century, of some type of constitutional government (e.g., "public officials" [*dêmarchoi*]; a "council of the people" [*bolê hê dêmosiê*]; "legal enactments" [*rhêtrai*]) most likely a broad-based oligarchy or timocracy of landowning farmers.[62] It is my belief that all those phenomena are *not* coincidental, but rather the natural economic, social, and political coalescence of early Greek agrarianism. Only in early Greece, did independent agriculturalists have free title to their plots, own slaves, and have absolute control of their communities.

This conjecture of the appearance of a "new man," in addition to a

---

*Such farms constituted "several different agricultural systems, depending on local conditions" (Isager and Skydsgaard 112). Yet uniformity, not regionalism, is more characteristic of Greece's agrarian regime during the *polis* period.

novel type of farming and the creation of private ownership of property, is confirmed when we look in the next chapter at another piece of literature, the *Works and Days*—an oral poem of Hesiod's composed about the same time as the *Odyssey*, but one drawn from a completely different social environment, where farmers are essential to the narrative of the poem itself, not incidental.

Chapter 3

HESIOD'S WORKS AND DAYS

The Privilege of the Struggle

Nature gave the ancient farmer the privilege of the struggle. Under the influences of climate and relief was evolved a system of tillage, which produced: (I) Winter grain crops maturing in spring or early summer. (II) Planted crops of olives, figs and grapes ripening in autumn without artificial watering. (III) Widely distributed summer crops of fruits, vegetables and fodder plants raised by irrigation, wherever springs and perennial streams were available. The immediate material gain of this triple system was a larger and more certain total harvest and a more varied food supply than the single seasonal cultivation could have yielded. More important, however, was the economic gain, because it meant improved economic methods. It involved increased application of capital for seed, manures and the construction of irrigation canals; and it demanded an elaborate and sustained system of farm work, in consequence of which the labor power of the community was kept employed all the year-round. The economy of national wealth and the gain in national efficiency were incalculable.

—Ellen Church Semple 1928: 155–56

I. Who Was Hesiod?

In my own remembrance of family dinners long past, grandfathers often extolled—or summarily dismissed—a man simply by the epithets, "he worked hard" or "he never worked at all." That criterion alone was to explain the appearance of his farm, the condition of his family, and the general reputation of his progeny. Sometimes this blinkered thinking could border on the idiotic, as when new barns or orchards were ascribed to years of patient labor rather than to a lucky inheritance, or when agricultural catastrophe and subsequent monetary ruin were explained as the result of "vacations and holidays," not the sudden appearance of a malignant tumor or the need to care for a bedridden, paralyzed daughter.

But both of these no-nonsense men were more often right than wrong: constant hard work inevitably was reflected in both the well-kept appearance and economic health of the farm; sloth was clear enough from either the sight of weedy, trashy ground or the more insidious, gradual extinction of the family estate. Xenophon's Ischomachos is made to say that success in farming is not so much mastery of agricultural practice—straight planted rows, careful sowing, proper fertilization—as simple hard work. "A man has neither olives nor figs," he states bluntly, "because he has not taken the trouble; he has done nothing to produce them."*

In farming bounty springs forth not merely from the richness of the soil, favorable weather, or even accumulated capital, expertise, and successful strategy, but also from hard work—and the *quality* of men who farm. One could also be labeled the son of someone who "worked" or "didn't work" as if the trait was simply heritable. Similar pejorative, but tellingly accurate, assessments of agrarian failure—"lazy," "loafer," "no-good," "moocher," "weak," "bum," "bad-seed"—until recently were

---

*Oec. 20.3–6. Not surprisingly, a modern anthropologist's examination of a farming community in southern Italy, consisting of homestead residences and intensive cultivation practices, concluded: "The hope to 'eat a piece of bread' far from the church bells depended also upon a local middle class of only middling wealth, and for the most part, mild entrepreneurial ambitions at least in comparison to the agribusiness of the more northern regions of Apulia. But above all, it depended upon, and fed, their extraordinary motivation to work until bones ached so as to make a step ahead for their children" (Galt 242; cf. Pl. *Resp.* 1.330B-C).

widely shared by society at large. With the rise of the modern social science parlance and the decline of an agrarian outlook, however, the more honest vocabulary so commonly used in agricultural disparagement has nearly vanished from common American usage.

New species of crops, farmhouses, and the use of slaves are only the outward manifestations of Greek agriculture. In themselves these practices cannot entirely explain the rise of Greek agrarianism and the early city-state, nor can they wholly account for its success. An equally important change at the beginning of the *polis* period was a transformation in the mind, a radical change of attitude, as farmers learned to invest their efforts in the land in an entirely novel way. This alteration in the Greek mentality involved a new ideology of work derived from land ownership, not tenancy. More specifically, it entailed an idea that manual labor, time spent on the soil, was both intrinsically ennobling, moral if you will, and a wise economic investment that would lead (not necessarily in one's own lifetime) to greater agricultural production and hence more wealth for coming generations.*

This obsession with hard work is entirely at odds with the "peasant" mentality ascribed to the Greeks by many scholars who point to the well-known aristocratic dislike of manual labor and widespread presence of chattel slavery in order to suggest that these two phenomena also help to explain the Greeks' reluctance to improve their own farmsteads materially.[1] But all this is quite wrong. Already at key places in Homer we have seen subtle changes in rural attitudes, primarily the image of Laertes on his hands and knees, weeding his orchard. In the *Iliad*, in the scene portrayed on the shield of Achilles, men are busy reaping grain, while young girls and boys gather grapes, all under the careful direction of the farm-owner who seems to orchestrate the efforts of his family and laborers (*Il.*18.541). Even the arrogant suitor Eurymachos's challenge to Odysseus to build fences and plant trees, and the hero's counterchallenge to test him first in a grain cutting and plowing match (and then only later in battle), are indications that agricultural toil was now be-

---

*There was a tradition that the Greek *polis* itself often intervened against the lazy and the unproductive, passing legislation that mandated employment, prosecuting any who were idle or unwilling to cultivate their plots, or who squandered their paternal estate. See, e.g., Plut. *Sol.* 31.5; Demosth. 57.32; cf. Isager and Skydsgaard 145–46, and the similar Roman yeoman statutes at Aul. Gell. *NA* 4.12.

coming both a test of manhood and a sign of good character. Eurymachos taunts:

> *Stranger, if I were to take you up, would you be willing*
> *to work for me on my outer estate—I would give you adequate*
> *pay—assembling stones for fences, and growing the tall trees?*
> *There I would provide you with an allowance of victuals,*
> *and give you shoes to wear on your feet, and clothing to put on.*
> *But since all the work you have learned is bad, you will not be willing to go*
> *off and work hard; no, you would rather beg where the people are, and so*
> *be able to feed that ravenous belly.*
> —(Od.18.357–64)

Odysseus in his response shows none of the absentee owner's distaste
for hard labor that he will later revert to in Book Twenty-four. Instead,
Homer portrays Odysseus almost as if he himself were a hardworking,
self-employed farmer, one who can find manly skill in the proper carving
of a furrow.

> *Eurymachos, I wish there could be a working contest*
> *between us, in the spring season when the days are lengthening,*
> *out in the meadow, with myself holding a well-curved sickle,*
> *and you one like it, so to test our endurance for labor,*
> *without food, from dawn till dark, with plenty of grass for our*
> *mowing. Or if it were oxen to be driven, those of the best sort,*
> *large ones and ruddy, both well fed with grass of an equal*
> *age and carrying power, and their strength is not contemptible,*
> *and there were four acres to plough, with the glebe giving to the*
> *plowshare. There you would see if I could carve a continuous furrow*
> —(Od. 18.366–76)

Despite these valuable glimpses of the new agriculture and ideal of
hard work, Homer's genre was epic; his aim was to glorify the martial
deeds of the heroic few, *not* the humdrum lives of the many. It is not surprising that in Homeric poetry about aristocrats in battle, there is precious little about the growing, contemporary culture of agrarianism, a
new creed practiced by those outside the traditional Dark Age ruling
elite. Homer composed for a conservative, aristocratic audience, who

preferred embroideries upon their own ancestral past to the stark realism of the present. No wonder that it was felt in later antiquity that the two poets represented the two poles of human experience, that Homer gave good advice for fighting, Hesiod for farming (cf. Plut. *Mor.* 223A).

For a much better presentation of the nascent agrarianism, one can fortunately turn to Hesiod, a near contemporary of Homer, but a poet of a completely different sort, who lived in Boeotia on the slopes of Mt. Helicon. Hesiod also composed orally and at about the same time (i.e., 700–675 B.C.). But fortunately for our purposes, Hesiod wrote not an epic of war centered on aristocratic figures, but an almanac of a rural society at peace. In his brief poem of some eight hundred lines, *The Works and Days,* which treats exclusively his contemporary age (the early seventh century), Hesiod is in some ways more historical than Homer, for his poem is not merely a treatise on a farmer's tasks (his *Works*) and obligations (his *Days*), but also a tract on the ideology of early Greek agricultural labor.

Keep in mind that Hesiod's poem is not fiction, at least not entirely. The poet's advice purports to be based on real farming experience. The *Works and Days* is a diatribe that springs from an apparently real dispute between the poet and his slothful sibling, Perses, over their inheritance.* The poem's frame of reference is the Hellenic countryside as seen by a bard who, unlike Homer, was probably himself also a farmer. Given the roughly contemporaneous dates of composition, we would expect in the *Works and Days* about the same picture of agriculture as in the *Iliad* and *Odyssey,* but presented in much greater detail, with considerably more empathy and knowledge of agricultural technique. Although both poets could draw on the emergence of intensive farmers in the description of their literary characters, it is much more vital to Hesiod than to Homer.[2]

Nearly all the structures of intensive farming discussed in the previous chapter are present in the *Works and Days,* and they explain why in the centuries to follow "the economy of national wealth and the gain in national efficiency were incalculable" (Semple 1926: 156). These practices confirm that Hesiod is describing much more systematically the same agriculture that appeared haphazardly in the *Iliad* and *Odyssey.* Al-

---

*See Will 1965: 551–55; Osborne 1987: 17.

though the olive, the so-called "first of all trees," is almost absent (only mentioned at line 522) from the poem, there is, nevertheless, as in the case of Laertes' farm, mention of many crops.*

"Cut all your grapes and bring them home, Perses," Hesiod warns his brother (611). Earlier he advises the farmer to prune the vines before the beginning of spring (570) and finish grape cultivation before the onset of summer (572). In addition, Hesiod frequently mentions live-stock (516, 590–592, 606–607, 775, 786, 790, 795; *Theog.* 22–23) and assumes that farmers grow grain (597–605), figs (680–81), and other fruit trees (22). Each crop, he says (in language remarkably similar to the description of the diversified produce on the estates of Laertes and Alki-noös), "produces a bounty in its *own* season" (393–94). Harvests are to be processed on the premises by the farmer himself, so Hesiod gives practical advice on the threshing and milling of grain, and the pressing of grapes into wine or, in contrast, their drying into raisins (597–615). Slaves are ubiquitous in the *Works and Days.* Like the family of Laertes' Dolios, they are considered essential to the farmer's varied regimen of tasks, in which both master and servant are expected to toil side by side: "Get to work, your slaves, yourself, everybody all together" (459, cf. 470, 502, 573, 597, 608, 766).

There is no exact description of the location of Hesiod's farm. But even if the poet exaggerated when he said that the general area of Ascra is "bad in winter, troublesome in summer, good at no time" (640), that description suggests that the farms in that hilly area incorporated some marginal land on elevated and difficult terrain.**

Hesiod reports that his father obtained the land after arriving as an immigrant from Cyme. As with Laertes' farm in the *Odyssey*, it appears that the family's fruit trees and vineyards were recently established on land previously underused or, more probably, not farmed at all. Like

---

*See Colum. *Rust.* 5.8.1 on the olive's importance. Its absence in the *Works and Days* results, I think, either from the higher altitudes of the poet's immediate environs on Mt. Helicon (i.e., about 1,500 feet in elevation), the fragmentary state of the text, or the embryonic condition of arboricul-ture in early seventh-century Boeotia.

**Modern scholars have, in fact, located the ancient site of Ascra (Snodgrass 1985: 88–95; 1987: 125; 1990: 132–33), the general vicinity of Hesiod's farm, on the slopes of Mount Helicon. Although the area is picturesque and fertile—near lies the legendary "Valley of the Muses"—the entire setting on a mountain is one easily reminiscent of Laertes' lower hillside estate on Ithaca.

Laertes, Hesiod's father no doubt reclaimed the Ascra farm only after great toil. Francis (291) correctly summarized the farm: "Hesiod's family had only recently migrated to Ascra, and probably lived under pioneer conditions as settlers on waste land; such conditions, however, seem to be favorable to that 'rugged individualism', often attributed to the American pioneer." At the date of composition of the two poems, both farms were understood to be no more than a generation old, *not* part of some aristocratic estate dating back to the Dark Ages.

Whether Hesiod actually lived on his property is never stated. But despite recent attempts to deny the existence of a Hesiodic homestead farmhouse* an isolated residence can surely be inferred from the poem. Hesiod, after all, mentions the evils of town, warning against loitering there far from the farm. Likewise, the presence of numerous farm animals (523, 554, 404; cf. 325, 376, 495), slaves, tools, wagons (420–435), and the advice to build "granaries" (503, cf. 411) suggest a rural, rather than an urban, home for an extensive agricultural infrastructure.

Nor can mention of residence "at the miserable village Ascra (*oizurê eni kômê Askrê*)" (640) suggest that his house was in town. All farmers, ancient and modern, identify their locale by association with the *nearest* town, without any implication that their house is actually inside the city, rather than merely nearby in the countryside. Moreover, Hesiod's frequent mention of neighbors is usually in an agricultural context ("Not even an ox would be lost, if there was not a bad neighbor," 348) and assumes the permanent residence of small farmers throughout the countryside. By employing the term "neighbor" in specific ways, he is unlikely to be referring to the occasionally worked ground of a nearby commuting peasant. Modern field surveys of the surrounding area also confirm that in the general vicinity of Ascra there is ample evidence of isolated farm sites. Finally, as in the Laertes passage in the *Odyssey*, there is no direct reference to the *size* of Hesiod's farm, but the assumption is that small agriculturalists like the poet must watch carefully the "bribe-swallowing barons" (*basilêas dôrophagous*), grandees who apparently favor only the very wealthy (39; 264–65).

Despite the poet's call for hard work in the pursuit of riches, there also

---

*See Osborne 1985: 15–16, but cf. the more realistic assumptions of Detienne 1963: 20, 27, and Snodgrass 1990: 132–33.

is affirmation that a life spent in honest toil is no disgrace if the farmer must be content with a smaller plot and dine occasionally on simple fare (40–41). At all times in the poem, private ownership and thus the theoretical ability of the farm to expand or contract are assumed.*

In the *Works and Days,* Hesiod exhorts the farmer to labor for profit, yet at the same time to see his farm as more than a mere livelihood. Crucial to that dual idea is work: Hesiod is obsessed with hard labor, distinguishing his farmers from peasants, who hope for little more than general subsistence.

The moral element in labor sanctions, but does not create the need for farm improvement and the quest for capital. Things are done on the ancestral farm that do not always make strict economic sense. Even today to survive, the family farmer may drive an extremely hard bargain over wages and sales. But his psychological and spiritual survival may also induce him to spend some of that precious hard-won capital in painting posts at the end of vineyard rows or planting ornamental trees along his alleyways.

A Greek idea of competition between agriculturalists emerges here, a common ideology arising from population growth and land scarcity: "Land hunger led to colonial expansion and wars between neighboring cities. For those who remained on the land, Hesiod understands the urgent need for efficient husbandry."** For Hesiod, farmers must strive against one another to produce the best crops in the most efficient ways possible, ensuring that "you may purchase someone else's land, and not have another buy yours" (341). He sees the entire world as one where "the potter is at odds with the potter, and the craftsman with craftsman, and the beggar is jealous of the beggar, and the singer of the singer" (25–26).

All this is healthy—and necessary. It is not merely the traditional negative jealousies of peasant cultures. Anthony Galt, who distinguished the small-farming community of Locorotondo in southern Italy from purely peasant societies, notes "small proprietorship and a dispersed settlement pattern"—and most importantly an attitude that "saw work as a value,

*Op. 37, 341; cf. Trever 158–59. For isolated farm sites in the environs of Ascra, see Snodgrass 1991: 132, 36; 1985: 88–95.

**Coldstream 1977: 368. For the ethic of hard work, cf. Detienne 1963: 55.

not as a necessary evil" (Galt 237, 238). This type of 'Good Strife' makes the farmer in Hesiod's poem envy his neighbor and presses him on to work harder to acquire greater wealth (23–24). In a phrase almost reminiscent of Adam Smith, Hesiod sings that the power of competition can "stir up even the lazy to work, for a man wants work once he sees his neighbor, a rich man, eager to plough, to plant and to put his house in good order" (20–22). Labor is now the ethical cargo of intensive agriculture; it is not a hindrance to increasing economic production. Hard work attains a moral dimension prefigured by the image of Laertes on his knees, Dolios and his sons mending terraces, and the countryside teeming with laborers on the shield of Achilles (*Il.* 18.540ff).

Hesiod believes that even the appearance of the farm is important to the community: weed-free fields, vibrant orchard and vine stock, and healthy animals. Good infrastructure prompts each farmer to want that ideal of agricultural excellence, and through the individual rivalry of landowners, the countryside of the *polis* as a whole progresses. Similarly, much later in Menander's *Dyscolus* (603–5), the successful farmer is described by the simple encomium "he is unmatched as a farmer"; in Menander's *The Farmer*, the aged agrarian will take time off from his vine digging only when he cuts his leg open and is forced to bed (Men. *Georg.* 65–66).

This Hesiodic idea of constant struggle, of work as intrinsically good, even moral, and bringing with it profit, is new to Greece. "Much then of the *Works and Days* may be seen as a rebuke of past practice," perceptively writes Thalia Howe. "Men are to give up the plundering and raiding (319ff.) of the past, and instead seek protection under a newer Zeus (1–10, 25–26), who protects the worker in the field (17ff, 398)." This moral and ethical element inherent in hard work, this "newer Zeus" is rooted in economic pragmatism. "Both the gods and men," Hesiod says, "are angry at those who are idle, living the life of the stingless drones" (303–4).[3]

Even today the attentive modern farmer must be up before dawn to ensure survival of his household, regardless of the tasks—or lack of them—at hand. Age-old wisdom, rooted in bitter experience, suggests that the lie-abed agriculturalist will eventually lose his farm. Whether his dawdling is due to drugs, alcohol, illness, or simple indifference, the continual late riser cannot, in my own experience, overcome such liability and stick to a steady regimen.*

This change in Hellenic outlook in the *Works and Days* largely explains why the agrarian revolution at the beginning of the Greek *polis* period was so successful. It was a transformation in ideology as well as practice. The occasional (and contemporary) emphases in the *Odyssey* on the work of Odysseus, Eurymachos, and Laertes reappear in Hesiod's world. Now the need for manual farmwork is not eccentric advice for rural success, but a tenet: a man should make a living from the soil on his *own*.

In the *Works and Days* strenuous labor can also lead to riches and prosperity. Hesiod, born into a changing world of rising population and diminishing arable land, does *not* see his agricultural experience as a static phenomenon, freezing the farmer into a particular status and class: "When a man adds to what he has, he keeps away bright-eyed hunger; for if you add only a little to a little and do this often enough, soon that little will become big" (361–63). Whether or not agriculture at this early stage actually offered much opportunity for radical advancement, for the "little" surplus (*smikron*) to become "big" (*mega*), is less important than the farmers' *belief* that eventually it did so: the pursuit of wealth and capital led to greater productivity throughout Greece and kept rural men busy reclaiming marginal land, planting trees and acquiring slaves, shifting to intensive agriculture in order to find rural independence and at times prosperity in supplying food to the growing surrounding community.

The nascent Greek city-state of this period may not have been guided in a formal economic sense—even later it rarely had an overriding conscious economic policy—but Greeks were now well aware of the source of capital and the value of surplus: "If there is desire for wealth in your heart, then do the following: Work with work on top of work (*ergon ep' ergô ergazesthai*)" (381–82). Hesiod believes this ethic can lead to 'surplus' and thus to profit: "For this is the way wealth piles up in the house." Even if there are many to feed, the poet says: "Zeus can provide easily the needed abundance for the greater number, for the more there

*Cf. the old Roman Cato (*Rust.* 5.8): "For this is the way farming is: if you do one thing late, you will do everything late (*Nam res rustica sic est, si unam rem sero feceris, omia opera sero facies*)"; and Columella (*Rust.* 11.2.80): "All things ought to be done on time, especially sowing. The old farming proverb says that early sowing can often deceive the farmer, the late sowing never—for it always turns out bad."

are, the more work there is, and thus the more the surplus (*meizôn ep-ithêkê*)" (377–79).

Hesiod's desire for intensive farming and its attendant wealth imply "a limited good," a prosperity that must come at the expense of others. Nor did he envision an endless stagnation in the productive capacity of the farm.* The *Works and Days* does not at all reflect the primitive state of agricultural production, an "embedded" way of peasant economic thinking aimed at ensuring self-sufficiency only, rather than family needs *and* valuable marketable surpluses. While competition between farmers is often—and sometimes exclusively—expressed in naked distrust of one another, in rivalry, envy, in obligated giving and reciprocity, these credos are *not* incompatible with a concurrent comprehension of market realities. Nor are they at odds with a sophisticated awareness of supply and demand, with a desire to pass on something greater than what one has received, which later became a common aspiration of most Greeks (e.g., Pl. *Resp.* 1.330B–D).

Envy is instinctual. It wars daily with rationality, reflecting the farmer's own ground-eye view of the immediate results of his own labor: success for him, failure for the man across the road. Even today, belying the popular image of the sophisticated agribusinessman, I know many farm families who care little for the statistics on the national output of their particular crops, who laugh at their ag-magazine's report of the county's yearly receipts, who pay no attention to nightly business reports, and who rarely dwell on the nation's balance of payments of agricultural trade.

Instead they keep their eyes glued to their neighbor. As Xenophon wrote, "You can tell by looking at the crops and trees of another man's land what the soil will and will not grow. . . . You can often get more accurate information from a neighboring plot than you can from a neighbor himself" (*Oec.* 16.3,4). Warily, farmers watch the land of kindred. Keenly they note a new barn, a vineyard's fresh stakes, a heavy grape crop, all seen as potential signals of their own demise ("It is not enough that I make it," a successful family farmer once admitted to me, "the

---

*On the limited good, see Millet 1984: 95. For a belief in the stagnant nature of Greek agriculture, see Finley 1973: 71; Starr 1977: 156–68; Jardé 194; Isager and Skydsgaard 191–98. But cf. Amouretti 1986: 239–55.

others, you guys, gotta fail"). For selfish reasons, men of this sort borrow thousands and work endlessly in order not to be left behind. This is not necessarily grandiosity or the symptoms of a fragile ego, not evidence either of a finite peasant world of petty men and limited good (though it can clearly be that as well). The overall efficiency and prosperity that result from self-interest have continually improved (in a strictly material sense) the lives of millions in this country, urban dwellers who consume the cheapest and safest food in the world. Envy, selfishness, and parochialism can all be—as any farmer knows—part of a sophisticated market system, rather than the baser traits of a subsistence peasantry.

What besides personal rivalry, as opposed to economic rationalism, can explain the sudden appearance in our vicinity during the late 1970s of thousands of acres of new vineyard trellises, cross-arms now nailed to each wooden stake? Agribusiness dogma would argue that the cost and upkeep of expensive, impressive, and productive trellising systems, replacing the plebeian single wire on a single stake of the past, would not ensure commensurate profit in increased grape tonnage and quality, would argue that the investment of the extra wood and wire depleted savings that families could have spent on leisure or recreation. But the specter of a neighbor's vineyard now suddenly elevated by a foot, its canopy widened by two, was too much for many Valley farmers to bear. And so field by field, entire vineyards were retrofitted with new crossarms, stakes, and wire—bringing improvement in quality and quantity of raisins to the industry as a whole.

What other than envy or individualism gone mad can account for a neighbor, veteran of two massive coronaries, in the midst of the raisin crash of 1983—when the idea of mutual aid, equipment sharing, grassroots group organizing, and collective lobbying made perfect sense—announcing instead that it was now simple Darwinism, him versus us? "You'll buy my place or me yours," he told me bluntly two years before his third, fatal heart attack. My last memory of him is his hobbling off, muttering a final "So it's either you or me—and it won't be me." For weeks on end we redoubled our efforts at tree and vine pruning, determined not to fall his victim.

Dawn in the new world of Hesiod's intensive farmer is no longer always the refreshing "rosy-fingered" maiden of a vestigial aristocratic society. In the seventh-century countryside, no longer depopulated but rather forced to question traditional practices of land use, the early morning takes on a different connotation: "Avoid sleeping until dawn" (Hes. *Op.* 574); now she "takes away a third part from work, and sets a man on his journey and advances him in his work" (579–80; cf. Starr 1977: 158–59). Over two centuries later, in Euripides' *Electra*, the small farmer—for all his humility—is at least allowed to boast of the same creed: "At dawn's light I put the cows to pasture and begin planting the fields" (*Elect.* 80).

Time in the countryside of the *polis* is not at all the Dark-Age time of serfs, peasants, and landlords, but instead the cosmos of individual property owners and self-employed farmers alone responsible for their survival or destruction. Thus the Aristotelian *Oeconomica* advises matter-of-factly: "Rising before dawn is most useful" (*Oec.* 1.1345a17). One may rest only during the scorching temperatures of the summer afternoon, well after six to seven hours labor since first light (e.g., Theoc. 10.50–51).

Greek farmers worked "all day long" (e.g., Hom. *Od.*13.31–34). In the Homeric hymn to Hermes, Apollo encounters a viticulturalist who has been digging in his small plot of vines "all day long (*propan êmar*) until the sun went down" (*Hymn. Hom. Merc.* 205–6). Plato later assumed that the care of wheat, barley, and vines consumed one's entire effort (*epimeleian pasan*; Pl. *Clit.* 408E6). The fourth-century playwright Menander's Sostratos says to the idle Daos: "Do you intend to stand around while we're working?" He adds that if the old farmer Knemon saw idleness, "right away he'd throw clods at you, and call you a lazy good-for-nothing" (*Dys.* 364–67). Although there was a romantic tradition in classical poetry that winter "was the time of laziness for the farmer" (e.g., Virg. *Georg.* 1.299), even then—as modern viticulturalists will attest—we should picture a busy season of fertilization, terrace repair, pruning, staking, trellising, and other maintenance operations vital to an intensive, diversified farm. To Hesiod it is simple: work at *every* season is the only, the necessary solution; each man builds for his future, giving his all until his health or youth is gone, his ethic absorbed by those who farm his plot in his aftermath.

There is a Greek notion of self-responsibility quite foreign to *both* the aristocratic and the peasant mind. To Xenophon, if a man knows no trade, he had better farm—or resort to the criminal life of stealing, robbing, or begging (*Oec.* 20.15). In Hesiod's new world there is no salvation granted by a wealthy patron or divine intervention, his belief in the justice of a "newer Zeus" not withstanding. Each farmer is on his own. Excuses and complaints are but the baggage of the perpetual victim, the whiner who seeks outside explanation of reason, or rescue from his own demise. Plagued with self-doubt, men such as these "turn their greedy thoughts toward the possessions of some other" (*Od.* 316), and thus become farmers who cannot and will not take care of their own livelihood (317). In Hesiod's stern code, these are men like his no-good brother Perses, who continually solicits aid to escape his own (inner) failure: "Perses, you fool, work for it; twice you may find help, and even perhaps three times, but if you bother them more, your begging will be in vain; your word-play will bring no profit" (401–3). In Hesiod's agrarian world a man cannot count on anything but himself. To seek outside support, to rely on another, invariably results in cruel disappointment. Such salvation is illusory—in the words of the old Greek agrarian proverb, "The vine-stake betraying the vine" (Arist. *Vesp.* 1291).

Euripides confirms this ethos was prevalent well into the fifth century: "A lazy man never makes a living if he is not willing to work" (*Elect.* 81). Labor on one's own plot confers dignity, sloth earns shame for weakness. "Work is no disgrace," Hesiod warns his brother. "The disgrace lies in *not* working" (311). Shame, Hesiod adds, "goes with poverty, but confidence with prosperity" (19). The agrarian chauvinism fostered in this early era became enshrined throughout later Greek literature: the commandment in the later Palantine Anthology is the stark: "Love the shovel and the life of a farmer" (*Anth. Pal.* 9.23).

Hesiod's credo is not one man's idiosyncratic upbraiding of an angry heir, but a reflection of the growing collective voice of the countryside, the universal religion of embattled men desperately working to grow enough food to supply the burgeoning population of Greece. Thus arose notions of an agrarian ideology quite apart from those minority voices springing up in nascent Greek city life (ironically, the very ones we usually hear in Greek literature). In Hesiod's poem there is superiority of the country over the city, where the "bribe-swallowing barons" hold sway—despite the mutual dependence of the one on the other. Hesiod advises the farmer to "pass by the blacksmith's shop and its crowded lounge" (493), and to marry a woman "who lives nearby" (700). Here we see amplified the implicit suggestion in the Laertes passage of the *Odyssey* that there *was* now a difference between life on the farm and life engaged in petty trade, day labor, or craftsmanship within the walls of the city-state. Competition between Greek farmers is designed to promote their common good (even when they themselves cannot always see it), and to set them apart from men who do not work their own ground.

Greek farmers appearing in the eighth century were *neither* subsistence peasants nor wealthy aristocrats, but rather something in between: the new *polis* agriculture created a new "class," a middling breed rare in agricultural history. Alert to evolution of class and status throughout this book, we must ask the same question in different guises: "Who was Laertes?" "Who was Hesiod?" And later: "Who were the *geôrgoi?*" "Who were the hoplites?"

At each stage of this study it is crucial to reemphasize the uniqueness of intensive agriculture in the long history of Greece and of the men who created that agrarianism. It is impossible accurately to gauge their numbers, possible only to approximate their *relative position between* a smaller entrenched elite and a slightly larger group below of landless poor, and some less successful subsistence "peasants." It is also difficult to postulate a neat, uniform agrarianism in all of the more than one thousand Greek-speaking *poleis*, city-states of all sizes of adjacent countrysides and urban centers. But we can distinguish a rough similarity in agricultural practice and farm life quite at odds with what preceded and succeeded the *polis*, or what was practiced in Sparta, Thessaly, Crete, and other atypical regions.[4]

It is easier to distinguish the farmers in the *Works and Days* from the wealthy, for clearly Hesiod feels a distinct antipathy for those who hold political power and have no need of manual labor. His vocabulary for the elites includes words such as "bribe-swallowers," "drones," and "fools," who do not know the inherent nobility of the just and honorable smaller portion (*Op.* 189, 264, 195, 207, 248), hawks that gloat over their seizure of a helpless nightingale (38, cf. 221, 264). Neither "have they ever learned how much better the half is than the whole," Hesiod says, nor "how much good there is in mallow and asphodel"—the working man's diet of the ancient Greek world (40–41). That proverb is not much different from that of the modern middling farmers of southern Italy, who likewise resent the rich: "All people," they insist, "are picked from the same plant." This uneasiness with affluence is *not* simply the traditional agrarian dislike for those in authority, but rather real disgust for the privileged who do not work hard on their own land.[5]

Much later Euripides' farmer in his *Electra* says something similar about the modest nobility of the agrarian life: once a man has eaten his daily bread, he announces, "you cannot really tell the rich and poor apart" (*Elect.* 431). Although the playwright Menander's farmers are not at all poor, his character Gorgias is still made to say: "It is not a pleasurable thing for me to enjoy wealth won by the labor of others, but only that which I've earned myself" (*Dys.* 830–31). At the beginning of the *polis* period, Hesiod sets the tone when he mouths none of the aristocratic mockery toward the less fortunate found in Homeric epic: "Never dare," he warns, "to ridicule a man for hateful, heart-eating poverty" (717).

The actual material circumstances of Hesiod's farmers confirm the poet's political and social outlook. Under his regime, agrarians must work, and work constantly. Surely that need for continual hard labor is why Aristotle in his *Politics* discounted farming as an occupation for his ideal, contemplative citizenry. Yeoman agriculture, noble as it might be in the philosopher's view, required too much work and provided not enough leisure for the development of virtue and participation in political life (*Pol.* 7.1329a2; cf. Eur. *Supp.* 420–23). Nevertheless, in the real world of the Greek *polis*, the middle group of agrarian citizenry usually, even on Aristotle's own admission, produced the most stable society (e.g., *Pol.* 7.1319a21–22).

Hesiod's farmers are not at all similar to the aristocratic Pindar's "noble souls," who have a life "free from toil and who do not torment the earth with the strength of their arms" (*Olymp.* 2.59–70), not at all similar to the aristocratic sixth-century Cretan landowner, Hybrias, who bragged that in his culture of lords, all serfs "fall down and kiss my knee, calling me master and great lord" (Athen. 15.695F–696A; cf. Willets 1963: 260–61). In the *Works and Days* that aristocratic snub of physical work is inimical to a people for whom famine is ever a worry (302–3).[6]

Hesiod is no aristocratic horse breeder. Although there are plenty of livestock on Hesiod's farm, all the animals are utilitarian. He tells the farmer to cut his timber in order to make his own plows and wagon (420–30), to manufacture almost anything he needs. Hesiod advises him to dress in sheepskin, a cape, and a felt hat, and, like Laertes, to strap leather hides on his feet (517–18; 539–46). (In contrast, at Sparta the absentee overlords forced the indentured helots to wear leather to brand them as *inferior* farm laborers, not possessors of rank and privilege [cf. Athen. 14.657C–D]). That image of a sunburned, leather-clad manual laborer (e.g., Theog. 54–57; Men. *Dys.* 416) portrays Greek farmers far better than finely clothed absentee lords, the wealthy upper crust who, Thucydides said, at one time in Ionia wore linen underwear and tied a knot of their hair with golden grasshoppers (Thuc. 1.6.2).

From now on throughout Greek literature, the farmer is to be a man of leather and hides, and one proud of his distinct weather-beaten look. In the *Dyscolus* of Menander, the status of the sunburned man can be surmised by the question: "Is he a farmer?" (754). Nor, as in the case of Laertes, is there any reason to believe that Hesiod's estate is large and bountiful. The evidence in the poem instead suggests that the farm is on less than prized bottomland and, given the few tools named, probably not much larger than five to fifteen acres.

On the other hand, it is also hard to agree with recent scholars' attempts to make Hesiod into a "peasant," unless one changes the popular conception of a peasant to our notion of an intensive small farmer, or a "better off" peasant. In regard to traditional definitions of peasantry, I have found *no* evidence that the *geôrgoi* of the Greek countryside by the fifth century (1) were frequently under debt obligation to the rich, (2) were without disposable cash, (3) were subject to an array of high rents and taxes, (4) were growers of food largely for subsistence without much regard for the market, (5) were lacking a strong and equal voice in political affairs, (6) were subject to military conscription without consent, (7) were liable to have their social status frozen indefinitely, (8) were without slaves, (9) were sharply divided from those higher up on the social scale by the size and nature of their farm holdings, (10) were without clear title to their farms, stock, slaves, and arms, or (11) were bereft of any chance for improvement and change in agricultural technique. Every one of these eleven characteristics was absent from the *polis* countryside. Instead, "independent," "intensive," "yeoman," or "middling" farmer much better fits the evidence.[7]

Although Hesiod's farm is not large, it apparently can support at least six people: the owner, his wife (695–701), at least one child (376–77), two or more male slaves (469–71, 502, 607–8), and a female servant (602–3). His farmer also owns oxen (404–5), mules, and slaves (459,

470, 502, 573, 608, 766), as well as his own farm equipment and house (405)—a sizable capital investment beyond the resources of the very poor (e.g., Will 1965: 547–48). Hesiod can conceive of his farmer freely buying the land of others (*ophr' allôn ônê klêron, mê ton teon allos*, 341). In fact, at no time in the culture of the *polis* were the majority of farmers legally trapped on their small holdings without recourse to buying, selling, renting, or leasing. Although there was strong social and familial pressure to retain the family plot (one of the chief tenets of agrarianism), the evidence still suggests that at all eras of *polis* history one could buy or sell farmland. It is nearly impossible to envision Greek homestead farmers as systematically being exploited by outsiders, or in possession of a distinct cultural tradition of victimization.[8]

Hesiod also contemplates maritime trade excursions as a way of profiting from occasional agricultural surpluses (618–35), and his farmers can even enjoy imported wine (589). Finally, he advises having only a single son, a probable reflection of worries over fragmenting the ancestral estate, thus reducing his heirs to the ranks of the poor—an idea quite at odds with the practice of the impoverished, who seek needed agricultural labor not in slaves or hired men, but in large families. This limiting of the farm family is different than the traditional notions of peasantry, but the preference for fewer offspring must also illustrate Hesiod's assumption that slaves are plentiful, affordable, and vital to the homesteader's operation. Clearly, the poet is addressing those who are *not* on the bottom of the social scale. His *Works and Days* is "a manual for the newly created economy of the tillers of the soil who were beginning to practice independent agriculture full-time and in great number."[9]

II. The Rise of the Agrarians

> The rich and the poor are not so removed from each other as they are in Europe. Some few towns excepted, we are all tillers of the earth, from Nova Scotia to West Florida. If he [the European] travels throughout rural districts he views not the hostile castle, and the haughty mansion, contrasted with the clay-built hut and the miserable cabin, where men and cattle help to keep each other warm, and dwell in meanness, smoke and indigence. A pleasing uniformity of decent competence appears throughout our habitations.
>
> —Hector St. John Crèvecoeur, *Letters of an American Farmer* (Letter 3)

Various later literary sources confirm Hesiod's initial picture of the emergence of small farmers who were neither wealthy aristocrats nor impoverished peasants tied to subsistence agriculture. Their vigorous presence is not a romantic abstraction, but a reality in the life of the later Greek city-state that explains much of the absence of class conflict between the rich and the poor throughout the ensuing four centuries of this study. The deterioration of just this group of middling farmers, in turn, accounts for the polarization in Greek society from the third century on, when the small and independent landowner was unable to survive, and the size of Hellenistic farms became much larger—even as the total arability of a city's surrounding lands (predictably) often declined. Throughout Greek literature of the *polis* period the challenge to the new farmer comes *not* mainly from the poor, with their litany of "redistribution of lands and cancellation of debts"—that agenda is usually characteristic of the fourth century and later—but from the entrenched wealthy, who resent the ambitious nonaristocratic landowner and "his pleasing uniformity of decent competence."

Right at the beginning of Greek agrarianism we see two phenomena in the agrarian sociology of the incipient *polis*. First, there is intense dislike on the part of the landed and wealthy elite for these upstart farmers, the *geôrgoi* who early in aristocratic literature are predictably dubbed the *kakoi*, the "bad," (in opposition to the *agathoi*, the "good" traditional aristocrats by birth), and second, recognition appears among more enlightened Greeks that the presence of an agrarian class of small farmers (properly called *hoi mesoi*, "the middle ones") was responsible for both the creation and preservation of the Greek city-state, and that their political agenda was both reasonable and proper.

In early Greek literature the *kakoi* (the "bad") and the *mesoi* (the "middle") are often *one and the same group*. The former is merely the pejorative label used by the wealthy to demean the once impoverished who are now in ascendancy.[10] The latter is either the self-nomenclature of the farmers themselves, or the label used by the few aristocrats and later philosophers sympathetic to their cause. At the most cynical extreme would be the (sixth-century?) reactionary poet Theognis (54ff.), who felt the agrarians had so successfully infringed the aristocratic domain, so completely replaced birth by material success in the growing *polis*, that they no longer were *kakoi*, or even *mesoi*. Now they wandered outside the walls of the *polis* with pretensions to actually being *agathoi* (the "good")!

The actual emergence of middling farmers explains in large part the Greek philosophical construct of moderation and "the golden mean," not vice versa. Aristotle recognized first the crucial role of the *mesoi* in the early *polis*, and second their relation to the birth of a more abstract philosophical and ethical notion of moderation: "In all city-states, then, there are three divisions of the *polis*: the very rich, the very poor, and those who are in the middle (*hoi mesoi*) of the two. Because it is agreed that the moderate way (*to metrion*) or middle (*to meson*) is best, it is clear then that it is most preferable to have the middle amount (*hê mesê*) of all fortunate things" (*Pol.* 4. 1295b2–6).[11]

A landscape of small family farmers, ancient and modern, usually results in a rural world of three, not two, classes. Greek agrarianism—the success and social stability offered by the creation of a large group of middling farmers—*antedated* the rise of conscious, written philosophical speculation. So it should be expected that an agrarian tradition informs a number of early Greek philosophers, men who drew on the emerging egalitarian landscape for their own views on natural harmony. Passages in Greek literature that connect farming to philosophy and early philosophers illustrate the original link between philosophical speculation and both agrarian ideology and the pragmatics of agriculture itself (e.g., Thales [Arist. *Pol.* 1.1259a10–12]; Empedocles [Theophr. *CP* 1.7.1]; "The Seven Sages" [Colum. *Rust.* 1.3.8]; Democritus [Diog. Laert. 9.48])—a very early tradition that *antedated* the later more systematic investigations of Xenophon, Plato, Aristotle, and Theophrastus.

Wealthier Greeks had no affinity for the emergence of *geôrgoi*. Anecdotes abound demonstrating the aristocratic dislike for the new type of agriculture that required hard work by the owner, leaving no leisure or time to engage in traditionally preferred hunting and athletic pursuits. Timaeus relates the disparaging jokes two wealthy Sybarites exchanged when watching farmers hoe the fields. Just watching them work makes the two wealthy men ill.*

---

*FGrH 566 fr.48. In Thessaly, which never really evolved from its status of Dark-Age aristocracy, farmers were not even allowed to use the marketplace, but were relegated to an inferior status, along with the landless and craftsmen (e.g., Arist. *Pol.* 7.1331a33–35). Surely the successful exclusion of such men reflects the absence of real agrarianism there and a disdain for the entire culture of small farming.

In contrast, Phocylides, an elegiac poet of the mid-sixth century, advises that his readers can find wealth in homestead agriculture: "See that you have a fertile farm, for a farm, they say, is a horn of plenty" (fr. 7.1–2). He was probably not talking about the estates of the landed aristocrats, for in another fragment he reminds his readers, "Much good is there to the middle-ones (*mesoisin*); I would wish to be midmost (*mesos*) in a city" (cf. Arist. *Pol.* 4.1295b30–35).

Around the same time at Athens we also see further reference to a rural group that was neither extremely wealthy nor reduced to abject slavery. In Attica there was an old tradition (going back perhaps to the end of the Greek Dark Ages?) that the officers of the citizenry were selected from the *eupatridai* (the nobles), the *geôrgoi* or *agroikoi* (the farmers), and the *dêmiourgoi* (the landless craftsmen) (Arist. *Ath. Pol.* 13.2–3; cf. Plut. *Thes.* 25.2). The terminology may be inexact. It may be too strict a tripartite social division for eighth-century Attica. Nevertheless, these categories echo a long-held belief that early in the history of the Greek *polis*, there were farmers who had carved themselves out a middle ground, neither wealthy nor poor.

The agrarian transformation was not uniform throughout Greece either geographically or chronologically. There were always (even in the late *polis* period) backwaters of reactionary horse raising and Dark-Age aristocracy. Yet it seems clear enough that Athens, at least by the early sixth century, while undergoing "a more or less anarchic system of individual transactions,"[12] was *not* in a period of agricultural retrenchment. Like hundreds of other *poleis*, Athens was struggling toward the formal political recognition of a true class of yeomanry, who owned their own plots and sought political representation equal to their economic success.

The lawgiver Solon appreciated the new realities when, at the beginning of the sixth century in Attica, he supposedly organized the Athenians into four census "classes" to divide political power and assess wealth according to the citizens' agrarian (and military?) status. The producers of 500 wet or dry measures of agricultural produce (the wealthiest so-called *pentakosiomedimnoi*), those who could show income of 300 *medimnoi* (the *hippeis* who composed the cavalry), and the 200-measure *zeugitai*, most likely our hoplite-farmers who "yoked" themselves side by side in battle, were all now allowed their respective magistracies and formally constituted the political body of the city-state.* They formed the ancestral constitution recalled so nostalgically throughout later Athenian literature. The fourth and last Solonian group of *thêtes*, mostly landless poor or impoverished subsistence farmers who could not rate 200 measures of annual produce (and perhaps originally were thereby incapable of buying armor), were still excluded from most formal political representation. Controversy surrounds the exact implications of these early census rubrics for economics, the military, and politics, but for our agrarian purposes the picture is clear enough: early Athenian society was defined exclusively according to agricultural production, not birth, and farming success was apparently the key to all political and military privilege.**

There now at Athens was formal recognition of a class of farmers quite *apart* from the poor below and the wealthy above. This middle grouping, this *zeugite* rubric of the 200–300-measure men who "yoked" oxen (or were "yoked" together in hoplite infantry service), suggests by 600 B.C. in Attica at least the entrenched existence of a militia of yeoman farmers.***

Quite naturally Solon ("a middle citizen" [Arist. *Ath. Pol.* 5.2–3; Plut. *Sol.* 14–15.1]) felt that he had deliberately positioned himself with his shield as a hoplite of sorts between the abject poor and the aristocratic rich. He writes (*Sol.* 4.5–8): "I provided the people as much privilege as they have a right to. I neither degraded them from rank nor gave them a free hand. And for those who already held the power and were envied for riches, I worked it out that they also should have no cause for complaint. I stood there holding my sturdy shield over both the parties."

At their root, these original social differentiations in early Athenian history may have been a product of locale as well. A little later, about

---

*E.g., Arist. *Ath. Pol.* 7.3–5; Plut. *Sol.* 18.1–2; Pollux *On.* 8.129; cf. Busolt and Swoboda 820–24.

**"It should always be remembered," wrote Louis Gernet, "that in principle, laws governing land ownership exist only for citizens, and inversely in some constitutions, it is almost a philosophical principle (as well as a condition in certain constitutions) that ownership of property be a prerequisite for citizenship. One should add that agriculture, valued more highly than other and more directly urban factors, is more closely connected with the nature of citizenship. In sum, the city-dweller as such has no real place in the *politeia*" (Gernet 1981: 314). See, too, Rhodes 137–46; cf. Patterson 180–82.

***On the general connection between farming and fighting, see also Arist. *Pol.* 4. 1297b15–28, 4.1291a31–33; Xen. *Oec.* 5.12–18; IG I³1.8–10; Starr 1977: 177–87; Finley 1981b: 124–25; O. Murray 120–152; Andrewes 1956: 31–42.

the time of the tyrant Peisistratus (mid-sixth century), we are told that rural interests in Attica were still known by their residence at the "Plain," "Shore," or "Hill" (e.g., Arist. *Ath. Pol.* 13.4; Hdt. 159.3). Even if such rubrics were not entirely historical, the conventional nomenclature at least reflected popular belief that the wealthier *agathoi* ("the good") had long been associated with the richest land of the "Plain" (the *pedion* probably nearest Athens). The "Shore" (the *paralia* or coastal area from Phaleron to Sunion) and the "Hill" (*huperakrioi* or *diakrioi*) distinguished poorer traders and farmers on less prized ground or even on rough terrain.[13]

Mere labels probably do not suppose strict historical distinctions in occupation or economic class. But they are at least another sign of a group of agrarians at odds with the wealthy holders of the old prized land near Athens itself. The geographical distinctions point to three, not two, social groups. Aristotle believed that Peisistratus "had made himself tyrant by raising a party against the men of the plain" (*Pol.* 5.1305a 23–24; 1310b 30–1).

There had long been strife between established estate holders on bottom land (perhaps owners of large herds and wealthy specialist growers of grain) and those who were becoming established as intensive farmers of diverse crops, often on land that could include rugged terrain. When Aristotle recalled the original creation of ten ruling archons at Athens (about 580 B.C.), he posited the presence of a middling group of agrarians between the aristocratic rich and landless poor. The ten officers, he wrote, were to be composed of five *eupatridai*, or nobles, three farmers (*agroikoi*), and two *dêmiourgoi*, or landless craftsmen and day laborers (*Ath. Pol.* 13.2).

Rarely in early Greek history was there anything like the "range wars" of the American West, but early on, large livestock owners were probably seen as a distinct group (e.g., Athen. 12.540d). It is reasonable to suppose that their interests often collided with the homesteaders—even though most farmers could own some livestock and most wealthy herdsmen could own some farmland. After all, the old-guard, livestock-owning elite descended from the decentralized and depopulated Greece of past centuries. They would wish to perpetuate their concentration on animals, and so would resent homestead farmers who opted for more efficient use of land and the curtailment of horse raising and cavalry. Aristotle, in his encomium of rural people, generally saw pastoralists and agriculturalists as different social entities (e.g., *Pol.* 6.1319a20–24). By the fifth and fourth centuries, animal-raising was a cash enterprise dominated by the rich who produced animals for specialized markets, for sacrifice and cavalry, and for the sporting tastes of an urban elite.[14]

The days of aristocratic horse rearing, for mounted raiding, and military cadres were numbered. Such practices were based on an underutilization of increasingly valuable farm ground. In turn, farming and rural infrastructure often precluded the unrestricted passage of large herds to and from mountain pasture, and intensive agriculture gave Greek farmers a modicum of social prestige entirely divorced from the mere possession of animals. Aristotle recounts in his *Politics* (5.1305a24–25) the curious story of Theagenes of Megara (625 B.C.?), the tyrant who slaughtered the cattle of the well-off (*hoi euporoi*), perhaps because they were wandering onto the property of others. Later, it is no surprise that in most literature of the *polis* the old hierarchy of pastoralism and cavalry was viewed as uncivilized, and compared unfavorably with agriculture and infantry service.[15] Some writers suggest that within these early *poleis* only five percent of the population may have held enough land to be called "aristocratic," whereas nearly half the citizen population qualified as hoplites. An *enormous* social transformation had obviously taken place in Greece, nothing less than the creation of an entire class, which through sheer preponderance of numbers overwhelmed the aristocratic culture of Dark-Age Greece.

Aristote's anecdote concerning Theagenes is part of a digression on early tyrants who championed the cause of the people—the people who, Aristotle tells us, "in those times lived on their farms (*epi tôn agrôn oikein ton dêmon*) busily engaged in their work (*ascholon onta pros tois ergois*)" (*Pol.* 5. 1305a18–20). The Athenian tyrant Peisistratus (mid-sixth century) especially was said to have deliberately encouraged rural residence and the farming of olives, going so far as to provide loans for trees and vines to broaden his support among rural farmers (Dio. Chrys. 7.107–8; 1.75.3; Arist. *Ath. Pol.* 16.3). From these random, but frequent, anecdotes about early Athenian history, a common theme emerges: a growing group of small farmers assumes political power and enjoys military status, quite distinct from either the poor or the wealthy elite. Small plots, not large herds or rich estates; infantry, not horsemen or skirmishers, agricultural competence, not birth, become the backbone of the Athenian *polis*.[16]

The Athenian leader Pericles at the outset of the Peloponnesian War remarked that most of the peoples of the Peloponnese were self-employed farmers (*autourgoi*), an indication they were neither absentee landlords or rich barons, nor peasants dependent on wealthy households or urban interests (Thuc. 1.139.2). In his report to his own people about prospective Athenian military strength at the dawn of the first Peloponnesian invasion (431 B.C.), Pericles (e.g., Thuc. 2.14) reviewed the forces in *three* categories: (1) cavalry (i.e., the wealthy), (2) infantry (i.e., the mostly farming middle), and (3) light-armed skirmishers and rowers (i.e., those without much property). Thucydides himself, when he lists the Athenian losses to the plague, catalogs the dead according to a three-part hierarchy: (1) 300 cavalry, (2) more than 4,400 hoplites, (3) significant numbers of the poor below (3.87).

The depiction of an agrarian hoplite group who did their own farm work alongside a few slaves, but who were neither extremely wealthy nor entirely poor, survived in Greek literature well into the fourth century, demonstrating the continued existence of a viable intensive agriculture during nearly the entire lifetime of the *polis*. In a particularly interesting passage in Euripides' late fifth-century tragedy, the *Supplices*, the Athenian hero Theseus is made to say that there exist three types of citizens: the rich are "greedy and of no use," the landless poor are grasping and easily led astray by evil leaders, but the "ones in the middle" (*hoi mesoi*) "are the salvation of the city" (238–42; cf. Bisinger 6).

Aristotle displays fewer of the aristocratic prejudices of Plato, and has a far clearer grasp of class distinctions and the role of property in the life of the city-state. He takes up the theme of the "middle ones" throughout his *Politics* (e.g., 4.1295a36–1296a22). He suggests that this identification and praise of those in between, although related to the more general Greek ideal of the "mean," also refers to a specific class, the landowning group of the *polis*.

This "class" is clearly *not* mercantile or commercial in the modern sense, but rather entirely agrarian, sandwiched between the few wealthy and the most numerous poor. Aristotle writes of middling farmers in realistic, rather than utopian, terms. He implies that agrarians of the middle had been widespread throughout the early *polis* history of Greece (although he saw them in decline during his own time at the end of the fourth century). The citizenry was divided into three groups: "the wealthy," "those without means," and the "middle ones" (*hoi mesoi*; cf. *Pol.* 4.1295b3–5; 1295b30–40), who were not pitted against either of the other two classes, and whose numbers resulted in a proportional stability in the *polis*. Aristotle earlier had said nearly the same thing: "some in the *polis* must be rich, some poor, and some in between" (*Pol.* 4.1289b33).[17]

His use of *mesoi* here refers explicitly to the owners of small farms: "When the farmer class and the class having moderate means are in control of the government, they govern according to laws; the reason is because they have a livelihood, and they are not able to be at leisure, so that they put laws in control of the state and hold only the minimum of assemblies necessary" (*Pol.* 4.1292b25–29). He is contrasting them with both the leisured, absentee wealthy and the underemployed landless. In a later passage, he concludes that those who hold property in moderation are the most stabilizing influence in the city-state (4.1295b29–31).

Aristotle goes on to reiterate that government of these middle ones is the best, but possible only when they are present in sufficient number to prevent class strife between the very rich and the abject poor (1295b40–1296a22). This observation implies, I think, that in his review of *polis* history he saw instability at the creation of the *polis* and then once more during the turmoil of his own time during the late fourth century. He apparently felt then that the *mesoi* were shrinking, and thus their erosion was leading to either extremely narrow oligarchical or excessively democratic regimes.* Finally, in his sixth book of the *Politics*, he once more confirms that the "middle ones" were, in fact, those who farmed on their own, and who provided the city-state with the social and political stability that led to the "best" type of government (1318b7–15).

> Since there are four types of democracy, the best of all is the first type, which was described in the preceding discourses [e.g., the farmer democracy of sections 1291b–1292b, cf.1295b]. It is also the most ancient of them all, although by the term "first" I mean first as a rubric used to classify the commons. Indeed, the best common people is the agricultural population

---

Pol. 4. 1296a24–26. See Lintott 1992: 126–67; Dawson 99–102, on declining *mesoi*.

(*geôrgikos dêmos*), so that it is possible to introduce democracy wherever the multitude lives by agriculture or by pasturing cattle. Not having a great deal of property, they have no time for frequent attendance at the assembly. Needing the essentials of life, they are always hard at work and do not covet the property of their neighbors.

Aristotle writes that this most stable form of government by small farmers had an ancient pedigree, and was to be associated with the foundation of the *polis*. He adds that in many states "in early times" an entire array of laws (restrictions on the size of land ownership, prohibition of the sale of farmland, legislation against borrowing against an estate, and rules of inheritance) existed that were "entirely fitting," and whose purpose was "to establish the agricultural nature of the community (*to kataskeuazein geôrgikon ton dêmon*)" (*Pol.* 6.1319a8; cf. Asheri 1963: 20–21). Clearly, Aristotle believed that the hardworking yeomen had formed the best constitutions in the Greek city-states, even though he worried that their farming responsibilities often had led them to be superseded by underworked radicals on both the left and right.

Finally, it should be no surprise that Aristotle (e.g., *Pol.* 4.1296a18–22) also believed that the best lawgivers—those who helped frame the constitutions of the agrarian city-states in the eighth and seventh centuries—emerged from "the middle group of citizens" (*tôn mesôn politôn*), men like Solon, Lycurgus, Charondas "and nearly all the great majority of the other lawgivers." The so-called Seven Sages of the seventh century saw the "mean" and "proportion" as integral in the holding of farmland (Colum. *Rust.* 1.3.8).[18]

It is just that rural middle group, the source of and exemplar for an entire society's "moderate" stance, that is under assault currently in the American agrarian landscape. Completely ignorant of Aristotle's warning, "we are rapidly heading toward a dual-sector system in which middle-sized family farms are all but eliminated, leaving a small number of huge superfarms and numerous small and economically unimportant, 'hobby farms.' The total number of farms is predicted to drop from 2.2. million in 1982 to 1.2. million in 2000, with just 50,000 superfarms accounting for 75% of the country's total agricultural production by the turn of the century" (Davidson 162). The Hellenistic practice of estate farming coupled with peasantry has taken over American agriculture.

But throughout the seventh century the *mesoi* proliferated. Inevitably, the farmers' growing economic power was reflected in their construction of the legal framework of the *polis*. Their later solid presence in the political life of the city-state proves that. Aristotle summed their importance up well:

> The lawgiver must always in his constitution take in the middle class: if he is making the laws of an oligarchy, he must keep the middle in consideration, and if he desires democracy, he must legislate to bring them in. And where the size of the middle class exceeds both of the extreme classes, or even one of them alone, then it is possible for constitutional government to be lasting. (Aristotle *Politics* 4.1296b35–39)

It is no surprise that modern political theorists have argued that democracy works only when there is a *prior* group of socially cohesive equals. In the language of the social sciences: "If horizontal networks of civic engagement help participants solve dilemmas of collective action, then the more horizontally ordered an organization, the more it should foster institutional success in the broader community" (Putnam 175). Translated that means representative and constitutional governments best serve the people. But they never emerge unless there is *preexisting* social and economic egalitarianism among the citizenry. In the ancient Greek world, as Aristotle saw 2,300 years ago, agrarianism provided that prerequisite "horizontally ordered organization." It made later democracy possible.

The initial appearance of Greek yeomanry drew both resentment and anger from the aristocratic elite, as the *geôrgoi* campaigned for additional political power to protect their economic advances, for a move from a birth elite to a landed, though broad-based, government. At this time of expanding commerce among the city-states there were also the ambitious engaged in rudimentary commerce and craftsmanship, especially the exchange and fabrication of clays and metals. But we should never overestimate their size or influence in the thousand or so agrarian city-states outside Athens and Corinth. In Greece of the *polis* period, the real political, social, economic, and military issues were always over land (e.g., Arist. *Pol.* 2.1266a37; Pl. *Leg.* 736E), not arising from commercial rivalry among a purported large class of manufacturers and tradesmen. Most of those who did live in town served the *geôrgoi* outside the walls in some way; farmers marketed their crops in exchange for livestock, slaves, building materials, clays, and metals provided by the more urbanized agricultural service sector. In short: "Ownership of land alone determined a man's political status and the city became officially subject to the countryside."*

Trade and business activity in general often revolved around the storage, transport, and exchange of foodstuffs. In the ancient world the great majority of the population always worked the land in some capacity, as free landowner, absentee estate holder, slave or serf, and thus most vague references to social turmoil during the *polis* period involved the ownership and control of agricultural property. In the *Politics*, Aristotle writes: "Some think that the proper regulation of property holding is most important, for the issue of property, they say, is universally the cause of class strife" (*Pol.* 2.1266a37–39). For what it is worth, much of middle and late fourth-century Greek literature has a romantic view of *polis* stability in the prior centuries (i.e., 700–400 B.C.). Isocrates believed that Greek society in the past had been balanced between wealthy and poor (*Aerop.* 7.31), a time when "moderation" was the key to social stability. Isocrates' obsession with the growing polarization in the fourth century between "poverty and wealth" (e.g., *Antid.* 15.142, 251) reflects his assumption that a substantial middle had existed earlier in most of the Greek city-states. Without the *mesoi*, the *polis* was not much more than "slaves and masters" (Arist. *Pol.* 4.1295b20–22).

After the establishment of the middling, stabilizing *geôrgoi* in the eighth through fifth centuries, there was rarely open hostility between the landless and the very wealthy until Hellenistic and Roman times.** Land redistribution schemes, confiscations, and proscribed gifts of farms to the community were all the (usually failed) efforts of the late fourth-century and Hellenistic Greeks to restore a long-lasting, stable property egalitarianism so characteristic of the earlier, lost culture of the *polis*.

Hesiod gives the first indication of the nature of this tension through

---

*Weber 1976: 174. See Morris 1991: 34–35; Salmon 1984: 404–6; and Finley 1973: 48–49, for the relative importance of agriculture and crafts in the early Greek economy. On the nature of those occupations in town which serviced the needs of farmers, see Engels 41–65.

**"The fifth, and first decades of the fourth, century were," the social historian Alexander Fuks wrote (41), "a time of balance. In this period there existed in most states of Greece a large and established rural middle class." Cf. Asheri 1966: 30–74.

his repeated attacks on "the bribe-swallowing barons" (*Op.* 38–39) who ostensibly cheat the small farmers like himself out of their legal property. In his *Works and Days* an apparently stable community of small farmers is envisioned, one with ill-will toward the aristocrats, only beginning to create a political program to ensure its continuance on the land. In much of the literature that follows Hesiod, strife concerning land use and land ownership intensified until it was resolved with the political ascendancy of the *mesoi.* "Class struggle" at this time was of course not a contest over the rights of slaves or over the interests of the poor, but rather involved the new farmers, men with growing economic clout and land but without noble birth. They were pitted against the old guard estate owners, the "*eupatridai*" or "*agathoi,*" well-born aristocrats who felt threatened by a more competent new agrarian class.

This tension is exhibited in a variety of ways in Greek literature, depending on the *polis* involved, the chronological period, and the political views of the author. Hostile thinkers refer to the homesteaders as "the bad (*kakoi*)." These are the disdained ill-bred upstarts, who, in the poet Theognis's words, "wore goatskins about their flanks and pasture like deer outside the city, and now they become 'good.' Who can bear it?" (frs. 54–57; cf. Starr 1977: 234 n.16; Figueira 1985: 128–29). Perhaps here Theognis is really objecting to the new farmers who, dressed like Laertes and Hesiod, rarely come into town, but "pasture like deer" on their isolated farms. The poet's attack on rustics and his natural affinity for the urban wealthy is a fine example of the anthropological observation that the wealthy of a society cluster in cities. In antiquity, the Greeks seemed to assume that the most prestigious land was contiguous to the *polis* proper*; at least initially the rural poorer residents were measured by their distance from the *polis* proper.

The real "good," Theognis goes on to say, are the well-born, adding "never yet have the 'good' ruined a city" (fr. 43). The implication is that the leather-clad farmers, who reside outside the city wall, are now no longer threatened by the "bribe swallowers," but rather have themselves nearly displaced the very wealthy from absolute control of Greek economic, social, and political life: "Many *kakoi* are rich, many *agathoi* are poor" (Theog. 315–17). Birth itself is no longer a guarantee of political

---

*Arist. *Pol.* 6.1319a10; Xen. *Vect.* 4.50; Diod. 12.11.1; cf. Audring 1989: 100–10.

power. "The noble marry the base," Theognis laments, "the base the noble. Wealth has confounded birth" (189–90). But it was not wealth, but work, that had confounded Theognis's ordered aristocratic world.

What has happened in the century and a half between Hesiod (700 B.C.), the budding voice of agrarianism, and Theognis (about 550 B.C.), the grouchy, besieged and hysterical reactionary? The small farmers have obtained political representation to match their economic clout. They have begun to fashion the city-state in the image of their own agrarian interests: "In most states the power of wealth could not be resisted: the economic revolution led *first* to social, then to political changes" (Whibley 78–79; emphasis added).

Sometimes the early *mesoi* accomplished this transformation through the so-called lawgivers, the legendary statesmen who Greeks of the *polis* believed had formed the constitutions of the nascent city-state to reflect its majority constituency. Too often scholars have seen these shadowy figures as constitutional philosophers, not primarily as pragmatic agrarian reformers. But Aristotle believed the early lawgivers had shaped their governments to ensure that the *polis* reflected the preexisting agrarian culture.

Most of these men remain hazy, near-mythical figures. Yet their laws have such a nearly uniform agrarian flavor that we can be sure they reflect real aspirations on the part of the early independent farmers. Philolaus of Corinth (about 730 B.C.?) had supposedly enacted regulations ensuring that the farms at Thebes might remain the same number in perpetuity (*hopôs ho arithmos sôzêtai tôn klêrôn*; *Pol.* 2.1274b1–6). The Corinthian Pheidon, "one of the most ancient of the lawgivers," purportedly argued that the population and the number of plots ought always to remain roughly equal (*Pol.* 2.1265b13–16).

An even more shadowy figure, Phaleas the Chalcedonian, advanced the concept that all the citizens of the *polis* ought to hold equal amounts of property (*Pol.* 2.1266a40–1266b6; cf. 2.1274a23–30). These early advocates of agrarianism are lost to the historical record as individual personalities, and we have no idea how their laws were passed, or the degree to which farmers themselves participated in the actual crafting of legislation. But their prominence and the advocacy of their programs do reflect two trends: the growing number of independent small farmers in Greece, and the concerted need to protect their economic gains from aristocratic backlash, especially any effort to separate farmer from farm.

The best-known figure between Hesiod and Theognis is Solon of Athens (about 600 B.C.), and his reforms need to be examined in detail. From a variety of literary evidence we can sketch a general picture of a group of farmers, "the sixth-partners" (*hektêmoroi*), who around 600 B.C. were under severe debt obligation to the wealthy, ostensibly owing five-sixths (rather than one-sixth) of their produce.[19]

The impoverished were no doubt failing new agriculturalists, who were either pledging their own newly acquired plots for capital, or working land in some type of sharecropping agreement with established aristocrats (see [Arist.] *Oec.* 2.1349a3–8, for the farmer's need for capital before planting). In any case, a century after the *Works and Days*, at Attica many of the *geôrgoi* seem not yet entirely successful and independent. In somewhat of an exaggeration, Plutarch tells us that Solon was presented with a situation where "all of the less well-off were in debt to the rich." Those struggling farmers must have been either farming land for the wealthy or paying up to five of six parts of their proceeds as rent (Plut. *Sol.* 13.1).

Aristotle appears to agree. He concludes in his *Constitution of Athens* that there was strife among the residents of Attica, that the existing constitution gave little heed to any but the rich, and that the whole countryside was under the control of a few wealthy men (*Ath. Pol.* 2.1; 4.5). This specter of a few nobles owning *all* of Attica is obviously an incorrect generalization: Solon never redistributed lands and yet later at least two thirds of Attica constituted small farms; few, if any, estates exceeded a hundred acres. The landscape *before* Solon must have *already* been populated by a great number of yeoman farmers.

Aristotle may have meant that some small farmers had not been able to make a living. To obtain necessary capital (for trees and vines, land reclamation, rural infrastructure), *geôrgoi* must have pledged any property they owned—even their own bodies—as security to the old landed nobles (e.g., Plut. *Sol.* 13.2). Ironically, in many Greek city-states there were rules prohibiting confiscation of weapons and farm equipment for agricultural debt, but the seizure of the debtor himself was apparently still allowable (e.g., Diod. 1.79.3–5), suggesting that debt bondage was sometimes the result of scarce capital and more plentiful labor. Solon's limiting of exports of grain while encouraging olive trading exemplified the populist checking of aristocratic landowners on richer bottomland while encouraging yeomen who were investing in trees and vines (e.g., Plut. *Sol.* 13; Arist. *Ath. Pol.* 2.2; Bravo 1983: 23–24)

Noteworthy is the limited program of relief for the abject poor, a debt-reduction scheme Solon, "in wealth and by occupation a member of the middle class" (e.g., Arist. *Ath. Pol.* 5.3; Plut. *Sol.* 14–15), supposedly advocated. Nowhere do we hear that Solon sought a redistribution of property or a general cancellation of debts. Wholesale confiscations took place rarely in the Greek *poleis* for nearly the next two and a half centuries. Solon himself was thus proud that "the wealthy suffered no harm" (fr. 5). Using the appropriate imagery of yeoman infantry, he says that he protected both sides of the quarrel with "a strong shield" (fr. 5).

His agrarian legislation outlawed debt slavery (the servile term "sixth-partners" [*hektêmoroi*] thereafter became obsolete), reconstituted census rubrics to allow smaller landowners to have a greater role in politics, and allowed the restoration of some small farms to their former owners (Arist. *Ath. Pol.* 6; Plut. *Sol.* 15.2–16.4), thus creating in one sense "the beginning of Athenian democracy" (Arist. *Ath. Pol.* 41.2). "The dark earth," Solon wrote, "whose mortgage stones fixed in so many places I removed. Once a slave, now she is free" (fr. 24). Solon's program was political recognition (1) of aristocratic excess and arrogance, (2) of a large number of poor whom he could not or would not help, and (3) of a sizable body of successful *mesoi*, who were now formally brought into the apparatus of Athenian government. Solonian legislation confirmed ongoing agrarian success: middling farmers' skills, not their birth, now brought political dividends.*

An enormous modern bibliography is devoted to the so-called Solonian Question, efforts to find out exactly what the Attic economic problem was, and how effective were the solutions. But the *majority* of independent *geôrgoi* of early sixth-century Attica were not necessarily affected, nor was the soil exhausted or the newly cultivated hillsides eroded from deforestation. The main beneficiaries may well have been those who already had carved out an independent stance from the wealthy.

---

*Of this group of hoplites James Holladay has correctly remarked: "Except for those at the very bottom of the census qualification, whose status might be precarious, the hoplites by definition possessed adequate land to support themselves and leave a little bit over. They were not economically depressed and they had shared the general political benefits arising from Solon's reforms" (51). See Starr 1977: 182–83; Spahn 139–60, Gernet 1981: 280–81, on the formal recognition of hoplite *mesoi*.

The crisis that arose was a *natural* evolutionary process of success and failure, a subtle transformation that occurs when there are fundamental changes in land use and a growing population. Political representation must make a correction and so catch up with economic influence; wealth must replace birth as a prerequisite for *polis* participation.

As small farmers rose out of the Dark Ages, a great number over some two centuries of intensified and diversified farming no doubt failed. (Later, Xenophon remarks: "Some farmers are so successful that agriculture provides them all they need, while others are so indifferent that farming is unprofitable" [*Oec.* 6.11]). Their land then came under the control of the more successful (not in every case the old, entrenched elite). Or, alternatively, the more desperate resorted to extreme measures—paying exorbitant rents, pledging their persons as security for debts—to continue farming. (In my own experience, once things go bad, farmers become increasingly frantic and look to all sorts of unrealistic mechanisms, hoping for one more year that may bring salvation; hence the modern farming proverb "never throw good money into a bad operation.") Some land may have been too poor to have been reclaimed and farmed in the first place (Plut. *Sol.* 22.3; cf. Plut. *Mor.* 147D) and, on the collapse of its owners, it simply reverted back to wild ground. Those failed *geôrgoi*, instead of being sent abroad as indentured servants, may have migrated abroad as experienced free agrarian settlers, as a part of a growing Athenian interest in overseas expropriation and conquest of lands (e.g., Plut. *Sol.* 8–9; Hdt. 5.54; 6.136). Although Solon probably accomplished little in alleviating the plight of the impoverished, he *did* codify the gains won by the majority of small hoplite-landowners, the *zeugitai* ("the yoked together"), by allowing them to hold office at Athens, by legislation protecting the family plot, and by ensuring those surviving, though encumbered, farmers that they could continue to work their parcels.[20]

Athens would not place agriculture under centralized government control to modulate the farming practice of its citizens. Nor would property primarily be owned by only the very rich. For the great duration of the *polis* period we do not hear of ongoing agrarian legislation in Greece, or of a series of controversial reform laws (such as at Rome during the early republic [e.g., Frayn 73–87]), to ensure agricultural egalitarianism and general equity in landholding.

Solonian census classification and economic and political reforms were not very beneficial to the landless or subsistence farmers ("the fourth class, the *thêtes*, had no share in any office" [Arist. *Pol.* 2.1274a22]). Failed poor were later described by Xenophon's Socrates: "Often when men farm the same type of ground, some become impoverished and say they were ruined by farming, while others prosper from agriculture and have everything they need" (Xen. *Oec.* 3.5). These successful agriculturalists were now formally incorporated by Solon into the Athenian political system and protected from aristocratic reaction. Later Athenians believed that Solon had established the tradition that orphans of those who fell in battle were to be provided with state support, another indication that the early lawgiver aimed the majority of his reforms at the hoplite-landowner (e.g., Diog. Laert. 1.55; Thuc. 2.46.1; Pl. *Menex.* 248e6–8; Arist. *Pol.* 2.1268a8–11).

It was now agricultural expertise, not mere birth, that brought one social prestige and political representation. For the first time in Attic history there was under Solon to be formal reckoning and clarification of the previously chaotic agrarian environment (a need "to define more precisely the user's rights, duties, and privilege" [Rihll 115]): farmers who proved themselves were now a protected species; marginal farmers who failed could never again seek government intervention to ensure their success, at least until the appearance of a much more radical democracy in the fifth century.

Solon provided a political framework to deal with new economic realities: a large group of nonaristocrats was to make up the governing council of Athens, a body that once granted representation was not radical but soon rather reactionary. It was not sympathetic to the landless and the failed, but rather protective of the newly successful. In the later history of Athens, the Solonian achievement—the "ancestral constitution" (*patrios politeia*) of hoplite landowners—was nostalgically recalled as the great property of yeomanry, contrasted at every opportunity with landless radical democracy. By the fifth and fourth century Solon was remembered as a broad-based timocrat by later hoplites and as the founder of democracy by more radical Athenians, but looked upon not at all favorably by aristocratic elites. In the fifth century the wealthy much preferred the earlier and harsher (and mostly mythical) constitution of Draco.[21]

After the emergence of independent landowners and their new ideology of hard work, any notion of landed titles was extinct. Vanished was the snobbery of horse rearing, gentry, chivalry, and pretentious manors, so common elsewhere across the Mediterranean and in Asia. In the early Greek community of southern Italy, "the picture of the rural society of Metapontum that begins to emerge does not support the theory of landed aristocracy. The surface distribution of the farmhouses with their related burial grounds leaves little possibilities for vast estates. It seems to have been a well-to-do, but also a remarkably egalitarian society" (J. Carter 1990: 430; cf. 409–10). *Polis* values were firmly established during the eighth and seventh centuries in many areas of Greece—primarily to serve agrarian "well-to-do, but also remarkably egalitarian" interests, that is, the interests of the hoplite *geôrgoi*. Save for a few reactionary states, serfdom and other forms of Dark-Age helotage vanished, superseded (ironically, or rather logically) by chattel slaves working alongside the owners of small farms.

I do not mean to imply that all Greek city-states followed identical patterns of agrarian development or that daily life was uniform throughout more than a thousand Greek-speaking communities. My point rather is that agrarianism is the *one* unifying *institution* that gave the early Greeks common ground, a shared ideology, an agreed-on notion of government, values, and war. Agrarianism *defined* the nascent *polis*, its beginning (and end), a community that from the outset "was not an agglomeration of traders and artisans parasitic on backward peasants" (Starr 1977: 100), but a community of cultivators and those who served agrarians. Thus the Greek city-state was born as a rural institution and as an agrarian ideology, not as religion, not as fortification, not as literature or philosophy or art, and not as an exact blueprint of the cultural life of the Greeks. The *polis*, in short, "was the creation of society; it was the servant of society, and not its master" (Engels 130), a necessary emporium and an assembly for its largely agrarian citizenry.

To understand fully this remarkable relationship between the manner in which Greek landowners farmed and the culture they created, it is necessary now to change radically our angle of vision. Our discussion must turn far from both agricultural technique and the politics of agrarian ideologies. We must learn something of the conditions under which Greek farmers of the *polis* actually worked.

Chapter 4

THE WAYS OF FARMERS

The history of agriculture was the history of mankind until the
nineteenth century. Historians have concentrated upon political
history, not upon the mundane and unexciting events of farming
life: even economic historians have shown more interest in the life
of towns and the fortunes of industry than the ways of farmers.
                                        —David Grigg 1982:15

I.

Farm residence, diversified crops, incorporation of marginal lands, slave
labor—these were characteristic of a new type of agriculture and agrarian ideology that arose in the eighth to sixth century in Greece. The description of the emergence of agrarianism (Chapter 1), the discussion of
infrastructures on the early Greek farm (Chapter 2), and the account of
its work ethic and the political dominance of a farming class (Chapter 3)
tell us little about Greek rural life. Too often when we speak of the rise
and fall of the small farmers in both ancient and modern society there is
the assumption that agrarianism, the rural chauvinism of homestead
farming, is inherently noble or worth preserving. But in order for any

who are not farmers to believe that, one must seek to glimpse the daily experiences and challenges of the ancient Greek farmer. Only in that way can we see what was unique about this new agrarianism, why it should have been intrinsically of more value than other types of farming. Only in that way comes empathy for those Greek *geôrgoi* producing food, fighting, and making laws under the most demanding of circumstances.

I attempt to sketch in human terms the environment of a Greek farm during the four centuries of the *polis* in Greece, avoiding a portrait drawn exclusively from the Attic countryside—a difficult task since nearly all Greek tragedy and comedy, as well as oratory, were produced at Athens. A paradigm is needed because the scholarly emphasis on the lack of uniformity in the Greek landscape and the tendency to avoid chronological or regional assertions or generalization can go too far. There *was* enough common agricultural practice in antiquity to speak of a "typical" Greek farm, even if bolstered by evidence from later literary sources and both modern and ancient agronomic analogy.

The ancients, of course, were quite aware of the vast local differences in climate, weather, and soils in Greece, and they knew the effects of regional environments on crop selection and maturity.* Nor should we forget the presence of a strong political consciousness and chauvinism in each of the city-states. Yet Greek literature does describe a natural homogeneity, an agricultural sameness that favors the growing of cereals, vines, olives, fruit trees, and pulses in most areas in Greece (e.g., Theophr. *HP* 8.2.7–11; [Xen.] *Ath. Pol.* 2.6), climatic, environmental, dialectal, or political differences notwithstanding.

One must not be utopian about the ancient Greek *geôrgoi*, not romanticize their code of behavior or social and political outlook. Paradoxically, the success and dynamism of the farmer during the age of the Greek *polis* were a direct result of his peculiar notion of exclusivity. Disliked by traditional aristocrats, small farmers had a large array of their own inferiors. These new agriculturalists saw little reason to offer scarce land and thus citizenship to the foreigners or resident aliens of their communities, much less to their own chattel slaves. City-states were always referred to *not* in the abstract singular, but concretely in the *masculine* plural. Athens was

---

*See Guiraud 548–551; for the idea of a general uniformity in ancient intensive agriculture, see Halstead 1987: 78.

usually dubbed *hoi Athênaioi* (literally "the Athenian men"), Thebes *hoi Thebaioi*, Argos *hoi Argeioi*; that is, Greek city-states were originally known by the men of the surrounding countryside, the citizens who owned property and who alone made the laws and fought the wars.

These *geôrgoi* were no friends of those who never acquired the skills, desire, or the opportunity to become successful independent farmers: the ranks of free but perpetually landless poor or those Greeks born into dire circumstances without political or social recourse, who either did not farm or farmed only sporadically. At least in the fifth and fourth centuries, such men at Athens rowed in the fleet, and at other *poleis* served as light-armed skirmishers outside the phalanx of landed hoplites (Arist. *Pol.* 6.1321a14–15). Incorporation of the Greek free landless into the body politic was the (revolutionary) achievement of Athenian democracy—and in that narrow sense it was ostensibly opposed by *all* landed interests. For all the Greeks without property, the new agrarianism offered little improvement over Dark-Age feudalism. In some sense agrarianism was antidemocratic, if by democracy we mean not constitutional government or elected assemblies *per se*, but simply government by all adult free natives, born of and residing in the *polis*.

Possessing a work ethic that is hauntingly similar to the modern "immigrant" philosophy of self-help, the Greek farmer saw little reason to extend social or political privilege to those who could not aid themselves. In the underworld of Homer's *Odyssey*, Achilles' ghost reflects the status of the propertyless when he says that he would rather "follow the plough as thrall to another man, one with no land allotted him and not much to live on, than be a king over all the perished dead" (Hom. *Od.* 11.489–91). Working for wages is unfortunate. But for the landless sharecropper working for wages is miserable. Later, the *polis* Greeks believed that the employment of the majority of the population out in the fields as farm laborers was a clear sign of a feudal or an aristocratic society, not a true community of yeomen (e.g., Plut. *Mor.* 291E).

Besides the landless poor, there were thousands of chattel slaves in the countryside throughout the Greek-speaking world. Their advance in real numbers into the *polis* community in the eighth through fifth centuries reflects the end of serfdom in Greece, and the rise of a broad-based and successful alternative to landed aristocracy. Slaves in large part were eventually responsible for the political and economic dynamism of the entire Greek agrarian movement itself. Despite the belief of many scholars that agricultural slaves were always and at every locale in Greece limited to "large estates," often, as seen in Chapter 2, the small farmer entered into a paternalistic relationship with his servant, working alongside him in the field and marching with him on campaign. "The heads of the families ate their crops and fruits at the same table with their slaves," the historian Philochorus writes, "with whom they had shared the labors of cultivation" (Philochorus 328 fr.97, in Macrob. *Sat.* 1.10.22).

Unlike later farm laborers on Hellenistic absentee estates, or chain gangs in the mines of the ancient world, slaves on small farms were—as captives go—undoubtedly treated relatively well and fed regularly, and their treatment became a real concern of the community. Nevertheless, slave *exploitation* was essential to the small farmer, and thus one must believe that nearly all servants attempted to flee in times of war or social chaos.*

In the farmer's mind all agricultural slaves were to be worked hard (cf. Aesch. *Ag.* 1044–45) and not left alone like (say) Alciphron's Noumenion who allegedly did nothing more than "eat and sleep" (Alciphr. 3.38). During the last years of the Peloponnesian War, Thucydides remarks that "more than two myriads" of slaves fled from Attica (7.27). These 20,000 deserters roughly approximate the number of small farms of Attica. Thucydides suggests that the servile losses from the farms in the Athenian countryside may well have been total. If there was any widespread dislocation in Attic agriculture after the war, it perhaps derived largely from the need to replace servile workers rather than from the loss of orchards or vineyards to Spartan ravagers.**

Rural women worked nearly as hard as the slaves, but they enjoyed little more freedom: marriages usually arranged, opportunity to travel off the farm rare, childbearing of utmost importance, legal protection secondary to spousal dictate. So Hesiod assumes, as farmers have so often assumed, that a wife is not much more than property. He urges that the grower of food "first get a house, and then a woman, and then an ox for the plough" (405;

---

*For slave desertions, see Thuc. 8.40.2; Ar. *Eq.* 20ff.; *Nub.* 7; *Pax* 451; cf. [Arist.] *Oec.* 1.1344b15–22; Hanson 1992: 227–28. On public interest in the welfare of slaves, see the examples at Dem. 55. 32–34; Pl. *Euthyp.* 4c; Xen. *Hell.* 5.3.7; *Oec.* 5.15–16.

**On the 20,000 agricultural slaves, see Hanson 1992: 225–28, and Hanson 1983: 142–43, for the effect of the Peloponnesian War on Attic agriculture.

cf. Arist. *Pol.* 1.1252b1–15), and Aristotle later sees scarcely any inherent difference among the three. Even Sappho, feminist poet of the early Greek world, revealed that the gulf between rural and urban, wealthy and yeomanry, transcended mere sex. Creature of an elite literary circle, she had disdain for the backward country woman, a "rural girl in farm-girl clothes, ignorant of the way to raise the gown over her ankles" (fr. 57).

Xenophon in his *Oeconomicus* has an elaborate schema for rural women. The (teenage) wife was to be responsible for all the indoor drudgery on the farm—weaving, food storage and preparation, raising children. The husband, "strong in the face of cold, heat, and campaigning, braver before physical threats," was to stay outside, the two together thereby making a harmonious team (*Oec.* 7.25–28). The later and derivative Aristotelian *Oeconomica* explicitly delineates that plan: "By nature men were made stronger, women weaker, so that by reason of his manly prowess he might be more inclined to protect the household, she, due to her timidity, supervise it. He brings in the necessities from outside, she protects what lies already within" (*Oec.* 1.1343b30–1344a4).

Numerous passages in Greek literature identify clear spheres of influence inside and outside the house, and we should understand that constant work outside was not normal for Greek women. The rare employment of wives and daughters among the crops was to the Greeks a sign of either unusual distress in the countryside or of a family's abject poverty. This ideology is not much different from the modern family farmers of southern Italy, whose philosophy of agrarian responsibility is summed up by the proverb: "The man by the shovel, the woman by the spoon."*

Such utilitarianism is not confined to the ancient Greek world or even to rural parts of southern Europe. It survives today anywhere independent farmers attempt to feed themselves from small plots. In the 1970s a neighbor lamented that he had paid his wife—she was in her late fifties at that time—"too much" to tie the canes on the trellis wires of his twenty-acre vineyard, "wages" that she in turn was to use to manage the family budget. In his mind, her work was little different from simple stoop labor, and thus must be paid at the going rate. Most in the

---

*Galt 193. See Brown 71–74, for the rarity of women in the fields, and cf. the apparently exceptional passages at Dem. 57.30, 45; Ar. fr. 339 Kock. Plato (*Leg.* 7.805E) seems to consider barbarous the Thracian custom of women in the fields..

vicinity saw the wife's presence in the vineyard as an embarrassing sign of the couple's reduced circumstances. In my own childhood the only liberated farm women (if we may use "liberated" for the exchange of the enormous responsibility of raising a family for the equally tiresome task of raising food) I saw were the few childless widows who chose not to sell out after the early death of their spouses. Their reward was the gradual, but grudging, respect of their neighbors and decades of the hard, brutal work that had killed their husbands. Odd women, I remember them as, excellent farmers all, in bib overalls and boots, hands rough, faces burned by the sun, and so out of place amidst the china and doilies of local teas and improvement clubs. In a play of Menander the competent and independent female guardian (*epiklêros*) of her own family's estate is ridiculed by her husband as a "witch," a pushy female who has taken over "control of the house, fields, and everything" (fr. 406 Kock).

Elsewhere Hesiod worries about bringing an attractive wife onto the farm ("Don't allow a woman with a showy ass (*pugostolos*) to deceive you with her pillow talk: she's after your barn" [373]). At the same time Hesiod frets over whether she might be homely, "a joke (*charmata*) to the neighbors"(701)! The *Works and Days* is replete with warnings about the danger a bad woman can pose to the survivability of the farm (703–5; "The man who trusts women," Hesiod says, "has trusted deceivers" [375]).

I grew up with the story of a cousin, who returned from pruning to find a stranger on the ranch "with"—as my grandfather put it—his wife. The story was retold repeatedly, partly to emphasize the need to marry wisely, partly to turn sympathy toward the victimized farmer, never to suggest that the relative in question—an arrogant, small-minded man—had probably bored his (urban-born and attractive) wife silly.

More than two centuries after Hesiod, Aristophanes combines the traditional agrarian mistrust of women with a similar suspicion of city dwellers. His citified wife is thus the worst of both worlds:

> May the matchmaker have perished terribly
> who urged me to marry your mother.
> For my agricultural life used to be the sweetest,
> one that was unwashed, without worry, unrestrained,
> one full of honey-bees, sheepfolds, and olive-pulp.

But then I married a niece of Megacles,
a rustic, wed to a town-lady
—proud, luxurious, extravagant.
  —(Ar. *Nub.* 41–48)

In the later utopian comedy, the *Ecclesiazusae*, Aristophanes has his character Chremes say that when the assembly was to vote on turning Athens over to the women, the shoemakers approved, "but the farmers (*hoi d' ek tôn agrôn*) grumbled their disapproval" (425–27). Alciphron has many letters reflecting the stock image of a miserable younger woman married to an older farmer who, in recompense for her unhappiness, depletes his carefully accumulated stores (1.27–28; 3.11). How often this was a real occurrence, rather than an imagined peril among the hidebound male farmers, we do not know. Ovid's later idealistic portrait of Philemon and Baucis, the contented rustic couple who, in blissful partnership, ate their own produce on wooden utensils, ignores—typically, given the agrarian romanticism of the Augustan age—the starkly utilitarian view of women that most Greek farmers held (*Met.* 8.640–80). After all, even today in the modern Greek countryside most women walk while their husbands ride the family donkey. Near Leuctra in central Greece, I once watched a man harrow five acres with a small tractor, his plump wife perched precariously to the rear on his spring-tooth to give it added weight over the clods. Oblivious, uninterrupted and, strangest of all, *quite content* with their respective duties, for an hour he dragged her around through the dust storm.

It is not enough to attribute the farmers' treatment of the landless, slaves, and women to the general climate of Greek culture—inasmuch as we are arguing throughout this book that *the foundations of Greek polis culture were agrarian*. That agrarian ideology of exclusivity, of the primacy of the free male landowner (who was to epitomize the entire community, urban and rural, of the *polis*) was a cause rather than a result of all Greek attitudes of social and political discrimination and privilege. Critics of the Greeks who fault Hellenic society for the narrowness and chauvinism of the adult, free male citizen, must locate their critique in the world of the countryside, rather than in the city, which is so overrepresented in literature. For most of the *polis* period in the great majority of Greek city-states, the chief unifying check on the participation of slaves,

the poor, foreigners, and women in politics was not necessarily philosophical, racial, or sexual bias. Those living on the ideological margins of
the Greek *polis* were stamped as second-, third-, and fourth-class groups
largely by their inability to own land, and thence have a claim on political or legal representation, economic importance, or military prominence. No surprise, then, that when a man was to be exiled from the
polis, and his citizenship to be stripped away, the state immediately
moved to confiscate his land.[1]

That the Greek *geôrgoi* were constantly opposed by the aristocratic
elite, and merely reacted in turn against the next lower rung on the social scale, is no explanation *per se* for agrarian exclusivity. Chauvinism
on the part of the small farmer ("A farm for a man is life's father, for only
land knows how to hide poverty" [Amphis fr. 17.2–3 Kock]) reflects the
utilitarianism that pervades all his social, economic, and political thinking—utilitarianism in the sense of doing everything he can to preserve
his small farm from the disasters, natural and man-induced, that daily
threatened his existence. Rarely in literature of the *polis* period is there
patent racism (slaves, after all, could be of any race or ethnicity, including Greek) or misogyny. Even hard-nosed Hesiod concedes that "a man
wins nothing better than a good wife (*gunaikos tês agathês*)" (702–3).
"Good" here means a woman who, though attractive, keeps her looks
from any but her husband in the privacy of his house, a woman who
works as hard as her husband without complaint or demand for anything
not crucial to the life of the farm.

The ancient Greek farmer unquestioningly assumed—*must* have assumed, if he were to survive—that the purpose of slaves, women, and
children was identical to his own: to farm under his direction, since
therein lay the time-proven formula of success and survival for all involved. The ties of these others to the *polis* derived from the farmer's
own claim as a landowning citizen—if he lost his ancestral plot, wife,
children, and slaves suffered as well. In some cases there surely were
genuine common interests. We hear occasionally of manumission of servants, of slaves who worshipped their master, of idealized lifelong marriages, where woman and man seem to be essentially a pair rather than
inferior and superior.

In *most* instances the farmer was absolute tyrant on his ground, and all
others bent their will to his directive. They were all, in a sense, *tools*, like

his wagon, livestock, and dog, whose reason to be was simply survival on the land. The new agrarianism, the rise of the small farmers, must always assume a *greater* number of slaves and women (in both relative and absolute numbers), must realize that the labor that created these fundamental changes in Greek society largely derived from yet another rural "other," who were always deemed unworthy to fight, own farmland, or make laws, men and women who remain in greater obscurity, even more forgotten than the largely nameless *geôrgoi* themselves. At the same time, understand this exploitation as a phenomenon apart from the distant and shady verandah. It is part of a brutal world where the small owners themselves labored to feed the community, their regimen interrupted occasionally by a short infantry campaign, where relief from backbreaking work meant only an opportunity to don bronze and die.

II.

The Greeks felt that their own climate was adverse and the soil poor. Land might produce only flowers and just about the amount of barley one had sown in the fall (e.g., Men. fr. 96 Kock). "Poverty and Greece," Herodotus says, "are stepsisters" (Hdt. 7.102; cf. Thuc. 1.2). Only a hostile farming environment could produce strong, vigorous, and intelligent citizens. In the Hippocratic corpus, hostile land—bare, without water, hot in summer, cold in winter (similar to Hesiod's description of Ascra)— produced men "by nature keen and eager to work, headstrong, self-willed and prone to fierceness, rather than to timidity" (Aer. 16.8–9; 13.24; Arist. Pol. 7.1327b26–31; cf. Plut. Mor. fr. 152). A favorite regional contrast was between the indolent Thessalians on rich land, and the more admirable hardworking, rock-farming Megarians (e.g., Isoc. 8.117–18; cf. 4.132).

Menander writes that "the land that produces poorly makes men courageous" (fr. 63 Kock). Milder climate and richer ground only spoiled farmers (e.g., Hdt. 1.143), and made the general population weak and soft (Theophr. HP 8.7.4). Agriculture in the Near East and Egypt, in the Greek mind, was always easy; farming there was characterized by abundant harvests, large estates, and the absence of the work required on the Greeks' own small plots (Theophr. HP 8.7.14; cf Hdt. 2.14). Xenophon apparently felt that when Greeks moved into the richer lands of Asia and prospered, it would demonstrate that any struggling kinsmen back home were themselves responsible for their own poverty (*An.* 3.2.26). Plato understood that climate and topography were critical to the moral formation of Greek citizenry, the presence of hard work creating strong bodies and souls (e.g., *Leg.* 5.747D–E). It is not necessary to ascertain the validity of this ancient belief (although, from my own experience of equating local soil types to farmers' characters, I believe it in part to be true), only to acknowledge that it was prevalent in ancient Greece. The Hippocratic corpus states that "some men's characters resemble well-wooded and watered mountains, others a thin and waterless soil, still others are like plains or dry bare earth" (*Aer.* 24.13).

In part, this bleak view of human character explains the Greek's peculiar, paradoxical, and ultimately agrarian view of the world—a world both hostile and dangerous that alone could certify his excellence by means of his mastery of it. Nature is harsh, not idyllic; man is brutal and cruel, not gentle. Constant farm work curbs the human appetite for sloth and luxury and so saves man: rugged land that is tamed in turn tames its master.

Two elements pervaded the ancient Greek agrarian mind: the specter of disaster and efforts to master that disaster. Here is the key to understanding all work, all routine of the ancient Greek farmer. Danger (cf. Plato's "the dreaded things in farming [*ta en tê geôrgia deina*]," *Lach.* 195B]) came in nearly any guise, human or natural. To the farmer, *all* humans, from his closest neighbor to his most bitter enemies, could pose risks. Why, if not to cause harm, would a man ever venture onto another's farm? Just as the farmer himself could pose hazards to others, so he knew well that another had the power to disrupt his agricultural regimen and hence destroy the livelihood of his farm. With the advent of the independent small farmer also arose a vast new network of like souls, the originals of the country neighbor, something far different from Mycenean or even Dark-Age communalism, when the countryside was less settled and the notion of private ownership of farms rare or nonexistent. Independence and private property brought agricultural productivity to Greece, but they also created never-ending quarrels over boundaries, water, and borrowing—the great triad of agricultural disputation that is the basis of so many private agrarian fights, ancient and modern, strife that once transferred to the community level became the natural catalyst for most wars.

There was the mundane challenge as a neighbor turned a flood course from his own land to the ground of another (e.g., Pl. *Leg.* 8. 844C; Ael. *Ep.* 6; Dem. 55.24–32; cf. Theophr. CP 3.6.3–4). Much worse in a Mediterranean climate, some stole communal irrigation water, diverting it to save their own gardens. I have had to padlock the irrigation gate on our own place to prevent the weekly theft of communal ditch water by an affable, smiling neighbor—a man I have known for thirty years, who considers himself a lifelong friend of the family: ideologically a kindred family farmer, prone to expound eloquently on the plight of the local farmer cooperative. He reminds of a fragment from Menander: "You pretend to be a rustic, but you are wicked" (Men. fr. 794 Edmonds). (My grandfather warred with him for the last twenty-five years of his own life and when he was eighty-six warned us of our own trials ahead with him.) When pressed about his "diversion" of summer water by the ditch tender who allots shares on the small community channel by careful regulation, the thief sheepishly replies: "You do what you have to do when the vines are thirsty." (No wonder that neighborly disputes over water among farmers in the countryside provide a key part of Plato's agrarian legislation in his *Laws* [e.g., at *Leg.* 844A–C; cf. Klingenberg 29–35; 66–116].) By most farmers on our communal ditch, he is generally avoided, though no one has considered moving, which was the case with Aeschines the Socratic, whom Athenaeus said was so hated that his neighbors abandoned their homes (612C; and cf. the fight over a farm at Hyper. fr. 36).

Although neighborliness was crucial to the farming community in general, to owners who shared a common political and social outlook, there was often an aloofness that prevented real friendship. Neighbors, after all, could do far more than divert water. They could also borrow equipment at the most inopportune time ("Two or three times you might succeed in requesting livelihood from them, but if you try it again, it will be for no use" [Hes. *Op.* 401–2]), essentially appropriating hard-won capital for their own needs at little or no cost. Thus arose the Greek proverb: "It is easy to say: 'Lend me oxen and a wagon'; it is easy to answer: 'I have work for my oxen' " (Plut. *Mor.* fr. 66). We lent our own vineyard wagons each raisin harvest for nearly thirty years to a hard-working neighbor who claimed that he could never afford to purchase his own. On his death, nearly a half million dollars were purportedly found in a shoe-box in his closet. For him the years of borrowing represented a carefully planned economy.

"The vintage is near," Alciphron makes his beleaguered vine grower remind his neighboring olive farmer in a desperate appeal, "and I have need of vine-baskets. Please let me borrow any extra that you have. I'll return them in a while. I too have more wine jars than I need, so if you need some, you're welcome. The old saying 'Friends have all things in common' should be especially true among country-folk." (Alciphr. 13.15). Even when there were surpluses on the farm and a desire to share the bounty with neighbors, self-interest usually ruled. The poor farmer in an anonymous fragment from Attic comedy complains that he digs and sows constantly, but still finds himself indigent; worse, he has lent out twenty *medimnoi* (measures) of barley, but received only seven in return (Anon. fr. 108–9 Kock). Often there was also a hidden pragmatic reason for apparent generosity. Another of Alciphron's farmers, who wishes to give away his young porkers, says, "It is fitting in the farmer's sense of fairness for those with surplus to share with friends," but then confesses that in reality he could not feed the new litter of pigs anyway since "my stock of barley is low" (Alciphr. 3.73).

'Neighborliness' to both the ancient and modern small farmer has no air of collectivization where all share land ownership and labor for a common harvest: that idealization belongs today to the realm of the university-run organic garden, in antiquity to the idyllic scene on Homer's shield of Achilles or to the romantic anecdote about the nobility of the Athenian statesman Cimon, who allowed anyone to pick fruit from his farm (Arist. *Ath. Pol.* 27.3–4). Aristotle saw the practical problems of sharing in his own Hesiodic-like suspicion of communalism (*Pol.* 2.1263a11ff.). He writes that if "in the enjoyment of produce and in the production of it, people are not equal, but unequal, then there must be complaint between those who enjoy or take a lot, but work little, and those who take less, but work more." He adds simply: "To live together and share all our human affairs is difficult."

Plato, outlining the agrarian legislation (*nomoi geôrgikoi*) in his *Laws* (8.842E-846D; cf. Pl. *Min.* 316E; Klingenberg 21–62), envisions a host of fights between farmers over: (1) boundaries, (2) general maliciousness, (3) bees, (4) carelessness in starting fires, (5) planting too close to borders, (6) irrigation and water supplies, (7) drainage and flood control, (8) theft of fruit, (9) trespassing, and (10) injury of property. His detailed description of probable disputes gives the impression that they were well-known in every Greek *polis* where the countryside was densely settled and farmed by tough independent yeomen, whose chief worry was their own crop. Plato's concern is no mere utopian fantasy. Many of his proposals resemble Solon's own rules regarding planting distances, property lines, and water disputes (Plut. *Sol.* 23).

In the real agrarian world, neighborliness refers to grudging respect and polite distance: "Play fair with your neighbor and pay him back with fairness—or better if you are able; that way if you ever have need again, you will find him always there" (Hes. *Op.* 350–51; and for other indications of "good neighborliness," cf. Dem. 53.4–5; Ar. *Plut.* 223–25: "my farm-companions [*sungeôrgous*"]). Similarly, various anecdotes in Greek literature attest that the value of a farm was either decreased or increased by the character of the neighbors (e.g., Plut. *Mor.* fr. 50).

There were genuine differences among agrarians, for private farmers devised their own particular schemes to survive (cf. Arist. *Pol.* 2.1263b25–26), no *geôrgos* having exactly the same soil, weather, health, or family challenges. Each day, each week, each year that a farmer worked his own peculiar piece of ground drew him not closer to others, as we would imagine among like kind, but rather a little more distant. No wonder the farmer is often portrayed as the eccentric of Greek comedy. No wonder in our first picture of neighboring farmers in European literature, Homer tells us that warring armies are like two men "with measuring rods in their hands" who fight over their respective property rights (Hom. *Il.* 12.421–22).

The self-interest of each agrarian was too often at odds with his neighbor's. "Ill-natured and envious is the eye of your neighbor, just as the proverb says" (Anon. fr. 440 Kock). The agricultural writer Varro (*Rust.* 1.16.6; cf. Colum. *Rust.* 5.8.7), in later Roman times, rightly observes that a neighbor's oak grove could kill olives (no doubt through soil transmission of oak-root fungus). Theophrastus (*HP* 4.16.5) earlier devotes a discussion to the compatibility (or lack of it) among particular neighboring species of trees and vines. In a single year I have lost nearly a hundred vines (two percent of the entire vineyard) to Pierce's Disease, a virus constantly transmitted by alfalfa hoppers from a nearby field. "Beg your neighbor to get rid of the alfalfa" is the only solution proffered by the local farm advisor, a county employee who acknowledged private-ly that in the real world a request like this was ridiculous. A radical change of farming strategy was, of course, too much to ask of any nearby farmer. Anthony Galt categorized the varying degrees of hostilities be-tween the modern farmers of southern Italy; the "most serious level of estrangement" was simply "*nen se trèmende chi m'bacce*—'they no longer look each other in the face'" (200). So it currently is with us and a neighbor to the east. He has decided to ignore an easement of fifty years and instead plough up a communal road. Embarrassed by our ostracism, he nevertheless loiters around our farm at persimmon harvest, begging in vain to borrow our tree props.

For their own survival, ancient Greek farmers could afford to make neighbors neither close friends nor real enemies. Hesiod concludes: "A bad neighbor is as great a pain as a good one is a blessing. A man who has a good neighbor has found a real possession. Not even an ox would die but for a bad neighbor" (*Op.* 346–49). Theophrastus suggests that occasional communal feasts in the Greek countryside were mechanisms for cementing neighborly ties (*Char.* 10.11), a tactic that indicates real tension.

Occasionally, the stakes of friendship were a question of life and death: "Please lend me twenty bushels of grain, to allow me to save my life, and the wife and children. When a good harvest returns, we'll repay you 'the same measure or better,' if our crop is abundant. Don't allow good neighbors to perish in hard times" (Alciphr. 1.24). More common is the stingy farmer portrayed by Theophrastus (*Char.* 10.13), who or-dered his wife not to lend salt, lamp wicks, food or grain for sacrifice, or even garlands or cakes, in fear that such small generosity would lead only to increased demands during the year. Theophrastus's better known "Boor" (*Char.* 4.10–12), once he lends out "his plough, basket, sickle, or sack, keeps up at night, remembering, and goes after it." Aelian's Dercyl-los at one point prays: "May never the ways of farmers be full of jeal-ousy" (Ael. *Ep.* 17)—after remarking on the fertility and bounty of Aischeas's farm nearby. Under the agrarian regime of the *polis*, the coun-tryside teemed with thousands of private agendas, each farmer in his own idiosyncratic way trying desperately to grow food in unique circum-stances.

Far more bothersome than neighbors was the occasional trespasser.

He was no mere rival, but a complete stranger who stole fruit or some-times engaged in senseless destruction. In a speech attributed to the fourth-century orator Demosthenes, the speaker brings suit, claiming in-truders have wantonly ransacked his estate (47.53–56). Here we learn that Greek farmers were particularly incensed at the loss of harvest or property to the vandal or the thief. Xenophon relates a ritualistic Thes-salian skit in which the two dancers reenacted a fight between a robber and a plowman for the latter's oxen (*An.* 6.1.1–13). Hesiod calls the more subtle rural burglar the "Day-sleeper" (*Op.* 604), the man who works at night on the property of those who work during the day. An an-cient commentator on a comedy of Aristophanes tells us that farmers often put sharp spikes amid their vines, to pierce the feet of intruders who raided their vintage (*Ach.* 230 and cf. scholiast).

Both the early Athenian lawgivers, Draco and Solon, purportedly made it a capital crime to steal grapes (e.g., Alciphr.3.40). That may in-dicate that theft was not unusual at harvest time. In Plato's ideal state there are various regulations, depending on one's social status (foreigner, slave, free citizen), concerning the legality of picking another's ripe fruit (*Leg.* 8.844E–845D), suggesting the problem warranted utopian discus-sion. Pollux compiles a list of prickly, thorny bushes and "all the other spiked objects placed among the crops for their protection." In southern Greece today practical cactus "fences" of nearly ten feet in height sur-round many vineyards.*

We saw earlier that the Athenian statesman Cimon was praised as the exception for allowing travelers to feed on his orchard's fruit—such largess apparently resulted from kindness rather than despair at keeping poachers out; at least it reflects the tension between grower and traveler over the potential theft of produce (Plut. *Cim.* 10.1–3). Few followed such a model of generosity. Theophrastus more typically caricatured the stingy farmer as one who would not allow travelers to pass through his fields, much less sample a fig or pick up fruit that had fallen to the ground (*Char.* 10.8). Suspicion and distrust of *any* intruder must by ne-cessity run deep for the homestead farmer.

A farm is quite different from a house in town. The urbanized fail to

*See Weaver 210. For ancient spikes among the crops, see Poll. *On.* 1.225, 10.131; Plut. *Mor.* 94E; Strato (*Ant. Pal.* 12.205.4); cf. Ar. *Vesp.* 449.

realize that to the agrarian walking through a vineyard or orchard is tantamount to the farmer's intruding into the town dweller's front yard. I lost my temper at an elderly man cutting through an orchard at harvest. Convinced he was intent on stealing fruit (no more than three or four dollars worth), I was on catching him humbled to learn he was entirely innocent—a diabetic attempting to get needed exercise via a country walk. But much worse is Menander's Dyscolus (109–21), who greets a visitor: "Damned man, so you're trespassing on my land. What's the idea?" He then proceeds to pelt him with a grape-stake, and chases him "throwing clods, rocks, and pears when he had nothing left." Later the playwright concludes: "Poor farmers are hot tempered, nearly all of them" (130–31).

The practice of transhumance was still known in many regions during the *polis* period. Oftentimes sheep and goats—as well as the herdsmen themselves—could consume produce on their trips to and from the mountains. So in both the Greek material and literary record, there is abundant evidence of fences on Greek farms, usually built of stone.* Hindrances could easily be made when clearing a field of large rocks for ploughing. But the ubiquity of stone and rock in the Greek landscape does not in itself explain the standard presence of small field walls.

Permanent rural borders are a reflection, I think, of both the independence and the fear (usually justified) of the Greek farmer. Demarcation is symbolic of the move toward agrarianism and intense identification with the land, ground that was not for mere sustenance, but instead *private* property to be passed on to kin for generations. The open Greek countryside was gradually becoming the rough private grid of a new class of farmers: "The way in which Greek farms were laid out must in many areas have resembled that of a dense patchwork, each subdivided by its plantings of vines, its rows of trees, its grain and bean fields and gardens" (Burford 1993: 110). Although fences could mark these property boundaries and ward off potential squabbles, they could only slow down, rather than keep out, intruders. Fenced borders were more to alert the stranger than to keep him away, and might stall the thief loaded down with produce.

Dogs, however, offered an even better method of protection from

---

*On fences, see Hanson 1983: 37–38. On transhumance, cf. Osborne 1987: 48–52; Shipley 17–19.

theft and attack ("Dogs," says Xenophon, "keep out the wild animals from the crops and sheep" [*Oec.* 5. 6]). On every farm, as now in Greece, pets guarded the house and fields,* "sleeping inside during the day to keep watch at night" (Varro *Rust.* 1.21). The dogs of the swine-herd Eumaios nearly tore apart the approaching Odysseus until their master "shouted at the dogs and scared them in every direction with volleyed showers of stones" (Hom. *Od.* 14. 35–36). These canines were not the aristocratic hounds, like Odysseus's old Argus and the elegant hunters on Greek vases, but rather more pragmatic watchdogs of the type Hesiod assumed every farmer to have: "And take care of the dog," he advised (*Op.* 604–5); "do not hold back on his food, or sometime a thief will carry off your belongings." Theophrastus's agrarian boor went so far as to bring his dog to the farmhouse door at every knock; holding him by the snout, he announced to strangers: "Here is the guardian of the farm, and of the man" (*Char.* 4). In one of Alciphron's letters about farmers, the farm-dog is so highly prized that he is invited to attend a rural feast along with his master (3.18).[2]

As Aristotle saw, the most serious of all human threats was not the occasional thief or the vindictive neighbor, but rather organized bands of raiders and brigands, or worse, the wholesale onslaught of enemy armies, belligerents who wished to destroy in addition to plunder. There was enough banditry even in the fifth and fourth centuries to make farm life somewhat perilous. Packs of plunderers who come across mountain bor-der passes, descend to farmland, and then flee are a common complaint in Greek literature, during both peace and wartime. That is precisely the scene in Aristophanes' *Acharnians*, when poor Lamachos is forced to march out on the snowy heights of Mt. Parnes to ward off a band of Boeotian marauders who threaten Attic farms up on the border (Ar. *Ach.* 1073–77; 1140–43). Surely farmers working border ground took the most losses, largely in stolen livestock and slaves (e.g., Paus. 4.18.1; *Hell. Oxy.* 12.3–5).

Raiders had not much interest in wanton destruction—that activity was more often aimed at drawing out enemy troops—but rather went after easy plunder. From numerous texts such theft seems to be a com-mon complaint of Greek farmers, and we sense that these references do

---

*See Richter 80–83; Walcott 1970: 97–98; Halstead and Jones 44; Burford 1993: 119.

not describe threats to uninhabited plots of commuting peasants, but rather to well-stocked, owner-occupied homestead farms (e.g., Thuc. 2.5.4; 2.5.5; 2.5.7; 4.103.5; 4.104.1; Hdt. 1.17; Polyb. 4.3.10; Xen. *Hell.* 6.2.6). In passages from Greek literature, the emphasis is usually both on the attackers' quick onslaught and the farmers' anguished and often futile efforts to mount a posse of sorts to retrieve their lost capital. After all, for those attacked, it must have been awkward to don heavy armor—shield, spear, helmet, and breastplate (the formal gear of the farmers' phalanx)—and expect to catch a quick-moving band of experienced robbers. Xenophon recommends that the farmer return the favor by simply plundering the food himself: "Often in war it is safer for one to maintain oneself with arms than to harvest food with farming implements" (*Oec.* 5.13).[3]

Ironically, much of the infrastructure stolen from farmers was, no doubt, simply reused by the attackers—often farmers themselves (e.g., Xen. *Oec.* 5.13)—on their own estates. The so-called Oxyrhynchus Historian tells us that during the last years of the Peloponnesian War (i.e., 413–404 B.C.) the Boeotians stole slaves, roof tiles, and other furnishings from the Attic countryside, as a byproduct of constant border raiding. This anonymous historian adds that predation was attractive since Attica at this time was the "most lavishly furnished" of any area in Greece. This prosperity in Attica grew because "whatever they took from other Greeks, they brought on to their own farms (*eis tous idious agrous*)" (*Hell. Oxy.* 12.4; cf. Hanson 1992: 217–18). That concluding and fragmented sentence is a much ignored passage, but it clearly implies that Athenian imperialism was not exclusively concerned with maritime trading and overseas profit, but could bring benefits to the farmers of Attica as well (cf. Dem. 21.167–68).

It was the invasion of entire armies, phalanxes of five thousand or more men which posed the greatest threat to rural inhabitants. Their mere presence on good farmland imposed serious losses, especially should their arrival coincide with harvest. Nevertheless, more than ten years ago I argued that, in fact, the entire strategy of crop destruction—the trigger for Greek infantry warfare of the *polis* period—*rarely* resulted in long-lasting economic catastrophe (Hanson 1983: 145–51). The inherent resiliency of trees and vines to cutting and burning, the short combustible period of ripening grain, the difficulty of organizing armed men into destroyers of orchards and vineyards during a brief invasion, the rough terrain of many Greek plots, and the effectiveness of local defense usually meant the farm was plundered, some of the stored crop lost, but the agricultural infrastructure *not* wiped out. The chief damage occurred when invaders caught an entire grain crop dry and thus combustible, but this required careful timing and even then was difficult, since grain is flammable for only an extremely short period and the harvests can extend for weeks in different locales. More often, as in the case of the Peloponnesian invasion of Attica during early summer of 431 B.C., prior word of a hostile advance meant the farming community could double their efforts to harvest at least a portion of the crop before the enemy's arrival.

Besides the loss of livestock, tools, and slaves—and often these too were evacuated—the greatest damage was psychological. This injury to the agrarian psyche cannot be overestimated. The sight of enemy patrols running free over farms must have been insufferable for yeomen, and it is surely for this reason that in Greek agrarian warfare until the Peloponnesian War we rarely hear of drawn-out sieges, where rural folk abandon their plots and withdraw to safe ground. The mere threat of agricultural devastation was usually enough to draw the farmers out, to marshal their phalanx, and to try the issue decisively. As we will see (Chapter 6, "The Ways of Fighters"), the *entire* development of infantry battle served to perpetuate the enhanced position of the farmer within the Greek city-state.

So far we have discussed only overt human destruction—that is, the physical harm that neighbors, thieves, plunderers, and soldiers could do to a Greek farm. But humankind is also capable of more insidious damage, acts of malice that can be far more deadly to the survival of the farmer. These psychological wounds are important in understanding the ancient Greek *geôrgoi*. Chief among the small landowner's worries were *members of his own family*. It was not enough that the *geôrgos* must work from dawn to dusk, and clothe himself in hoplite armor to risk his life; every bit as perilous to the family estate was the family itself (cf. Hesiod's warning: "If trouble strikes your house, neighbors will come in their bedclothes, but family members will dress up" [*Op.* 344–45]).

Unlike the traditional mentality of the peasant who seeks as many children as possible to aid in farm work, the intensive Greek agriculturalist, who had access to slave labor, sometimes (like the modern farmer) saw multiple offspring, in particular daughters, as real liabilities to his consolidated holdings. In the *polis* period, when population was gradually rising while available land was continually dwindling, inheritance of the patrimonial estate was often the chief crisis in the life of any farm family. Without any constant tradition of primogeniture—the Greeks felt that all male offspring should have the opportunity to own farmland—the family plot theoretically could be divided by two, three, four, or more sons, jeopardizing the survival of the property, brother fighting brother over his own small allotment. That scenario forms the dramatic context of the *Works and Days*, where Hesiod's brother, Perses, has apparently bribed the local magistrate into unfairly granting him the bulk of the family land (*Op.* 27–41; cf. Walcot 1970: 77–93; and Hom. *Od.* 14.207–10; *Il.* 12.421–22), resulting in Hesiod's long diatribe against the injustice.

Later in Greek literature there is ample reference to blood feuds between brothers over the inheritance of the ancestral property (e.g., Xen. *Mem.* 2.3.1–10; Is. 2.28). Daughters, of course, cost the farmer expensive dowries and, if there were no surviving sons, brought sons-in-law into the family who might not always have similar regard for the so-called family plot. No wonder that Hesiod bluntly advises: "There should be only a single son (*mounogenês pais*) to look after his father's house, that way wealth will increase in the home. But should you leave behind a second son, take care that you die old" (*Op.* 376–79; cf. Xenocr. fr. 97).[4]

There has been little discussion of a dilemma of near-equal gravity, the childless farmer who has no heir to assume control of the traditional estate. Although we hear that the sterile grower could pass on his farm to whomever he wished (e.g., Is. 7.30; Dem. 43.75), there was a real loss of accumulated expertise: the break between father and son reduced productivity in the life-cycle of the farm. A modern example reflects this process. In the middle and late 1970s the condition of our own farm after nearly a century was precarious. My grandparents were in their eighties, one daughter was dead, another an invalid, the third employed off the farm. The old man's four grandsons were in college, with no apparent desire to retain the home place. The farm was overgrown with weeds. The equipment had been stolen. Repair, replanting, and maintenance had been ignored by a succession of hired hands, who looted infrastructure and planned their own regimen in open defiance of the patriarch. To watchful neighboring farmers (potential buyers all), this was clear enough proof of the moral inferiority of our clan, who "had gone off and gone bad." Only the sudden reappearance of my brothers and cousin restored the farm to its past productivity (despite repeated mistakes and near disasters). Only in the last two years of my grandfather's life—his eighty-fifth and eighty-sixth years—was the accrued damage of a decade and a half gradually reversed.

Many family-owned farms, ancient and modern, have gone through this "life cycle" of decay and renewal. Youth haphazardly awaits its turn, as the farm totters during the transition from one extreme of expertise without bodily strength to the other of hardiness without wisdom, the dangerous disequilibrium of "an old man's wisdom" and "a young man's muscles" (Aesch. *Sept.* 622). If a generation is skipped, the farm's survival rests on the ability of the elder (in just a few years' time) to transfuse his lifelong proficiency into the grandson before unchecked youthful exuberance proves fatal. Youth, after all, brings prerequisite strength and energy to farming, but it can also create fatal recklessness. Most middle-aged and elderly farmers lament their lost vigor while laughing about the stupid decisions they made in their twenties and thirties.

Besides concern over brothers, wife, sons, daughters, and in-laws, problems with inheritance, and property distribution, the farmer's own health was a chief problem. Often he delayed marriage until his thirties (Hes. *Op.* 700–701; Pl. *Leg.* 4.721B; 785B; *Resp.* 5.460E; Arist. *Pol.* 7.1335a6) and did not inherit until even later. Much of his family-raising and hard work, both often extremely stressful, was done in his late thirties, forties, and fifties, not in his teens and twenties. For many, the brutal regimen simply broke their health in a few years. These are daily occurrences on any farm, past or present, and more than anything else threaten the existence of the small agriculturalist. No surprise that Hesiod has elaborate advice on proper clothing to prevent exposure to the cold in winter or to avoid sunstroke in summer.*

***Op.* 504–60; Walcott 1970: 26–27. On the life-cycle of the farm, see Gallant 1991: 11–34; 17–21.

Throughout later Greek literature we hear of freak accidents. (Agriculture traditionally has been statistically the most dangerous occupation, with the highest instances of accidental death and injury) Accidents and injuries must have been common among folk who lived and worked the majority of their lives outdoors. For one Antipater of Sidon there is a poignant epitaph, lamenting his death when he stepped on a snake while protecting his crop from birds (*Ant. Pal.* 7.172; cf. Hom. *Il.* 3.35–36). The Roman agronomist Columella assumed ("as generally happens," *quod accidit plerumque*) that someone on the farm would be injured by the end of any given day (*Rust.* 11.1.18). In Menander's *Dyscolus*, Kleainetos gashes his leg open while digging in his vineyard, and "by the third day the old man's wound became swollen, and fever took hold; he was extremely ill" (*Dys.* 46–51). From the same play, we also learn that back injuries were a frequent occurrence while laborers were digging around vines (*Dys.* 533–38; cf. 372–73).

A hobbled farmer threatened the viability of the farm itself. Medicine was rudimentary and palliative—reduction of swelling and the staunching of bleeding—and as in the case of Kleainetos, completely ignorant of prophylaxis and treatment against bacterial or viral infection. In family farming, ancient or modern, there is no sick leave, no paid disability, no work that can be postponed until the return of health. Medical attention for trauma is often distant and an expense the farmer cannot afford.

On the farm, animal and human waste—and thus infection—was ubiquitous. Aelian relates the tale of Hemeron, who, like Menander's Kleainetos, cut his leg on a rock only to have "inflammation take him and his groin swelled up" (Ael. *Ep.* 2). Nor must we forget military service, for which the small landowner was eligible as a hoplite until his early sixties. A war wound, although not fatal, might cause later disability and ruin the agrarian's ability to plough, prune, or cultivate. Plenty of references exist in Greek literature to hoplites who are wounded or covered with scars (e.g., Xen. *Mem.* 3.4.1; cf. Hanson 1989: 210–18). In this context (see Chapter 6), the exigent nature of Greek infantry battle of the agrarian *polis* is easily understood.

Not all sickness is purely physical. Cardiologists in nearby Fresno expect between August and October to perform many heart bypasses on stressed grape-growers; their pumps have a predictable tendency to collapse during the tension of harvest. The sheer isolation of farm life, the constant repetition of technique, the ever-present fear of every conceivable natural and human danger, also played havoc with a man's mind.*

There must have been plenty of instances in which the line between eccentricity—innate to most small homesteaders—and madness was crossed. Where self-reliance is at a premium, where challenges are unique, the sheer ingenuity and independence of the Greek farmer encouraged aberration and occasional derangement. The agriculturalist, ancient and modern, unceasingly seeks to go beyond mere rote and custom in his cultural practice (cf. Theophr. *CP* 3.2.3), desires to expand on the accumulated expertise of generations in order to *know* precisely what causes his crops either to die or to thrive. Unfortunately, that quest for a rational explanation of an irrational process, for the secret to success and failure is mostly futile: exact knowledge of plant biology and of crops' reactions to outside stimuli is beyond the capabilities of mere agronomy. The endless and doomed contemplation of absolute agricultural science in an environment of solitude often pushes the farmer over the brink.

The late fourth-century playwright Menander saw potential for comic relief in this phenomenon. His play the *Dyscolus*, or "Curmudgeon," features a misanthropic Attic farmer who seeks refuge from society on the slopes of Mt. Parnes, despising all social intercourse. Elsewhere we hear of even more bizarre behavior: Aethiops of Corinth (about 730 B.C.?) who sold his right to land at the new colony at Syracuse for a fruitcake (Athen. 4.167D; Archil. fr. 216); the Corinthian who gave up his vines for philosophy (Arist. fr. 64 Rose³); the philosopher Kelanthes who "for the sake of philosophy" cultivated and irrigated his garden incessantly (hence he was dubbed "the Water-Pump") (Diog. Laert. 7.168–69). Alciphron also takes up the theme of the misanthropic Timon (apparently a stock character in earlier Attic literature) and makes him into a recluse who hits passersby with dirt clods (Alciphr. 3.34).

Why should we not hear of mental instability associated with agricul-

---

*For all the glorification of the farm's solitude ("How sweet for the man who hates worthless ways is solitude, and for that man wishing no evil, a good-producing farm is all that he needs" [Men. fr. 466 Kock]), the isolation took a toll. Cf. the example of the despondent farmer who lost his animals and so hanged himself on a wild pear tree (*Anth. Pal.* 9.149). In my own locale, suicide among agrarians is not uncommon.

ture? Farming requires solitary hours of repetitive work that not merely invites philosophical speculation but often demands continuous self-criticism and self-doubt, attempts to blame or exculpate oneself for the vagaries of nature. Without much interaction or conversation with others on the farm, these musings can drive a farming man, or any other man, nearly mad.

Consider the dilemma of the modern raisin grower, instructive of the timeless need for balance in the unbalanced environment of agriculture. At summer's end, does he hold off picking his grapes until his crop reaches full maturity (20 to 22 degrees, Brix), ensuring a top quality, *heavy* raisin (raisins are sold by weight)? If so, in most years this mandates patience (especially for the grower of a lush, extremely productive but late-maturing vineyard [cf. Colum. *Arbor.* 3.2]), a long wait for harvest until September fifth or even later, and a subsequent drying period of at least twenty-one days. California grapes once picked for raisins are left exposed to the elements. They dry naturally in the sun on paper trays atop terraced earth between the vine rows (in contrast to the more conservative and smaller-scale Greek method of transporting the grapes to protected drying sheds and platforms). "Left naked one high" on the tray is the Fresno parlance: a whole year's work absolutely vulnerable to the weather until dried and collected out of the field in October.

For the farmer who seeks the best quality of raisins, and thus the best price, the cost of delaying his grape harvest for a week or two (until mid or late September) is often one he can ill afford to pay (cf., "If he waits for the full ripening of the grapes, he may forfeit the vintage (*amittat vindemiam praecoquem*)" [Colum. *Rust.* 3.21.5–6]). For each day that the grapes are left to ripen on the vine and to gain sugar—and hence weight—the chance of fall rains increases commensurably. For each of those days the drying time on the ground lessens, as the daylight hours wane, the darkness lengthens, and the humidity rises. Each day that the grapes stay on the vine unpicked gaining crucial sugar, the chances *decrease* that the fruit will ever dry into finished raisins.

"Have 'em all in the sweatbox by the equinox," my grandfather used to say of the need to get the raisins dry, out of the field, and boxed by around September 21, "and you'll usually make out all right." Hesiod advised picking in September: "When Orion and Seirios arrive in the middle of the heavens, and rosy-fingered Dawn looks on Arktouros, then cut all the grapes and bring them home (*tote pantas apodrepen oikade Botrus*)" (*Op.* 609–10). (Compare the similar advice on harvesting from the modern dry technical manual: "Harvesting should start when the grapes reach 22° or 23° Brix or September 1, whichever comes first. If the grapes have not reached Brix by September 1, it is an indication that the vines are carrying an over-crop and measures should be taken to correct the condition in future years" [Winkler et al. 653]).

The scholarly advice that "measures should be taken to correct the condition in future years" is no solace to the poor farmer on the brink of disaster on the first of September with an enormous and immature crop, with berries still unripe from a cool summer and with too many clouds now in the sky. For him it is not the "future years" of the university raisin manual that matter, but the here and now of overdue bills and a mortgage to service. Thus now he has no choice but a throw of the dice. For this gambler who wishes—*must* wish—top quality *and* maximum returns (the ideal but impossible combination) on his year's work *in lieu* of absolute safety, who must therefore wait too long, the ruin of an unseasonable fall rain is often total: financially a catastrophe, humiliation psychologically.

"I ran out of heat" a broken man of seventy remarked to me in October 1982 as I surveyed his 120 acres of stinking, fermenting wet grapes submerged in a sea of muck and worms—for a three-quarters dried grape is still a grape, never a raisin. Given a good inch of rain it is soon little more than a putrid mass of mold. Years of capital investment were no more than distillery material and z-grade mix for the local cattle feed lot. Theophrastus (CP 5.15.3) warned of "carrying out agricultural procedures at the wrong moment."

Is it then wiser to play the odds conservatively, to cut your grapes much earlier, in the second or third week of August? This early picking, of course, greatly increases the chance that the raisin crop will be harvested. Grapes will dry quickly on the sizzling summer tray, given the hundred-degree searing heat of the August dog-days. Here, as every farmer knows, is the trade-off. Often early-picked grapes are immature. Without much sugar, they scorch in the sun. They fail raisin quality tests. They weigh little. They make a red, not a purple, raisin. They bring in some cash. But often it is far less cash than is required to pay the year's expenses. So some farmers prefer the chance of September "mush" to the certainty of August "rocks." "You'll need a tarp on your semi to hold those Wheaties from blowing plumb off" a bothersome farmer once scoffed when, stung by the previous season's late harvest and subsequent total loss to rain, we in our twenties picked too early on August 19. The grapes, without much sugar that year, turned into weathered flakes, not really raisins at all. Fifty to seventy tons evaporated ("Your kid's new clothes just dried up too," the old pest gibed). A fourth of the grapes that year were immature, sour in August, they were little more than water and skin.

The perfect equilibrium (the Greeks' *to meson/to metrion*) is the farmer's ideal. But if he is to survive, he must learn that the balance between good production and reasonable safety is never ascertainable until after the fact. During the harvest and the ensuing wait as the grapes dry, excellence is fickle. The "right" decision changes hourly with the weather. A rain scare on a September afternoon, a storm that threatens to annihilate every tray of grapes on the ground, turns the early harvester, who picked in August and has his now dried poor-grade raisins in the barn, into a genius, the late gambler, with green sweet grapes vulnerable on the dirt, into an abject greedy fool; all this will be confirmed by the night's downpour or be erased from the mind as a strong wind—without any explanation or inherent logic, much less "fairness"—blows away the threatening clouds.

In the clear, cloudless heat of morning, yesterday's wise man is seen as panicky. Given the new forecast of days of good drying weather ahead, he appears to have harvested immature grapes needlessly early, and thus to have given up for no good purpose tons of would-be raisins. He is, in short, a hothead who bolted too soon, scorned by the late harvester, a man who is now suddenly transformed from greedy and reckless into a paragon of wisdom and steely nerve.

These images, these thoughts, these realities—for they are in the last analysis, like the weather, real enough—change, day in and day out within an agricultural community, until the harvest is finally played out. The whole daily, hourly process is repeated silently, often unobserved by others in a man's family, pounding in a farmer's brain, year in, year out. Small wonder it is that the pacing, frowning farmer has a reputation for instability. In Aristophanes' *Plutus* the character Cario meets an unknown Informer and asks him his occupation: "Are you a farmer (*geôrgos ei*)?" The Informer replies: "Do you think I am as melancholy mad as that?" (902). Menander observes: "The life of farmers has sweetness—by creating hopes to meet the pain" (fr. 641 Kock). In despair over an entire irrigation system washed away, Alciphron's farmer simply sighs: "I must try another sort of life" (3.13).

Equipment and infrastructure are the tools a farmer uses to produce his crop; but appurtenances in themselves can often cause worry and pose considerable trouble. Like the weather, they can become hostile, wound, or maim a farmer and confound his carefully thought-out plans. Almost everything an ancient Greek farmer used or consumed on his plot was of his own fabrication, its maintenance his own responsibility. There is little evidence that there was an extensive urban industrial or manufacturing stratum at agrarian *poleis*.* Water, food, and sewage disposal were his first concerns. The presence of a nearby spring, river, or lake was essential to his survival, and consequently there are plentiful references, as we have seen in Chapter 2, in the epigraphical, archaeological, and literary record, to mechanisms—wells, ditches, cisterns—for obtaining water on homestead farms. Food for the winter—both for consumption and to exchange in the local market for cash—had to be stored in bulk, and to be kept free from spoilage and insect damage, not to mention theft or destruction by intruders. Ancient agricultural handbooks are replete with advice on how to prevent loss of stored crops, and suggest that farmers' problems often *began* rather than ended at harvest; insects, fungi, and rodents could attack stored grains and fruit (e.g., Plut. *Mor.* 219C1; Theophr. CP 4.15.3–16.4).

Sewage was less of a problem. Farmers simply constructed privies, often fashioning them in such a way that feces could fall into mounds and be collected as fertilizer for the fields, despite the disease that incorporation of human waste into the food chain can cause (cf. IG II² 2496; Pliny *HN* 17.6; Theophr. *HP* 2.7.4; Men. *Dys.* 584–85). Often these piles were veritable compost heaps, where straw, leaves, weeds, rotten food, wine, and every kind of refuse was dumped to be collected later

---

*See Gallant 1991: 121; cf. Plato on the more utopian idea of a specialized agricultural implement industry (*Resp.* 2.370C).

when decomposed into fertile soil additives (e.g., Semple 1928: 134–36; White 1970a 127–135; cf. Varro *Rust.* 1.13.4).

Most tools, like the farmer's infantry spear, were made of wood with iron heads and thus of simple, durable construction (e.g., *Anth. Pal.* 6.104). Nevertheless, a plough or wagon could often break at the most crucial time, causing the farmer to lose critical hours in its repair. Simiche, the slave-farmworker in Menander's *Dyscolus*, was sure of punishment when he lost the farm's shovel as he was trying to fetch a dropped bucket from the well (584–85). Hesiod, forever the pragmatist, therefore urges having spare implements on hand: "Have two ploughs on hand, and work over them at home, one jointed, the other all one piece. This is by far the best thing to do; for if you break one, you can still put the oxen to the other" (*Op.* 432–33).

Although most tools pale in complexity compared to modern equipment, their construction and upkeep was a constant task: "Fool, there are a hundred pieces of lumber in a wagon. Be sure to have these at home beforehand" (Hes. *Op.* 456–57; cf. Men. *Dys.* 375; Colum. *Rust.* 11.1.20). No doubt the poet realized that there was an ever-present temptation to "get by" with a single set of tools or to borrow implements from a neighbor. That was surely a shortsighted policy, for the salvation of a crop otherwise lost would more than pay for investment in good equipment. Independence, self-reliance, and responsibility are the key, traits to reappear throughout Greek military and political life. There is none of the palace decision making and bureaucratic overregulation found in the Linear B tablets of past Mycenean times.

Because the *polis* farmer lived on his ground, the house, as well as fences, terraces, pens, outbuildings, and "barns," required constant maintenance—and became instant, visible reflections of the farm family's relative success or failure within the general agricultural community. The repair of field walls and terraces was apparently the work Homer envisioned Laertes busy with in Book Twenty-four of the *Odyssey* (*Od.* 24.224). Later lease agreements on stone tablets always were careful to stipulate that the renter return the property as it was or much improved. The fear of a caved-in roof during a storm, a washed-out terrace taking part of the orchard, animals escaping through defective fencing (cf. Lys. 7.4.9–11) all explain the farmer's inability to rest, and his obsession with keeping busy year-round to prevent catastrophe.

III.

"In farming most things are impossible to know in advance," Xenophon sighs. "Sometimes, hailstorms, frost, droughts, rains, blights and other things ruin plans which were otherwise well thought-out" (Xen. *Oec.* 5.18). Natural, not human-induced catastrophe, was the most feared ("The year bears the crop, not the soil," Theophr. *HP* 8.7.6; cf. Guiraud 486–90), confirming the traditional image of the farmer battling against the elements (e.g., Pl. *Resp.* 7.527D).*

My concerns here, however, are much more narrow and mundane: What did the farmer do; what did he think when confronted with natural disaster and how did constant worry affect his overall outlook? The agrarian ideology of self against nature is crucial to understanding the political and military mentality of agrarianism, and thus the entire cultural history of the ancient Greek *polis*.

By "natural" threat I mean any slight deviation from the normal ecological environment to which the agriculturalist has grown accustomed. Chief among the elemental disasters was sudden rain, not merely the deluges that erode soil and damage infrastructure, but the more serious unseasonable downpours right at harvest. Those storms could be lethal, wiping out days or months, even years of work. Besides preventing access to the fields and damaging terraces and ditches (e.g., Alciphr.3.13; Theophr. *HP* 8.6.5–7), rainfall could soak ripening cereal stalks, split harvestable grapes, tree fruit, and olives, and rot drying raisins and figs (e.g., Xen. *Symp.* 2.25; cf. McDonald and Rapp 55). Less dramatic, but equally injurious, were storms at key times of planting or pollination. Continuous rain while fruit trees are in bloom can prevent fertilization and result in the absence of an entire year's crop; "some permanent crops," says Theophrastus (*HP* 4.14.8; cf. *CP* 2.9.3–4), "such as trees and vines, if rain falls on them as they are dropping their blossom, also lose their fruit." If they occur right after planting, rain and accompanying humidity tend to rot seeds in the ground, ruining chances for germi-

---

*Gallant (1991: 113–42) has devoted a great deal of discussion to ancient agrarian responses to natural crises: the collecting of wild flora, hunting, fishing, selling and slaughtering livestock, the relinquishment of slaves and property, marrying off or sending away a daughter, or embarking on military service or other outside employment.

nation. Plato once made a rhyming pun on this ubiquitous dual worry of the farmer over soils and seasons by dubbing it *hôra kai chôra* (Pl. *Hipp.* 225B–D).

What was the Greek farmer's response to a disaster? In essence, there was little, if anything, he could do after the fact. Much effort instead was put into forecasting doom.* Aelian (*NA* 6.16) wrote that "dogs, oxen, swine, goats, snakes, and other animals have a prescient knowledge of impending famine, and also they are the first to know of an approaching earthquake. They can foretell fair weather and the fertility of crops. Though they have no share of reason, nevertheless, they do not make mistakes in the phenomena mentioned above."

At other times, wild plants, not animals, could give some indication of the crop year. Theophrastus purportedly thought that farmers might look to the health of nearby oak and mastich trees to receive some idea of the upcoming yield of their grain crops (Plut. *Mor.* fr. 17). Often the best caution was simply to begin harvest a little early, sacrificing some quality in the produce, but increasing the odds that the entire crop could be gathered in the shortest period of time. The *geôrgos* was constantly apprehensive, continually examining plants and animals for some clue, some help in warding off disaster.

Given the Mediterranean climate, downpours could sometimes be beneficial (cf. Plut. *Mor.* fr. 68). The absence of rain was almost always a greater problem to Greek farmers (e.g., Theophr. *Char.* 3.3). Here, I mean both the "mini-drought" of a few weeks or months, or even a year or so, which retards plant growth and cuts into the size of the harvest, as well as the far more lethal climatic aberration, when little if any rain appears for years at time, where entire vineyards and orchards might die.

Peter Garnsey notes that in the years between 1931 and 1960, there was a twenty-eight percent chance that the annual wheat crop of Attica could have failed. In such atypical cases, farmers faced the real chance of food shortages. Temperatures—usually associated with July and August—can today in Greece exceed 100 degrees Fahrenheit for weeks at a time. Since plentiful winter and spring rains are usually absent, there is no surplus moisture stored in the soil for the wheat or barley to draw on.

---

*E.g., Hes. *Op.* 448–50; Arist. *HA* 597a23; cf. Brumfield 21–23 and especially the story of Thales' forecast of the size of the next year's olive crop in Arist. *Pol.* 1.1259a7–20.

The danger is not confined to cereals. As grapes ripen, especially in the early stages of development when their sugar content is low, they often are sunburned, the more exposed clusters shriveling up altogether. (As I write this paragraph, we have lost this week about twenty tons of immature grapes to four continuous days of 110-degree heat.) The same is true of other tree fruit and olives. Produce on drought-stricken trees and vines, with little foliage, is often scorched and ruined. Farmers impatient to sow grain might find their cereal crop lost at the very beginning of the agricultural year with the absence of fall rains.

The presence of a *variety* of crops and species ensured that all fruit on the farm was not in the same vulnerable cycle. Smaller immature berries and clusters cannot weather a sudden spate of excessive temperature as well as grapes on the verge of harvest. There are a few examples in the agricultural treatises of rudimentary attempts to spread dirt or clay over produce (*hupokonisis*), and other efforts to deflect heat (e.g., Colum. *Rust.* 4.28.1; 9.2.60; Theophr. *HP* 2.7.5; *CP* 3.16.3; Xen. *Oec.* 19.18–19). This was no doubt a desperate move by the farmer to try something, anything, rather than allow his crop to shrivel and vanish before his eyes, inasmuch as protective coatings—today everything from talc to polymers is employed on vegetables, tree fruit, and grapes—provided little real defense. One of Alciphron's letters illustrates the dilemma: "There's a drought here now . . . and the soil is parched. All our sacrifices to Zeus of the rain-storms are in vain" (Alciphr. 3.35). The comic playwright Philemon's farmer compares his farm to a doctor who feeds him like an invalid, concluding, "I fear that his treatment will soon make me a corpse" (Philemon fr. 98 Kock).

Natural shade—we frequently hear of individual trees and entire groves appearing in almost a divine context in Greek literature—was essential to the small farm, requiring the planting of laurel, mulberry, fig, or other species with large canopies wherever possible. Far more important for combating drought and heat, however, were cultivation practices such as continued pulverization of the soil, which increases the carrying capacity of the ground during spring storms, or the use of straw over bare earth to conserve moisture. Irrigation, as we have seen, was essential during summer for gardens and the survival of young trees and vines.[5]

Frosts, wind, and hail could destroy crops, usually without warning in early spring: "The violent hailstorm has cut down the standing grain, and there is no hedge against famine."* So too in a Homeric simile a sudden gust blows down a carefully nurtured olive tree (Hom. *Il.* 17.53–58). For frost prevention it was important to have sealed ground, not freshly cultivated earth that exposed roots and did not absorb day-time heat (Theophr. *CP* 5.13.1). Sometimes vines were buried to prevent cold damage (Theophr. *CP* 5.12.6), or stones were put under the ground to transmit stored heat to roots (Theophr. *CP* 3.20.5). These nuances in cultivation practice might save an entire crop. I have seen a freshly disked vineyard lose its entire grape crop to a March frost, while a neighboring plot with sealed ground suffered no damage.

But the best protection was to spread risks by incorporating different species. In areas of violent gusts, windbreaks of poplars or other fast-growing, upright trees might cut down on some damage, but such plantings brought an entire array of problems of their own, from reducing available soil moisture for the crop, to attracting bird and insect pests, to shading out crops at the edge of the fields. Ironically, occasionally harsh winds could prove of some value, if the air movement occurred during grain winnowing (*Ant. Pal.* 6.53).

Insects are a constant pest in Greek literature. Grubs, coddling moths, locusts, mites, worms, grasshoppers, and beetles were the bane of any farmer (cf. Theophr. *CP* 4.14.1–5; *HP* 8.10.1–3). When Dicaiopolis in Aristophanes' *Acharnians* compares an army to a "swarm of locusts," he is surely drawing on a danger known to all Attic growers (*Ach.* 150). Elsewhere in Attic comedy we hear that pests could devour greens and thus raise the price of vegetables in the market (e.g., Alexis fr. 15.12–15 Kock).

The ancient practice of diversified crops must have mitigated some disasters. Flare-ups of insects, when natural hunters—birds and other insects—lose control of pest populations, occur when there are no alternative habitats nearby to encourage predator growth. The rise of intensive, diversified agriculture probably made Greek farmers of the *polis* innately *less prone* to locust and grasshopper swarms or to sudden destruction by spider mites. Like attempts to combat other natural disasters, there was little the ancient Greek farmer could do to kill insects on

---

*Alciphr. 1.24. On ancient attempts to prevent weather damage to crops, see Bintliff and Snodgrass 154; cf. Theophr. *CP* 5.13.7; 5.12.2–13.2; *HP* 4.14.5–6; and the bizarre practice at Paus. 2.34.3.

a large scale once they infested crops in numbers, despite the mention in our agronomic texts of a variety of innovative attempts at eradication.

The imaginative ways in which independent farmers attempted to combat birds and insects are striking. Aelian relates (*NA* 3.12) the romantic story of the residents of Thessaly, Illyria, and Lemnos who fed locust-eating jackdaws at public expense. That way, "the clouds of locusts are sizably reduced, and the produce of these peoples remains undamaged" (cf. Ar. *Aves* 588–90). Ancient agronomy, following Aristotle's lead, believed in spontaneous generation of insects on plants; although wrong in its explanation for the explosive growth in insect populations, that belief *could* lead to careful cultural practices that would diminish insect habitat (Theophr. CP 3.22.3–23.1).[6]

Birds were less dangerous than insects; they could, however, attack all three legs of the intensive farmer's triad: grain, tree fruit, and grapes (e.g., *Anth. Pal.*7.172; Theopompus *FGrH* 115 fr. 274). Aristophanes' comedy the *Birds* plays on just that fear throughout, as the nightmarish cast of airborne pests threatens to eat the grain, grapes, and olives of the Athenians unless they are enthroned as masters (227–245; 1119–1125). Theophrastus (*HP* 8.6.1) tells us that bird pests usually ate the grain as soon as it was scattered. Much earlier Hesiod advises the farmer to have a young boy follow behind to throw dirt over the seed to prevent its loss to birds (*Op.* 470.). Aelian (*NA* 17.41) also felt that incursions of field mice and sparrows had as serious effects on grain production as drought or frost. Occasionally, we hear of rudimentary ways of fighting back, such as spreading sticky substances ("birdlime") on fruit-tree branches where pests landed (e.g., Alciphr. 3.30; Eur. *Cyc.* 433; Athen. 10.451D; for the ancient viticulturalist's use of herbs and animal products to fight mildew, ants, mice, and worms, see. Colum. *Arbor.*13–15), or planting honey cakes in the field to lure birds away from freshly scattered seed (Aelian *HA* 17.16).

There were frequent attacks by wild animals such as boars and deer, another indication that Greek intensive farming had encroached on hillsides near mountainous and uncultivated areas. Homer tells of the enormous boar Artemis sent to tear up the "tall trees" (Hom. *Il.* 9.533), a beast that was elsewhere rightly known as "the tireless destroyer of vines" (*Anth. Pal.* 6.169).

In the struggling farmer's thinking, anything that walked or flew was a source of potential trouble better off dead. I have shot gophers and squirrels at regular intervals, in the field, beside the road, even on the house lawn. When pressed by urban friends to justify the gratuitous slaughter, I have searched for all sorts of excuses, from the fear of plant damage to their tunnels' undermining irrigation ditches. But the true reason is the dislike of any creature that dares to pose a threat, however remote, to a carefully planned agricultural regime. Alciphron's letters are replete with references to foxes who chew grapes and gulp down entire clusters (e.g., 3.22), varmints who repeatedly escape efforts to trap and kill them. In one incident, the farmer's dog, instead of the fox, falls victim to poisonous baited meat. We also hear of one Greek farmer who boasted that he "had knocked out the brains of a rabbit." Another dedicated a hedgehog to the gods, "its body full of sharp spines, a grape-eater, the destroyer of sweet vineyards, caught all curled into a ball rolling among the grapes" (*Anth. Pal.* 6.45; 6.72; 6.169).

Fungi, viruses, and bacterial infestations were common, and much more baffling than animal attack. Theophrastus lists a variety of diseases of viticulture—scab, mildew, bacterial fire blight, bacterial cancer, necrosis, sun-scorch (*CP* 5.9.1–12.1; and esp. 5.10.1–3; *HP* 4.14.1–10). Long experience in cultural practices (pruning, cultivation, pulling leaves, etc.), as well as additional fertilization and irrigation, might dramatically reduce outbreaks (cf. Theophr. *CP* 3.22.1–2). In some cases, we hear of bizarre remedies: burying stones, ashes, and iron, which theoretically could rectify deficiencies in micro-nutrients such as boron, zinc, and potassium. But without proper knowledge of botany or biology, most farmers blamed crops lost to disease either on the gods or on their own failed efforts at anticipating disaster. The poor farmer of the comic playwright Apollodorus of Carystus lamented that whereas others had vinegar-fig trees, which produced sour fruit, his farm was even worse: it produced bad grapes from the "vinegar-vine" as well (Apollodorus fr. 25 Edmonds).

As if natural calamity were not bad enough, the absence of crop damage was just as serious: there was the final irony that the complete want of disaster in any given year and the subsequent production of bounty could prove disastrous by creating a local market glut and diminished value for produce. Of course, the ancient Greek economy during the *polis* period was relatively unsophisticated. But its backwardness in comparison to modern capitalist systems has led too many scholars to downplay the importance of exchange, supply, demand, profit, speculation, and investment altogether when examining ancient economic life.* In the case of farmers of the Greek city-state, we know from a wide variety of literary sources *throughout* the *polis* period that a rudimentary food market operated on the local level, and that an oversupply of agricultural commodities could spell for producers as many problems as scarcity. This is exactly the situation Xenophon describes in his *Ways and Means* when he writes: "When there is a glut of wheat or wine, the prices of crops are cheap, and the profit from growing them vanishes, causing many farmers to give up" (*Vect.* 4.6–10). It is likely that this basic cycle of supply and demand, and consequent profiting in foodstuffs, emerged early in the history of the *polis*, providing a real incentive for intensive-farming *geôrgoi* to plant crops and take risks beyond the needs of their own immediate households.[7]

In this regard there are plenty of anecdotes from later sources demonstrating the desire of early Greeks to exchange and sell food. Besides the story of Solon's visit to Egypt for trading purposes (Arist. *Ath. Pol.* 11.1–2; Diog. Laert. 1.26; Plut. *Sol.* 2.7), there is a tradition that the philosopher Thales sometime in the seventh century acquired as many olive-presses as possible in anticipation of a bountiful harvest at Miletus and Chios, when processing equipment would be especially valuable (Arist. *Pol.* 1.1259a10–21). Greek literature is replete with stories of excess agricultural profits in times of scarcity, and more commonly financial disaster during periods of overproduction.**

Because of the perilous environment, the farmer's ideology of the need for hard work is not merely reasonable, but vital. Moreover, the threat of catastrophe—man-made, animal, insect, climatological, and meteorological—explains two other characteristic responses of farmers: repetition and a reverence for tradition. Agriculture and its practitioners are—*must* be—conservative. Experimentation in life-style, work ethic,

---

*E.g., Mickwitz 588–89. See instead Engels 24–25, 135–142.

**[Dem.] 42.20–31; Diod. 16.83.1; Xen. *Hell.* 6.1.11; *Oec.* 1.5–8; *Vect.* 4.6–7; [Arist.] *Oec.* 2.1347a25–35; see too Pritchett *War* 5.471–73; Skydsgaard 1992: 11; Jameson 1978: 91; Kent 308–12; Pritchett 1956: 190–91; Osborne 1991: 133–42; and cf. especially Engels 24–25; 135–42.

and daily routine can, if proved to be unwise or unsound, cause famine and disaster. "Farmers as a class," K. D. White concludes of agriculture in antiquity, "tend to be conservative in their outlook, suspicious of new methods, and generally adverse to experiment" (1970a: 48–49).

The safest course was simply to follow, religiously and without question, the example of previous farmers, that is, of one's father and grandfather. Much of Hesiod's emphasis on time and the calendar (i.e., his *Days*), on unswerving attention to detail, derive from the *fear* inherent in farming. In the chapters to follow, we see that it is just these characteristics of intensive, property-owning farmers—discipline, bonds to family and friends, affinity for hard work, steadiness in the midst of disaster—that explain the undeniable courage and military prowess of the Greek phalanx of the *polis*.

Even in the modern mind of the farmer, replete though it be with knowledge of pollenization, fertilization, and plant physiology and pathology, an irrational terror of crop failure (cf. Plato's "the fears of farmers" [Pl. *Leg.*10.906E]) always remains: in the case of the perennial cereals, fruit, and vegetables, that the seeds will not sprout, not germinate, not mature, not be fertile, not produce normal fruit. With permanent crops that fear only intensifies, fear not merely over a year's work, a season's harvest, but rather over a life's investment in orchards and vineyards.

The life of the intensive agriculturalist is one of unending fretting over disease and threats to the very life of the tree and vine. I have seen an entire plum orchard, six years of meticulous care invested in its establishment, felled by bacterial cancer in the space of a few weeks, verdant young trees transformed into hideous scorched sticks (cf. Theophr. *CP* 5.11.1–2). There is no palliative treatment other than to tear out the stumps, burn the wood, fumigate the ground, and then plant new stock, preferably a different species that will not similarly fail.

On an intellectual level this gnawing, ever-present concern over total destruction is absurd. The likelihood especially in modern times—with fumigants, fungicides, fertilizers, herbicides, and insecticides—is greater that harvests will appear, not fail, that orchards and vineyards will thrive, not die. But emotionally, spiritually the anxiety has an undeniable logic. Most farmers, both ancient and contemporary, are a season or two away from oblivion—financial ruin in the case of the modern grower, for the *geôrgos* of antiquity starvation. Plato, for example, speaks of the farmer made "helpless" by one bad season (*geôrgon chalepê hôra epelthousa amêchanon theiê*, *Prot.* 344D).

Even more important, the growing of food in a Mediterranean climate involves a transformation of the most radical kind, materially, aesthetically, substantively. From bare ground to a solid carpet of grain, from barren, sickly wood to an enormous canopy of leaves and fruit, the changes over the course of a season are startling. A visitor in January once asked as he looked out my kitchen window at sixty acres of vines where the grapes were. He nodded in disbelief when assured that the short, gnarled, and paltry-looking naked stumps would in a mere nine months' time each produce fifty pounds of quality grapes fresh, ten pounds of raisins dry, and provide seven-foot high, quarter-mile long continuous canopies of green foliage.

The more I explained to the guest the marvelous step-by-step changes that would soon take place in the vineyard, the more I too wondered, doubted, worried whether it was still possible, whether the eighty-year-old vines were this year at last too enfeebled to produce yet another crop. By the end of our conversation, I began despairing—praying to Demeter or Dionysos as it were—that we would have anything to harvest, any crop at all to pay off bills and accumulated debt, to provide food and shelter, so unimpressive to me too were the barren vine stumps of five generations of men seen in the midst of winter. No wonder Xenophon remarked on the uncertainty in agriculture: "You might plant a field well, but you will not know who shall harvest the fruit" (*Mem.* 1.1.8). Similarly, the Attic dramatist Philemon has his character say, "The farmer always is rich—the coming year" (Philemon fr. 82 Kock). Menander simply concludes, "The life of the farmers has pleasure in soothing over the pain with hopes" (Men. fr. 641 Kock).

The only solution to this agricultural anxiety, as Hesiod knew, was fidelity to things that worked in the past, precise attention to dates and repetition, avoidance of anything novel that might bring on disruption of past success. What else can explain the notebooks my grandfather kept for nearly half a century, detailing the weather, stage of fruit development, prices, and work being done on that particular day on his farm, despite the presence of modern weather forecasts and innumerable published guides on everything from farm management to plant pathology?

Terrified that the great chain of agricultural knowledge accumulated over generations might be broken (he had three daughters, but no son), daily he left an account of the yearly farming cycle—all in hopes of preserving his expertise should one of his ignorant progeny ever take his place. A typical diary entry in his sixty-sixth year on a July day in 1956 reads:

Tuesday, July 31, 1956

Clear, mild, about normal

Manuel is using the Laikham weed-cutter in vineyards. Vernon is picking Hale-peaches with Otis, Delmas, J. D. Pinner, and Joe Carey. Barr Packing Co. sent seven men to strip Late Santa Rosa plum trees. Homer is irrigating eight acres of girdled vines every other middle. I am irrigating short Thompson vine rows between the ponds, and the short North and South rows. It has been a month of very uneven temperatures, very hot and sultry and very cool. Pests have been very bad, especially red-spider. For Gower nectarines: vapotone by aeroplane, then Orthotran by sprayer. For vines: Malathion 4% plus Aramite 4%. Mildew has been very bad all over the county. Our place is comparatively clean. I am going to change to Anchor Brand sulfur in hot weather.

If a vine is pruned correctly, then that process must be repeated constantly, *on an ancient farm as many as two thousand times per acre.* This is completely alien to the modern urban gardener or backyard fruit grower, this concept of scale (cf. Plato's comments on farming versus the fantasy of farming, Pl. *Phaedr.* 276B). Most clever and experienced horticulturists can devise creative and organic strategies to produce a tree full of peaches or a few boxes of tomatoes for the summertime table. To apply that strategy to even five acres of peaches (anywhere from six hundred to two thousand trees depending upon the spacing), to two to three acres of tomatoes (six to eight thousand plants), when production of fruit or vegetables involves one's survival on the land, is a different matter altogether.

Duplication of traditional technique on a large scale without alteration assures the farmer uniformity of result throughout the field. By the same token, herein lies potential catastrophe as well! The agrarian is no weekend gardener, who can afford to err on a few sickly tomato plants or a weak stand of corn. A single initial mistake will be repeated through-out the farmer's field, ensuring that the problem must affect all his har-vest—and thus his very livelihood.

As an example, after deciding a weak Santa Rosa plum orchard need-ed nitrogen (it is the most sensitive of all plum species; cf. *HP.* 2.7.4: "Manure does not suit all trees the same"), I foolishly opted for the cheapest formulation, ammonium sulfate, rather than calcium or even ammonium nitrate. After carefully working in a pound around a tree on the one-acre orchard, I repeated the process on all 121 trees to guaran-tee that *all* would receive exactly the same, "proper" amount of nitro-gen. A week later, each Santa Rosa sapling shriveled and burned, the orchard in its entirety exterminated through excess nitrogen, the process of fertilization killing, not saving, the trees in methodical order (cf., Theophr. *CP* 5.15.3: "destruction through an excess of food [*huper-bolê trophês*])." All the trees died in an identical manner, all because of the mistaken activity of a mere two hours.[8]

Throughout Greek literature we hear constantly of the glories of the old family estate, of the precariousness of an old fig tree, of the wisdom of the patriarch. These paeans originate in the farmers' need for conser-vatism and ritual repetition, strategies and ideologies possible only when a man owns his own land and seeks to pass it on improved to his own kin. Often an individual history of a family farm emerges quite as impor-tant as that of the nearby community. Thucydides describes the displea-sure that the rural folk of Attica felt on being herded into the walls of Athens at the beginning of the Peloponnesian War, suggesting that many had viewed the famous fifty years of Athenian expansion and im-perialism since the Persian Wars (i.e., 480–431 B.C.) quite narrowly, sole-ly as it affected the rural prosperity of their farms, not as it influenced the building program of Pericles or the subjugation of errant subject states in the Aegean. Thucydides (2.14–16; cf. *Hell. Oxy.* 12.3–5) fur-ther elaborates that the farmers of Attica were angry at abandoning their homes and adopting new habits of life in the city in 431 B.C., espe-cially since they had only recently become reestablished after the evacu-ation of Attica during the Persian Wars (480/479 B.C.).

That same close identification with the ancestral estate is illustrated in Aristophanes' *Peace.* The protagonist, Trygaios, yearns to see his small farm and the fig tree that he had planted as a young boy (557–63), an event in his own life far more memorable than the contemporary rise of the sophists inside the walls of Athens. Why would this not be so, when these are men and women who preferred not to sell or move, but had every intention of dying where they were born, who would rather have farmed the poor land of their fathers than the better ground of some stranger? Frequently there is reference not merely to the bounty of the farm, but to the aesthetics of groves, vineyards, and flowers (e.g., Ar. *Pax.* 577; *Ach.* 996–99). That suggests the ancestral plot could be a thing of beauty in addition to a means of survival.

From the omnipresence of danger, the consequent fear of disaster, and the response of conservatism and repetition, ultimately there emerges in the farmer's mind the realization that all his efforts are aimed at equilibrium, at some type of counteraction to an original action. He needs to react to disequilibrium, natural or man-made, while ensuring that he does nothing to upset the fragile symmetry crucial to agriculture. The notion of the "golden mean" ("nothing too much," "nothing in excess") is a hackneyed enough theme in Greek literature. But its roots surely are, like nearly every other element of Greek culture, agrarian. They derive out of the necessities of intensive Greek agriculture of the *polis*. The philosopher and agronomist Theophrastus wrote of the uncertainty and nuance inherent in farming: "Many things are in dispute; in some, the dispute is a simple question of yes or no; in others it is a question of better or worse" (*CP* 3.2.4). Similarly, Xenophon's Ischomachos says: "The God does not regulate the year on a fixed schedule: so, in one year it is best to sow early, in another very late, in another at mid-season" (*Oec.* 17.4).

Rather than searching out this trait of moderation and flexibility inherent in every aspect of Greek rural life, a vivid sense of the need for "balance," for the "middle" (*to meson; to metrion*), for a perfect harmony (cf. Pl. *Amat.* 134E; *Symp.* 187A), can be gained by looking carefully at the actual production technique of a single crop, such as grapes. "The farming of the vine," Columella (who wrote more about viticulture than any other extant Greek or Roman agronomist) reminds us, was "more complicated than that of any other tree" (*Rust.* 5.7.1). The early Greek poet Alcaeus more bluntly wrote: "Plant no other tree before the vine" (fr. 342 [Z18 Page]). Perhaps the time and attention required in the Greek vineyard explains the Aristophanic description of the small farmer as "vine-loving" and Peace herself as "giver of grapes" (*Ach.* 495). So axiomatic was the connection between the *polis* and viticulture that the Greeks often saw the absence of the vine in other places as a confirmation of barbarity (cf. Diog. Laert. 1.104–7; Antiphanes fr. 56 Kock; Hom. *Od.* 9.133).

The Greeks of the *polis* saw the world about them as a series of cultivated rings, concentric circles of civilization. Those peoples (mostly Greek) who cultivated grains, trees, and vines in a stable setting belonged at the core of all civilization and culture; those without fruit-bearing, cultivated lands were regarded as little more than satellite barbarians at the outer orbits of human habitation. These marginal peoples obviously lacked the prerequisite agricultural environment for the creation of *polis* values. So viticulture, in a manner not characteristic of either cereals or even olives, sharpened the identity of the grower and helped to spawn the new agrarian ideology of the ancient Greek countryside in the time of the *polis*.[9]

A brief review of the vine's cultivation will demonstrate why this was true. I will describe the pragmatic challenges involved in ancient Greek viticulture to illustrate the inherent difficulty in production and the expertise required to ensure a crop. The successful propagation of the vine demanded moderation and harmony—the mean that appears categorically at the source of Greek political thought and culture throughout the life of the city-state. The *mesoi* were the middle people of the *polis;* they took on that role and adopted that outlook because they and they alone were also those who sought daily just that balance in the growing of food. When they trudged into the city it was their experience as farmers, as small but permanent growers of trees and vines, as yeomen combatants against nature—not their knowledge of literary texts or philosophical paradigms—that they drew on to craft laws, fight wars, and manage the community: in effect, to create what we now call Western civilization.

IV.

Given a choice in location,* the ancient Greek small viticulturist had to consider the vagaries of temperature, exposure, altitude, available moisture, and soil conditions. The *geôrgos* knew well enough that vines theo-

---

*The site of the vineyard was limited originally to the rugged terrain of one's own small farm and thus further reduced by rocks (e.g., Theophr. CP 3.6.5) or stumps (Lys. 7.14).

retically survived almost anywhere in Greece (e.g., Weaver 207–8, fig. 1). But the key was to plant his vineyard where natural factors tended to maximize production and quality while minimizing risks and expenditures (e.g., Pliny *HN* 17.19; Varro *Rust.* 1.25–27).

Those Greek farmers whose hereditary plots were blessed with greater natural advantages—all other factors being equal—enjoyed greater success ("success" being defined as consistently higher yields at less labor and cost). We should never underestimate the role that inheritance plays in farming, ancient or modern. Often a man is stuck, for good or ill, with the land he inherits, which can determine the degree of his family's future agricultural success for generations. An anonymous comic fragment sometimes attributed to Philemon realistically urges: "It is better to lend to the land than to the man" (Philemon fr. 216 Kock). Unfortunately, modern lending agencies often feel the same way, concluding that the clever raisin farmer on a sand hill is a worse risk than the talentless grape grower on deep loam. Logically, Plutarch listed good land as the primary ingredient to farming success, followed by the skill of the cultivator and the quality of his seed (Plut. *Mor.* 2B).

Exposure to dry summer winds (e.g., Theophr. *HP* 4.14.2, 10; Colum. *Rust.* 5.5.15) depleted soil moisture and increased water requirements; hot gusts occasionally burned off leaves and tender clusters. On the other hand, the farmer had to be just as chary of low ground. Unusually depressed terrain, although sheltered from wind, drew in cold heavy air and decreased nighttime temperatures and so allowed otherwise tolerable frosts (Theophr. *HP* 4.14.6, 13) to devastate an entire year's crop. Flatland or gullies also caused problems of drainage—crucial for all *vinifera* grapes—during unusually wet years (Theophr. *HP* 4.14.8; *CP* 3.6.3–4; 3.12.1; cf. McDonald and Rapp 55).

In addition, the ancient Greek viticulturalist had to contend with a complex of decisions beyond mere questions of elevation and exposure. Soil quality in relationship to vine variety was crucial for successful grape growing: "It is very important to consider the variety and characteristics of the vine in consideration with the area you wish to plant" (Colum. *Rust.* 3.1.4). Deeper, fertile soils on the plains, such as sandy and clay loams, produced the heaviest crops. But that was not always preferable for wine varieties. Unlike raisin or fresh grape production, where greater cluster size and quantity were preferred, wine grapes often produced superior vintages on rocky, sandy (e.g., Virg. *Georg.* 2.346; Colum. *Arbor.* 3.6), or even infertile soils, which tended to check productivity and overall vine vigor. Harvested yields were low there, but proper sugar and acidity levels (depending on the type of wine desired) were more easily obtainable. There is a general mean in grape farming between quantity and quality of production; unfortunately, one is usually at the expense of the other.

For a modern parallel, nothing is as frustrating as the current predicament of the wine grower of the central San Joaquin valley in California. Nowhere is land richer, the growing season longer, irrigation more plentiful, the continual heat more predictable. Vineyards tower on seven-foot stakes and produce huge crops of over fifteen tons of fresh grapes per acre. Yet often that massive vintage goes without a buyer. Even in good times prices scarcely cover production costs. More often, the grape harvests of most wine varieties are used as juice or sweeteners, and for blending purposes in jug wines.

Instead, fine wineries prefer that the identical species be grown near the coast, especially to the north in the Napa Valley of California. Cooler temperatures, poorer soils, rugged terrain, and the absence of frequent irrigation all work to produce a scrawny vineyard—pathetic to the trained eye—which produces a crop of between one and six tons per acre, less than half the tonnage possible in the hotter, more fertile Central Valley. Nevertheless, these grapes are eagerly purchased by connoisseurs and sell for premium prices, because the more stressful environment on the hillsides actually produces far finer taste.

Similarly, growers in early Greece must have soon learned that once-barren hillsides, unwanted and uncultivated by Dark-Age aristocratic landowners, actually offered an ideal opportunity for skilled vine growers (e.g., Colum. *Rust.* 3.11.1–3). In fact, as pointed out earlier, such *eschatiai* were more suitable for grape production than previously prized plains. The key was that the initial planting of the vineyard involved a delicate *balance*. The farmer had to be careful not to opt for either extreme, and instead to be aware that conditions adverse to full production ironically could prove hospitable. So the growing practice of viticulture in the early *polis*—much more so than livestock raising or grain growing—must have reordered Greek values and contributed to the peculiar Greek notion of harmony and moderation: fertile bottomland could produce too many leaves, too few sweet grapes. Excessive fertilizer, overabundant leaves and clusters were to be avoided. Hard work, not natural bounty was to be lionized. The vintage should be large enough to produce a reasonable amount of wine for the next year, but not so large as to delay maturity or ruin wine quality.

Because farms were extremely small, because land, at least initially, was not frequently exchanged and sold, and because grape production was less sensitive to radical market fluctuations, most Greek farmers were tied to their ancestral estate. That is, *geôrgoi* worked the same ground, their *klêros* that had been passed down within their families since the early years of the *polis*. Because the Greek viticulturist could not, as the modern agribusinessman can, easily liquidate holdings and transfer capital to more favorable sites, success depended on one's skill in overcoming intrinsic natural disadvantages, often varying within the confines of the small ancestral plot. "There is no advantage in fighting against the god," Xenophon makes Ischomachos say in the *Oeconomicus*, "one is not likely to obtain a better yield from the land by planting trees and vines and sowing grain of the type he wishes, rather than those crops which the land itself prefers (*ho ti hê gê hêdoito*) to bring forth and support" (*Oec.* 16.4).

Lacking choice of location, the layout of the vineyard was a crucial expression of vine expertise. Labor expenditure and costs were directly proportional *to the number of vines, not the size of the acreage* planted. As a general rule of viticulture, the most desirable spacing scheme was one that required the least number of vines per acre (and hence the least number of vine rootings and stakes at planting, and, later, mature vines for pruning) without reducing the size of the potential crop. The great diversity in vine spacing that existed in antiquity must illustrate the absence of any uniform practice.* Divergences show significant regionalism (e.g., Theophr. *CP* 3.11.2–4) and reflect farmers' attempts to discover the optimum ratio between vine density and maximum production, given the specific grape variety and soil conditions of each individual vineyard. Balance and harmony between the soil and the number of vines planted per acre were crucial.

---

*Up to two thousand vines per acre; e.g., Kent 291 n. 173. See also White 1970a: 236–37; Pecírka and Dufkova 161; Guiraud 482–84; cf. Weaver 207–8; Colum. *Arbor.* 4.2–5. Amouretti (1988: 12–13) discusses the importance of local conditions.

In general, poorer soils required more vines per acre (and thus more work), richer ground, fewer vines, to achieve identical crop production—an indication of how the fertility of the ancestral estate might affect generations to come. Grape vines on poorer soils achieved smaller trunk size, and thus more stock had to be planted per acre to produce adequate canes, leaves, and grapes (Theophr. CP 3.7.2). Even in contemporary agricultural practice, it is poignant to see families on poor soils struggle constantly in their fields, while a few miles distant, the less industrious prosper on the inheritance of their deep loams. Modern experience demonstrates that density of plantings can be reduced substantially on extremely rich soils without crop loss, and at a saving of labor and management.

An alternative strategy mentioned by some of the ancient agronomists was to plant closely on rich soils and sparsely on weaker soils (e.g., Theophr. HP 2.4.6; 2.5.6). Apparently this was an effort to maximize capital and labor where returns were greater and to minimize costs on inherently unproductive ground, not "to throw good money after bad." Mastery of the nuances in viticulture is a far more complicated proposition than cereal or livestock production, and could have been accomplished only by men who were independent property owners, responsible for their own success or failure, plying their craft over generations of success and failure.

Other important factors besides soil quality affected vineyard layout and initial planting. The occasional desire to cultivate with oxen between vine rows (probably rare in Greece with the advent of available slave labor) mandated wider spacing and thus a smaller number of vines per acre (e.g., Colum. Rust. 5.5.3). At times grapes were probably interplanted with grain and other annual crops (e.g., Theophr. CP 3.10.3–8), and thus allowances for ploughing would reduce vine density. Another consideration was the choice of nursery stock (e.g., Theophr. HP 2.2.4; 2.5.3; CP 3.5.1–5; Xen. Oec. 19.8–14). Rootings (the prior year's grape cuttings that had developed a root system during the year in the nursery) were more expensive (Colum. Rust. 3.3.12), but guaranteed a much lower rate of failure at transplantation than cuttings planted right from dormant canes (Theophr. HP 2.2.4; CP 3.5.3). Mere cuttings, however, which saved time and expense, were occasionally preferred for planting on deep, rich soils, and resulted in a tolerable rate of success (Colum.

Rust. 5.5.7–10; *Arbor* 3.1–4; Theophr. *HP* 2.5.3; *CP* 3.2.7; 3.3.1; 3.4.2; 3.5.3). Layering, the burying of a dormant cane (e.g., Colum. *Rust.* 4.15; Pliny *NH* 17.96; Theophr. *HP* 2.1.3; *CP* 3.5.1, 3.11.5), was the quickest, surest way to propagate new vines (bearing in the second year). But it was possible only to replace missing vines in a mature vineyard, because layering requires the presence of established vines nearby.

Much can be lost in the falsely economical effort to save expenses in the new vineyard by using cuttings instead of more established one-year grape rootings. It is an enticing choice that the wise farmer should shun. A neighbor in February 1990 planted a forty-acre vineyard in cuttings (about 24,000 rootless vine canes). He avoided the nearly $10,000 cost of nursery rootings by spending a few hundred dollars in the labor of putting into the ground foot-long lengths of dormant vine canes cut from his nearby mature vineyard. But when the hot temperatures of May arrived, the whole enterprise turned into disaster. Forty percent of his parched rootless sticks had failed to leaf out, making the cultivation, irrigation, and fertilization of the nearly half dead vineyard pointless. He lost the whole year—his entire investment of labor and capital. An embarrassment to his neighbors, he disked up the abject field and began the process all over with *rootings* in winter 1991.

The ancient Greek viticulturalist had to choose the proper grape varieties and had to know widely diverse soil, temperature, moisture, wind, and altitude variants. At planting, the farmer decided between cuttings or rootings and then selected a vine density that best suited his conditions to achieve the highest returns at the lowest expenditure. Ancient leases, which required tenants to plant vines at prescribed distances (e.g., *SIG*[3] 963), probably reflected the wisdom of the lessor concerning the precise nature of the land (e.g., Xen. *Oec.* 16.3–5). Such regulations were aimed at ensuring adequate production over the long term by demanding closer plantings on weaker soils—a strategy that required more time and expense on the part of the tenant.

As a general rule, larger crops resulted in poorer quality grapes (Theophr. *HP* 2.7.2);* and greater susceptibility to insect damage—factors rarely identified in any of our sources. The key again, as with vine-

---

*Poor grape quality usually entails less sugar, lower acid, smaller berries, more failed bunches at mid-season (i.e., "water berries" or drying of the tips of the clusters).

yard site selection and planting, must have been proper balance: the viticulturalist always desired the largest crop possible without loss of quality. Precise equilibrium was, as in modern times, always sought but rarely found, given the vicissitudes of weather conditions and incomplete understanding of vine physiology. The "right" strategy can be approximated only in hindsight, in careful retrospection once the crop year is over. Yet long experience in principles of dormant cane pruning (e.g., Colum. *Rust.* 4.9–23; 11.2.16; Theophr *HP* 2.7.2; 4.19.6; Cato *Rust.* 32; *Geopontica* 5.23; Brumfield 38–40) and later spring cluster, leaf, and shoot thinning (Colum. *Rust.* 5.5.14; Varro *Rust.* 1.31.2), must have succeeded in modifying crop size and quality to a significant degree.

The more buds that were left on dormant vine wood (as evidenced by the number and length of remaining canes/spurs after pruning), the more fruit clusters emerged. But light pruning also increased the chances that the large crop would fail to achieve maturity before autumn rains (e.g., Colum. *Rust.* 11.2.61), if ever, and at the expense of weakening the vine itself (Theophr. *CP* 3.15.5). That had negative repercussions for future crops: poor fruit-bud formation the next year. On the other hand, severe pruning or later overthinning of fruit clusters unnecessarily reduced the size of the crop and spurred rank vegetative growth (Theophr. *CP* 3.15.5), as the vine overcompensated for reduced fruit demands.

Nothing, I think, is as disappointing or as embarrassing to the grower as a lush, vigorous leafy vineyard with little fruit. In 1982 a proud neighbor overpruned, overwatered, overfertilized, overtrellised, and overthinned his grape crop. At harvest, local farmers came by to marvel at the beautiful vineyard with no fruit (cf. "luxuriant tendrils" [Colum. *Arbor.* 3.2]). When a raisin grower places his harvested grapes on the ground to dry into raisins, for all around it is an instantaneous referendum on his entire skill as a farmer (e.g., Xen. *Oec.* 15.11–12). One simply looks down the row and sees—or does not see—trays of drying grapes. There is in farming, unlike many modern professions, no recompense "for growing canes and leaves"—no livelihood in elegance masking unproductiveness.

Dormant winter pruning required real expertise. Although pruners normally left the same number of buds as the year before on mature vines, the more skillful vine dressers occasionally were able to tailor cuts to individual vine needs (e.g., sick or weakened vines demanded more severe pruning; hardy stumps, suggesting tolerance for more clusters and canes, needed less cutting. They also sought to anticipate upcoming crop size. Cognizant of a prior short yield (and vine tendency to bear robustly when a past crop has been unusually light), the experienced pruner expected greater fertility in that year's dormant buds. He left either fewer or shorter canes to avoid overcropping (which could harm the vine itself, cf. Theophr. *CP* 2.11.3) and thus poor quality grapes. "When the vine is pruned with equal regard for its own condition and for the year's production of fruit," Theophrastus advises, "it will have long life and will always be fruitful" (*CP* 3.14.5).

By contrast, the past year's large harvest suggested reduced vine fruitfulness the next season: the exhausted vineyard takes a "rest" for a year. This cycle presented the opportunity for the skilled pruner to leave more buds than usual via longer or more numerous canes. He expects that the vineyard will react to last year's bounty by producing a greater ratio of sterile buds (which would bear leaves only).

Should the pruner have erred in anticipating crop size (common enough, since the grape was not as predictable as the olive in its cyclical pattern of fruitfulness), and discovered that by late spring too many of his extra buds formed clusters, a return trip through the vineyard to snip off young bunches and pull leaves could still adjust crop size (e.g., Varro *Rust.* 1.31.2). After a heavy vintage, the vine dresser leaves a larger number of canes the next winter: if he guesses right, he has a good crop; if too many grapes appear, he can simply pull them off. The best way to spot a poor pruner after the fact is simply to watch his rows nine months later during harvest: they either have too few grapes or too many of poor quality. But, then, of course, the damage has already been done.

Too-severe pruning could obviously not be remedied by later thinning. The fear of destroying his own crop (much worse than natural disaster for his psyche) often led the viticulturalist to cut canes conservatively, especially given the prospect of spring frosts or hail that might diminish crop size. Conservative pruning accompanied by corrective spring thinning of grapes required greater labor expenditure and distinguished intensive, small-scale viticulture. It also signified a larger ideology of viticulture, a way of thinking that stressed the permanence of the vines, the need for proper balance in their cultivation, and the recognition that deviance from past practice might disrupt the natural process of growth and renewal—all traits, as we will see, that left a large (and conservative) imprint on the character of the farmer, and thus of the entire Greek *polis* itself.

Timing of dormant vine pruning was also vital, and illustrated the need to achieve a critical equilibrium between two extremes (e.g., Theophr. *CP* 3.2.3, 3.15.1–5). The agricultural writers list various ideal periods, ranging from October to March. In this connection it was important to understand that the earlier the pruning, the earlier also the subsequent spring bud-break. Late pruning (February–March) could have been advantageous where spring frosts were frequent, and where vines had little difficulty reaching maturity in the fall. In other words, the presence of unpruned canes during much of the fall and winter caused the vine to *delay* spring budding until safer warmer temperatures were more likely.

Early pruning (November–December) to achieve an early harvest was advantageous only if spring frosts were rare and the farmer expected fall ripening to be difficult or weather uncertain. The fear of late-maturing grapes was nearly proverbial (Alcaeus fr. 11a). In any case, the early-pruning viticulturalist had to wait until late October or early November when the first fall frosts brought on vine dormancy. Only then could he be sure that his selected canes or spurs were "winterized" and were not among the few that died back over the dormant months. The wait for fall frosts and rains that stripped leaves also made the pruner's task far easier. On two occasions I have seen an overeager farmer struggle with the bothersome task of pruning leafy canes in November, only to have a sudden frost destroy many of those still green—taking away the source of his upcoming crop in a matter of hours.

There is, do not forget, always a diametrically opposite alternative in farming, the optimum choice elusively in between: pruning had to be completed before the twentieth or so of March, when buds began to swell and leaf out, when contact with the canes could have bruised or injured new growth (cf. Colum. *Rust.* 11.2.16). Cuts in late March also could ooze when the vine broke dormancy, increasing susceptibility to grape pathogens (Theophr. *CP* 3.15.1–2). Tasks that normally were to be accomplished *after* pruning but *before* bud-break (i.e., replacement of stakes, tying canes to supports, cultivation) could not be delayed. The picture that emerges from even a small Greek vineyard is clear: constant decisions, endless searching for the precise but always elusive equilibrium between multifarious choices, the need for constant attention and labor, and reverence for ancestral practice. Much different from cereal or livestock production, these complexities in viticulture and arboriculture help explain the new intensified Greek agriculture of homestead residencies, slave labor, incorporation of rough terrain, and mastery and control of food processing.

Time and capital invested in vine staking and trellising, digging and cultivation, thinning, suckering, and girdling, fertilization, windbreaks, and occasional irrigation improved both crop size and quality, and thus kept the farmer busy all year long.* Letting the vine simply sprawl unchecked over the ground (as is common in Greece today), or propped on short sticks required little capital, and provided leaf exposure as effective as more complex support systems. But that way bunches also came into contact with the earth, ensuring rot and easy access to fruit for rodents and other pests (Varro *Rust.*1.8.1, 5–7; Theocr. *Id.* 1.4).

Trellising eliminated that problem. The horizontal training of vine canes on cross-arms, trees, ropes, wicker, or other supports also increased yields through greater leaf exposure to sunlight and ventilation of mature clusters, and made harvest earlier as well (Hom. *Il.* 23.564–65; Varro *Rust.* 1.8.3–5; Pliny *HN* 14.3; 18.35; cf. Amouretti 1988: 12–14, 15, fig. 1). Pliny observes of the advantages of trellising, "The vine does not overshadow itself and is ripened by constant sunshine; also, it is more exposed to currents of air, and so more rapidly rids itself of dew; trimming and other operations are also carried out more easily" (Pliny *HN* 18.165). Trellising, of course, also required much more capital, labor, and maintenance than mere staking.

Digging, besides improving penetration and collection of water and stimulating new root growth (Colum. *Rust.* 2.2), aided nitrogen fixation through greater aeration around the roots. In addition, cultivation of the vineyard deprived overwintering insects and worm larvae of easy ac-

---

*On these tasks, see Colum. *Rust.* 4.12; Pliny *NH* 18.16.5; Varro *Rust.* 1.8.1; Plut. *Mor.* 4C; Colum. *Rust.* 4.8.1; Pliny *NH* 17.140; *SIG*³ 963; Ar. *Pax* 1148, *Aves* 1432; Varro *Rust.* 1.31.2; Colum. *Rust.* 5.5.14; Men. *Dys.* 584–85; *SIG*³ 963; Xen. *Oec.* 16.12. On the modern Greek practice, cf. Weaver 209.

cess to the stump and destroyed perennial, noxious weeds. Depending on the variety (i.e., table or raisin), girdling (which must have been known to the ancients, despite the tradition that it was "discovered" in 1833 by accident on the Greek island of Zante [e.g., Weaver 213]) augmented fruit-set and enlarged berry size. But girdling cuts—stripping the bark and cambium layer off in a ring around either the canes or stump—must not penetrate beyond the cambium layer if vine injury is to be prevented. Timing is crucial. Girdling at the wrong cycle of vine growth had little effect on size or quality, and could occasionally have had harmful results (e.g., Weaver 213).

Thinning of leaves (rather than the more radical and difficult additional summer pruning of canes and spurs) would have improved grape color and maturity, and was of value in mold and rot prevention (Colum. *Rust.* 11.2.61). Suckering removed unwanted shoots from the stumps, kept roots below the surface, and preserved the original vine shape. Irrigation, never as rare as usually assumed in ancient Greece, must have produced dramatically higher yields and lessened overall temperature and insect stresses. In turn, the application of water created new problems of weed control, excessive humidity, vastly increased labor and capital costs, and could be detrimental to grape quality (e.g., *Theophr.* CP 3.8.4, 3.15.1). But addition of water was critical for the establishment of new vineyards, where young vines did not have the root capacity to find and tap existing soil moisture.

Applications of nitrogen (through legumes or manures) produced markedly higher yields. However, fertilizer use must have been properly timed (i.e., in the fall or winter) so that nutrients were absorbed at bud-break rather than later in the summer when a sudden uptake of nitrogen might have caused rapid vegetative growth at the expense of berry ripening. "With the vine in any case," observed Theophrastus, "manure is to be put on every three years—or even at greater intervals—because the vine cannot take more frequent manure; and water is no help as it is with trees, but the vine burns and then dies" (Theophr. CP 3.9.5). Manures had to be incorporated quickly into the soil upon spreading to prevent nitrogen loss. They also usually increased unwanted weed growth.

The Greek farmer strived to discover the point at which vineyard expenditures resulted in optimum yields, to avoid both neglect, which impairs returns, and "overfarming,"* which brought no economic benefit for the additional time, labor, and capital investment. In ancient Greece of the *polis*, however, for a variety of reasons formal economic theory was not always followed by the homestead farmer. First, labor was usually provided by either family or slaves. Hours spent in vineyard tasks did not necessarily "cost" the farmer anything. In fact, continuous activity in the fields was probably preferable to idling, which in the farmer's eyes was a source of discontent and trouble. Second, because the viticulturalist usually lived on his farm, his land was essentially an extension of his house and home. Effort spent, for example, to ensure absolutely weed-free fields or to replace old props (beyond what was necessary for successful grape production) was no different from whitewashing the home or tending the garden.

In other words, the well-being and even the appearance of the vineyard reflected the social status of its owner, justifying additional labor and expense not directly commensurate with increases in grape quality or production. Social pressures may have induced the intensive-farming *geôrgos* to keep busy in the vineyard—fertilizing, propping, digging—in a manner *not* seen previously in the Greek countryside and surely *not* typical of market-oriented vineyards of imperial Italy. No wonder that the individualism, self-reliance, and pragmatism of the viticulturalist distinguished all of Greek culture, itself fundamentally an agrarian society of small proprietors, not of nomadic shepherds, indentured serfs, or extensions of a central palace.

This cursory description of ancient Greek grape growing reveals sophisticated agricultural technique, complex knowledge of viticulture, and ongoing debate about soil science, pruning, grafting, species improvement, trellising, and plant and animal pests. Their insight into and philosophical contemplation of agriculture strengthens the picture of the *geôrgoi* who built the *polis* : they were not subsistence peasants but an independent keen-eyed yeomanry constantly intent to improve their small plots, and pass on to the next generation greater value than they had themselves received. Once their agrarian outlook is understood, their peculiar approach to military and political life makes perfect sense.

---

*Cf. the Roman proverb: *nihil minus expedire quam agrum optime colere:* "nothing is less efficient than to take care of a farm too well" (Pliny *HN* 18.38).

PART TWO

THE PRESERVATION OF AGRARIANISM

❦ ❦ ❦

But the fundamental equivalents are there. . . . There is a combination of intensified land use, improved military organization, and enhanced ideological legitimization, however different the forms which they take. In none of them is the explanation to be found by isolating trade, warfare, religion, population growth, or anything else as the cause of the transition to statehood. It is to be found by ascertaining how there came to be built up a sufficient accumulation of power of all its three separate but mutually reinforcing kinds.

—W. G. Runciman 1982: 377

Chapter 5

BEFORE DEMOCRACY

Agricultural Egalitarianism and the Ideology Behind
Greek Constitutional Government

I. Small and Equal Farm Size

Anyone for whom seven acres are not enough is a dangerous
citizen.
— Pliny, *Natural History* 18.4

The family farm is the final stronghold against oppression, whether
economic or political, and no tyranny or "ism" will ever thrive in a
country that grounds its agriculture on that base.
— Statement of the American Farmer's Union, 1947

In prior chapters we have explored the emergence of a new Greek agricultural technique and the creation of a novel but growing class of farmers who incorporated hillsides, lived on their farms, employed slaves,
and planted trees and vines (Chapters 1 and 2): an economic renaissance among the Greek city-states that shifted power from aristocracy to
broader-based landed timocracies and constitutional governments
(Chapter 3). The success of intensive, homestead farming in Greece
made the spread of agrarianism inevitable between the eighth and fifth

181

centuries, producing the rise of the *polis* and the accompanying political empowerment and control of a novel farming class.

But to ensure the survival of the new Greek *geôrgoi* there must have existed also something more than phalanxes, institutions besides magistracies, political offices, and the like. Most basic for the early Greek agrarians was something not entirely political or military, but instead a unifying community ideology, well beyond the notion of the Hesiodic concept of hard work, an ideal that could be shared by all citizens of the *polis*, and enshrined even later among those—merchants, craftsmen, traders—who themselves were not directly tied to the land. So what arose at the beginning of the Greek *polis* period, then, was a concept that survived in some form to the end of the fourth century and indeed in a sense even into our own times: a belief that there should be *no* large farm property, *no* radical inequality in the holding of rural property, and, by extension, no extremely rich or poor citizens in the *polis*. This constraint against enormous acreages was entirely moral; had there been ethical or political support for latifundia, the advance of Greek agronomy and the presence of large pools of slave labor made the farming of immense estates entirely practicable.

All the farmers of the neighboring community were to hold land roughly similar in size. Among this broad agrarian class of Greek *mesoi*, land should ideally be passed down through the family without alienation. The ancestral property (*klêros*) belonged to a family (*oikos*), not a single (and unpredictable) individual to do with it as he pleased. The few holders of large fortunes, even those nonpropertied rich involved in trade or mining, should be subject to a variety of restrictions and limitations, preventing accumulated capital from being expressed in large landed estates.

In Chapter 3 I presented an account of how the new agrarian *mesoi* gradually emerged as a distinct class to assume power in the Greek *polis*. Middling farmers, then, were there *first*. They were not creations, not the products of Greek politics and government, but rather the necessary prerequisites for constitutional institutions.[1] So we must first establish what was the ideology behind the political movement of the early *polis* period, examine why in early Greece "the outlook for collective actions" was *not* "bleak." What did these middling farmers *want* out of the constitutional framework of their new city-state?

In the fifth century, particularly at Athens, we see considerable cash holding in mining and trading, and instances where some farmers had become dispossessed, whereas others had become undeniably wealthy. Equal farm size in and of itself is not always a guarantee of landed egalitarianism. In agriculture the *quality*, rather than the quantity, of farmland is the real key to productivity. Ten acres of bottomland near the walls of the *polis* were more productive than larger farms on more distant upland slopes. In agriculture, it is always preferable to produce the crop on a small but rich farm rather than on a large, poor estate. What is striking here is not merely that some Greek farmers prospered while others failed—that is to be expected given the wide discrepancies in natural agricultural talent and luck once private-property-holding farmers were outside the control of kings and lords. Rather, the question arises, *why* and *how* did the exemplar of static property equality—even among those whose ancestral plots were on poorer soils and who had a real need for additional land—endure for nearly four hundred years?*

Even at the end of the fourth century there remained many in the Greek city-state (some of whom were no longer themselves active farmers) who still entertained these notions of equality in landholding. They venerated the old idea that a man was entitled to a piece of ground where he could live and work, from which he could raise a family and fulfill military, social, and political obligations, and which he could pass on *improved* to his heirs. Quite simply, during the lifetime of the Greek *polis* there were rarely, *if ever*, corporate, absentee farms encompassing vast tracts of unbroken farmland. Out of that agricultural reality arose a more general shared notion for the first time in Greece: the farm-owning citizens of a community should all have roughly the same measure of wealth. The agricultural grid of the countryside should resemble something like the even rows and files of a cereal field.[2]

Even today that ingrained desire for privately owned farms of roughly equal size remains strong, although the old eighteenth- and nineteenth-century notion of a community of agricultural equals has long since disappeared, and the American government has for quite some time given up formal protection of the family farm. *Half* our nation's

---

*Differences in farmers' wealth and farm quality: Xen. *Oec.* 6.11; Xen. *Oec.* 16.3–5; cf. Eur. frs. 195, 742 Nauck. Cf. Pl. *Leg.* 5.745D–E.

food, after all, is grown on only *four* percent of our farms, the largest ones, of course (Davidson 35). On the eastern side of the San Joaquin Valley of California, even though the whole notion of family farming and agrarian values is in its final death-throes, among farm families the ideal still remains that farms "should" be between forty and two hundred acres per person.

However sprawling the conglomerate enterprise of 1,000, 10,000, 30,000, 50,000 acres and more becomes, however shiny the fleet of new trucks and tractors, however numerous the array of college-educated agricultural managers, however impressive the corporate logo, the complimentary stationery, pens, hats, and calendars, an intrinsic distrust still resides in the heart of every real farmer. There is an inherent dislike for bigness. Uneasiness arises with conglomeration and absenteeism when applied to the land, despite the general American fascination in recent decades with wealth, financial power, and ostentatious display of riches.* "Speculators" are essentially all who do not live on and work the land they hold title to.

Whence does this suspicion of corporate farming among family farmers and their associates derive? Why does it linger? It is not, as Strange points out, merely the envy of success, the covetousness of the bounty of others, "the parochial jealousies of a backward suspicious people." It must be a remnant of the ideology of farming that predominated in this California valley in the century between the 1870s and 1970s, of the romantic notion of centuries-old traditions in the West that roughly identical farms— small vineyard or orchard, farmhouse, water tower—ensured a community of equals, of hardworking peers, of a culture intrinsically practical, fair, and stable, the prerequisite for democratic government, the cement that prevented the few from preying on the many.

---

*"The natural aversion agrarian communities everywhere seem to have for absentee ownership of land," Marty Strange has written, "is therefore more than the parochial jealousies of a backward, suspicious people. It is based on their heritage of experience that when land accumulates in the hands of speculators, people who depend on working the land for their living are sure to suffer" (Strange 171). "The family-size farm," wrote Secretary of Agriculture Henry Wallace, nearly a half century ago, "owned by the man who operated it, was the ideal of our land-settlement policy. But we failed to safeguard the ownership of the land which was homesteaded to such an extent that a large proportion of our best farm land fell into the hands of speculators and absentee landlords" (cf. Griswold 165)

To those of this agrarian stamp, the conglomeration of land was a perversion of the ideal. It was the work of men who had nonlanded wealth, government connections and wily tax lawyers—men who had not merely bent, but rather abolished altogether, the old unwritten rules. In an ancient context, such landlords were men like the millionaire of second-century A.D. Roman Greece, Heroides Atticus, or even the less ambitious Cicero, and Cato, *not* like old Laertes, Hesiod, or the nameless growers at Metapontum in southern Italy. Large-scale entrepreneurs who saw the land solely as a business venture, they were men more imperial Roman than *polis* Greek.

During the raisin crash of 1983, a labor contractor for one of the nearby large farms (about ten thousand acres of trees and vines) lamented to me that the company was forced to cut piece-rate harvest wages by about twenty percent (a reasonable decision given the *sixty percent* decline in the price of raisins). Despite a general recession and the precariousness of his own managerial job, he said of his employers: "I hope the sonnabitches go belly up." When the owner of thousands of acres gouged the local Federal Land Bank for nearly thirty million dollars in bad loans, some of the cooperative's members—we who, remember, ourselves would pay for that disastrous folly through larger assessments and higher interest loans on our own debts—nevertheless were glad to see the would-be magnate's empire broken up and sold off parcel by parcel.* Similarly, the grandson heir to a squandered corporate enterprise of our locale was generally acknowledged to be better off once his inheritance crumbled and he was forced to sell down to his own forty acres and to peddle his own produce at farmers' markets.

Quite simply, the widespread distribution of farmland into numerous hands also makes economic as well as social sense. J. L. Davis, for example, in studying the rural archaeology of the Cyclades islands during the Ottoman period in Greece, felt that single-family small farmsteads were crucial to an intensive use of the land: "The way in which agricultural production has been organized seems rather to have reflected changes in the distribution of land ownership: viz. at times when an elite minority has controlled the economy, many factors have operated to *constrain* the

---

*That 1987 bailout of the American farm credit system cost taxpayers nationwide four billion dollars, see Davidson 183 n. 13.

intensification of subsistence agriculture."[3] In other words, absentee magnates do not tolerate a developed countryside peopled by independent yeomen.

Greek literature shows a clear pattern of agrarian legislation and practice (about 700–550 B.C.), ensuring widespread landed equality (by about 550–400 B.C.), followed by worries that the idea of agrarianism was under attack (400–300 B.C.), culminating in the gradual erosion of autonomous communities of independent small farmers altogether (300 B.C. and after).

This Greek desire for equality of landholding and preservation of an independent farming class is expressed throughout the *polis* period in at least *five* ways. *First* and most important, is the evidence of *fact*: the actual conditions of landowning, the size of farms as expressed in the literary and epigraphical record, oratory for the most part, and leases and sales recorded on stone. These artifacts reveal a consistent pattern. In nearly every instance where land is mentioned in fifth- and fourth-century Greece (there are "precisely five land figures," wrote M. I. Finley [1981b: 64], "in the whole of Athenian literature"), we hear most often of farms from ten to twenty acres, occasionally larger estates between fifty to seventy acres, but in almost *no case until the Hellenistic and Roman Period* (300 B.C.—400 A.D.) of anyone's land extending over one hundred acres.

Consider the three largest farms known at the close of the *polis* period in Athens of the fourth century, when the size of farm plots slowly began to increase. Although all of these properties were owned by wealthy men, they were, nevertheless, *not* large in either relative or absolute terms. The so-called estate of Phainippos due east of Athens at Kytheros in Attica was probably less than one hundred acres. The next largest farms known are the approximately seventy-acre ancestral estate of the infamous Alcibiades who helped wreck the Athenian Empire, and land of about the same size bought by one unknown Aristophanes in the 390s B.C. At the end of the fifth century, mention is made of a forty-five-acre plot of Lysimachos on Euboea and a fourteen-acre farm in the Athenian Plain.

So strong was the egalitarian spirit that even during the erosion of the agricultural *polis* in fourth century B.C. at Athens when we hear of complaints about the size of farm plots, there were still apparently *no* large

holdings. The strange reference in Plato's *Theaetetus* to "a myriad *plethra*
(about 2,225 acres) or still more," like the much later expression "many-
acred" (*poluplethrotatos*), seems to be entirely in the realm of speculation
and fantasy and not to belong to the historical city-state during the *polis*-
period.[4]

Earlier in the Homeric poems, the estate of Meleagros was probably
not much more than fifty acres (e.g., Semple 1928: 152), and the plots of
Laertes and Alkinoös, as we have seen, were much smaller still. Four
acres sometimes appears in the Homeric poems as an ordinary grain field
or orchard (e.g. Hom. *Od.* 7.113, 18.374). Perhaps the typical impression of the later rural populace is found in a fragment from the comic
playwright Anaxilas of the fourth century. In his play, one character
asks: "How are you? But how lean you appear." The agriculturalist
replies, "I am coming apart, because I farm a little plot in the country"
(Anaxilas fr. 16 Edmonds). Theoretically some wealthy Greek landowners may have had several such "little plots" spread throughout the countryside surrounding the *polis*. But we have no figures in extant sources
for any large property holders who own more than a hundred acres of
farmland.

Archaeology tends to confirm the evidence of ancient Greek literature. The arable terrain (encompassed by present-day remnants of a
field wall) that surrounds the affluent "Cliff House" estate in southern
Attica reveals a farm of about fifty acres. Nearby, Hans Lohmann
thought that he detected from rural structures and traces of walls and
boundaries the farms of the very wealthy in southern Attica. Predictably,
most "wealthy" plots were of about fifty to seventy acres. In similar fashion, on the island of Euboea rural field walls suggest farms a little larger
than twenty acres. Even though the more substantial farmhouses are
most likely to survive in the archaeological record, the evidence
nonetheless suggests that these more impressive "estates" never encompassed large acreages during the *polis* period. That the ancient Greek
farm was typically surrounded by a field wall is another reflection that
these plots were designed to be autonomous, clearly delineated, and not
easily conglomerated.

Although it is possible, and even probable, that many of the wealthy
occasionally owned two or more parcels in different districts of Attica,
and that these farms could change in size over generations, it again is

significant that no single plot ever reached manorial status, and rarely exceeded one hundred acres. M. I. Finley observed: "There is good reason to believe that 45- and 70-acre holdings, though not unusual, were above average." Those scholars who believe that there were numerous "big" farms in Attica refer largely to acreages between seventy and a hundred acres, not estates in the hundreds, much less thousands of acres.[5]

There must have been an enforced code of the Greek *polis*, a social ethic at work that discouraged the accumulation of property. How else can we explain why the inherited rich, the more gifted *geôrgoi*, the more successful in commerce and mining, all failed to accumulate vast tracts, failed to transfer their off-farm capital into landed estates—phenomena that were commonplace after the demise of the free and autonomous Greek *polis*?

When the *polis* had a chance to intervene formally in the distribution and sale of farmland, the community preference for small farm plots is often made explicit. Documents on stone—usually lists of public land sales—confirm the absence of large holdings. In fifth-century Attica at least, there seems to have been some (albeit vague) notion of an "average" size hoplite farm, which the *polis* at least assumed was the proper size for its landholding citizenry. The Russian scholar V. N. Andreyev reviewed inscribed records of the sale of public lands at Attica. He discovered that forty to sixty *plethra* (i.e., 8.9–13.3 acres) composed the standard size plot, and that these parcels were sold publicly at *about the same price per unit of land*. That seems a reasonable-sized estate for hardworking yeomenry. Given the techniques of intensive agriculture, homestead residence, diversified crops, and slave labor, *geôrgoi* could manage a good enough livelihood on a "normative" hoplite farm of between ten and twenty acres.[6]

The rare wealthy Athenian landowner probably owned no greater than four to five times more land than the average yeoman. So Attica of the *polis*-period was an entirely *different* society from either imperial Rome, the Hellenistic world, or modern America, where farms, both nucleated and scattered parcels, of 50,000–100,000 acres are occasionally known, 5,000–10,000 times larger than the plot of the typical hoplite *geôrgos*.[7]

Osha Davidson points out how different is the current American farm-owning pyramid: "5% of American landowners own 75% of our land, and the bottom 78% own just 3%. The figures are even more unbalanced in many regions. For example, the top 5% of landowners own 90% of privately owned land in Hawaii, Florida, Wyoming, Oregon, and New Mexico, and hold 80% of it in Washington, Utah, New York, Nevada, Maine, Louisiana, Idaho, California, and Colorado. In looking at these figures, it is instructive to note that on the eve of the revolution in Cuba, the largest 9% of all landowners held 62% of that country's land, while 66% owned 7%" (35).

Unlike Greece, these are not percentages of the citizenry as a whole, but only of those Americans who already own farmland. Such a concentration of American property-holding reflects a growing monopoly of the production of food itself. By the late 1980s, for example, 4.1 percent of American farms produced nearly half the food and a third was grown by 1.2 percent. The Department of Agriculture estimates that by the year 2000 *half* of the nation's nourishment will come from *one percent* of existing American operations (Strange 41). If the ancient relationship between landowning, farm size, and the nature of the surrounding community is still of any relevance, then America surely has just about abandoned a *polis* type of rural social organization.

To return to Greece of the *polis* period: on the Aegean island of Melos, the hoplite figure of between forty and sixty *plethra* (about 8.9–13.3 acres) per farm reappears, confirming the ubiquity of the ancient agrarian ethos of property egalitarianism. Thucydides says the Athenians divided the island among five hundred settlers after the conquest of 415 B.C. If there was arable land of about 27 sq. km. (6,671 acres), each new Athenian landowner would have had a farm of a little over twelve acres, the new community mirroring the existing pattern in Attica itself. The size of these farms in Greece during the age of the *polis* was a world away from imperial Rome or Hellenistic Egypt, where estates of many thousands of acres belonging to an individual owner were common, a trend contemporaneous with growing abandonment and depopulation of the countryside.[8]

A *second* manifestation of equality in landowning—that is, same-sized holdings of *moderate* size (*metria ousia*; Arist. *Pol.* 2.1266b28–31)—is reflected in early legislation of the Greek *polis* and discussed at length in philosophical discourse. This promotion of agrarianism suggests that the appearance of medium-sized Greek farms of roughly the same area in extant literary, archaeological, and epigraphical sources is no accident. We hear of continued—and, at the end of the Greek city-state, beleaguered—efforts to maintain an agrarian system. Although the more drastic agrarian advocates in the early and final stages of the *polis* may have promoted land confiscations and communistic redistribution schemes, these extreme measures were apparently *not* comprehensive or well thought out. Indeed, they were rare among the early city-states.*

More frequent between 700 and 300 B.C. were moderate, conservative state efforts—in addition to social pressures—to ensure that the agrarian ideal remained strong. According to Aristotle (*Pol.* 2.1266b14–20; cf. 5.1307a29–31, 6.1319a6–10), Solon had purportedly passed laws that restricted the size of farms at early Athens: "There is," Aristotle wrote in his *Politics*, "Solon's legislation and that of other states which prevents an individual from acquiring as much land as he might desire (*nomos hos kôluei ktasthai gên hoposên an boulêtai tis*)." Aristotle goes on to expound on the Greeks' ideology of agrarianism. He apparently could recall a number of shadowy figures from the nascent era of the *polis*, all of whom sought first of all to ensure that farms were roughly of equal size—an extraordinary visionary stance not emulated on any large scale since.

Aristotle is not talking about new colonies or *poleis* sprung *ex nihilo*. He means city-states that grew slowly out of the Dark Ages, communities where there still must have remained a number of old wealthy estate owners among a larger group of more dynamic small farmers. "Pheidon, the Corinthian," he says, "who was one of most ancient lawgivers, believed that households and the citizen population ought to remain at the same numbers—even though at the beginning everyone did not own equal-sized allotments" (*Pol.* 2.1265b13).

Early Greek yeomanry was faced with a dilemma. There was preexisting inequity in landowning. Yet because of the natural growth and success of intensive homestead farming, most Greek agrarians naturally became a conservative people, eschewing radical, forced confiscations of the lands of the wealthy. Much less did farmers favor the communalism advocated by the poor.**

---

*See Lacey 333–35; cf. Arist. *Ath. Pol.* 12.3; Theogn. 345–47, 1199–1202.

**On the reluctance for confiscation and shared ownership, see Pl. *Leg.* 3.684D, 5.736C; Arist. *Pol.* 5.1305a2; Isocr. 12.259; cf. Figueira 1984b: 198–200.

Instead, we see a general social ethic at work, backed by state intervention in inheritances and concern with farm size, in order to ensure
that gradually the territory around the *polis* came to be owned by a citizenry of middling farmers. The changeover from Dark-Age pastoralism
to a grid of equal-sized hereditary farms was difficult. Even more trying
was the effort to preserve that exemplar in the late fifth and fourth centuries when the growth of commerce in the Mediterranean and nonlanded wealth from outside Greece severely altered the native agrarian
patchwork. Nevertheless, it was just that agrarian ideal of the early *polis*
that persisted in the minds of most Greeks, prompting both Aristotle
and Plato to champion farm-owning egalitarianism during their own
troubled times of the fourth century. Property legislation must have varied widely by locale in detail and emphasis, depending on the relative
success of yeomanry at any given region in Greece.

In this regard Aristotle makes it clear that the accepted notion of agrarianism posed problems of application. It was, after all, easy to found new
poleis on egalitarian principles, but a quite different matter to break up the
estates of the wealthy in existing communities once a new group of agrarians came on the scene. "Phaleas, the Chalcedonian [late fifth century?],"
Aristotle wrote, "was the first one to devise this expedient: he said that
the property of the citizens ought to be equal, and he believed that this
would not be difficult right away among those city-states in the process of
foundation, while among those city-states already settled it would require
more effort (*ergôdesteron*)" (*Pol.* 2.1266a39–1266b6; cf. Métraux 212–17).

"More effort" sometimes had involved the earlier struggle (see Chapter 3) between *kakoi* ("the bad" upstarts) and *agathoi* ("the good" entrenched aristocracy). The inequity fostered in the pastoral systems of
the Dark Ages did not vanish overnight. Aristotle refers elsewhere to
earlier agrarian legislation whose primary aim was to fix the number of
farms in a perpetual state of equality through either birth control, inheritance, or statutes against selling the ancestral estate.*

Aristotle concludes that since agrarian democracy was felt to be the
most stable form of government, "some of the laws established in many
communities in early times were completely practical, either outlawing

---

*E.g., *Pol.* 2.1266a–1274b; cf. Asheri 1966: 16–21; Woodhouse 74–87; Starr 1977: 150–52; Burford
1993: 16–17.

the ownership of a certain amount of land under any conditions, or else forbidding the ownership of a certain area between the citadel and the city." He adds: "In early times there was also in many city-states even legislation which outlawed the sale of original land allotments, and there is said to be a law established by Oxylos with the same effect, outlawing loans secured on a certain part of a man's land" (*Pol.* 6.1319a13). The philosopher was also impressed that at the conservative community of Aphytis on the isthmus of Pallene in Macedonia "everyone was engaged in farming (*pantes geôrgousin*")" (*Pol.* 6.1319a15–18)—a region, not surprisingly, known for its practice of viticulture (Theophr. *CP* 3.15.5).

Besides citing early examples of agrarian legislation in the Greek city-states, both Aristotle (*Politics*) and Plato (*Laws* and *Republic*) discuss ideal aspects of landowning in Greece—inasmuch as farmland is the basis of any theoretical discourse on the utopian community (e.g., Pl. *Leg.* 5.736E; Arist. *Pol.* 2.1266a37; cf. Morrow 74–92). But their theoretical position is often problematic (do they always, often, or never reflect, or react against, contemporary conditions?). Their philosophical thinking is also often colored by their own varying degrees of sympathy for, distrust of, or hostility toward the status of fourth-century Athenian democracy, and, in contrast, toward the presence of tyrannies and monarchies creeping in from the margins of the Greek world at the waning of the *polis* period.

Although Aristotle and Plato, in their notions of ideal government and the proper class and status of the citizenry, champion equitable property-holding regimes where landowners themselves should *not* do the actual farmwork, it is clear that the three-century-old Greek notion of egalitarian agrarianism—under attack in their own times—is *never* challenged.* Both philosophers assume that the accumulation of land by the wealthy is injurious to the *polis*. Even Plato, who believed strongly that the gifted should be rewarded accordingly, nevertheless advised that *no* citizen should ever be allowed to acquire land that would result in his farm being five times larger than the smallest in the city-state (Pl. *Leg.* 10.744 E–745A). In his view, even the best growers should not have all the advantages (cf. Pl. *Gorg.* 490E). Perhaps Plato based his thinking

---

*See Morrow 103–12; Isager and Skydsgaard 123: "In the ideal state envisioned by Aristotle, all citizens, as mentioned above, were to start with equal plots of private land".

on the actual pattern of landholding in Attica, where we have see that hundred-acre farms were generally unknown. In fact, the rarer forty-five- to hundred-acre "estate" of the rich Athenian was not much larger than five times the size of the "average" hoplite plot of about ten or so acres.[9]

In Plato's view, only with equal lots worked by citizens of roughly similar status can the twin evils of poverty and abundant riches be avoided. He summed up the *dêmos*, the backbone of his stable *polis*, as "the third group; they farm their own soil (*autourgoi*), they own moderate property (*ou panu polla kektêmenoi*), and they give no offense to anyone. Whenever they come together, however, they are the most numerous and carry the most influence in the assembly" (*Resp.* 8.565A). This Platonic ideal of agrarianism, based on the actual environment of the traditional Greek *polis*, never really vanished from the Western philosophical tradition. In late-eighteenth-century England, for example, William Ogilvie, like Aristotle and Plato, advocated an equitable distribution of farmland among the citizenry, including rules concerning inalienability, inheritance, and fragmentation (e.g., Montmarquet 165).

Aristotle is both more explicit and more pragmatic than Plato (or any other thinker in antiquity) in his conception of agrarianism. He criticized the agrarian programs of earlier lawgivers and philosophers such as Plato, *not* on the basis of their morality (he was largely in agreement with their conservative aims), but rather of their practicality. Aristotle, the supposed author of treatises on 158 constitutions of various Greek city-states, went further than any ancient thinker in pondering the growing problem of inequality in Greek landowning and its effect on the vitality of the *polis*.

In Aristotle's view the ideal was not merely make all the plots equal, but rather also to insist on a properly moderate (*tou mesou*) size, plots that would result neither in excessive luxury nor in abject poverty.* At the core of the problem, Aristotle believed, were the gifted rich and the talentless poor, men whose natural abilities, or lack thereof, needed to be

---

*"Aristotle recognizes," wrote L. B. Carter, "that the possessor of property has a calming and sobering effect, conducive to a state of *apragmosunê* (quietism), which in turn brings a quieter, more stable society, and there does not appear to be any historical evidence for extreme poverty among farmers in Attica in the Classical Period" (95).

moderated by education to preserve the harmony and balance of the *polis*. In his view the Greek *polis* must "teach those that are the respectable by nature that they are not to desire excessive riches, and to prevent the base from having the ability to do so" (*Pol.* 2.1266a38–1267b19). Aristotle seems to champion the cause of some sort of middle group, which both the wealthy and the poor are to emulate.

Was this class a historical fact in Greece? Apparently it was, for Aristotle makes its presence explicit in Book Six of his *Politics*. There he states clearly that the best commoners are "the agricultural population," the ones who own property of moderate size, a community based on an "agrarian democracy" of sorts (*Pol.* 6.1318b10–12). Although his notion of constitutional government or "polity" is fraught with contradictions (it is often unclear whether it is more oligarchical than democratic), there is no doubt that as Aristotle looked back on nearly four centuries of *polis* history he believed the "middle constitution" had been the best form of government, in large part precisely because it was the product of a large middle landowning class, the class which farmed and bore hoplite armor (*Pol.* 2.1265b29).

Furthermore, Aristotle was apparently worried in his own time that agrarian *poleis* were moribund. That may explain his nostalgic look back to earlier lawgivers and advocates of agrarianism (e.g., Pheidon of Corinth, Phaleas, Philolaus of Corinth, Solon, Charondas, and Oxylos), and the more conservative rural city-states of his own times (e.g., Aphytis, Thebes, Mantineia, Malea), which were committed to maintaining a static landowning pattern among the citizenry.[10]

A *third* type of evidence also reflects the Greeks' interest in property egalitarianism and small farm size. At the beginning of the *polis* period, and later throughout the seventh to fourth centuries, we see frequent agrarian colonization around the Greek-speaking world. The creation of new city-states *ex nihilo* was a utopianism far more concrete than any ideal community of Aristotle and Plato. The evidence of colonies can be a valuable indicator of an early Greek agrarian ideology. Surely the formal organization of colonists and their creation of equitable plots and a complex social structure presupposes the *prior* formation of a *polis*, and suggests a preexisting, ongoing agrarian ideology.

Predictably in the cases where pristine land overseas was divided up among the colonial populace, there seems to have been a preference for standardized allotments involving rectangles of land of around fifty *plethra* (about eleven acres). This practice may suggest that farm plots between forty and sixty *plethra* (8.9 and 13.3 acres), the so-called exemplary hoplite farms we discussed earlier, were being duplicated afresh in early colonies. Is that coincidence further evidence of a preexisting ideal size for citizen farmers throughout Greece?

The entire Greek science of "geometry" or "land measurement" (Ar. *Nub.* 202–4) no doubt grew out of this need to allot precisely equal parcels in the land of these new communities. Xenophon's Socrates says that the purpose of "geometry" was to ascertain the *size* of the plot in order to calculate the potential yield (*Mem.* 4.7.2). Standardized rectangular plots of about the same size appear in the Crimean Chersonesos and at Halieis in the southern Argolid region. In southern Italy at Metapontum, already by the sixth century all new land had been equitably parceled out. Usually a farmhouse and family tombs occupied each plot; farms in Greek Italy, as at Halieis, were of standard square or rectangular shape, ranging from 16.3 to 32.6 acres in size. The supposed Panhellenic colony at Thurii (443 B.C.) under the direction of Pericles of Athens, was in theory a utopian enterprise (Hippodamos, the father of municipal planning on a grid system, supposedly planned the layout of the settlement), where all Greeks might start out anew with equitable farm plots.[11]

Because most colonists sought to establish new communities according to traditional "basic principles," their efforts to parcel and distribute land take on great importance. Were they not in some sense "cloning" the imprint of their mother city? That is, would-be *geôrgoi* were seeking to reproduce—or given this second chance, to perfect or to improve on—an agrarian ideology they had seen at home. In colonies, there were none of the problems (as Aristotle realized) of Dark-Age holdovers, aristocratic horse-breeders who were resistant to reformulating the land of their ancestors along newer agrarian principles.[12]

These landowning patterns are more than just the result of the neatness of planned surveying that facilitates real-estate transaction. Instead, they are an effort by the Greek *geôrgoi* to start afresh with one family per farm of about the same size. They wanted no repetition of the struggles at the end of the Dark Ages between the upstart *kakoi* and the privileged *agathoi*. No wonder that early Greek folk wisdom of the seventh century, collected in the sayings of the so-called Seven Sages, advised: "Measure and proportion should be applied to all things. These precepts not only should be directed to those who are about to embark on other enterprises, but also to those who are to obtain farmland (*agrum paraturis*): they are not to acquire any more than reason allows (*ne maiorem quam ratio calculorum patitur*)" (Colum. *Rust.*1.3.8).

Besides extant records of Greek farm size, philosophical discussion, and colonization schemes, a *fourth* sign of the ideology of property egalitarianism and the ubiquity of small farms is the negative example: simply the absence of class conflict over farm property. In the period 600–400 B.C. there are only a few instances among the Greek *poleis* of any widespread policy to cancel debt and redistribute farmland more equitably. Does this calm not suggest that yeomen were numerous, increasingly satisfied, and influential? The silence about landed revolution implies that agrarianism once established remained prevalent, that most farmers were not falling victim to greedy land-grabbing elites or incurring debt to wealthy urban proprietors.

"The classical age," Alexander Fuks has written, "was a time of balance and tranquillity. The social polarity was relatively small. In most of the Greek states there existed an agricultural middle class, numerically large and firmly established. The social question, and with it the aspirations for economic-social change, was only a marginal matter in the life of classical Greece." Even in the aftermath of the twenty-seven-year Peloponnesian War (431–404 B.C.), agrarianism was still the glue that held even volatile democratic states together.*

Fifth, there is evidence in Greek literature of a centuries-old distrust of the wealthy, an uneasiness with riches even though the bent of most of our surviving Greek authors is aristocratic and thus should reflect those particular private, rather than public, interests. Even Plato saw that social unrest was caused by strife between the wealthy and the poor, brought on by the accumulation of wealth by the few and loss of land by the many. In a memorable passage in the *Laws* (5.736C–E; cf. Fuks

---

*See Fuks 12–17, who counted about seventy cases of social-economic conflict in the Hellenistic age as compared with about six such cases in the classical period. See also Asheri 1966: 21–24; Andrewes 1971: 229: "Less radical reformers, like those who were vocal at Athens and elsewhere at the end of the fifth century, saw the mass of hoplites as a foundation on which to build a stable constitution."

172–89), Plato envisions a solution where the wealthy forgive debt and distribute their (excess) land to ensure that moderation takes hold over the polarized commons.

The idea that those with larger holdings (still small by the standards of the later Hellenistic Age) should share their property and forgive debt was deeply ingrained in Greek culture (e.g., Democr. fr. B.255 D–K; cf. Cole 120–22). According to Aelian (VH 14.24), sometime in the growing tension of the mid-fourth century one Theokles and one Thrasonides of Corinth voluntarily remitted debts of the less fortunate and so escaped the wrath of the *dêmos*.

There has also been research by historians of ancient Greece into "reciprocity and obligation," a social ideology where the well-off could be seen as legitimate only if they put their wealth at the disposal of the community and in particular the poor. In the nostalgic literature of the fourth century, Isocrates felt that the *noblesse oblige* of the wealthy had been a key to past Athenian success, circulating private accumulated capital to serve the greater needs of the state. He believed that in past times farms had been rented out on moderate terms or given to those less fortunate. Whether such beneficence was historical or not, it at least suggests that by the fourth century, when there was a growing polarization between rich and poor, a perception existed that there had once been a social contract of sorts among the citizens of the *polis*.[13]

Greek sumptuary legislation that discouraged ostentatious displays of wealth, and general public censure of the manifestation of riches also derived from the countryside. These laws extended the fundamental belief of the Greek *polis* that all lands were to be about the same size in perpetuity. Guy Métraux correctly saw that landholding had an enormous effect even on the parsimony of private Greek building practice: "Architecture *and land use* went hand-in-hand with politics in the earliest periods of Greek history" (97; emphasis added). Agrarian thinking fostered an egalitarianism manifested in the vast difference between individual and communal structures: "The Greeks were at pains to give state projects a splendid character and this could only be achieved by encouraging architectural simplicity in the private sector" (Métraux 97).

Important here is to recognize that this uneasiness with wealth in the private sector, this social pressure against large estates, is *not* merely the clamor of the landless poor who demand redistribution of land and cancellation of debt. That scenario is reserved for the more frequent class struggles of the Hellenistic and Roman Periods, when the number of the propertyless grew enormously. Suspicion and dislike of landed riches naturally emanate from the *middling* farmers themselves, a vigilance on their part toward any who would attempt to consolidate land at others' expense (cf. Men. *Dys.* 284–88). Leases of farmland owned by temple estates, while in later times sometimes let out to wealthy landowners, rarely were extended for more than ten years. This prudence on the part of religious authorities gave little chance or incentive for the tenant to make permanent improvements or to assemble various plots into vast tracts (e.g., Kent 243–338). "It became clear," V. N. Andreyev has written about the tradition of farm ownership (even at Athens, the most innovative, liberal, and in some sense anti-agrarian of the Greek city-states during the *polis* period), "that under normal conditions the concentration of land ran into a strong barrier" (23).

Even more important than this "strong barrier," we rarely hear of a property tax in Greece, at least not a permanent, institutionalized fee on the holding of farmland, one that might transfer capital from the countryside to the city. When at Athens an emergency war tax (*eisphora*) was levied in the late fifth and fourth centuries, it was most often on the capital of the largest properties, usually burdening few other than the rich liturgical class. In contrast, Dionysius, tyrant of fourth-century Syracuse, was infamous for funding his massive mercenary armies by looting temples and taxing property up to twenty percent of its value per annum. Within five years the citizenry had paid out to the state its entire net worth.

The huge armies, public works, and royal courts of the Hellenistic age (far in excess of anything present at Athens) required tribute and taxes on the countryside and the presence of serfs on royal and sacred lands—all relatively unknown earlier in the *polis* period, at a time when the hoplite farmers themselves were architects of their own financial policy. There is no evidence that many farmers of the city-state had direct, normal tax obligations through assessments either on the value of farmland or on annual revenues from crop production. Greek thinkers of the *polis* correctly saw that taxes would not spur productivity (as is sometimes wrongly argued), but rather tend to depress production and impoverish the agrarian population.[14]

In a general portrait quite relevant to Hellenistic, Roman, and even modern times (but clearly *not* applicable to the Greek *polis*), Joseph Tainter points out (quite frighteningly to my mind):

> Organizational solutions tend to be cumulative. Once developed, complex social features are rarely dropped. Tax rates go up more often than they go down. Information processing needs tend to move in only one direction. Numbers of specialists ordinarily don't decline. Standing armies rarely get smaller. Welfare and legitimatizing costs are not likely to drop. An ever increasing stock of monumental architecture requires maintenance. Compensation of elites rarely goes down. What this means is that when there is a growth in complexity it tends to be exponential, always increasing by some fraction of an already inflated size (Tainter 116).

There was almost no military parasitism during the lifetime of the autonomous Greek *polis*. The phenomenon is common in the later Greek and Roman world, when farmers were conscripted for long periods of military service to fight in distant wars, which often left them little defense or security for their own small plots. Liturgies, private patronage, group meals, public sacrifices, public pay, ostracism, exile—in addition to the standard agrarian legislation about farm size and inheritance— were all in their original, and often exaggerated, form *polis* devices to circulate wealth among the greater citizen population, to prevent, in other words, "certain forms of dependency."[15]

Both political and religious authority in most Greek city-states was colored by agrarianism. Political leadership and cult figures were careful not to infringe the economic and social position of the small farmer. Public properties, for example, at least at Athens during the life of the *polis* never grew beyond more than five to ten percent of the total arable land available. Land for religious sanctuaries was always dubbed "a slice" (*temenos*), never the "whole"; the gods' property, not that of individual farmers, was to be "cut out" of the grid.

It would be odd if other Greek city-states had publicly owned a greater degree of land than at Athens, given the preponderant nature of Athenian bureaucracy and governmental infrastructure. Even rents to farmers from temple estates under the *polis* were relatively cheap, and the money often recycled back to the rural population in the form of public sacrifices and banquets. Sometimes the gods' lands in time of need might be rented out to the less fortunate, or even informally farmed by the poorer usurper without immediate penalty. In general, the sacred properties required much of the same agricultural regime common to the yeomanry of the agrarian community: diversified crops, on-the-farm buildings, intensive labor and capital investment.

No religious cult could develop an elaborate priestly caste, which needed to be subsidized through tithes, taxes, or mandatory donations. No sizable body of *polis* land was needed to support unproductive religious grandees, as was the case with Hellenistic monarchs and later Christian dignitaries. When Greek religious sanction of the free *polis* did intrude into the life of the farmer, it was not in the form of land confiscation or mandatory tithes, as in the parasitism on agriculture characteristic of later religious bodies in the West. The *polis* gods and the servants of the gods (e.g., Theophr. CP 2.7.5) were usually conciliatory and concerned with practical agriculture and the well-being of those who actually farmed.[16]

Agrarian city-states of free farmers were reluctant to engage in massive temple construction or other public works projects that diverted capital into nonproductive enterprises, activities that would have forced agrarians to pay taxes and cough up scarce capital from their farms. Most grandiose religious building in Greece occurred at maritime states such as Athens and Corinth, whose commerce allowed the expenditure. Even there little option existed for landed assemblies to siphon off monies from the countryside. Aristotle felt that the pyramids in Egypt and the massive erection of the early grand temples in Greece were the devices of tyrannical regimes, which desired to keep the populace both busy and impoverished (*Pol.* 5.1313b19–28)—in implicit contrast to agrarian city-states of the *polis* period, where farmers were protected from oppressive taxation and forced labor.

This general idea of equality of farm size soon permeated the entire fabric of the city-state well beyond the notion of landholding. R. A. Padgug, despite his often doctrinaire Marxist orthodoxy (e.g., his use of "commune" for the early agrarian *polis*), saw clearly that later egalitarian Greek institutions had grown out of the original interest in equitable landholding.

A strong emphasis on equality therefore re-emerged, both as the memory of an earlier institution as well as a method of preserving the restored commune itself by preserving its members as members. The political aspect of this equality was its clearest expression. The development of the assembly as the chief governing body of the territorial state, the use of the lot as the means of fulfilling offices, as well as related political institutions, were not in themselves new. Rather they were rivals of older communal institutions, reworded and given new meaning in the democratic *polis* (Padgug 101).

As an example of agrarian equality, of "older communal institutions" transplanted throughout the citizenry, Herodotus relates that the citizens of the Aegean island of Siphnos divided equally the revenue from their mines (Hdt. 3.57). Conversely, only with difficulty did Themistocles convince the Athenians to build a fleet from the public wealth of the silver mines at Laurion. It was naturally assumed in the early Greek city-state that the equitable and more traditional practice was to give every full-grown citizen ten drachmas from the bullion mined out (Hdt. 7.144), to allot monies on an egalitarian basis identical to the grand tradition of dividing up the countryside into equal-sized properties.

Small and equitable farm size inculcated a number of values in the citizenry and created a shared vision of what a Greek city-state might be. In the early agrarian *polis*, modest, equal-sized plots ensured that all Greek citizens would have to work with their own hands. All would look at the ensuing (mostly natural) challenges pragmatically, rarely theoretically. All would acquire capital largely through their own sacrifice and toil. All would rely on their own resolve and bodily strength to reclaim land or ward off invasion. All would be secure in the thought that a whole cadre of like citizens was presented with about the same challenges, with about the same opportunities to succeed or to fail.

II. The Nature of "Agricultural Government"

The best people is the agricultural population
—Aristotle, *Politics* 6.1319a

Besides the social protocols and occasional legal sanctions against the accumulation of land, early farmers quite soon sought more formal political power to ensure that the owners of small plots, the *klêroi* of the *polis*, could set the policies and direction of their agrarian communities. The

ideology of and social pressure for small, equal-sized farms were transformed into formal law. As we have seen in Chapter 3, throughout seventh and sixth century Greece, there was a gradual retrenchment on the
part of the old landed aristocracies, themselves anachronisms from the
pastoral baronies of the Dark Ages. In their place, broad-based timocracies, governments of property owners, based on wealth rather than absolutely on blood, gradually appeared. We must remember that the birth
of constitutional government in the West was *not* an Athenian invention of the fifth century. It was a much earlier outgrowth of agrarianism,
a prior effort to formalize and protect a landed egalitarianism.

Sometimes this transition to constitutional government was through
the agency of intermediary tyrannies. Much more often it occurred
through more or less peaceful evolution. In any case, by the sixth century, Greece as a whole—Athens, Elis, Corinth, Thebes, Argos, and
throughout the Greek islands—was a region of city-states where the
farmers of the surrounding countryside chose their leaders by popular
acclaim. "Almost all states by 500 B.C. were oligarchical in structure and
remained so. Very few were still aristocratic in the full sense of that
term."* It was these middling communities (*tois mesois*) "of equals and
peers (*ex isôn kai homoiôn*)" (e.g., Arist. *Pol.* 4.1295b26) that Phocylides,
the sixth-century Milesian poet, had in mind when he wrote that in
contrast to the Near Eastern palace, "the law-abiding *polis*, though small
and set on a high rock, outranks senseless Nineveh" (fr. 4).

At the end of the seventh century in Athens, the career of Solon and
his so-called legislation, as we have seen earlier, reflects a society in the
midst of transition. It is difficult to generalize about the totality of agrarian reform attributed to Solon—laws regulating the export of olive oil, the
planting of olive trees, the distribution of landed inheritance, and the
like. But the traditional stories of his program do reveal comprehensive
shifts in the Athenian economy, the planting of diversified crops, the
plight of small farmers, the creation of nonaristocratic wealth, along with

---

*Starr: 1986: 93; cf. Salmon 1984: 233–37; Ehrenberg 1937 149–53; Larsen 28–29. "By the fifth
century B.C.", wrote G. E. M. de Ste. Croix, "when rule by hereditary aristocracies had become rare
in the Greek world, the members of the governing class who alone possessed full political rights in a
Greek oligarchy would be defined by a property qualification" (1972: 35; 98–99). On the presence
of egalitariaism and equality prior to democracy, see Spahn 174–82.

the necessary and concurrent efforts to broaden the political basis of an evolving society along nonaristocratic lines. To Solon, the "*dêmos*" was now to be the large group of citizens, quite distinct from the aristocratic elite. This new agrarian majority was to form the backbone of the *polis*.*

It may be that the rise of an agrarian constituency in Attica, as elsewhere in Greece, began even much earlier than Solon (i.e., about 600 B.C.), for Solon's agenda seems more reactive than visionary. The so-called Draconian constitution at Athens (i.e., 620 B.C.), for example, *if* historical, apparently provided citizenship to "those who could provide arms" (Arist. *Ath. Pol.* 4.2), a catch phrase throughout Greek, and especially Athenian, history to signify representative government by hoplite landholders (as opposed to *either* earlier narrow aristocracy *or* later radical democracy [e.g., Thuc. 8.92–3; 8.97.1; Arist. *Ath. Pol.* 33.1; Xen. *Hell.* 2.3.48]).

What should we call early agrarian governments of the seventh, sixth and early fifth centuries? Oligarchies? Timocracies? Democracies? Hoplite constitutions? Agrarian governments? Ancestral constitutions? Aristotle, writing late in the fourth century, was also perplexed by this admittedly gray (and changing) area between broad-based farm-owning "polities" and the later more radical democracies of his own time. After correlating the rise of hoplite infantry with the development of early Greek representative government, he writes: "Therefore, what we now label constitutional governments (*politeias*), the men of the past called democracies, but the early constitutional governments were of course oligarchical and royal, for, since populations were small, the middle class was not large" (*Pol.* 4.1297b24–7).

Even though Aristotle thought Solon had founded Athenian democracy (*kai dêmokratian katastêsai* [*Pol.* 2.1237–8]), these original evolving polities, based on the expansion of a rural middle group (*to meson*), were never in truth democracies in the fifth-century Athenian sense. At least they were not popular constitutions where rule was by the entire *dêmos*,

---

*"The clear and definite impression of Solon's usage of the term *dêmios* [the adjective] is that for him it signified neither the total community (*polis*) nor the 'the commons' or 'the masses,' as the term was used later, but the citizenry exclusive of the minority that was in a position of power and control. *Dêmos* [the noun] in Solon has no undercurrent of contempt or sense of innate inferiority and it includes more than the poorest citizens" (Donlan 1970: 391).

propertied and propertyless citizens alike. Instead, the native-born under "constitutional government" (*politeia*) who held no land were without much right to political participation.

It was quite easy in the later Greek world to distinguish advocates of extreme oligarchy, rule by only the few, from proponents of extreme democracy, rule by any and all whose parents were native-born free adult males (cf. Plato's "two cities" of rich and poor [Pl. *Resp.* 8.551D, 8.552B–D, 8.544C]). But this frequent notion of a binary opposition between rich and poor is usually the stuff of political polarization and crisis. Then it is natural to describe all the citizenry split into two opposed camps, the *mesoi* joining one of the two sides as the critical player in an alliance of the moment. Outside of stasis and revolution (e.g., Thuc. 3.82), recognition of a middling group is, as we have seen earlier (see Chapter 3), apparent in Greek literature, even if there was genuine confusion about how to label precisely such agrarian and moderate representative governments.

A great number of factors entered into the equation: the *number* of people who participated in government, the economic class of those enfranchised, the *intent* of the governing constitution, and the type and nature of civic courts and institutions (i.e., use of lot, pay for service, voluntary contributions). David Asheri, at least, thinks most broad-based oligarchies of middling farmers in the Greek world were known formally as "moderate constitutions." They could be best distinguished by their original legal agenda, an array of agrarian laws attempting to preserve land egalitarianism: (1) limiting sale or leasing of land to prevent land concentration; (2) single heirs to prevent division of ancestral lots; (3) limitation on dowries and heiresses. These legislative acts were "characteristic of moderate constitutions directly interested in the maintenance of a large and fixed number of citizens on their respective estates."[17]

For some flavor of the politics of the Greek agrarian movement, we can return briefly to Aristotle, who, as we have seen, took up the question at length in his *Politics*. Although his purposes were philosophical, rather than historical or even ideological, his is nevertheless a gifted analysis of three centuries of earlier Greek political development. At least at one point Aristotle felt there had been among the city-states *four* different spectra of democracies, and also *four* distinguishable forms of oligarchy. From his lengthy discussion, it seems clear that when middling farmers were in control of a Greek *polis*, government was broad-based: it was representative of the economic interests of most of the citizenry; it was designed to follow the dictates of law; its legislation was primarily concerned with preservation of static, fixed plots among the landholding population. That was the entire principle behind agrarian constitutions.

Aristotle must hedge in defining precisely the differences between the inexact rubrics, "oligarchy" and "democracy." Either word could at times describe the agrarian government that he called "polity" (*Pol.* 4.1292b11–12; cf. Busolt and Swoboda 310–16; Whibley 107–11). In reality, *before* the fifth century there was probably little, if any, difference in the use of the Greek words *dêmos* (literally "the people") and *oligoi* (literally "the few," but in actuality the middling landowning citizens of the *polis* ([Plut. *Per.* 11]), simply because the gulf between a landless urban mob and a reactionary, wealthy few was *not yet manifest.* "Oligarchies," for all their ostensibly antidemocratic property qualifications, in the Greek early *polis* were still the "rule of the people," and "the people" was the broad base of hoplite yeomanry.

So the very concept of "oligarchy" would have been foreign to a member of the agrarian *polis* before the fifth century. Even as late as the fifth-century at Athens, a *polis* that enfranchised its large group of landless *thêtes*, the word "*dêmos*" could still include the middle class of hoplites.* These considerations led the constitutional historian J. A. O. Larsen to call landed Greek constitutions with a property qualification not "oligarchies," but rather "timocracies," governments by those who owned some land (Larsen 32–33). In many city-states that could mean a substantial group of native-born residents. Aristotle himself said that "timocracy desires to be government by the mass, and all within its property qualification are equal" (*Eth. Nic.* 8.1160b16–20).

So under the original notion of agrarian oligarchy/timocracy/democracy/polity, the term *dêmos* actually meant the native-born resident citizenry who owned land and formed the popular government. *Dêmos* was

---

*Patterson 76; A. M. Jones 1957: 90; Andrewes 1971: 210. For what it is worth, before the fifth century the word *oligarchia* did not even exist in the Greek vocabulary (Donlan 1970: 381–82). For the rough equivalency of *dêmos* and *polis*, cf. Meiggs and Lewis 8; Donlan 1970: 386–87; Lewis 1990: 261–62.

in some contexts nearly the same term as *polis* itself. The "people" and the "city-state" at this earlier time both meant the landowning citizenry, *not* necessarily including its native-born free, but disenfranchised, poorer residents. The later reinterpretation of *dêmos* as *everyone* born into the *polis*, landed and landless alike, was the creation of fifth-century Athenian democracy, which even then often tended to see the term as inclusive of the hoplite middle.

Keep in mind also that the "new" Greek oligarchists of the late fifth and fourth centuries—and the novel creation of the word "oligarchy" itself—were quite *different* from the old agrarian, moderate lawgivers. Dangerous men like Critias (460–403 B.C.) at Athens were *not* of the same temper as the earlier Solon or Philolaus of Corinth. Although tyrants of Critias's ilk might later call themselves "oligarchs," they were, in fact, bent on a more aristocratic, narrow, and patently antidemocratic regime (e.g., Dawson 26–29; Ostwald 475–90). They usually had nothing in common with the yeomanry, present or past, who had built the *polis* and created broad-based agrarian governments. Just as *dêmos* became in the fifth century a more expansive term to mean those who supported the new concept "*dêmokratia*," so at that same period the rubric *oligoi* regressed to signify a narrow aristocracy, which was now likewise given the novel rubric "*oligarchia*" (cf. Donlan 1970 382–83). Neither *dêmokratia* nor *oligarchia* was an apt description of agrarian governments, which were broad-based timocracies/polities with a low property qualification.

No wonder that Aristotle's review of some three centuries of changing political nomenclature is confused.* Nevertheless, in his sometimes contradictory scheme of political analysis, the notion of agrarian democracy fits best somewhere in his first category of democracy and his corresponding first type of oligarchy: "There is one kind of democracy where office holding is based on property-qualifications, but these requirements are low" (*Pol.* 4.1291b38–41). Later, he elaborates that "when the farmer class and the group which possesses moderate property are in control, the society functions according to law" (4.1292b25–29; cf. Busolt and Swoboda 354–59). He finally (*Pol.* 6.1318b10–1319a19) con-

---

*"Aristotle himself found the two-regime (democracy/oligarchy) scheme inadequate and potentially misleading" (Ober 1990: 123).

cludes that the first type of democracy is "the best" and "the oldest (*ar-chaiotatê pasôn*)"—and one reflective of "an agricultural population" (*dêmos ho geôrgikos*). I do not think that Aristotle could call agrarian government the "oldest" if the notion of a middle class of small farming, arms-owning citizenry was a mere philosophical "construct."

We also know of a variety of words in a sixth-century Greek context denoting "equality" of some sort (e.g., *isonomia, isêgoria, isos damos, and isokratia*). Such nomenclature probably suggests that the formal concept of civic egalitarianism was taken for granted among those of the landed classes well before the appearance of Athenian democracy in the fifth century.

So Aristotle knew that the "first" type of early agrarian democracy was *not* radical democracy along the Athenian model of the late fifth and fourth centuries. He acknowledges that in one sense it had been essentially a benign "first" type of oligarchy: "In the cases where more men own property, but less of it and of not a great extent, then this is the first type of oligarchy." The chief difference between oligarchy and democracy in Aristotle's view is the extent of a property qualification (cf. *Eth. Nic.* 8.1160b15–21): the stiffer it became, the more oligarchic the *polis*, the less restrictive the property requirement, the more democratic the city-state. Aristotle confesses that he does not know the precise standard that might ideally result in the largest body of hoplite landowners running the government (*Pol.* 4.1297b1–5).[18]

Aristotle's agrarian government is clearly to be distinguished from his other three types of more restrictive and repressive oligarchies, where property qualifications are high and birth comes in to play. Those constitutions were not agrarian. They resulted in rule of the rich alone. In contrast, Aristotle says that his favored first oligarchical type, like the first brand of democracy, allows law to be supreme "since there is a great number of men who participate in the government" (*Pol.* 4.1293a14–20). This broad-based body was a type of government that he later (*Pol.* 6.1320b22–26) seems to feel is nearest to real constitutional government ("polity").

In sum, Aristotle's review of Greek constitutional history suggests an affinity for representative government based on a low property qualification. He champions constitutions that enfranchise a near majority of the male adult (hoplite-armed) population. In his view that was something possible only when there was a vibrant agrarianism and thus a preponderance of small farmers. This was a populace which in turn legislated to ensure continued property egalitarianism. It was the rural population in short that made the *polis* "great" (*megalê*, Arist. *Pol.* 7.1326a23–25), and that had been there from the beginning of the city-state (*Pol.* 7.1318b8; cf. Whibley 22–24).

During the first two centuries of the *polis*, when broad-based agrarian constitutions were normative, in Greek literature appears a strong *anti-aristocratic* flavor. Attacks on the wealthy elite show the rise of yeoman ideology and imply "that the basis for social change was deeply rooted in a firm sense of identity and self-esteem of the peasant class, and, further, that a feeling for justice, equality and common dignity formed a stratum of democratic orientation which found constant public expression during the seventh and sixth centuries."*

Perhaps to the modern mind, especially in the 1990s when the triumph of democracy appears to be widespread and enduring, agricultural government, agrarian "timocracy" with a property qualification, seems illiberal in its restrictiveness and discrimination against the landless poor. This exclusionary nature of agrarian government is quite undeniable. It is entirely in line with our portrait so far of the rise of intensive agriculture and the accompanying creation of a new chauvinistic class of agriculturalists. These were farmers neither extremely wealthy nor poor, who often composed only a third to half the citizen population (cf. Ps. Her. Att. *Peri Pol.* 30–31).

But envision agrarian "democracy" within the context of the times. If representative government is defined merely by the requirements of voting and participation in officeholding—forgetting for the moment such legislative rights as free and unlimited speech, an absence of censorship, juries, fiscal accountability, subsidies for governmental participation, and the use of lots in magistracy selection—then the only form of government *more* representative of the people seems to be radical democracy of the type that emerged at Athens in the late fifth and fourth centuries. There every Athenian born to citizen parents who were Athenians (regardless of wealth or property holding) was entitled to participate in the assembly. But herein also rises a paradox in our discussion of

---

*Donlan 1973: 154; for anti-aristocratic passages, see Tyrt. 9.1–12; 9.13–22; 9.23; Callinus 1.6–21; Archil. fr. 22, 94, 97; Xenophanes 3; Hipponax 16, 17, 24A, 24B, 25, 29, 39, 42D.

the comparative equality of ancient governments. Under Athenian democracy, as under agrarian democracy, slaves, resident aliens, and women were also disenfranchised.

In the case of Athens, discrimination was very, very widespread indeed. Given the nature of the Athenian economy, restrictions may have affected three-fourths of the *adult resident* population. Citizens at Athens numbered between 40,000 and 50,000 persons during the fifth century, whereas adult resident aliens (about 10,000?), slaves (about 80,000–150,000?), and adult women born to two Athenian parents (about 40,000–50,000) totaled well over 150,000 persons. No more than 40,000–50,000 adult *citizens* directed affairs out of a total of perhaps nearly 200,000 adult *residents* of Attica.*

On the other hand, it is conceivable that in many agrarian city-states (see, e.g., Arist. *Pol.* 6.1318b23–1319a14; cf. Thuc. 1.141.3) where there were few, if any, resident aliens engaged in commerce, where manufacturing was rare, where slaves were primarily agricultural (i.e., not more than 15,000 chattels in all of Boeotia; cf. Buck 160), and thus not needed for manufacture or mining, *as great* a proportion of the adult resident population participated in government as under so-called radical democracy at Athens. Could agrarian government be as democratic as "radical" Athenian democracy?

The example of the conservative Boeotian regime at Thebes offers an illustration. It was a confederation of surrounding *poleis* in the fifth century traditionally considered backward, conservative, and oligarchical, with a strong agrarian heritage (e.g., Arist. *Pol.* 2.1274a32–1274b10; cf. Thuc. 4.76.2, 5.31.6). The government in Boeotia was apparently careful to discriminate against its landless residents, who were not allowed full rights (e.g., *Hell. Oxy.* 11.2). The presence of a property qualification at first glance seems to have produced a far less egalitarian society in Theban-controlled Boeotia than the democracy across the southern border at Athens. Aristotle says that at Thebes anyone who was active in trade or menial labor (*Pol.* 3.1278a25–26, 6.1321a29–30) within the

---

*See Gomme, *Comm.* 2:34–39; 1933: 25–26; A. M. Jones 1957: 165; B. Strauss 78; cf. M. H. Hansen 53–54; 90–94; Guiraud 156–59; Busolt and Swoboda 187–89; 764–66. For those eligible and ineligible to participate in democracy at Athens, see A. M. Jones 1957: 75–96; M. H. Hansen 61–64; 94–96 Harrison 187–99; 165–76.

last ten years was barred from participation in political life. That policy would have disenfranchised thousands at Attica. No wonder Euripides in his play the *Supplices* presents the Theban viewpoint as largely unsympathetic to the political acumen and capability of the working poor (Eur. *Suppl.* 420–22).

Thucydides (4.93.3) wrote that at the battle of Delium between Athens and Boeotia (424 B.C.), the more than 10,000 Boeotian light-armed troops present there (mostly poor or landless?) outnumbered their fellow 7,000 hoplite infantry and 1,000 cavalry—those fighters engaged in farming who enjoyed full citizenship. These numbers probably mean that in the fifth century on any given day a muster of the various contingents of Boeotian military manpower (perhaps two-thirds of all available troops) reflected the oligarchical restrictions of participation in government. The make-up of the Boeotian army reveals that about half the male inhabitants were denied full citizenship rights. That is, about 12,000 adult residents were full citizens qualifying for hoplite service, but more than 15,000 adult males fought outside the landed phalanx (cf. Busolt and Swoboda 564–65). The latter group presumably did not meet the property qualification for full citizenship privileges.

Yet appearances can be deceiving.* The property requirement for those to serve as hoplites nearby at the Boeotian town of Orchomenos was apparently quite low, about forty-five measures (*medimnoi*) of yearly agricultural produce (e.g., Poll. *On.* 10.165). If that census figure is at all reflective of Boeotia as a whole, the Theban confederacy was again a broad-based "oligarchy." All but the smallest farmers had a say. Curiously, the forty-five *medimnoi* of annual agricultural produce is about a fourth of the old Solonian agrarian *zeugitai* qualification at Athens (two to three hundred *medimnoi*), a much steeper census which traditionally marked the cut-off point for enjoyment of *full* political rights, even under the democracy.

Ostensibly it may have been easier to qualify for hoplite military service in Boeotia than at Athens. And there is no reason to believe these

---

*Larsen notes that "even the simple fact that the Boeotians possessed representative government has been noted only by very few" (40), and adds that the confederacy was "one of the best illustrations we have of Greek moderate oligarchy" (Larsen 32). "A little under half the population would have had *full* rights" under the constitution (Moore 129; emphasis added).

census rubrics were always static. Aristotle believed that successful agricultural years allowed more small farmers to meet property and wealth qualifications and so enter the political framework of some agrarian *poleis*. That implies that the property qualification was low enough in many Greek city-states to allow the less fortunate farmers an opportunity to acquire full privileges. At the beginning of the Peloponnesian War (431 B.C.) the Thebans could make a vigorous defense of their Boeotian confederacy as an *oligarchia isonomos* ("an oligarchy of political equality"; cf. Thuc. 3.62.3), a broad-based timocracy where all citizens had rights under the law (although not full access to all offices), quite in contrast to the narrower government (*dunasteia*) that for a time had run things there during the Persian Wars (490–479 B.C.).*

How many did *not* have full citizenship rights (i.e., eligibility to hold all elected offices and participate in all municipal councils) under the agrarian confederacy led by Thebes? Start with the 15,000 or so light-armed troops who did *not* fight as hoplites. Add their wives and the spouses of the enfranchised 12,000 hoplite farmers. Finish with (say) between 12,000 and 15,000 agricultural slaves who worked on the citizens' farms. All these marginalized groups add up to a *total* of about 50,000 to 60,000 *dis*enfranchised free and slave adult residents. The full-citizen hoplites (about 12,000 hoplite farmers) composed about twenty percent of the total *adult* resident population of Boeotia (i.e., 60,000–70,000).

So in the total resident adult population, Boeotian citizen-hoplites were no more an exclusive percentage than the combined propertied *and* propertyless citizens of the radical democracy across the border at Athens. That democratic system went one step (but only one step) further to incorporate the free landless as citizens.

How could a property qualification at Boeotia still result in as egalitarian a society as that at democratic Athens? Clearly, we must look at the actual social and economic conditions under which the Greek agrarian city-states operated before we label them less egalitarian than more

---

*That interim rule was an aristocratic deviation from the normal "ancestral constitution" that had championed the cause of middling Boeotian farmers (e.g., Paus. 9.6.2). Except for a brief period during the Persian Wars and later during Athenian intervention (e.g., Thuc. 1.108; cf. Busolt and Swoboda 358), the constitution of Boeotia seems to have been unusually stable and broad-based throughout the fifth century. For flexibility in the property assessment, see *Pol.* 5.1306b11–16; *Ath. Pol.* 7.4; *Rhet.* 1387a21–26; cf. [Dem.] 42.4; Pl. *Leg.* 5.744C; 745D; Rhodes 145–46.

radical democracy at Athens. The conservative character of the agrarian economy, its closed, insular nature, must be considered in any discussion of Greek constitutional government. Agrarian "democracy" in theory was not quite democracy as defined by the Athenian model. But because it did not encourage the presence of disenfranchised resident aliens (metics) or slaves engaged in workshops, trade, or mine work, agrarian governments may have been about as representative of its surrounding adult resident population—citizen and noncitizen—as radical democracies. Agrarian economies without large navies and merchant ships simply did not draw in foreign residents and nonfarm slaves in large numbers, populations who by any Greek standard were always shut out from participation in government.

Locale may also have been important. In the typical agrarian-based *polis* such as Thebes, disenfranchisement from full citizenship was by statute: those who did not produce enough harvests or who did not own land at all were prevented from holding magistracies and in many places from voting. Yet in a radical democracy such as Athens, marginalization of segments of the population might take still place for reasons quite distinct from property holding. Farmers in the unusually large expanse of Attica, who might live fifty miles or more from Athens proper, surely would not need to attend the assembly or serve on law courts as frequently once there was an ever-ready and enfranchised urban poor (cf. Larsen 3; but cf. Markle 161–65). Ironically, a representative or timocratic council such as an elected or allotted *Boulê* could be more representative of the total Greek citizen body than the radically democratic assembly. The democratic *ekklesia* purportedly was open to all adult citizens—but in reality only to those with easy physical access to the assembly grounds.

Although the degree of agrarian participation in Athenian democracy is hotly contested by modern scholars, the ancients at least were aware that farmers were reluctant to undergo time-consuming, bureaucratic governmental responsibilities in Athens proper. Aristotle makes the point that farmers live scattered throughout the countryside "and do not meet or feel so much the need for meeting in the assembly" (*Pol.* 6.1319a30–36). Apparently "they have more pleasure in their work than in taking part in politics" (*Pol.* 6.1318b 9–27). Once there was established a constantly politically active body of poor at Athens, agrarians' reluctance to trudge into the *polis* might explain the feeling in Greek literature that the landed hoplites at Athens had not the same say in assembly decisions as their roughly equal-numbered counterparts, the landless *thêtes* who rowed in the fleet.

A final consideration concerns logistics. Democracy at Athens was more direct than representative. In the fifth century it required the physical presence of about six thousand citizens in the *ekklesia* to approve or reject decrees. No more than a fifth (of some forty to fifty thousand citizens at Athens in the fifth century) would vote on any given legislation. Any suggestion in our sources that this minority pool of direct participants was repetitive, static (e.g., more urban and poor than rural and middling), and not entirely representative of Attica as a whole, takes on important significance.[19]

Agrarian governments were theoretically somewhat more restrictive by insisting on a moderate property qualification, but met less frequently and reflected more the consensus of their smaller and more homogeneous body of farmer-citizens, so the actual number of Greeks who were deciding state policy may have been *no* smaller, *no* more exclusive than under democracy. In the ancient Greek world radical democracy apparently functioned by direct vote in town in the open-air assembly. That forum at Athens on any given day thereby eliminated four fifths of the Athenian citizenry from face-to-face legislative deliberation.

Agrarian egalitarianism throughout all the Greek city-states was the foundation of Athens' innovative step in enfranchising her landless native-born residents. The Athenians were *not* creating *ex nihilo* a new democratic ideology as has been argued recently (cf. Arist. *Pol.* 2.1273b38–39)—the year 1993 was, after all, the 2,500-year anniversary and celebration of Cleisthenes' democratic reforms of 507 B.C. Instead, democracy in the Athenian sense was a modification of prior broad-based, agricultural timocracy. It was a moderate extension of a long tradition of agrarian values to an additional group who did not hold land—a move itself not nearly revolutionary enough to transform the *polis* to meet the complex economic and social challenges of the fourth-century Mediterranean. No wonder Aristotle writes that "democracy is only a small deviation from polity (*hê dêmokratia epi mikron gar parekbainei to tês politeias eidos*)," and that often landed "timocracies pass into democracy (*timokratias eis dêmokratian*)" because "they are very similar (*sunhoroi gar eisin hautai*)" (Arist. *Eth. Nic.* 8.1160b18–22; cf. Larsen 40).

The general democratic nature of *all* the agrarian Greek city-states—agrarian polities and radical democracies alike—is what led W. G. Runciman quite correctly to see a general, uniform *polis* ideology of egalitarianism, one which for so long prevented power in Greece from accumulating in specialized and entrepreneurial hands:

> *Poleis* were all, without exception, far too democratic. Some, of course, were more oligarchic than others. But this meant only that their government was in the hands of a relatively smaller number of relatively richer citizens, rather than a relatively larger number of relatively poorer ones. In terms of a close concentration of economic, ideological, and coercive power in the hands of a compact, self-reproducing elite, no Greek *polis* ever came anywhere near the degree of oligarchy which characterized the institutions of both Rome and Venice during the period of their achievement of world-power status. In no Greek *polis* did there ever form a nobility or patriciate with an effective monopoly of the means of production, persuasion, and coercion and the capacity to transmit that monopoly to its chosen successors (1990: 364–65).

III. The Idealization of Yeomanry

> There are many sorts of profession. The practice of medicine is good for a man of suitable station. Petty trading is contemptible. Nothing is better, nothing provides such good living, nothing is more worthy of a free man, than farming.
> —Abbot Emo of Wittewierum (Gronigen, Netherlands, A.D. 1221 (in. Slicher van Bath 1963:194)

"Agriculture is a humane (*philanthrôpos*) and gentle art (*praeia technê*)," as Xenophon's Ischomachos puts it (*Oec.* 19.17). These commonly espoused sentiments, from both wealthy and poor Greeks of the city-state, cavalrymen and hoplites, suggest that agrarianism was also preserved in the culture of the *polis* by a moral force, one in addition to the establishment of agriculture-based political institutions or social, legal, and ideological pressures to ensure equality of landholding. There was an ethos of the land, a near-religious feeling among the Greeks that yeoman agriculture, manual work on one's own farm, was morally uplifting and essential to one's character. After all, the common word for landed property, *ousia*, also came to mean "being" or "essence" (cf. Arist. *Pol.* 2.1266b19). To the Greeks the two were inseparably linked.

At the beginning of Greek literature, Homer, as we have seen, makes the shade of Achilles reflect this growing ethical notion of property holding. To the hero's mind the only thing worse than being landless was to work as a hired hand for a landless man: "I would rather follow the plough as thrall to another man, one with no land allotted him and not much to live on, than be a king over all the perished dead" (Hom. *Od.* 11.489–91). Oddly enough, by the fifth century all members of the city-state—the landless poor, the urban craftsman, and the occasional wealthy horse-breeder—accepted the agrarian ideology that those who owned and worked their own ground held the moral high ground and were the glue that held the *polis* together. At Athens the audience who enjoyed Aristophanes' rustic agrarian plays, *Peace, Acharnians, Ecclesiazusiae,* and *Thesmophoriazusae*— drama that often was anti-urban, anti-elite, anti-intellectual—must have been in some part nonagrarian!

For the life of the free *polis*, this affinity for the land was a powerful force. Although more subtle than political representation or military power, it tended to check corporate and absentee agriculture, while championing the yeomanry of the middling farmers. Agrarian themes in Greek literature from the seventh to the end of the fourth century are clear. Agriculture was a "natural" occupation (cf. Pl. *Leg.* 10.889D). It required exploitation of the earth—not of other citizens. Simplicity and honesty were instinctively inculcated through hard work. People engaged in politics out of real need, not to create careers or accumulate riches. Farming outdoors contributed to a healthy physique. It curbed sloth, resulting in a population that wished peace, but was formidable in war, in contrast to the lazy, cowardly urban mob.

Even those few very rich who had no intention of working their ground themselves, and whose practice of landholding was antithetical to small farming, praised yeomanry. The author of the *Oeconomica,* wrongly attributed to Aristotle (*Oec.* 1343a25-b2), believed agriculture was "the best occupation" because it was "just," an occupation "not at the expense of others." Aristotle himself, despite his obvious awareness that farming demanded technology and could be at times quite lucrative, nevertheless still maintained that agriculture was the most natural of tasks (*Pol.* 1.1256b10–22). It was inherently noble work aimed at meeting essential needs, not at obtaining superfluous profits. In his *Rhetoric* Aristotle says explicitly that people honor those who are gallant, free, and just. In that group of the best citizens the farmers are the most conspicuous, "those who work on their own farms" (*Rhet.* 2.1381a21–24).

Similarly, Xenophon goes on at length that "the best life" is farming, which gives the body "the greatest degree of strength and beauty (*kallista te kai eurôstotata*)." The entire farming community was the backbone of the state, since farming made "those who work the soil brave, the best citizens, most loyal to the *polis*" (*Oec.* 6.9–10), an occupation that seemed to make its adherents "the most noble in their habits (*ta êthê gennaiotatous*)" (*Oec.* 15.12).

Plato says nearly the same thing. In his view, the ownership of the family plot was the only mechanism by which the citizen could fulfill his political obligations and thus practice virtue (*Leg.* 5.741B). Menander writes likewise: "For all humans the farm is a teacher of virtue and of the life devoted to freedom" (fr. 408 Kock), a sentiment echoed by a contemporary comic poet, Philemon: "A farm is the best gift a man could have" (fr. 105 Kock).[20]

Aristophanes makes this idealization even more explicit throughout his fifth-century Athenian plays. His comic farmers are peace-loving, independent, and completely self-reliant. "Looking out at the countryside," sighs Dicaiopolis, the farmer of the *Acharnians* who is cooped up in Athens during the initial evacuations of the Peloponnesian War, "loving peace, hating the town, desiring my country village which never ever cried out 'Buy charcoal' or 'Buy vinegar' or 'Buy oil'; it knew not at all 'Buy,' but instead produced everything itself" (Ar. *Ach.* 32–36). In Aristophanes' view, the farmers of Attica represented a pristine life-style that was inherently ennobling, one derived from the early days of the Greek *polis*, now under assault at Athens from growing urbanization, overseas imperialism, and welfare radical democracy. In his play the *Peace*, "peace is most welcome to the farmers," who walk back to the countryside, phalanx-like, their mattocks and pitchforks on their shoulders, like hoplite arms gleaming in the sun (*Pax* 549, 556–57, 564–67).

This heartfelt love of farming was not just a romantic notion, unlike the much later genre of pastoralism—that artificial, rosy picture of the countryside drawn by a bored and urban elite. Farmers in fifth- and fourth-century Athenian drama symbolize and embody the inherent dignity of the entire (vanishing) agrarian *polis*. "The farmers do the work," wrote Aristophanes bluntly (*Pax* 511), "no one else." These same *geôrgoi*, he says later in the same play, "are most wise" (603), hardworking men sometimes known elsewhere in literature as the "good farmers" (*agathoi geôrgoi*; Lys. 20.33). The comic poet Philemon makes his farmer say: "Out on my farm digging the earth I have found the answer—peace" (Philemon fr. 71.6–8 Kock). So it is in Greek tragedy; the noble farmer of Euripides' *Electra* is made to declare: "The yeomen alone preserve the land" (Eur. *Orest.* 920). Zethos in Euripides' lost play *Antiope* claims that only in cultivation of the earth can a man find true wisdom (fr. 188 Nauck).

Informal and *ad hoc* as these idealized sentiments were, the exaltation of agriculture reveals a fascinating distrust for just those activities—specialization, bureaucratization, social stratification, and taxation—that usually create (and topple) complex societies (e.g., Tainter 193–216). So there is a gut-instinct characteristic of agrarian sentiment in Greek literature that residence on the farm, simple comportment in dress and behavior, intensive small-sized cultivation, yeoman control of warfare, and brusqueness and rapidity in government are all essential to the survival of Greek *polis* culture.

The effect that agrarianism had on the economy at large, in preventing specialization and complexity, has not gone unnoticed by scholars. Historians have been quick to detect a "primitiveness" in the nature of Greek economic thinking, a society based more on a desire for equality and stability than for real productive growth. As I stated earlier, this "backward" interpretation of the Greek economy has been greatly exaggerated. Farmers *did* know profit and loss, supply and demand, prices dependent on scarcity and surfeit. But this knowledge is not incompatible with the Greeks' simultaneous notion that agriculture, like war, was not a mere profession, but an opportunity to prove moral excellence as well.*

The ethical element inherent in farming did create a moral economy of sorts in which the possession of equal-sized plots, not capital formation

---

*See Detienne 1963: 54; Isager and Skydsgaard 200: "a curious mix of gift-giving and a market economy"; cf. Engels 24–27.

alone, was given social and cultural prominence. Agrarianism was an ethical force in the *polis* from which business and profit as ends in themselves took on "unnatural" connotations, explaining why nakedly commercial activity was shunned until the late fourth century, and even then considered "deviant." Profit seeking was largely the work of foreigners and resident aliens (e.g., Gernet 1981: 318)—men properly to be denied the right by the agrarian *polis* to own land, fight in the phalanx, or vote in the assembly. That creed explains why the destruction of Greek agrarian thinking in the Hellenistic Period, the end of yeomanry in the late third and second centuries in Greece, may for all of its inequality and widespread impoverishment have created much greater wealth in the economy overall. The dismantling of *polis* egalitarianism allowed more selfish and unblinkered bright minds to seek out and to create capital—albeit to be enjoyed by an increasingly smaller privileged elite.

This emphasis throughout classical literature on the moral superiority of agriculture is not only based on the observation that farming is an activity closer to nature than trading or commerce. At times the working of the soil, as the Greeks knew, could be seen as unnatural and dependent on man-made, not natural, forces. I think, in the context of the Greek *polis*, the purely philosophical idealization of agrarianism prominent in the Greek literature of the fourth century also derives from three historical facts: (1) the realization by all Greeks of the *polis* that their collective and cherished institutions of the city-state arose as part of the early movement toward small, private, and equitable ownership of farm plots; (2) the fact that the majority of *polis* dwellers were directly connected to the growing of food, and felt that local self-sufficiency in food production (*autarkeia*) was essential, even when in some cases it no longer made strict economic sense; and (3), the fear that in the fourth century some communities, most notably Athens, had developed social and political practices inimical to traditional *polis* agrarianism.

Agrarianism was not merely an ethos confined to the country chauvinism of the *polis*, but the ethos from which most other Greek values can be traced. Because both Aristotle and Plato (and most all Greek political thinkers) believed, unlike modern theorists, that government's real role was to improve the nature of mankind, the occupation and life-style of the citizenry became of utmost importance. As long as a large segment of the population worked and owned their own farms, agrarianism, the *polis*, and Greek culture itself, were all in good hands. Patience, frugality, practicality, and communality among the citizenry were the natural harvests of the rural creed. That explains why the philosophers saw that anything that undermined agrarianism—large farms, city life, hired labor, mercenary service, sea power, and participation of all citizens in politics regardless of property ownership—soon eroded the original concept of a *polis*. Such anti-agrarianism may have led to capital formation, greater democratization, and rapid urban growth, but it also changed the Greek character in ways we moderns might uniquely appreciate. Critics of Plato and Aristotle find their thinking illiberal, reactionary, and backward. But they have not refuted the philosophers' basic connection between agrarianism and the stable Greek state. And they have not shown that the Hellenic character and ethos were the unique products of an urban, democratic, and imperialistic Athens, rather than the earlier bounty of the ten-acre farmer, hoplite, and council member. So if we now object to the view of Plato and Aristotle, it may be because we have lost empathy with the horny-handed farmer himself and his cargo of self-reliance, hard work, and a peculiar distrust of rich and poor alike.

Chapter 6

THE WAYS OF FIGHTERS

Not finely roofed houses
Nor the stones of well-built walls
Nor even canals or dockyards
Make the *polis*, but rather men of the type
Able to meet the job at hand.

—Alcaeus (28a)

I.

There is a long tradition in the West that good infantry, indeed the best infantry, was always made up of the men who worked the countryside. The theme is ubiquitous in Greek literature (e.g., Xen. *Oec.* 5.4–5, 6.6–7, 9–10; [Arist.] *Oec.* 12. 1343b2–6). It is echoed constantly by later Roman authors who looked fondly on the Greek exemplar. "Our own ancestors," wrote Varro (*Rust.* 3.1.4), "with good reason sent their citizens from town back to the countryside, for during peacetime they were fed by the rustic Romans and in war defended by them." Vegetius could remark as late as the fourth century A.D.: "I do not believe that there has ever been any question that the rural folk are the best equipped for military service" (1.3; cf. Pliny *HN* 18.26). In modern

221

times, sociologies of battle in this country have usually argued that our best ground fighters have risen out of the conservative rural territory of the American South and Midwest, where tradition, family values, and acceptance of discipline remain strong.

Yet the original purpose of agrarian infantry in the West was *not* to storm cities, *not* to gain advantage over foreign troops, *not* to protect the Greek *polis* from outside challengers—although agriculturalists were to do exactly that superbly time and again—but rather to fight each other, farmer against farmer, and thereby to protect their property and their community. In the process they helped to establish agrarian control of the political life of their respective city-states. Much has been written about the tactics and strategy of Greek infantry during the lifetime of the *polis*. Journal articles continue to seek out unappreciated maneuver and articulation on the part of hoplite phalanxes in set battles of the fifth and fourth centuries, forgotten Cannae-like tactics at Marathon (490 B.C.), or unnoticed reserves and a revolutionary *en echelon* advance more than a century later at the battle of Leuctra (371 B.C.).

In the end, however, the search to find a military revolution in hoplite battles of the fourth century is more often futile. True, there were rudimentary set-moves of phalanxes by this time, especially at Sparta and Thebes. However, except for strengthening the wings or increasing the depth of a phalanx, a formidable simplicity persists throughout the warfare of the *polis* that continues to baffle and frustrate even the most ingenious military historian. The relative absence of many specialized contingents, the seemingly unintelligent deployment of existing cavalry, the general avoidance of missile troops and siegecraft, the reluctance to integrate light and heavy infantry before the fifth century, all at times drive the armchair strategist of Greek warfare in desperation to hasten to the military drama of Philip and Alexander, and therein to study the richer complexities of Macedonian battle.[1]

This amateurism of the hoplite phalanx, this abject absence of military science itself until the fourth century (which makes Greek hoplite warfare of the city-state less interesting to the professional battle scholar), ensures that the warring of Greek *poleis* is all the more fascinating for our own purposes. Those are to investigate this most curious subordination of warfare to a larger agricultural agenda. Greek fighting of the *polis should never be discussed outside the context of farming.*

In the last analysis, like the rise of small farming itself, the collision of hoplite phalanxes is a human story of muscular strength, physical endurance, and resolute nerve—the Thebans wrestling at Leuctra (e.g., Plut. *Mor.* 639), the Spartans biting and clawing at Thermopylae (Hdt. 7.225.3), the great bodily pushing at Coroneia (e.g., Xen. *Hell.* 4.3.19). Greek warfare before the fifth century is not a tale of evolving technology or of intellectual brilliance. The hoplite battlefield was simply the agrarian *polis* transferred in mass to a place of killing and death, an agricultural community that had frozen technological development and tactical experimentation for over two centuries.

Of course, Greek infantrymen appear as graceful warriors on fifth-century red-figure and black-figure vases, and as formidable professionals on monumental sculpture of Panhellenic temples and treasuries (see Anderson 1970: pls. 3, 6, 9, 15). Hoplite warfare can even be termed "glorious" by the lyric and elegiac poets ("men perish by war, cowards by disease," *Anth. Pal.* 7.234, 7.233; Tyrt. 12.13: "the noblest virtue"). Is there not also an undeniable sophistication to hoplite weaponry, as the double-gripped shield and double-pointed spear attest (e.g., Hanson 1991b: 67–74)?

But clashes between massed columns of armored amateurs were more an unglamorous saga of small farming men—burial remains tell us that the soldiers averaged around five feet six inches in height and about 140–150 pounds. The combatants were stout agrarians of all ages, killers of an afternoon whose prime objective—whose only directive in the beginning—was to battle other farmers over disputed ground. No wonder these agrarians called their hoplite fighting "threshing it out" (Tyrt. 19.16). No wonder Homer compared two opposing masses of armed men to "two lines of reapers, who facing each other, drive their course all down the field of wheat or of barley" (*Il.* 18.68–69; and cf. 19.221–26).

Through the appropriation of *polis* fighting, Greek agriculturalists emerged in the first two centuries of the *polis* to assume a monopoly over the life of the city-state. These yeomen were not men mounted on horses, above the filth and brutality of infantry fighting on feet, knees, and belly. They were not hired thugs, psychotics, or crazed beserkers (e.g., Lazenby 1991: 107–8), the red-eyed deviants that modern societies wheel out in time of crises, only to closet when the dust settles, "but rather men of the type able to meet the job at hand" (Alcaeus 28a), who produced the food, made the laws, and fought the wars of the Greek city-state.

As we have seen in the last chapter, a code of social, political, and ethical thought was necessary to embody the gains of new agriculturalists, and to express exactly what the Greek farmers were. That agrarian vision of the geôrgoi, once discussed, debated, and articulated was expressed ideologically in legislation and geographically in a patchwork of farms upon the landscape—and then ultimately preserved militarily from reactionary challenge, from within and without individual city-states. Reform through legal, political, or ethical recourse is rarely entirely peaceful. Lasting agrarian change must be ensured by force and by threat of force—and thus ultimately by possession of arms.

We must therefore investigate how it was that the Greek farmer found himself as a hoplite in control of the battlefield, in the seventh through fifth centuries, and thereby was able to protect and promote his novel ideas of agrarian government and property egalitarianism. The process begins with the creation of new weapons. They were tools entirely antithetical to the previous equestrian and aristocratic supremacy of Dark-Age clans, appurtenances also superior to the missile weaponry and inferior body protection of the poorly equipped Greek foot soldiers of the pre-*polis* era.

The basic components of classical Greek infantry armament that appeared at the end of the eighth century—bronze helmet, body armor, greaves, round shield, and thrusting spear—were in fact known in some form or other to the earlier and mostly elite Mycenean and Dark Age Greeks, and also to alien Eastern and European peoples well *before* the appearance of the *polis* (e.g., Snodgrass 1964b: 37–68, 72–90; 1967: 59–60; 1971b: 33–50). Yet between 725 and 675 B.C.—an era roughly contemporaneous with Laertes' farm and the world of Hesiod—there was an evolution and modification of these earlier weapon designs into a far more codified, heavier collection of bronze and iron arms and armor: (1) a double-grip, concave, round shield; (2) a "Corinthian" helmet that covered nearly the entire face and head; (3) a "bell" corselet of solid bronze; (4) pliable, laceless greaves for the knees and shins ("protection against spear and stone" [Aesch. *Sept.* 676]); (5) a spear with both an iron head and a sharp bronze spike at its butt; (6) short secondary sword, should the spear shatter. This distinctive ensemble, labeled by modern scholars the "hoplite panoply," was the more or less exclusive armament of the farmers of Greece for the next two hundred years of the *polis* period (i.e., 700—500 B.C.). Even thereafter, with modification and transformation in the fifth and fourth centuries it was tied inextricably to the agrarian populace of Greece.

The problem for our purposes is to chart the cause and effect of the new arms (which are first attested in Greece between the late eighth and middle seventh centuries archaeologically, iconographically, and in the literature of contemporary lyric and elegiac poetry), not merely in a military sense, but in a social and political context as well. Quite simply, does the rather sudden appearance of these new hoplite arms, and the subsequent fighting in massed array explain how the new farmer class seized control of Greek political life? Do these innovations in arms tell us how *geôrgoi* took land or influence away from entrenched landowners? Or, in contrast, is this so-called hoplite reform in armament *not* the catalyst for agrarian change and the rise of a new breed of agrarian, but merely a reflection of the successful property owners' emerging muscle, of their desire to fabricate new equipment and arms to protect their novel way of rural life?

Or do hoplite equipment and the phalanx have no relationship at all with farmers and the rise of agrarianism? Do they illustrate instead the evolving military tastes of traditional aristocratic landowners, the landed barons who, through some hundred years of social and economic assimilation, slowly incorporated other less fortunate men into their ranks? If that third premise were to be true, there would be no need for the present chapter in this book. These questions—endlessly debated by classical scholars throughout this century—*are* important because they represent sharply alternative views of early Greek history, and thus contradictory notions of the relationship between early Greek agriculture and the emergence of the Greek city-state.

To some historians, it was not new farming strategies, as I have argued repeatedly in this study, but rather brute force that brought agrarian change, as if military power could exist in a vacuum quite apart from economic prominence, as if a panoply could somehow guarantee farming success. To other scholars, there is absolutely *no* connection at all between agrarian change at the beginning of the *polis* period and the rise of new military practice, as if fundamental and concomitant changes in military practice and farming—the two most important duties of a Greek—had no connection with each other or the rise of the *polis* itself.

I believe in a much different scenario: the *prior* transformation in agricultural practice (as discussed in Chapters 2 and 3) resulted first in successful economic challenges to traditional aristocratic interests. Then this material evolution of the countryside—from pastoralism and aristocratic control of cereal estates to a network of agrarian city-states surrounded by small farms—gathered force as successful independent farmers framed a new social ethos and political ideology (seen in Chapters 4 and 5). That momentum made possible, even demanded new methods of waging wars over entirely new objectives. It led to the formal creation of hoplite weaponry and finally face-to-face, near-ritual duels between agrarian phalanxes.

In sum, yeomen emerged from the anonymity of the old mass to reinvent the Greek phalanx as the private domain of heavily armed, mutually dependent small farmers. This "invention" of hoplite warfare was not some utopian enterprise, the "construct" of some agrarian conspiracy. Instead imagine its birth far more pragmatically, as the result of one group of agrarians, perhaps first on the island of Euboea or in the Peloponnese at Argos in the late eighth century, reinventing and rearming the "phalanx" and thus finding themselves invincible on the battlefield. Other agricultural communities were also forced to go "hoplite" to defend their property. Soon the entire conglomeration of agrarian *poleis* learned that only a phalanx of armored farmers in careful files could save the honor and property of their respective city-states, once agrarians over the border invaded their territory. The military efficiency of hoplite rectangles and the growing economic and political clout of small parcel owners worked hand in hand to ensure agrarian control of the *polis*.

Currently, the more influential scholarly hypothesis of the social and political environment of early Greek hoplites correctly stresses that the introduction of "hoplite" equipment was a half-century or longer process (i.e., about 725–675 B.C.). Helmets, breastplates, and double-gripped shields gradually began to appear on proto-Corinthian pottery of that period, in private burials, and as votive offerings at the Panhellenic sanctuaries.*

---

*"In this stage there was as yet no crystalized formation or form of tactics; indeed, there was no standardized panoply, either of armour or of offensive weapons" (Snodgrass 1965: 113). For a rejection of social and political change connected with a dramatic hoplite reform, see Snodgrass 1965: 110–116; Snodgrass 1991:18–20; and cf. Snodgrass 1980: 103–4; Greenhalgh 71–74; 151–55.

Greek hoplite equipment was more likely fabricated before, and quite apart from, the tactics of the phalanx. The birth of the Greek phalanx of the *polis*—the formation to which this heavy equipment was ideally suited—in this view, should not necessarily be either simultaneous with, or even necessarily dependent on, hoplite arms and armor. No intrinsic connection need exist between new hoplite weapons and phalanx tactics, separated as they were by many decades.

To support this (*nonagrarian*) interpretation of early Greek military history, it is pointed out that archaeological finds prove the presence of many items of hoplite equipment—helmets, greaves, shield bosses, spear-heads and -butts—in the last quarter of the eighth century, but there is no corresponding pictorial evidence on vases or references in literature to true phalanxes until much later, perhaps not even until 650 B.C. Seventh- and sixth-century Greek vase painting and poetry are the only media in which early phalanxes might appear. Contemporary burials and surface finds cannot shed light on tactical formation. Panoramic temple friezes were rare, and historical writing was simply nonexistent in the seventh century.

How does this theory of initial separation between panoply and phalanx fit into our matrix of agricultural change and the rise of the *polis?* How would the idea apply to the notion of radically new strategies of farming at the end of the eighth century, to the world of Hesiod described in Chapter 3? In this scholarly interpretation, neither weapons nor tactics suddenly changed the status quo of the population in the Greek city-states. New weapons and tactics are not the property of any novel "class." Novel shields, helmets, and breastplates instead reflect throughout the seventh century the continuing influence of traditional propertied and mounted aristocrats. These horse-riding elites gradually incorporate the less well-off farmers to walk alongside themselves to battle. Only slowly are farmers to be equipped with protection and weapons akin to their horse-owning superiors. Military transformation, then, is incremental. It is without radical social repercussions (e.g., Greenhalgh 151–55). Tactics and technology are *not* inseparably related in the early military history of the Greeks.

Others have espoused a so-called sudden change to the Greek phalanx idea, the dramatic and exciting notion of an abrupt social transformation brought on by force of new arms and tactics throughout most of Greece.

This theory takes nearly the opposite view from the "gradualists."* These social historians concentrate on the peculiar shape, the great size, and the considerable weight of the three-foot, double-gripped, concave shield. In their eyes, this new hoplite protective device is tantamount to one of the great revolutionary breakthroughs in Greek history. It is an innovation quite capable of tactical determinism in its own right: "The change was relatively sudden and due *imprimis* to the widespread adoption of what became regarded as the hoplite accouterment *par excellence*, the shield with *porpax* [arm-band] and *antilabe* [hand-grip]" (Cartledge 1977: 20). Its adoption, along with other items of the hoplite panoply, around 700 B.C. could only have signaled an abrupt transformation in Greek infantry fighting itself, since such equipment could be used only in massed formation: any solo fighter with heavy bronze body armor and clumsy shield would be a lumbering, easy target.

According to this school of technological dynamism, new hoplite equipment literally demanded the new tactics of the phalanx (but cf. Cartledge 1977: 20–21). The employment of new arms and formations in turn allowed a new group of Greek revolutionaries (controversy rages about their precise status) militarily to seize control of municipal life, to take over, in other words, the nascent Greek *polis*. This way of thinking, this advocacy of the so-called hoplite reform, gives primacy to force of arms. It oddly does not seem to allow for either the preexisting military expertise of mass fighting or prior agricultural success of its wearers.

To summarize the two schools: the former group of skeptical historians sees gradual changes in Greek battle weaponry (725–675 B.C.), a much later phalanx that follows only around 650 B.C. or after, and no accompanying social revolution caused by either novel weapons or tactics. There was, in these gradualists' opinion, instead a slow evolution of inclusion in early Greece. More and more citizens of the *polis* could afford armor and were thus invited into the phalanx. Perhaps they were even recruited by aristocrats or the very wealthy—men who alone would have had the initial wealth to fabricate arms, who had themselves first devised the phalanx tactics, purportedly seeing at first few social, political, or economic implications or upheavals through massing in column.

---

*Social and economic changes brought on by changes in tactics: Cartledge 1977: 20; Lorimer 76–138; Detienne 1968: 140; Nilsson 240–41, 248.

Agriculture is rarely discussed in this scenario. The impression left is that hoplite fighting had little to do with the rise of Greek yeomanry.

The latter determinist hypothesis argues precisely the opposite. These scholars envision a brilliant breakthrough in technology and tactics. Discovery of the hoplite panoply very quickly in or near 700 B.C. mandated revolutionary phalanx tactics. Both the new hoplite equipment and its proper use in the phalanx are indicative of an undeniable military surge forward. It is the first push of a potent, new landowning class.

There is a problem with both theories which directly affects our interest in the origins of Greek agrarianism. Both schools of scholarly thought postulate that new battle tactics, whether at 700 or 650 B.C., *followed* the adoption of novel equipment. Shield, breastplate, helmet, and spear came first. Fighting in mass followed. Both schools argue in bipolar terms. They either accept or reject a military revolution of the have-nots against the haves. Both schools would not necessarily see hoplite equipment as a reflection of the preexistence of a new agrarianism, already well on its way in the era of Laertes and Hesiod around 700 B.C.

Chronology—difficult to ascertain when our sources are so meager—is crucial to both hypotheses, although in diametrically opposed ways. Both groups of scholars see new hoplite equipment *first*, novel phalanx tactics *second*. They disagree, I think, only on the interval in, and the relationship between, the emergence of the hoplite panoply and the creation of the Greek phalanx.

But on examination there simply is not enough proof in the few contemporary literary and artistic genres available at the time to determine whether the phalanx though unrecorded (or even undetected by us moderns) did not exist earlier (i.e., before or about 675 B.C.). Just because painted vases of the early seventh century do not show the unmistakable presence of opposing Greek phalanxes does not preclude prior fighting in mass. Early proto-Corinthian vase painters may not have had the technical capacity to show such intricate designs, or their painted images of one or two warriors ostensibly dueling may be in fact simply phalanx conventions: the contemporary audience, unlike us historians today, may have known that such representational imagery really stood for massed phalanx warfare.

More important still, there *are* numerous references in Homer's *Iliad* (i.e., about 700 B.C.) to mass fighting of infantry. Recently, many scholars have suggested that these passages are historical and thus must reflect phalanx tactics of some type *before* the complete adoption of the hoplite panoply. That is, Homer, by at least around 725–700 B.C., knew phalanxes to be common military formations in the Greek world, even before their later characteristic hoplite weapons came firmly on the scene.*

Most likely a less rigid style of massed attack had already been present in the eighth century. Earlier mass tactics could have existed apart from formal hoplite equipment. John Salmon in another context puts it more eloquently: "The phalanx was not yet known in its later form; but early phalanx warfare might well have taken a slightly different form without being different in nature. A phalanx has two essential features: its cohesion and its relatively large size; both can be achieved without following the later canonical pattern closely." Later in Greek and Persian history armies mass in column, and they fight as "hoplites" without what is usually termed the hoplite panoply, without "the canonical pattern." It is easy to imagine that earlier Greeks of *all classes* in the late Dark Ages fought in mass with a variety of weaponry and armament, perhaps led on by mounted barons who might themselves seek out and then joust with one another.[2]

If an early Greek phalanx did not require hoplite technology, was the inverse true? Could a man equipped solely with the seventy-pound bronze panoply of the hoplite fight in *any* formation? Could a man in heavy armor battle in small groups or alone outside the phalanx in all sorts of terrain? Consider carefully the particular elements of the hoplite panoply, especially the concave wooden shield. Seventy pounds of arms and armor were difficult to wear and somewhat expensive to fabricate. They were also disadvantageous for fluid fighting and individual combat. The image of a metal-encased pikeman scrambling alone over rocks, darting across a plain in groups of twos and threes, or perched on a massive charger is unconvincing.

Why would mounted duelists or light-armed skirmishers, men who, in this view, *never* fought in mass, suddenly pay for the novel hoplite designs—weapons that were no better (and often a great deal worse) for their looser method of fighting than their current lighter and less expen-

---

*See Latacz 46–49; Pritchett *War* 4.30; Delbrück 1975; but cf. van Wees 1986: 286. On difficulties in realistic artistic portrayal of phalanxes, see Cartledge 1977: 21; Pritchett *War* 4.41; Salmon 1977: 91; cf. d'Agostino 68–70; Ahlberg 49–51.

sive brands? Why would Greeks fabricate weapons disadvantageous to existing methods of combat, weapons whose ideal use was as yet *unknown*? Aristotle at any rate saw that the hoplite panoply had improved existing battle formation and was not viable outside mass tactics: "Without cohesive arrangement (*aneu suntaxeôs*) heavy armament is useless (*achrêston to hoplitikon*)" (*Pol.* 4.1297b20–21). Hoplite weaponry must have been designed precisely for "cohesive arrangement."

The Greek hoplite panoply that emerged at the end of the eighth century offered new advantages to phalanx warfare *alone*. New weaponry must be seen as a specific invention—an agrarian invention—aimed at improving the *preexisting* conditions of massed warfare. Heavy bronze arms are evidence of a technical response to a precise military need. That need was to fight more efficiently in mass as infantry—as Greeks and other peoples *had done for centuries*. Farmers, as all other Greeks, had fought in a phalanx of sorts, but as their numbers and wealth grew, they soon reequipped and redefined it. In the process Greek warfare itself was reinvented in agrarian terms.

Later the hoplite panoply was nearly always connected with massed tactics. The reverse—phalanxes or rather mass conglomerations of infantry always composed of hoplite-equipped warriors—was *not* true. Tactics more often *create*, rather than merely respond to, weaponry.* Is it realistic to suppose that the Greeks created their peculiar hoplite weapons without knowing how to use them in their proper tactical context? Wiser it is to believe that the experienced mass fighters of early Greece simply sought out better tools.

Of the general group of massed infantrymen, by 700 B.C. it was the growing number of *geôrgoi* who now began to have the technology, capital, and desire to acquire improved weaponry. This reshaping of mass attack into ordered phalanx assault was a momentous change. Like farm residence, grafting, the rise of viticulture and arboriculture, and slave labor, it was every bit as important, I think, as the contemporary intellectual ferment of the late eighth and seventh centuries, when the rise of natural inquiry and the creation of philosophy and poetic genres began.

---

*See Hanson 1991: 74–77. For the use of the panoply with massed attack, see Plut. *Phil.* 9; *Flamin.* 8; Paus. 8.50; Xen. *Mem.* 3.9.2; Diod. 23.2.1; cf. Arist. *Pol.* 4.1297b20–25; Eur. *Herac. Fur.* 185ff.

The diversion of bronze from use in aristocratic cauldrons to hoplite armor is a reflection of this across-the-board reordering of Greek values. Metals in Greece were no longer to be used by only the wealthy for decorative and ceremonial utensils. They became the wider property of the agrarian community to protect farmers as they headed into battle.* In some sense, the entire existence of individual expression and philosophical speculation in the newly literate *polis* depended on the ranks of its bronze-clad yeomen.

Consider further that the hoplite's curious "butt spike," the reverse point at the end of his spear, as well as the dramatic concavity of his shield, offered few advantages to men who fought alone or skirmished in small groups. But those two strange pieces of equipment do reflect the needs of men in the middle and rear of a mass formation,. They might now serve phalanx-fighters who often had never engaged the enemy first-hand themselves. These agrarians, who were behind the initial fighting ranks, needed a point on the butt end of their upright spears to slam into the wounded or dazed enemies at their feet, as they trampled over them in their push forward.

The newly created deep concavity of the shield also served the mass of farmers. It allowed these middle and rear hoplites to rest their shield-carrying arms by allowing the shoulder to be tucked under the rim, relieving from the arm sixteen or twenty pounds of weight. As farmers "hung" their concave shields on their shoulders, and pushed into the men ahead, their arms were rested until their turn in the fighting at the front came up. Only then were the fighters required to thrust and parry with both their shields and spears.

Similarly, the hoplite's "backplate"—the rear portion of the bronze cuirass—and the heavy Corinthian helmet (which had no orifices for hearing and nearly curtailed vision) must be seen also as technological improvements to the existing manner of fighting in a confined mass. Many soldiers would not often have confronted the enemy head on, but rather pushed blindly into the backs and sides of comrades ahead. Spear butt, concave shield, and backplate do not protect men in isolation or even men at the head of a column. Instead they are designed for the

---

*See Snodgrass 1980:105–6. The diversion of bronze toward weaponry marked "a technical development of new arms and armour which could not be arrested or ignored" (Holladay 1982: 99).

great majority of fighters in the middle of a phalanx, who push on the backs of comrades ahead, who walk over fallen enemies at their feet, who must maintain the great weight of their shields when no enemy is at their face—those fighters who want something better than their existing arms and armament. The revolution in equipment had in mind not merely the fighters at the front, but the far greater number of men in the middle and rear of the column as well.

This sequence of military development—traditional loosely organized mass fighting made more effective by the introduction of specifically designed weaponry—suggests that the farmers in the ranks were by the end of the eighth century emerging as a group distinct from the landless *and* the elite, striving to change the dynamics of infantry warfare. *Geôrgoi* now were codifying by trial and error, gradually regularizing the battle crashes of the past into more formalized affairs between organized and armed phalanxes of exclusively agricultural heavy infantry. As the numbers, social prestige, and economic security of the middling farmers grew, rich and poor Greeks gradually were pushed off to the sides and rear of the phalanx, to the physical and ideological margins of the battlefield. Codified weaponry of the agrarians helped, along with protocol and custom, to crystallize the rather chaotic mass (and mess) of the past.

Envision earlier Dark-Age warfare as a conglomeration of fighters, armed with spears, javelins, swords, various types of shields, and mostly fabric or composite body armor. Clans would fight generally in massed, but unorganized, attacks. Armament might vary by locale, reflecting the tastes and relative wealth of the particular region. Horses were at a premium (Arist. *Pol.* 4.1289b33–41), and used either to fight with other mounted elites, to lead the loosely defined pack into battle, or to charge into and pursue the throng of pikeless, unarmored serfs.

Is there any reason to believe that the impoverished Greeks—those without any farmland at all—would have the organization or capital to forge hoplite weaponry, and would then arrange themselves into revolutionary bodies of phalanxes, formations designed to battle on and over farmland *they did not own?* If the have-nots had set the military agenda of the city-states, we would expect mountain skirmishing and missile volleys to have been characteristic of Greek warfare as a whole. Mountain passes, I think, would have been closed, not open to the passage of agrarian infantry of the city-state. The lightly clad guerrillas of other contemporary cultures would have struck terror into adversaries, not peculiar farm folk covered in bronze, who were so distinctive and preeminent in song and art.

Through the four hundred years of the *polis* period, the poor never achieved military parity with their social betters. They were in many maritime *poleis* traditionally reduced to rowing in the fleet. In the more numerous landlocked communities without navies, they skirmished as "the naked" or "the light" (*gumnoi, psiloi*) before and after battle when the heavy infantry was not in the killing zone. Only at Athens after the Persian wars did the possession of an oar, rather than a panoply, bring some prestige. That suggests that among most agrarian *poleis* (and at Athens herself until the fifth century) hoplite warfare was never in the interest of the landless, who had little armor and used "slavish" weapons like the javelin, sling, and bow (e.g. Xen. Cyr. 7.4.15).

At the other extreme, was the creation of the hoplite panoply simply a manifestation of traditional aristocratic control? Was it a sign of the continuing power of Dark-Age estate holders who began to wear the new equipment on their horses, and who sought better protection in their private duels and jousts or who served as a privileged mounted hoplite corps at the head of poorer followers (e.g., Snodgrass 1965: 114–15; cf. Salmon 1977: 94–95)? The panoply does not appear to be designed for horsemen. It seems more fitting for infantry in close array, often in great numbers. These heavily protected phalanxes were intrinsically anti-cavalry. They were invulnerable to charges of horsemen. Greek horses lacked the size, power, and armor to crash against a wall of spears. Their aristocratic riders were without stirrups, protruding lances, and the rigorous training of later medieval knights.

Mounted hoplites taxiing to the battlefield only to dismount and join the ranks of similarly clad infantry has the taste of the ceremonial, if not the ridiculous. If an historical occurrence (cf. Detienne 1968: 119–21; d'Agostino 80–82), it was surely only a transitional phase as aristocrats quickly were denied control of phalanx battle altogether (e.g., Arist. *Pol.* 4.1297b18–24). We hear in Greek literature of no new *heavy* cavalry, of no revolutionary mounted, armored aristocratic class in the late eighth or early seventh century who could as cataphracts now tear through the ranks of the unarmored peasantry. The marginalized nature of Greek cavalry suggests that the panoply was originally designed and used for quite different infantry purposes. Early aristocrats (mounted or not) who wore such equipment were at best a transitory phenomenon.

Later on the hoplite class (*zeugitai*) was apparently separated from horsemen (*hippeis* and *pentakosiomedimnoi*) on census rubrics (e.g., Arist. *Ath. Pol.* 7.3–5; Plut. *Sol.* 18.1–2; Poll. *On.* 8.129–32). At Corcyra during the Peloponnesian War hoplites joined the poor and clubbed and stabbed to death the wealthy (Thuc. 4.47). At Athens hoplites were never ideologically akin to the wealthy. Even when authors wish to lump the two groups together in antithesis to the landless who were off the hoplite register (e.g., Thuc. 6.43.1), the rich and farmers are spoken of as *distinct*, rather than identical (e.g., [Xen.] *Ath. Pol.* 1.2; 2.14; cf. Xen. *Hell.* 2.3.48). By the late fifth and fourth centuries there are even complaints that hoplites were not at all rich and were greatly put out by the need to go on campaign (e.g., Dem. 24.11; 21.83; Lys. 16.14). In colonization schemes the wealthy were expressly excluded, the *polis* emphasizing that hoplites and landless *thêtes* alike needed the exclusive opportunity to win new land (e.g., *IG* I³ 46.43–46).

In a strictly military sense, did not the introduction of heavy bronze weaponry by massed infantry seal the fate of horses and consequently the aristocratic horse owner? Land was now permanently to be devoted to the intensified growing of grain, trees, and vines, not left open for mono-cropped cereals or grazing. A diminution of the importance of horses in the city-states is seen clearly in the fifth century, when the wealthy cavalry were more horse prancers before and after the hoplite crash than real chargers. Throughout Greek history, cavalry service was considered unwelcome "elitism." Like bowmen on the other end of the social scale (Hom. *Il.* 2.385–87; Thuc. 4.40), horsemen were often ridiculed and pilloried in Greek literature (e.g., Lys. 16.13, 14.14; cf. Starr 1977: 135–36), as either the pretentious or the timid who chose not to serve with the "mass" (*to plethos*). Even at Sparta, Xenophon, himself a pony man, claims that only the "weakest in strength and the least eager for glory (*hoi tois sômasin adunatôtatoi kai êkista philotimoi*)" mounted horses (*Hell.* 6.4.11). To reassure his hoplites when faced with foreign mounted adversaries, he could scoff that "no one has ever lost his life in battle from the bite or kick of a horse, but it is men who do whatever is done in battle" (Xen. *An.* 3.2.18). At the end of the fifth century, when Xenophon's Greek mercenary hoplite army in Asia was in dire need of cavalry protection, a veteran of the Ten Thousand could ridicule, rather than envy or admire, his mounted commander (*An.* 3.4.47–48).

That dismissive view of cavalry was why the wealthy aristocratic Mantitheos at the battle at the Haliartos River (395 B.C.) chose to face danger as a hoplite, rather than serve "in safety" as a horseman (*tois men hippeuousin asphaleian einai;* Lys. 16.13). In the revolutionary times of late fifth-century Athens, it is interesting that hoplite landowners, for all their supposed conservative sympathy with reactionary and wealthy aristocrats, never joined attacks against the democracy for long.* Athenian elite right-wing revolutionaries were usually cavalrymen (Xen. *Hell.* 2.4.2–7, 2.4.24–27, 2.4.31–32; 3.1.4; Arist. *Ath. Pol.* 38.2), who often expelled hoplites from their small farms (e.g., Xen. *Hell.* 2.4.1). The mounted warriors ubiquitous on Greek vases of the sixth century (Greenhalgh 84–145) were adopters, not originators of the hoplite panoply.

Praise for mounted troops in Greek literature usually springs from envy of their wealth and their exalted economic status as horse raisers, not from any perceived value to the *polis* of their military contribution— which, despite recent scholarly revisionism, was normally relatively marginal. The Greek *polis* was one of the few societies in the long history of Western civilization where horsemen, and the entire accompanying elite culture of horse raising, were deliberately relegated to minor roles in formal infantry warfare, once more reflecting the Dark-Age demise of the livestock monopoly and the rise of a more productive farming majority.

This chauvinism of the earlier hoplite is *not* to say that later on when Greek armies were confronted by foreign challenges, or ventured overseas in difficult terrain, cavalry and archers were not vital to the preservation of infantry. Should the protective mechanism of agrarian protocol be left behind in Greece, real support against nonagrarian hillmen, skirmishers, slingers, and archers was needed for the vulnerable phalanx. My point is not to deny that horsemen and missile troops—through

---

*See Markle 158–59; de Ste. Croix 1981: 292; A. J. Holladay 1982: 103. Of fifth-century Athens, Anthony Andrewes observes: "The noticeable social gulf here was rather between the middle class and the really rich, roughly the division between hoplites and the cavalry" (1971: 232)—a sentiment anticipated by Aristotle in his *Politics* (4.1289b35–40), who remarked that "it is not an easy thing to raise horses unless one is rich"

their mobility, speed, rates of fire, and power—enhanced infantry, but simply to assert that in Greece proper, until the Peloponnesian War, landed infantrymen developed a "system" that deliberately made missiles and mounted warriors incidental to success in battle. The system reflected contemporary social, economic, and political aspects of agrarianism.[3]

Later, as Greek hoplites and mercenaries ventured into Asia Minor, Italy, and the East beyond the protection and protocols of the old agrarian *poleis*, horsemen and archers became essential (and reflected the reemergence of a powerful and wealthy elite, a growing underclass, and the corresponding decline of an agrarian middle). But these subsequent developments only highlight just how unusual were the circumstances in Greece during the few centuries of agrarian infantry dominance. Then the occasion, terrain, status, armament, and tactics of interstate warfare followed a prescribed agenda. It is no accident that cavalry and skirmishers, slingers, and archers—valuable military assets entirely antithetical to yeoman infantry—came either from the two extremes of *polis* society or from outside the Greek city-state altogether.

As Aristotle in retrospect saw (*Pol.* 4.1297b16–24, 28), at the beginning of the *polis* the decline of both skirmishers and cavalry left the *mesoi*, the middling landowners, as both the wearers and beneficiaries of hoplite armor: "And indeed the earliest form of government among the Greeks after monarchy was composed of those who actually fought. In the beginning that meant cavalry, since without cohesive arrangement, heavy armament is useless; and experience and tactical knowledge of these hoplitic systems did not exist in ancient times, and so power again lay with mounted horsemen. But once the *poleis* grew and those with hoplite armor became stronger, more people shared in government."

Aristotle depicts a sequence where wearers of hoplite armor *refine* (rather than invent) the mass (already on the scene, but "without cohesive arrangement" and void of hoplitic "experience and knowledge"). Infantrymen use their armor and tactics to enhance (not to establish *ex nihilo*) their rising status within the *polis* (cf. Salmon 1977: 95). In the later Greek history of the sixth, fifth, and fourth centuries, the fighters of the phalanx were always associated with the landed class of small farmers (e.g., [Arist] *Oec.* 1.1343b2–7). There is no reason to suppose that conditions were different at the very inception of such weaponry at the end of the eighth century.

So the "hoplite reform" was not quite a reform in a tactical sense. Call it instead a "hoplite reflection" or even a "hoplite acceleration"—military transformation as illustrative of ongoing changes in the economy of the Greek world. Strictly speaking, the appearance of standardized weaponry at the end of the eighth century was not a grab for agrarian power, but a shield to protect that power. It was the technology, not the tactics *per se*, that was new. Dark-Age soldiers had fought loosely in mass formation for many years in ancient Greece, in most cases under the direction of aristocratic leaders and clansmen. Gradually the spread of diversified, intensified farming created a shared ideology of new landowners, men in the ranks who no doubt had begun to accumulate capital from their farming success. With the same ingenuity by which they devised new approaches to traditional land use, the planters of trees and vines began to fabricate bronze weaponry to improve their performance in the traditional mêlée of Greek battle.

At first hoplite armies would have been relatively small and made up of the more successful yeomen. As agrarianism spread ("once the *poleis* grew and the wearers of heavy armor became stronger" [Arist. *Pol.* 4.1297b23–24]), the tactics and strategy of Greek mass warfare itself— as Aristotle also saw—were transformed, not always by deliberate attempts to attack the wealthy aristocrats, but rather more often by success that made the wealthy somewhat irrelevant in the *polis*. Hoplite martial prowess made both the wealthy with horses and the poor with missile weapons odd men out in the newly reformulated "mass." That body was to follow agricultural rules and protocols, which were now to ensure the growing control of an agrarian middle (Arist. *Pol.* 4.1297b24–25), the city-state's "constitution of hoplites" (Nilsson 246–47). Although neither horsemen nor archers could ever stop a Greek phalanx, their presence in considerable number in combined operations could still complicate and sidetrack the quick resolution of a purely infantry collision. No wonder they were to be discouraged whenever possible in formal wars between Greek agrarian infantry.

For the first time in the history of the West, shock fighting took on social and economic implications. One group of particular combatants in their new armor soon dominated the battlefield. The reconstituted "hoplite phalanx" was thus the old Dark-Age wine in new agrarian flasks. In the period innovative agricultural strategies were gaining momentum—

tree and vine grafting, homestead residence, slave labor, diversified crops, incorporation of marginal land, on-the-farm storage and processing—farmers also sought to consolidate, reaffirm, and accelerate their efforts at agrarian government through a radical remaking of traditional Greek mass warfare. Infantrymen, for one of the few times in the annals of military history, were absolute architects of their society's military doctrine.

They applied their grid mentality of property holding to the old pack of Greek fighters, creating neat files and columns (i.e. Aristotle's "cohesive formation" [*suntaxis*], "experience" [*empeiria*], and "tactical knowledge" [*taxis tôn toioutôn*]). There was to be a new phalanx, with all the farmers absolutely equidistant from one another, completely dependent on the shields of others, and identically armed. A checkerboard of near identical farmers there was to be in the countryside, on the battlefield, and in the council hall. From that agrarian phalanx evolved an entire protective mechanism of rules and practices that ensured the importance of *geôrgoi* in the nascent community for nearly three centuries. In short: "The Greek *polis* in its characteristic form is not imaginable without the hoplite army" (Nilsson 245).

Although at some city-states tyrants at the head of a phalanx could bring about a dramatic end to old aristocracies, as we have seen in Chapter 3, more often they simply were not needed. Farmers themselves, through their own agricultural expertise and agrarian ideology, had ensured their economic, political, and military superiority. The transformation to broad-based timocracy and agrarian democracy was far more frequently accomplished without the aid of a strongman.

The hoplite appropriation of the old motley phalanx guaranteed that for at least the next three centuries Greek farmers would not be summarily mustered for extensive campaigns of aggressive despots. They would not face forced conscriptions. They would not pay property taxes on their land for the construction of military engines and mass armories. They would not allow military technology to siphon off agrarian capital. They would not provide percentages of their harvests to support an extensive caste of professional generals, standing armies, or military dynasties.

Some have argued against this agrarian genesis of hoplite battle. The doyen of Greek military archaeology, A. M. Snodgrass (1965: 114–15), once felt that farmers "would have no vested interest in war; on the contrary, it would be a double menace to their property, possibly leading to its devastation and certainly requiring their own absence from it." But the point was not a choice to have war or not have it. The dilemma is to determine who is to control, who is to decide, who is to wage the inevitable organized killing—a phenomenon not parenthetical, but, as the Greeks knew during the lifetime of the *polis*, innate to human society (e.g., Pl. *Leg.* 1.626A; Heracl. fr. 53; Anon. fr. 846 Kock).

Almost any other form of conflict was more inimical to farmers' interests than hoplite battle. "Should we not reject any suggestion," Yvon Garlan writes, "that a mode of combat is nothing but a fortuitous combination of autonomous, heterogeneous forces, technical, economic, social, and political?" (Garlan 1975: 125). War must be legislated (as history teaches us) if destruction of property and person is to be curtailed, held within "reasonable" limits so the culture can survive. If not the farmers of ancient Greece, who then should determine when, where, and how agrarian men were to fight, to kill, and to die? The wide-open Hellenistic age of great navies, mercenaries, artillery, siegecraft, heavy cavalry, missile troops, and light-armed professionals—the period when hoplite monopoly of warfare was broken and far more nonfarmers perished—did not enhance the status of independent and small food producers, but rather eroded it.

For one of a very few times in history, during the Greek *polis* period military conscription was not a club that the wealthy used to beat down the rural populace in order to further their own interests in private squabbles or overseas extravaganzas. Hoplite armies served no master but themselves. That notion of citizen control over the military and private control of arms is—along with decisive battle, constitutional government, private land ownership, and notions of egalitarianism—yet another important legacy of Greek agrarianism of the *polis*.

No wonder Aristotle in his *Politics* equated hoplite militias with the very success of the city-state: "a *polis* that sends out great numbers of base men (*banausoi*), but few hoplites (*hoplitai*) is incapable of being great (*megalê*). For a great *polis* is not the same thing as one with a large population" (*Pol.* 7.1326a23–25). Aristotle, who best of all ancient thinkers understood the equation between yeomanry, constitutional government, and hoplite warfare, felt the agricultural class was the best population, and, once armed, it alone made the *polis* "great." No wonder, "originally only the heavy-armed hoplite was the true citizen soldier" (Ehrenberg 1951: 300).

"Throughout Greek history," Paul Guiraud writes, "the relationships between peoples frequently depended on the status of territory and the requirements of the agricultural class" (Guiraud 615). But agrarian control over politics and warfare came at a price: farmers, after all, who for their own militarily sound reasons had excluded others from the battlefield, must themselves then take on the sole risks of killing and dying. After the creation of the hoplite panoply, for nearly two and a half centuries (700–480 B.C.) hoplite battle *was* Greek warfare. Small farmers altered all organized killing between city-states in their own image and thus protected their creation of Greek agrarianism.

I am not suggesting that hoplite warfare was absolutely predetermined in some unspoken Panhellenic fashion, that it grew out of mutual and near-conspiratorial efforts of farmers in all Greek *poleis* to form consciously a private agricultural monopoly that excluded the marginalized (e.g., foreigners, slaves, women, and the poor)—although the result of agrarian battle was to do precisely that. Armies are formed to fight. They are not models. They are designed to conquer their foes. And so they reflect first of all the particular interests and skills of their own citizenry. Imagine, then, a more haphazard hoplite genesis: a few early Greek agrarian city-states fielding superior troops of newly armed hoplite infantry as part of an effort to gobble up some borderland of their neighbors. Because no other tactical formation, no other military armament, no other method of group muster could withstand a hoplite phalanx— given the terrain and the existing social and economic realities of an ascending Greek agrarianism—all other Greek *poleis* were forced either to adopt hoplite warfare (i.e., rearm and reorder their mass attacks) or to submit to terms if they were to protect the integrity of their hard-won patchwork.

This military reality cemented the economic and political dominion of small farmers as hoplite battle became Greek warfare. Hoplite phalanxes spread because they were unstoppable on the battlefield, and tactical manipulation, ambush, and surprise were—and are—difficult enterprises. But the composition of the ranks and the choice of the killing field was determined by an underlying agrarian mentality, which in the beginning was prerequisite for cohesive heavy infantry.

There are no real detailed Greek prose accounts of hoplite battle in the two centuries before the battle of Marathon (490 B.C.). Fighting in Homer and in early lyric and elegy can appear ambiguous and difficult to place in a precise chronology and locale (although recent scholarship is more confident about the presence of massed fighting of phalanxes in these sources). The extant remains of early bronze panoplies, however, are numerous. The later Greeks themselves also believed that phalanx warfare had a long tradition before the fifth century; and anecdotal accounts of apparent hoplite battles of the seventh and sixth centuries abound in Greek literature. It is incorrect, then, to believe that land warfare before the fifth century is obscure and inaccessible to generalization.

Nearly all Greek landowners were heavy infantrymen, or *hoplites;* most hoplites of the early phalanx were in turn landowners. The agrarian nature of hoplite warfare is a fact assumed throughout Greek literature. "It is often the case," Aristotle could still say at the end of the fourth century, when mercenary armies were on the rise and the census rubrics of the old agrarian *polis* were often neglected, "that the same men are to be both hoplites and farmers (*hopliteuein kai geôrgein symbainei tois autois pollakis*)" (Pol. 4.1291a31–33; cf. 4.1297b15–28). Both he and Plato seem to treat as either utopian or outside the culture of the Greek *polis* (i.e., at Sparta, Crete, Thessaly) the strange idea that those who actually work the soil themselves and those who fight should be *different* groups.[4]

Most revealingly, at the very beginning of the Greek *polis*, the hero Odysseus knows well the normative synergism between fighting and farming (e.g., Hom. *Od.* 18.366–86). Naturally, then, he must reject that ethic when he lies that he is from Crete, an area of the Greek world that never completely adopted city-state culture (Hom. *Od.* 14.216–29). The late fourth-century Athenian ephebes, young warriors who took up the shield and spear to patrol the countryside, still swore to protect "the wheat, the barley, the vines, the olives, and the figs" (Tod 2. 204). Xenophon felt there was always an intrinsic historical relationship between farming and the cohesion of the phalanx: "Farming teaches one how to help others. For in fighting one's enemies, just as in working the soil, it is necessary to have the assistance of other people" (Xen. *Oec.* 5.14). He adds that because farmers are in top shape, mentally as well as physically, once attacked they should go on the offensive as well—ravaging the similar farmlands of their oppressors (*Oec.* 5.13). Here Xenophon makes the direct connection between their wartime gear (*hopla*) and their peacetime farming implements (*geôrgika organa*). They are the private tools the agrarian uses to work and to protect his property. Just as the hoplite commander exhorts his infantry, so too, Xenophon says, the farmer directs the slaves who work beside him (*Oec.* 5.16).

On the other hand, craftsmen and nonagrarians reputedly made poor soldiers (e.g., Xen. *Oec.* 4.3). In Euripides' lost play *Antiope*, the tough rural Zethos is made to rebuke his more refined, musician brother Amphion for his ignorance of farming and fighting. "You wouldn't know what to do with a shield," he says in disgust to his nonfarming sibling (fr. 185 Nauck). His implication is that only those who farm really know how to fight. At some agrarian regimes craftsmen were shut out of political and military life entirely (Arist. *Pol.* 3.1278a25–26; 6.1321a29–33). Later I shall suggest that the eventual inclusion of these nonfarmers in the phalanx was symptomatic of the decline of the agrarian *polis* itself.

In Aristophanes' *Peace*, the craftsmen sell the *geôrgoi* swords, spears, and shields as well as pitchforks and agricultural implements; they needed both (*Pax* 545–53). The farmers thank the goddess Peace, who has taken away their "helmet-crests and Gorgon-emblemed shields," allowing them instead to go back to their farms with "spades and mattocks" (560–65). When the comic poet later wishes to ridicule the utter uselessness of hoplite weaponry during peacetime, Aristophanes conjures up agricultural metaphors: spears as vine-poles and trumpets as weight-scales for figs (*Pax* 1245–65), the traditional "swords to ploughshares" metaphors of agrarian infantry.

Understandably much of the battle parlance of the Greek phalanx—"horns" of "yoked" men who "threshed it out"—came from agriculture or rural life, not urban experience (Tyrt. 19.16; cf. Pritchett *War* 2.190; Whitehead 1981: 282–86, and Colum. *Rust. Praef.* 1.13–15). Indeed, "phalanx" itself, denoting the ranks of heavy infantry in battle order, probably derived from the Greek word for "beam" or "log," a logical assumption if most of its fighters lived in the country. In an anonymous comic fragment there is the natural military image of a "division of farmers" (*hê tôn geôrgôn taxis*; Anon fr. 382.2 Kock). And men who went out to work the fields could most naturally be compared to an army on the move (Plut. *Mor.*175A).

It was this unique symbiosis between agriculture and warfare that explains why Greek authors often commented on the productive potential of farmland *not* in terms of soil, arability, or mere size, but simply by the number of hoplite infantry a region might theoretically support (e.g. Arist. *Pol.* 1270a17–32; Plut. *Mor.* 413F-414A; cf. *FGrH* 115 fr. 225; Dem. 23.199). In Greek eyes, the land alone produced infantry.*

For nearly three centuries of the *polis* period (700–400 B.C.) the two ideas of heavy infantry and land ownership were in the majority of Greek city-states inseparable, tied inextricably in a material, logistical, geographical, tactical, strategic, and ethical sense to the lifeblood of the *polis*. Seldom at this time do we hear that phalanxes are to protect the walls or the houses of a *polis*. Never do we read that craftsmen, potters, and shoemakers make the most effective fighters or that the best armies simply derive from the most populous city-states.

II.

Just as in Chapter 4 we saw the pragmatic challenges confronting the intensive farmer at peace, we must now look at how these same farmers preserved their culture on the battlefield, how they reconstituted Greek warfare, and so learn just how steep was the price of their agrarianism. The field of the *geôrgos* was a far different place than the interior of a phalanx. But that military formation reveals the same characteristics of the new agrarian mentality, the same patience, the same self- and group-reliance, the same muscular strength and steely nerve shown by the planters of trees and vines. If in peace the Greek *polis* was an *agrotopia* for like-minded equals, in war it became a *thanatopia* of similarly armed hoplites massed in column.

Materially, the hoplite panoply, as we have seen, was crudely simple. Each farmer supplied from the wealth of his small farm his own breastplate, helmet, spear, shield, greaves, and short sword, some seventy pounds of wood, bronze and iron—half his own body weight, load

---

*When Plato complains in his *Republic* about the lack of military training among the armies of the Greek city-states, he first of all centers his criticism on the traditional amateur status of yeomanry: "Is it so easy" he sarcastically asks, "that one who is working the soil can at the same time also be a soldier?" (Pl. *Resp.* 2.374C).

enough to exhaust a man, even a hardworking man, in less than an hour. The ensemble probably cost 100 drachmas, about the price of an agricultural slave. Imagine slave and panoply as the two essential military possessions of every Greek *geôrgos*. In Greek literature and from the evidence of extant panoplies, three elements ring true about the equipment: that it was unwieldy, even damaging to its wearer; that its use ostensibly required little practice or professional skill; and that it offered superior protection.

Xenophon's Socrates is made to say of the breastplate, "a wonderful invention," but then he learns from Pistias the armorer that it is very difficult to achieve "a good fit," one whose weight is to be properly distributed over "the collar-bone, shoulder-blades, shoulders, chest, back and belly" (*Mem.* 3.10.9–14). The shield had to fit the arm length and body size of the wearer (e.g., Xen. *Mem.* 3.10.12). There are plenty of occasions in Greek literature where it simply flies off the arm of the hoplite, given its awkward size and cumbersome weight (Hanson 1989: 65–71). "Large shields," the Greeks knew, "made infantry slow to move" (Diod. 15.44).

Both the importance of the shield (e.g., Plut. *Mor.* 220A) and its absurd size and shape made it the general trademark of hoplite warfare itself. The word "hoplite" was derived from *hoplon*, another name for *aspis*, the round, concave shield. The depth of the phalanx was calibrated not by "men" or "spears" or "swords," but almost always as "shields" in depth (e.g., Xen. *Hell.* 6.4.12). No wonder the distinguishing mark of heavy infantry was a shield (Pl. *Leg.* 6.756A), which additionally suggests, as we will see, that the mentality of the hoplite was largely defensive, not offensive.

Bronze armor, without recourse to ventilation under the Mediterranean sun, without orifices for hearing, without interior padding to cushion the shock of deadly blows to the head, was designed solely to allow the hoplite to reach his opponent and deliver death or mayhem to the man at his face, all within the space of a few minutes. Hoplite armament was simply agrarian pragmatism—like the leather protection of old Laertes—in its most lethal manifestation. Offensive weaponry—the spear mostly—required little expertise ("There was little chance," Xenophon's Cyrus dryly remarked, "of missing a blow" [*Cyr.* 2.1.16–18]). Polybius seems to agree when he points out in his famous comparison between the Roman legion and the later Macedonian phalanx that each legionary had to face ten spearpoints protruding from the ranks (18.30.3). The problem for the killing apparatus of the phalanx was always too much supply (of the competing spear thrusts) for the limited demand (of front-rank targets).

Despite the frequent breakage of the spear and cracking of the wooden shield, most of the hoplite's equipment was durable and reliable in combat. There was little room inside the phalanx to employ anything like the battle-ax, halberd, or long sword.* Armored farmers were simply "pole-men," whose muscle rather than technique was key. All motion in the phalanx was frontal, not lateral. This preference for the spears—clumsy and nearly useless for the soloist, but for synchronized companions an invincible wall—is significant: the spear's use for the Greek, as for the Swiss, implies military cohesion; cohesion reflects social unity, and unity an individual like-interest. The hand-held lance, not the bow, not the horse, not the sling, was until the appearance of mass-produced firearms a lasting trademark of yeoman infantry: if Greek farmers could achieve the unity and cohesion of massed columns, on the battlefield they inevitably found unmatched power in their wall of razor-sharp poles.

For nearly all of the farmer's life, his defensive and offensive weaponry was of little utilitarian value on his plot. It was essentially worthless for hunting. The panoply was absurdly inappropriate against the trespasser or nighttime renegade. Unlike the frontiersman's flintlock, the hoplite's breastplate and spear nearly always collected soot over the hearth, seeing little or no peacetime action (Ar. *Ach.* 279). Aristophanes says that in periods of peace, the great round shield could just as well serve as a lid for the farmer's well (fr. 295 Kock). Less kindly, he joked that the breastplate doubled as a chamber pot, helmets as medicine boxes, spears as vine-poles, and trumpets as scales (*Pax* 1228, 1249, 1254, 1261).

But once donned in the hour of battle, the hated panoply was well worth its cost, for it often saved the life of the farmer. Even if the shield

---

*For shield breakage, see Hanson 1989: 65–88; and for broken spears, cf. the numerous examples on the C-painter (e.g., Hackett 75). On the absence of ax and halbert in the phalanx, see Anderson 1991: 25.

was penetrated, the two to ten millimeters of the hoplite's bronze breast-plate ensured safety from nearly any projectile (Gabriel and Metz 58–71; Hanson 1989: 70–71), ensuring that, unless a man lost his arm, leg, face, or head he could get in close to wreak havoc and push back his foe.

A chief drawback to the panoply's use was simply carrying the monstrosity into battle, for the ensemble equaled nearly half a man's weight (see Hanson 1991b: 78 n.1), and was awkward—bothersome in shape and design, not easily transported unless worn, not worn easily for more than a few hours without exhaustion. No wonder Euripides remarks that "the hoplite is a slave to his equipment" (Eur. *HF* 188). At the battle of Nemea (394 B.C.), where nearly fifty thousand hoplites may have collided (cf. Lazenby 1985: 128–29, 136), imagine that *nearly eighteen hundred tons* of bronze weaponry were needed just to allow the fighting to proceed, the tools of the killing trade themselves a monumental problem in logistics.

The infantryman brought along his slave to carry his weapons—easy for one accustomed to the backbreaking job of digging around vines—until nearly the last second before his charge. Servile labor in Greece thus was not merely a sign of intensive agriculture, but an indication of "intensive" battle as well. Incidentally, those scholars who deny the presence of slave labor on the small farms of ancient Greece, claiming that agriculture could not keep servants continuously employed, often overlook their essential presence on the Greek battlefield. They are obliged to find ample reference in Greek literature that hoplite attendants, if not slaves, were hired workers or male underaged kin.

One could argue that without slave attendants to carry the hoplite's cumbersome panoply, war between phalanxes would never have taken place, farmers would have not reached the battlefield, and the whole agrarian element in Greek warfare would never have originated. To the Greeks it was a sign of a radical change in war making, of growing distance from landed militias, when any army carried its own provisions and arms. Philip's mobile professionals in the Macedonian phalanx, who marched with reduced armor and without individual attendants (e.g., Front. *Str.* 4.1.6; Polyaen. *Str.* 4.2.10), presented an unusual—and terrifying—challenge to parochial defenders of the *polis*.

The advantages and the drawbacks of the hoplite panoply can only be understood as a reflection of the peculiar ideology of its wearer—an ideology at its inception almost exclusively agrarian (see Hanson 1991: 3–11). Hoplite weaponry's great size and weight reflected the notion that infantry battle was to be decisive—that is, short and brutal for all involved. This idea is in perfect harmony with the farmer's general disgust for inaction and nuance, for protracted quarreling and continual haggling, for a view of the natural world largely shaded gray, not black and white. For the agrarian pragmatist, it was better to use his own hands to kill face-to-face, without guile, without delay.

Interruption of the hoplite's summertime harvests was thus deliberately brief. Like his farm's prosperity, success in war now depended largely on his own muscular strength and unshakable nerve, not on time wasted away from crops in mastering the bow or sling, not on following protocols devised by others—i.e., the more wealthy without empathy for agrarian ideology. Xenophon in his *Oeconomicus* argues that the artisans who master a craft and live inside the *polis* are more cowardly folk than the farmer. In times of war they would simply vote to stay inside the walls and not risk any danger at all (*Oec.* 6.6–8).

To impatient militiamen nothing was as crucial as the short campaign. Take a man away from his land for years on end—as the later Roman experience shows (e.g., Wolf 66–67)—and the entire agrarian structure of the community crumbles. Others left behind with much different views about landowning fill the political void. Changes occur in the economical management of absentee plots, while the professionalized army increasingly shows itself bent on overseas conquest, a notion entirely antithetical to an amateur agrarian militia. The weight and difficulty of the panoply *did* serve the interests of farmers. Physically, hoplite armor sharply limited the ambit of war and the type of man who could endure such a burden. It is no surprise that in the new war making of the fourth century and later Hellenistic era, the panoply was severely reduced, as both space and time, terrain and recruitment, expanded enormously beyond the realm of agriculture. Battle, like the size of agricultural property, became much larger—and more lethal to the old idea of a *polis*.

Although the cost of hoplite weapons has often been exaggerated, their composition and construction in the first two and a half centuries of the *polis* did reflect an expense beyond the means of the slinger, stone thrower, javelin carrier, archer, or light-armed skirmisher, men who likewise needed extensive training and time to master the accurate delivery of airborne projectiles. Even if poorer men might acquire heavy weaponry, they were usually bereft of slave-attendants, and thus would be exhausted carrying their own provisions and panoply, struggling to keep up with their agricultural betters. The possession of burdensome weapons, and the accompanying invulnerability of men so equipped in mass, surely were signs of a larger hoplite snobbery as well. The landless and the less affluent Greeks could not afford heavy armor. They could not engage as meaningful combatants, and could thus have less say—as Aristotle saw (*Pol.* 4.1297b23; *Ath. Pol.* 4.2–4)—in the management of the *polis* itself.

Greek battle gear was simply the wartime reflection of a yeoman's plot. Both were beyond the reach of the poor, both nearly uniform-sized possessions of a larger matrix of kindred agrarians, both requiring back-breaking toil ill-suited to nonfarmers. If the countryside was to be a patchwork of roughly similar farms worked by leather-clad yeomen, the phalanx was an analogous grid of identically bronze-clothed fighters. Whether a farmer looked over at his neighbor's plot, or over at the man next to him in battle, or over at the agriculturalist seated next to him in the assembly, the unique egalitarianism of the agrarian *polis* was continually reemphasized and enhanced.

There was, as we have seen at the beginning of the city-state, also a growing disinclination for cavalry. Horses—ponies or nags is a more appropriate description, given their small size—required too much upkeep for all but the richest (e.g., Davies 1971: xxv–xxvi). The encroachment of farms made the grazing space around most Greek *poleis* precious. In any case, yeomen preferred more economical slaves and oxen for their own agricultural work. Rich mounted warriors could do little anyway against the raised pikes of armored infantry ranks. At Plataea (479 B.C.) not many more than three hundred Athenian hoplites for a while stood off repeated attacks of thousands of Persian cavalry (Hdt. 9.21–23) who, despite their ferocity and numerical superiority, could neither easily bowl them over nor break into their sea of spear tips. The absence of large breeds of war-horses, stirrups, and plentiful grazing land—the usual assets of the later terrifying knight—all allowed the Greek agrarian hoplite to enforce his own brand of chauvinism. For that price of military and political exclusivity, small farmers of all ages everywhere were willing to acquire strange weapons, to form ranks side-by-side, to endure a bitter but brief killing spree, to spend an afternoon entombed nearly insensate in bronze, battered by brief but furious storms of enemy iron.

The key to this ideology of the yeoman hoplite was, like his clear title to his own plot, his private ownership of these peculiar arms (e.g., *IG* I³ 1.9–11). Not only were military exclusivity and social prestige ensured for "those providing their own arms (*hoi kektêmenoi ta hopla*)" (e.g., Arist. *Pol.* 3.1279b4–5; cf. 7.1329b37–38), but more important, until the fifth century, the state normally did not stockpile shields, spears, and panoplies or create armories. That absence of an early *polis* hoard of weaponry meant campaigning was under the control of agrarian councils (e.g., *IG* I³ 105.34–35). They alone had the *physical* mechanisms to fight. The rise of public ownership of arms and armor in the fourth century and later—equipment far more varied, expensive, and sophisticated than the near obsolete seventy-pound panoply—along with the growth of skirmishers and mercenaries, *was entirely anti-agrarian.* It contributed in no small measure to the decline of the hoplitic code—and thus of the agricultural *polis* itself. Before the fourth century, owners of their own panoply are synonymous with owners of farmland, synonymous with the citizenry itself.

Classical scholars have occasionally branded the hoplite ideology as "elitist." They are correct if they mean exclusive. They are far off the mark if (as I suspect) they mean an engine of privilege. "Elitist" in that sense rings false for *mesoi* farmers, yeomen who did their own work, who sought constitutional, rather than hereditary, government, who had no love for the aristocratic horse breeders above them, and who were not at all members of that leisured and liturgical class.

Military historians, I think, should be wary of intruding the old dichotomous class struggle—poor/rich, mass/elite, exploited/exploiter, powerless/powerful—into the sociology of Greek *polis* warfare. Why not brand hoplite warfare for what it really was: the military reflection of the origin of European agrarianism, the genesis of a broad-based and entirely novel yeomanry, one neither wealthy or poor, in its pure form the private property of *geôrgoi, mesoi, autourgoi,* and *zeugitai*—all various names for the agrarian middle?

Logistically, it was critical that the farmer-hoplite fight in person, briefly and decisively on the battlefield, free from obstacles and encumbrances (cf. Ober 1991: 173–79). That way he would neither squander his year's produce nor surrender control over the conduct of war to a professional corps of besiegers, artillery officers, wagon masters, field engineers, and other support staff. The elevation of nonfighters could have destroyed the amateurism of Greek battle (Anderson 1970: 44–53; Hanson 1983: 74–75), because they are inevitably organized by, and feel loyalty to, the few wealthy men on top. Costly distant campaigning, drawn-out sieges, and elaborate fortifications were frowned upon until the tragedy of the Peloponnesian War; they are remarkably absent from Greek fighting before the late fifth century.

The entire idea of a walled *polis* was one many Greeks were never entirely comfortable with (Arist. *Pol.* 7.1330b33–1331a19; Pl. *Leg.* 6.778D-779B; Plut. *Mor.* 190A; 210E27; 212E; 215D; 221F6). Military architecture shifted the Greek mind from pitched battle on and over farmland into the complex world of elaborate fortification, military professionalism, and accompanying high taxes. Extension and elaboration of war making were in the agrarian hoplite's mind the unpalatable preference of men who wished to fight year-round. They sought to decide battle through technology, machinery, and sheer numbers rather than with nerve and bodily power, to venture on some extended *anabasis* in search of glory and gold, to kill rather than to farm, to stay abroad rather than to return to the *polis* of their birth, to import food from overseas rather than to grow it at home.

Thucydides' Pericles summed up well the parsimony of agrarian ideology: "Yeomen farmers (*autourgoi*) are a class of men that are always more willing to serve in person than with money; confident that they will survive battle, they are not at all convinced that their own money will not prematurely run out" (Thuc. 1.141.5). Sensitive to this reluctance of farmers to muster for distant expeditions, over half a century later Demosthenes tried to persuade the Athenians to march out to prevent the Macedonian conquest of Olynthus. He was still forced to acknowledge in the twilight of Greek agrarianism that "if you yourselves were forced to serve abroad for thirty days, and you took from our countryside the supplies needed for the campaign, I suppose that the farmers (*tous geôrgountas*) among you would lose more than you spent on the entire previous war" (1.27). Hoplite warfare was delimited by the harvest requirements of its armies of farmers, restricted usually to the late spring or summer, just after grain reaping, but before grape and olive picking, when the countryside was dry, and passes free of mud and snow (e.g., Dem. 9.48–50; Hanson 1983: 30–35; 43–44, 137–51).

Nor was there either a real science of siegecraft, *poliorcetics* (literally "*polis*-works"), the traditional nightmare of the logistician, in Greece before the fifth century, or artillery before the fourth. Unlike the engineer, the artillery technician, the paid mercenary, or the rower in the fleet, each Greek infantryman brought his own rations—usually a mere three days' supply (Plut. *Mor.* 349A; Ar. *Ach.* 197; *Pax* 312; *Vesp* 243; cf. Pritchett *War* 1.32–44)—carried by his own transport, the slave from his small farm. A small flock of sheep or goats usually followed the army, not so much for meat rations while on the campaign, but rather for the knife across the jugular for intermittent sacrifice and augury (e.g., Paus. 9.13.4–5; e.g., Jameson 1991: 198–99). We see here agrarian individualism at the core of early Greek warfare: private slave, private arms, private food. All ensured farmers' control over the apparatus of war making and made the appropriation of monies from the countryside unnecessary.

Paths through the mountains of Greece were rarely garrisoned (Ober 1991: 174–75). For enemy farmers or hired poor to guard them would require time and extensive provisions (and was not really militarily feasible), and so defeat the purpose of decisive battle. Conflict would be prolonged into a series of random hit-and-run skirmishes: indistinguishable, unheroic, and unheralded killing in the high crags far from home. A bronzed hoplite would be shamed into lumbering by himself over rocks and gullies to dodge missiles and arrows from his more nimble social inferiors. No wonder that occasional guarding of passes in the fifth century (see de Ste Croix 1972: 106–47, 192–94; Hanson 1983: 74–85), with good hoplite infantry slaughtered in the trees and hills by their social subordinates, brought a rare burst of emotion from the otherwise somber Thucydides. Of the Athenian hoplites who were butchered in the mountains of Aetolia during the Peloponnesian War, he wrote: "They were many and all in the prime of life, the best men (*beltistoi andres*) that the city of Athens lost in the war" (Thuc. 3.98.4): brave men forced into the wrong place at the wrong time.

In contrast, the hoplites' ideal battlefield was easily accessible right across the border: a day's march out, a day's fighting, and a day's trek home. It has been suggested that Greek city-states sometimes reciprocally made roads—many of them still observable—that led right up to their borders to facilitate movement of phalanxes between territories. This network was not foolishness. Communities of small farmers strived to ensure that disputes could take place, not avoided, and hence be settled quickly and decisively by pitched battles (Ober 1991: 179; cf. Vanderpool 237–40). In sum, during the great age of the hoplite from the seventh to the mid-fifth century, if a man was not killed or wounded, war was *terribile dictu* cheap: it cost him scant time, money, or produce.

Nowhere can this agrarian ideology of Greek warfare be better illustrated than in the arena of hoplite battle, the "smoothest and fairest plain" (Hdt. 7.9.2) where sides squared off. All conflicts were on evacuated and often harvested flatland. Usually this meant level or undulating cereal ground (e.g., Thuc. 4.93–96), rather than on the uplands of olives and vines or dense scrub (but. cf. Xen. *Hell.* 4.2.19). The farmland of Greece was the only place where cumbersome formations of heavily armed and slow-moving infantry could maneuver with any degree of success. Any deployment on broken ground, on small hillsides, in dense vegetation, was phalanx suicide and so recognized by every hoplite (Xen. *An.* 4.8.0; 4.2.12; Thuc. 3.98.2; 4.29ff; cf. Plut. *Flamin.* 8.2–4). Once the respective phalanxes had lumbered into position, terrain was never much of a concern. By mutual agreement, hills, gullies, ravines, forests, and swamps were to be avoided (e.g., Polyb. 18.31.11). Like the landless poor and other assorted missile troops who often appeared suddenly in such places, these natural "obstacles" (in both a physical and psychological sense) could only prolong the conflict and defeat the purpose of the tried hoplite ritual (Ober 1991: 173–188).

The historic physical limitations to battle—terrain, weather, provisions, and distance—were, for one of the few times in Western warfare, deliberately made secondary considerations. The concern for hills, temperature, precipitation, and food belong to the military cosmos of the fourth century and later, when these extraneous factors appear ubiquitously in the historical record and military manuals.

Most disputes from the eighth to fifth centuries were fought over marginal land on the border between *poleis*, another indication that the stakes involved in the killing were agrarian, not urban.[5] The boundaries between *poleis*, though usually mountainous, undulating, and only vaguely demarcated, were nevertheless felt to be sacred to the entire population of the city-state. Poor farming land was valuable more for its psychological than its agricultural importance. Perhaps that concern with ownership of the land explains the simile in Homer's *Iliad* comparing opposing armies to two men in dispute over a farm boundary, with rulers in their hands (Hom. *Il.* 12.421–24). Much has been written about plunder and booty in early Greek warfare, but it is hard to see much real profit in a hoplite army's acquisition of a neighbor's scrub land on the border.

For another city-state to encroach on frontier ground or, worse yet, to expropriate this public no-man's-land, was an affront to the entire community, men who as individual growers had carefully refrained from incorporating disputed land onto their own plots (Pl. *Resp.* 2.373D–E). That ground was left unfarmed as a buffer zone reassured the local agrarian community that their own plots were safe from hostile intrusion.*

The few peaceful resolutions of disputes over ground ("There is an accord," wrote Aelian [NA 5.9], "between the people of Rhegium and Locris that each has access and can farm the land of the other") are the exceptions that prove the rule: Greek border areas were the fuses that ignited most hoplite wars. The Spartan commander Lysander purportedly replied to the convincing argument of an Argive delegation over their disputed border: "He who is the master of the sword talks best about the boundaries of land" (Plut. *Mor.* 190E3). For the Spartans the state's borders were understood simply "as far the spear can reach" (Plut. *Mor.* 210E28). No wonder the Spartan Polydorus purportedly remarked that he had battled the Argives over their common border, and not besieged their *polis* proper, "because I came to take territory (*chôran*) not to capture a city" (Plut. *Mor.* 231E3).

The main fight between phalanxes was normally down below on good flatland, in the interior territory of one of the belligerents. The same battlefields must have been visited and revisited generation after genera-

---

*"The protection of the plains," writes Robin Osborne, "demanded the protection of the borders; training the citizen soldier involved stressing the importance of the marginal land at the edge. Because borders figured so prominently in the life of the citizen, disputes about borderlands were not simply disputes about the defense of the territory, but about the defense of the whole citizen body" (1987: cf. 149; 1992b: 380).

tion, inasmuch as only a few plains in Greece serve as strategic nexuses between the major city-states. How else can we explain the repeated hoplite engagements in the same Argive, Corinthian, and Mantineian plains? Consider the striking proximity of battle sites in the "dry plain of Boeotia" (Aesch. *Pers.* 806)—a veritable Spartan, Athenian, and Theban slaughterhouse—over a two-hundred-year period. There, only a few miles separate the battlefields of Plataea (479 B.C.), Tanagra (458 B.C.), Oinophyta (457 B.C.), Delium (424 B.C.), Haliartos (395 B.C.), Coroneia (first: 447 B.C. / second: 394 B.C.), Tegyra (377 B.C.), Leuctra (371 B.C.), and Chaironeia (338 B.C). Epameinondas, the fourth-century Theban general, labeled that plain "the dancing-floor of war" (Plut. *Mor.* 193E18). But for the farmers who would kill in Boeotia, not dance, "blood alley" would have been a more appropriate name. For the Athenians butchered there at Chaironeia by Philip II in 338 B.C., their mortuary epigram simply called the well-trodden killing fields "famed": "Time, the all-surveying deity of all kinds of affairs for mortals / Be a messenger to all men of our sufferings / How striving to save the sacred land of Greece, / We died on the famed plains of Boeotia" (e.g., IG II^2 5266; *Anth. Pal.* 7.245).

The whole point of early Greek agrarian warfare, as I have said, was to save the lives and property of its farmers, to curb defense "expenditure," and all the while to satisfy the human need for brutal bloodletting, reducing battle in Pindar's words (fr. 15) to "a thing of fear." Therefrom all strategic and tactical thinking was derived: deliberate agrarian attempts to find an elusive equilibrium between brief, but real wars, and a prosperous, lengthy "peace" between Greek *poleis*. That critical balance—the mean at the heart of agrarian life—alone must explain the often misinterpreted remark of the Cretan lawgiver in Plato's *Laws* (1.626A; cf. Anon. fr. 846 Kock). "Peace," he said, "is merely a name; in truth an undeclared war always exists by nature (*kata phusin*) between every Greek city-state." But until the Peloponnesian War, Plato's "undeclared war" (*polemon akêruktos*) was distinguished only by an occasional hoplite battle, which for most small landholders meant an afternoon of hard fighting and thus peace enough for the city-state to prosper.

"Strategy" is Greek for generalship. In reality for the invading army it amounted to little more than collecting and deploying the various contingents of the alliance, choosing the route and time of the invasion, and, if need be, organizing a provocative, rather than destructive, attack on the cropland and farmhouses of the invaded agriculturalists. Xenophon said it consisted mainly of the right way to march out in formation, the proper manner to post sentries, and the best approach in crossing passes (*Oec.* 20.6–11). The Spartan king Archidamos on the eve of the first great invasion of the Peloponnesian War (431 B.C.) initially refrained from attacking Athenian farms, hoping that the enemy, in the cherished tradition of hoplite warfare, would be provoked into marching out in column. "The reason why Archidamos stayed in formation at Acharnae during this invasion," Thucydides writes, "rather than descending into the Athenian plain, was said to be for the following reason. He expected that the Athenians might possibly be tempted by the great numbers of their young and the unexampled efficiency of service to come out for battle and try to stop the ravaging of their farms" (Thuc. 2.20.1–2).

Provoked agrarians could occasionally choose to ride it out safely behind the town's walls (the art of siegecraft was still in its infancy). Wisely (but less courageously) they might allow a brief, and usually benign, ravaging of their farms (e.g., Xen. *Hell.* 4.4.16; 6.5.15–20). Besides marching out to battle heroically in the plains or, less commonly, eschewing pitched battle altogether and retreating to endure a siege behind strong walls, there was also a third, less reputable choice: abject capitulation. That was the position of the cowardly but prudent viticulturalists of Akanthos in northern Greece, farmers who simply folded and thereby let the invading Spartans inside their walls, rather than risk loss of access to their upcoming vintage (Thuc. 4.84.1–2; 4.88.1–2; and cf. Hdt. 5.34.1; 6.101.2; 6.109.1).

More often, as even the fifth-century Athenians' opposition to the evacuation policy of Pericles revealed (e.g., "It seemed likely that the three thousand infantry of the deme of Acharnae would refuse to submit to the ravaging of their farms, and would force the rest of the Athenians to march out for pitched battle" [Thuc. 2.20.]), hoplite farmers wished to battle. Except for the Athenians during the Peloponnesian War, most Greek city-states before the fourth century chose to face the invader (e.g., Thuc. 5.64.5–65.2). Immediately, the decision was made to muster all the able-bodied landowners, to preserve their pride and the sanctity of ancestral plots, to march out in the close columns of the phalanx, and to meet the trespassers in a single pitched battle.

"Agriculture," the Aristotelian *Oeconomica* says, "inures men to exposure and toil, and gives them the strength to face the perils of war; for the property of farmers alone lies outside the walls of the city" ([Oec.] 1.1343b5–7). Xenophon, in a note of agrarian Darwinism, also stresses the inherent link between free agriculture and hoplite bravery: "The land stimulates farmer to fight for his country since nature raises the crops out in the open for the strongest to take" (*Oec.* 5. 7). Usually the assembly of property owners (i.e., the "strongest," the hoplites themselves) determined the response of the *polis.* For much of the life of the Greek city-state until the Peloponnesian War, there was never a separation in political and military representation. There was no ominous gulf between those who say "fight" and those who really do fight, the phenomenon that has undermined Western societies from the agrarian crises of the third to first centuries B.C. at Rome to the American tragedy in Vietnam.

Agricultural damage—the specter that drew out the phalanx—was limited by the natural toughness and ubiquity of the vine and olive, rough terrain, the difficulty of catching moisture-laden grain at its combustible stage, the inherent simplicity and resiliency of labor-intensive, but capital-scarce farms and, last, the very incongruity of clumsy hoplite infantrymen or vulnerable skirmishers taking on the role of day laborers hacking at vines and trees (see Hanson 1983: 37–63).

Completely absent from the mind of the seventh- and sixth-century hoplite "strategic" planner (besides the notion itself of a "planner") was any intention of genocide, of scorched-earth retreat, of mass conquest and expropriation, of terrorism, or of indiscriminate murder and hostage taking. All that belonged either to ancient legend of the pre-*polis* era or to Greece during the later fifth and fourth centuries B.C.—when the agrarian protocols eroded and those on the margins of traditional yeomanry sought to end the old ideology of the *polis.*

Nor, aside from the unusual Spartan subjugation of Messenia, was there much consideration of permanent occupation or mass enslavement. Cleomenes of Sparta was considered mad for his ghastly incineration of his trapped Argive adversaries at Sepeia (494 B.C.; Hdt. 6.80–85; 7.148). Herodotus's peculiar and ironical description of the "battle of the fetters" (550 B.C.), when the Spartans brought along chains to shackle their Tegean opponents (unsuccessfully, as it turned out), suggests that enslavement of neighboring defeated Greeks was the exception, not the rule during the seventh and sixth centuries (Hdt. 1.66). Early aberrations in the hoplitic code, not surprisingly, are often associated with Sparta, whose atypical professional military was always in danger of going beyond the pale of accepted agrarian practice.

Wide-scale massacre and sale of conquered peoples inside Greece became commonplace only in the later fifth century during the nightmare of the Peloponnesian War, when the landed monopoly of Greek warfare eroded for good. Examine the staggering numbers of enslaved listed in W. K. Pritchett's monumental *The Greek State at War, Part V* (Pritchett *War* 5.505–41) to see just how different the fourth through second centuries were from the practice of the earlier *polis*. While our surviving literary sources differ, it still seems to me reminiscent of the killing and savagery of the nineteenth century giving way to the horrific extermination of the twentieth. Treatises such as the *Cavalry Commander* of Xenophon or Aeneas Tacticus's *Defense of Fortified Positions*—strange "how-to" manuals for the non–hoplite—were thus naturally suited to fourth-century military practice. They reflect an evolving contemporary military ideology for a more complex, nonagrarian-thinking *polis*; the old hoplite monopoly of the fifth century had been shown to be largely irrelevant during the Peloponnesian War, and was only sporadically resurrected in its aftermath.

"Tactics," as the historian Xenophon says, were "only a small part of generalship" (*Mem.* 3.1.6). To infantrymen of the *polis* period they seemed nearly as one-dimensional as strategy. Tactics addressed only the basic "problem" of Greek battle of the city-state: the collection of all the combatants as quickly as possible into a confined space. "An ordered army," Xenophon wrote, "is the finest thing to see for friends and the most terrifying thing for enemies. . . . For when armies march in order, though there be tens of thousands of them, they all march calmly as if they were one man; the empty spaces are always filled by those who are coming up from behind" (*Oec.* 8.6–7). Xenophon adds: "Without formation, an army is a confused mass, easy pickings for enemies, for friends a disgusting sight, utterly useless (*achrêstotaton*)" (*Oec.* 8.4.).

Plato wished that in his utopia Greek armies could at least practice mustering and march out one day a month (*Leg.* 8.829B). In a formal sense, Greek tactics of the *polis* also consisted of not much more than determining the proper, although elusive, ratio between breadth and depth of the phalanx (usually stacked eight shields deep, but no greater it seems than fifty), and the placement, always somewhat political, of the particular allied troops on the proper wings of the army. Drawing up the phalanx was considered the "acme of the art of war" (Plut. *Phil.* 14.5).

Occasionally, the stronger, better fighters needed to be identified and placed at the front and rear to stop any stampede from either direction, and to urge on the weaker farmers in the center (e.g., Xen. *Mem.* 3.1.7–11). Ambushes and deception were considered "trickery" outside the realm of early *polis* warfare. Often there was more simply a moral, rather than legal, restraint on ruse: anything but stand-up gallantry went against the entire Greek heroic code. During the warfare of the *polis*, there were none of "the charts and diagrams for the illustration of tactical doctrine" so common in Hellenistic times (Plut. *Phil.* 4.5).

To the modern military mind, very little was left to chance in hoplite battle. Most often it was simply a case of winning the fray with your strong right wing—"horns," as the agrarian infantrymen called them—before suspect and less reliable allied militias on the left collapsed—sometimes, as in the case of the so-called tear-less battle (Plut. *Ages.* 33.3), before even meeting the enemy. Most rudimentary tactics that did emerge were simple, rather than complex, variations of head-on assaults in column (e.g., Xen. *Lac Pol.* 11.5–10; *Cyr.* 2.2.6–10). Given the absence of reserve troops, specialized units, the surprise attack, the night engagement, and the concealed ambush, there was no desire until the fourth century for elaborate pre-battle tactical planning or even real battlefield command. An Alexander, Napoleon, Patton, or Rommel might have sent cavalry to punch holes in the enemy phalanx, javelin throwers and archers to hammer at his wings, followed by light infantry feints, encircling columns, and surprise attacks in the rear, all preliminaries to the main assault held in reserve, awaiting the opportune moment of enemy weakness. But to the *polis* Greeks before the Peloponnesian War, these generals would have been a distasteful bunch, tinkerers and manipulators afraid, at first sight of the enemy mass, to grab the shield and run with their men to death.

So the chateau general, the bloated grandee, and the armchair know-it-all, as we understand them, were virtually nonexistent. Archilochus (fr.114), the seventh-century, anti-aristocratic lyric poet, spoke for all when he said that his battle leader must be only "short and bandy-legged, firm set on his feet, full of heart and courage." He ridiculed—as agrarians always do those in ostentatious positions of authority—any who would have pretensions about command, the wartime counterpart to Hesiod's "bride-swallowing barons."[6]

The sense in Greek literature before the fourth century is that the "general" himself is not much more than a hoplite, a battlefield leader who fights along with his men. He is neither a wealthy land baron nor a professional graduate of years of tactical and strategic training. Elevation of the *strategos* above his followers was somehow seen by the *polis* Greeks as nonegalitarian and—given the absence of real tactical and strategic choice—silly as well. There seems to have been an entire absence of overall battlefield control in early hoplite warfare. Often individual contingents formed up the ranks as they pleased, with little regard for the repercussions on their own allied columns on their left and right (e.g., Thuc. 4.93; and cf. Xen. *Hell.* 4.2.13; Thuc. 5.68).

I know of no sculpture, no artwork before the fourth century glorifying a general as the "man on a horse." The rural chorus in a lost play, the *Demes*, by the comic playwright Eupolis, complains bitterly about the farmer-hoplites who voted in the losing generals at the battle of Mantineia (418 B.C.): "I pray that whoever picked men like that to hold the office, may neither his flocks or fields ever bear fruit" (fr. 110B, 11–12 Edmonds). There was a notion—one no doubt often quite true—that even at the end of the fifth century the general was a farmer, not much different from his men. Common in the literature of war is a chaotic scene where agrarians openly challenge authority, berate their generals, and offer unsolicited advice before, during, and after battle. Xenophon complained that hoplites were among the most insubordinate (*apeithestatous pantôn*) of all troops (*Mem.* 3.5.19).

This image of a "soldier's general" has been challenged by scholars who argue it was—and has been throughout Western battle practice—but one of many "masks" of command. But no evidence exists to show that before the Peloponnesian War Greek hoplite generals wore many other masks. Rarely was a general mounted, isolated to the rear, or free of the fighting itself. Debate over the battle activity of hoplite "commanders" is academic quibbling: whether the "general" fights and dies exposed in the front rank, or is surrounded by more seasoned contingents stationed a few ranks behind the initial collision. In Plato's *Ion*, Socrates shows that Ion's claims of mastering all of Greek tactics from intimate acquaintance with Homer are fatuous. But in his classic refutation, Socrates never suggests that the "science" of generalship is any more complex that it had been centuries in the past.[7]

Dionysodorus complains in Xenophon's *Memorabilia* that some at Athens felt one could simply assume command without any military experience at all—suggesting through his invective that this was often precisely the case for much of the life of the *polis* (*Mem.* 3.1.2–7). Socrates is therefore made to say that "to be eager for victory (*philonikos*)" rather than to have made formal study is crucial in generalship (Xen. *Mem.* 3.4.3). Theoretically, the seer who accompanied the army may have had as much authority in directing the time and occasion of battle as the general himself, for if the sacrifice "revealed" unfavorable omens, the battle might be delayed, and in rare instances postponed altogether.*

Strategy, tactics, and generalship were not merely rudimentary. They were deliberately made nonessential in war between two opposing phalanxes, inasmuch as they were all antithetical to farmers' interests. Greek agrarian warfare, as it was originally conceived, was not so much atactical or astrategic, as it was *anti*-tactical, *anti*-strategic. It was not primitive but sophisticated when one appreciates its underlying conventions.

Farmers during the *polis* period were not to be fodder for aristocratic careerism. They were not to be sent abroad to fight wars for which they had no desire, much less political or economic interests. They were not to be bled white paying taxes for professional armies. They were not to incorporate landless and alien skirmishers and mercenaries merely to achieve military diversity and flexibility. Instead, for one of the few occasions in the history of the West, rural folk, independent and autonomous citizens of more than a thousand Greek communities, set their own mili-

---

*See Pritchett *War* 1.109–115; 3.47–153; for actual instances, see Jameson 1991: 219–21. Plato claimed by law the soothsayer was subordinate to the general, which reflects the normal influence the seer had on the troops (Pl. *Lach.* 199A.)

tary agenda, and would not be conscripted from their farms to serve the big men of the city.

Once hoplite battle commenced, killing was equally economical. Columns of bronze-clad infantry, as Xenophon himself witnessed at Coroneia (*Hell.* 4.3.19), "collided, pushed, fought, killed, and died," seeking always to collapse the opposing phalanx before exhaustion set in—usually within an hour under the summer Mediterranean sun. Pushing with the shield (the *ôthismos*) while stabbing with the spear required little weapon training or skill. Success instead came from a steady nerve in the face of what Sophocles called the "storm of the spear" (*doros en cheimôni*)" (*Ant.* 670), what Aeschylus, veteran of Marathon, knew as "the air made insane by the shaking of the spear (*doritinaktos aithêr epimainetai*)" (*Sept.* 155).

The tragedians' images make perfect sense when we remember that the jostling and bobbing spears of the first three ranks of the phalanx (hence the metaphor of the porcupine's rising quills [e.g., Plut. *Arist.* 18.2]) all could impale the oncoming adversary. Often on Greek vases (e.g., Ducrey 49, 240) the gaping wounds on a fallen soldier suggest that at least a few fighters ended up as pincushions of sorts, soft meat thrown against dozens of sharp skewers.

When I speak of "pushing" in Greek battle, I mean just that. It is not some metaphorical expression to connote movement of men forward, but actual leaning into the man ahead, applying real pressure with the shield to his shoulder, side, and back. Similarly, references in Greek literature attest to "hand-to-hand" and "shield-to-shield" combat. These phrases suggest literal not symbolic brawling and wrestling (Thuc. 4.96.2; Tyrt. 11.31–34; Diod. 12.70.3; 15.39.1; 15.87.1; cf. Hanson 1989:154–56;171–84). Perhaps when offensive weapons failed or pressure simply made their use problematic, agrarians resorted to their hands and teeth, and again the farmer's strength and endurance were critical. Is it any surprise, then, that Thebes, the agrarian *polis* par excellence, favored attack with massed columns of sixteen, twenty-five, and fifty shields deep, secure in the thought that their tough yeoman could break through any wider enemy formation column before being outflanked or caught in the rear?

In the mind of every farmer there was an overriding desire not to play the coward before lifelong friends and family posted at his side, his "compatriot farmers." "A strong arm can bear the spear thrust no better than a weak one," Euripides says, "it's a man's courage and nature that make him what he is" (Eur. *Elect.* 389–90). An ideology of agrarian solidarity was reflected in both the massed nature of the columns—brother, father, son all together (e.g., "Every living thing fights better in the presence of offspring" [Pl. *Resp.* 5.467B])—and the interdependence spawned by hoplite technology, something impossible using the tactics of the long line or hit-and-run skirmishing. Greek literature reflects precisely that idea: men carried their shields "for the sake of the entire line" (Plut. *Mor.* 220A; Thuc. 5.71; and especially Plut. *Pel.* 1.5). Aristotle concluded that militias of amateur farmers were far more courageous than hired mercenaries: "Infantrymen of the *polis* think it is a disgraceful thing to run away, and they choose death over safety through flight. On the other hand, professional soldiers, who rely from the outset on superior strength, flee as soon as they find out they are outnumbered, fearing death more than dishonor" (Arist. *Eth. Nic.* 3.1116b16–23).

Ideally, all farmers who threw down their shields and ran away were punished, since the first duty of a hoplite "was to protect rather than inflict injury on the enemy" (Plut. *Pel.* 1.5; cf. *Anth. Pal.* 7.230). Euripides laments that the hoplite "is slave to his weapons since he might die if the man to his right proved a coward" (*HF* 185). "Farming," Xenophon says of agrarian militia, "educates one to help others. In fighting (*ienai tous polemious*), just as in the working of the soil (*tês gês ergasia*), it is necessary to have the assistance of other people" (*Oec.* 5.14). Given the shared agrarian ideology of the *geôrgoi*, their adherence to uniform and egalitarian notions of property holding (e.g., "The ideal of timocracy is government by the mass of citizens, and within the property qualification all are equal" [Arist. *Eth. Nic.* 8.1160b18–20]), it is hard to envision for long armed farmers of this brand as small groups of mounted knights. Nor would Greek agrarians be comfortable as isolated contingents of professional garrison troops, or as a long solitary line of bowmen and slingers, much less as mercenary killers. It is far more understandable that each plot in the countryside around the *polis* was mirrored by a slot in the phalanx.

For that task of lining up together in massed rank for a single, decisive battle, even the old (e.g., Andocides' "the aged men arming for battle") and occasionally the unfit could still offer service. Dispense entirely with the idea that the ranks of the phalanx were composed of elegant youths of the type so often portrayed on Athenian red- and black-figured vases. At the end of the fifth century they seem almost effeminate in their slenderness. That is aristocratic idealization, akin to Plato's glorification of hoplite infantry, rather than a ground-level snapshot of the men who went to war.[8]

It is sometimes popular in the age of "gender studies" for scholars to insist that the sleekness and artwork of the Greek panoply are reflections of male rituals reflecting sexual ambivalency, more akin to the search for masculine identity or even fashion than simple killing. But a few ornate and tasteful Greek breastplates in the museums or references in literature to occasionally decorated panoplies (Xen. Mem. 3.10.14) should not mislead us—any more than the stylish gray uniforms and plumes of Confederate officers who led their grizzled troops to mass butchery and dismemberment. Aeschylus emphasizes that even the young "man-boy" Parthenopaios, the down-cheeked warrior, who might have appeared nonthreatening, was "not at all maidenish like his name" (*parthenos* means maiden or young girl). Instead, he attacked Thebes as a "savage with a terrible eye" (*Sept.* 536–37), with "a cannibal sphinx on his shield" (541). Earlier in the same play, *Seven Against Thebes*, Aeschylus has Eteokles say, "I am not afraid of whatever a man wears. Images don't inflict wounds. Crests and bells can't bite without a spear" (*Sept.* 397–99).

So despite soldiers' interest in a neat appearance (e.g., Xen. *An.* 3.2.7; Hdt. 7.208; Thuc. 6.31), hoplite battle entailed real killing, where spears, not images, "bit." It was an ugly thing. Grubby-looking farmers were of all ages. They were men who, like Aristophanes' old "gray-haired" Acharnian hoplites, may have looked gnarled and aged, and complained of stiff limbs (*Ach.* 210–20), may have been near blind and fat (Plut. *Mor.* 192C3; 235F62), but whose backs and legs were used to the rigor of constant farm chores: "all old men, close-grained and stubborn, made of ilex and maple wood" (*Ach.* 180–82; cf. Hanson 1989: 89–95).

From personal experience, I have learned that farmers and farm laborers in their fifties and sixties—often with paunches and arthritic joints—possess an uncanny strength. That power belies their appearance, and certainly is unmatched by the young urban jogger or novice iron-pumper. So accustomed are we (like urban Greek artists) to associate youth and beauty with physical excellence, so confident are we in relying on the gadgetry of the fitness industry to achieve a muscular physique (like the aristocrats at the *polis* gymnasia), that at first glance this assertion that real power can lie hidden within a sorry agrarian frame, in "the horny handed farmer" (Val. Max. 7.5.2), seems ludicrous. But the bodily strength and combative skill of the potbellied cultivator might not be entirely physical. Perhaps his power derives too out of the experience of repetitive labor and the discipline—physical, mental, spiritual—needed daily to endure hostile weather and constantly boring but nevertheless dangerous tasks of agricultural solitude?

How else can I explain why when I was in my late twenties, friends visiting from the city, expert runners, bicyclists, and weight lifters all, often tired after pruning a row of vines, or a large plum tree, becoming winded, bored, and indignant? They—all around my own age—were left far behind by seasoned men in their fifties without sculpted muscles, ugly men of alcohol and tobacco, who could not jog a mile without collapse. Inexplicably there seems to be muscle after all in a farmer's ungainly belly and back, ugly muscle though it may be, every bit as strong as elegant muscle.

Xenophon contrasted the agrarian physique with the "ruined bodies and enervated souls" of the urban craftsmen, who could never match the farmer-hoplite in bodily strength or nerve. How could they, when none toiled in the fields or risked their livelihood out beyond the walls (cf. *Oec.* 6.5–10)? Elsewhere, he says: "Farming keeps the body in shape for the infantryman (*geôrgia . . . pezê sphodron to sôma parechei*)" (*Oec.* 5.5). Herodotus tells the story of Cleobis and Biton, who, when oxen were not to be found, yoked themselves like animals to a wagon and drew their mother five miles into Argos. Not surprisingly, he tells us they had been farming in the fields (Hdt. 1.31).

A set of pre- and post-battle rituals reemphasized the static, artificial nature of phalanx warfare. Usually battle took place after a midday meal, when hoplites relaxed, drank, gamed, or slept. Then, rested and fed, both sides squared off on a small plain and proceeded to eye one another for minutes on end. Meanwhile, the "general," ancient historians claim, strutted down the line delivering his customary harangue. Given the many instances where battle seems to interrupt his speech midsentence, we can imagine how boring and stereotyped the address was to the armored men waiting in the sun primed to fight. How thousands confined in armor (without earholes) and arrayed in the open (skeptical farmers all) could hear the single voice of their commander, we are never told.

A seer appeared. He usually offered up a preliminary sacrifice of one of the animals. If battle seemed "wise," he confirmed the "favorable" signs. Xenophon saw the inevitable link between agriculture and phalanxes, the similarity between the uncertainty of farming and the risks of fighting: "The gods are lords of the operations in farming no less than they are of warlike actions. Those who are at war try to win over the gods before fighting, and consulting them by means of sacrifices and auguries as to what they should or should not do. In regard to farming, do you suppose that it is any less necessary to propitiate the gods?" (*Oec.* 5.19–20). Both phalanxes then walked to within bow-shot, often screaming the war cry "*eleleleu*," "*alala*," or other queer sounds so familiar to country folk acquainted with animal noises.[9]

These rituals must not conjure up an image of choreographed columns artfully colliding ("a walking tour ending up in a combat" [Adcock 82]). Just because an occasional poet termed fighting "glorious" is no reason to assume that it was anything other than what Pindar called "a thing of fear" (fr. 15), "a graceless and unimaginative affair in which weight of numbers counted for as much as, if not more than, skill in the manipulation of spear and sword" (Cartledge 1987: 44). The sculpted frieze on the Siphnian treasury at Delphi shows clearly enough the tumble and melee when heavy infantrymen collided (e.g., Hurwit 297–98). On other stone reliefs and in ceramic portrayal, stumbling, tripping, and the smashing of prostrate hoplite bodies seem commonplace (e.g., Ducrey 48, 212, 244–45, 255 258). The phalanx was above all a terrifying example of pure military efficacy, a formation unstoppable and unassailable in confining ground, one never conquered through direct assault, one to be defeated only by finesse, ruse, and the manipulation of terrain—and then only after its agrarian fighting components had vanished.

In minutes armed men crashed together, running "the stadium dash" of about two hundred yards between the two phalanxes (Plut. *Mor.* 846E; Hanson 1989: 138–51), striving to battle one another on top of farmland. The Spartans alone adhered to the older hoplite protocol of walking, not running, into the enemy spears. For the defenders it was often the same soil they and their neighbors had worked a few days before. For the invaders, the farmhouses, orchards, vineyards, and stone field walls were largely identical to their own plots back home. Blinded by the dust and their own cumbersome helmets, farmers stabbed away with their spears, pushed on ahead with their shields, and, failing that, grabbed, kicked, and bit, desperately hoping to make some inroad into the enemy phalanx, usually having little idea whom they had killed or wounded.

Remember that Tyrtaeus, the seventh-century war poet, called the killing "threshing it out" (19.16). To men accustomed to the brutal farm work of converting wheat and barley to flour and gruel, killing in bronze armor was not a singularly demanding task. Xenophon made the same agricultural connection and once compared the pile of dead hoplites to "heaps of wheat" (*Hell.* 4.4. 12; cf. Aesch. *Pers.* 818). Aeschylus likewise envisioned the huge hoplite shield as a large threshing-floor (Aesch. *Sept.* 489), a flat surface where bodies, like grain, were to be smashed.

Visually, acoustically, aromatically, and physically hoplite battle was a nightmare of an hour's blurred images, glimpses through small slits in bronze helmets of maimed limbs, trampled bodies, whirling spear-tips and sword blades, shouts, shrieks (Arrian's "impediments in the air" [*Tact.* 27]), and sobbing, where the stink of sweat and excrement was intensified by the claustrophobic environment of pressed flesh and hot bronze armor (Hanson 1989: 135–218; Lazenby 1991: 91–102). The poet who portrayed the bloodsucking Fates gnashing their white fangs, whirling above the slaughter ([Hes.] *Scut.* 248–57), no doubt drew on the recollection of all veterans of hoplite slaughter.

Few agrarians were killed outright in battle. Fewer noncombatants were ever in danger. But those unfortunate farmers who went down, did so in gruesome fashion. Exposed limbs, groin, neck, and face were ripped apart by spear-tips. Bones and flesh were stomped by hundreds of heavy feet. For all the kindred agrarian ideology of the various city-states, in hoplite battle itself there was never any quarter given in the phalanx, never any hesitation to stab and cut stunned adversaries. Bloodletting, the art of tearing apart flesh and breaking bone, was no strange sight to farmers who butchered their own meat and hunted game.

There is nothing but disdain in Greek literature for the rare "tremblers," "shield-casters," and "spear-tossers."* These were runaways and simple fainthearts, agrarian turncoats all. Theophrastus's archetype coward is one who smears the blood of another on himself (*Char.* 25.4–6). Eupolis's lost fifth-century comedy, *The Shirkers,* portrayed the evaders as lacking sex altogether, cowards neither men nor women (fr. 31 Kock). Plato imagined in his *Laws* that the best conceivable punishment for those who flung down their shields, who sought a shameful retreat rather than a glorious death buried beneath their pursuers, would be to have them somehow changed from men into women. More realistically he suggested a fine of one thousand drachmas (Pl. *Leg.* 12.944B–945A), a sum equal to about half a typical hoplite's total worth. At Sparta, infantry runaways (and the definition of "runaways" was not very forbearing) were simply stripped of citizenship and drummed out of the community of warriors (cf. Plut. *Mor.* 191C10).

Very soon (cf. Pritchett *War* 4.46–51) the conflict was over as one group of farmers collapsed. Sometimes they were gradually worn down from the front rank backward, more often broken suddenly in a terrified scramble at the rear under the pressure of the accumulated shields of the adversary. Both pursuit and slaughter—the only real opportunity for *class* warfare in the first two centuries of the agrarian *polis* as both wealthy horsemen and landless poor could now slay with ease isolated hoplite farmers straggling home in dejection and confusion—usually ceased at the nearby foothills. The rare protracted retreat at Delium (424 B.C.), when the Boeotian conquerors at twilight rode down and hunted out panicked Athenians for miles was thus a particularly infamous—and ominous—episode in the history of Greek warfare. Numbers of distinguished and elderly Athenian hoplites were uncharacteristically chased, caught, or killed outright.*

Plato, no doubt thinking of the gallant behavior of Socrates at the Athenian debacle at Delium, wrote in his *Laws* that one of the worst

---

*Plut. *Ages.* 30.2–4; *Mor.* 193E18; *Lac. Pol.* 9.4–5; Ameipsas fr. 17 Kock; Hdt. 7.231; Hanson 1989: 64. In Attic comedy and occasionally in oratory flight in battle is a stock charge, not much different from allegations of passive homosexuality.

**The disastrous retreat lived on as an especially nightmarish event in the collective memory of the Athenians; cf. Thuc. 4.96; Diod. 12. 70.4–6; cf. Pl. *Ap.* 28E; *Lach.* 181A; *Symp.* 221A; Plut. *Alc.* 7.6; *Mor.* 581.

things a citizen might do was to act with cowardice in retreat (*Leg.* 12.944C–D). The runaway, Plato says, gains through his flight "a disgraceful life rather than a blessed death by gallantry." Much more often, nearby rough terrain, the absence of a true cavalry, and an unspoken dislike of spearing fellow Greeks in the back kept the losers' fatalities well below fifteen percent. "It is a shameful sight," Tyrtaeus (11.17–20) writes of the tragic scene of hoplites impaled from the rear and scattered over the battlefield, "when a dead man lies in the dust, driven through from behind by the stroke of an enemy spear." The runaway, like the man who lost his ancestral estate, had shamed his family and community, and so lost his spot in the grid whose conservation was critical to the life of the community.

Nearly always both groups of farmers accepted the verdict of battle and felt no need to prolong the bloodletting: "It was not a Greek custom to murder those who had already yielded in battle" (Plut. *Mor.* 228F30). At Sparta discipline was so firm that hoplites in the midst of battle could cease their slaughter immediately upon hearing the call to cease fighting (Plut. *Mor.* 236E71). Postbellum disputes over rotting corpses and the erection of trophies (e.g., Thuc. 4.97–101) were characteristic of the Peloponnesian War and later, when the protocols of decisive battle and agrarian warfare were unwinding. But in the mind of the early farmer-hoplite of the eighth to fifth century, what would be the point of further disputation, when all landowners had carefully followed the rules, when none had recourse to any "extenuating circumstances" other than their own failure of bodily strength or nerve? For a farmer who had no one other than himself to blame for a paltry crop, military defeat was naturally explicable solely through self-censure.

Once the citizen body of these agrarian governments had been repulsed on the field of battle, who in the *polis* could second-guess the military efficacy of its yeoman members? Hoplite defeat, like a bad harvest, logically spelled the collective failure of the entire agrarian infrastructure of the particular city-state. Sometimes battle failure understandably led to wide-ranging political settlements (cf. Hackett 78–79), far out of proportion to the actual expenditure and depletion of human lives (for the most part agrarian) and accumulated capital. Aristotle saw infantry defeats as a major cause of subsequent changes in government (e.g., *Pol.* 5.1302b29–1303a20). Fifth-century challenges to, and revivals of, agrarian oligarchy in

Boeotia usually followed the outcome of dramatic hoplite battles (e.g., Thuc. 1.108, 113). The inability of Athenian yeomen to check the on-slaught of Xerxes helped to give ascendancy to the "trireme crowd" for the next 150 years. After all, farmers had taken the defense of the *polis* into their own hands, and thus were to live with the prestige of victory, the ig-nominy of defeat, or, worse, the exposure of inadequacy.

An immediate truce was thus customary. Real depression could ensue when hoplites learned of their losses in dead and wounded. The farmers' wagons doubled as hearses and ambulances traversing the battlefield loaded up the dead and incapacitated. We only occasionally hear of the sun-baked and bloated corpse. There was even the more bizarre, though utilitarian (in the agrarian sense), idea that rotting human cadavers could increase soil fertility. Most often the dead farmers, though stomped and speared by foot and iron, were stripped, identified, and sent back for burial.[10]

We scarcely know of head-hunting, scalping, or even mutilation during the formal warfare of the *polis*. It was a startling enough contrast that sun-burned farmers who grew food for their fellow citizens were now doing their best to extinguish, not nourish, human life. Under normal circum-stances corpses were cremated and their bones sent home. On some rarer occasions they were interred in mass right on the battlefield (see Pritchett *War* 4.94–100)—unless the ever ubiquitous, ever busy farmer ploughed too much of the flat killing ground (so perhaps the epigram: "The ploughman's iron has rolled me out of my tomb" [*Ant. Pal.* 7.175–56]).

Both armies of agrarians, victorious and conquered alike, returned to their small farms and friends. Most captives in Greek warfare derived from the fall of cities, *not* from defeated hoplite armies (Connor 15). Victors erected a battlefield trophy and collected the defeated's spoils for thanks offerings or profit by sale (Pritchett *War* 2.246–75; Lonis 129–43). The permanent stone monuments that dotted the countryside, the garish display of loot at the Panhellenic sanctuaries, were not mere reflections of the frequency of agrarian warfare, but instead real tokens of hoplite ubiquity that presented themselves at nearly every place and occasion (cf. Hdt. 1.34; Ar. *Ach.* 279; Pl. *Leg.* 887D–E; Arist. *Ath. Pol.* 42.3). These commemorations were, in other words, both advertise-ments for, and reflections of, hoplite agrarianism (e.g. Jackson 232–42). They were signs of the moral superiority of citizen yeomenry, who mustered willingly—unlike their nonagrarian contemporaries in Lydia and Persia (e.g., Hdt. 1.76–77)—to preserve their own farms and homes.

Even in maritime states like Athens, the commemorative apparatus of the *polis* was all hoplite. Battle dead—at sea, in passes, on horses—were memorialized largely in hoplite terminology and imagery (cf. Loraux 161–64, 91–92). Hoplite iconography was all-encompassing. Just as infantry battle had been preluded by viewing hoplite statues and votives at Panhellenic sanctuaries, then sanctioned on the spot by peripatetic seers, so it was officially ended by a formal exchange of the dead, and solemnized by trophies and dedications—all a clear message to the entire community of hoplite omnipresence and agrarian exclusivity.

This is the picture of formal Greek warfare between free landed infantry of the city-states that arose at the beginning of the seventh century. It was a system of fighting among independent farmers seen *nowhere* else in that Mediterranean age. Its ethos is typified best by Tellus the Athenian, whom Solon claimed to be happiest of all men, since after producing sons and grandsons, he died gallantly on the battlefield during a successful border war against Eleusis (Hdt. 1.30).

III.

Greek hoplite battle between phalanxes before the Peloponnesian War was predictable in time, place, sequence, and aftermath of infantry fighting. This prompts us to ponder just how one particular Greek hoplite phalanx in a climate of utter violence *actually defeated* its adversary. Can some general trend be detected to explain the outcome of a typical hoplite battle? Perhaps no more than in European warfare of a later age, but to my knowledge such a query has never even been raised, much less answered, about hoplite fighting. The question goes right to the heart of Greek warfare in general. Like the hoplite protocols themselves, the etiology of victory may once again illustrate the agrarian foundations of the entire practice, cementing the notion that the primary concern of Greek combatants of the early *polis* was agriculture.

Was victory between Greek phalanxes achieved through one army's preponderance of muscular strength? Steadfast nerve? Maneuver and articulation? Strategic and logistic superiority? Supremacy of numbers? Blind luck? Advantage in weaponry and military technology? Since there are accounts from historical sources in various degrees of detail of some twenty or so major hoplite battles between 650 and 338 B.C.—the period roughly contemporaneous with the life of the free Greek city-state—the question is perhaps resolvable. But it remains partially shrouded in an agrarian morality that transcends questions of simple military efficacy.

Because there was no real military science in the great age of hoplite battle, there is no need to discuss Greek warfare in anything like traditional military terms. "Breakouts," "articulation," "maneuver," "preparedness," "mobilization," and "assets" are all terms, I believe, that do not belong in the world of hoplite battle. Its conflict knew no "theaters," "fronts," "reserves," or "salients." These are modern concepts that have few equivalents in the Greek military mind (much less in the ancient Greek vocabulary; cf. Hanson 1991: 8–11).

Even in a simple contest of brute force, was there superior skill, size, or strength among the farmers of any one particular hoplite army? Herodotus believed the Greek successes at Marathon (490 B.C.) and Plataea (479 B.C.) against the Persians were in part a result of their superior training and armament (Hdt. 9.62.4, 9.63.2; cf. 5.97.1, 7.211.2; Diod. 11.7.3; but cf. Lazenby 1993: 256–261). Even if true, Herodotus's logic cannot be directly applied to the wars of phalanxes, fought, after all, almost exclusively between fellow landed Greeks, homogeneous infantrymen of the *poleis* who worked on similar farms, who were armed identically, and battled almost entirely alike, who observed religiously the formal regulations of Greek military practice.

That uniformity may explain why even later military analysts of the Hellenistic and Roman periods seem confused about how and why a Greek phalanx engineered the defeat of its particular adversary. The first-century A.D. tactician Aelian (*Tact. Praef.* 146) drawing on sources going back at least to Polybius (second century B.C.), and perhaps incorporating a tradition rooted in phalanx warfare of the early *polis*, could only list (without qualification) a gamut of possible explanations. Aelian's puzzlement might suggest that few Greeks themselves knew which factor in a phalanx battle was the most influential in eventual success.

All battles are decided *either* because of the strength of forces in infantry or cavalry; *or* because of the superiority of forces in tens of thousands or thousands; *or* because of the morale of the men; *or* because of the physical strength of men; *or* because of training, *or* because of the skill of the tactical deployment, *or* because of terrain, *or* because of the suitability of the occasion [emphasis added].

On occasion, the farmers of Hesiod's Boeotia were known to be especially physical, excelling in combative sports; their conditioning reflected their general reputation in antiquity as doughty rustics and the widely held acknowledgment that size and strength were important in hoplite battle (e.g., Aen. Tact. 1.3–5; Andrewes 1981: 1–3). Pericles in his disparagement of Boeotians compared them to oak trees (Arist. *Rhet.* 3.1406b). In general, the Greeks felt that athletic prowess and skill in wrestling enhanced hoplite combativeness (e.g., Pl. *Leg.* 7.830C–831B.; *Lach.* 182; Athen. 629B–C; Lucian *Anach.* 24, 28; and see Pritchett *War* 2.208–45). Plato could envision fighting as "the avoidance of blows and missiles by swerving, ducking, jumping, and crouching" (e.g., *Leg.* 7.815A), although fluid motion was perhaps not typical of men wearing seventy pounds of armor, who struggled simply to remain standing while stabbing and pushing in the crowd. Commanding physicality is the effect Aristophanes is creating when he brings onstage a no-nonsense farmer from Boeotia in his *Acharnians* (*Ach.* 860–910).

Plutarch (a native of Boeotian Chaironeia not far from Thebes) went further. He explicitly correlated Boeotian ferocity and muscular power to military prowess: "The Spartans at Leuctra," he says, "were overpowered by our men, who were experts in wrestling." Elsewhere he notes that the Thebans had little patience with the unfit (Plut. *Mor.* 639E). Diodorus apparently drew on the same lost source as Plutarch (most likely the fourth-century B.C. historian Ephorus), for he points out on several occasions that it was the Thebans' bodily strength that wore down their Spartan counterparts (Diod. 12.70.3; 15.39.1; 15.87.1; cf. Xen. *An.* 3.1.23). Was the well-known national characteristic of Theban armies to stack their phalanxes especially deep (e.g., Thuc. 4. 93.4; Xen. *Hell.* 4.2.13, 18; 6.4.12) designed to capitalize on the accumulated thrusting power of unusually strong men, to break down shallower lines through the group strength of hardy farmers?

Is it no accident that the Theban reputation for individual strength is usually found in a fourth-century context, implying that the conservative, landlocked armies of Boeotia were still composed almost exclusively of farmers, although in other *poleis* there had been a steady erosion in the exclusive farmer/infantryman equation and thus a general decline in the fighting corps of the *polis?* At Athens, the incorporation of the unfit, nonagrarian, and privileged into the ranks was a source of constant complaint for philosophers and comic poets. They felt mongrelization of the phalanx had eroded hoplite prowess (e.g. Pl. *Resp.* 8.556D-E; Xen. *Mem.* 3.5.15; Ar. *Ran.*1087–96).

Nevertheless, outside of Leuctra—a battle that has baffled modern commentators (cf. Hanson 1988: 190–92)—we have no tradition that Boeotian physical strength is to be associated with their particular battle successes (at Tanagra [458 B.C.], first Coroneia [447 B.C.], and Delium [424 B.C.]). At Leuctra (371 B.C.) most scholars usually discount Plutarch's explanation of muscle. They cite instead a variety of other causes (e.g., cavalry tactics, an oblique attack, and massed column on the left wing). None of them have anything to do with the bodily strength of the victorious Thebans and their allies.

But the Thebans and their confederates were *not* always victorious in battle. Armies from Boeotia apparently lost to the Athenians at the shadowy battle of Oinophyta (457 B.C.). They were fought to a standstill by the Spartans both at the second battle of Coroneia (394 B.C.) and at second Mantineia (362 B.C.)—not to mention their disgraceful and failed efforts to aid the Persians at the battle of Plataea (479 B.C.), where they were, in fact, repulsed on the left wing by the Athenians.

Nor elsewhere in narrative battle accounts involving Spartans, Corinthians, Argives, Athenians, and others is the superior strength of particular hoplites distinguishable, much less determinant. The impression in our literary sources until the fourth century is that most hoplite armies were uniformly composed of farmers, roughly indistinguishable in body size, strength, and equipment. Their similarities explain in part the alarming hoplite propensity on both sides for simple misdirection and misidentification in battle (cf. Hanson 1989: 185–193).

For explanations of continued hoplite success one must look predictably enough to the Spartans, the sole professional soldiers of the eighth to fourth centuries, the "craftsmen and technicians of military science" (Plut. *Pel.* 23.4; cf. Xen. *Mem.* 3.9.2). Supported by an entire population of individual servants or helots, they alone were free to engage in constant drilling, group messes, and a life devoted to the bar-racks. Through such extensive training, they produced uniquely skilled fighters, like those found in no other national army. "Not by caring for our fields," Plutarch tells us the antiagrarian warriors bragged, "but rather by caring for ourselves did we acquire those fields" (*Mor.* 214A72).

Spartan success was derived not merely from their experience in han-dling the spear and sword. Plato in his *Laches* reminds us that there was little real value in set moves or *hoplomachia* in phalanx warfare. He sug-gests instead that the simplicity of crowded hoplite crashes left no room—or need—for formal weapon techniques (192E–194A). Other anecdotal literary evidence seems to confirm the idea that there was not much to be gained by extensive individual training with spear and shield (see Anderson 1991: 28–32).

Many ancient sources (e.g., Thuc. 5.66–71) do speak of Spartan ex-cellence at marching and drill, at group movement under the terrifying conditions of massed combat. They suggest that the one army of profes-sionals in Greece, *of nonfarmers,* alone held battlefield superiority, the true "artisans of war and servants of Ares" (Plut. *Comp. Lyc. et Num.* 2.6). Spartan hoplites seem to have brought a real zest to the muster, singing as they lumbered out to the battlefield (e.g., Dio. Chrys. 2.59). In phalanx battle much must have rested on just this ability to march in deliberate set order, without allowing fatal gaps to appear between ho-plites, without flinching at the moment of collision, something difficult for most agrarian amateurs, who between campaigns rarely practiced forming up with their tribesmen and neighbors. The Spartans alone by the fifth century still anachronistically walked across no-man's land slowly to the music of pipes, in John Milton's words, "to the sounds of flutes and soft recorders" (cf. Adcock 8), forfeiting entirely the advan-tage of momentum at impact, which a running charge might add (e.g., Thuc. 5.70; Plut. *Lyc.* 22.2–3).

The Spartans' deliberate walk must have had a chilling effect on their adversaries. The unfortunate Athenian general Cleon ran away at Am-phipolis (422 B.C.) once he saw the distinctive shields of the approach-ing Spartans. No wonder, Plutarch says, their onslaught—highlighted by long hair and crimson cloaks—was always "at once awesome and terrify-ing" (e.g., Eupolis 359 Kock; cf. Plut. *Pel.* 17.6; Xen. *Hell.* 4.4.10). Such well-trained killers were they, that even in the most desperate circumstances, Spartan hoplites were able to stay calm and keep good order (e.g., Xen. *Lac. Pol.* 11.7). That is why Herodotus makes the renegade Spartan king Demaratus say to the Persian king that "as individual fighters they are as good as any in the world, but when they fight in a group they are the *best* in the world" (Hdt. 7.104.4). The passage emphasizes that group drill and training at Sparta were perhaps more important than individual skill and bodily strength.

Yet even the Spartans, the most successful of all Greek infantry, the sole army of professional nonfarmers, *were not invincible.* Scholars who repeat the legend of Spartan invincibility forget just how often their phalanxes were beaten back at their own game of infantry battle (much more often than in the case of the Thebans). They lost decisively at the battles of Hysiae (669 B.C.), Tegea (560 B.C.), Haliartos (395 B.C.), Tegyra (377 B.C.), Lechaion (390 B.C.), and Leuctra (371 B.C.). Spartan hoplites came away less than triumphant also at Coroneia (394 B.C.) and second Mantineia (362 B.C.). Herodotus says that in early campaigns during the sixth century against their immediate neighbors, the Tegeans, "they met with nothing but defeat" (Hdt. 1.67). It is not exactly true to suggest that their skill in hoplite drill and unit cohesion were absolutely critical, that Spartan expertise and discipline routinely defeated all comers (e.g., Plut. *Mor.* 241B4–5).

Other factors must have at times mitigated their advantage in drill and discipline. Pericles was *not* completely exaggerating when he reminded his Athenian audience during the first year of the Peloponnesian War: "And if with relaxation rather than work, and with natural, rather than enforced, courage we nevertheless are willing to hazard dangers, that is only to our advantage, since we do not have to toil *needlessly* in advance of the hardships to come and yet still face our struggles with *just as much daring* as those who are always in a state of preparation for them" (Thuc. 2.39.4; emphasis added).

If drill did not always guarantee battlefield supremacy, then what does explain the Spartans' own occasional setbacks against purely agrarian militias? More important, since we are investigating universal causes for the success or failure of hoplite armies, what accounts for the outcome of the many battles between the other Greeks, instances where Spartan professionals were not present (for we hear that no other Greek *polis* until the late fifth and fourth centuries followed their lead and instituted drill on any wide scale)? Although the degree of hoplite training is still controversial among classical scholars, no evidence has been adduced to show that phalanxes before the late fifth century were routinely mustered to engage in lengthy marches and mock battles, as later mercenary forces were.

The key to success in warfare of the agrarian city-state cannot be found in traditional military exegesis (i.e., strategy, tactics, and logistics). Nor is victory always attributable to superior strength, skill, or battle experience on the part of the infantrymen of any particular *polis*. Is triumph a question simply of superior force, of greater numbers of hoplites assembled at any given battle?

Here too problems arise. The location of hoplite battle (small plains surrounded by rough terrain) and the absence of second and third stages of fighting, gave little opportunity for the application of preponderant infantry forces—reserves, second armies, combined contingents, feints, and ambushes. Because only the first three ranks could reach the enemy at any given time, and because it is not at all clear that even unusually deep phalanxes always caused a proportionate increase in thrusting power (e.g., Pritchett *War* 1.134–43; Hanson 1988: 193–207), the sheer numbers of bodies present at a hoplite battle—either *in toto* or concentrated at a given point—may have been only of secondary importance.

In any case, most opposing Greek phalanxes were roughly the same size. Even on those rare occasions when one side outnumbered its adversary, victory was not automatically achieved. There are examples of outnumbered hoplite armies defeating their opponents decisively. The victorious Thebans at Leuctra (about 6,000–7,000 men) may have numbered many thousands less than their Peloponnesian counterparts (i.e., 10,000–11,000; cf. Anderson 1970: 196–98). In other engagements such as Delium (424 B.C.: 7,000 Boeotian hoplites and 10,000–12,000 auxiliary troops vs. 7,000 Athenian hoplites and an unknown number of auxiliaries [Thuc. 4.93.3–4.94]), and Nemea (394 B.C.: 23,000–25,000 Peloponnesians vs. 24,000–26,000 Athenians, Argives, and Boeotians [e.g., Xen. *Hell.* 4.2.9–11; Diod. 14. 83.1]), it is uncanny just how evenly matched both sides actually were. At the battle of second Coroneia (394 B.C.), Xenophon (*Ages.* 2.7–9) says precisely that. The Thebans and Spartans, he believed, were about paired (i.e. about 20,000 men each; cf. Anderson 1970: 310 n.18).

This rough numerical parity at hoplite battles gives credibility to the traditional idea that the Greeks were quite fearful of the hegemony of any one *polis*, constantly changing allegiances and trading sides throughout the fifth and fourth centuries. All were efforts, reflecting the agrarians' similar ideological discomfort with the accumulation of farm plots, to prevent the overwhelming numerical preponderance of force on any one side. The egalitarianism of the agrarian grid was superimposed by the citizenry onto the larger interrelationships between the city-states themselves.

Was victory in hoplite battle, then, determined by the rule of the inexplicable, of chance and blind luck? The Spartans under Leonidas suffered betrayal at Thermopylae (480 B.C.), and were fatally attacked from the rear through no fault of their own (Hdt. 7.212–14). Otherwise, they might have held off the invasion of Xerxes for days on end. At Leuctra (371 B.C.) some pre-battle drinking and the unfortunate collision of cavalry and infantry (Hanson 1989: 126–31; Anderson 1970: 213–15) apparently doomed the Spartan rightward advance—a tactic so very successful against Theban troops more than twenty years earlier at Nemea (394 B.C.)—at the outset. That unfortunate confusion explains in part their shocking defeat at the hands of Epameinondas and his Thebans. Leuctra was a battle where, according to the Spartan apologist Xenophon, "everything turned out wrong for the Spartans" (*Hell.* 6.4.8–15; cf. Hanson 1988: 205–7).

Plain bad luck may account for the Athenians' fate at Delium (424 B.C.), where all imaginable catastrophes took place (Thuc. 4. 94–96). After mistakenly fighting their own troops, the Athenians compounded their failure—this time fatally—by wrongly surmising that a few enemy cavalry sorties on the horizon signaled an entirely new enemy force, "the sudden appearance of them starting a panic in the already victorious wing of the Athenians." On the edge of victory, but quickly bewildered and terrified, the Athenians fled the battlefield altogether. "The intelligent Athenian hoplites," Sir Frank Adcock summarized of Delium, "had put two and two together and made it five" (Adcock 85).

Nevertheless, "luck," confusion, and misdirection in themselves cannot explain most hoplite victories (e.g., Hanson 1989: 185–93). More often in hoplite battle, there is truth to the dictum of von Moltke that "luck in the long run is given only to the efficient." This is especially true among the ancient Greeks, where the sheer uniformity in numbers, armament, tactics, terrain, and command eliminated the unplanned and unexpected from most "normal" hoplite battles.

The only other common factor that can adequately account for Greek hoplite success or failure is nerve (cf. Pl. *Lach.* 193D). Here, I think, lies the real secret of Greek warfare of the *polis*. In the last analysis, battle was for the farmer a war of the spirit, as was his effort to conquer nature, to reclaim land, and to draw a living from the earth (e.g., Xen. *Cyr.* 3.3.19; cf. 2.3.11). The desire to push ahead, facing the "storm of spear," not to flinch, not to leave one's assigned place in the file or line, are, of course, frequently described in Greek literature. They are the ancients' desiderata of survival within the phalanx.

Under close examination, these are the same emotions, the same skills so explicitly outlined by Hesiod in his outline for agrarian success: hard work, honor of community, willingness to sacrifice and face the unexpected danger, concern for past social and religious custom and tradition.*

Here one wonders how, and under what precise conditions, that superior, victory-giving morale—itself an offshoot of the solidarity of the farm-owning classes of the *polis*—was achieved by any *one* particular agrarian city-state? The hoplite armies of the *polis* almost all lacked real uniforms, medals, rank, military advancement, cash bonuses, and other traditional forms of group and individual combat rewards and punishments. The few prizes for valor that appear in Greek literature were given to the strong and reliable who upheld the line, *not* to the Homeric few who waded out in front of their comrades (Pritchett *War* 2.276–90). Only in non-*polis* societies—Scythia, Persia, Thrace, Carthage, Iberia, and Macedonia—do we hear of state decorations for military valor and special recognition for killing individual opponents (e.g., Arist. *Pol.* 7.1324b.10–24).

I have argued in *The Western Way of War* that both alcohol and the presence of the hoplite "general" in the front ranks were strong combat

---

*E.g., Hes. *Op.* 303–19; 342–44; 397–401; 410–14; 495–500; 707–14; 722–24; 822–28. "Ultimately," the British expert of Spartan military practice John Lazenby has remarked, "the single most important factor in a hoplite battle was undoubtedly what Napoleon thought, many centuries later, counted for three-quarters in war: morale. "Lazenby 1991: 104; cf. Lazenby 1993: 258–61; cf. Hanson 1989: 117–25; 219–26.

incentives, and that an even more important part of morale was regimental *élan* (Hanson 1989: 117–25). Most hoplite armies were arranged in formation by tribal and family affiliations. This form of muster guaranteed that farmers fought in a manifestly public way, given the close order of the phalanx, with lifelong friends and family at their side, and men like themselves in the front and rear. Fellow soldiers, Plato says, come together as they observe each other in actual battle (Pl. *Resp.* 8.556D–E).

The farmer in battle was no different from the man back on his land: fearful, proud, determined that his orchard and vineyard be as well kept and productive as his neighbor's, he carried into the phalanx a strong ideology of individual chauvinism mixed with group concern. Sociologies of battle tell us that in the final seconds before combat, men choose to face down the enemy rather than to run, not out of some abstract notion of God or country, but instead from the fear of playing the coward in front of their own small group, of "not wanting to let 'one's mates down' " (Lazenby 1991: 107; Hanson 1989: 123–25).

But the *esprit de corps* of this unique regimental system of the Greeks (akin to the tactician Aelian's "suitability of the occasion" and "morale of the men" quoted earlier) explains only the generic success of hoplite armies—why almost all Greek phalanxes of the *polis* period charged together, rather than disintegrated in panic at the outset. The flight before the battle even begins (e.g., Thuc. 5.10.8; Xen. *Hell.* 4.3.17, 4.8.38, 7.1.31; Eur. *Bacch.* 303–4), although well known in Greek military history, is the exception, not the rule. What accounts for the superior morale of any one agrarian army at any one time? Under what conditions did one network of family and friends, one body of ancient Greek agrarian neighbors, push their similarly armed and identically arranged adversaries off the field of battle?

The answer, I think, is tied directly to the agricultural basis of the city-state, detected in the agrarian ideology of the combatants themselves. More precisely, the key to success of these citizen militias often depended on *where* the battle took place, whether hoplite-farmers came out of their walls on the defensive to protect their own cultivated ground at their feet, or battled as invaders on the flatlands of another. Even though most fighting began over borderlands, rarely did the actual killing occur there in the highland passes and plateaus. More often one army went down into the immediate interior of another *polis*, where the prerequisite level surfaces for phalanxes were found. Except for an occasional fight on neutral ground, on most hoplite battlefields at least one contingent of the army felt at home.

Athenians, Thebans, and others (even Spartan farm overlords) in most of the major engagements over a two-hundred-year period were vastly different—that is, inferior—soldiers once they left the borders of their territory, once they lost their "home field" advantage, as it were, and marched into the countryside of the enemy. Even in the fourth century, when Greek hoplite battle was often being replaced by more frequent raiding and skirmishing, and when the ranks of the phalanx proper were not always composed exclusively of farmers, the traditions of agrarian identification with the homeland still permeated the military forces of the entire *polis*. Logistically, strategically, psychologically, and spiritually the hoplite phalanx of the Greek city-state was not well suited for lengthy invasion or continual aggression.

The Thebans, until the Panhellenic defeat at Chaironeia against Philip and his Macedonians (338 B.C.), lost few of the numerous major hoplite battles that were fought *within* the confines of their native Boeotia. The horrendous struggle at second Coroneia (394 B.C.), although an especially violent confrontation with the Spartans, a few miles from Thebes herself, was essentially a toss-up; neither phalanx achieved a clear-cut victory (Xen. *Hell.* 4.3.22–23; Plut. *Ages.* 18). Apparently, the Thebans were defeated in their own territory by the Athenians only at Oinophyta (457 B.C.), a little-known affair largely left unrecorded in our literary sources (Thuc. 1.108.2). Some citizens were also repelled earlier as traitors alongside the Persians at Plataea (479 B.C.).

Contrast these rare losses with their unrivaled record of successes against a series of Athenian invading armies at Tanagra (457 B.C.; Thuc. 1.108.1), first Coroneia (447 B.C.; Thuc. 1.113), and Delium (424 B.C.; Thuc. 4.96–97), and against the Spartans at Haliartos (395 B.C.; Xen. *Hell.* 3.5.22–4; Plut. *Lys.* 28–29), Tegyra (375 B.C.; Plut. *Pel.* 16.1, 17.3–4), and Leuctra (371 B.C.; Xen. *Hell.* 6.4.16–26). *All* these Boeotian victorious battles were fought within walking distance of Thebes.

The Spartans were *never* defeated in their native Laconia during the eighth through fifth centuries. Until Epameinondas' invasion of 370 B.C. their countryside was thus epitomized as "unplundered" (e.g., Plut. *Ages.*

31.1–2). Although Spartan hoplites often had dramatic success abroad, it is notable that their only real defeats, at Hysiae (699 B.C.), Tegea (560 B.C.), Thermopylae (480 B.C.), Haliartos (395 B.C.), Lechaion (390 B.C.), Tegyra (375 B.C.), and Leuctra (371 B.C.), were all in battles fought away from the vale of Laconia.[11]

The Athenians, it is true, put their faith in their navy by the fifth century, and were quite successful both in purely naval actions and in a number of amphibious assaults and small-scale raids. But in major infantry conflicts of hoplite phalanxes, they too had little luck beyond their borders. Athenian defeats at Tanagra (457 B.C.), first Coroneia (447 B.C.), Delium (424 B.C.), Amphipolis (422 B.C.), Mantineia (418 B.C.), Assinarus River (413 B.C.; Thuc. 7.84–86), and Nemea River (394 B.C.) contrast markedly with a few surprising foreign victories.* Perhaps the Athenians, in their failure to march out against the Spartans during the five invasions of the Peloponnesian War (i.e., 431–425 B.C.) deliberately ignored the tradition of Marathon—the only major land battle of the *polis*-period fought on Attic soil. In that battle their hoplite infantrymen fought superbly and victoriously on their home ground against overwhelming odds.

There are occasional exceptions to this tendency for a decisive advantage to go to the defending phalanx of agrarians. Obviously the success of the invaded *polis* over the aggressors was not guaranteed in every fight, as is clear from the battles of Oinophyta and second Coroneia. Those were occasions where the Thebans were not able to defeat invading armies decisively.

Some Greek encounters were also fought on neutral ground belonging to a third *polis* (e.g., Amphipolis [422 B.C.]). In other, rarer instances it was simply difficult to determine which side had actually won. At second Coroneia (394 B.C.) and at second Mantineia (362 B.C.), the invading Spartans (394 B.C.) and invading Thebans (362 B.C.) *both* gave a good account of themselves, but ultimately failed to rout the defending enemy decisively from the battlefield. After second Mantineia the historian Xenophon in the last lines of his *Hellenica* remarks of the battle's inconclusiveness that "there was even more uncertainty and confusion in

---

*Such as Oinophyta (457 B.C.), Sphacteria (426 B.C; Thuc. 4.6–15), perhaps not properly a hoplite battle, and first Sicily (415 B.C.; Thuc. 6.70).

Greece after than before the battle " (Hell. 7.5.27). Both Spartans and Thebans not surprisingly erected victory trophies (Xen. Hell. 7.5.26).

It is instructive, in this regard, to examine both the battles of Leuctra (371 B.C.) and second Mantineia (362 B.C.). The combatants—Spartans and Boeotians—were identical. The tactics at both engagements were about the same. There is no evidence that preponderance of numbers affected either engagement. What is clear is that both aggressors failed to win the respective battles outright. The Spartan invaders failed at Leuctra, the Theban nine years later at Mantineia. Does this not suggest that both Thebans and Spartans were more effective hoplites when they fought on their own ground, in sight of their native polis (see Hanson 1988: 204–7)?

Because in the fifth and fourth centuries many Greek hoplite armies were increasingly composed of a wide variety of allied contingents, and because the ranks were no longer exclusively composed of farmers, the entire notion of locale itself was often problematic. Battles such as those fought at Mantineia (418 B.C.; 362 B.C.) took place on ground that could be seen as both home and foreign turf to different groups of hoplites in the same army. In 418 B.C. the Mantineians allied themselves with the Athenians and the local Argives against their neighbors, the Tegeans, and the rest of the nearby Peloponnesian allies. The Athenians were thus relatively distant foreigners fighting alongside the native Mantineians to ward off Peloponnesian invaders—who themselves were near neighbors.

All the same, during the three-hundred-year history of hoplite warfare, in the great majority of significant and recorded land battles, there is an undeniable pattern that defending hoplite infantry usually repelled the invaders. This tendency reflects, I think, their stubborn Greek agrarianism in defense of their homes. Out of some twenty-one major pitched Greek battles, in at least sixteen there was a clear-cut decision involving hoplites battling to protect their home ground against an army of invaders. In the other five engagements, the outcome was ambiguous, the battle was on neutral ground, or the presence of several allies clouded the definition of native territory.

If one focuses on the decisive sixteen conflicts between attackers and defenders, in twelve of these battles the defensive hoplites were victorious, a seventy-five percent frequency.[12] The reason for the success of defensive troops—in a world of infantry battle that typically saw no fortifications, dug-in installations, or augmentation by civilian troops and scouts—may be more than the intrinsic military advantages that accrue to the defense.

Hoplite battlefields were usually uniform courts of killing. Flat, treeless, and without hidden and unknown obstacles such as gullies and ravines (for an exception, see Thucydides' remarks on the peculiar significance of watercourses and hills at Delium [Thuc. 4.96]), these were places where the defenders' superior knowledge of terrain did not necessarily give them the advantage once the invaders had arrived in the small plains of the invaded. Polybius remarked that this rare ground was the only suitable stage for hoplite battles, adding that "it is almost impossible or, at any rate very rare, to find an area of countryside of say about two or three miles, or more, that contains no obstacles" (18.31.3–5).

Nor did a "home field" offer much advantage in logistics. Until the Peloponnesian War, few Greek armies planned lengthy expeditions. Once hoplites arrived in foreign territory they usually left within a few days. The army relied almost exclusively on the rations each man brought along, occasionally rifling an abandoned farmhouse or stealing any ripe grain left unharvested.

Finally, in the great age of hoplite warfare, local civilian guerrillas posed little threat. Almost all fights took place openly in the countryside. From the land outside the city proper slaves, the poor, women, children, and the aged either were evacuated to mountainous or foreign ground, or were housed behind the walls of the *polis* (Hanson 1983: 87–101). The image of house-to-house fighting where civilian noncombatants throw roof tiles and box in the bewildered enemy stragglers on twisting streets belongs to the Peloponnesian War and after (e.g., Plut. *Mor.* 228E). Even then such urban guerrilla fighting was always the exception—as the rare, nightmarish struggles inside Plataea (429 B.C.), Olympia (364 B.C.), and Argos (272 B.C.) attest (Thuc. 2.4; Xen. *Hell.* 7.4.28–33; Plut. *Pyr.* 34.1–3).

The superiority of Greek infantrymen fighting on home ground is explicable primarily as a spiritual advantage. Most farmers today cannot leave their farms even for a much-needed few days of vacation. Anytime my grandfather, who was born, lived, and died on the same farm, left his acreage, he was nearly overcome with unhappiness and worry The brightest moments of his rare one- to three-day excursions were the last miles home. Only then was he sure he had made it back. Only then did he miraculously snap out of his despair.

All farmers struggle with that agrarian anchor. They call home after a few miles on the road, afraid things have irrevocably changed in the minutes since their departure, convinced that (often spectacular) sights elsewhere are never as moving as those on the (often dreary) home place. So a chorus of Theban natives sings of their nondescript but native plains: "If you give up to the enemy this deep soil of ours, what land on earth would you ever find better?" (Aesch. *Sept.* 303–5).

No wonder the tactics, strategy, and even the technology of hoplite warfare of the *polis* were inherently protective (cf. Plut. *Pel.* 1.5). Large shields, heavy breastplates and helmets, and spears of moderate size reflected these values—precisely the opposite mentality of pike-wielding, lightly protected, and aggressive Macedonian phalangites, rootless men often with no farm of their own, who predictably added ten feet to the hoplite's spear but reduced the shield's area by two-thirds.

Polis warfare was an integral system never designed for absolute conquest, perhaps not even intended for serious invasion. Troops, apparently small farmers all before the mid-fifth century, were superb infantrymen when they fought for their families and on their home ground. They were less reliable when they saw themselves far from their *polis* as invaders—that is, as crop destroyers, farm-trodders, agrarian killers of their social counterparts. Xenophon feels it necessary to remind his reading audience (who apparently would feel otherwise) that in wartime farmers should not merely be defensive, but instead should go on the offensive against someone else's farm (*Oec.* 5.13). Again, it was left to Macedon to transform the phalanx—introducing light armor, long pikes, diminution of baggage carriers, integration of crack heavy cavalry and light-armed troops—from a defensive to an offensive force. That was only possible, I believe, because those troops—barons, serfs, laborers, mercenaries, and thugs—were not middling agrarians from autonomous *poleis*.

Hoplite-farmers, as the spread of their standardized equipment and protocols throughout the Greek *poleis* attest, shared a vague "agrarian consciousness," a common enough notion of agricultural chauvinism. In wartime, the native ground could even be personified as one with its ho-plites: "the soil," Aeschylus writes, "grieves for the men it loved" (*stenei pedon philandron*) (Aesch. *Sept.* 901–2). In his *Persians*, he makes the ghost of King Darius says of the Greeks that "the land itself fights on their behalf" (*autê gar hê gê xumachos keinois pelei*)" (*Pers.* 792; cf. 796–97).

This rural identification with native farmland made most men hardly sympathetic to the notion of neglecting their own crops (e.g., Thuc. 3.15.2; cf. 1.141.3,5: 1.142.7), in order to march out and destroy the property and lives of those who labored much like themselves. The ten-dency arose in the first two and a half centuries of the *polis* for short campaigns and the absence of any lasting damage to the agricultural in-frastructure of their adversaries (Hanson 1983: 145–51).

Even as late as the fifth-century battle at Delium (424 B.C.), the The-ban general Pagondas only with difficulty prompted his Boeotian con-federate army to march a few thousand yards beyond their border into Attica. He believed that it was necessary to punish a retreating Athen-ian army of invasion, which had just days earlier affronted the sovereign-ty of Boeotia by occupying her temple to Apollo at Delium. Even though the ensuing battle was clearly to be defensive, fought to keep aggressive armies out of his native Boeotia, Pagondas was still faced with a dilem-ma: the retreating Athenian invaders were now no longer invaders, but technically right on or across the poorly demarcated and undulating Boeotian-Attic frontier. To protect their own land, the Boeotians might have to go a very short distance *beyond* the limits of their native ground to provoke a fight.

This possibility clearly bothered both Pagondas and his men. Boeot-ian discomfort is good evidence that Greek hoplite troops had much greater spiritual confidence when they were fighting inside their own frontier. Thucydides makes Pagondas address the problem head-on in a pre-battle harangue to his hoplites: "Boeotians, the idea that we should not fight the Athenians, unless we square off within Boeotia itself, is a concept that should never have been entertained by us generals. It was to hurt Boeotia that the Athenians crossed the frontier and constructed fortifications in our own country" (Thuc. 4.92.1).

His Athenian counterpart, the general Hippocrates, was similarly aware of the traditional association between hoplite phalanxes and agrarian conservatism. He worried about the morale of his own invading army, even though it was probably no longer composed exclusively of farmers. Knowing that his Athenian hoplites had first ventured into Boeotia to harm enemy territory (and were therefore the aggressors of this particular campaign), he was also aware that his army had now made its way safely near or back over the ill-defined border. The trick was somehow to explain to his Athenian phalanx that a prior offensive intent was now transformed into "defense": "You must not think that we are going out of our way to run a risk in the country of another. The battle will take place in their territory, but in fact it will be for our own" (Thuc. 4.95.2). Perhaps the invading Athenians in the ranks who had just stepped over the border into Boeotia did not believe Hippocrates' sophistry that they were in Attica fighting for their homes. In any case, within a few minutes they were defeated decisively *inside* Boeotia.

Whether the two opposing generals—given the problems of acoustics—actually gave these speeches in 424 B.C. is also not clear. But two ideas do emerge from Thucydides' narrative: (1) the historian at least believed that location was crucial to the morale of the respective armies; and (2) whatever the actual relationship of the battlefield to the official border between the two Greek *poleis*, the nature of the campaign made it clear that both sides—victorious Boeotians and defeated Athenians—knew the Athenians were in truth the invaders. Elsewhere, Athenian hoplites on most other extended campaigns outside Attica, in Aetolia (426 B.C.), at Amphipolis (422 B.C.), and over the two years in Sicily (415–412 B.C.), were lackluster (e.g., Thuc. 3.94–98, 5.6–11, 7.11–88). If there were any bright spots among Athens' expeditionary forces, they usually involved mercenaries and light-armed troops, typically during the fourth century when the two were synonymous.

As in so many other spheres, the later years of the Peloponnesian War (431–404 B.C.) saw a revolutionary departure from past infantry practice. The introduction of sieges, mercenaries, night attacks, ambushes, and hit-and-run raids involved a host of different combatants, men of every class and status who had no common agreement of what war should be. But even after the Peloponnesian War (which we will see was the great turning point in the history of Greek warfare), traditional hoplite battles were not forgotten. Although no longer the absolute rule in Greek warfare, landed infantry and the collision of ground troops of the old school continued to provide a decisive outcome in many campaigns. We still hear of many brutal stand-up encounters in the fourth century. To the extent that the reactionary belligerents chose to send phalanxes of small farmers into battle, anachronistically or not, the old thinking still applied. Most hoplite collisions, as two centuries before, usually continued to turn out favorably for the invaded, less so for the aggressor.

As Aristotle puts it of war between the Greek city-states: "It is fitting to engage in military pursuits (*tôn polemikôn askêsis*) not in order to enslave those who are not deserving of slavery, but first of all so that men themselves might not be enslaved by others" (*Pol.* 7.1333b39–41). Plutarch says about the same thing. In Greek battle "not to suffer harm" rather than "inflicting injury" was the first concern of the soldier, of the general, and of the officials of the *polis* itself (*Pel.* 1.5). Ancient authors attest that the phalanx was a terrifying formation, but it was a body of men whose chief interest was to protect and defend, not to attack and slaughter.

Agriculture emerges as the underlying basis, the entire foundation of Greek warfare during the life of the *polis*. Hoplite armies, after all, were more than militarily efficacious. They arose in the late eighth and seventh centuries in order to ensure the existence of the small plots of a growing class of agrarians, to cement the ideology of the early *polis* itself. Excluding both the rich and the poor, phalanxes of farmers created a system in which their own mutual interests might transcend *polis* boundaries. When natural disputes arose over poorly defined borderlands, farmers agreed to decide the matter themselves—but usually in a manner that would ensure to all parties a battle both brief and decisive. In this way, the protocols of early hoplite conflict never endangered agrarian primacy in the respective Greek city-states, but rather enhanced it.

For much of the early *polis* period a hoplite farmer of Attica had nearly as much in common with his Boeotian counterpart across the border as he did with either the Athenian aristocrat or the landless laborer. That sense of agrarian solidarity forms the dramatic context of Aristophanes' play the *Acharnians*, a comedy produced during the Peloponnesian War (425 B.C.), in which an Attic farmer makes private peace treaties with fellow agrarians of other city-states in open opposition to official Athenian policy. It is argued in the play that the farmers of Attica have greater affinity with "foreign" rustics than they do with their "kindred" inside the walls of Athens (Ar. *Ach.* 859–957).

Only with agrarianism in mind can we explain why both the wealthy and the poor were insignificant in battle, why farmland was often attacked yet rarely damaged, why plains, not passes were the loci of killing, why heavy armor was worn in the scorching heat of the Mediterranean sun, why shields were big but spears relatively short, why battle was brutal yet rarely catastrophic in terms of casualties, lost time, and monetary expenditure. Although invasion of the flatland of an enemy was usually needed to settle ownership of contested borderland—itself often inferior ground—most paradoxically of all, even here a natural check on belligerency was present. Most armies of small farmers usually proved less enthusiastic, and less capable fighters once they left their own familiar ground and assumed a role at odds with the entire defensive and protective ideology of agrarianism.

Hoplite armies—by challenges to local sovereignty, through the instigation of gifted and ambitious political leaders, in anger at religious affront, from desire for additional land, in answer to aggrieved allies—could often go way beyond the border. But in doing so farmers inevitably lost the moral high ground—and this was recognized in diminished spirit on the battlefield.

Chapter 7

THE ECONOMY OF AGRARIAN WARFARE

There was no war by land, not at least by which any hegemony was acquired; there were many border contests, but of foreign expeditions designed for conquest there were none among the Hellenes. Indeed, there were no subject city-states under the control of the great city-states; thus these Greek states did not unite as equals for allied expeditions; instead, what fighting there was at this time consisted merely of local fighting between rival neighbors.

—Thucydides 1.15

The Greeks of the past did not even choose to defeat their adversaries through deceit, thinking instead that there was nothing glorious or even secure in military successes unless one side killed the enemy drawn up in open battle. Therefore, there was an agreement not to employ unseen weapons or missiles against one another, but they decided that only hand-to-hand fighting in massed column was the true arbiter of events. For that very reason, they made public announcements to each other about wars and battles in advance, when they would decide to enter them, and even concerning the places where they were to meet and draw up their lines.

—Polybius 13.3.4

We have examined the codified and predictable nature of Greek agrarian warfare in the *polis* period, how it enhanced independent farmers and made agricultural territory critical to the outcome of hoplite battle. But during the fifth and especially in the fourth century, the traditional agrarian rules of hoplite warfare were gradually bypassed (see Chapter 8, "Hoplites as Dinosaurs"). The phalanx itself no longer always played the decisive role between warring Greek city-states.

During the fourth-century and subsequent transformation in the conditions of the Greek city-states, many Greek authors belatedly recognized the value of the hoplitic regulations of centuries past. They often pointed out nostalgically that for more than two centuries the early *poleis*, in accordance with some unwritten "laws of the Greeks," had been able to restrict most conflicts to a single, though frightful, collision of hoplite heavy infantry.[1] These later writers, at least, thought the warfare of an earlier time (the seventh through fifth centuries) had been extremely economical. They (correctly) felt it had been responsible for the general stability of the early Greek *polis*.

The actual costs of Greek warfare have usually been discussed by scholars only for the fifth and fourth centuries, and largely in association with Athens: either the complex financial arrangements that supported her navy and expeditionary hoplite forces during the Peloponnesian War, or the squabbling over the necessarily reduced funds allotted to her defense during the fourth century.[2] Rarely is Panhellenic military outlay reckoned for the period of the early Greek *polis* (700–480 B.C.). For that era there is little record of credits and debits on the balance sheets of *polis* treasuries. Nor was there a need for property and produce taxes so crucial for later military expenditure (e.g., Thomsen 136–41). Instead the agrarian monopoly of the Greek city-state was at full force both in war and at peace. It discouraged any type of mobilization that required burdensome levies on its farmers—who, after all, themselves composed the councils of their respective governments.

The acquisitive, positive, income-producing aspects of early Greek warfare—the much-discussed raiding and plundering of cattle, people, slaves, and agricultural produce—have received far more attention than the negative considerations, the collective expense in money, time, and lives incurred by Greek society during wartime from the first appearance of the hoplite until the invasion of Xerxes (700–480 B.C.).[3] The scholarly emphasis on plundering, raiding, and piracy has, I think, led to a mistaken impression that Greek warfare between state armies was somehow exclusively an income-producing enterprise (e.g., "in some sense war will be by nature an acquisitive art" [Arist. *Pol.* 1.1256b23–24) rather than (at best) an income-redistributing—and far more often an income-destroying—phenomenon. Careful examination of military expenditures of the early city-state reveals that the small farmers who arose at the end of the eighth century crafted a warfare whose innate frugality explains in part the growth of the new agrarianism *and thus the continued existence of the Greek city-state itself.*

Literary, epigraphical, and archaeological evidence concerning Greek warfare before the Persian invasions (490–480/479 B.C.), as we have observed, is unfortunately meager. This explains the silence of modern scholars concerning military expenditures at the beginning of the *polis* period. A word of caution about the ancient evidence for this chapter is needed: there is, I repeat, *no* detailed prose account of *any* hoplite battle in Greece until Marathon (490 B.C.), at the end of the era under review. From references in later literature, lyric and elegiac poetry, vase painting, and archaeological excavation, we can nevertheless infer the earlier shadowy engagements must have been largely similar to their fifth-century successors. For questions of armament, generalship, casualties, and hoplite fighting itself, some literary evidence is legitimately drawn from the later times of the fifth and fourth centuries.

Remember that Herodotus makes the Persian Mardonius (dramatic date 480 B.C.) relate his own familiarity with the peculiarities of hoplite warfare (apparently gained from his entry into northern Greece in 492 B.C.; cf. Hdt. 7.9). Mardonius's knowledge of Hellenic warfare must imply that the historian and his (later fifth-century Greek) audience were assuming a long tradition of hoplite fighting *before* the Persian wars. The property classification at Athens for infantry service, and the laws regarding the abandonment of rank in the so-called Solonian legislation, derive from the early sixth century. These statutes imply an early tradition of battle between columns of heavy infantry dating well back to the seventh and sixth centuries (e.g., Plut. *Sol.* 18.2; Arist. *Ath. Pol.* 7.3).

In addition, Sparta—as elsewhere in the general study of the social and economic history of the city-states—poses special problems and deserves careful discussion. Yet Spartan hoplites, once they reached the battlefield, curiously were armed and fought (i.e., hoplite panoply, phalanx) almost exactly like other Greeks. Depending on the specific context and level of investigation, her soldiers were at once both unrepresentative of Greek military practice and characteristic of general hoplite infantry fighting.[4]

I.

Most early city-states of the Greek mainland possessed only a few military ships of any sort. Given the agrarian character of the *polis,* and the general distrust of farmers for the sea, the majority of Greek farming communities was suspicious of extensive organized navies in the seventh and sixth centuries. We can therefore dismiss the notion that extensive commerce and overseas involvement, not the agrarianism indigenous to Greece herself, sparked the so-called Hellenic renaissance of the eighth century.[5]

Since fighting on the water was relatively unorganized and naval expenditure was sporadic in most early *poleis,* capital expenditure allotted to armaments was primarily limited to land warfare. With the relative absence of chariotry, missile troops, large organized cavalry contingents, artillery (e.g., Plut. *Mor.* 191E), and siege engines, the technological costs of land fighting between 700 and 480 B.C. for most Greeks were essentially focused on the early hoplite panoply. The costly purchase and labor-intensive fabrication of enormous timber and bronze siege-engines and fleets were almost entirely absent in Greece before the Persian Wars (Meiggs 116–37; 154–59).

Classical scholarship has usually believed Greek armor to have been exorbitantly expensive. It has described, I believe wrongly, hoplite fighting as "elitist." In this view, only the well-to-do of the *polis* could afford heavy armor. The wealthy forged hoplite battle to exclude and to oppress the landless poor, who were given no say in the defense of their communities. But the initial outlay of bronze was *not* enormously costly. Individual purchase of arms actually proved an economical investment for the entire untaxed agrarian community: the hoplite panoply allowed a brand of warfare that was unusually cheap in nearly all its manifestations, beginning with the weapons themselves.

In almost all cases the cost of infantry arms was met *entirely by the individual farmer himself*. Only much later in the fifth and fourth centuries, and perhaps in the case of Sparta (e.g., Cartledge 1977: 27), do state subsidies appear for public ownership of arms and armor—usually under very unusual conditions, such as repair of weapons while on the march, gifts to orphaned offspring, or training arms for young Athenian recruits. Mass state-sponsored and tax-supported fabrication of weapons quite clearly belongs to the late fifth and fourth centuries and later, when Greek city-states and wealthy men devoted huge sums to equip foreign and mercenary soldiers. Public intrusion into the supply of weapons marked the end of traditional Greek agrarianism.[6]

The small landowners of Greece alone, no doubt for the first time in the West, shouldered the collective expense of military technology. In the first two centuries of the *polis* period the state essentially contributed nothing toward the production of military equipment for its defense. These self-armed infantrymen were not, as in the Dark-Age past, a few wealthy cavalrymen who fielded their own horses, but hundreds of soldiers who comprised the complete defense of the community. Remember, whatever the outlay of the *geôrgoi* for their hoplite armament before the Persian Wars, that expenditure has to be weighed against the virtual absence of state taxes for public armories, ships, and dockyards. Farmers bought their own arms, but no defense budget siphoned off the produce of their farms.

The actual cost of the hoplite panoply before the Persian Wars is a controversial subject. It goes to the heart of the much-debated sociology of the early Greek *polis*. Much of the evidence for the value of bronze, iron, and wood used in arms is found only in late fifth- or fourth-century inscriptions (e.g., Pritchett 1956: 178, 306–8; Pouilloux 371–79, lines 11–21). Rarely, the cost of arms is mentioned in Attic comedy where the intent (e.g., Ar. *Pax* 210–64), as in the case of references to farming implements (*Pax* 1203–5), is probably to exaggerate the price.

In the earliest surviving Athenian decree of the late sixth century, Athenian settlers on the nearby island of Salamis are to provide their own arms up to the value of thirty drachmas (restored reading see Meiggs and Lewis 14; IG I³ 1. 8–10)—an amount that would have been rendered largely irrelevant if the actual costs of procurement had greatly exceeded that figure. Conjectures of seventy-five to one hundred drachmas for the panoply of the fifth century and later seem reasonably correct.[7] They weaken the traditional emphasis on the steep expense of hoplite weaponry. Most farmers would invest an equal or greater amount in a slave attendant or an ox. The wage of a day laborer in the fifth century was at most around one drachma a day, suggesting that infantry armament then was worth about three months "salary" of the poorest.[8]

Ownership of the hoplite panoply became simply a device, like similar restrictions on the voting franchise, used by the agrarian community to limit participation in the phalanx to those who were middling farmers. Originally at Athens those were the *zeugitai* of the early sixth century with an annual income of two to three hundred liquid or dry measures of produce. Perhaps (although there is scarcely any evidence) later in the *polis* agricultural harvests were converted to net cash holdings of 2,000 drachmas.* Hoplite arms in themselves were only general, not precise, reflections of economic status.

Some residents of the Greek *polis* who were landless, or who possessed plots too small to grow enough produce to qualify for heavy-infantry service might, nevertheless, theoretically have had the resources to acquire hoplite arms. But barring national emergencies, under the strict agrarian protocols of the early city-state, they would have been discouraged (but probably later not prevented) from fighting in the phalanx proper. Instead they were relegated to the light-armed band of skirmishers, or, in the case of some later maritime *poleis*, served as rowers on triremes.

It is wrong to suggest that the high cost of infantry armament always sharply limited participation in Greek hoplite warfare. Hoplite-farmers themselves set arbitrary limits on military service tied to their importance as food producers of the *polis*. During the heyday of the phalanx (i.e., the first two centuries of the *polis* period), the *geôrgoi* wanted non-property owners to be excluded from infantry service, Greeks who might have otherwise been able to acquire the necessary accoutrements. It seems unlikely, therefore, that farmers themselves were exhausted financially by the purchase of the required hoplite bronze, iron, and wood. Ownership of arms was denied to the poor, not the middling Greek.

That the hoplite panoply was not unduly expensive when measured

---

*That would be equal to about forty *plethra* of land (about nine acres), i.e., forty *plethra* at fifty drachmas per *plethron*.

against the landed wealth of the hoplite class may be borne out also by the traditional frequency of arms abandonment on the field of battle.* There are also references to thousands of helmets, shields, breastplates, greaves, spears, and swords stockpiled at the Panhellenic sanctuaries. We also hear of the apparent ownership of duplicate sets of arms, while there is occasional later mention of entire armies of non-hoplites outfitted in mass.[9] Hoplite arms and armor were always plentiful and accessible in the Greek *polis*.

Even the original cost of arms and armor—tied to the price of bronze and the fabrication—is *not* the sole indication of the expense of military weaponry. Far more subtle considerations concerning the use and durability of this equipment need to be taken into account. The following criteria reinforce the idea that the early hoplite-farmer's outlay was extremely economical.

Hoplite weapons and armor were uniform in design. Despite occasional regional modifications (e.g., the "Boeotian" or "Attic" helmets of the fifth and fourth centuries), most offensive weapons and body armor were nearly identical in shape, size, and function throughout Greece (see Snodgrass 1967: 50–71). This military sameness is, I think, clear evidence of a common agrarian culture. Argives, Corinthians, Spartans, Athenians, Thebans, and the farmers of other city-states used essentially the same equipment in the early *polis* period. Whatever the protestations in poetry that the enemy's property "is no good," whatever the Spartans' supposed lack of interest in the equipment of "losers," whatever the philosophical admonitions against stripping other fallen Greeks, every infantryman's weaponry, friend's or foe's, was for the most part seen as identical to one's own—and therefore quite valuable. That technological uniformity in form and function had important economic ramifications.

Hoplite armament was interchangeable. The equipment of the defeated army could be reemployed—or sold—by the victors, thus reducing financial losses in wars when we consider the network of Greek city-states as a whole. The uniformity of design also ensured a ready market for used arms at nearly any location. At least some percentage of

---

*See the poet Archilochus: "So what does it matter? Let the shield go; I *can get another one equally good*" (Archil. 5; emphasis added; cf. Alc. 54; Hdt. 5.95.1; Ar. *Vesp* 22).

captured arms was always recycled, either through outright adoption by the victorious side, or by sale to hoplites on the open market.[10]

There was never a weapons race among rival agrarian city-states, each side seeking to discover some ingenious technological—and inevitably transitory—advantage over its adversaries. Although individual modifications and alterations of the standard panoply reflected personal tastes and accumulated combat experience—different crests, emblems, helmets, absence of greaves, incorporation of precious metals and bright colors and the like (e.g., Hanson 1989: 58–59; Pritchett *War* 3.259–61)—the early Greeks apparently "agreed" to codify weaponry beyond national boundaries. This understanding froze weapons development. It eliminated costly periodic redesign and retooling, and it allowed armorers to concentrate their efforts solely on efficiency in production. Workshops quickly mastered basic patterns and purchased wood, resins, leather, iron, and bronze in bulk.

Often there were real worries expressed that one city-state's arms fabricators might supply the infantry of another, something only possible if their respective armies were outfitted in similar fashion and if soldiers bought their arms on the open market.[11] Under the rules of traditional Greek agrarian warfare, there was little need for craftsmen and designers to incorporate new materials or technologies, to seek new arms markets, or even to worry about competition and profit. To paraphrase Henry Ford, hoplite-farmers everywhere might have any shield they wished, as long as it was big, concave and round. Any other type of weaponry would change the nature of the agrarian phalanx and thus disrupt the formal collision of Greek heavy infantry in column.

The panoply was static in design for nearly two centuries. In the early *polis* period (700–500 B.C.), although gradual modifications in helmets and body armor did occur (e.g., elimination of thigh and shoulder guards), there was essentially no obsolescence in arms—the traditional inflationary bane of modern military procurement. A hoplite shield used at Olynthus in 348 B.C. would have looked roughly the same as that used by Archilochus three centuries earlier (Snodgrass 1964: 65 n. 110). The hoplite panoply could be produced in roughly the same manner generation after generation. Only around the time of the Persian Wars (490, 480/479 B.C.) did the bronze breastplate and helmet become superseded by lighter and less cumbersome models.

There is no reason to doubt that when the infantry veteran had died or (more rarely) reached the "retirement" age of sixty-two, the panoply was handed down, father to son (e.g., Plut. *Mor.* 241F17). Perhaps in certain instances a son might have problems fitting into his ancestral breastplate, helmet, and greaves (Snodgrass 1967: 91–93). In addition, the length of the spear and the diameter of the shield apparently depended on the hoplite's height and arm length. But Greece was largely a homogeneous society and diets were constant generation to generation. Unlike modern American culture, where both the occasional differing races of parents and excellent nutrition, together with medical improvements, can result in offspring of quite different size from their parents, there is reason to believe that many young Greek hoplites *could* fit into their father's arms, just as medieval knights did later on. Small adjustments in helmet lining, the shield strap, and spear length surely were not difficult to make. Hoplites wore a tunic beneath their breastplates, and its thickness might be adjusted to correct small intolerances. Imagine some innate flexibility designed into the panoply despite its metallic construction: over the potential forty-year tenure of some hoplites, many would need to adjust their armor to their changing girth. How many veterans of sixty today can fit into the uniforms of their twenties? In actuality a hoplite's son, not the father himself in his forties, fifties, and sixties, might better match the soldier's own lost youthful physique.

As I pointed out earlier, the acquisition of hoplite arms *per se* was not an automatic guarantee of qualification for service in the phalanx of the *polis.* Infantry service depended on the possession of enough income from agricultural property. If in the early Greek *polis* a farmer met the census rubric, he purchased the hoplite panoply. If he could not meet the qualification, he was not allowed to buy or otherwise obtain heavy arms (which were not necessarily beyond his economic reach). There would be no suggestion that a son was trying to bypass the eligibility requirement for phalanx service by taking over the ancestral arms of his father. If a young man's own worth met the eligibility standards set by the *polis,* he could simply save the purchase costs for new equipment. Wherever practicable, hoplite arms were inheritable. Obviously, not all hoplites wore their father's equipment, especially when father and son might serve side by side for years.

In an economic sense, the uniformity of battle weaponry *reduced* the

Greeks' overall military expenditures: any one set of arms could outlast its original purchaser. Whether inherited by kin or taken by the enemy, the used hoplite panoply could enjoy continued utility and save its new owner cash outlay. Weapons—like farm tools—were passed on from one farmer to another, generation to generation.

Hoplite equipment was extremely durable because of both its metallic construction and the peculiarity of its usage. Bronze greaves, corselets, and helmets could all absorb repeated blows. They could be patched or reworked when damaged. Without moving parts, Greek armament had a "shelf life" of literally centuries. A dramatic example of the panoply's durability occurred in 379 B.C. when some Theban patriots overthrew the Spartan garrison, occupying their citadel by arming themselves with the old votive arms hanging up in the sanctuary stoas (Plut. *Pel.* 12; Xen. *Hell.* 5.4.8). For these brave fighters, the random size and the advanced age of the weapons were apparently no obstacles at all.

When there is mention in Greek literature of ruined weapons, it is usually the spear and shield—the two components of the hoplite ensemble made mostly of wood.[12] Although both shield and spear were prone to damage and frequently appear splintered on vase paintings, they were also relatively cheap to replace, requiring little, if any, new metalworking (e.g., Hanson 1989: 65–88; Blyth 5–21). Often weapon repair consisted simply of the fabrication of new wood shield cores and spear shafts, and the reuse of the appropriate bronze and iron fittings.

Finally, the nature of hoplite battle can also explain in part the long life of the panoply. Most of the infantrymen were stationed in the middle and rear ranks. These fighters might not necessarily even meet the enemy. Their task was to push on their comrades' backs, creating forward pressure while preventing retreat.[13] Extensive equipment damage, then, was often confined to the first three ranks of the phalanx. They were the men whose spears alone could initially reach the enemy and whose defensive armament was in turn targeted in the initial crash. Modern simulations and calculation of the effectiveness of ancient battle gear suggest that rarely could the spear—or even arrows—do much serious damage to the Greek hoplite shield or breastplate (Gabriel and Metz 58–71). The breastplate's and helmet's quarter- to half-inch bronze protective cover virtually ensured that all weapons were turned aside from the flesh. The rarer occasions when body armor and helmet

were penetrated probably occurred when the hoplite stumbled, his stationary, prostrate body then targeted by repeated two-handed jabs of
butt spike, spear tip, or sword.

There was rarely in hoplite battle a mandatory expenditure of offensive weaponry. With the slinger, bowman, and javelin thrower largely removed from the field of infantry battle, hoplites might incur absolutely
no damage to or loss of their offensive equipment—in line with the
pragmatic, parsimonious image of agrarian rustics. Unlike the inherent
waste of missile warfare, Greek infantry substituted "recyclable" muscular strength to power the spear or sword. Both seldom left their wearers'
hands. Because weaponry was purchased privately, there was inherent
self-interest in its upkeep and preservation.

II.

In the early *polis* period (700–480 B.C.) none of the agrarian combatants
received *any* state pay or even subsistence support, in either cash or provisions (e.g., Arist. *Ath. Pol.* 27.2, 24; cf. Pritchett *War* 1.27, 3.29;
Michell 361)—a stance wholeheartedly approved by the reactionary
Plato in his *Laws* (cf. Morrow 191–92). In other words, as in the case of
hoplite equipment, the Greek city-state contributed essentially *no* monetary outlay to the cost of warfare. Nor was the farmer obligated to supply his own hoplite arms—relatively inexpensive as they were—as an
indirect form of taxation. Rather individual weapons outlay was a necessary means to ensure that there was no real financial obligation imposed
from above in the form of property taxes, forced military conscription, or
land confiscation. Private panoplies were far more economical, efficient,
and practical than tax-supported armories.

In fact, any money paid for hoplite military service before the Persian
Wars was confined solely to foreign mercenary service. We hear of a few
early adventurous hoplites in pay of distant lords in Asia and Egypt (e.g.,
Parke 3–14). In the case of Athens—and there is no reason to believe
she was atypical—formal wages for hoplite service were probably not introduced until the mid-fifth century (Arist. *Ath. Pol.* 27.2; cf. Pritchett
War 1.3, 7, 11; cf. Jameson 1980: 220–21).

Hoplite amateurism was entirely in line with the agrarian distrust of
standing armies and the expense they incurred. Pericles reminded his

democratic and imperialistic Athenian audience at the beginning of the Peloponnesian War (dramatic date 431 B.C.) that their enemies to the south had no stomach for the costs of war. People like the agrarian Peloponnesian allies of Sparta, who were personally engaged in direct cultivation of the soil, he felt, simply did not have the necessary public capital for fighting. Pericles concludes that "independent farmers (*autourgoi*) are a type of men who are always more eager to serve in person rather than to pay cash" (Thuc. 1.143.2–3), suggesting that even as late as 431 B.C. formal infantry salaries were a bothersome (and relatively recent?) phenomenon in most Greek city-states.

The fifth- and fourth-century rise of *polis* fleets represented a dramatic shift from private to public expenditure on arms, from moderate to enormous outlay for defense forces. Nowhere was this redirection in emphasis more notable than at Athens after the Persian Wars: "Hoplite forces were recruited from the more well-to-do citizens who could meet armed at their own expense. On the other hand, the naval defense, which certainly could not be ignored in view of Athens' geographic position, entailed considerable expenses" (Thomsen 136).

III.

As Pericles tried to make clear when he pointed out the drawbacks of yeoman militias among the city-states of the Peloponnese, someone does pay for military service: if not the *polis* itself in cash, then the individual hoplite in time lost from farm work. But in the two centuries that saw the rise of hoplite warfare (700—480 B.C.) and the emergence of Greek agrarianism, the time devoted by farmers to campaigning was short, and therefore the collective burden on the "economy" of the city-states minimal.

Hoplite battles were themselves singular and brief. They were also not frequent before the fifth century. Little travel or auxiliary campaigning was required. In peacetime there was rarely weapons practice, drill, or other military training—scant time needed, then, save for actual battle. W. K. Pritchett, for example, has collected the evidence for the length of actual hoplite encounters. In all cases they transpired in an afternoon, in an hour or two at most. Rarely, if ever, were initial conflicts followed by second engagements (*War* 2.46–51; Hanson 1991: 78–79), a practice that makes perfect sense when we envision hoplites burdened with seventy pounds of equipment under the Mediterranean summer sun.

Much has been written about the *frequency* of one-day "wars" among the Greek city-states. The idea is widespread that the Athenians were at war two out of every three years in the fifth century (Chamoux 162; de Romilly 1968: 20; Zimmern 354). Yet if we review Greek history before the Persian Wars, there is good reason to believe that major wars between *poleis* in this murky period were infrequent. In contrast, the later period between 480 and 338 B.C. is an era of near-constant fighting in a variety of theaters. Between 650 and 480 B.C. at Athens there appears nothing like the subsequent lengthy Persian Wars, the Egyptian campaign, various invasions into Boeotia, the Argolid, and the islands, and the "First" and "Second" Peloponnesian Wars.

The Athenians' incessant bellicosity alone accounted for nearly fifty years of continuous hostility in the fifth century (though much of it—predictably, given its frequency—was on sea or between light-armed troops). Athenian deviance from agrarian military protocol was constantly resented by her reluctant allies, who, like the similar Peloponnesian satellites of Sparta, had no belly for constant campaigning and time away from their plots (Plut. *Cim.*11.1–2; *Nic.* 9; Thuc. 3.15.1, 3.16.1–2). In contrast, throughout early Greece as a whole, outside of the shadowy Lelantine War (post 700 B.C.?), the Argive catastrophe at Hysiae (669 B.C.?), Sparta's Messenian civil conflicts, the brief Sacred Wars, and the struggles between Elis and Pisa over Olympia, there were not more than a dozen important campaigns in the historical record involving the major Greek city-states in more than two hundred years.

Conflicts of the era were brief day battles between neighbors. They arose over contested border ground. They reflected the agrarian interests of the hoplite-farmers who preferred system to chaos in the resolution of conflict. Hoplites were the same farmers who in peacetime fought with one another constantly over the exact borders of their own individual plots (Thuc. 5.41.2–3; Pl. *Leg.* 5.745; 842E-843A; *Resp.* 2.373D–E; Arist. *Pol.* 7.1330a4–23). Perennial rural "hot spots," like ancestral property quarrels between farm families themselves, flared up again and again throughout Greek history.[14]

This large body of evidence must have led G. E. M. de Ste Croix to remark (after careful rejection of the so-called commercial causes of early Greek warfare): "Quarrels about the ownership of land, especially border land between two states, were the principal causes of war between Greek states and were universally recognized as such."* If there were Greek overseas expeditions before the Persian Wars, they may often have been the sporadic, private campaigns of mercenaries and tyrants, not official and public musters of yeoman farmers. Warring was common enough to cement solidarity among the hoplite agrarian class, but not so frequent as to retard their steady economic and political ascendancy within the *polis*.

Why should there have been any great mobilization in warfare between contiguous agrarian states? Distance from farm to the battlefield was short: a brief march of a day or two out and back for the column of small landowners (e.g., Ar. *Pax* 1183). Fighting over the border was one of the most economical aspects of Greek campaigning, certainly reflective of the whole practice of early Greek warfare. Each side often traveled about the same distance to the rough midpoint between their respective city-states in search of a flat plain below the mountains—border disputes being theoretically the shortest distance for all involved. The battle at Delium (424 B.C.), for example, was fought near or right on the borderground between Athens and Thebes. Most city-states, as we have seen, possessed roads that led out to mountain borders and then often continued into foreign territory. It has been argued that these routes were military, rather than commercial, in nature (Ober 1991: 174–79). Because siegecraft and similar tactics of delay were frowned on by the landowning militias of the early city-state, overland networks were not merely designed to facilitate the transport of a *polis* army, but perhaps to encourage hoplite battle itself.

Wars of this type curtailed, rather than augmented, defense outlay. Often both neighboring city-states in an eerie harmony of sorts finished their roads right up to the approximate mountain boundaries. Either side could easily invade the other's territory if a dispute arose: any "war" would be brief, decisive, and fought openly between agrarians, essentially eliminating the tactical choices of the invaded, eliminating the need

---

*de Ste. Croix 1972: 219–220; cf. Frost 293; Rhodes 217. "No regular mobilizations," Frank Frost soberly surmises of Athenian military practice in the seventh and sixth centuries, "seem to have taken place" (Frost 283).

for skirmishers, siege engineers, and mountain garrisons. If identification of the militarily utilitarian nature of these ancient roads is correct (e.g., Ober 1991: 178–79), there is yet another implication that the ideology of the Greek hoplite-farmer transcended formal borders.

Despite the clear chauvinism of the respective city-states, I have argued that farmers in the early agrarian *poleis* may have had almost as much in common with their counterparts across the mountain as with landless craftsmen or urban traders in their own city-state. Of agrarian fifth-century Thebans and their rural kindred souls across the border in Attica, Max Weber remarks: "Theban 'democracy' was based on hoplite yeomanry which achieved the unification of Boeotia and then sought peace just as did the farmers of Attica under their 'oligarchic leaders'" (1976: 216).

The pervasive power of agrarian ideology persevered even into the times of rural transition in the middle and late fourth century. It surely engaged both Plato and Aristotle. These two reactionary thinkers worried that farmers in the countryside might in their own self-interest see no reason to fight their counterparts across the border. They might not be willing to sacrifice their farms and persons in order to save the general population of their own *polis*. Both philosophers urged citizens of the *polis* to have dual residence, houses both in town and out on the farms (Arist. *Pol.* 7.1330A14–23; Pl. *Leg.* 5.745; cf. Bisinger 31–32). Ties would be cemented between farmers and their urban counterparts. In time of war the landed would not find accommodation with the invaders at the expense of their landless inside the walls. Conservative philosophical concern suggests that in the aftermath of the Periclean strategy of letting invaders into Attica during the Peloponnesian War (431–421 B.C.; 412–404 B.C.), utopian thinkers felt that farmers were growing increasingly frustrated with the radically democratic tendencies of Athens.

Outside of Sparta, hoplites spent little time training for war. Although much has been written about *hoplomachia* (the hoplite "war-dance"), the military flavor of many athletic events, and the continual calls in utopian literature for more formal battle preparation, the Greeks themselves at least believed for most of the *polis* period that war really was more a question of courage than of skill.[15] That scholars must search for a military component in ritual dance and athletics is, I think, a tacit admission that formal training for Greek hoplite battle *per se* was essentially absent.

Training, after all, might have taken up more of the farmer's time than war itself. But Greek hoplites normally devoted not more than a week or two of the summer campaigning season to actual marching and fighting, activities that were predicated on slack periods in the agricultural calendar. The need to work hard on the farm explains why Greek land warfare before the late fifth century seems essentially defensive in nature, why fighting on home ground was important to the morale of the hoplite. Intensive farm labor and close attention to a variety of crops also reveal why hoplite war making was not designed for extensive mobilization, annexation, or outright conquest. Thucydides believed that the original members of the Delian League, even in the exhilaration of their success over the Persians, were nevertheless "reluctant to go on campaign" (1.99.3). Outside of outright battle, most (non-Spartan) hoplites were always at work on their farms rather than drilling on the parade ground.[16]

This made Plato urge more formal muster and drill among the Greek city-states (Pl. Leg. 8.829 B; cf. Xen. Mem. 3.12.5)—drill that in actuality must have only infrequently taken place in open-air fields and sanctuaries (e.g., IG I³138; Ar. Pax 353–56; Jameson 1980: 224–25). Throughout later Greek literature there is explicit fascination with the disciplined mercenary band (e.g., Front. Str. 3.12.2; Polyaen. Str. 3.9.35) and the ubiquitous suggestion that these professional, highly trained corps were essentially unknown among hoplite armies of the past (cf. Parke 78–79).

IV.

Almost all figures for hoplite battle casualties (unlike modern practice, confined to the dead rather than inclusive of wounded) derive from the fifth and fourth centuries when detailed accounts in the historical record first emerge. Peter Krentz, who collated some seventeen major pitched hoplite battles from Acragas (472 B.C.) to Leuctra (371 B.C.) in the texts of the major Greek historians, found a surprisingly consistent hundred-year pattern: ten to twenty percent (fourteen percent on average) losses to the defeated phalanx, three to ten percent (five percent on average) killed among the hoplites on the winning side (Krentz 1985: 18). Even during the frequent warmaking of the turbulent fifth century, battle fatalities per single hoplite engagement were *light* and a state's annual battle dead bearable—as long as these engagements were fairly rare.

Entire encirclement of ancient Greek armies was quite the exception. At Marathon in 490 B.C., the Persians had found themselves cut off and nearly surrounded in enemy territory, a rare phenomenon that explains their extraordinarily high number killed (6,400 of perhaps an original 20,000 men—or roughly thirty-two percent of their original force). In battle exclusively among Greek hoplites there is simply nothing like the total destruction of thousands. We hear of no battlefield death traps such as the Roman holocaust at Cannae (216 B.C.), where 50,000–70,000 (Polyb. 3.107.9–15, 3.117.1–3) of the roughly 80,000 or so in the legions (as high as an eighty-eight percent fatality rate) went down between the Carthaginian pincers at day's end (at the rate of well over one hundred a minute). Even cursory examination of battle fatalities of the Hellenistic and Roman wars reveals that nearly always forty percent of defeated armies in those times perished (e.g., Gabriel and Metz 83–87), the day's slaughtered customarily, rather than unusually, ranging in the tens of thousands.

The problem in assessing both the relative and the absolute severity of infantry casualties in Greek hoplite warfare is the *change* in hoplite practice during the fifth century. After the Persian Wars, when the Greek agrarian city-state was in the midst of enormous transition, faced with novel challenges and opportunities, hoplite battles—both the major collisions and the smaller and less well-known confrontations— were *not* necessarily rare.

To take a theoretical example: if an infantry force during this era fought one out of every two years (to use a more conservative figure than the famous "two out of three" years at Athens in the fifth century, a young farmer, twenty-one years of age, could potentially be called up twenty times before his sixtieth birthday. If he experienced an equal number of winning and losing battles, there was roughly a ten percent chance he would lose his life in any one encounter. By age forty a hoplite could expect a theoretical certainty of death in battle.[17]

The casualty figures for Greek hoplite dead are suggestive, but remain only rough estimates. Not all hoplites were called up for every campaign. Minor battles might have required only a few hundred infantrymen out of thousands eligible on the muster lists. The average life expectancy for

Greeks in general was probably only between forty and forty-five years anyway (e.g., Gallant 1991: 20).

Understandably, at the beginning of the Peloponnesian War, *both* sides—Sparta and her Peloponnesian allies, Athens and her imperial league—looked forward to the fighting; the reason, Thucydides tells us, is that the youth of both alliances "had *little* experience" with war (Thuc. 2.81). The historian is correct. From 453 to 433 B.C., outside of a major hoplite battle or two, there had been a twenty-year period of general tranquillity in landed warfare among the city-states (e.g., Gomme *Comm.* 2.8–9).

It is possible to make a rough estimate of the *total* fatalities in Krentz's seventeen major hoplite battles during this hundred-year period (472–371 B.C.). By adding together the dead of each Greek hoplite battle recorded in Krentz's survey, we obtain a cumulative sum of about 24,000 total Greek fatalities in these major engagements. That is an *astonishingly modest* number in comparison to Hellenistic and Roman figures! In Hellenistic and Roman times, the total fatalities of a single day's battle such as Issus (333 B.C.; about 50,000 dead), second Chaironeia (86 B.C.; about 100,000), or Munda (45 B.C.; about 100,000–120,000) might within a few hours exceed the old Greek hoplite total from over three centuries. Just as later (Chapter 9) we will see that once the city-state unraveled, the size of Greek farms grew enormously while the total population in the countryside actually shrank, so in the military sphere, once the agrarian hoplite vanished the number of deadly engagements increased dramatically and the fatality ratios soared.

These numbers of Greek fatalities *are* considerable when one remembers the much smaller populations of the landed hoplite class in the Greek city-states.* Total infantry dead in these two centuries was actually somewhat higher than Krentz's figures, since characteristically ancient historians often recorded no losses on the winning side (for example, at the battles of Himera, Locris, Syracuse, Miletus, Ephesus, and Phlius). At other significant encounters (e.g., Tanagra, first Coroneia, Oenophyta), chronicles lacked any precise reckoning of the dead at all, and are therefore absent from Krentz's survey.

---

*E.g., 10,000–20,000 eligible hoplites on the infantry muster rolls at (only) the largest *poleis*, usually a little less than half of the citizen population; see de Ste. Croix 1981: 283; perhaps only 100–800 eligible for hoplite service at the "average" city-state (Ruschenbusch 1985: 258–263).

In the case of fifth-century Athens, Barry Strauss (75–76, 80–81; 179–82) computed fatalities that were not exorbitant. He calculated that the 5,470 total hoplite dead of the twenty-seven-year Peloponnesian War represented a quarter to a third of her total original infantry strength in 431 B.C. Even this seemingly impressive total represents an average of only 202 hoplites killed per year *during the entire war,* a figure matched by not much more than a minute's work in the major Roman and Hellenistic encounters. In comparison with the plague and natural causes, those hoplite dead were *not* an alarming figure. Given expected rates of replenishment in this period, the between 5,000 and 6,000 infantry losses would not have inevitably reduced hoplite strength *per se* during the nearly three decades of war. And in the first two centuries of the *polis* period when hoplite battle was far more infrequent, there are many reasons to believe that battle fatalities for Greek agrarian infantry *were even lighter.*

The near-uniform adoption until at least 520 B.C. or later of the so-called bell corselet (as opposed to later composite and fabric models), greaves, Corinthian helmet (cf. the later vulnerability of the small, conical headgear, the *pilos*), and occasional auxiliary armor (thigh, ankle, stomach, and shoulder guards) suggests that earlier Greek hoplites originally were far better protected against attack than their successors—as we see from the vast discrepancy in casualties in the Persian Wars between the Greeks and their lighter-clad Eastern adversaries (e.g., Hdt. 5.49, 97; cf. Snodgrass 1967: 92–94; Anderson 1970: 24). In fact, Greek bronze protection was all but impenetrable from most projectile and hand-weapon attack (e.g., Gabriel and Metz 56). The thickness and extent of the panoply, coupled with the rarity of auxiliary skirmishers and light-armed troops who could wreak havoc in retreat, argue for even a *smaller* percentage of individual battle fatalities than the ten-percent figure of the later fifth and early fourth centuries. Clearly, farmers of the early *polis* knew that when they invested in full panoplies of bronze, battle dead were to be few.

Second, early Greek hoplite warfare, as distinguished from its practice in the latter fifth and fourth centuries, was an altogether *slower* affair. It was waged between lumbering, fully-armored farmers who walked rather than ran together. Herodotus (6.112; cf. Ar. *Ach.* 698) says flatly that Marathon (490 B.C.) was the first occasion (in the then two-hundred-year history of hoplite fighting) where Greek hoplites *ran* at the enemy! Even if Herodotus's statement were not strictly accurate, it still reflects a general Greek belief in the fifth century that in the two centuries preceding that battle most agrarian armies met at a much slower pace (Delbrück 72–90; cf. Hanson 1989: 135–170). Other suggestions that before the fifth century the flute played a greater role in hoplite battle (e.g., Anderson 1970: 293 n. 64) also argue for the marching rather than running nature of Greek hoplite armies. That observation is borne out by the greater weight of the early hoplite panoply (protection that incorporated cumbersome thigh and shoulder guards, as well as more plate, rather than composite armor).

In general, velocity, the centuries-old twin of lethality, seems to have been absent from the Greek battlefield before Marathon (490 B.C.). The sheer slowness of encumbered farmers was an integral part of early agrarian warfare. Lumbering rather than sprinting hoplites may explain why in the first two centuries of the *polis* there were fewer casualties than even in the relatively nonlethal hoplite battles of the fifth and fourth centuries.

Finally, not only were fewer hoplites killed on early Greek battlefields, but also, as we have seen, there were most likely far fewer battles between 650 and 480 B.C., largely because of the absence of hegemonic leagues that so often in Greece after the Persian conflict drew many smaller *poleis* away from purely agrarian concerns (i.e., local borders) into lengthy, drawn-out wars for spheres of political influence. Although figures for total infantry losses are, of course, unattainable before the Persian Wars, the hoplite battle dead between 640 and 480 B.C. may have been only a fraction of the cumulative fatalities later, in the century-and-a-half era before the battle of Chaironeia (338 B.C.). Even that later 150-year period of battle fatalities (480–338 B.C.) pales in comparison to the Hellenistic and Roman infantry butchery to come. Just as farmer-hoplites during the lifetime of the *polis* kept the size of farm property largely equitable and small, so too in war were they favored a system that ensured few big armies, few big slaughters.

In the case of Athens, there is good reason to believe she lost more hoplites during the twenty-seven-year Peloponnesian War (431–404 B.C.) than in the entire two centuries before the Persian invasions. Modern scholars who have surveyed her military activity before the Persian

Wars are struck by the relative absence of any real organized military structure, or indeed of any serious wars (e.g., Frost 292). The early scarcity of military activity implies that Athens, before she became the bellicose, maritime giant of the fifth century, was essentially identical to other agrarian city-states in her military practice in the seventh and sixth centuries. That was a time when small groups of farmers spontaneously marched out to settle border disputes simply, through short but decisive pitched battles. Border disputes were resolved, agrarian identity was solidified through group sacrifice, and the number of actual killed was quite small. It may be disturbing for modern historians to acknowledge the inescapable conclusion here: the conservatism of agrarian timocracy did not lend itself to the adventurism and the mass killing spawned later by more radical government. The propensity for greater slaughter in ancient Greece is to be associated with the dynamic rise of landless democracy in general and in fifth-century Athens in particular.

There is a tradition accompanying some of the accounts of Greek battles before the Persian invasion of Xerxes (i.e., 700—480 B.C.) that implies fatalities were incredibly light, or that there was at least an acknowledged concern on both sides to limit casualties. One thinks of the prohibition of missiles loosely associated with the so-called Lelantine War, the early tradition of *monomachia* or ritualized battle between two chosen fighters, the agreement to settle the Argive-Sparta dispute over Thyreatis borderland through a matched battle of 300 "Champions", the Spartan notion that they could bring along enough fetters to enslave their Argive adversaries, and the legendary 192 dead at Marathon, the 300 Spartans killed at Thermopylae, and the 159 Greek fatalities during the central engagement at Plataea (479 B.C.)—the latter battle was the greatest assemblage of hoplites in the military history of the Greek *polis*. Only around 1,000 -2,000 Greek hoplite infantry died in pitched encounters inside Greece during the entire Persian Wars.

Even the one military disaster of any magnitude (at Sepeia, 494 B.C.), by its very notoriety in Greek literature for the trickery, sacrilege, and massacre on the part of the Spartans *after the battle itself was over* (Hdt. 6.19, 6.75.3–83, 7.148.2; cf. Karavites 122–23), is the exception that proves the usual Greek rule of the age to limit the human costs of war. Even in the fifth and fourth centuries when the horizons of Greek warfare were drastically expanded and stand-up encounters between larger armies much more common (e.g., Delium in 424 B.C.; Mantineia in 418/362 B.C., Nemea in 394 B.C., Coroneia in 394 B.C., Leuctra in 371 B.C.), hoplite fatalities were not catastrophic. In none of the battles named above were there ever more than four thousand combined dead. This economy in human expenditure is quite in contrast to the Hellenistic casualty records of the third and second centuries. Then battles and sieges often degenerated into the mass slaughter of tens of thousands in the space of hours.[18]

V.

Most studies of Greek generalship before Alexander have centered on either preeminent fourth-century commanders such as Agesilaus, Epameinondas, Pelopidas, and Timoleon, or the more notorious leaders of quasi-professional "*condottiere,*" men like Iphicrates, Chabrias, and Chares. In the fifth century before the Peloponnesian War and the advent of new auxiliary contingents and tactical opportunities, however, most historians recognize that "generals" usually fought in the midst of their troops, without much responsibility or opportunity once battle began.[19]

Controversy over the standard view of the hoplite general fighting *always* alongside his men—whether in the front rank or in the center of the phalanx (e.g., Wheeler 1991: 135–154)—is confined to the fifth century and later, reflecting the growing sophistication and complexity of hoplite battle, when an occasional general may have been outside the first initial charge of the opposing front lines (e.g., Plut. *Pel.* 1.5–2.4). Even at that time, nevertheless, it was standard practice for most battle-field commanders to stand with their men at some point in the battle (see Pritchett *Topography* 8: 62–63).

During the first two centuries of the *polis* period those anonymous battle leaders uniformly took an inspirational role. Early Greek "generalship" was inherently amateurish. It was without lengthy tenure. It was bereft of extensive command staff and intrinsically *dangerous.* Even the famous commander Epameinondas of Thebes (who later died heroically at the battle of Mantineia [362 B.C.]) served in the ranks as a mere hoplite when his tenure as general was over (e.g., Plut. *Mor.* 797A-B). As a result, there are subtle, but unmistakable, *economic* implications in the brief, primitive, and lethal nature of hoplite command, emphasizing the agrarian genesis of hoplite warfare, and more specifically, the small landowners' desire to prevent a professional officer corps from interrupting their own rural routine.

Simply put, a permanent drone class of military professionals was never subsidized by any of the agrarian city-states. Outside of Sparta, there was essentially no permanent general staff. Even under that military system, generals were given little if any formal training in either strategy or tactics (cf. Lazenby 1985: 24–25). Throughout Greece, there was no array of officers who had to be paid, fed, and housed year round by the citizenry, no cabal that might wrestle away civic control of the war-making arm of the *polis,* no constant pressure for military intervention from a prepared army organization. Amateurism, like the hoplite's notion of private weapons and decisive confrontation, was essential to the prominence of Greek yeomanry within the city-state and it was often to be enshrined as a cornerstone in the later Western military tradition.

Nor is there evidence of a Greek salaried officer corps, much less higher officer pay, before the Persian Wars. Given the later military history of the West, the military nonprofessionalism at all levels of Greek war making was agrarian egalitarianism in its more radical manifestation. It was an extraordinary development in its own right, one quite in contrast to Near Eastern and Mycenean palace practice of past centuries. At Athens the board of generals seems not to have existed before 501/500 B.C. (Arist. *Ath. Pol.* 22.2; Rhodes 264–65). Nor was there an extensive and expensive civilian bureaucracy involved in military, financial, and logistical planning for the first two centuries of the *polis.* In strictly financial terms, "officers"—or more accurately "battle leaders" within the phalanx itself—cost the state absolutely *nothing.* Between 700 and 480 B.C. in most Greek city-states (quite unlike the centuries-old practice in Asia and Egypt) military professionals and warrior-princes with elaborate and permanent retinues did not exist.

In a more abstract sense, there was also little opportunity for a cult of personality. Because most generals would either die (Hanson 1989: 107–116) or retire after one or two battles without much continuity in command structure, rarely could a single stalwart mind envision and plan a series of conquests or lengthy campaigns. There were no Alexanders or Hannibals in the agrarian Greek *poleis*. Outside of the political-military activity of a few early tyrants (e.g., *FGrH* 90 F57.5; 105 F2; 324 F6; cf. Arist. *Pol.* 5.1305a8) and some gifted fourth-century captains (e.g., Epameinondas, Pelopidas, Iphicrates, and Chabrias) there were virtually *no* sustained military careers. The practice was characteristic of an agrarian society that had always in earlier times been skeptical of kings in battle (e.g., Arist. *Ath. Pol.*3.3).[20]

Personal advancement, enrichment, fame, and fortune—the entire engine of military adventurism—and thus any chance for costly military outlay, were precluded by hoplite agrarianism. In both the early and later Greek character there is a strain of open disdain toward generals (Archil. 114; Ar. *Ach.* 965; *Pax* 172–75; Xen. *Anab.* 3.4.46–48; Plut. *Mor.* 188E). By the fifth century there was an insistence on hoplite activism—even in the Spartan army—in command decisions (Thuc. 5.7.2; 5.65.6). Until Miltiades' apparently disreputable (but understandable) effort to secure personal credit for the splendid Athenian victory at Marathon (Aeschin. *In. Ctes.* 3.186; cf. too *IG* VII 2462 for complaints over the attention given to Epameinondas after the Theban victory at Leuctra), there does not seem to be a *single* named general associated with any pre-Persian War battle victory. Cleomenes' win at Sepeia (7.148; Paus. 2.20.8)—consisting of the post facto murder of nearly the entire hoplite class at Argos—was notorious. It gained him infamy, not glory from the incineration of his trapped adversaries.

VI.

So hoplite warfare emerged as an agrarian enterprise, one made up of farmers fighting on farmland over disputed borderland. Their battles were not designed for aggression or sustained expeditions. From an exclusively agricultural point of view hoplite warfare was an extremely *frugal* enterprise. Few, if any, significant wars on land took place. Most smaller disputes were usually between neighboring city-states, whose hoplites killed each other over small tracts of border ground. Those lands, ironically, were not always significant in purely agricultural value, but were important to farmers as symbols of agricultural prestige, beneficial to the growing agrarian chauvinism of the community at large, and reflective of individual agrarians' own endless haggling with neighboring farmers of their locale.

Greek armies of the pre-Persian war era—if one can even use such a dramatic term as "armies"—were typically small bodies of extremely heavily armed farmers. They met each other at a walk, and then struggled for an hour or so to push their adversaries off the field of battle. Once the system of hoplite warfare took hold in the late eighth and seventh centuries, the traditional social and economic expenditures of fighting, so common earlier in the palace economies of the Near East and in Egypt—property taxes and rents, technology, soldiers' salaries, extensive fatalities, lost agricultural productivity, lengthy training and preparation, permanent officers and planners, destruction of entire cultures, unity of political and military authorities—were minimal. Indeed, they were often nonexistent throughout a vast area of the Greek-speaking world, a break between Western and Eastern practice that cannot be strongly enough emphasized.

Simple durable weapons were largely codified for nearly two centuries throughout the insular Greek city-states. The extensive and unmatched protective cover of such bronze armor, the deliberate exclusion of missile weaponry, cavalry, skirmishers—all the usual sources of fatal motion and speed on the battlefield—and the accompanying rules that limited fighting in a concrete and moral sense, reduced drastically the number who were killed in any given battle. Like restrictions against land accumulation and political aggrandizement, warfare of the *geôrgoi* strove to ensure the equilibrium of the agrarian patchwork. So unlike their more sophisticated successors, Greek hoplite landowners of the seventh and sixth centuries were fighters of a day. They were not habitual trained war makers.

There was neither a priestly class of unproductive military professionals nor an otherwise unemployed military intelligentsia. The formal study of tactics as an academic enterprise did not even exist before the late fifth century. Finally, agricultural devastation was a trigger rather than the goal of invasion. Plunder and booty were incidental, not essential, to the mobilized army's existence, at least until the fourth century. Formal hoplite battle left relatively little imprint on the local civilian environment. I do not intend to minimize the brutality of early battle. One need only to read of the poet Tyrtaeus's "beating waves of assault," "the dead man in the dust," "toe-to-toe and shield against shield," the hand "holding the bloody groin," or glance at early Corinthian vase painting to recoil from the mayhem and bloodletting among those in the front ranks. For those few hundreds and occasionally thousands of combatants, battle was an especially horrific experience (cf. Hanson 1989: 152–209).

If such a picture of the economy of agrarian warfare appears too neat, one must examine carefully the erosion of military practices in the ensuing two centuries of the *polis* period (480–338 B.C.), the so-called Classical Age of Greek history, to understand the deliberate economy of the original hoplite system. To fathom the catastrophe of the Peloponnesian War and its legacy of constant warring in its fifty-year aftermath, contemplate the later Greeks' elimination, element by element, of the original agrarian protocols. That disastrous chain of events led the late-fifth-century historian Thucydides to remark of the new fighting that war now was "not a matter of heavy weaponry, but of money (*ho polemos ouch hoplôn to pleon alla dapanês*)" (1.83.2).

Reduce and modify the hoplite panoply. Incorporate costly cavalry, missile troops, artillery, and light-armed skirmishers on a widespread basis. Introduce state pay for military service. Erode the predominance of set land battles and heavy infantry through frequent, lengthy, and often indecisive raids, sieges, and ambushes. Elevate the navy to coequal military status, and transfer the cost of armament from the individual (for his panoply) to the state (for triremes, dockyards, fortification, artillery, and naval crews). Create clear distinctions between soldier and general. Allow battle leaders authority for extended command. All are prescriptions for "a war of money" and its accompanying detritus: extensive civilian and military deaths, neglected farms, steep taxes on the countryside, empty treasuries, the cycle of repeated conquest, enslavement, and revolt.

That cargo belonged to Greece in the late fifth and fourth centuries (see Parke 228; Garlan 1975: 17; Pritchett *War* 5.505–541). It was relatively absent during the period before the Persian Wars. Even Sparta's decline in a political and social sense was a direct aftermath of the Peloponnesian War—a conflict that forced her to embark on costly naval and mercenary operations for extended periods outside Laconia, a period that did not allow her to decide wars through a day's fighting against an agrarian phalanx, and so preserve her peculiar inward-looking social structure.

A few examples of Athenian military costs in the fifth century show the horrific expense involved once farmers lost control and hoplite battle was superseded as the decisive mechanism for deciding entire wars. The Athenian siege at Samos (441 B.C.; Diod. 12. 28; Thuc. 1.17) purportedly required at least 200 talents (1.2 million drachmas, roughly equivalent to 1.2 million man-days of paid labor). The real cost of that campaign may have been ten times that sum (e.g., Kagan 37; cf. Meiggs-Lewis 55). Samos was a pittance, however, compared to the costs of sieges at the outbreak of the Peloponnesian War and later.

The two-year encirclement at Potidaea (432–430 B.C.; Thuc. 2.70; cf. Diod. 12.46) drained ten times that earlier outlay, over 2,000 talents (12 million man-days of labor!). The great Athenian debacle on Sicily (415–413 B.C.) cost much more than that figure just to pay the naval and land forces for each year there (cf. Boeckh 395–96). Thucydides remarked that the original armada that left for Syracuse took "many talents" from the city (6.31). Donald Kagan argued that in order for the Athenians to fight the Peloponnesians in the new fashion of total war beginning in 431 B.C., 2,000 talents were needed *each year*, a figure that would exhaust Athens financially in about six years (Kagan 37–40).

These are monetary figures alone and thus exclude the enormous costs in lost equipment, time, and casualties required in distant sieges and campaigns that often do not show up in the records of state expenditure. Thucydides reminds us that of the more than 40,000 combatants (citizens, foreigners, metics, and slaves) who departed for Sicily "few out of many returned home" (Thuc. 7.87). Compare all these costly examples to a theoretical muster of an agrarian fifth-century phalanx of 5,000 combatants. They would cross the border, fight, and return home, bringing along their own three-day sack of rations and their attendants. Campaigning in this style might expend no more than 30,000 drachmas (5,000 hoplites plus 5,000 attendants for three days at one drachma per day).

Two other factors complicate the idea of an early conscious, Panhellenic attempt to limit the costs of warfare. First, social and religious historians argue for the primacy of ritual and cult, not the less sophisticated, less theoretical notion of agrarian pragmatism, as the real motive forces behind the Greeks' codified system of battle. Actual fighting in this view was incidental to pre-battle animal sacrifices, displays of youthful masculinity, exhibitions of engraved artwork on breastplates and helmets, expressions of adult male solidarity, and ceremonial boasting through trophies, votives, and dedications, as if war was not over land but a mechanism solely of cultural expression.

But is not this argument grounded in the admission that all such customs and rules merely reinforced the privileged position— that is, the economic status—of the hoplite landed class? How might rites of passage for young adults and other religious practices serve society as a whole when restricted to a segment of the adult male population of farmers? Do farmers seem the type of folk to elevate the style of fighting over the substance of killing? When we see an occasional design on extant Greek armor, remember that this artwork was incidental, not essential, to the protective capacity of the bronze—the real, the only reason for the panoply's existence.

Unlike later (Hellenistic and Roman) peasantry, Greek hoplites of the city-state were never at the beck and call of a tax-collecting, elite class who favored mobilization of armies for their own selfish squabbles or because of a private desire for loot from overseas expansionism. Even perfunctory analysis of war making in Greece of the Hellenistic and Roman Period shows this difference clearly. After the fourth century the frequency of campaigns increases. Money needed for technology and manpower rises. Time spent away from agriculture is considerable. Disruption in the countryside due to military appropriation of farmland is habitual. Civic and personal indebtedness is commonplace. Taxes become frequent. Capital shifted from local agrarian communities to larger urban bureaucracies grows. Clearly, Greek hoplites of the *polis* were *not* peasants traditionally defined as "under the leadership of aristocratic, urban or other classes" who show "submissiveness to political rulers," and thus become resentful pawns of ambitious warlords.*

This strikingly independent agenda of the original hoplite-landowner is not necessarily made explicit in the rare contemporary sources between 700 and 480 B.C., given the preponderance of pictorial and archaeological evidence and the absence of comprehensive literary

---

*Francis 292–93. For steep taxes collected from the countryside to pay for centralized government, see Alcock 29–31; A.M. Jones 1974: 82–89; cf. Pritchett *War* 5. 438–504; Day 236–9; Duncan-Jones 122–42.

accounts before the Persian Wars. Even the few contemporary literary references of the early *polis*-period—essentially epic and lyric poetry and fragments of philosophy—naturally do not reveal the special economic advantages that accrued to the hoplite class. Instead these accounts predictably stress the *general* Panhellenic religious, social, and political functions of warfare. They record the outward heroic manifestations that institutionalized and legitimized early hoplite fighting to all, rich and poor, in the Greek world.

Nevertheless, subsequent (and admittedly reactionary) Greeks of the fourth century later decoded the narrower purpose of their landed ancestors' system. Once agricultural warfare was lost, succeeding embattled and impoverished generations of Greeks usually emphasized quite clearly the real economic and political advantages that had once accrued from the heroic hoplite creed of their fathers.

Thucydides (1.15) in sharp contrast to the strategic practice of his own age (431–404 B.C.), saw that in prior times there were no military confederations, no campaigns of conquest, and no extended wars on land (*kata gên de polemos . . . oudeis*). Conflict in the old *polis* essentially had been reduced to brief border disputes. "Nothing," the distraught orator Demosthenes (9.48) warned his mid-fourth-century audience of complacent Athenians, "has been more revolutionized and improved than the art of war. I know that in the old times," he continued, "the Spartans, like everyone else, would devote four or five months in the summer to invading and ravaging the enemy's territory with hoplites and citizen militias, and then would go home. They were so old-fashioned—or good citizens—that they never used money to buy advantage from anyone, but their fighting was fair and open (*all' einai nomimon tina kai prophanê ton polemon*)."

Polybius (13.3.2–4) nostalgically emphasized the simplicity of past hoplite procedures—no deceit, no missiles, no surprises, no manipulation of terrain. All that explained to him why their fighting was a far simpler and nobler business than war in his own second-century Greece. The general Greek sentiment about the purity and simplicity—and thus the economy—of original hoplite battle explains the constant irritation in our later sources for anything that allowed "good" hoplites to be killed by artillery or hand-propelled missiles, by anything other than the muscular strength of a like landed class.[21]

More interesting still, many fourth-century Greek thinkers genuinely worry over the growing costs of non-hoplitic warfare, the capital needed for sieges, raiding, and fortification that were all divorced from agrarian infantry battles (cf. Ober 1985: 87–100). Aristotle in his *Politics* relates the story of Eubulus, the Bithynian banker who offered a besieging general Autophradates the opportunity to receive cash in lieu of his siege costs. "Eubulus," Aristotle says, "asked him to figure how much time it would take to besiege Atarneus [on the coast of Asia Minor], and then to calculate how much would be his expense that he would incur for that period. For he said he was willing for a sum somewhat smaller than this simply to evacuate Atarneus at once" (*Pol.* 2.1267a32–36).

In consideration of just that increasing cost of warfare, Xenophon asks in his fourth-century treatise on state expenditure, the *Ways and Means*, whether war now always made strictly cost-to-benefit sense. "Someone might ask me," he speculates, "that even if a *polis* is wronged, should she then remain at peace with the aggressor? No, of course not. But I do say that we should have better luck against an enemy, if we first of all provoke no one by doing wrong ourselves" (*Vect.* 5.13). Aristotle in his *Rhetoric* emphasizes the new civic concern over the economic aspects of the ever more complex war making, over Thucydides' "wars of money." He says that citizens now discuss in the assembly income and outlay, war and peace, defense of the countryside, and the problem of food supply (*Rhet.* 1.1359b-1360a)—topics far more complex than mustering the citizenry of farmers to march out in column for a few days, topics now necessary for *polis* defense, but completely antithetical to the entire agrarian ideology of the city-state.

W. G. Runciman (1990: 355) also focuses on this paradox in the new defense strategy of the fourth century: "Without the financial resources, how could a *polis* build the fortifications and hire the mercenaries? But until the mercenaries could find some other livelihood than war, how could they be prevented from depleting the resources of an overwhelmingly agricultural community? And unless they could be enlisted in the service of a tyrant capable of establishing a securely legitimated monarchy for which they could furnish the standing army, how could they be prevented from drifting from one paymaster to another, and, as Isocrates complained, assaulting whoever they ran into on the way?"

Second, some scholars argue that the absence of complexity within early Greek warfare was not a deliberate effort to curtail military expenditure. Rather it was merely reflective of the embryonic state of development of the *polis* when agrarian populations were smaller and without the capital, experience, or knowledge to advance military science and practice. But even if one accepts the now generally suspect view that "archaic" Greek culture and institutions were less sophisticated than what evolved in the later fifth and fourth centuries (or in the *earlier* bellicose Near East and Egypt), hoplite battle is surely an exception. Weaponry, tactics, and strategy showed little, if any, elaboration for more than four hundred years. So static was the method of fighting that had emerged at the beginning of the eighth century, that the agrarian protocols of the phalanx remained nearly impervious to the other undeniable cultural, political, and economic transformations of the age.

That is why the hoplite phalanx itself functioned relatively unchanged even through the progression of tyranny, oligarchy/timocracy, and democracy—all forms of government under which Greek hoplites fought. Hoplite battles were celebrated in early lyric poetry or late fifth-century tragedy, and hoplite warriors were identifiable both on proto-Corinthian and, two centuries later, red- and black-figure Attic vases. Pitched agrarian battle could involve a few hundred men or many thousands. It adhered to a code of fighting perfect in its conception and single-minded in its appropriate design and purpose. No wonder George Grundy correctly declares: "The hoplite phalanx was of such a nature that any great elaboration of tactical design in its evolution was practically impossible" (Grundy 267).

Major changes in Greek warfare during the fifth century and later, as we will see in Chapter 8, "Hoplites as Dinosaurs," were *not* alterations in the formation and application of the hoplite phalanx itself. They were not, as Grundy rightly saw, "great elaboration of tactical design." Transformation involved incorporation of *other* forms of fighting that eventually did not change battle very much between phalanxes *per se*. The phalanx simply became more marginal, more vulnerable to outside attack—and in the end nearly irrelevant. The reactionary nature of hoplite warfare, the insular world of two columns colliding, explains why classical scholars can legitimately describe the environment within a phalanx, its activity on the battlefield, in nearly uniform terms throughout four centuries, *even though the larger conduct of Greek warfare itself changed enormously in just that period.*

Historians of ancient Greece must reinterpret the role of early hoplite warfare. Far too much emphasis has been devoted to circumstances surrounding the origins of the system—the so-called hoplite reform (which, as we have argued, was *not* a dramatic reform at all)—without corresponding appreciation of the economic ramifications of that code for two hundred years of Greek history. Do not be carried away by notions of the "primitiveness" of the Greek economy to such an extent as to believe the ancients had no idea of profit and loss, income and outlay. Economically the Greeks may not have acted in a purely capitalistic mode in the modern sense, forswearing business ventures, corporations, and other activities aimed primarily to enrich a few visionaries who sought goods and money above all. But the farmer-citizens of the *polis* were conscious of how a market worked, of debits, incomes, and expenditures (e.g. Engels 24–27; 131–42; Cohen 11–12).

The early agrarian Greeks' social and political considerations were grounded in the secure knowledge that their peculiar method of fighting was economically frugal. Hoplite battle was *not* a mere epiphenomenon of religious and cultural expression, nor a ritual involving unsophisticated fanatics. In a large part it was a conscious mechanism to reduce defense expenditure among the farmers of the emerging Greek *poleis*. "They also engaged in hostilities," W. G. Runciman remarks of early Greek city-state formation, "with one another which were sufficiently frequent and serious to encourage a sense of political identity *without* being so destructive to inhibit the emergence of states" (Runciman 1982: 366; emphasis added).

Hoplite war by its conservation of the lives, property, and capital of the Greeks is a testament to the brilliance and tenacity of the small landowners of Greece. Hoplite protocol seems to me in large part responsible for the stability of the agrarian city-state, and thus for the entire fruition of Greek culture itself. How odd that in the largely unknown valleys of mainland Greece, rural folk, isolated and forgotten by the more turbulent world of the Mediterranean, invented Western warfare as part of the discovery of politics itself. If landed councils were to survive, were not to be swept away by marauding hordes or by the megalomaniac vision of an Eastern lord or Macedonian thug, Greek warfare had to be both ferocious and reasoned, both capable of annihilating foreign challenges and yet calibrated to spare rival city-states.

While scholars are taken with the Greek invention of political science, and while I have emphasized thus far the critical role of the agrarian patchwork, neither *polis* nor countryside was possible without a competent army in service to both. Every bit as important as constitutional government and agrarian egalitarianism was the Greek invention of military protocol, the revolutionary idea that armies were to serve people, not people armies.

Part Three

TO LOSE A CULTURE

The essential basis for the ancient city was, we have seen, a community of small farmers who were free and who owned their own land. Although the historical evolution of the Greek cities and of Rome soon changed this original social structure, nevertheless the citizen soldier who owned his land remained the social ideal for antiquity

—C. Mossé 1969: 49

Chapter 8

HOPLITES AS DINOSAURS

In a process of gradual separation warfare became divorced from the farmland and from the farmer, and the Greek city lost its essential identity.

—Robin Osborne 1987: 164

Greek "warfare" was not the same thing as Greek "battle." Infantry battle between phalanxes still continued throughout the slow decline of the free city-state well into the middle and later fourth century, as the famous murderous encounters at Coroneia (394 B.C.), Nemea (394 B.C.), Leuctra (371 B.C.), Mantineia (362 B.C.), and Chaeroneia (338 B.C.) attest. Those battles, fought magnificently with largely agrarian infantry and seemingly oblivious to the military revolutions of the times, were in themselves not much different from hoplite fighting of the seventh century. The arrangement of spearmen in columnar formation was commonplace even during the subsequent Macedonian period in Greece, as the engagements between heavy pike-bearing phalangites at several later clashes confirm (e.g., Sellasia [222 B.C.], Cynoscephelae [197 B.C.], Pydna [168 B.C.]).

Technically, the charge of a phalanx, whether armed with the traditional hoplite panoply or, in the third through second centuries, modified tactically and equipped with the Macedonian *sarissa* (the fourteen-to-twenty-foot

327

pike) and lighter body armor, remained an option for Greek military commanders well into Roman times. The sheer power of that massed formation is what impressed the Roman general Aemilius Paulus at the fight at Pydna: "He considered the formidable appearance of their front [the Macedonian phalanx], bristling with arms, and was taken with fear and alarm: nothing he had ever seen before was its equal. Much later he often used to recall that sight and his own reaction to it" (Plut. *Aem.* 19.3). On occasion later Roman legions themselves abandoned their accustomed grace and fluidity, their cohorts coalescing both horizontally and vertically to achieve the greater force of attack in column. The legacy of phalanxes remains with us in the West today, seen in our preference to fight it out quickly, brutally, and, at all costs decisively, a military spirit that arose originally in the Greek countryside.*

"Warfare" is usually a much more inclusive term than "battle." It not only suggests the myriad rules, regulations, and practices that surround conflict, but, far more important, "hoplite warfare" denotes the supremacy, the exclusivity, of infantry battle between small farmers as the only real means of resolving conflict between the Greek city-states of the early *polis* period. For the insular world of the hoplite to make any sense, for his *polis* to remain agrarian, his peculiar showdown between rows of armored farmers could not be simply *a* theater of operations. It had to be *the* theater of most military conflict. Battle, as in the seventh and sixth centuries, had to remain the equivalent of war.

Anything less would call into question the premise of the closed system of agrarian monopoly: land-based timocracy, agricultural self-sufficiency, egalitarianism in property holding—a system that had remained absolutely unquestioned for more than two centuries (700–490 B.C.). In its pristine state, hoplite fighting of these two centuries might properly be labeled the "first stage" in the evolution of Greek *polis* warmaking. But soon after the Persian wars (490, 480/479 B.C.) the elements of agrarian and hoplite supremacy began to erode throughout Greece. The reason is easy to see: the unique conditions of relative historical isolation that had marked the peculiar birth of the city-state came abruptly to an end.

---

*On occasions where legions fought as phalanxes, see Strabo 7.3.17; Caes. *Bell. Afr,* 15.3; cf. Wheeler 1979: 314–18. On the Western preference for decisive battle, see Hanson 1989: 218–28.

I. Hoplite Warfare. The Second Stage (490–431 B.C.)

Until the fifth century, the parochialism of hoplite agrarianism was rarely questioned by the Greeks or anyone else. As we have seen in the last two chapters, the conventions of the seventh and sixth centuries ensured that war between the Greek city-states was decided by a day's battle between farmers, and *only* by a battle between farmers. Hoplite fighting was a brutal necessity to cement agrarian control of the Greek *polis*, its military frugality crucial to rural tranquillity and prosperity and paying real dividends to Greek civilization at large. The first real challenge to this military culture came with the Persian invasions of 490 and 480 B.C. Until then, Greece had been left largely alone from foreign belligerency. Before the fifth century, hoplites were more likely to be found overseas than foreign troops to be present inside Greece. Greek heavy infantry who had not become successful landowners during the early evolution of the city-state were often prized as mercenaries abroad in both Asia and Egypt, where their unusually heavy armament, shock tactics, and reputed nerve could provide foreign despots with small elite contingents.

The battle of Marathon (490 B.C.) was the first ominous warning of the vulnerability of agrarian infantry. The dramatic Athenian victory ended a startling period of Greek isolation, when her city-states knew little about the military and political challenges beyond their borders. Miraculously, for more than two centuries (700–490 B.C.) the farmers of Greece had been left alone to devise their own curious notions of war and warrior, in an unreal parochialism that belied the potential turmoil of the eastern and southern Mediterranean.

Ostensibly, the Marathon revealed the supremacy of landed troops, the difference between men who were armored and those who were not, between men who were shock fighters and those who had no belly for the collision of flesh and bronze. It was the hoplite army of Athens, not her light-armed troops (essentially nonexistent at the time), not her horsemen nor her rudimentary navy, that defeated Darius I at Marathon. Heavy infantry it was also (not cavalry, not javelin throwers) who had lumbered after the Persians and hacked away at them even as they sought escape in their ships. Heavy hoplite infantry had killed nearly 6,400 of the invaders, all at a loss of a mere 192 men. Until then,

Herodotus says, the Greeks had been afraid even to look upon Persian soldiery; "until then to hear the very name of the Medes had brought terror to the Greeks" (6.112). Understandably the Spartan late arrivals after the battle sought permission from the victorious Athenians to march out onto the battlefield of Marathon simply to gaze on the rotting eastern corpses. After that experience, few Greeks feared to fight, much less to look upon, Asian infantry.*

Marathon confirmed the earlier success of Greek hoplite adventurers abroad and set a pattern that was unaltered for the next two centuries: any time Greek hoplites faced foreign adversaries in a head-on collision on flatland, the enemy was found wanting, creating a growing sense of infantry superiority among Greek military observers (cf. Xen. *Hell.* 7.1.38). Do not, however, be misled by the heroism of the Greek victory, nor by the ebullient accounts in Herodotus and Aeschylus that Marathon was proof of the martial invincibility of two centuries of Greek military tradition.** Days before Marathon the Persians *had* successfully besieged the Greek *polis* of Eretria (490 B.C.) on the island of Euboea opposite Attica (Hdt. 6.101), bringing to bear a multifarious force of siege engineers, marines, light-armed troops, cavalry, and missile throwers. The hoplite infantry of Eretria, descendants of a gallant martial ethos dating back two centuries to the great battle on the nearby Lelantine Plain (about 700 B.C.), chose to stay inside their city, rather than fight outside against this new type of war ("they had no intention," Herodotus notes, "of marching out and offering battle").

Only the Persians' unwise deployment of troops on the coast of Marathon—their cavalry seems to have played no decisive role—and their loss of nerve in an amphibious landing near Athens herself ensured defeat. Furthermore, *no* Greek allied hoplites, except the brave Plataeans, came to Athens' aid. No community of Greek farmers thought it necessary to fight overwhelming odds when their own lives

---

*See various passages in Herodotus: for Greek parochialism, Hdt. 1.29–30; 59; for Greek views of those who were not armored and who did not relish shock warfare, Hdt. 5.49.5; 7.211.2; 9.62.3–9.63.3, cf. 6.112; for primacy of heavy infantry at Marathon, Hdt. 6.113–117; cf. Wardman 49–52; for late Spartan arrival at Marathon, Hdt. 6.120.

**On the Greek ebullience after Marathon, see Aesch. *Pers.* 25–32; 52–57; 85–86; 147–49; 278; 728–29; 817; on the Persian cavalry at Marathon, see Hignett 1963: 68–70; Lazenby 1993: 60–61.

and property were not in immediate danger. Was Marathon not proof that agrarianism had created common values and ideologies, identical armor and tactics, but no real federal spirit that went beyond the parochial squabbles of hoplite amateurism? The Ionian revolt of Greek cities on the western coast of Asia Minor (499–494 B.C.) had garnered *little* infantry support from the agrarian city-states of mainland Greeks, despite constant pleas for assistance.

In the peculiar mind of the hoplite-farmers in most Greek city-states, to die for a few acres on their own border made far more sense than to perish far away in a crusade to keep "Greece" free. The Milesian Aristagoras, complaining of agrarian parochialism, pointed out to the Spartans that they, the neighboring Argives, and the Arcadians battled only over "strips of land." These Peloponnesian city-states were simply not aware of, or interested in, more important fighting over "gold and silver" across the sea alongside Aristagoras's Ionian Greeks against the Persian overlords.*

The victory at Marathon was proof of sorts that hoplite battle in its purest form was *not* intended for wartime alliances or for the extension of force beyond one's immediate borders. Agrarianism was a very reactionary ideology that grew out of an exclusive need to protect an insular farming community, one that won battles like Marathon through "sheer guts and chance" (Lazenby 1993: 80). But when thrust into the challenges of the greater Mediterranean, "guts and chance" could just as often turn into appeasement.

The peculiar tactical choices of the Persians to fight on a small, flat plain, not the inherent and undeniable superiority of Greek heavy infantry, explain in some part Marathon's outcome: "failed mostly by his own fault" later Greeks conceded of the Persian defeat (Thuc. 1.69.5). The battle gave warning that in the future there were to be real tactical and demographic limitations to the Greeks' exclusive reliance on hoplites, and thus—in the new context of the Mediterranean world itself—real limitations to the entire notion of *polis* agrarianism.[1]

Other challenges were not addressed by the blinkered ideology of hoplite battle. Heroic though it was, the victory at Marathon was not proof that the entire Greek agrarian way of war could continue to function unin-

*For the Ionian revolt, see various passages in Herodotus: Hdt. 5.49–50, 6.7, 44, 49; cf. 9.6.

terrupted and unquestioned, once Hellenic city-states became interactive in the complexity of politics and wars to their east, south, and west. The technology of the phalanx was designed perfectly for the brief moment of fighting on flatland, in an abbreviated campaign of a few days, between tough farming men who shared the same idea that all killing should start and cease with the presence or absence of heavy infantry. Greek hoplite armies, despite the Athenians' superior courage at Marathon, were vulnerable in multitudinous ways to outside attack by any opponents who found their rules of killing patently absurd. These hoplite regulations applied to no one except the small farmers of the Greek-speaking world.[2]

Greek armies, as we have seen in the last two chapters, at this time had no real logistical support. They had no mechanism for subsistence beyond a few days other than sporadic foraging and organized plundering. Without naval coordination, without talented and professional officers, without the incorporation of specialized contingents, there was little chance that Greek hoplites in the first two decades of the fifth century could prevent determined outside aggression. How, without supporting contingents, could they take the offensive on difficult ground or against continual hit-and-run assaults of well-led, integrated mounted and missile troops? Hoplite weaponry was largely useless at sea, a liability on rough terrain. What had appeared in hoplite warfare to be economic and frugal (see Chapter 7), in this quite different and brutal context of simple military efficacy became backward and unsophisticated.

But to shift hoplite warfare away from agriculture, away from its intrinsic parsimony, to meet novel challenges abroad, to turn the undeniable Greek genius loose in devising military technology and innovation, was tantamount to transforming the foundations of the Greek city-states, calling into question the social and political monopoly of the small landowner himself. (There was not even formal Greek military science written before Xenophon [about 400–360 B.C.], although the genre, predictably, soon was to be extremely popular in the Hellenistic age.) Any revolution in Hellenic war was an admission that the Greeks were ready to open their system up and thereby to sacrifice their splendid form of military isolation, their relatively humane hoplite institutions—all in exchange for greater wealth and political power overseas. Understandably, paid killers and mercenaries like Xenophon's ten thousand, not mobilized *polis* militias, devised ways to use hoplites in Asia.

That dilemma was brought into even sharper focus ten years after the initial Asian probe at Marathon. The Persian onslaught (480–479 B.C.) under Xerxes, son of Darius I, was altogether different from the prior incursion—and more important, dissimilar to *every* Greek battle of the past two centuries in a strategic, tactical, and logistical sense. The Persian army was prodigious. It was no amphibious corps of a few thousand adventurers. An entire city of sorts methodically gobbled up Greek territory as it inched its way south. Even discounting Herodotus's vastly inflated figures, the enemy must have descended into Greece well over 100,000 strong.[3]

Their intent, as the veteran Aeschylus reminds us in his play the *Persians,* was not to inflict a tactical defeat on the battlefield as past hoplite armies had done. The Easterners aimed at no less than the total enslavement and subjection of a race ("They threaten to yoke in servitude Hellas" [Aesch. *Pers.* 49–50]), an idea either for or against which *no* Greek phalanx—except the Spartans in Messenia—had ever yet battled. To prepare for and to fight total wars—as the Spartans had also learned in Messenia—had dire consequences for the agrarian ideology of the *polis.*

The Persian invaders quite naturally scorned "the laws of the Greeks." In their eyes *polis* borders were abstractions and local sovereignty irrelevant. They incorporated ambush, bribery, and deceit, recruiting mercenaries and other Greeks into their service. Persian forces marched into Greece in a multiplicity of guises. They had heavy infantry of course, but also equally powerful naval, cavalry, and missile contingents. The new message of warfare *inside* Greece was clear. When pressed, some Greek farmers would ally themselves with barbarians against other Greeks. Even the patriotic Greek defense was "limited to a minority of states" and "a fragile affair," composed of "under forty states" whose "loyalty was not constant" (Lazenby 1993:253).

Nor would hoplites any longer be a sufficient protective force for the *poleis.* Numbers, sailors, tactics, fortification, evacuation, strategy, trickery, and subterfuge were all needed against these new enemies—and needed quickly. Almost overnight they entered the mainstream practice of Greek warfare. Any landed conservative in the city-states still calling for a single hoplite conflict of the old style, for yet another Marathon to bowl over inferior infantry of the East, was not merely misguided but nearly lunatic.

As the Athenians would prove through their evacuation of Attica itself, the hallowed ground of agriculture (and hence by logical extension farmers themselves) could in theory become irrelevant to the survival of the *polis*—an entity that was to be reformulated for a time in many minds not as the land, but rather solely as the people. The objective for the Greek defenders was to annihilate rather than simply defeat the enemy on land and sea by any means possible that kept population—not land, not temples, nor even agrarian pride—intact.

The centuries-old notion of Greek agrarianism, I believe, never quite recovered from the invasion of Xerxes. Herodotus's famous observation in his history (written about 430 B.C.) that the Persians had thought Hellenic warfare "absurd" (9.7.2) may in part reflect the Greeks' notion of Herodotus's own time: the exclusivity of the hoplite, in their eyes, was already being seen as a glorious, but antiquated, institution.

"New" men arose like Themistocles of Athens and the even more unsavory Spartan commander Pausanias.* These generals understood—even preferred—the Persian concept of total war. In that sense, they were more Eastern than Greek. The legacy of these captains is not the heroic last stand of the Three Hundred at Thermopylae. Nor was their reputation derived from the stunning infantry victory a year later at Plataea (which was fought by the Greeks only after the Athenians, Quisling-like, threatened to make a separate peace [e.g., Hdt. 9.6]).

Their contributions were the wholesale evacuation of the Athenians from their city. They were part of the naval triumph at Salamis by landless Athenian sailors, and the subsequent pursuit by the more adventurous Greeks of the defeated Persians by land and sea. All these developments—for the farmers of Greece disturbing trends cloaked in the general ebullience of national victories—marked the first real departure from and hence challenge to hoplite warfare. Greek naval mobilization was, after all, a dramatic shift from private to public armament, from inexpensive mustering to capital-intensive production.

Plato, the would-be protector of conservative agrarian values, understood that. Over a hundred years later in the fourth century, in a review of past *polis* history, the philosopher saw the importance of Salamis (480

---

*Appropriately nicknamed "Odysseus" (Plut. *Mor.* 869A; *Them.* 10.6; Paus. 10.15.5; Thuc. 1.138.3). On Pausanias, see Thuc. 1.128–35.

B.C.). But he advanced the feeble argument in his *Laws* that the land victories at Marathon (490 B.C.) and Plataea (479 B.C.) had really saved Greece. The victorious sea-battles were not merely less significant, in his view, but actually "had made the Greeks *worse* as a people." To Plato, the deleterious social ramifications of an ascending landless navy who welcomed constant service outweighed simple military efficacy (*Leg.* 4.707C–E). In his *Gorgias*, Socrates does not think the Athenian leaders of the post-Persian Wars, those who built the walls, docks, and ship-yards, were even worthy of the name of "statesmen." They had, after all, made the citizens "worse" (Pl. *Gorg.* 515C–519A). Hoplite battle, as an element of agrarianism itself, had a strong ethical element. It was a means to preserve the culture of the polis and maintain the morality of its citizens. Unlike sea battles, a single collision between phalanxes improved the character of the city-state's populace. It was a way "to make the Greeks better" (*beltious tous Hellênas poiêsai;* Pl. *Leg.* 4.707C).

The landless *dêmos*, Aristotle also thought, "being responsible for the naval victory during the Persian invasion, became taken with itself and chose worthless demagogues whenever the more respectable opposed their policy" (Arist. *Pol.* 2. 1274a13–16). Understandably, Plato, Aristotle, and later right-wing thinkers saw Salamis as a turning point. The victory there, in some sense an unfortunate "accident" (*sumptômma*), marked not merely the rise of Athenian naval power, but a critical change of direction in the *entire culture* of the Greek city-state. In this philosophical view, victory at sea could only give prestige to the landless rowers, and thus power to radical democracy, not to a property-based oligarchy or timocracy.* People who are paid to fight prefer to fight, regardless of the effects of constant warring on their community.

The price of those victories, as Plato knew by the fourth century, had been the slow erosion of the old code of the hoplite. Ascendancy followed for the landless who were bound to inject their own nonagrarian values into the social and political fabric of the Greek *polis*—something that could eventually nullify the pristine equation of small farmer/infantryman/lawmaker of the city-state. Even earlier, Aeschylus had clung

---

*Pl. *Leg.* 4.707A–D; 706B–C; Arist. *Pol.* 4.1304a20–25; [Xen.] *Ath. Pol.* 1.1–2; Plut. *Them.* 7,19; Isoc. 8.48,64,69,75,79,101. To the philosophers who viewed battle as natural and inevitable, *how* the Greeks fought was more important than *why* they entered a particular war.

to the myth of hoplite superiority when he wrote that Greece's was a victory of "the Dorian spear" over the Asian bow—as if the heroic stand and assault of the Spartan hoplites at the battle of Plataea (479 B.C.), not the seamanship of his own democratic compatriots, was proof of the superiority of the Greek landed infantry (*Pers.* 816; cf. *Pers.* 85–86; 147–49; 238–45). But both Aeschylus and Plato later realized that the status of hoplites—and all that went with it—was *not* enhanced during the Persian Wars, despite their spectacular success at Marathon and Plataea.

Polis political ferment about the Greek victory over Persia is seen in the fabricated saga that hoplites had actually played a "decisive" role during the sea battle of Salamis, by spearing drowned Persian sailors (Fornara 51–54). Aristotle even thought that if navies were necessary for the survival of the *polis*, there must be found some mechanism to avoid enfranchising the landless, the so-called sailor crowd (*ho nautikos ochlos*). In his view, they did not deserve citizenship. Triremes could just as well be manned by agrarians in their off season (*Pol.* 7.1327b8–16).

Even at the two pitched hoplite battles of the Persian Wars— Marathon (490 B.C.) and Plataea (479 B.C.)—despite the enormous disparities in casualties, the margin of Greek victory was slim, and the verdict for a time in doubt. It is forgotten just how hard-pressed the Greeks were at Plataea, a battle where the Persian use of cavalry, manipulation of terrain, inclusion of Boeotian Greeks, and incorporation of archers and fortified positions confused and stymied the defending Greek infantry for days. The reluctance of Greek hoplites to abide strictly by their old protocols in the face of such an enormous and variegated force illustrated the newfound poverty of their old agrarian ritual. The initial and wise Spartan reluctance to face the various Persian masses on unfavorable ground prompted their commander Mardonius to poke fun at the Greeks' abandonment of their old way of deciding wars. In a mock challenge of sorts, he called the bluff of the Spartan contingent at Plataea:

> Lacedaemonians, you are said to be bravest of men by those who live in these parts, drawing praise because you never run away from battle, nor leave your rank, but instead stay put until you die in your places or you destroy your enemies. But there is not one bit of truth in all this. Before the

battle has even begun, before the two sides have met in the hand-to-hand, we have seen you running away and pulling up from your deployments, as you try to have the Athenians make the first trial against us, while you yourselves fight against our slaves. In no way is all this the work of brave men. And so instead we have been deceived in our appraisal of you. For according to general report, we expected that you would send a herald to us, proposing that you would fight us Persians one-to-one. And we for our part were ready to do just that, but now we have surmised you are doing no such thing. Indeed, you are instead cowering in fear before us. Now, since you do not offer up any challenge, a challenge we shall offer to you. Since you are reported to be the bravest of your people, why do not we fight one another in equal number, you on behalf of the Greeks, we for the barbarians? And if it seems wise also that others should join in on the fighting, let them do just that after we are through. But if it should seem better that we two alone should decide the entire issue, let us then fight it out; whichever side should win, these men will win the battle for all of the respective armies.*

No wonder one of the old die-hard Spartan regiment commanders, Amompharetos, later refused to budge when ordered to make a tactical withdrawal by Pausanias to more favorable ground. Like many other Greek hoplites, he must have wished to take the Persian Mardonius up on his demeaning dare of ritual battle. The Spartans' (primitive enough) adoption of an articulation of forces, tactical feints, and rearrangement of troops were all blasphemous to the creed that men in bronze should draw up, charge, and fight until one side collapsed, nothing more, nothing less.[4]

The final victory over Persia at Mycale (479 B.C.) on the coast of Asia Minor reveals a similar challenge to hoplite dominance. While neighboring Greek hoplites in Ionia had played a role in the battle's outcome, troops from the Greek mainland and the islands had to be transported there by sea. To reach the battlefield, marines and amphibious troops were dependent not merely on their armor-carrying agrarian slaves, but also on the *free* poor who powered the triremes of the *polis*. That combined naval-infantry operation at Mycale set the example for the Greeks in the Aegean for nearly 150 years.

In the aftermath of the Persian invasion and defeat (479 B.C.), there was,

---

*Hdt. 9.48. For Plataea, see Hdt. 9.45–66; cf. Wardman 56–59; for Myclae, see Hdt. 9.90–107.

as is so common after any great social and cultural upheaval, a conscious and deliberate reactionary return to normality. We hear of a series of fifth-century "wars" among Greek city-states decided in the old agrarian way by single traditional standoffs between willing city-states at Dipaea (471 B.C.), Tanagra and Oinophyta (457 B.C.), and first Coroneia (447 B.C.).

But stones were thrown into the private hoplite pond by the Persian experience. The multifarious lessons of the invasion of Xerxes rippled out in a variety of unpredictable manifestations—all eventually lethal to the hoplite agrarian code. The Persian Wars marked the most significant event in Greek history. Not only was foreign tyranny repelled in 480/479 B.C., but just as important, the military and agrarian protocols of the city-states were shown to be wanting, and from then on were irrevocably altered. In short, just as the second World War ended the isolation and parochialism of American society, so too the Persian Wars drew Greece into the maelstrom of the Mediterranean and in the process overturned the accepted norms inside the *polis* itself.

Finally, these military challenges of the age did not reflect prior or even concurrent social instability within the Greek *polis*. Before 490 B.C. farming chauvinism and agrarian government were normative ideologies, and navies organized of the politically estranged were rare. The Persian invasions were not consequences of prior assaults on the cosmos of the agrarian *poleis*, but rather were catalysts of change.

From this point on, a cyclical pattern—military novelty, conservative reaction, then greater change—prevails in the Greek city-states, reflecting the new ambiguous cause-and-effect relationship between Greek warfare and social transformation: at periods in the fifth century martial challenges question traditional Greek social and political values; at other times, preexisting tensions within the *polis* become manifest only on the battlefield.

II. Hoplite Warfare. The Third Stage (431–404 B.C.)

The two victorious city-states of the Persian Wars, Athens and Sparta, had both learned of the attractions of hegemony. As would-be Persian dynasts, they were beginning informally between 480 and 460 B.C. to align the other Greek *poleis* into two opposing armed leagues. The reactionary Spartan idea that *polis* culture really meant a utopia of friendly unwalled communities,* all deliberately vulnerable to the march of a hoplite phalanx (hers being, of course, preeminent) was never in the mid- and later fifth century taken too seriously outside the Peloponnese. Despite her excellence in infantry, Sparta was never a shining example of Greek agrarianism. She was, after all, a somewhat deviant *polis;* the equation between free food-producer, lawmaker, and hoplite had been retarded through the presence of various castes of indentured servants and a general repugnance for farm work on the part of her elite paramilitary Spartiate warriors.

The bipolarity caused by the rift between Athens and Sparta in itself need not have been injurious to the fragility of this Greek way of war. After all, constant tension between matched powers can promote a conservative, even reactionary stability all around. Unfortunately for the agrarian culture of the old Greek *polis,* however, Athens and Sparta were both atypical—and powerful—city-states (a fact which in itself suggests greater economic and military power might ensue if mainstream agrarianism was *subverted!*). The two were communities unlike Argos, Thebes, or even Corinth and Syracuse, and unlike the hundreds of smaller, lessknown agricultural *poleis.* In their radically different views of society, both Sparta on the right of the agrarian norm and Athens to the left did ironically share at least one notion: free agriculture, the *polis* of small independent landowners, and traditional agrarianism itself were no longer to be necessary for the military, social, political, or even economic life of Greek communities. Both city-states realized that full-time farmers in a phalanx were a hindrance to the projection of offensive power, which had suddenly become attractive in the Mediterranean vacuum created by the retrenchment of Persia.

The numerous subjects of the growing Athenian maritime empire, an inheritance from the Persians, were in one sense like the indentured helot servants at Sparta. Both Athenian and Spartan underlings ensured that their respective masters could fight year-round if need be, without worries over lost time on the farm or the requirement—physical, spatial, spiritual—to enshrine agriculture, and the preservation of those who farmed, at the center of conflict. There was a tradition at Athens that

---

*On this theme, see Thuc. 1.90–93, Cf. Plut. *Mor.* 190A: "Is not a wall a dwelling place for women?"

some twenty thousand of her citizens gained an off-farm livelihood from the defense of the empire, capital acquisition that was directly or indirectly involved in military expenditure.[5]

Equally injurious to the hoplite monopoly, both Athens and Sparta in the years after the Persian Wars possessed no mechanism for ending their growing rivalry decisively and quickly. Neither side—Athens less than Sparta—would adhere to the old hoplite constraints, which defined war making as single pitched battles. Like their ancestors at the battle of Salamis, the Athenians of the mid-fifth century had the constant option, and the inclination, to withdraw from the challenge of pitched land battle in order to put their confidence in their fleet, and to transform her hoplites into a completely new type of soldier. The arch-conservative of the fourth century, Plato, complained of this new practice in his *Laws*. He disliked intensely the idea that hoplite marines had become accustomed to jumping on shore and then running back at full speed to their ships: "And they see no shame in not dying gallantly in rank when the enemies attack" (Pl. *Leg.* 4.706B–C).

Like their own infantry predecessors at Thermopylae and Plataea, the Spartans unimaginatively thought they could wait until an adversary inevitably chose to face their own feared professional hoplites. Triremes did not pose much threat to landlocked Laconia and her environs in the Peloponnese, and the Spartans had others to work their ground back home should a new war call for campaigning beyond a few days' march. Sparta's chief worry in the new strategy of hegemonic warfare was to convince her traditional agrarian allies throughout the Peloponnese to leave their farms to march alongside her in a grand invasion to the north.

Both cultures could prevent losing a war. But neither Athens nor Sparta knew how to win such a novel conflict quickly and decisively. The progression and escalation of their fighting took it at each step, in each year of their twenty-seven-year ordeal, further and further from the old agrarian ideal of war as a single infantry encounter. At war's end, Sparta had fashioned a competent navy, and Athens had developed effective seaborne infantry forces.

As each *polis* sought to increase its navies and its non-hoplite land forces, heavy infantry in phalanxes became more and more marginal. The phalanx was always incidental, never essential, to ultimate victory. At Athens the decline of traditional hoplite infantry was acknowledged by historians and became a favorite topic of late fifth-century and early fourth-century conservatives.[6] Aristophanes railed against the youth of his day who could not even hold their shields chest-high, and Andocides remarked that now old men were forced to fight, while young men made speeches (Ar. *Nub.* 987–90; Andoc. *Alcib. 22*). It is no surprise that in Aristophanes' *Frogs* (about 405 B.C.) the old veteran of Marathon Aeschylus is made to long for the Athenian hoplites of the early fifth century, "six-foot noble men" who "breathed spears and white-crested helmets," so unlike the "runaways, market-loungers, scum, and trouble-makers" of the poet's own day (*Ran.* 1014–16).

The great sea-battles of the Peloponnesian War were often fought between ships manned not merely with the poor, but also powered by mercenary, resident alien, and frequently slave rowers. This shift posed the embarrassing challenge to the hierarchy of any *polis* with a substantial navy: if sea-power, not hoplite infantry, was now critical for victory, if the disenfranchised or less prestigious rowers were to be crucial for the salvation of the *polis*, why should hoplites enjoy greater political privilege and social esteem ?[7]

Almost all the major battles of the twenty-seven-year Peloponnesian War were fought either at sea or close to the shore, and required traditional land powers, such as Thebes and Sparta, to build navies themselves—with all the accompanying social repercussions in their respective city-states, with all the problems of raising capital and levying taxes for public armament and extensive crews. Mindful of that erosion in the hoplite ethos, Argos once proposed to Sparta in the middle of their long conflict (418 B.C.) that both sides might resolve their dispute over the borderland of the Thyreatis by an old-style formal pitched battle, with pursuit of the defeated not being allowed into the interior of either country. But the Spartans initially considered the notion "silly" (*môria*). The proposal was never adhered to by either side (Thuc. 5.41).

If Argos and Sparta—conservative military regimes *par excellence*—could not turn the clock back on Greek warfare, no other *poleis* had much chance. Sparta by the end of the Peloponnesian War was plundering, raiding, and using non-hoplite troops as frequently as any other Greeks. The great majority of her rowers were either slaves or hired mercenaries.

Even the projection of military power on land during the Peloponnesian War was often just as antithetical to the exclusivity of hoplite battle. Expeditions composed not only of heavy infantry, but also of light-armed skirmishers, javelin men, and archers were sent far from the old killing grounds of the past. These mongrel forces were deployed in the most unlikely of places: the rigorous terrain of Aetolia, the wooden brush of Pylos and Sphacteria, the siegeworks at Plataea, and on the islands of Lesbos, Melos, Sicily, and elsewhere. In these environments hoplite phalanxes, drawn up and fighting strictly in the old style, were almost useless. In the Peloponnesian War alone there were at least nine major occasions for the use of siege engines, and even more frequent expensive and lengthy circumvallations of fortified cities and citadels. Since both Sparta and Athens deemed it worthwhile to fight on novel and unusual fronts, the acquisition of light-armed skirmishers, mercenaries, sailors, and besiegers were all necessary.[8] Save for a few isolated small battles (e.g., Solygeia, first Syracuse [Thuc. 4.42; 6.69–70]), hoplites held center stage only at the dramatic encounters at Delium (424 B.C. [Thuc. 4.89–101]) and Mantineia (418 B.C. [5.68–74]).

Both antagonists of the Peloponnesian War also possessed men for the times, a generation of especially gifted, enterprising, and original thinkers, eager to put into practice their unusual theories that grew out of the Persian experience. Here I do not mean the imaginative Themistocles, Cimon, and Pausanias, veterans themselves of the Persian wars, or even Pericles, the strategic successor to Themistocles. I refer to a host of less well-known, but far more capable second- and third-generation military minds, who saw martial opportunity not merely on the periphery of infantry battle, but rather altogether outside the traditional amateurism of hoplite practice. These were captains like Brasidas of Sparta, who in the company of hardened veterans and enfranchised helots organized real strategic campaigns up and down the Greek peninsula. Demosthenes of Athens mastered the art of the light-armed skirmisher and mountain guerrilla. Gyllipus, Lysander, and succeeding Spartan naval commanders integrated both sea and land troops, and employed slaves and mercenaries in a series of campaigns far beyond the borders of Laconia. Finally, Alcibiades, student of Socrates, saw that the new war involved few of the old ideas worth fighting for, least of all the preservation of the insular (and boring) world of the Greek agriculturalists, who had held together the fabric of the Greek city-state for so long.[9]

The hoplite remained the martial ideal. But from 431 B.C. on, most fighting was increasingly far less heroic, fought more at sea, around city walls, and in rough terrain than on "the smoothest and fairest plain." In his speech to the Athenian assembly on the eve of the disastrous expedition to Sicily, Alcibiades reminded the audience that throughout the Peloponnesian War Greek city-states had usually lied about the size of their hoplite forces—in reality they always had turned out smaller than they had boasted (Thuc. 6.17.5–6). The phalanx was something every *polis* bragged about, but sailors, mercenaries, and skirmishers were now more likely to see action.

The brightest minds in the Greek *poleis* welcomed, rather than resisted, the military revolution that destroyed the older hoplite proviso, a revolution that was necessary to wage war on a Mediterranean scale. This willingness to take up the challenge of overseas campaigning makes perfect human sense. For in the old world of amateur farmer-hoplite, there had been no place for military ingenuity and preeminence, no outlet for talent on the confined battlefield of a few acres. Command had brought no commensurate social status or opportunity for wealth. Is it surprising that under the changing conditions of the late fifth and fourth centuries these generals of (mostly poorer) light-armed troops were themselves from the wealthier classes? Like the landless men they led from the opposite end of the social scale, the upper echelon had little vested interest in maintaining the exclusivity of hoplite battle and the middling farmers who fought with it.

Somehow, for more than two centuries, the farmers of ancient Greece, in their inherent dislike and distrust of command structure and military hierarchy, had foreseen that the genius of the gifted when misapplied to the battlefield could result only in glory for a few, death for many, and expense for all. The orator Demosthenes pointed out the failings of generals in his own era during the mid and late fourth century when the military mean, like its agrarian twin, was on the wane. Athenian commanders were now to be put on trial numerous times for graft and sedition, "but not one of them," Demosthenes complained, "dares risk death in battle against the enemy. No, not even once." He nostalgically concludes: "Generals should die fighting the enemy (*apothanein machomenon tois polemiois*)" (Dem. 4.47). Generals now, like large estate owners, had other agendas outside the blinkered world of the farmer-hoplite.

III. Hoplite Warfare.
Its Fourth and Last Stage (404–338 B.C.)

In the aftermath of Athens' defeat in the Peloponnesian War (404 B.C.), there was, as after the Persian Wars, a reactionary revival of the age of pitched battle. In the early fourth century farmers, after all, still constituted the bulk of most Greek city-states' citizen population. Phalanxes were always terrifying military spectacles. In the post-war exhaustion, disputes over border territory and local hegemony reappeared as part of the military landscape of the *polis*. Perhaps the internecine slaughter of the Peloponnesian War was seen by many Greeks as the tragic consequence of deviance from hoplite battle.

But, as with the hoplite battles of the post-Persian War era nearly a century earlier, the *second* return in the first half of the fourth century to military conservatism of landed infantry was also largely illusory. True enough, major hoplite battles such as Nemea (394 B.C.), second Coroneia (394 B.C.), Leuctra (371 B.C.) and Mantineia (362 B.C.) were classic, stand-up affairs—*all* predictably involving the red-cloaked Spartan mossbacks. The literary descriptions of these antiquated encounters within the pages of Xenophon, Plutarch, and Diodorus provide our standard accounts of what the older, unrecorded contests of the previous three centuries must have been like. *As isolated events in themselves,* these hoplite battles must have been largely unchanged from their original form.

But during the fourth century as a whole, hoplite clashes were the exception, not the rule, of Greek military conflict. Fighting on land became far more expansive, as tedious as it was inconclusive. Even in the aftermath of the Peloponnesian War, even in the general disgust at the slaughter that the "new" warfare had brought, hoplite decay nevertheless *accelerated!* The more the fourth century Greeks fought and killed savagely, barbarically and without honor for things other than farmland, in places other than on farms, with men other than farmers, the more untenable the primacy of farmers became!*

---

*Although the decline in dedicatory hoplite panoplies at the Panhellenic sanctuaries in the aftermath of the of Peloponnesian War could reflect the general dislike of killing other Greeks (cf. Jackson 243–47), the sheer scarcity of military votive offerings may also simply suggest the real absence of captured full panoplies—and thus the rarity of major hoplite battles altogether.

Entrepreneur warriors of the fourth century fought and even lived abroad.* They plundered to pay their mercenary troops, and employed without distinction heavy and light infantry, missile men, marines, and naval contingents as the particular occasion demanded. Their more random and frequent slaughters lacked the formality and solemnity of the old hoplite clashes. These engagements also gave little opportunity or need for public commemoration or the Panhellenic dedication of votives. What was there worth commemorating? After all, under the prior dominant military ethos, on-again, off-again fights in a complexity of environments were hardly honorable or worthy of remembrance. The javelin wound through the brush, the anonymous arrow taken on the rampart, the rock to the face at the bottom of a canyon were not at all like the hoplite's sea of spears, farmers head-to-head, friend and family at the side, flat, clear ground beneath the feet. But the incessant skirmishing and plundering did offer some opportunities for cash and the accumulation of both personal power and prestige.

Between Mantineia (362 B.C.) and Chaironeia (338 B.C.) there was apparently no major hoplite encounter in Greece. The twenty-four-year hiatus was marked by unending light-armed skirmishing, trickery, mercenaries, sieges, fighting at sea, civil insurrection, and simple capitulation. After the establishment of the Athenian ephobia in the later fourth century—the formal training of Athenian youth for guard duty and rural patrols—each youth was to said to have sworn that he would protect the wheat, barley, vines, olives, and fig trees of Attica. That declaration of agrarian fealty would *not* have been necessary under the old hoplite code. Then all citizens took for granted that the defense of the *polis* was simply the defense of farmland.[10]

The introduction of special training and service for Athenian youth in the fourth century was ironic. The more reluctant Athens became to send out in pitched battles an agrarian hoplite infantry (who required essentially no training), the more it devoted scarce resources to drill and march its young patrollers. The statesman Phocion's complaints about Athenian reticence in opposing Philip reflected the financial complexity

---

*Such as Conon, Iphicrates, Sphodrias, Chabrias, Chares, Charidemos, Agesilaus, Pammenes, Diopeithes, and Timoleon. See, for example, Plut. *Mor.* 126E; Dem. 9.48; and Pritchett *War* 2.59–125; Parke 73–97.

of Greek warfare, once its agrarian core of doughty farmers was lost. He advised that the Athenians could make war on the Macedonians only when "I know that young men are ready to do their military service, when rich men are ready to pay their taxes, and when orators are ready to avoid embezzling public funds" (Plut. *Phoc.* 23). As we will see in the next chapter, Athens was deliberately attempting to mold her hoplite forces to a role more in tune with democratic thinking, more flexible in meeting diverse foreign challenges—that is, *away* from a traditional agrarian mission to fight pitched battles on and over farmland among like communities. But, as we will also learn, to alter the military tradition of the *polis* often encouraged avoidance of military service, comprehensive taxation, and the prominence of capital in military planning. Change the military arm of the city-state to meet new challenges, and the entire ideological framework of the *polis* fell apart.

Notice that hoplite battle—rare as it was becoming in the latter fourth century—essentially changed little over some four centuries: *no* formation, foreign or domestic, could yet withstand the direct onslaught of a phalanx. As we have seen, the heavily armed Greek infantryman on the field of Leuctra in 371, once he squared off in the phalanx against a similarly arranged adversary, would have felt at home—strategy, tactics, and spirit—among the ranks of his ancestors at the battle of Hysiae (669 B.C.). The evolution in Greek warfare on land from the fifth century onward was largely a result of incorporation and adoption of other more specialized forms of fighting and a consequence of an enormous increase in military manpower. Even conservative Xenophon's fourth-century ideal was not just a rectangular box of brave farmers, but a composite army where "hoplites, cavalry, peltasts, bowmen, and slingers march in complete harmony to the orders of their leaders" (Xen. *Oec.* 8.6; cf. Plut. *Mor.* 440B).

The mechanics of hoplite battle, perfect in form and spirit at birth for its stated objective, changed little. They were simply bypassed. Ultimately the agrarian phalanx was made irrelevant, as the mission of Greek soldiers was transformed from fighting over contested borderland to all-out war with foreign invaders, would-be conquerors, plunderers, and pirates over cities, booty, tribute, taxes, and spheres of economic and political influence. In this regard, the Greek agrarian militiaman was increasingly shown wanting in two important ways: (1) the style of fighting in the phalanx was now too one-dimensional, and required augmentation and support from a variety of other forces who were not always citizens of the city-state; (2) for the sheer numbers that were required on the various fronts in the constant fighting of the fourth century, the supply of small farmers in the Greek *poleis* was simply not enough to meet the demand.* Of this new compartmentalization and specialization in Greek warfare, Xenophon could observe that the fourth-century Spartan phalanx was still preeminent among any foolish enough to meet it in pitched battle with hoplite spear and shield. But he conceded that even the Spartans would now have little success against Scythian bowmen or skilled Thracian targeteers (*Mem.* 3.9.2–3).

Another closely connected sign of the revolutionary military upheaval in the fourth century—one with fundamental ramifications for the autonomy of free and agrarian citizen militias—was the steady decline of private ownership and individual control of battle weaponry. As the hoplite's farm no longer guaranteed social, economic, and political superiority, so too his panoply lost its exalted status. The rise of the mercenary movement and the decline of yeoman phalanxes led to mass arming of paid infantry armies by the state. Sometimes we hear of confiscation of private citizen arms, the creation of vast armories, or the wholesale on-the-spot outfitting of entire armies. Possession of a agricultural plot no longer gave the farmer either the sole economic ability to buy the panoply or the social privilege to do so. As early as the late fifth century Hermocrates at Syracuse had advised that his Sicilian *polis* equip those who were without hoplite gear (*paraskeuasôsi to hoplitikon hois te hopla mê estin;* Thuc. 6.72.4), as if this largess were now to be expected. The fourth and third centuries saw only increases in this trend, as the phalanx took on a professional, nonagrarian character.[11]

Hoplite phalanxes pristine to the outside observer, on the inside by the fourth century were experiencing an insidious incorporation of noncitizens and mercenaries into their ranks (cf. Parke 46–48). This hybridization might explain the reluctance of infantry in the fourth centu-

---

*John Lazenby remarks of the eclipse of the conservative Spartan phalanx in the fourth century: "The truth of the matter is not that Sparta's army at last failed her, but that after her defeat of Athens in 404, she overstretched herself, and so called upon her army to perform too many tasks for which it was not well fitted, against increasingly bold and enterprising enemies" (Lazenby 1985: 40).

ry to march out over borderland to determine an entire war. Farmers probably continued to make up the majority of fighters in the phalanx, but, given the demands on manpower, others were there as well, at democratic Athens most particularly. Athenian diversity apparently reflected the growing irrelevance of the old farm-based census rubrics and revealed the *de facto* divorce between social and military status, the increasing unimportance of land ownership as the key to the city's defense. No development was more lethal to the notion of the city-state than the end to the yeoman/infantryman equation.

Isocrates believed that it was easier in the fourth century to gather an army of outsiders than it was to muster a force from the *polis* proper (cf. 8.41ff.)—an indication that there were many Greeks who fit not at all into the old agrarian hoplite rubric. Those who did were increasingly either unable or unwilling to shoulder alone the defense of the city-state. Xenophon, in his *Ways and Means* (about 355 B.C.), urged that resident aliens no longer be used for Athenian hoplite service. Harkening back to Athens' glorious infantry past, he advised: "The *polis* would benefit if the citizens served with one another in the army rather than with others such as Lydians, Phrygians, Syrians, and barbarians of all types—of whom a significant portion of the resident alien population consists. Besides the advantage of not using these people for military service, it would also in its own right be a fitting thing if Athenians should believe it better to fight their battle themselves rather than relying on the help of foreigners" (*Vect.* 2.3). In fact, at Athens in the late fifth and fourth centuries, resident aliens and foreigners took an increasingly important role in the city's land (and naval) defense—even though they usually did not own land and did not enjoy full citizenship rights.* In his *Hiero*, Xenophon even advised putting mercenaries at the front of the phalanx (10.6). Both their training and their expendability made them the most likely candidates to face the greatest dangers. In the new *polis*, the safer middle and rear ranks, not the cutting edge, were the preferred spots for scarcer citizen soldiers.

There is also evidence that land ownership, membership in the so-

---

*Whitehead 1977: 29–30; 82–83. Paul McKechnie (79–100) found ample evidence of disconnected men in fourth-century Greece. He devoted an entire study to the "outsiders" who had no real citizenship or affinity with a particular *polis*.

called *zeugitai* class at Athens—even as early as 440–430 B.C.—was no longer any guarantee that one fought as a hoplite. Why else would defense taxes at Athens be assessed on a man's military occupation—cavalry, hoplite, archer—rather than on his more formal census classification (*pentakosiomedimnoi, hippeis, zeugitai, thêtes*)? Why else would troops at Athens on the eve of the Peloponnesian War be described solely in military rather than economic rubrics?

How else could someone as urbanized and reputedly poor as Socrates have fought as a hoplite at the battles of Potidaea, Delium, and Amphipolis? Similarly, in the comic playwright Aristophanes' *Peace*, the Attic *geôrgoi* complain that they are singled out for the most frequent hoplite duty, while their urban counterparts manipulate the muster rolls, and so serve less. Aristophanes adds that the city folk are largely "shield tossers"—yet another probable indication that by this time the Athenian hoplite phalanx was composed of both landed and nonlanded (Ar. *Pax* 1181–90).[12]

This conversion from an agrarian to cash qualification to no qualification at all must have been nearly ubiquitous by the fourth century when the phalanx became even more composite. Then the orator Demosthenes warned his Athenian audience in his *First Olynthiac* that an expedition abroad for thirty days would especially hurt "those of you who are farmers." He was in fact probably acknowledging that not all in the hoplite ranks were so employed (1.27). Plato also complained about the absence of formalized hoplite training, arguing that it was illogical to expect a farmer or cobbler simply to pick up a shield and become a soldier that day (*Resp.* 2.374D). He, at least, must have felt that farmers *and tradesmen* had been doing precisely that for years as hoplites. Aristotle in his *Politics* acknowledged that because of the inflation and the increasing monetization of the *polis* economy, the old property qualifications had to be continually readjusted (5.1308a35–40). His concern suggests that, even for political and social purposes, stratification of the citizenry by wealth was becoming increasingly complex.

In some cases by the late fifth and fourth centuries, when men were needed quickly, even these nonagrarian cash standards for Athenian hoplite service were either unenforced or not uniformly applied. That may be why we hear of hoplite infantry armed and outfitted either *publicly* by Athens and other *poleis* or by wealthy private citizens. There was also the

notion on certain occasions in the ever-growing complexity of the Peloponnesian War and its aftermath, that one's social status or economic condition did *not* always determine one's role on the battlefield. Plato remarked
of the wide variance in social and economic background in the ranks:
"Very often a tough, sunburnt poor man (*penês*) is stationed in battle
(*paratachtheis en machê*) along side a shade-reared wealthy man (*plousiô*)"
(*Resp.*8.556D). The egalitarian ranks of the old agrarian phalanx were
rapidly vanishing as centuries of tradition and stability were abandoned.

Fluidity and imprecision in recruitment may be further reflected in a
variety of circumstances. There were occasional calls to "make the *thêtes*
into hoplites" (Antiphon fr. B6). Various references appear to metics
and foreigners who served in the Athenian army as hoplites with heavy
armor. The reverse also occurred, those above thetic (landless) status
being used as rowers on ships. There was an apparent absence of class
distinction for entry into the Athenian ephebia, where all citizens became "hoplites" of sorts by the public gift of the shield and spear. Slaves
were mustered on both land and sea. Wealthy knights (*hippeis*) served on
foot as hoplites and even as light-armed troops and rowers at sea. Specialized and better trained contingents (*epilektoi*), not mustered militias,
were a commander's first choice of troops.[13]

In theory, at late fifth-century Athens, census rubrics and economic
status still determined political and military service. In practice, ambiguity and improvisation were the norms. Athenian heavy infantry was by
the late fifth and fourth centuries no longer necessarily a social institution *per se*. More often the phalanx was a purely military asset, one outfitted with available armor and manpower, increasingly without special
cultural or political significance, one open to those who were not citizens and those who were not landowning yeomen (*zeugitai*).

If, in a crisis, the Greek *polis* of the fourth century needed hoplites, it
could (most drastically) either buy the arms and outfit the available men
without precise reference to formal census registers, or it could induce a
rough muster among the general population based on simple age groups
rather than careful attention to the accuracy of those enrolled on the
hoplite catalogues. As the agrarian exclusivity of the *polis* army further
eroded, hoplite service was probably more and more idealized (and, as
Alcibiades saw, exaggerated) by all classes—*pentakosiomedimnoi, hippeis,
zeugitai,* and *thêtes*—and increasingly the private domain of none.

Although the democracy at Athens may have been the most anti-agrarian of the city-states and sought deliberately to integrate hoplite-landowners into the more egalitarian fabric of her military forces, there is no reason to believe that other *poleis* did not similarly adapt to the tactical, strategic, and manpower challenges of the new Greek warfare in the fourth century. Agesilaus in Asia Minor had wealthy men supply both a rider and a horse to form his cavalry contingent, not surprising when the Spartans had been employing slaves and mercenaries in their fleet for years.*

This growing separation between farming and infantry service is well illustrated much later by a poignant letter of Alciphron: "Do not go off on military service, boy, but come back to us and enjoy a life of peace. Farming is safe and without danger. It has no armed bands, ambushes, or phalanxes" (Alciphr. 3.16). And he captures well the post-*polis* separation between farmer and hoplite with the description of the braggart soldier who bores the rural folk with tales of gore and killing (3.36).

Menander (who often idealized the waning agrarian code of his times) in the late fourth century had also written in a lost play that "man's true goal is excellence in war, farmer's work is that of a slave," which also suggests the increasing gulf between the two occupations (fr. 647 Kock). The old nexus between agriculture and warfare was ending in the *polis*. To the agriculturalist, farming should have "no phalanxes." To the warrior, the "farmer's work is that of a slave." More and more the disequilibrium resembled the atypical communities such as Sparta, Crete, and Macedonia where yeomanry had long been disconnected from fighting, where city-states had been retarded for centuries.

A few anecdotes about the usual relationship between agriculture and warfare in those environments recall their long time perversion of traditional *polis* values. The early Cretan poet Hybrias had bragged that in his "great spear and sword lies my wealth, and in my fine shield, a screen for the body. With these, I plough; with these, I reap; and it is with these I trample out sweet wine from the vine." So far, so good. The lyric poet Archilochus, after all, had said about the same thing (e.g., fr. 2). But then Hybrias adds something quite peculiar: "It is for these that I

---

*Xen. *Hell.* 3.4.15; Welwei 195–97. Their phalanx of Peloponnesian allies had traditionally been composed of nonagrarians (e.g., Plut. *Mor.* 214A72).

am called master of the serfs, who dare not endure the spear and the sword and the fine shield, a screen for the body. All fall down, grasping my knee and calling me master and Great King" (Athen. 15.695f–696a). Despite the social conservatism of Plato and his disapproval of the fourth-century *polis*, the philosopher had a natural affection for radically authoritarian regimes like those found in Hybrias' Crete. In the *Republic* the penalty for the soldier who deserts his post is *reduction* to the farm-working class (Pl. *Resp.* 5.468A; cf. Arist. *Pol.* 6.1328b6–24)!

Military service was often employed in nonagrarian regimes to preserve serfdom. It did not ensure freedom for the toilers in the field. An anecdote about the youth of the secret police (*krupteria*) at Sparta is grisly: "The young Spartan *krupteria* actually went through the fields where the helots were working and killed the strongest of them" (Plut. *Lyc.* 28.3–5). Excellence in farming was rewarded with murder by those who had no occupation at all other than war (e.g., Plut. *Mor* 214.A72). A Spartiate himself might be prohibited by law from tilling his own ground. At Crete farmers and soldiers were such separate entities that the former were not even allowed into the gymnasia. Despite the vaunted reputation of the Spartan phalanx, by the fourth century perhaps less than ten percent of its men were full Spartiate citizens, a society that fielded no troops at the Greeks' last gasp at Chaironeia (338 B.C.).*

Whenever, wherever *polis* agrarianism was retarded, armed militias were not composed of free citizen agriculturalists, and so soldiers served as a repressive, not a liberating, force for those Greeks who actually produced food. This Spartan, Cretan, and Thessalian tendency—rejected by most of the normative city-states in the *polis*-period—was in Hellenistic times soon to be characteristic of Greece as a whole. From a fragment of the historian Theopompus, who like any Greek was concerned about the traditional bridge between farming and fighting, we are told of the Macedonian cavalry: "I believe that the Companions, who were not more than 800 in number at that time, enjoyed the produce of more land than 10,000 owners of the best and most extensive land in Greece" (FGrH 115 fr.225; cf Glotz 1927: 341). Dark-Age horse culture loomed again on the Greek horizon. Not only was farmland to be used

---

*For Cretan farmers, see Isager and Skydsgaard 149–53. Cf. Lazenby 1985: 58, for the composition of the Spartan army.

less intensively in an agricultural sense, but militarily it was less productive as well. Land was to produce eight hundred knights—not its true potential of twelve times that number in tough yeomen infantry. And so the historic relationship between farming and fighting was lost, as Greek infantry could no longer be counted on as a stabilizing and egalitarian force in the countryside.

One reason for the collapse of hoplite warfare was the inherent limitations—in actual numbers and tactics—of self-armed, small farmers as sole protectors of the evolving Greek city-state. Throughhout this account I have rejected the seemingly most obvious cause of hoplite decline, the advent of the fearsome horsemen of Philip II and his professional phalangites or the rise of an isolationist "defensive mentality" among the "exhausted" Greeks themselves. Ostensibly, the *polis* hoplites who went down like magnificent stags on the battlefield at Chaironeia (338 B.C.) signaled the end of the free city-state, and with its demise, the obsolescence of the hoplite phalanx itself.

Philip's professionals, infantry with frightful pikes of fourteen feet and more, and cavalry who chose to fight year-round if possible, doomed the hoplite code and the hope of the city-state itself. But surely the advent of Macedonian phalangites was also symptomatic, the last, fatal expression of the more serious virus deracinating Greek agrarianism. The phalanxes of Thebes and Athens nearly won at Chaeroneia (338 B.C.), but such a victory in itself—Demosthenes' views notwithstanding—would *not* have ensured the end of the Macedonian threat and the continued autonomy of the city-state. The problem lay inside the Greek *polis* itself, *not* at Macedon. It was arguably no greater a danger to southern Greece than were the unsuccessful Persian invaders of years past. This growing crisis of the Greek city-state was inherently structural and thus inevitable. It was not solely generational, much less the product of a corrupted fourth-century citizenry: Greek city-states had needed for decades in the fourth century a great number of paid men to fight long and hard in a variety of corps; but to do that, they had learned, undermined their entire ideology of the citizen hoplite, the backbone of the *polis* system itself. The hoplites that battled Philip at Chaironeia were just as brave as their ancestors who slaughtered the Persians at Plataea; but the hopes and responsibilities of the city-state were no longer in their hands alone.

The moment agrarian heavy infantrymen lost their supremacy in the Greek mind, social, political, and economic prestige was bound to be given to any who took their special place (e.g., Pl. *Leg.* 4.706C–707D; Arist. *Pol.*7.1327b3–17). Here the dilemma was that on the new battlefield thousands, not one particular class or military corps—horsemen, light-armed, technicians, mercenaries, missile men—might enter the fray in lieu of the phalanx. These men usually wanted cash, not the public's thanks, commemoration on stone, or a few words of stirring eulogy at year's end. There was neither to be a royal *polis* of loyal wealthy cavalrymen nor an egalitarian patriotic society of rowers and skirmishers, but simply no *polis* at all. The chaos of the battlefield reflected the social disequilibrium within the disintegrating agrarian city-state. Isocrates (4.146) remarked that the Ten Thousand Greek mercenaries who marched into Asia at the end of the fifth century—military and logistical innovators *par excellence*—were not so much selected for their nerve, imagination, and skill as much as for their own unsuitability as citizens in their home *poleis*, men left entirely out of the traditional agrarian matrix. Once agrarian militia ended—as it had to end in the complex economy and society of the fourth-century Mediterranean—the entire protective mechanism of the Greek city-state lay wide open.

Philip—no agrarian adherent of the traditional city-state—had a natural affinity for picking and choosing a multitude of militarily efficacious corps, for transforming diverse units into a coherent military whole. In the strict military sense, that conglomeration of diverse fighters was for a time successful. It resulted not only in increased tactical and strategic options, but also in the short term succeeded in unifying diverse classes and statuses into a loyal mass without the landed chauvinism of the hoplite census. His fighters were not a *polis* now, but one enormous quasi-Dark-Age clan, a Grand Army on the move whose motley, mongrel underlings swore devotion to their king, a man of mythic stature rather than of commonplace agrarian proportions. Macedonian battle success did not derive, as is sometimes argued, from emulation of the culture of *polis* infantry. Its dynamism grew out of a complete repudiation of Greek yeomanry, a rejection not only of big shields, short spears, and hoplite snobbery, but a repugnance for the ideology that the battlefield should enhance and reinforce agrarian egalitarianism itself.

The central cause of the decline of hoplite warfare had little to do with braver or more bellicose foreign enemies. The problem lay, as we will explore further in the following chapter, with the inherent limitations of the Greek city-states themselves as players on the wider panorama of Mediterranean life, with the sheer stasis, with the very rigidity of the *polis*.

But was that dilemma not always the price of Greek agrarianism?

Chapter 9

THE EROSION OF THE AGRARIAN *POLIS*

The picture which emerges from our analysis of the distribution of the population, land, and wealth in the Classical Period, does not reveal the existence of an "aristocracy" and the gross social inequalities that such a term implies. The society which made maximum use of the land and brought it to peak production was one of small- or medium-sized farms and citizen-farmers—as close, perhaps, to the Jefferson ideal as the ancient world may have come. Its precipitous decline was probably not the result of the class struggle, nor may it have been entirely due to outside political forces beyond its control, but rather—as our detailed analysis of agricultural changes and the shifting settlement pattern suggest—in part at least to a failure to understand completely the potential and the limitations of the land itself.

—J. Carter 1990: 441

I. The Paradoxes of Greek Agrarianism

The Greeks themselves during the period of the *polis*—Hesiod, Herodotus, Plato, and Thucydides here mostly agree—saw their own existence as a small part of the inevitable rise and fall of states. Nor was their cyclical view simply one of pessimism. It was more than the "golden-age" idea that past communities were "better" than present Greek societies. This notion of the creation/maturity/decline of states was akin to the natural process of birth, maturity, and death. "All Greek authors," wrote the French historian Jacqueline de Romilly (1977: 19), "considered the rise and fall of a state just as they would consider the rise and fall of an individual person. The pattern of rise and fall has nothing to do with states as such, nor did the Greeks conceive any difference in nature between states and individuals."

De Romilly's correct observation does not mean that ancient historians and philosophers were completely ignorant of the influence of criteria such as finance, military expenditures, and demography. She suggests, I think, that all such data were seen by the Greeks merely as symptoms of this larger, this inevitable natural cycle of aging within a community, not as perceived catalysts, or causes in themselves, for social decay.

That cyclical notion is inherent in agriculture and so in an agrarian society at large. As a man's back weakens, his muscles fail, his nerve and spirit break with age, the decline shows immediately in the farm. Things are not done as in the past. Weeds grow. Trees and vines lose their productive edge. House, barn, and fences become unkept. True, the next generation is eager to inherit and may remedy the decline. But one life of the farm (to the aging farmer its best life), an entire cycle in its history has ended, will not come again. For the mature agriculturalist who sees firsthand this natural process of erosion daily—in himself, his family, his neighbors—the entire world outside takes on a similar pattern. The community, the state, the country, like himself, will grow old, the ongoing and predictable deterioration clear for the keen eye, the inevitably agrarian eye, to see.

In our literary sources, fourth-century Greek authors can comment on excessive defense spending or the growth of noncitizen populations. But these observations are *not* presented as analysis of erosion. They are sometimes confirmation of the senility of the Greek *polis*, a natural epilogue to the youthful exuberance of past times. It is unlikely that any ancient Greek thinker, in a systematic sense, discussed social, political, and economical phenomena that might account for the decline of the *polis*, although many Greeks—orators and philosophers mostly, especially during the fourth century—were quite aware that the three-centuries-old agrarian economy and social structure of the city-states were in a real state of crisis.

In a political sense, indigenous hoplite-farmers throughout the fifth century had been losing their exclusive importance to a growing minority in the Greek *poleis*, men who shared neither their agricultural background nor their agrarian vision of what a Hellenic city-state should be. Once the dominant class in the community by both their numbers and their status as the sole producers of food, the recalcitrant *geôrgoi* still in the late fifth and fourth centuries assumed that *all* Greek residents, landless and foreigners alike, would continue to accept their peculiar ideology that locally grown produce was the lifeblood of the *polis*, that wealth, social prestige, and political privilege were inseparably tied to something as pedestrian as a ten-acre farm, that naval power, mercenaries, foreign expeditions were *not* a necessary part of the city-state's military and political agenda, that money divorced from land was no sign of success, and that all residents shared in their glory of the phalanx lumbering out to reclaim lost border ground.

With the break-up of the Persian hold over the Aegean and the eastern Mediterranean world in the fifth century (i.e., 480–431 B.C.), and with the increasing disintegration of imperial control in Asia itself during the fourth (404–323 B.C.), things changed. As we have seen in the last chapter, many in the Greek city-states first learned of a wealth *beyond* their borders, and of the opportunities for Greek economic and military practice *beyond* the egalitarian sanction of the *polis.*

For these ambitious and aggressive non-landed, non-hoplites, there was a growing realization that food, like soldiers, could also be imported from abroad. Many Greeks knew that greater profit now lay in disreputable marketing and trading, rather than in the tedious growing of harvests. Seamanship and the navies that protected merchant vessels in the Aegean were now seen as important assets of commerce. Equal wealth was found from trading, mines, crafts, and in the region-wide exchange of natural resources such as clays, stone, metals, woods. A few years of hired killing in Asia could earn far more for a warrior than a plot of grain, vineyard, and orchards in Greece. Residence outside the Greek patchwork was not stifling, but lucrative, to those of the non-hoplite class (see, e.g., Rostovzeff 1941: 1.99ff; Garlan 1975: 103; Kinkel 66–68). In strictly financial terms, the end of Greek agrarianism, the diminution of the small hoplite farm as the key to social, military, and political privilege, resulted in much *greater* capital formation and wealth circulating in Greece, the Aegean, Italy, Sicily, and Asia Minor at the end of the fourth century and on into the third (cf. Pritchett *War* 5.468–71).

All changes in the delicate equilibrium of the Mediterranean tugged from both above and below at the old middle group of Greek small farmers. M. I. Finley saw these ultimate—and fatal—contradictions of the agrarian *polis* once it was placed within the wider backdrop of the Mediterranean: "Profound structural changes followed, in the land regime as in other respects. Urbanization created new uses for land and wealth, introduced chattel slavery, made possible the existence of classes (and even of considerable wealth) not tied to land, and eventually fostered a considerable monetization of the economy. . . . It is no coincidence that the various examples given by Aristotle in the *Politics*, of communities which were still struggling (or had only recently abandoned the effort) to preserve more archaic property regimes, were without exception drawn from the more backward, non–urban Greek regions" (Finley 1975: 159).

The generations of the fifth and fourth century in the less "backward" Greek *poleis*, so castigated in conservative literature of the times (e.g., Andoc. *Alcib.* 22; Ar. *Nub* 987–99), naturally began to question the viability and honor of intensive agriculture itself. True, uneasiness on the part of some folk is always inherent in an agricultural society. I can attest to that from my grandfather's lectures about the evils of the nearby town and his quiet disdain for those who would not live on or work their soil. Even if inappropriately labeling ancient Greece a "peasant society," E. K. L. Francis was at least correct in identifying the blinkered and confining mentality of agrarianism. He saw the stifling impact it has on its own who choose not to accept its limitations: "This does not necessarily mean that individuals would not emerge in peasant societies whose mental pattern leads in a different direction and who cannot adjust themselves to tradition. However, for them there is no room or outlet within the closely knit community. We must presume that these will eventually be cast out, and compelled to seek a living in some way other than agriculture" (295).

What was different in the fifth and fourth centuries was that now greater opportunity arose for the traditionally rebellious and dissatisfied Greeks, for those ever-present agrarian misfits with a different "mental pattern." At last they could achieve considerable nonfarming success, acquiring enough capital to make the old agrarian protocols appear nonsensical. Hesiod's age-old advice to marry at thirty, to acquire a wife, ox, and slave, and then, through the avoidance of debt and the sea, to find at near senility security in the soil seemed increasingly impracticable, if not silly—given the realities of a Mediterranean-wide economy and a near limitless theater of wars, sieges, and plundering expeditions. Instead, many fifth- and fourth-century Greeks no longer minded at all being "cast out"—once they saw money and economic influence awarded to those outside "the archaic property regimes" without land, without heavy hoplite armor, indeed without even formal citizenship.

Just as the phalanx remained largely unchanged—and thus was bypassed—in a sea of complex, revolutionary military changes, so the fourth-century Greek *polis* itself seemed frozen, still operating on political premises that were becoming increasing irrelevant to a growing nonagrarian but capable and influential resident population. Hence the innovative, though inevitably futile, practice in the twilight of the free city-state of awarding grants of citizenship to some wealthy benefactors who were not native-born residents (cf. Pecírka 1963: 201). But the deep structural problems of the Greek *polis* could not be solved by the expansion of citizenship to only a few prominent foreign men, whose talents more often incurred private envy and suspicion. Much more was needed.

Even noncitizen foreigners and slaves who had joined in with Athenian patriots to rescue their democracy from the so-called Thirty Tyrants (i.e., 403 B.C.) were probably *not* guaranteed citizenship for their valiant efforts, as Athenians in the subsequent calm quickly tried to renege on promises of citizenship grants. No surprise that at Athens—and it was perhaps the most democratic of the Greek city-states—any attempt to expand the franchise was usually met with stern conservative opposition. Reactionary proposals (albeit usually from extremists rather than *mesoi* farmers) were made to bring back an even narrower agrarian republic of landowners (cf. Ostwald 500–509).

The Greek world of the late fifth century and fourth centuries, for all its vast military, social, and economic upheaval, was still extremely conservative *politically*. There was no chance that many metics, foreigners, freedmen, or exceptional slaves—whatever the warranting circumstances—would ever be formally included in the *polis*. Far more likely, even in troubled Greek democracies, nonlandowning citizens might themselves be threatened with a loss of their citizenship: the ideology of the obstinate polis looked *backward,* not forward, to meet the changing cultural environment. Of that old and unsolved problem of most gifted resident-aliens lacking citizenship—and thus the chance for property ownership—A. R. Harrison notes of democratic Athens: "This incapacity, extending as it did to metics, had far-reaching effects on the economic structure of Athenian society, since it meant that the very men who were the backbone of the trading and banking community were precluded from owning, and therefore borrowing or lending on the security of, land" (237). A small farm was no longer a guarantee of financial success, no prerequisite for military service, but it was still mandatory for social status and political power.

The proper question is *not* why and how the agrarian *polis* eroded in the fourth century. Rather it is how was such a rigid entity inviolate *so long,* immune from the turbulent fifth- and fourth-century history of the eastern Mediterranean, a political brontosaurus born completely in answer to agrarian problems germane to a Greece of centuries past (cf. Starr 1977: 34)? Economics and fighting, both Mediterranean phenomena beyond the control of the *polis,* might change radically in the late fifth and fourth centuries. Yet the beleaguered Greek city-state wherever possible still stuck to its anachronistic social and political protocols born two and three hundred years earlier.

Hoplites were *not* pushed off their farms in the fourth century by grasping land barons. Nor were they displaced by the agricultural devastation (greatly exaggerated) incurred in the Peloponnesian War (as has sometimes been simplistically argued). Rather, increasingly in the late fifth century, agrarians became caught within their own confining rules. After more than two centuries of unquestioned prominence, the farmer/hoplite/landed citizen found himself more and more in a classic "no-win" situation. Small, intensive growers still owned and worked land in the fourth century out in the Greek countryside (cf. Snodgrass 1990: 128), but their absolute importance *inside* the *polis* was being lost.

By removing all others from the battlefield (and from a real voice in the *polis*), the Greek *geôrgoi* were simply captives of their own success at creating an exclusive egalitarianism. The landless (both the traditionally impoverished and the newly affluent "backbone of the trading and banking community") became increasingly more numerous than the hoplite insiders, as their *polis* system took on the appearance of a benign but anachronistic apartheid. "The increasing size, and economic importance, of the community of Greeks living outside the cities," Paul McKechnie writes, "created during the fourth century a mass of economically active people who had nothing to gain from the continuance of the system of making political decisions by a majority vote of citizens." These private clubs, McKechnie rightly adds, became increasingly irrelevant: "Once there was a significant number of free people outside the system of democratic or oligarchic government, and some of them were educated, articulate men who could have been influential had they been allowed to become involved in government, objections could arise to the position which closed associations of citizens held as governing bodies in the Greek world" (McKechnie 10).

Native Greek farmers of the *polis*, "the closed associations" of "the system," offered no mechanism for political integration once the floodgates of military and economic opportunity burst open. Entertaining no unifying ideology other than the possession of equal plots of land and the rigid desire to possess, to protect, and to perpetuate that agrarian ideal, Greek hoplite landowners themselves had little taste for opportunities opening up in the Mediterranean. They had scant business sense, no desire or ability for political innovation, and were bereft of military visionaries: hoplite agrarians possessed no appeal to any other outside their own (shrinking) egalitarian sphere. There was little to offer "the mass of economically active people," little hope either that *poleis* could grow into super city-states and still retain their characteristic informality, distrust of government, and immediate, almost hourly connection between voting, fighting, and farming. That self-contained autonomy in part explains Aristotle's reactionary and largely sympathetic treatment of hoplite agrarianism, why he felt the ideal *polis* should *not* have a large population, why it should be self-sufficient, with most of its natural resources at hand (e.g., *Pol.* 2.1265a13; 3.1276a29; 7.13261–b). As M. I. Finley noted, (1975: 159), Aristotle's favorite examples in his *Politics* are isolated, conservative Greek polities, which lay in the backwaters of Greece (and thus had been less exposed to upheavals of the contemporary conditions of the late fourth century). Similar favorites in the *Poli-*

tics are ancient lawgivers who attempted to preserve a simple agrarian state (e.g., *Pol.* 2.1274a22–1274b26, 6.1319a14–16).

But land once parceled, even if equitably so, and doggedly retained, is a limited, a finite commodity. Membership in the Greek agrarian grid was not a currency well suited as the *conditio sine qua non* of citizenship to a growing and evolving populace, a populace increasingly eager for the roll of the dice offered by military adventures and foreign commerce (cf., e.g., Padgug 92–93; 100–104). Thomas Jefferson, in the romantic and often blinkered tradition of Western agrarianism, long ago lamented this intrinsic, unsolvable problem of landholding as the only key to citizenship: "I think our governments will remain virtuous for many centuries; as long as they are chiefly agricultural; and this will be as long as there shall be vacant lands in any part of America When they get piled up upon one another in large cities, as in Europe, they will become as corrupt as in Europe" (cf. Griswold 31).

In sum, the Greek agrarian city-state had been able to fashion an unusually egalitarian social, political, and military system, but one (like many modern liberal states) closed to the larger, ever present (and growing) world of have-nots surrounding the *polis*, the other who desperately wanted the economic and social advantages of *polis* life. Herein lay the dilemma. To open up the discriminatory gates of *polis* citizenship was—as modern states have also often discovered—to corrupt the carefully constructed equilibrium and the unifying agricultural heritage that had evolved over two centuries of agrarianism. For the Greek *geôrgoi* to refashion the traditional *polis* for *all* residents might just as likely lose it for everyone. The economy of the city-state would remain agricultural but the ethos of the people would no longer be agrarian.

Nowhere can these paradoxes of ancient Greek agrarianism be seen more clearly than at Athens. It was the one Greek city-state that sought (ultimately unsuccessfully) to transform the agrarian ideology of the traditional *polis* to meet the new needs of the fifth- and fourth-century Mediterranean world. At Athens local hoplite farmers through a variety of mechanisms were won over to the idea of radical democracy—a government that in the fifth century relinquished its property qualification for most offices, built a navy, created an empire, and sought substantial outside sources of food and capital.

II. Rethinking the Greek Polis

i. The Athenian Reformation

To enfranchise as full citizens those who did not hold land, to mobilize serious military forces other than columns of landed infantry, to import food from outside the farms of their own Attic citizenry, all that could call into question the old agricultural protocols of the Athenian *polis*. But such a modification of *polis* ideology was needed in the fifth and fourth centuries, if the city-state were to survive as an *autonomous* entity within the growing complexity of Mediterranean empires and nations.

Athens altered the economic, political, and military triad upon which the city-state was based in the fifth century (e.g., [Xen.] *Ath. Pol.* 1.2, 1.7–9, 2.1–6, 2.14–16; Plut. *Them.* 19). By moving to the left she avoided some of the inherent, unresolved inconsistencies of the normative agrarian Greek *polis*. At the same time, that shift helped to accelerate the city-state's (inevitable) decay. As we have seen, the wars with, and eventual victory over, Persia (490, 480/479 B.C.), and the subsequent creation of a maritime empire presented economic and political possibilities unimaginable in the sixth century, offering Athens resources beyond the capabilities of most other *poleis* (Thuc. 1.89–96).

Athenian imperialism hastened the democratization process begun by Cleisthenes (507 B.C.). It enhanced social groups who held no land. Twenty thousand citizens now worked outside of agriculture (e.g., Arist. *Ath. Pol.* 24.3; Ar. *Vesp.* 709). Beside conferring prestige on landless *thêtes* who had served so well against Persian ships (c.f. Meier 555–60; 579–98; Momigliano 1–7), the formal creation of a vast navy from the tribute of allied states turned Athenian attention permanently seaward (Thuc. 1.99.1; Plut. *Cim.* 11), away from purely landed aspirations. The erection of the long walls and the fortification of the Athenian port at Piraeus only cemented this new reliance on naval, rather than infantry power alone (Thuc. 1.107.1–108.1, 2.13.7). Citizens of Athens in a psychological sense walled themselves off from their own farmland to connect with the sea.

Grain as early as the mid-fifth century was now imported in sizable quantities into Piraeus. Despite the controversy over the exact date and degree of dependence on overseas foodstuffs, Athens' well-known concern for foreign supplies represented an ostensible interest in food pricing, availability, and commerce at odds with the old idea of absolute landed self-sufficiency.[1]

Finally, the exploitation of the silver mines at Laurion in southern Attica, the growth of some small factories in Athens, and the manning of a huge Aegean fleet drew nonagricultural slaves into Athens proper in enormous numbers. With them came the metics. They were an unblinkered and gifted group of resident alien businessmen, bankers, and traders, a shadow city of outsiders who had no part in the functioning of democracy, no formal political rights in the *polis*. Surely that demographic reality made the traditional notion of a city-state of agrarian peers problematic.

By the fifth century, there were somewhere between 10,000 and 40,000 metics (adults and children), and between 80,000 and 150,000 slaves.[2] As if the official attempts at diversifying the economic, political, and military resources of Athens were not enough, this more insidious, less organized migration of foreigners and slaves into the *polis* further diminished the classic exclusivity of the hoplite landowner at Athens (e.g., Plut. *Per.* 12; [Xen.] *Ath. Pol.* 1.10–12). By the middle of the fifth century, we are not sure how many residents were *not* middling agriculturalists of Attica. It is a safe guess that at least half the citizens might no longer possess a hoplite-sized farm—that is, land that would have met the traditional yeoman census. Of the total resident population of adults in Attica (citizen men and women, metics, and slaves), hoplites liable for military service probably constituted no more than a tenth (i.e., about 20,000 hoplites out of a total adult population in Attica of perhaps more than 250,000). Yet the entire ideology of the Greek *polis* had once derived from just that increasingly small minority.

A ten-acre farm and its native proprietor were finite commodities. Cash and the foreign-born in the late fifth and fourth centuries were not. Every person, every drachma brought into Athens in some sense eroded the exclusive hoplite/citizen/landowner trinity. That centuries-old entity could cope with the slow economic growth and static military conditions of the seventh and sixth centuries far more successfully than the expansion and monetization of the fifth-century economy. The traditional economic structures of the *polis* had been in some part ethical. They were predicated on the innate moral superiority of yeoman agriculture over all forms of commerce and nonlanded capital.

The result of what we may legitimately now call the "Athenian experiment," this catalyst of *polis* deviancy among the Greek city-states, *should* have been, I think, constant friction between old guard hoplites and newer landless residents and citizens—with occasional outright fighting between the two groups as landed broad-based oligarchy and timocracy sought to suppress landless democracy, as farmer fought wage earner for the soul of the community. Radical democracy of the Athenian kind, after all, was inimical to much of the concept of broad-based agrarian timocracy we have seen in this book. No matter how *low* the property qualification for full citizenship under egalitarian agrarian governments might extend, did not Athenian-style democracy go even further? Ostensibly (though not always in practice), Athens put a man with little or no land on roughly *equal* political and military footing with a farmer-hoplite (e.g., Arist. *Pol.* 4.1292a10–12, 4.1293a1–13; [Xen.] *Ath. Pol.* 1.2.)—a citizen whose plot had provided the fountainhead of family privilege for generations. Cash, a far more fluid and volatile standard of privilege than land (e.g., Arist. *Pol.* 5.1308a35–1308b8), could quickly widen the gulf between wealthy and poor, and destroy the agrarian middle.

But between 507 and 338 B.C.—the establishment of Athenian democracy and the end of Athenian autonomy—often convolution, *not* revolution, marked Athens. As democratic institutions took hold after Cleisthenes (507 B.C.), the agrarian exclusivity of Attic farmers was transformed or at least partially reinvented. Although there was always growing tension between Athenian landed and nonlanded, no overt fighting broke out between hoplites and the poorer during this long process of democratization. What occurred at Athens throughout the fifth and into the fourth century was actually a gradual diminution of hostility between the two groups, yeomen (*zeugitai*) and landless (*thêtes*). Farmer-hoplites increasingly *accepted* the tenets of Athenian democracy, as the Athenian *polis* apparently tried to bend that it might not break, reinventing the nature of the traditional whole that it might at least save some of its parts.

How and why could so-called radical democracy at Athens ever become palatable to hoplite-farmers? Democratic government was a revolutionary institution. Did it not threaten the old economic, political, social, and military domain of small landowners?

The answer lies in the unique inclusiveness of Athenian democratic ideology. The Athenian *polis* took special care not to marginalize but rather to incorporate *geôrgoi*—still a real power in most Greek city-states—into the cultural life of a reformed *polis*, even when novel democratic institutions were at odds with the traditional farming agenda of Attic hoplites. Just as important, however, hoplite-farmers came to learn that their own social, economic, and political status could (for a time) be enhanced under Athenian democracy, not inevitably diminished as the orthodox view sometimes maintains. If Athenian farmers could give up their belief in traditional agrarian exclusivity, some growers might find even greater profit—at least in the immediate short term.

The challenges to hoplites at Athens were not unique. They were reflective of larger military and economic processes ongoing in the fifth-century Mediterranean itself, fundamental changes that questioned the entire Panhellenic notion of past centuries that a *polis* was an egalitarian institution confined to small landowners.[3] By the late fifth century cash was frequently acquired through innovative agricultural practices such as leasing and specialization for local markets. Worse for the small Athenian farmer, capital could often be found outside agriculture altogether from mining, trade, and banking. Aristophanes' Blepyros, in the *Ecclesiazusae*, points out the odd phenomenon that some wealthy now "have silver and gold, but own *no* land" (*Eccl.* 601–2). This "new social reality," Edward Cohen remarks, saw "the rise of a new 'mixed' Athenian establishment, which was infusing the traditional Athenian upper classes with wealthy resident foreigners, former slaves, naturalized citizens" (88).

The novel divergence between property owners and the creators of commercial capital soon raised the specter of cash-wealthy—but land-poor—men of talent and vision. Quite naturally, under the static existing system of agrarian values, these upstarts were either looked at with mistrust and envy by yeomanry, or, in the case of resident aliens, denied proportionate social and political opportunity altogether. In most Greek *poleis* this discrimination was expressed by the absence of something as basic as a ten-acre farm. Cash brought a man economic might. But land was still the key to political and social status inside the *polis*.

The *poleis* throughout Greece—and Athens most of all—after the Persian Wars were subject to a variety of challenges and opportunities, for which their traditional and inflexible infrastructure of the past two centuries was ill-equipped. These growing tensions in many city-states became manifest in the fourth century when we hear of a number of serious civil outbreaks.[4] Social tensions among the Greek *poleis* can be traced to a fundamental and growing inequality between propertied and propertyless, as the rigidly egalitarian institutions of the past broke under new economic realities and were no longer able to maintain for the resident population a flexible and moderate alternative.

ii. The New Athenian Military

As the hoplite phalanx was becoming more and more irrelevant in late fifth and fourth century Greece, Athens successfully sought to refashion the entire role of the heavy-armed hoplite. Of course duty outside formal phalanx battle ended the hoplite's role as exclusive protector of the *polis*. But fighting away from the mass also gave Athenian agrarians new responsibilities, albeit in much different roles. During fifth-century Athenian democracy, hoplite infantry were used *more* frequently than during the period before the Persian Wars under either agrarian oligarchy/timocracy or Peisistratian tyranny (i.e., 700–480 B.C.)—although in guises entirely antithetical (and so in the long term disastrous) to the entire notion of traditional one-day, agrarian wars.

Despite the emphasis on naval operations in the Athenian Empire, there were plenty of occasions throughout the fifth century when autonomous hoplite forces played a less dramatic, but nevertheless vital military role in the defense of the *polis* as amphibious troops and besiegers.[5] The ever-conservative Aristotle may have had these hoplite operations in mind when he complained that constant infantry service abroad had incurred high casualties among the landed, and in his opinion strengthened the aspirations of the poor at home (e.g., *Ath. Pol.* 26.1; *Pol.* 5.1303a7–10). Although these battles outside the agrarian arena were part of the process (discussed in the previous chapter) that precisely destroyed hoplite warfare in Greece, at Athens her heavy infantrymen were nevertheless not left idle. They were used outside pitched battles and integrated into the city's multifarious defense forces. The dismantling of *polis* agrarianism at Athens was an insidious process. It incorporated farmers themselves as agents of their own eventual demise.

There are, as we have seen, numbers of anecdotal passages in Greek literature attesting to the growing friction between landed conservatives and the naval mob. Under closer scrutiny these concerns are usually the disenchantment on the part of the more wealthy at Athens. There was probably not much complaint from the Athenian hoplite farmer himself, who, after the Persian Wars, increasingly was seeing his traditional military interests oddly protected by democratic change.[6]

A much more accurate representation of grass-roots Athenian hoplite ideology is found in Aeschylus, and even in the conservative comedy of Aristophanes and the often bitter drama of Euripides (cf. Spahn 8–9; Eur. *Suppl.* 238–45). These playwrights had no real sympathy for aristocratic (or Spartan) oligarchs, but rather praise for the egalitarian nature of Athenian democracy. They acknowledge the great contribution of the rowing-class of Athenian poor. But they see in it no obstacle to their innate pride in the achievements of their own class of hoplite farmers in both a military and agricultural sense.[7] The integration of moderates such as these into democracy, and those whom they represented, is in stark contrast to the single-minded, reactionary shrillness of the Athenian fourth-century philosophers. Those elite dissidents idealized the Athenian hoplite class of which they were not a part in either sympathy or practice (de Ste. Croix 1972: 183–85, 355–76; L. B. Carter 97–98).

During the late fifth century, as I suggested in the last Chapter 8, only a few hoplite armies collided head-on in the thousands. At Athens, however, hoplites were still busy for a while yet. There were numerous occasions when hoplites marched out on infantry expeditions and attempted to engage the enemy (not always successfully) in decisive encounters. Here one thinks of the twice-yearly invasions of the Megarid, when the Athenian hoplites mustered in full force during the Archidamian War (Thuc. 2.31, 4.66.1; Plut. *Per.* 30.3). Two thousand hoplites also marched north against Spartalos in 429 B.C., forcing the Chalcidian infantry into the city proper, and then falling back before enemy missile troops and cavalry sorties. Deployed traditionally on flat ground against an enemy who had no intention of deciding the issue with similar heavy infantry, over 430 hoplites perished (Thuc. 2.79.7).

Athenian hoplites also played a vital role in more complex, combined operations during the Peloponnesian War. These were situations where they were transported by sea and then expected to occupy ground alone or seek out enemy light and heavy infantry. Although ostensibly marines in the sense that they arrived in enemy territory on ships (cf. Jordan

193–95), rather than by land, it is better to describe these hoplites as "expeditionary forces." Often their activity was far from the coast, independent, and not always supported by combined naval strategy.

A good example is Demosthenes' ill-fated Aetolian campaign (426 B.C.). After landing near Oeneon in Locris, he set out into the rugged terrain of Aetolia with a combined force that included three hundred Athenian hoplites, "all," Thucydides says in a rare note of poignancy, "in the prime of life." One hundred twenty perished, "the best troops of the Athenians that fell in the war" (Thuc. 3.98.4). At Solygia (426 B.C.) Nicias fought a traditional hoplite battle against the Corinthians before withdrawing his army to his ships off the coast (Thuc. 4.44.6; Diod. 12.65.6). Later, Cleon's attack on Amphipolis was spearheaded by twelve hundred hoplites and a fleet of thirty ships (Thuc. 5.2.1). The most infamous example of a hoplite army transported in mass is, of course, the disastrous Athenian expedition to Sicily, when "few returned home." There the combined allied force may have numbered between 40,000 and 50,000, including *at least* 2,700 Athenian heavy infantry, and many more thousands in allied hoplite companies. They fought an initial decisive and successful action against the Syracusan heavy infantry and for most of the later campaign stayed primarily on land (Thuc. 6.43; 7.20, 87.6; Diod. 13.2.5, 8.7, 9). These were all examples of Athenian infantry deployed beyond the arena of the set pitched battle.

Hoplites in the fifth century were used by the democracy in even smaller numbers as amphibious marines in the classic sense, or as more daring seaborne raiders (e.g., Pl. *Leg.* 4.706B–C). During the Archidamian War, they skirted the coast of the Peloponnese, disembarked, ravaged, and plundered (e.g., Thuc. 2.17.4; 2.23.2; 2.25.30; 2.26; 2.32; 2.56; 2.58.1). In the wake of enemy reprisals, they unheroically fled to the safety of the ships (and the safety provided by landless rowers). Although these troops rarely formed up in the phalanx for decisive, single battles, rarely sought out their enemy counterpart or engaged in drawn-out sieges, there is little doubt they were employed as hoplites proper. Agrarians equipped for head-to-head collisions (although perhaps now in lighter composite armor) now preferred the cowardly but effective skirmishing of their social inferiors.

More controversial still is the actual status of the trireme's standard seaborne contingent of ten *epibatai*, the naval "marines" permanently attached to Athenian vessels independent of any hoplite forces being transported from theater to theater. Given their exalted status in the literary and epigraphical sources, the nature of their training and armament, and their apparent recruitment from the hoplite muster roll, it is logical—if these strict census differentiations still always applied in the late fifth and fourth centuries—that most *epibatai* should not have been landless *thêtes*. Marines were often those who were eligible and liable to see service as hoplites proper (cf. Jordan 184–202; Gomme *Comm.* 2.42, 80, 271, 367). From the record of their employment during many naval engagements, Athenian marines were not mere adornments. Often they became the decisive element in battle as both naval boarders and defensive troops who kept the enemy from gaining access to the decks of their own ships. Even more striking, on some occasions in the Peloponnesian War, farmers may have not fought as hoplites at all, but rather served as rowers in the fleet alongside the landless.[8]

What we see at Athens during the entire course of the fifth century is not quite—as so often is argued by the Old Oligarch, Plato, Isocrates, Aristotle, Plutarch, and others—an abridgment of the hoplite presence. It was more complex than that. There was actually increased opportunity and need for infantry service, albeit in *new* and untraditional ways. Although these novel military roles in the long run were dooming agrarian warfare in Greece, in the short term, they were not immediately injurious to Athenian yeomanry itself. This integration and complementary nature of Athenian hoplites and rowers was exactly what Pericles was referring to in his funeral oration when he bragged that the Athenians were usually successful at war because of "simultaneous attention to the navy and the expedition by land of its citizens to many lands" (Thuc. 2.39.3), a practice that "made every sea and land the highway of our daring" (Thuc. 2.41.3; and cf. especially 1.142.5). Agrarians were now in service to an empire, not simply devoted to the sanctity of their ancestral borders.

Elsewhere, among other Greek democratic and maritime powers, there was nothing approaching the Athenian balance in naval and land defense. Hermocrates of democratic Syracuse blamed the Sicilians' initial loss to the Athenian phalanx on his own citizens' utter lack of familiarity with hoplite warfare (Thuc. 6.72.3–5)—a testament to how far some democratic seafaring city-states by the end of the fifth century had strayed from the old hoplite protocols. The number of conventional single-day encounters that were purely hoplite in character may have decreased under Athenian democracy, but the occasions where fighters saw some type of hoplite service surely multiplied. This ubiquity of heavy infantry was due both to a greater frequency of war making during the fifth and fourth centuries (as opposed to seventh and sixth), and the expansion of the Athenian hoplite horizon to include these new responsibilities as marines and as seaborne hybridized troops.

Even the notorious (from a farming point of view) Athenian policy of avoidance of pitched battle in Attica during the Peloponnesian War (e.g., Thuc. 2.14.1; 2.21–22; Plut. *Per.* 33.7) did not ensure the destruction of native farms by enemy ravagers. While forced evacuation of landowners inside the walls of Athens should be seen as democracy's rebuke of traditional Greek agrarian ideology, it was still not necessarily fatal to Athens' own indigenous hoplite farmers. The issue is surely more complicated: Athens sought to protect her agriculturalists in novel ways that were compatible with her new democratic, rather than past agrarian, thinking.

The five enemy invasions between 431 and 425 B.C.—and even the Spartan occupation of Decelea outside the walls of Athens (413–404 B.C.)—did not irrevocably harm Athenian farms. Planting continued throughout the Archidamian War, and perhaps sporadically even during the occupation of Decelea. Serious damage to capital crops such as trees and vines did not occur. Many farmers never evacuated their families to Athens at all (Hanson 1983: 111–43). Other Athenian land forces were not idle in Attica; they did not allow ravagers to attack with impunity the property of fellow hoplites. The democracy took pains to ensure that cavalry patrols, light-armed sorties, and overseas actions were designed to relieve pressure from local farmers' property (e.g., Thuc. 2.19.2; 2.22.2; 7.27.5; cf. Xen. *Hipp.* 7.4; *Vect.* 4.47; cf. Bugh 81–119).

Most rural folk surrounding Athens were completely opposed to the evacuation, an affront, they felt, both to their hoplite pride and to the integrity of their property (e.g., Thuc. 2.20.1–2; 2.21.3; 2.59.1–2). But the real suffering of Attica's agrarians was the great plague of 430 B.C. inside Athens, not enemy ravagers (e.g., Thuc. 3.87.2; cf. Hanson 1983: 126–27). Understandably, we hear of no organized, sustained hoplite resistance to Pericles' strategy of forced evacuation. There was little, if any, civil insurrection over his policy—a plan that the historian Thucydides (no radical democrat) felt made for good strategy (e.g., 2.61.2; 2.65.7, 13).

Periclean defense was, in fact, palatable enough to its citizens (even if strategically unsound) partly because of the belief of Attic hoplites in their leaders' promise to protect their farms by means other than pitched hoplite battle—a promise for the most part kept. In an ironic sense, if any profited from the radical, anti-agrarian strategy of deliberate avoidance of hoplite battle in Attica—the old Persian War ideology of Themistocles promulgated by Pericles and his followers—it was the Athenian farmer-hoplite (even if not always the wealthy cavalry elite)!

Surely, in a strictly cost-to-benefit sense (excluding psychological considerations of the martial credo of the hoplite), pitched battle in 431 B.C. on the Athenian Plain between Athenians and the Peloponnesian invaders would surely have led to at least one or two thousand dead Attic farmers (out of a ten- to twenty-thousand-man infantry force in the field)—and a greater loss of military prestige among local landowners. The Peloponnesian and Theban invaders may have marched into Attica in 431 B.C. with perhaps forty thousand men (cf. Plutarch's improbable figure of sixty thousand; Hanson 1983: 123 n. 38)—the largest assembled hoplite force since the combined Greek army at the battle of Plataea in 479 B.C.

Under imperial democracy Athenian hoplites for a time enjoyed bizarre trade-offs: highly visible military service, but an actual avoidance of all-out (and lethal) battle between national armies in Attica; evacuated farms but little long-term destruction of the Attic countryside. Pitched battle in Attica and constant protection of isolated homesteads ostensibly were the hallmarks of hoplite agrarianism. But by the late fifth century, they were also the very military situations where high hoplite casualties were certain, and probable the defeat and accompanying loss of agrarian repute before formidable Peloponnesian and Theban infantry.

At the beginning of the Peloponnesian War, the nonlanded and poorer Athenian *thêtes* were about equal in number to the other citizens who fought in the phalanx (about twenty thousand men each). By 404/3 B.C. at war's end it was a completely different story. During the twenty-seven years of fighting, landless *thêtes*, the supposed beneficiaries of Athenian liberalism, died more than twice as frequently as hoplites, the purported losers under radical democracy (e.g., B. Strauss 5, 58, 71, 75–76, 80–81,

179–82). If the Peloponnesian War was a tragedy for all Athenian citizens, it became an abject slaughter of its landless population.

The multifarious use of Athenian hoplites as amphibious troops was a dramatic marriage of traditional infantry and growing naval power. Aside from the acknowledged advantages that mobile infantry brought to the defense requirements of the Athenian empire, there were also less apparent social and political benefits to democracy as well. Landowners were transported by, and could fight alongside with, their social inferiors. This blurred traditional census rubrics. It cemented the notion—as the shared experience of danger offered by military service so often does—of political equality (e.g., Arist. *Pol.* 6.1321a17–19).

The role of heavy infantry at Athens was not quite rejected altogether in the fifth century, but rather transformed. This revolutionary development tended to strengthen the social foundations of Athenian democracy, just as it undermined agrarian protocol. It went forward apparently *without* much objection from farmers themselves—despite the knowledge that the precious equation between small landowner and heavy soldier was now gone.

iii. The Expansion of the Athenian Economy

All produce, home-grown and imported alike, in the fifth and fourth centuries was now in even greater demand at Athens; foreign supplies only helped assuage the increased appetite for a variety of foods among the growing Attic population. The notion that Athenian democracy paid little heed to the hoplite agriculturalist, or did not require his local foodstuffs, is simplistic. This need for foreign supplementation might just as well argue for increased local demand. Importation was not designed to replace domestically grown food. "Those of you involved in mining," the speaker of a Demosthenic speech against Phainippos (about 320 B.C.) reminds his audience, "have experienced setbacks, but you farmers are profiting beyond what is fitting" (42.21; cf. Diod. 18.18.6). Xenophon's Ischomachos says: "No business gives greater returns than farming " (*Oec.* 20.22; cf. Pritchett *War* 5.471–73).

The dynamism and growth of Athenian democracy surely enhanced the economic position of the local Attic farmer in a strictly financial sense. Ironically, at just the same time it was *ending* his traditional and privileged role as single food guarantor of the *polis:* short-term monetary enhancement for individual growers, long-term destruction of the old agrarians as a class. If Athens was ultimately destroying Greek agrarian ideology, that upheaval was part of a more immediate effort to protect her farmers as citizens at large, by extending Athenian custom and practice beyond agriculture and the original confining ethos of the *polis.* Attic cultivators seeing monetary gain in the fifth and fourth centuries, forsook long-term (and parochial) interests. Greek farmers, much like their modern counterparts, always seemed to have a special fascination with sudden, unexpected riches, even when they eventually destroyed their agrarian tranquillity (e.g., the story at Hdt. 7.190.1).

We have argued that the farms of Attica were not really sacrificed during the Peloponnesian War, and that, despite the rhetoric of Attic comedy, local agriculture was not destroyed. In the ensuing fourth century, Attica spent vast sums on interior fortification, to keep secure the countryside of Athens (cf. Ober 1985: 51–101). This military conservatism was not so much a reaction to the agrarian damage of the Peloponnesian War (which we have suggested was in fact minimal), as much as an acknowledgment of three new realities: (1) the need to curb the overall defense expenditure and avoid costly offensive campaigns (e.g., Lys. 34.10; Lycurg. *Leocr.* 1.42–43); (2) the realization that the Athenian hoplite phalanx, in its changing composition and spirit, was no longer eager to face down enemies in the old style of pitched battle (e.g., Ar. *Eq.* 1369–71; Xen. *Mem.* 3.5.19; cf. [Xen.] *Ath. Pol.* 2.1)—fights that in themselves were becoming increasingly rare in Greece; and (3) the presence of an enormous (and expensive) variety of military contingents on the evolving Greek battlefield.

The increasing appearance of mercenary bands and organized groups of light-armed raiders demonstrated that peril lay not in organized columns of heavy infantry, but in war waged by any means at an enemy's disposal. In this context, expensive rural construction made some sense. It at least showed the democracy's intention not to neglect the Athenian landowner. The new pragmatic and self-interested Athenian hoplite wanted the psychological security of keeping foreign armies off his farm—without the need to march out to meet the aggressor in a pitched battle. To a large extent the democracy—through roads, forts, rural patrols, and garrisons—eagerly granted him his wish.[9]

More than thwarting agricultural loss, radically democratic government, ostensibly hostile to broad-based, agrarian timocracy, brought clear profit to the farmers of Attica. This paradox manifested itself in a number of ways. At its most basic it was simply a question of greater opportunity for theft. After describing the Theban plundering of rural Attic estates, the fourth-century anonymous Oxyrhynchus Historian explains that this was possible because the Athenian (democratic) countryside was "the most lavishly furnished" in Greece (12.4–5; cf. Thuc. 2.14–16). His commentary on the wealth of the Attic countryside ends in fragments. But a partially restored phrase concludes: "whatever they took [when fighting] from the Greeks they brought into their [own] fields." The subject of that incomplete sentence is unexpressed. It almost surely must be the Athenians: apparently Attic farmers in the fifth century often took rural property from conquered subjects and then reemployed it on their own farms. This pilfered cargo resulted in an agrarian infrastructure that was the most "lavish" among all the Greek city-states. The Thebans at the end of the Peloponnesian War then replundered what the Athenian farmers themselves had plundered. Here we should imagine stock, slaves, tools, woods, and metals, items the Athenians had probably looted from years of overseas campaigns and local intrusions into nearby agrarian Megara.[10]

When the right-wing thinker of the fifth century, the so-called Old Oligarch, believed that Athens' wealth in part derived from the sea, he perhaps was thinking of both plundered and legitimate riches of every type that came into the Piraeus—and then were dispersed throughout Attica (2.7, 11). The impression is that beneficiaries of Athenian maritime power were the farmers of Attica.

Less overt than simple theft and plunder must have been more insidious private dealing by Athenian officials. These were opportunists who found ample opportunity to acquire cheaper products across the Aegean, even after the formal end of the empire. In a fourth-century oration of Demosthenes, Meidias is accused of diverting ships while on official Athenian business to pick up stock and slaves for his farm back in Attica (Dem. 21.167–68; Plut. Mor. 785C). That charge of seizing property and using it for one's own needs in Attica must have been a frequent complaint (Dem. 51.13; cf. Dem. 4.24, 45, 47; 8.24).

Equally important to Attic farmers was the introduction of pay for hoplite military service, probably sometime around the mid-fifth century—a phenomenon, as we have seen, entirely inimical to agrarian warfare. Military compensation was no doubt welcomed, not rejected, by Athenian farmers themselves. In the agrarian twilight of the fifth and fourth centuries yeomen were quickly learning of the immediate cash benefits this new democracy had to offer. Monetary incentive lies behind the purported (and, in the traditional agrarian sense, blasphemous) advice of Aristides after the Persian Wars that the Athenians "should strive for hegemony, and after coming in from their farms, live in the city. For that way there would be compensation for everybody: for those who were serving in the army, for others who were posted as frontier guards, and in general for those attending to public affairs" (Arist. *Ath. Pol.* 24.1–2; cf. Plut. *Arist.* 22, 25). Thucydides believed at any rate that one reason the army supported the daring expedition to Sicily was the steady wage in the short term, and the chance to obtain enough capital to fund their pay in the future (Thuc. 6.24).

Under the traditional agrarian regime of the past two centuries, the Athenian farmer had left his plot, formed up in the phalanx and advanced the *polis*'s claim to a strip of disputed borderland—inferior farmland ironically involving more a question of community prestige than a source of agricultural bounty. Most losses during afternoon wars in both time and lives were the agrarian community's alone. Now the burden was shifted to the entire *polis*. Should Athenian farmer–hoplites fight, they were to be paid. The money was to come not from taxes on their property or harvests, but from overseas tribute and commercial excise revenues.

Under Athenian democracy the burden of *polis* defense not only was shared with the landless, but also could prove (for a time) much more lucrative to the landed. Was this not a small price for the short-sighted (or realistic?) agrarian to pay for the loss of his agricultural exclusivity? Given the mobility of ships and government support, many Attic farmers now would be salaried to range over the Aegean and even into the Mediterranean as far as Egypt or Sicily, and in the process be given greater opportunity to carry valuables back to their own ground. The tradition that Attic agrarians had enjoyed state pay from both military and public service under the Athenian democracy led Plutarch to say they had been "corrupted" by Pericles' offers of cleruchies (settlements abroad), theater subsidies, and jury pay (Plut. *Per.* 9.1). Plutarch may have been correct. All were activities that took a man away from his farm and curtailed the city's reliance on his ability to grow food. That surely constituted "corruption" in the old agrarian sense.

Even if Plutarch exaggerated and, in fact, many rural Athenian hoplites rarely found opportunities for state cash, generous *polis* entitlements to others (Aristides' "everybody") could only expand the economy. "Trickle up" economics, as it were, enhanced the assets of those who were not poor to begin with. Athenian expansionism was not a zero-sum format where someone's gain was another's loss. It was an *inflationary* process that actually benefited most involved. Throughout the fifth century at Athens, the number of those citizens meeting the hoplite census (now probably a cash rather than a farm production requirement) increased, as urbanization and the monetization of the economy accelerated (e.g., Patterson 67–68).

Incidentally, in my own experience, market growth and an expanding economy have always enriched grumpy agrarian mossbacks. Neighboring farmers in our own locale continued to groan all through the inflationary 1970s that "everyone was getting big in farming," that "you could now leverage your way into riches without knowing anything about agriculture," that "foreigners and outsiders were buying up land," that "you can buy anything on credit," that "costs were going sky-high." Despite their genuine agrarian revulsion at the increasing speculation and investment in agriculture and their realization of the growing dangers of outsiders to family farming, this was precisely the period when conservative growers eagerly made their most profits, enjoyed their greatest advances in net worth, and enjoyed their most sustained prosperity.

In the case of Athens, imperialism and an expansionary market economy brought profits to local Attic farmers. These developments were welcomed—even though they soon would spell the destruction of the old agrarian Greek city-state. Of that late fourth-century crisis of the *polis*, Jan Pecírka correctly saw its genesis in the transformation of the fifth-century Athenian economy: "In no case, however, can we say that the origins of this "crisis" of the "community of the citizens" should be sought in the fourth century. Its roots go back to the Athenian Empire of the fifth century" (1976: 29).

iv. Political Conciliation

The creation and evolution of democracy through the fifth and fourth centuries have traditionally been interpreted as a political affront to the power and privileges of the old hoplite regime in Athens. Any extension in political participation was antithetical to the traditional guarded influence of the farming class, and a challenge to the foundations of the traditional agrarian *polis*.

There is much truth to this notion. Cleisthenes purportedly brought in non-Athenians and freed slaves to be enrolled in the citizen rosters of the newly constituted demes (Arist. *Pol.* 2.1275b34–40; cf. *Ath. Pol.* 21.4). The introduction of ostracism (e.g., Plut. *Arist.* 7.3–8; Philochorus *FGrH* 328 fr. 30; Arist. *Ath. Pol.* 22) forced any prominent figure to weigh very carefully the jealousy and hostility of his social inferiors.

In the 460s B.C., in the wake of increased naval prominence and growing imperialism, the popular leader Ephialtes also reduced the power of the aristocratic Areopagus to not more than a homicide court for murdered Athenians. The transference of its formidable political influence to the Athenian landless assembly, the council, and the law courts was traditionally felt (perhaps wrongly) to have been practicable only when Cimon, accompanied by four thousand conservative hoplites, was away from the city, engaged with the Spartans in suppression of her helot revolt. Pericles' subsequent inauguration of pay for citizens' public service, his building program, and his reliance on an Athenian naval presence of at least 330 ships were seen as efforts to increase the power and visibility of the landless *thêtes* at the expense of the rich and the middling hoplite classes—developments whose continuance by the reconstituted democracy of the fourth century only made things more difficult for local farmers.[11]

Confirmation of agrarian hoplite resistance on the political level to the expansion of Athenian democracy should be apparent in the only real revolutionary movements in the history of Athenian democracy: the oligarchical insurrections of the Four Hundred in 411 and "The Thirty Tyrants" in 403 B.C. During the turbulence of the Peloponnesian War and its aftermath, the populace was exhausted and suspicious of the democratic government which had lost their empire. The extreme rule of the so-called Four Hundred, ostensibly a revolutionary body of Athenian elites, gave way after only four months to one Theramenes and his more moderate followers. They proposed that Athenian citizenship be based on the ability to afford the hoplite panoply (rather than on possession of land alone). That change resulted in a group called "The Five Thousand," but which more likely included nine thousand or more (Thuc. 8.97.1–2; Arist. *Ath. Pol.* 33.1–2; Lys. 20.13; cf. Busolt and Swoboda 69–70) who would succeed the failed rightist cabal.

In 411 B.C., then, the environment at Athens seemed ideal for a return to broad-based agrarian timocracy of the old style (cf. Thuc. 8.97.2; Arist. *Ath. Pol.* 33.2) discussed in Chapter 5. Permanent overthrow of radical democracy and a return to "hoplite democracy" along the lines of Aristotle's ideal "polity" or—better yet—a regression to Solon's reforms of nearly two centuries prior, could recreate a sixth-, rather than a fifth-century, Athenian *polis*. Moderate leaders and a middle constitution of largely agrarian holders of heavy weaponry could once again hold sway (see Whibley 192–207; de Ste. Croix 1981: 605–6; 30, 31; Ostwald 384–95; cf. Bisinger 44–45).

Yet the fortunes of the so-called Five Thousand transitional reformers in 411 B.C. were no more successful or lasting than those of the more reactionary Four Hundred revolutionaries earlier in the year. Why was this so? Neither insurrectionary group could count on the support of Attic hoplite agrarians. Just as the "hoplites" (or whoever the men of the Five Thousand actually were) had been instrumental in dethroning the ultra right-wing Four Hundred (e.g., Thuc. 8.92.4; 8.98.1), so many of these hoplite landowners in power now actually acted as custodians for, *not* usurpers of, democracy. When the danger of aristocratic revolution was over, in a matter of months power returned from hoplites of the Five Thousand to the original radically democratic government.

While the exact sequence of political events of the year 411 B.C. has been continuously debated, in both stages of the revolution Athenian agrarians openly opposed the wealthy aristocratic Four Hundred. They also had little enthusiasm for the idea of a permanent hoplite government of Five Thousand—even though that latter body probably would have been composed of men identical to themselves. Clearly, the gradual erosion of the old tenets of Greek agrarianism was proving lucrative to Athenian *mesoi*. By 411 B.C. farmers knew well that radically democratic government and Aegean imperialism both could pay dividends (at least for a while) to landowners in Attica.

Little need be said of the more radical and murderous aristocratic coup that ensued in 403 B.C. at Athens. Then Attic hoplites were even less sympathetic to the wealthy ideological zealots on their right.* Democratic resistance to the rightists—with recent losses in the Peloponnesian War of landless rowers at sea, and the navy demoralized over their defeats—once more counted on moderate hoplites, now led by the hero Thrasyboulos. His efforts culminated in a dramatic hoplite battle at the port of Piraeus, where the radical oligarchs led by the aristocratic Thirty Tyrants were routed, and democracy for a second time in a decade restored.

Nor in the aftermath of the Thirty's downfall did the Athenian citizenry have any sympathy with aftershocks of anti-democratic fervor, like the so-called farmer proposal of one conservative Phormosios. He wished to confine citizen rights only to those who owned land (rather than Theramenes' earlier idea of restriction on the basis of arms). That reintroduction of a property qualification (*politeian mê pasin alla tois tên gên exousi paradounai*)—the backbone of the old agrarian *polis*—would have disenfranchised some five thousand Athenian citizens immediately (Dion. Hal. *hypoth.* on Lys 34). Yet it failed to become legislation. Apparently, the Athenian hoplite constituency had no desire to balkanize a society in which they had done quite well, and which they had just defended with their own lives (Markle 158–59; de Ste. Croix 1981: 292).

By the mid-fourth century even the Reaganesque reactionary Isocrates could bristle at the thought of a property requirement to restrict participation in Athenian democracy (Isoc. 4.105). A return to Greek broad-based and timocratic agrarian oligarchy, "hoplite" or "farmer" democracy—roughly akin to Aristotle's "polity"—seems to have been often considered, but found to be without much grass-roots support among Athenian hoplites themselves. What explains, then, this remarkable political loyalty of hoplite landowners to Athenian democracy, a government that had done so much to transform—and in a long-term sense to destroy—the Greek agrarian *polis*?

After a century of gradual dilution of their old agrarian privileges, at the end of the fifth century, Athenian hoplites fought unwaveringly on

*They were largely cutthroat dreamers who had expelled hoplites from their farms (e.g., Xen. *Hell.* 2.4.2, 4–7, 24, 26–27, 31–32; cf. 3.1.4; Arist. *Ath. Pol.* 38.2).

behalf of democratic institutions. In the fourth century they continued their staunch support. The military and economic explanations for the attractiveness of Athenian democracy to the agrarian hoplites of Attica have already been offered. Keep in mind (as we saw in Chapter 8, "Hoplites as Dinosaurs") that military service itself in Greece was changing so much that, at least by the middle of the fourth century, a man's equipment and manner of fighting were no longer always an accurate representation of his social status: many hoplites may not have been farmers and some may not even have owned their own arms.

The landless at Athens had suffered an inordinate number of casualties during the Peloponnesian War, diminishing in the years right after the war the revolutionary fervor from a growing underclass. Aside from military and economic self-interest—and the gradual irrelevance of the hoplite census itself—there were also political reasons that show precisely how Athenian agrarians had been transformed through the fifth and fourth centuries. As defenders of Athenian democracy, Attic farmers no longer adhered strictly to the agrarian ideal of phalanx battles, property qualifications, and self-sufficiency in food production.

First, old-style agrarian timocracy, as I have argued in Chapter 5, "Before Democracy," was in itself the forerunner to Athenian democratic government. The original hoplite reaction against the wealthy landowning clans in the seventh and sixth centuries—whether dramatic or insidious—had instilled in Greek farmers no love of aristocrats. Instead they had a natural affinity for representative constitutions. The innovative decision to expand the franchise to an additional class of native-born residents was in some sense a far less radical move for hoplites than their own destruction of hereditary aristocracy and monarchy centuries earlier. The heritage of Athenian democracy can be traced directly back to agrarian timocracy of the seventh and sixth centuries. Farmers themselves were the original architects of all Greek constitutional governments.

No wonder that those earlier agrarian oligarchies (wrongly, Aristotle felt) had dubbed themselves "democracies," a logical enough notion when political participation was considerably broadened to include a sizable group of like-minded farmers (e.g., *Pol.* 4.1297b24–26). Similarly, Herodotus argued that once the democratic regime of Cleisthenes was established, the Athenian land army had fought far better than under

Peisistratian tyranny (Hdt. 5.78)—another suggestion that even at the beginning agrarians had felt more at home with democratic government than with narrow authoritarianism.

When cornered, the reactionary Four Hundred of the revolution of 411 B.C. sought vainly the protection of a "Five Thousand" hoplite constituency. The former believed that a broader-based agrarian constitution might garner considerable support among the farming citizenry, and thus stave off popular reprisals from the landless *dêmos*. Most revealingly, the aristocrats of the Four Hundred, like their ancestors centuries earlier, cynically had little real empathy for the idea of a genuine "hoplite" polity. They thought "that so many sharers in power would be essentially the rule of the people (*antikrus dêmon*)" (Thuc. 8.92.11).

The rightist Four Hundred were absolutely correct in their belief that the succeeding Five Thousand hoplite representatives would be more palatable to the Athenian democrats as "essentially the rule of the people." But they were entirely wrong on the more critical issue: the political traditions of agrarian, broad-based oligarchy had now at Athens become distant echoes of a century past. They were no longer viable. They were completely extinguished, never to be permanently resurrected. If Attic hoplites did not wish agricultural government, no wonder they had even less desire to protect aristocratic autocracy in its attack on landless democracy.

For agrarian militiamen of Athens, too much popular government was not nearly as evil as none at all. During the life of the autonomous Athenian democracy no property qualification along the old Solonian lines, flattering though the proposal might be to farmers, was reestablished to disenfranchise the landless. "Many of the hoplites," G. E. M. de Ste. Croix has remarked of these two Athenian right-wing revolutions at the end of the fifth century, were "inclined to waver—as one would expect of *mesoi*—but eventually [came] down firmly on both occasions in favour of the democracy" (1981: 291–92).

Second, for all the complaints of later elites, the public symbolism and popular ideology of Athenian democracy during much of the fifth century was all hoplitic, not, as we usually assume from the complaints of rightists such as the Old Oligarch and Plato, exclusively dominated by themes of the landless. The conservative Plutarch thought that Cleisthenic democracy, far from marking the beginning of radical democracy, had actually been "an aristocratic regime" (*Cim.* 15). The fifth- and fourth-century military muster lists (*katalogoi*) that listed Athenian citizens in their demes for military service—even if more and more symbolic than regulatory (cf. Boeckh 652–53)—were essentially hoplite registers. They omitted poor *thêtes* altogether, men who, incidentally, no doubt aspired to become yeomen *zeugitai* (i.e., to possess some capital and own land) whenever they could (Thuc. 6.43.1; Ar. fr. 232 Kock; Andrewes 1–3).

Class differences remained under Athenian democracy, but as is usually the case where cash, rather than birth and property, reigns, they were more along emulative American, rather than resentful European, lines. The Athenian poor often envied the *geôrgoi* and thus sought to reconstitute hoplite ideals, not destroy them entirely.

Officially, the magistracies and major public offices at Athens were rarely until the fourth century opened to the landless. They remained the domain of the upper three classes, of which the yeomen *zeugitai* were by far the numerically superior.[12] For what it's worth, the Athenian orator Lycurgus during the late fourth century thought it important to mention an old precedent where the proposer of legislation had to prove land ownership (*Leocrc.* 22). There is a reference in another fourth-century orator, Deinarchus, that Athenian generals purportedly had to have landed property inside Attica (in *Dem.* 1.71). These are echoes that—even under democracy—property still continued to lend symbolic prestige and social status. The transformation of the agrarian *polis* to a landless institution was spiritually and psychologically incomplete.

The occasional call to "make the *thêtes* into hoplites" (e.g., Antiphon fr. B6; cf. 6.12, 21, 35), in the strictly political (rather than military) sense of granting all citizens in democracy equal access to office holding, was also a phenomenon of the late fifth and fourth-centuries, a time when class distinction and the census rubrics themselves were becoming ever more incidental. We never hear of a wish "to make the hoplites into *thêtes*." Ideologically, hoplites were made to feel that the landless *thêtes* were becoming more like themselves, rather than vice versa. This "big-tent" notion that others were brought up, rather than insiders pulled down, was critical to the Athenian *polis* transformation.

Infantrymen, not (the militarily more important) rowers, were frequently portrayed on Attic vases. Dramatists and historians lauded infantry service. Public sculpture and painting emphasized hoplite bravery (e.g., Paus. 1.15.1–3; 10.10.4; Nep. *Milt.* 6.3–4; Aeschin. *In. Ctes.* 3.186). Popular myth magnified infantry prowess. Hoplites were commemorated in public decrees, casualty lists, and in public orations (see. Loraux 161–64; 170–71; cf. 151). When the Athenians wished to punish and humiliate their captured adversaries they voted to cut off the prisoners' right thumbs, making them incapable of using the hoplite spear, but not the oar—even though the greater military threat to Athens at the end of the Peloponnesian War was from enemy triremes, not landed hoplites (Plut. *Lys.* 9).

Just as the growth of Athenian democracy had reconstituted the need for infantry and enhanced the private prospects of many farmers, so too it deliberately cultivated hoplite tradition and pride. Athens gave its landed infantry a sense of magnified (if not always lasting) political preference as well—*even as the whole exclusionary and parochial ethos of the agrarian hoplite was itself slowly eroding* (cf. Fornara 51–54; Wardman 59–60). This ideological deference to hoplites in the fifth century can also explain why their continued incorporation and loss of independence at Athens went on unheeded during the fourth century. Hoplitic symbolism was adopted by the democracy for all occasions. This was not a device to divide, but rather one to unify the various elements of the multifaceted democracy.

Third, the large number of slaves and resident alien metics at Athens, and the careful restrictions between citizen and noncitizen, also helped to draw hoplites into line with democratic thinking. The inclusion of landless into the Athenian citizenry hardly exhausted the group of social and political inferiors. Hoplite landowners still realized that democracy provided sharp demarcations between free and slave, citizen and noncitizen, male and female, and even at times propertied and propertyless. Adult Athenian males who enjoyed voting privilege and full access to political office were still a distinct minority of the adult resident population of Attica. Inclusion of the landless at Athens in the citizenry may have resulted in a no more egalitarian society than existed during more conservative agrarian regimes. Those rural city-states of Greece, as we have seen in Chapter 5, may have insisted on the tradition of a property qualification for their native-born, but they were also simply without large numbers of disenfranchised aliens and slaves engaged in trade, commerce, and mining.

At Athens there were also instances—military service, colonization schemes, cleruchies—where yeomen and propertyless shared common enterprises and aspirations. Athenian farmers were not routinely ostracized. They were not as a group singled out and hauled into court, or subjected to land confiscations and redistributions. Emulation and admiration, not class warfare, was the rule. Athenian hoplites' political loss was completely relative, never absolute. If it was to be a question of political diminution, it occurred through the sharing, not the curtailment, of rights and privileges.

What are we to make of the baffling relationship between Athenian farmers and democratic government? How did such a marriage affect the evolution of the Greek city-state as a whole? We have seen that during the fifth and fourth centuries the old rigid structures of the agrarian *polis* were gradually transformed on a variety of fronts, without much opposition from farmers themselves. Hoplite service was no longer always a peculiarly agrarian experience. Nor in itself did it now comprise the totality of Greek warfare. When the national interest in the early fifth century (490–479 B.C.) called for a new theory of defense, replete with social ramifications, hoplites at Athens were presented with the dilemma of the old warrior Ajax, to change or die—and quite readily attempted the former.

The expansion of the Athenian economy, the growth of the fifth-century population, and the increasing bureaucracy of government in the fourth—all fatal to the centuries-old idea of *polis* agrarianism—actually for a time enhanced local Attic agriculturalists. Through frequent paid military service and overseas plunder, cash and capital accrued to farmers in an increasingly complex and market economy. The veneer of hoplite ideology in turn was preserved in the hearts of all Athenians, and politically its yeomen representatives may often have continued to receive preferred treatment over those without property—the supposed beneficiaries of the new radical democracy. No surprise it is that hoplite farmers always supported, never attacked, democracy in time of crisis.

This metamorphosis of hoplites into democrats, this abandonment of the entire concept of the exclusivity of hoplite-landowners—timocratic oligarchy, phalanx warfare, agricultural *autarkeia*—was made possible not through coercion or revolution. It was accomplished by seduction and ratified through the manipulation of symbols. That should remind us all that in a sea of economic and social change, agrarianism cannot be saved simply through the undying spirit of its farmers.

The end of traditional agrarian privilege at Athens for a time provided farmers greater agricultural income, continued prestige, and less exposure to peril. In place of the monopoly of agriculture arose a somewhat more flexible and stable *polis* for the new conditions of a rapidly changing Mediterranean—as the relative immunity of Athens to the Greek revolutionary fervor of the fourth century demonstrates. Nowhere else among the Greek city-states was the endangered hoplite class so supportive of, and protected by, the aspirations of the landless citizenry. Athenian aristocrats may have lamented the loss of the hoplite ideal, but many hoplites themselves must have actually welcomed their change into loyal democrats. Athens extended the egalitarian idea of agrarianism to all its native-born residents, and sought to refashion hoplites not as exclusive protectors of agrarianism, but rather as defenders of the new democratic order in the late fifth and fourth centuries. All that brought her a century of calm, but it also accelerated the destruction of the traditional Greek *polis*.

v. Athenian Aftermath

Athens went farther than any other community in transforming the old agrarian *polis*. But the Greek city-state was not saved by Athens—as the decades after the battle of Chaironeia show (338 B.C.). This "failure" of Athenian democracy—if we can dare label the inability of a state to obtain perpetual autonomy a "failure"—was due to two reasons. First, as we saw in Chapter 5: "Before Democracy," Athens still found no way to incorporate the resident aliens, wealthy foreigners (metics) or any other not born to native Athenian parents. Those were often just the people so vital to the economy of the fourth-century Greek world. The marginalized were every bit as important—in fact, they were more vital—to the city as the enfranchised native *thêtes*. Even when the poorer landless were brought into the Athenian *polis*, the total number of adult residents outside the city-state's citizen rolls may have been as great at Athens as at other more conservative agrarian communities—rural communities who were far less engaged in trade and overseas contacts. In this political sense, if continued survival, autonomy, and independence within the dangerous world of the fourth century were the simple goals of the Greek *polis*, Athenian democracy did not go far enough in redefining the relationship of citizen and noncitizen. It did not end the importance of land in the new environment where far greater capital could be made away from the farm; it did not jettison the cumbersome baggage of agrarian prestige and landed egalitarianism. Was it not suicidal to transform the economic and cultural foundations of the Greek *polis*, without a simultaneous and *complete* overhaul of the political framework of the city-state itself?*

As is the case with most would-be revolutionaries—Russian communist reformers of the late 1980s are good examples—who enact only half-measures, Athens' attempts to rework her farmers into the city-state, for all the resulting (temporary) social stability of the late fifth and fourth centuries, actually may have done more in the long run to destroy the tenets of traditional Greek agrarianism than any other force of the time. The move away from land-based agricultural governments, the turn away from wars of a day by phalanxes, the reinvention of agrarian timocrats into farmers as democrats, the reliance on trade, overseas imports, and a navy, all intensified the complexity of the fourth-century Greek world. Athens helped to make the old agrarian *polis* more and more anachronistic. Her democracy offered in recompense only a partially reconstituted city-state: she had helped to destroy the old agriculturally exclusive world, but she had not completely prepared the *polis* for the new cosmology of the Mediterranean.

Athens, as the most powerful of the Greek city-states, essentially had two choices in the widening horizons of the fifth century. She could have retained her agrarian traditions, by foregoing active participation in the eastern Mediterranean in the wake of the Persian defeat. She might have played a prominent role in Greek unification around agrarian principles, creating some federated fortress Greece, a defensive alliance of autonomous agricultural city-states, a democratic and Ionian mirror image of the Peloponnesian League under Sparta.

---

*As Jan Pecírka correctly formulated the dilemma: "The economic and political evolution of Athenian society outgrew the framework fixed by the *polis* . . . the framework of its economic and political principles, the framework of its social structure and inherited moral values and political behaviour" (1976: 19).

Alternatively, after taking up an activist and internationalist stance, Athens, like Rome later, could have moved beyond all resemblance to her agrarian genesis, a landed tradition that was so inimical, so disadvantageous to her new cosmopolitan position. Instead, Gorbachev-like, she did neither. She wished to have it both ways: to be a *polis* and simultaneously a commercial and military force in the affairs of the Mediterranean, to give land prestige and yet host thousands of landless.

That was impossible. The two were inherently contradictory. The status of locally owned property still lingered at democratic Athens; the restrictions on citizenship to the native-born were normally in force; the veneer of agrarian egalitarianism and envy of the more successful were only enhanced under democracy. All that was the cargo of the old agricultural Greek *polis*. It should have had no logical place in a new, greedier world, where foreign trade and capital acquisition were necessary elements of state policy, not targets of moral censure.

Athens in the fifth century had forcibly exposed the fragile and parochial agrarian ideals of Greece to the storm of the Mediterranean at large. Through her complex financial and commercial interests, Athens simultaneously sought to extend, to transform, to improve on, and so to preserve the egalitarian heritage of agrarian ideology. Is it not tragic that in that very process she also hastened on the destruction of the entire economic, military, and political premises of the traditional Greek city-state?

III. Elsewhere and After

Agrarian pauperism was the cancer of Greece in Hellenistic times.
—Glotz 1967: 348

I think one may conclude, from the accumulation of individual instances, that the trend in antiquity was for a steady increase in the size of landholdings; not a simple straight line upward, as much an accumulation of scattered, sometimes very widely scattered, estates as a process of consolidation; but a continuing trend nevertheless.
—Finley 1973: 102

If Athens could not reinvent the city-state to meet new social and economic challenges and opportunities, no other Greek community could.

But we should not dwell on this end of the autonomous agrarian *polis* in the fourth century. No state, no political entity exists in perpetuity. Consider the great duration of the Greek city-state over four hundred years, its success, and the lasting power of its ideas.

To illustrate the contribution of Greek agrarianism from the eighth to end of the fourth centuries, examine alternative, non-*polis* Greek communities by locale. Throughout the four centuries of normative *polis* culture, there were always other areas in the Greek speaking world—Thessaly, Crete, and Sparta come quickly to mind—where the city-state never quite evolved from the Dark-Age clan to a community of agrarian equals. In those places, instead of agrarianism, we see indentured servants, large estates, an absence of broader political representation, and distortions of the idea of infantry militias (cf. Busolt and Swoboda 284–88). The sociologist E. M. Wood saw this clearly. Her "peasant citizen" at Athens is, in fact, essentially the same as our yeoman farmer:

> One way of defining the significance of the peasant citizen (and increasingly also the artisan citizen) might be to consider this phenomenon against the background of other peasant societies, beginning with the communities of early Greece before the advent of the *polis*, and those Greek states which never saw the full development of either the peasant-citizen or large-scale chattel slavery, notably Sparta, Thessaly, and the city-states of Crete. In all these cases, agriculture and production in general were dominated by people who were politically subject to or juridically dependent upon privileged classes or a central authority to whom they were obliged to render tribute and/or labour services in one form or another (Wood 83).

For these nonagrarian areas in Greece, the failure to emerge along *polis* lines was a product of choices made in the eighth and seventh centuries. Problems of food supply and land use at the end of the Dark Ages were *not*, as in the case of the normative Greek *polis*, resolved through a movement of sizable numbers of the population to intensive agriculture and the incorporation of marginal lands at home and subsequently colonies abroad. In the case of Sparta, the brutal conquest of neighboring territory and the imposition of serfdom on populations indigenous to both Laconia and Messenia occurred (cf. Busolt and Swoboda 663–70).

True, there was a tradition that the Spartiates themselves held equal shares of land, and in their name allotted similar-sized farms to helot families. But this was not quite an affirmation of broad-based agrarianism. Instead it was a peculiar *distortion* of the ethos of small farming. Although early Sparta was not completely indifferent to the development of intensive agriculture, hoplite warfare, and nonaristocratic government in Greece of the eighth and seventh centuries, her helot "problem" led to bizarre mutations in the agrarian ethic.

A small body of hoplite equals ("Similars") did emerge at Sparta. They did fashion among themselves representative government of sorts, and did hold about equal-sized plots. But given the need for constant surveillance of thousands of subjugated peoples, Spartiates turned to an oppressive militarism. Males did not farm. They trained constantly for battle. In Thessaly also, the old Dark-Age regime of aristocratic horse owners and dependent serfs was never quite dethroned. No wonder it boasted that its indentured peasants could be drafted onto triremes in mass (Xen. *Hell.* 6.1.11). Set against this class of serfs was a tiny group of rich landowners. The Thessalian Menon from the area around Pharsalus supposedly helped to equip an entire Athenian army and three hundred horsemen from the wealth of his own private estates.[13]

Outside the Greek *polis,* ubiquitous expansive estates, serfdom, and manorial agriculture had been commonplace for centuries. In these areas where small-scale privately owned plots were rare, the whole notion of agrarianism never quite caught on. Its accompanying appendage, the Greek *polis,* also was never fully developed.* In other words, many oriental states and village communities had not shared the Greek experience—its "liberation of agriculture" and concomitant rise of the *polis.* It is not unfair to say that they had not progressed too far beyond the palace mentality of centuries past. Scholars who advocate an Eastern heritage for Greek culture should confine their arguments to the pre-*polis* era. They can legitimately claim an Asian or African pedigree for Mycenean bureaucracy and perhaps

---

*"While in ancient Greek society the city (*polis*) was the center of an agriculturally cultivated or pastured territory and the seat of individual landowners with at least formally equal rights and duties (*koinonia tôn politôn*), the basis of production in the old Oriental societies was the village community, which had above it . . . the despot or a temple or some other governmental owner of their means of production, especially of the land" (Kreibig 6).

even the Dark-Age lord, but not for the etiology of the unique Greek city-state.

Examine eras in Greek history which did not see small farmers and hoplite warfare, those times both before and after our *polis* period between 700 and 300 B.C. The manorial nature of the Greek Dark Ages gradually reasserted itself in Hellenistic and Roman times—*in the exact areas where the old agrarian polis had once held sway.* Specifically, in Hellenistic and Roman times, either cultivated lands coalesce into larger blocks or enormous numbers of scattered farms come under the ownership of one man. Crop raising falls into patterns of monoculture. Formerly good agricultural land is abandoned altogether. Rural settlement and population decline—in some aspects the Dark-Age situation before the advent of the *polis.*

It was not confined to a single locale.[14] Conflict between rich and poor within the *poleis* is understandable when the old agrarian protocols against accumulated wealth withered away. Although in fifth- and fourth-century literary, epigraphic, and archaeological evidence there appears no Greek farm larger than one hundred acres, that is no longer the case in the third and second centuries (Finley 1981b: 65; cf. Guiraud 391–99). Then the sources attest both to much larger estates and to excessive tribute imposed on diminishing numbers of smaller farmers, an age where the infusion of nonfarm capital into the community must have severely disrupted the old agrarian regime.

Gallant (1991: 188–193) has compared two Greek *poleis'* respective financial obligations during the fifth century and later during Hellenistic times. Under the regime of the Hellenistic despot Lysimachos (306–281 B.C.) the Aegean island of Amorgos and the Ionian city of Miletus needed between forty-five and thirty-six percent of their cultivable area to pay for tribute, more than double the amount required by the earlier "oppressive" Athenian empire. Obviously, the degree of rural exploitation increased in these communities once the structures of the old agrarianism—and Athens was herself far more imperialistic than most of her contemporary city-states—withered away. Hellenistic dynasties required far more capital for military expenditures and urban interests than was true of past Greek city-states. When they looked for revenue for their palace, their garish siege engines, and their hordes of mercenaries, they looked to an increasingly vulnerable countryside. In the third and second centuries exploitation of farmers was far easier without the presence of agrarian legislation, the popular representation of landed councils, strong infantry defense forces, and the ethos of past agrarian chauvinism.*

Archaeological field surveys of modern Greece have also suggested that many regions were undergoing fundamental structural changes at the end of the fourth century, accelerating their evolution away from the culture of yeomanry by the third century.[15] That is when continual non-hoplite warring and the resulting taxes on both land and produce by nonrepresentative and nonconstitutional governments eventually caused a depopulation of the countryside. It was an environment increasingly devoid of farmhouses and the traces of intensive agriculture. After the fourth century, the growing *absence* of rural infrastructure in Greece implies an ongoing erosion of the traditional city-state, a waning of the old underlying agrarianism.

Farm residence was on the decline in many regions. In the transition to large estates, overseers and bailiffs more frequently occupied the traditional family farmhouse.** A little to the north of Attica in Boeotia "by late Hellenistic times, there is an initial fall-off in the number of occupied sites, and second a tendency for occupation to be concentrated in the larger centers" (Bintliff and Snodgrass 145). The southern Argolid and Messenia area in Greece generally reveal about the same striking pattern (van Andel and Runnels 1987a: 110–17, 162; MacDonald and Rapp 146). In the Greek settlements of southern Italy after the fourth century, "the numerous country roads . . . fell out of use and were grown over as the countryside reverted to pasture land" (Carter et al. 309; Carter 1990: 409–10; 412).

Besides the accumulation of properties into larger estates, there was also, paradoxically, a rise in brigandage among the scarcer isolated farms once the ethos of the small landowner was cracked and the ever vigilant

---

*"Because the local elite no longer needed to look solely to the community for legitimation of its power, the community lost the leverage it used to have over them. Instead power devolved downward from the king to his "friends" and others, and thus communal accountability dissipated" (Gallant 1991: 195).

**Xen *Oec.* 12.3; Langdon and Watrous 170. Of the deme Atene in southern Attica, Hans Lohmann has remarked: "At the end of the 4th century B.C. there was a sudden collapse, the valleys became depopulated and barren and none of the numerous farmsteads was to survive considerably into Hellenistic times" (1992: 56).

agrarian vanished. Paul Guiraud, who a century ago noted this phenomenon, thought that the continual warring, increased class strife between rich and poor, and the subsequent assumption of power by Hellenistic authoritarian regimes lay behind the general agrarian decline (e.g., 1893: 398–406). This destruction of small farming and agrarian ideology is also expressed in a variety of Greek literary sources in Hellenistic and early Roman times. Lament over the decline in the countryside is much more than mere formulaic *topoi* in Greek literature (e.g., Alcock 47–48; cf. Day 231–38).

The evidence in Greek literature for these later changes is anecdotal and found in a variety of sources. A few examples will suffice. They generally confirm the record of archaeological survey mentioned earlier. In the Roman period the topographer Pausanias remarked that Aetolia, never a shining example of intensive agriculture, was now abandoned and uncultivated altogether (Paus. 8.24.11). Strabo said that by the first century B.C. Arcadia, a little farther to the south—once the home of solid hoplite infantry—was in large part relegated to pasturage (8.8.1; cf. 9.2.25; 9.5.12; cf. Polyb. 4.73–74). Polybius remarked of early second-century Greece in general: "In our own times some cities have become deserted and agricultural production has declined, although neither wars nor epidemics were taking place continuously" (36.17.5).

Plutarch (*Mor.* 413F–414A) only slightly exaggerated the vast difference between the Greek countryside during his own time (the late first and early second century A.D.) and the earlier agrarianism of the *polis* era, when he remarked that "the whole country of Greece could hardly field 3,000 soldiers, which is the amount that the Megarians alone sent forth to Plataea" (i.e., 479 B.C.). In the Greek mind, wise use of the land increased rural population and produced stout infantry; concentration in farm owning and extensive agricultural practices resulted in the very opposite, in a near absence of agrarian pike-men. In a famous passage in Dio Chrysostom, who lived about the same time as Plutarch, there is a reference that Thessaly was desolate and Arcadia depopulated (33.25). Of a city in Euboea, Dio also says in a discussion of the hazards of large estate farming that two-thirds of its surrounding countryside were unused and unfarmed (7.33–34; 38). Lucian, writing of Attica in the second century A.D., could be amused at men who claimed to own the entire countryside surrounding small villages (Lucian *Ic.* 18).[16]

Under the agrarian patchwork of the old Greek *polis* period there was *nothing* approaching the estates of the third-century B.C. farm of an Apollonius at Memphis (6,500 acres) or an Heroides Atticus (worth in cash about 2.5 million drachmas [enough wealth to qualify 1,250 farmers under the old 2,000 drachmas hoplite census of past centuries]). By the second century A.D. Heroides owned a great part of the deme of Marathon—the fifth- and fourth-century B.C. haunt of hundreds of hoplite farmers.*

Under a corporate agricultural regime, close attention to farming detail and any notion of independence by the farmworkers themselves were impossible. In Ptolemaic Egypt, for example, peasants in some type of share cropping arrangement farmed the enormous estate of one Apollonius. They complained to their absentee owner of the problems in working such a vast property: "There are lots of mistakes in this business of the ten thousand *arurae* [about 6,800 acres?], because there is no intelligent person to manage the agricultural work. Call some of us up and listen to what we have to tell you" (Rostovtzeff 1922: 75). At Hermopolis in late Roman Egypt a list of farm owners shows that the wealthiest 3.5 percent owned 53 percent of the surrounding countryside; the poorest 47.5 percent had only 2.8 percent of the land (cf. Duncan-Jones 138–39).

Unlike the agrarian regime of the *polis*, Hellenistic agriculture under the Ptolemies, Seleucids, and Attalids was often "subject to most detailed bureaucratic planning, at every level: what seed was sown where, what dues were paid by the lessees, and when—every step in the procedure, from the renting of royal storehouse equipment to the assessment of harvest returns, was subject to scrutiny by a swarm of local or governmental officials" (Green 368; cf. Kreibig 6–26). We should imagine there were "lots of mistakes" in farming when "detailed bureaucratic planning" intervened "at every level."

In the aftermath of the *polis* period, the paradoxical situation arose that as the number of Greek farms shrunk and the surrounding countryside became less cultivated and less inhabited, the actual size of remaining farms *increased* enormously. With general decline in overall

---

*Cf. Finley 1973: 100–101; Day 231–38; Jardé 119; the dedications of Heroides at the Panhellenic sanctuaries rival the aggregate contributions of entire city-states of the sixth through fourth centuries.

population, with more and more land vacated, it would seem a logical step for the absentee wealthy to curtail labor and capital investment in agriculture. They preferred instead to seek profit in large, extensively farmed estates managed by overseers and manned by servile gangs or serfs.

Incidentally, despite popular supposition, the concentration of American farmland into vast corporate tracts has not led to greater agricultural productivity per acre (cf. Strange 78–103). As in the case of the ancient world, less efficient farms arose and a decrease in rural population continued. In the experience of one modern rural sociologist: "The most important concomitant of large-scale operations is the composition of the population it produces. With a given amount of available land, the larger the farming units are, the fewer will be the number of farm operators" (Goldschmidt 218).

Drawing on comparative data of similar complex societies, Joseph Tainter located in the countryside the eventual collapse of the entire oppressive Roman bureaucracy. Farmers increasingly in the second through fourth centuries A.D. had lost control of their production, and thus were squeezed by exorbitant taxes. These monies were *not* recirculated, and hence brought little productivity in return to rural parts. Tainter's general economic analysis of rural depopulation in the later Empire conforms to the ancient literary and archaeological evidence discussed earlier about Hellenistic Greece:

> Three explanations are commonly offered for the abandonment: soil exhaustion, labor deficiencies, and barbarian raids. None of these is really satisfactory .. . . Contemporaries attributed it to overtaxation, and there is much to recommend this interpretation. The expensive government and military of the Dominate are clearly implicated. . . . Under these conditions the cultivation of marginal land became unprofitable, as too frequently it would not yield enough for taxes and a surplus. Hence, lands came to be progressively deserted. Faced with taxes a small holder might abandon his land and go to work for a neighbor, who in turn would be glad of the extra agricultural labor. A patronage system developed where powerful local land-holders extended protection over peasants against the government's demands.[17]

Even if all this has the air of the abstract, of the grand theory of rise and fall, the general lessons we must draw from ancient Greek agrarianism are unmistakable. Privately held small and equal-sized plots, homestead residence, intensive production strategies, wide-scale private ownership of individual slaves, farmer control of food storage and processing, freedom from excessive taxation, and strict agrarian control of war making and politics all led to social stability in the ancient Greek world. They resulted in a countryside and rural community—the *polis*—immune from exploitation by outside powers, in a laboratory for intellectual and artistic renaissance well before even the rise of Athenian democracy. Behind them all lies the agrarian creed of egalitarianism for the landed and the dispersion of wealth and capital throughout a broad middle group of citizens. These are the *only* conditions out of which successful broad-based constitutional government can arise. For citizens to care about the future of their own community and believe in their own abilities at directing it, a large body of them must have acquired the prerequisite confidence and expertise through their own private economic and military success. In a preindustrial society, that can best occur among a like group of yeoman militiamen, who develop shared values and a common culture through their private, though nearly identical struggle. Ten thousand men each farming ten acres, alike pruning vines and picking fruit, each proud of his private slot in the checkerboard of the phalanx, bring to government that priceless balance of individual responsibility and group concern. None can survive without another, yet none look to another for survival. Disturbing as it might be to modern intellectuals in the university, it is not an exaggeration to say that our entire Western literary and philosophical tradition arose on the backs of a very peculiar and previously unseen sort of farmer.

The problem (tragic to my mind) is that such systems, like the Greek *polis*, often unfortunately grow up in isolation, and then tend to be closed, overly conservative and reactionary societies. They cannot respond to sudden infusions of wealth and population, forces disruptive of the traditional one-to one equation that was between land and social/political/military status. To reinvent itself, as Athens more than any other city-state attempted to do, required a *complete*, not a haphazard move beyond agrarianism. That was something too much to ask even from radical Athenian democracy. The Greek *polis* was, in short, "hostile to the concentration of power into the hands of any single person, family, or group except for limited periods and for limited purposes as endorsed by the citizen body as a whole" (Runciman 1990: 366). The agrarian egalitarianism that had for centuries prevented exploitation against its own also frowned upon the infusion of noncitizen talent—a resource that could prepare the Greek city-state for new challenges ahead.

The central thesis of this book has been the rise of a remarkable agrarian culture in Greece. Its political, economic, and social system for nearly four centuries gave rise to a steady prosperity. In turn, farming success provided the leisure, capital, and ideology of what we now know as *polis* culture, the fountainhead of Western civilization. More specifically, it seems to me the Greeks discovered that the inherent basis of economic development and social stability revolved around three general concepts.

First, a private system of land ownership encouraged productivity and rewarded innovation among its native-born citizens. Farm ownership introduced the idea that human excellence is fostered by individual, *not* corporate, *not* state initiative. This original move toward privately held, intensive agriculture provided in most areas a surplus of food production. It freed a sizable minority for commerce, small crafts, and government bureaucracies. The last point is especially important. The freedom of the Greek *geôrgoi* from property and income taxes should never be forgotten. During the late Hellenistic and Roman periods in Greece, the countryside was continually vulnerable to blanket taxation, funds that were often raised by local authorities and then *transferred* to distant dynasts, further weakening the rural economy. Of the assumption of Roman control in Greece, Susan Alcock also points out that the result was an acceleration of trends begun earlier during Hellenistic times, a "higher level of systematic, regular and direct taxation. These could be augmented by other extraordinary levies. Most taxes were required in cash, and the province as a whole suffered a net loss of revenue to the central authorities."[18] The more subsequent generations of Greek farmers were taxed, the more they disappeared—and the less money was raised as inefficient estates took their place.

Authoritarianism in Hellenistic and Roman Greece surely did not result in increased agrarian efficiency to meet outside demands. It did not evoke an efficiency spawned by necessity and the trickle-down effect of enrichment for the few. In post-*polis* Greece outside dynasties only increased the ongoing decline in rural population, and they ended most equitable distribution of farm property.[19]

Second, and even more important than private farm ownership and freedom from government interference in any appreciation of contributions of the agrarian Greek *polis*, were the real efforts to deal with the inevitable inequality that arose out of an entrepreneurial system of agriculture. Men and women are not born of equal talent or opportunity. Hence, accumulated wealth, and the power of that wealth, for much of the life of the agrarian *polis* were carefully scrutinized. Originally popular government grew up as a precise response to the needs of small farmers, as a mechanism to protect their agricultural achievement and cohesive middle identity. Soon a whole set of sometimes creative, sometimes bizarre, ultimately confining institutions—liturgies, land inalienability, restriction against nonagricultural activity, scrutiny of public officials, laws of inheritance—followed. While land was seldom on any wide scale confiscated or redistributed—to do that would shake the confidence of those who were devoting labor to improving their own small parts—a social ethos nevertheless arose that frowned upon the accumulation of farm property and wealth (cf. Isager and Skydsgaard 128–29). Amid the agrarian ordeal of the seventh through fifth centuries, the truly successful landowner was not encouraged to gobble up his neighbor. To act so brought stricture rather than admiration. Instead, his public donations and services that recycled his expertise and his capital through the community brought him praise, rewards, and adulation.

The leisure and wealth that derived from agricultural productivity of the *polis* of the seventh through fourth centuries were in a social sense not predatory. Agrarian capital was channeled back through the foundations of the city-state, reappearing to support what we now would call Greek culture—civic buildings in stone, public architecture, painted pottery, literary and philosophical pursuits. In the present century-long debate between capitalism and collectivism it is striking how often we have forgotten this contribution of the agrarian Greeks.[20] The agrarian Greeks' major accomplishment, after all, was the unique balance and harmony between individual excellence and corporate well-being, an equilibrium between private enterprise and social stability.

Besides the wider economic development spawned by intensive agriculture, and the accompanying political mechanisms to protect middling farmers, the third and final component of the Greeks' success was the limitation of warfare. The construction of rules and regulations sharply *curtailed* the amount of capital and labor devoted to war making and, most important, diminished the degree of human and material suffering caused by battles, which could be frequent but not costly.

Do not underestimate the importance of hoplite frugality. There does seem to be a sharp break in the military practice of the Greek city-states before and after the period of the free *polis*. Expenditures for both aggression and defense historically can devour the accumulated wealth and leisure of most societies. But in Greece from the early seventh to the late fifth century a mechanism was found to relegate costs to an insignificant portion of the agrarian community's outlay: the same *local* control of land tenure that preserved the agrarian grid also governed the composition and conduct of the phalanx.

As this book has argued, all these *polis* structures were the work of an ideology of agrarianism, of farmers who emerged out of the Greek Dark Ages with a new egalitarian ethos at odds with the traditional notions of both the rich and the poor. Just as the appearance of new intensive agriculture, ideas of egalitarianism, and hoplite warfare explain the rise of the city-state, so the deterioration of those institutions and the demise of their creators reflects the erosion of the *polis*. Specialization in agriculture, the elevation of cash and commerce over small farming, increases in the size of individual estates, growing disparity between rich and poor, the appearance of mercenaries, and cavalry and specialized troops involved in extensive and constant campaigning, are all interrelated. They are characteristic of the Hellenistic Greek world and beyond. They are emblematic of the end of the city-state of middling farmers—and all that went with it.

An aerial photograph of a Greek "city-state" circa 250 B.C. would *not* necessarily appear dissimilar to one taken a century and a half earlier (i.e., 400 B.C.). Walls, temples, and houses after all would be about the same. On closer examination, municipal institutions would seem roughly identical: young ephebes, cults of the Olympian gods, philosophical schools, public records on stone, civic boards and regulatory bureaucracies. Linguistically as well, the populace of the later Greek community spoke more or less identical Greek to that of its ancestors. Organized learning and intellectual investigation went on; academics thrived. Examine standard modern surveys of the disintegration of past empires and cultures: the Greeks are conspicuously absent. In neither Joseph Tainter's *The Collapse of Complex Societies* nor Yoffee and Cowgill's *The Collapse of Ancient States and Civilizations* is the Greek *polis* even discussed.

So the notion of an "end" of the city-state, of Greek culture of the *polis*, should not conjure up images of a holocaust or Armageddon, the specter of shaggy barbarians and livestock in the agora of an abandoned community. The Greek *polis* never achieved a level of uniformity or complexity comparable to other imperial or palatial systems. It never experienced a cataclysmic social and cultural demise. Much different and far more complex societies (such as in the Near East and in the New World) often are decapitated and collapse in isolation (without, as in the case of the waning Greek *polis*, a Rome or Macedon nearby), no competing power primed to take advantage of the exhaustion (cf. Tainter 201–4). Utter confusion reigns for centuries in their wake. Depopulation and widespread impoverishment are the predictable reactions to prior overspecialization and bureaucratization. Cataclysms of this magnitude are far removed from the erosion of the Greek city-state.

Nevertheless, by the third and the second centuries the Greek *polis* was clearly lost—if by "lost" we mean the old equation of small landowner/hoplite infantryman/citizen. Lost was the idea of a free man within an autonomous city-state, a recipient of the cultural dividends that arose from that matrix. "The *poleis* which survived and indeed flourished in the Hellenistic and even Roman periods," wrote W. G. Runciman (1990: 348), "were, therefore, *poleis* in name only: they were urban communities with a life of their own, but not 'citizen-states' in the sociological sense." The curious Greek experience with agrarian egalitarianism was over by the third century B.C. "The 'political' life of the Hellenistic city was essentially determined by two contrasting facts: the lack of real power and the insistence on autonomy. As there was so little power, the autonomy more often than not was only nominal, and at any rate remained a purely parochial affair. There were no true heirs to the political citizens of the classical age" (Ehrenberg 1951: 372).

With the demise of the inward-looking, stodgy yeomen, enormous wealth and poverty ensued. The Greek-speaking Hellenistic world could now use the Hellenic genius without ethical constraint. It could leave the West with affirmation of the now popular "diversity," not unity, with urban cosmopolitanism, not patchworks of homestead farms, with bizarre siege engines, elephants, and packs of hired killers, not ephemeral boxes of bronze-clad farmers. Theirs was a realm of potentates and their tiny cabal of "friends," not agrarian councils of dour husbandmen, "their facial expressions like sour vinegar" (Ar. *Eccl.* 289–292).

Chapter 10

EPILOGUE

World Beneath Our Feet

If agrarianism is to survive, as I believe it can, it will serve as a different sort of a record: not of mass changes in the lives of the many, but of the persistent counterpressure of those few who choose to go in a direction of their own.

—James Montmarquet 1989:248

The earth bears everything and takes it back.

—Euripides *Antiope* (fr. 195 Nauck)

I. The Other Greeks

The Other Greeks has offered an alternative, nearly exclusively agrarian account of four centuries of Greek social, political, and military history (700–300 B.C.). Systematic emphasis on the countryside, as I argue in the Introduction is the most effective way to understand the ancient Greeks and the creation of the city-state. But it is an approach often neglected in this country, both because of the current directions of formal *American* academic research, and the more alarming and growing ignorance of agricultural life within our very culture.

405

Fundamental changes in the way the early Greeks grew food (Part One, The Rise of Small Farmers in Ancient Greece) were, I think, the causes of *all* subsequent cultural development in the West. There was a direct, not an incidental, relationship between the origins of our own intellectual heritage and the nearly forgotten yeomen of the Greek city-state. At the end of the Greek Dark Ages, population pressure and problems in food supply prompted a radically different approach to farming, a reordering of the Hellenic countryside characterized by decentralization, by local efforts at employing greater labor and infrastructure to produce a much wider and more productive variety of crops. The Mycenean palatial lord and the later Dark-Age baron, for all their respective degrees of political authoritarianism and oppressive economic exploitation, were *not* efficient food-producing organizers. For the next four centuries anything resembling those past societies was *not* to be resurrected as a permanent fixture in the Greek landscape.

Instead, now in relative (and unusual) isolation from the wider fabric of eighth to fifth century B.C. Mediterranean history, small, independent agriculturalists were free to coalesce as an entirely novel farming class in Greece. This so-called *mesoi* group of yeoman landowners grew food far more effectively than in the past. By the end of the sixth-century as many as a third to half of the free residents of the Greek *polis* considered themselves hoplite-landowners, not landless poor, not indentured serfs, not impoverished gardeners, not wage earners, not leisured rich horse raisers nor owners of large herds. The appearance of successful yet middling farmers marked the *creation* of European agrarianism as we have known it since. The ancient Greek agricultural community now believed that the land surrounding their growing communities, their *chôra*, should remain privately and perpetually in the hands of farm families, rural property to be divided more or less equitably and permanently among these citizens of the nascent *polis*.

Herein (see Part Two, The Preservation of Agrarianism) arose *all* subsequent Greek military and political development for the next two centuries (700–500 B.C.), institutions that are rarely—if at all—discussed in connection to agrarianism. So we should now reconceive the *polis*, constitutional government, the origins of individualism and Greek warfare itself as efforts to perpetuate independent landowners as exclusive citizens of the city-state, endeavors not so much to empower farmers as to create a larger and responsible community of equals. All were institutions utterly unimaginable without the supporting infrastructure of an agrarian middle. The continual erosion of hereditary aristocracy in the seventh and sixth centuries was thus, on a political level, followed by something entirely unprecedented in Greek history, the appearance of real constitutional government. But these broad-based "oligarchies" were not narrowly restricted to cabals of wealthy elites. Indeed, they were not, I think, "oligarchies" at all.

Typically, agrarian "polities" or "timocracies" incorporated a wide body of farmers, whose councils in turn sought to ensure the property-owning status of their successful agrarian constituents. The degree of democratization of these Greek agricultural governments of the seventh through fifth centuries—women, slaves, foreigners, and the landless were all marginalized—was normally regulated by size of the property qualification. Yet that requirement was quite often low. It might extend to owners of less than fifteen acres of farmland. In other words, Greek constitutional and representative governments did not appear *ex nihilo* at Athens. These breakthroughs were not the labor of political theorists, philosophical schools, or even of pragmatic politicians such as Solon, Cleisthenes, or Pericles. Popular government, as Aristotle saw in his *Politics*, was made possible only through preexisting egalitarian thinking, the pragmatic day-to-day experience of a cadre of independent and small farmers throughout the Greek city-states.

The simultaneous Greek military revolution of the early seventh century is explicable only by this rise of agrarianism, not merely by the technological dynamism of the hoplite phalanx, terrifying though it was. The new technology of hoplite weaponry in the late eighth and seventh centuries gave both power and order to the traditional "phalanx" of massed but loosely organized Dark-Age fighters. Just as new agrarian political and economic ideologies enhanced the agricultural evolution of the times, thereby ensuring a parquet of independent yeomen, the rules of military engagement (the third leg of the agrarian triad) now legitimized the grid of hoplites in the phalanx. Regulation born of agrarian thinking determined the place, time, object, sequence, and aftermath of Greek battles between the *poleis*.

In this manner, the ancient Greeks found a way to curb defense outlay without risking security. They discovered a means to distribute land equitably among a sizable group of citizenry without confiscations or the destruction of individual initiative. They established a political forum that regularly and peacefully resolved questions of social power and control, without authoritarianism or revolution. These three military, economic, and political challenges have undermined most societies since. Equality, responsibility, and cooperation explained a Greek farmer's slot in the phalanx, his parcel of land, and his seat in the assembly.

But there were intrinsic ideological and practical *limitations* to the entire practice of Greek agrarian egalitarianism—and so to the whole notion of the Greek *polis* itself (see Part Three, To Lose a Culture), should the city-state ever find itself in an environment different from the insularity of its agricultural birth. The idea of rampant equality in politics, battle, and farming among a static population of landowning yeoman was clearly reactionary. Agrarianism reflected the peculiar, confining circumstances of the genesis of the Greek city-state in the eighth and seventh centuries. Therefore it was vulnerable to subsequent demographic changes and integration with the surrounding Mediterranean economy.

Once Greece, driven on by Athenian imperialism, reentered the main fabric of Mediterranean history after the Persian Wars, financial, military, and political challenge and opportunity tore at the very premise, the basic tenets, of the traditional agricultural life of the *polis*. Fourth-century thinkers like Plato and Aristotle, so troubled by the growing diminution of agrarian conservatism in their own times, so disturbed by the increasing number of nonlanded residents and the amount of capital outside of farming, naturally put egalitarian landowning at the center of their reactionary philosophical utopias.

Hoplite warfare was not suited for distant campaigning. Its peculiar economy and its rules of engagement were largely absurd to foreigners, who fought on variegated terrain with completely different notions of war and warrior. Archers, rowers, slingers, cavalry, mercenaries, and light-armed troops, after all, were intrinsically valuable military assets, regardless of their relationship to the Greek landscape or the sociology of the *polis*. Similarly, self-interested Greeks of talent and vision, nonlanded men, who could create capital well enough off the farm, had no place in the agrarian matrix of the *polis*. It was an institution that once it had "evolved out of the confusion and depopulation which had followed the collapse of the Mycenean system was positively disadvantageous in the wider environment which they themselves had helped to create" (Runciman 1990: 350).

In a complex Mediterranean (and ironically increasingly Greek!) world, commerce, trade, and military adventurism—endeavors of "the wider environment"—all demanded status commensurate with new economic clout. As the number of the new practitioners grew, the yeoman class increasingly became unable to retain its own traditional agenda—an ideology that had been so beneficial to the past insular culture of Greece as a whole. The structures of the Greek agrarian *polis* could not live with fundamental change nor by the fourth century survive without it.

The Hellenistic world and Rome as well, we are now constantly reminded, was more multicultural, dynamic, and wealthy. States were far better adapted to capital formation, commerce, and the vast extension of military power, far more flexible in the granting of citizenship and the marshaling of large, diverse, and lethal armies. But was this not all at a *price?* After the fourth century, there was chaos in the Greek Aegean. Individualism had gone mad, a product of growing political turmoil, increasing inequality, the loss of social cohesion, and enormous military expenditure among the city-states—just the perennial problems which the blinkered world of Greek agrarianism for nearly four centuries had assiduously sought to address.

Outsiders might become citizens in such new states, but for what purpose? Citizenship in a *polis* was now to offer little guarantee of egalitarianism. There were to be few protections from the exploitation of wealthy and urban interests. After the demise of the polis individualism for a time might be enhanced, but the community as a whole lost. And in the end there was no individualism.

Greece in some sense may have also been a more exciting, more adventurous place after the fourth century. Then military service, citizenship, commerce, land ownership, farm production, and accomplished foreigners were all to be seen in pragmatic rather than in ethical terms. This change in values and outlook, however, surely was at an enormous social, political, and economic cost for Greek landed and landless alike. Agrarian protocol had both empowered and disenfranchised many Greeks. But the city-state had also created an undeniable equilibrium in some ways beneficial even to those without land. Manipulation by a large group of small farmers could never be as encompassing or as severe as the exploitation engineered by a tiny cabal of imperial elites. With the demise of the farmers' *polis,* the concept of egalitarianism vanished for nearly everyone, citizen and mere resident alike.

Agriculture itself, the narrower practice of food production in Greece, continued for a brief time mostly unchanged. But farming in Greece, after the fourth century was now more and more conducted on entirely different ideological premises once the autonomous *polis* was lost. Those shifts in Greek attitudes by the third and second centuries eventually did have enormous pragmatic ramifications for all involved: growing depopulation in the countryside, specialization of crops, decline in farm residence, enormous increase in farm size, growth of mercenaries, continual warring among professional armies, transference of local capital, an end to regional community autonomy, the impotence of representative assemblies, serfdom and peasantry replacing widespread ownership of chattel slaves, and growing rural impoverishment along with enrichment of an urban elite.

That full account of Hellenistic farming and fighting has *not* been adequately chronicled. No books have been devoted to Hellenistic warfare or agriculture. But a comprehensive study of both would explain much of the Greek-speaking world after the *polis*—and it would dim considerably much of the luster that the Hellenistic age now enjoys.

II. The Populist Legacy

We should not assume, however, that Hellenic agrarianism was ever entirely uniform. It did not encompass all of Greek life in every locale from the end of the Dark Ages to the rise of the Hellenistic monarchies. Large territories—Sparta, Thessaly, Crete—never, or at least only piecemeal, adopted the inclusive agenda of intensive, privately owned agriculture, broad-based oligarchy by property qualification, and hoplite warfare.

At the other extreme, some *poleis* to the left of the agricultural exemplar, such as Athens, often at the forefront of Mediterranean history in the fifth century, gradually sought to evolve and to transform the agrarian ethic among their landed and nonlanded citizens alike. Athenian democracy resulted in innovative, but at times clearly *anti*-agrarian, political practice and military strategy. The Athenians and their imperial democracy, in short, helped bring the wider Mediterranean world to the very doorstep of the Greek *polis*. Through extension of citizenship to the landless, urbanization, fortification, diminution of agrarian warfare, creation of a fleet, and reconstitution of the ideological basis of its middling landowners, Athens attempted both to save the idea of the city-state as a viable political institution, and yet to end the hegemony of the old agrarian *polis*. True, that contradictory effort led to a cultural explosion, to a vibrant, very brief artistic and intellectual renaissance at Athens unimaginable among her more pedestrian agrarian neighbors. But her piecemeal attempts at city-state transformation ultimately *failed*. Athenian imperialism only made the survival of the Greek city-states' ideology even *more* problematic.

One third to one half of the adult male native population within most Greek city-states never owned adequately sized land in the first place. They never voted in the assembly, never fought in the hoplite phalanx, never entered into the small farmers' matrix, and so benefited only indirectly from the trickle-down fruits of hoplite agrarianism. At best, these Greeks on the edge might possess insubstantial plots. They enjoyed only partial political privileges, and were drafted as prestigious infantrymen only in dire circumstances. A comprehensive history of those marginalized Greek peoples also has yet to be written.

But Greek yeomanry, even if these farmers were not preponderant in absolute numbers, was clearly the dominant culture of ancient Greece. Hoplite cultivators did establish the social, political, economic, and military foundations of most Greek city-states—and hence the general fabric of the life and thought of the *polis* itself. Nonagrarians in the *polis* adopted the farmers' values and laws, not vice versa. If we now wish at last to trace the origins of the so-called Greek legacy, the genesis of our own contemporary Western culture, we must look to the unique circumstances in the early Greek countryside, not simply to Athenian democracy.

There are, as I see it, at least twelve fundamentals of Western civilization that originated exclusively in the agricultural practice of the *polis*. They have rarely, *if ever*, been acknowledged in their proper agrarian pedigree as the discovery of farmers, not urban intellectuals:

1. Private ownership of land
2. Free choice and independence in economic activity

3. An economic mentality that sought to improve productivity
4. Liberation from oppressive and capricious taxes and rents
5. Constitutional government based on local representation
6. Chauvinism of a cohesive middle stratum, neither wealthy nor poor
7. Notions of egalitarianism and equality of property holding
8. Private ownership of arms
9. Citizen composition of amateur militias
10. Absolute subservience of military organization to civilian political control
11. Desire to limit and control defense outlay
12. Preference in warfare for decisive engagement and frontal assault

These Western ideals, so cherished and taken for granted so long in America, all grew out of a purely practical, utilitarian—and inevitably agrarian—environment. The autonomous and agrarian Greek *polis* itself vanished in the Hellenistic era. But that disappearance was due to complex phenomena that finally exposed the city-state's fragile cargo of agrarian exclusivity and structural rigidity. Most of the city-state's ethical and moral values, however, transcended the confining nature of its late eighth-century birth. They could be applied perfectly well to any subsequent culture with the prerequisite courage and necessary imagination. For a civilization in crisis such as our own, there *is* value in discovering the ideological foundry from which first emerged much of what we take for granted, much of what we have always assumed to be a *non*-agrarian heritage.

Is there not merit now for Americans to discover from the Greeks why, in the words of Max Weber, "the prevailing life-style was marked by great simplicity, and this was true of the creative figures of Hellenic culture in the period of its greatest achievements"? "Greek art in particular," Weber adds, "was not stimulated in any way by a demand for material luxuries" (Weber 1976: 200). And should not our generation seek to know why private lavish dwellings were "a clear violation of a building ordinance intended to enforce a social principle, that of the equality of property among members of the landowning class" (Métraux 96)?

The pragmatic, egalitarian, and common-sense values of the Greeks,

I repeat, were not the harvests of nostalgic philosophical utopias. Hellenic culture did not originate from the work of ancient theorists or rhetoricians. It was not the result of intellectual discussions over power and gender in dialogues, plays, and orations. E. M. Wood, despite wrongly calling Athenian hoplite-farmers "peasant-citizens" nevertheless makes a perceptive—but nearly neglected—observation: "Many of the cherished ideals of Athenian culture, and even some of its most exalted notions of Greek philosophy may owe their origins to the experience and aspirations of the Attic peasantry" (Wood 126). The "ideals" and "exalted notions of Greek philosophy" were the direct result of the birth of European agrarianism.

The learned practitioners of nuance and criticism, the urban cultural fora, now and in the past, are mostly unconcerned with and incapable of creating a just and viable society of equals. They usually do not believe in, do not live among, do not work beside, do not marry among the great middle group of ancient and modern citizenry, the people who day by day, nearly unconsciously craft the culture and create the values in which they live. Most theorists and intellectuals are also at a distance from nature and the harsh pragmatism that she instills in all those who attempt to grow food in a hostile environment, unforgiving of either error or misfortune, unconcerned with excuse or special pleading. As stated in the Introduction, I see a disheartening—and continuing—tendency on the part of current American classicists to think and write too exclusively about this intellectual few of the Greek *polis*, thinkers who rested on the shoulders of the unknown giants in the forgotten countryside.

Is that late twentieth-century academic fascination with the political theory and literary criticism of a small cadre of ancient writers not explicable, when we consider that the modern American scholar of this era—himself dependent on the bounty of a vibrant middle-class—often has no appreciation, no affinity, no affection for the very culture that has produced and now protects him? To understand the other Greeks, American classicists, however imaginative and erudite they may be, must change more than their approach to classical scholarship. They must end more than their preoccupation with texts, theories, and rhetoric. They must radically shift their focus from the confining world of graduate seminars and panel discussions to the popular arena of poorly educated undergraduates and the ignored majority of middling readers. Only thus can the concerns and aspirations of the forgotten present illuminate a neglected past.

Clear proof of the dominant role of yeomanry in Greek cultural history is, as we have also seen, the negative argument, the fact that most of their values—despite the continued (and growing!) presence of the Greek philosophical schools, libraries, and organized intellectual research—vanished from common practice, both chronologically and regionally, once the agrarian middle of the Hellenic city-state disappeared. That (very provocative) book which chronicles the peculiar affinity of ancient Greek academic (as opposed to original) thinking for monarchy, tyranny, and authoritarianism also has not yet been written.

To the modern literary, philosophical, and theoretical historian of the 1980s, the despotic Hellenistic world was an intellectual feast of increasing diversity in philosophical approaches, of growing organization and sophistication of academic enterprise and inquiry. It was a thinking-man's gala, a multicultural pandemonium much in vogue now in the university. But the post-*polis* was a world—like ours—roughly contemporaneous with the period in which rural life and the majority of citizenry was rapidly vanishing as independent and powerful forces for political, social, and military autonomy and egalitarianism. It was, after all, farmers, not urban savants, who had kept the culture of the Greek city-state alive.

Gloriously informed investigation, brilliantly reasoned contemplation among introspective literati, and far-seeing theories of the Greek *polis* were not the creators, not the catalysts for the extension of pragmatic Greek values. They were the logical fruit of the groundwork of agrarians, Greek farmers who are now all but lost to the European historical record. The efforts of these *geôrgoi* provided the capital, the security, the freedom, the entire backdrop for a curious few to enhance, to question, to nuance, and to transform their own fundamentally sound agrarian political, social, and military thinking—this urban intellectual renaissance reaching a crescendo in the late fifth and fourth centuries B.C., just as the old supporting framework and *safety* of egalitarian agriculture was collapsing. No wonder once the cohesive middle was lost, constitutional government and local autonomy never really returned to Greece.

So I argue that you must change your accustomed impression of the ancient Greeks. Do not envision them as distant geniuses or robed intelligentsia. They are *not* "the famous 'creative minority,' an aristocracy of intellect and morals, an upper class, not mere individuals, of a higher level of intellectual and moral education" who alone "create true and eternal things" (Ehrenberg 1951: 373). The Greeks are not a few beard-ed stone heads. Their culture instead is the inevitable consequence of a strong middle group of independent farmers, who alone had the talent, courage, and vision to construct a society in their own image, confident that from that creation would inevitably flow the best of human talent and aspiration.

Appreciate that agrarian genesis of Western values. Seek to preserve a remnant of it in your own experience, and with it find some protection for, some anchor to, your own precious but now precarious political, eco-nomic, social, and military heritage, some understanding that the free individual does have responsibility to his community.

This effort at populism, academic "vulgarization" if you will, is, I think, *urgent* now to the preservation of Classics as an academic disci-pline in this country. Despite strong class enrollments, despite integra-tion within the general education framework of the university, the study of classical antiquity is under assault throughout the United States. If we professors do little to convince the public of its value, its usefulness, it will surely vanish altogether as a formal academic discipline.

To take but one example, at my home teaching institution, California State University, Fresno, in the summer of 1992 (six months after the Classics program received national recognition), the university of nearly twenty thousand students in the face of budgetary reductions advocated *first* of all eliminating *every* class in the language and culture of Greece and Rome, and *all* courses in humanities from Homer to the Renais-sance. This decision (only partially rescinded when funding was re-stored) was agreed to by the chairman of the Literature Department, reluctantly sanctioned by the dean of the School of Arts and Humani-ties, but originally made *by the vice-president and president of the university.* Why would the humanities, and Classics in particular, be the *first* disci-plines to be stripped from a university curriculum?

We academics, I think, are in large part culpable. In the United States—out of timidity, self-interest, or both, it must be admitted forth-rightly—we write ever more about ever less for ever fewer. The enormous industry—there is no other word for it—of our American university is now at a critical juncture, faced with a dilemma it seeks to avoid, but can-

not. The 1980s saw in this country a growing number of people simply uninterested in reading history and literature. Many are openly hostile to
learning and intellectual life in general. The next stage in the erosion of
American learning is even more frightening. If the literacy, if the inquisi-
tiveness of the general populace continues to diminish at present rates
(and is there reason to believe that it will not?), most Americans by the
end of the 1990s will not merely be uninterested in, but actually *incapable
of*, absorbing a challenging book. In times of economic stagnation taxpayers will no longer contribute to what they neither understand nor wish to
understand. How many university-based journals, how many academic
press books pile up on the table of the nurse, cook, or plumber, much less
of the doctor, stockbroker, and lawyer? How ironic it is that hours released
from the university classroom during the 1980s subsidized so much of this
specialized, often counterproductive research; how ironic it is that we academics ignored what might have saved us, in order to indulge in what now
surely is destroying us.

Our problem in Classics in this country is *not* really how many women
or people of Asian, African, or Hispanic heritage choose to learn or not to
learn Greek and Latin. It is the nearly unsolvable dilemma of class and
status that affects us all, not the simpler and solvable issues of race, gender, or ethnicity. For too long our pool of prospective classics students and
scholars of both sexes and all ethnicities, has been stocked by those with
traditional and narrow academic interests, those with little knowledge of,
much less experience in, the beleaguered social and economic life of the
society in which they *now* live: men and women who exclusively read and
write books of theory and criticism largely about those of the past who
wrote books, men and women who have either no ability to or no interest
in communicating their expertise to the public at large.

In a larger sense, the hour of reckoning is ominously near for all the
disciplines lumped under the rubric "humanities." The growth of com-
puter networks, electronic mail, and extensive data banks—ironically all
projects welcomed by scholars—are double-edged swords. Can such
technology also not make the whole notion of esoteric, university-press
publications obsolete undertakings, and even more the ubiquitous academic journal? Both species of university endeavor, after all, are unnecessarily expensive. They are often inaccessible—in style, spirit, and
interest—even to the few on campuses who read them. Will not some

clever student in frustration (with no interest in seeing the emperor clothed) soon ask the dreaded question: is there a need for such scholarship at all to be presented in printed or book form, much less any reason for the accompanying old lie that many can, or will wish to, read it? Surely, if academics are to continue to write for and squabble only among themselves in obtuse language, on topics unintelligible to the public, why not turn the entire enterprise over to the machines—compiling, concording, communicating silently over optic cables between proud university towers? As priestly sects of bibliographers and tabulators cloistered at terminals, we will type on keyboards in esoteric tongues. Unknown by and unimportant to the mob below, we will very quickly be left adrift, less important to society than the Linear B scribes or hieroglyphic masters of the past.

Financial support is required by the entire enterprise of recent academic publication—primarily the effect of the tenure policies of most American universities that value minuscule teaching responsibilities and sheer quantity of output over quality, independence, and originality of research. But the public *already* has passed judgment. They no longer read any of what we write. They are convinced that we are neither willing nor able to teach undergraduate students the fundamental elements of Western culture. Soon they will no longer subsidize what they see as an increasingly expensive and irrelevant fraud.

I no longer entirely believe in the traditional scope and presentation of much of academic research in the humanities, at least as it is practiced now in this country. Nor do I have much confidence in the methods accompanying that inquiry, nor even in the present environment in which such work takes place. In their present evolved forms, these scholarly practices at times deliberately limit, rather than encourage, access to literature and history. Both traditional *and* revisionist disciplines, right and left, in my view, have become ever more elitist. They are *not*, as they must now be, populist.

Finally, a word is needed for beleaguered American graduate students of Greek culture who now contemplate an academic career in the twilight decades of our profession in this country. If we are to study a culture that evolved from middling agrarians, the writing of ancient history, your work and life's vocation, at this penultimate but exciting hour must satisfy more than ever at least four criteria.

1. Should not Greek and Roman history be *accessible*—in language, style, and spirit—to all those who labor *outside* the university? That is a difficult task. Disdained by your professors, it is now unwelcomed even by your peers.

Academic populism requires creative talent. It is more than mere erudition. But it is an approach which until recently has had a long and glorious tradition. Adopt it. Seek to recapture your independence and your audience, and discover an affinity with your ancient subjects of inquiry. You can rescue your profession from the theorists and specialists. They can be formidable critics in talk, bitter in brief repartees, but their teaching and writing have not stopped the decline of their own discipline. It will be tragic if you alone are to inherit the bitter harvest of what they have sown.

2. The study of antiquity must, if people are to read it, also raise broad, important issues of the past, big questions that are invariably cultural, social, and economic, and thus help to make sense of traditional political and military concerns. This demands that the historian must generalize. He must risk exposure to the myriad corps of specialist critics, the "millions of ants" whose censure can be disheartening, vehement, and ceaseless.

3. Ancient history's intellectual framework must also be rooted firmly in classical scholarship, supported by direct citation of ancient texts, inscriptions, artifacts, coins, vase paintings, and the like. Nearly always this requires the historian to free himself from rigid dogma and purely ideological concerns. He must confess unfashionably that there is an agreed-upon, indisputable body of knowledge, a corpus of information largely immune to personal distortion and prejudice. In other words, there *are* facts, *facta* and *dicta*, things that were actually done and said.

The incorporation of models and analogy, the judicious use of theory is on occasion valuable for the historical reconstruction of antiquity, given the paucity of primary sources. The work of M. I. Finley has often been a testament to successful use of these methods when applied to the ancient world. But their employment must succeed, *not* precede, must enhance, *not* replace, must clarify, *not* obfuscate a mastery of original data. Theory is the capstone to years of philological and historical study. It is not the foundation. Nothing is so embarrassing, nothing so transparent, nothing so silly, as to witness the young "theorist" of the ancient world bereft of a pragmatic foundation in classical scholarship.

4. Equally important, historians of Greece and Rome must now also draw on their imagination and—if they possess it—their emotion. They must make the effort to recapture, or better to recreate, the spirit and the *ordeal* of the past. Scholars must try with any and all means at their disposal to provide a glimpse of what life was like, what it meant to the people of antiquity—and why we should now care. The historian who ferrets out good and evil, who spots timidity and gallantry, may be opinionated—even biased. But he is not necessarily therein inexact or inaccurate—if his evidence is presented openly for scholarly examination. The infusion of passion and fervor, as classicists as ideologically and methodologically diverse as Peter Green, Robin Lane-Fox, G. E. M. de Ste.Croix, and Bernard Knox have shown, stirs controversy. It repels tedium and can parry the monotony inherent in the assemblage of literary, archaeological, and epigraphical data. It can also save a near terminal discipline for another generation.

III. World Beneath Our Feet

A final word of caution is also needed about the current position of *American* agrarianism. The time is late. The obstacles are many, the stakes high. The future is bleak—if it is from farmers, a particular type of farmer, that much of our cherished heritage was once sprung, and is preserved. The story of Greek agrarianism and thus of Greek history itself is of utmost importance to any who seek to arrest the decline in American culture.

To take one small, but not unrepresentative, example: at a slow but unending pace, concrete, asphalt, rye grass bury the farms of the Santa Clara and San Joaquin Valley, in megalo*poleis* such as San Jose and Fresno, currently the third and fourth largest metropolitan areas in California—if we dare use the word *poleis* for unchecked urban sprawl. To walk over this ground, to shop, or to eat, is to walk among detached and unknown souls, themselves residents of no more than a decade or so. Like urban outsiders in the Hellenistic city, they have no intention of remaining or dying where they live, much less perishing where they were born. The arrival and departure of so many of these continually transient, disconnected people, citizen and noncitizen alike, are predicated simply on the endless pursuit of cash and status. The culture that they create is one for the most part of irresponsible individualism and unchecked materialism, ostentation for the more successful, envy for those below, of self-interested and obedient response to authority, the wellspring of, the lifeline for, all their financial advancement.

Of the uncanny similarity between modern American culture and life in Hellenistic post-*polis* times, Peter Green alone observes:

> I could not help being struck, again and again, by an overwhelming *déjà vu*, far more than for any other period in ancient history known to me: the "distant mirror" that Barbara Tuchman held up from the fourteenth century A.D. for our own troubled age is remote and pale compared to the ornate, indeed rococo, glass in which Alexandria, Antioch, and Pergamon reflect contemporary fads, failings, and aspirations, from the urban malaise to religious fundamentalism, from Veblenism to *haute cuisine,* from funded scholarship and mandarin literature to a flourishing dropout counter-culture, from science perverted for military ends to illusionism for the masses, from spiritual solipsism on a private income to systematic extortion in pursuit of a plutocratic dream (Green xxi).

Buried beneath the concrete and asphalt of our present suburbs is the ghost of another somnolent and shadowy world. It is a discarded universe of past farms and lost agrarian communities, whose shared memory and silent values are now nearly gone from American culture. For the most part this sudden, but catastrophic conversion of thousands of acres into shopping centers, highways, and housing tracts in California—and the rest of the nation—is a phenomenon of the last twenty years, a transformation whose consequence very few have fully grasped. We know in California (where so much of our national policy and social future originates, where less than one-half of one percent in the state are farmers, a dwindling population itself three times *smaller* than the crescent number of state residents on food stamps [Scheuring 383]) that agrarianism in purely social terms is preferable to corporate agriculture. Communities of small farmers have a stability and a human infrastructure superior to that of the agribusiness town. We realize that the certain destruction of half of the state's original agrarian landscape will finally turn out to be environmentally unfortunate.

Studies decades ago proved that the towns of the western side of the

San Joaquin Valley of California (the Hellenistic model) that had grown up as a result of corporate agriculture, lacked the stabilizing "culture" of east side valley communities (the *polis* model)—hospitals, PTAs, Little Leagues, community bands, service organizations, home ownership, newspapers, churches, small businesses. The latter were places where farmers had staked out parcels of twenty, forty, and eighty acres, not vast absentee tracts in the thousands (Goldschmidt 279–343). Two case studies in Walter Goldschmidt's classic 1947 study were the corporate-farming town of Arvin ("practically no paving, street lights, or sidewalks . . . slow in getting adequate water and sewage facilities" [Goldschmidt 216]) on the corporate southwestern side, and Dinuba (on the same avenue eight miles to the east from our own farm) on the family-farming east side of the San Joaquin Valley. "Dinuba residents," writes a recent sociologist reviewing Goldschmidt's work of nearly a half century ago, "also had a higher standard of living than did residents of Arvin, and in addition had more control over community decisions: those decisions were more commonly made by local popular election in Dinuba and by county officials in Arvin. Greater social stratification was found in the community of large farms, and greater economic and social homogeneity of the entire population existed in the town of the small farms" (cf. Davidson 67).

Nor have things changed under the absentee and estate agriculture of central California. Often I drive over to visit the towns of Five Points, Mendota, and Huron in the corporate-farming western side, the Hellenistic world of the San Joaquin Valley. The contrast with the eastern side, the small-farming communities of Reedley, Dinuba, Selma, and Kingsburg, which are themselves quickly disappearing as farm communities in their evolution to suburban commuting hubs of Fresno, is still striking. An article by Richard Street in the March 17, 1990 issue of the conservative *California Farmer* (its logo: "The Business Magazine for Commercial Agriculture"), entitled "Agriculture's Wild West Town," notes of the west-side town of Huron: "That Huron is not a particularly good advertisement for the community-building qualities of Westlands [the federal water district that supplies the corporations] becomes apparent to anyone walking the town's streets. Huron has no Catholic Church, no fast food franchises, no chamber of commerce, no Little League, no Boy Scouts, no high school, no newspaper, no PTA, no

Lion's Club, Kiwanis Club, Rotary Club, or any other kind of club. It does, however, have 13 bars."

In sum, in strictly scientific terms, California corporate agriculture had led to rural depopulation and a less intensive, less productive use of land similar to Greece in the post-*polis* period: "The data demonstrate that where the towns are surrounded by large farms, the population per acre declines. . . . It is of particular importance to remember that, though the number of people supported is greater, nonetheless, the average income in the small farm town of Dinuba is appreciably greater than in the large farm community of Arvin, and they have a higher standard of living" (Goldschmidt xli).

Anyone with any sense, of any political persuasion, can sense the difference in values between family farming and agribusiness, between a rural sociology of three, rather than two, classes (cf. Goldschmidt 58–63), between a settled and a sparse countryside, between a *polis* and a palace or fiefdom. The philosophy of farmhouses, diversified and permanent crops, trees and vines, generation-upon-generation in the same house, for all its parochialism, its blinkered limitations, its inflexibility, its frequent boredom, still clearly lends stability to a society at large. The notion continues to provide value, a *middle ground* to a community, in a way that open, vast acreages managed from afar cannot.

But the sad history of complex societies, ancient and modern, argues that bureaucracies grow, never shrink. Unproductive citizens multiply, rarely wane. Taxation, urbanization, and specialization are the harvests of elite legitimizing, nuancing classes—government, insurance, advertising, law, finance—who feed and clone from ritual, regulation, and regimentation. Family enterprises give way to corporate and governmental entities; in their wake mercenary enlistment, personal service, and public subsidy are offered to the landless and jobless detritus. Rural becomes urban, farmers suburbanites, as popular culture overwhelms agrarianism, never vice-versa. Even language is refashioned to convince that work is drudgery, simplicity boredom, charity entitlement, words themselves reinvented so that capital accumulation might become "success," chaos "diversity," selfishness "freedom," and failure "victimization."

Could not, one asks, America at this late hour reverse that Hellenistic trend and relearn harder rural values that were with us at the beginning? The task is not, as in the case of the early Greeks, the physical challenge of scarce treasure, scant resources, poor soil, insufficient labor, or foreign invasion. We have the capital, the land, the people, and the intelligence. But a rendezvous with simplicity and self-reliance entails starker psychological and ethical burdens where physical work would be respected, public service rewarded, and military duty required.

There is no hope that the family farm will return in the next century. Subsidy for corporate farming will only increase as technology, not agrarianism, is seen as the solution for the food crisis to come. The thug and the financial pirate alike will not be reinvented as the local peach farmer or hardware store owner. But again could not we, one demands, at least adopt the *spirit* of the early Greeks and the contemporary farmer, at least transfer the values of the departed to post *polis* America? We could. But we will not, for we have not the courage. That renaissance involves an entire rejection of what we now hold so dear, a return to what we clearly despise: a common culture of peers, life away from the vortex of pelf and publicity, a firmness with the poor as well as the wealthy. Could we really imagine a United States where public assistance for being unproductive is eliminated, for the welfare mother and corporate irrigator alike, for the dank tenement and the tasteful vacation home, for the corner loiterer and futures speculator? Could we envision Los Angeles and New York as failures of the human spirit, worthy of no dole, no handout, instead to clone Fowler, Exeter, Kingsburg, and other small east side agrarian towns as the closer ideals of the Greek *polis*? Do we want through incentive and fine a state where all citizens must be reeled in to vote on their local and national affairs, a community where the cargo of bankruptcy, divorce, and illegitimacy draws stern rebuke, not state sanction? Do we really desire an "intrusive government" that would tax annuity, interest, and dividend only to subsidize family-based construction, manufacturing, and agriculture, a government that does not call stasis "stability" or rising employment "inflationary"? And can the eighteen year old forego his semester of sociology at the local JC, the more eager Ivy League tyke his first cog on the cursus honorum for a year of shared military service, where all in the American phalanx learn that they are, for all their strange hue, residents of the same land, speakers of an identical tongue, fierce protectors by birth or choice of a long and distinguished cultural heritage?

In that American *polis* one could not complain of big government but pocket as relish his social security; could not desire to stand tall without

TABLE 1

Differences Between Arvin and Dinuba

	Arvin	Dinuba
1. Environmental Factors		
1. Land:		
(a) Area served	64,000 acres	43,000 acres
(b) Land in farms	46,000 acres	34,000 acres
(c) Intensive uses	22,000 acres	24,000 acres
(d) Land of soil classes 1 to 3	59,000 acres	31,000 acres
2. Water		
(a) Source	Pumped	Surface supplemented with pumps
(b) Cost	$6.92 per acre	$4 per acre
3. Other resources:		
(a) Minerals	Oil leases, general	None
(b) Recreation	Little or none	Little or none
II. Cultural and demographic factors:		
1. Popultion of community	6,000	7,400
2. Cultural Origins:		
(a) American Origin	88 percent	81 percent
(b) Native Californian	4 percent	19 percent
(c) Dust Bowl migrants	63 percent	22 percent
(d) Median length of residence	less than 5 yrs.	15 to 20 yrs.
3. Educational attainment (average for family heads)	7.6 yrs.	8.4 yrs.
4. Economic status:		
(a) Median income bracket	$1,751–$2,250	[same]
(b) Wage labour as proportion of family heads	81 percent	49 percent
III. Historic factors:		
1. Age of community (as of 1944)	31 years	56 years

	Arvin	*Dinuba*
2. Decade of major growth	1930–40	1910–20

IV. Agricultural production factors:

	Arvin	*Dinuba*
1. Value of production (1940)	$2,438,000	$2,540,000
2. Type of farming:		
(a) Proportion irrigated land in orchard and vineyard	36 percent	65 percent
(b) Proportion in row crops	41 percent	11 percent
(c) Proportion in cotton	29 percent	7 percent
(d) Proportion of farms in fruit	35 percent	79 percent
(e) Proportion of farms in field crops	40 percent	17 percent

V. Farm organization factors:

	Arvin	*Dinuba*
1. Tenure:		
(a) Tenancy	42 percent	14 percent
(b) Absentee ownership	36 percent	16 percent
2. Labour requirements:		
(a) Man-hours of labour required	2.9 million	3.5 million
(b) Requirement for hired labour	2.3 million	1.4 million
(c) Minimum labour requirement as percent of maximum	25 percent	20 percent
(d) Maximum outside seasonal workers required	1.175	1,595
3. Size of farm operations:		
(a) Number of farms over 160 acres	44 percent	6 percent
(b) Acreage in farms over 160 acres	91 percent	25 percent
(c) Average farm size	497 acres	57 acres
(d) Average value of production	$18,000	$3,400

From W. F. Goldschmidt, *Small Business and the Community: A Study in Central Valley of California on Effects of Scale of Farm Operations*, in C. V. Blatz, *Ethics in Agriculture* (Moscow, ID, 1991), 210–11.

sending his only son into harm's way; could not talk of values only to strip the assets of his demented paterfamilias, parking him in a subsidized convalescent bed. He could not lecture on responsibility behind his gadgeted estate; could not call work his day's hedge, wager, and gamble, and could not equate living long with living well nor confuse uncreased skin and firmer flesh with probity and character. And so we would come to learn, as the Greek *geôrgos* and the American farmer have, the bitter lesson that total freedom is chaos, that what is legal is not always moral, that we are by birth, training, or character neither equal nor inherently good, that to vote, to work with one's hands, to defend the state, to raise a family, to pass on something better, that to repair not scavenge and cannibalize the wreckage of neighbor and friend, that to do all that and break no statute, undermine no covenant, is, after all, life's work, nothing more, nothing less.

But far from being saved by agrarianism, agrarianism has been ruined by us, as the farm has become more like city, not city like farm. So that equation between small farming and the creation of agrarian egalitarianism, that effort at establishing overall political and social equity out of rural values, is now, I am suggesting, in some sense irrelevant. For the last fifty years the family farm and small rural community remained a reassuring, dreamy image for the American public, never a pressing political concern: "Rural communities are just dim blurs along the gleaming superhighway that carries us into what we tell ourselves is an ever brighter future" (Davidson 71; cf. Strange 239: "The affection some of us feel for the family farm is about as deep as our affection for the unspoiled Garden of Eden").

I say the lessons of agrarianism are now in some sense irrelevant because the choice that faces us now in America is *not* any longer entirely between agriculture run by corporate culture, and viable farming run by individual families. That battle to have 50,000 instead of 500,000 farms has essentially been lost. The issue now is the very existence of agriculture as we have known it in this country. In the past, the economic or social historian might chronicle the rise of *latifundia* and the subsequent demise of yeomanry through a variety of locales and ages, citing a wide diversity of cause and effect relationships—soil practices, irrigation, state policy, military service, infusion of nonlanded wealth and capital, climatic changes, social and political upheaval, emergence of new social and religious organizations, and transformations in social and ethical values.

Agriculture arose and was transformed, leaving its mark on the culture itself: *polis* culture versus Hellenistic clientage, yeoman Roman republicanism set off against Italian manorialism. Historically there has been a cyclical sense of agrarian rise, fall, and reawakening, as societies themselves waxed and waned. The nation of small farmers idealized by Jefferson slowly gave way in this country during the Industrial Revolution and the World Wars to a growing network of agribusiness. In turn, farming corporatism itself seemed recently checked by its frequent wastefulness, occasional disregard for the environment, and growing dependence on expensive crop, water, and financial subsidies. To the naive and perpetually optimistic, it seemed challenged by an inevitable return to smaller and more responsible land strategies.

So it seemed. In reality there was *no* brake in the 1980s on agribusiness. In that decade, small family farms continued to erode. With them went beneath our feet communities of independent farmers and businessmen. "Today our family farmer is in jeopardy," writes Jay Staten, "the production of food is not. Because there is always food at the local supermarket, we may ignore or underestimate or not notice the issues connected with the loss of the family farm. The future of farming has political, economic, and moral ramifications. Those ramifications may be invisible or unimportant to the majority. They will not be unimportant to our children. Who will produce their food and at what cost? Who will own the land? How much government control and support will be involved? Our actions or lack of action today will decide the answers to those questions" (Staten 225).

What has caused the end of family-based agriculture? Population growth and technology on a scale heretofore unforeseen have disrupted the old cycle of agrarian death and renewal in midstream. In this new paradigm, *the entire premise of producing food from the soil is being redefined.* It is most unlikely that in our lifetime the limitations of corporatism will result in a return to yeomanry and the culture that arises when small farmers work their own ground.

The rise of corporate farming was not thrust onto family farmers—at least not entirely; the allure of immense size came just as much from *within* the agricultural community as from the market pressure without.

Agribusiness emerged on two fronts, one political and completely pre-dictable: the farmer's turn to a comfortable conservatism. The other was more personal, but in itself entirely human as well: private greed and in-nate materialism, a notion of self over community.

First, as in the case of the Greek hoplite, the modern American farmer of the past two centuries—cultural conservative and rural prag-matist that he was—had a natural distrust of the foreigner, of cities, of cultural change, of the entire notion of social progress itself. For the agrarian intellectual in the guise of populist democratic legislator, who sought to engender a notion of stewardship, land preservation, environ-mentalism, widened marketing opportunity, and small cooperative ef-forts among farmers, the shortsighted agriculturalist had nothing but disgust. Too often in his mind (often *correctly*), utopians seemed bent on organized unions. They liked centralized bureaucracies. They envi-sioned agrarian ideals as part of a much larger movement toward redis-tribution of income and the end of private property. To the agrarian, as to the ancient *geôrgos*, all this was anathema.

It was an idealized regime, one that threatened the yeoman's absolute freedom to farm in the way of his ancestors, to rely on the old rather than the new prejudices of habit and custom. In desperation, American agriculture—the small farmer squeezed between poor commodity prices and continually higher costs—in the post-war era turned ideologically instead to the businessman, the agro-corporation, and the political pro-fessionals who were bought and sold to *protect* them. But to the agrarian, agribusiness offered only a shared social conservatism, the veneer of the old cherished idea of American values and patriotism. That corporate package, as the farmer has finally now learned, was for the most part a lie that had ramifications for us all far beyond the confines of the rural landscape.

For these large-farming men believed not in agriculture, but in agribusiness. They championed not an agrarian community, but a few clever, rather than rugged, individuals. Mouthing conservative shibbo-leths, they instead radically and systematically transformed the very eco-nomics of small farming. Corporatism saw agriculture, as it saw everything else, as a business to be run, a profit to made or lost, land to be sold off or reacquired as market investment strategy and financial planning dictated. Never was it to be a noble enterprise with a distinguished social pedigree from the dawn of Western civilization, much less a catalyst for rural social development, and *not at all* the linchpin of our cultural legacy.

American government, Democratic and Republican alike, in response offered its bureaucracy of support to agribusiness. Subsidies, tax exemptions, retailing incentives, insurance, advertisement, marketing, and chemical and biological research poured into this new brand of American agriculture. Employees of the Department of Agriculture nearly outnumbered family farmers themselves. Enormous investment kept depressed both farmers' returns and the cost of food for the consumer (the profit for these conglomerates, after all, was in the processing and marketing, not the growing of harvests).

The strategy of the American government served only to destroy, rather than to promote, family-owned agriculture. It rewarded mostly the prominent and visible practitioners of scale. These were conglomerates that could lose money in the actual growing of food, but stay profitable through crop subsidization and the entire mechanical process of bringing produce to the consumer. Jay Staten concluded of this present marriage between government and corporate agriculture:

> The "independent" farmer that prevails in the minds of most Americans is a dying breed. Tomorrow's financially secure farmer will be process-oriented— taking inputs and redefining them into expected outputs. The decisions of the farm sector will be made beyond the farm gate. Farmers will most likely make their production decisions based on forward contracts made with food processors. More and more, the farm products will be controlled by the processing industry and made possible by the farm-supply industry; the consumer will have less to do with the type of product made available. This is despite the increase in consumer involvement in the safety of those products (Staten 212).

That the suffocation of agrarianism has social, political, and ethical ramifications well beyond the mere economics of farming is, I suggest, not confined to ancient Greece. A near half-century ago Walter Goldschmidt felt that eventually American corporatization of the farm would transcend agriculture and begin to affect us all. "The examination of the treatment of the Arvin-Dinuba study, however, tells us what this industrialized agriculture does to our national life. It shows how knowledge gets suppressed and truth distorted, how bureaucracies are entered and destroyed, how national policies are subverted, and the character of our nation reshaped" (487).

The decline of American agriculture was not merely a lapse in political judgment. It was not a mistaken alignment on the part of farmers with those conservatives who sounded kindred, but acted in a way revolutionary and entirely antithetical to agrarian ideology. To be fair, the mistake also lay in the dark heart of the American small farmer himself. He too saw the specter of riches and expansion. Soon he was nursed on the promise of efficiency, unknown profits, large houses, pressed uniforms, and bright tractors. He was, in other words, greedy.

In place of a vineyard that had been his nursery to an entire way of life, he saw half-mile rows of laser-leveled land, with thousands of shiny metal stakes, absolutely straight and in-line, all designed and guided by a manager who computed chemical and fertilizer schedules from the cab of a new pick-up. This abject capitulation of modern farmers to the narcotic of agribusiness, to the "process-oriented" mentality, led James Montmarquet to abandon *all* hope for the present agricultural community, to look instead for some utopian (and, I think, frankly impossible) emergence of a new American grower, one cast in the noble but lost agrarian tradition:

> Rather than educating the sort of people who happen to be farming, fundamentally what we need to do is to attract a different sort and, in the ways I have suggested, a better sort of individual to farming. We need to attract educated young people from both rural and urban backgrounds, young people with a capacity to learn farming but not necessarily with a farm background, young people whose idealism and whose naturalistic interests could bring about a genuine renewal of rural life and culture in the United States (Montmarquet 245).

The more sober historian, however, can see that the status of agriculture in this country has reached its penultimate stage, quickly to be replaced by the science of "food production," far distant from "naturalistic interests." Soon, I am afraid, the name "agriculture" will be abandoned by these new practitioners of food production, who see themselves in no way necessarily connected with either "land," the *ager*, or its "culture" (*cultura*). These are men who believe that there is presently "excess production capacity" and that there are now "too many farmers" (cf. Comstock 31).

Forecasters instead optimistically envision genetic engineering, newly designed crop species to thwart the elements, frosts, insects, and idiopathic crop failure, the centuries-old banes of the wily agriculturalist. Generations of pragmatic expertise are to be replaced by textbook formula and business acumen. Enriched water, scientifically blended fertilizers, and varieties of interactive herbicides are to be tubed intravenously through the soil to the "plant's" roots on precise computerized schedules. Land, and animals designed and then cloned for the machine, are to be cultivated and harvested in large factory-like settings, run by an efficient cadre of elite engineers, economists, and responsive employees. The whole complex—and ultimately vulnerable—enterprise is to be capitalized through the profits of insurance and investment strategy, with financial gain its only motive.

"Farm" size is to increase even more radically. Farm settlement will become ever more nucleated. Crops will be more specialized, labor more rare, and the total acreage of farmland in the United States always more reduced. All this will be packaged for the consumer through the promise of cheaper food and expanded urbanization onto prime farmland. It will all be debated, nuanced but ultimately legitimized by the usual array of subsidized social and natural scientists.

This description is no brave new world. It is a scenario unfolding now, right now in our midst. Its next stages are proudly outlined in current agribusiness publications. Its ultimate evolution is under cheery discussion in university agriculture, biology, engineering, economics, sociology, and business departments, whose staffing and buildings grow as farmers and farms shrink. Farmhouses, sustainable agrarian communities, small plots, independent viable agricultural operations, crop diversity—all will become rarer. Ultimately they will be the stuff of pastoral literature, nostalgic film, and the occasional agrarian activist's call to resurrect an ideology that is to be no more.

To this growing American agribusiness of the Hellenistic and imperial brand, much hostility is now being expressed. Publications worry about our present food supply. As calls to arms, they identify and assail the costly prerequisites of corporate farming: the environmental hazards of mass applications of synthetic chemicals into a fragile landscape, the eventual exhaustion of soil and water through nonsustainable agricultural practices, the specter of sudden agricultural catastrophe through fuel or fertilizer shortages, soil salinity, or mutated plant pathogens, and the growing pollution of the air and scarcity of water once farms are turned into housing tracts. They point out that the loss of crop diversity and farm decentralization will eventually make these complex food systems—that is, *all of us* as well—as vulnerable to sudden collapse as the palatial agricultural economies of the pre-*polis* past.

But my own anxieties are now more about the immediate present, concerned more with people. I worry most about the men and women who farm, the present-day *geôrgoi*, and the culture they create, the fragile American *polis*, the continuation of three classes rather than two and the community values that we all now profess to hold so dear and that appear always to be the egalitarian precursors to democratic institutions.

My fear is not whether we will have a sizable presence of family farmers, but whether we are to have *any* farmers at all! I have tried in this survey of Greek history to answer the usual challenge posed by the growing number of American anti-agrarian historians and social scientists, who ask. "If we are to be persuaded that now when family farms are so few in number we have a moral obligation to save them, advocates must explain why this is so" (cf. Comstock 97).

To explain "Why is this so?" I end this book with a second question, rather than a simple reply. In the next century—now a mere few years distant—when this present, this awful cycle comes to its ultimate fruition, a far more critical issue in America will remain unsolved: *where* will be the needed counterpoint to our amoral philosophy, to our national ethos? *Where* will be the singular critic, the often unpleasant individual, the cratered veteran of a continual, a personal struggle with nature, the cultural dissident who will still choose to go it alone in order to protect the old notion of a community, who will have innate distrust for authoritarianism, large bureaucracy, and urban consensus? *Where* will be the person prerequisite to, the exemplar for, democratic and egalitarian government?

As the Greeks tell us, he always argues for, continually insists on, a military, a political, an economic community of autonomous *middle* citizenry. His is the now increasingly rare voice that says no to popular tastes, no to the culture of the suburb, no to the gated lodge. He can always tell those of us of a different brand, an aggressive and materialistic urban stripe, how far adrift we have become from that ideal. His is the voice that can say finance, insurance, advertising, and law—the great tetrad of the last decade, the ever "increasing costs of legitimizing activities" (Tainter 116)—are not the real work, the true production, the noble professions of our nation.

What other profession is there now in this country where the individual fights alone against nature, lives where he works, invests hourly for the future and never for the mere present, succeeds or fails by his *own* intellect, physical strength, bodily endurance, and sheer nerve? In what other vocation now does an American care so little about his own appearance, about the type of car he is to drive, about the title of the job he is to enjoy, about the status of his associates, and so much about the promptness of his action, the unambiguity of his intent, and the value of his promised word?

Will our contemporary and abstract policy-making or learned philosophical discussion, will the novelists among us, will the American university professor and consultant of the day, will the institutionalized scholar, government planner, and academic theorist on the Left and Right, will they provide the needed counterpressure, the necessary barricade to the growing tyranny of a uniform, materialistic, urban, selfish, and ultimately Hellenistic culture?

Or at long last, when we seek in vain for our lost American *polis*, will we look for it amid the ghosts of our own *geôrgoi*, now gone to a world beneath our feet?

APPENDIX

Farming Words

Geôrgos does not simply mean "peasant." A subsistence farmer was
a geôrgos; but so was a rich landowner like Iskhomakhos, the hero of
Xenophon's Oikonomikos. If you are a subsistence farmer, you will
tend to see your interests as being the same as those of the gentleman farmer. Consequently, the vast majority of the citizen body . . .
will have tended to share the same values and aspirations
—Todd 1990: 160

Just as Greek agrarianism argues for a new concept of chronological
unity in *polis* history, so too the literary evidence rejects the traditional
notion of a countryside divided between wealthy owners and impoverished workers, and instead argues for a new Greek, the family farmer.
Since many classical scholars ask that for every Hellenic institution and
idea there be a corresponding word in the Greek language, we must examine the vocabulary of ancient agriculture. If there were middling
agrarians in ancient Greece, not just peasants and lords, surely the
Greeks had names for them.[1]

The standard inclusive word in Greek after Homer for farming is *geôrgia*, derived from a combination of *gê* ("land" or "earth") and *ergon*
("work"), resulting in the notion of "land-work," on nearly the same
principle as Latin "agricultura" and English "agriculture." It refers nearly

435

exclusively to the growing of cereals, vines, trees, and vegetables, but on occasion, like its Latin counterpart, *geôrgia* can refer to animal husbandry. Unlike "farming" in English, however, rarely is *geôrgia* used metaphorically in the wider, nonagricultural sense of "employing" or "using" (e.g., Dem. 25.82). It is instead almost exclusively in the Greek mind associated with the direct growing of food.

The Greek language, however, more than Latin and French, and even English and German, has an ability to form a variety of verbs, adjectives, adverbs, and nouns from a single stem, using standard prefixes, suffixes, and other common rules of word formation.[2] *Geôrgoi* is the conventional Greek word for "farmers." It is used often in this book in its transliterated, but untranslated, form to mean precisely that. Its verbal derivative, *geôrgeô/geôrgein*, means "to farm"; the adjective *geôrgikos* denotes "agricultural," the diminutive noun *geôrgion* "field," and so on. A related verb, *geôponeô/geôponein* (see Eur. *Supp.* 420–22), "to labor in the field" is used rarely of farming. Like similar antiquated English expressions (e.g., "to toil" in the fields), it is usually found in an exclusively poetic or archaic context.

Our ancient agrarians also show up with other names. That multiplicity of expression is quite logical, given the predominance of agriculture in the life of the Greeks from the eighth to fourth centuries B.C. Greek has an entirely separate family of agricultural terminology, but one which, by its association with *agros* ("field," "land," "earth"), a near synonym for *gê*, often means nearly the same thing. *Agros*, however, itself has quite an expansive range of meanings. At its broadest, it refers to the countryside around a *polis* (e.g., Pl. *Leg.* 9.881C). More often it can mean particularly a single farm.[3]

Is there a shade of difference in these two standard families of related words *geôrgia* and *agros*, as is the case between the English "agriculture" and "farming"? Sometimes distinctions exist, but they are of a completely different nature. They derived from the notion that *agros* ("field," "land"), far more frequently than *gê*, carries the additional connotation of "wild" or "untamed" land. Hence *agroikoi*, more than *geôrgoi*, can sometimes mean "rustic" or "boorish" (e.g., Ar. *Nub.* 628; Isoc. 5.82.2), quite apart from, or in addition to, merely "farmers." Perhaps *agroikoi* also was an earlier term, one derived originally from a more aboriginal sense of Greek rural workers, before the institutionalization of the agrarian culture of the *geôrgoi* during the *polis* period in Greece.

As might be expected, then, *agroikoi* during the *polis* period can on occasion be a term of endearment (i.e., "country folks"). More often, given the bias for urban life in surviving Greek literature, *agroikoi* becomes a word of rebuke and disdain, stronger than merely "rustics," approaching more the English "boors" or the American "clods" or "hicks." Usually, however, both the positive and pejorative nuances of *agroikoi* are easily identifiable from the context of the passage. They cause little confusion when the author means something other than mere "farmers" (i.e., *geôrgoi*).[4]

The rich variety of these general agricultural terms, unlike present-day American English, reflects the importance of land in the Greek vocabulary. This is further confirmed by a near infinite variety of more specific words in Greek referring to particular *types* of agricultural measurement and farm property.[5]

The astounding assortment of farmland terminology is not alone attributable to the long history and evolution of the Greek language. Nor is the abundance of the Hellenic agricultural vocabulary due merely to dialectal and poetic usages. Instead, all these precise words illustrate the ubiquity of farming in the lives of the ancient Greeks; there were as many words for types of farmland as there are now for kinds of automobiles.

But the real crux in Greek vocabulary usage arises when ancient agriculture is discussed in a context *other* than strictly the cultivation of the soil. That is one of the central issues of this book: passages in Greek literature concerning agriculture that reveal social, economic, and cultural ideologies, reflecting, for example, the particular nature and size of the farm, or the class and status of either its workers or owners. In modern English usage, we know well enough now that "big," "large-scale," "corporate," or "factory" farm and related parlance of American agribusiness are used to denote large acreages, absentee ownership, lack of farm-owner residence, and the involvement of outside managers, shareowners, and partners. These operations usually derive their capital from industry and finance quite apart from agriculture.

Corporations see the cultivation of the soil strictly as a business enterprise, a percentage return on invested capital or a method of diminishing tax liability, rather than a way of life. Often the American agricultural terminology denoting this "bigness" in farming is used ideologically and in a pejorative context (oddly, often by those who themselves benefit from, or are employed in, the corporatization of agriculture). The usage may be deliberately set in opposition to "yeomen," "homestead," "small," or "family" farms and farmers. Those smaller entities are thought to operate in nearly the opposite manner from that of corporations and vast estates: "family" rather than "corporate" still suggests that the production of food and the culture surrounding that activity in and of itself are as important as profit and loss. "Family" farmer implies that the owner lives on and works the land, which itself is of only moderate size.

The Greeks, unlike us Americans, in the *polis* period *lacked* just such a demarcation in their vocabulary usage. Herein lies a variety of problems that have plagued classical scholars. For without clear rubrics in the ancient language to distinguish the sociology of agriculture, how can we determine class and status in the ancient Greek countryside? How do we know who the other Greeks were?

But is the concern for a precise, specialized vocabulary of ancient Greek agrarianism sometimes not exaggerated? Is there not a reason for the vagueness of the Greek language in this area, a reason *why* the Greeks, who developed a rich terminology of differing soils and property types, did not during the *polis* period also create a commensurate complex vocabulary for the various statuses of people who worked that ground?

Although the absence of class distinctions for farmers in the Greek language of the *polis* is not proof in itself of a uniformity in agricultural status, of a sameness that blurred class differences, it is nevertheless suggestive. I believe I am faithful to the evidence of Greek literature in referring often to a particular and dominant brand of ancient Greek farming of the city-state between 700 and 300 B.C. as "small" or "middling" (owner/operators of ground from about ten to seventy acres), or "intensive" (the devotion of capital and labor to increase production), or "new" (farmers after the Dark Ages), or even "homestead" (the presence of a house on the farm), or, more confidently still, "yeomen" (those who own and cultivate their own small plots, in both a relative and absolute sense). These English rubrics are usually mutually *inclusive* terms and, I believe, can be justified by our Greek historical sources as well. The Greek *polis*, remember, lacked words on the two opposite ends of the scale for "extensive," "wealthy," "large," or, in contrast, "tenant," "poor," and "peasant" farmers. Why might this be?

It reflects the notion, I think, that the Greeks in the *polis* period more or less envisioned *all* who worked their own land as more similar than dissimilar. They were seen as a roughly homogeneous group of *geôrgoi*. That, of course, is not to deny at all the presence of many poor and wealthy farmers in the ancient Greek countryside, the existence of both small plots and larger acreages, the *occasional* (and mostly later) use of *geôrgos* for the narrow act of working the soil regardless of social status.

Instead, the blanket usage of *geôrgoi* between 700 and 300 B.C. among the city-states to denote all who worked their *own* ground suggests that rubrics denoting class and status are *not* emphasized in our sources. This reflects the Greek view that there were *not* extremely wide discrepancies in the nature of land holding or even in agricultural outlook for much of the *polis* period. During Hellenistic and Roman Greece, however, *geôrgos* can include almost anyone who is employed in agriculture, from slave to absentee landlord.

So *geôrgoi* to a Greek of the city-state between 700 and 300 B.C. was a clear enough label that needed little elaboration. It is one that I often use *without translation* throughout this book. After all, we know of *no* farm at any time in Attica of the *polis* period that exceeded one hundred acres. Outside the feudal worlds of Thessaly, Crete, Asia Minor, and the Black Sea region, no estates are found anywhere in the period of the *polis* in Greece. Corporate manors are instead much more characteristic of Hellenistic and Roman times, and perhaps earlier as well during the Mycenean era and the subsequent Dark Ages.

I argue also that after the Dark Ages, the cultivation of vines, olives, and cereals was predominant and practiced in an intensive manner. *Geôrgia* ("farming") throughout four centuries often carried a generic meaning that cereals, trees, vines, and gardens were farmed intensively on small private plots. No huge estates were run by slave gangs for absentee owners until much later. In other words, there is a logic to the idea that the word *geôrgia* and its cognates could at least for a time serve well enough in most city-states for the activity of the *entire* rural population who worked their own soil (e.g., Arist. *Pol.* 6.1319a7–20).

So although we know there were wealthy and poor farms, some acreages larger than others, Greek, nevertheless, possesses *no* precise agrarian word for "baron," "estate," or "manor," much less "large-scale" or "corporate." No modification of, or addition to, *geôrgoi* ever appears to express great landed aristocracy—never, for example, *megaloi* (big) *geôrgoi* or *plousioi* (rich) *geôrgoi*.[6]

Even specific words referring to "large" farmers illustrate more similarity than dissimilarity to those lower on the agricultural social scale. The vocabulary used to describe the wealthy elite is always expressed in a social and an aristocratic sense, "the good," "the well-born," "the beautiful," rather than in a strictly agricultural framework. The closest we hear of an agricultural hierarchy in the *polis* is at Attica under the old agrarian census of the Athenian legislator Solon (about 600 B.C.). There, for example, the *pentakosiomedimnoi* ("five-hundred-measure men") were originally the wealthiest Athenian landowners, whose estates could produce five hundred measures of dry or liquid agricultural produce. The next lowest classes, the *hippeis* ("knights," who produced three hundred measures), the *zeugitai* (the "yoked," who harvested two hundred measures), and the *thêtes* ("laborers," "menial workers") were merely differentiated by levels of agricultural production (themselves *not* at wide variance between the respective classes). They were *never* separated by agricultural technique nor even choice of crops. Under this Solonian system of social classification there were no implications that some Greek farmers were outright barons while others, in contrast, were serfs or debtsmen: the few "five-hundred-measure" men at Athens held ostensibly little more than twice what the great middle group of *zeugitai* possessed.

A vocabulary of agricultural impoverishment was found in the few non-*poleis* societies at all times in Greece (e.g., *heilôtai* at Sparta, *penestai* at Thessaly), and no doubt commonly most everywhere during the Dark Ages. But again, in our *polis* period, words such as *hektêmoroi* ("sixth-partners," denoting a rental agreement), or *pelatai* ("clients") seem either to have gone out of usage during the sixth century or, once the *polis* was fully established, to have retained a deliberately archaic flavor.

The absence of precise vocabulary for the wealthy estate or corporate farm, as we have thus seen in the case of "farm/farmhouse" is no final argument that such operations did not exist (though I know of no confirmatory evidence of their existence), only that the Greeks never felt a need to differentiate and specify these farmers in their agricultural terminology. The title of a lost play of Aristophanes', "The Farmers" (*Hoi Geôrgoi*), or Menander's later "The Farmer" (*Ho Geôrgos*) would carry no ambiguity about the drama's content. The characters, the audience clearly would know, were all farmers who did their own labor on their own small plots. They would not be portrayed as indentured servants, nor be depicted as wealthy, absentee estate barons, nor as seasonal wage laborers.

The so-called Old Oligarch ([Xen.] *Ath. Pol.* 2.14) of the later fifth century, an anonymous right-wing propagandist, similarly was *not* thinking of the wealthy *or* the impoverished when he thought it necessary to explain that the ideological stance of *hoi geôrgountes* ("the ones who farm") was often opposed to the landless poor. Isocrates, on the other hand, said that the farmers "were not at all wealthy" (7.49). Clearly, "farmers" could be seen at different times by different Greek authors legitimately as *neither* impoverished *nor* wealthy.[7]

I think that these binary delineations—rich/poor, mass/elite, propertied/propertyless, oppressor/oppressed, exploiter/exploited, peasant/landlord—are better avoided. It is wiser to return to pedestrian, and in a sense old-fashioned, agrarian terms (often employed by astute Greek historians of the late nineteenth and early twentieth centuries) such as the English "middle"/"middling"/"yeoman." These nouns and adjectives, as I hope I have shown, much more accurately reflect Greek vocabulary usage and the actual sociology of the ancient Greek countryside during the time of the *polis*. Then the issues of class and status were more complex since there was a large group of agrarians sandwiched between the small group of aristocrats on top and the numerous landless poor below.

This general linguistic notion that farming in Greece could emerge in most places as an owner-operated, family-owned enterprise, its laborers engaged in working their own plots of cereals, vines, and trees on an intensive scale, receives some confirmation from two other peculiar but emphatic words in the Greek vocabulary that are sometimes used of farms and farmers. The general term *autourgos* (*autos* [self] + *ergon* [work]), although not a common term in Greek (it appears only a few times in the history of the language), does mean literally "self-worker." It sometimes appears in an agricultural sense interchangeably with *geôrgoi* to refer to farmers in general, emphasizing that they do their own manual work.

Pericles supposedly labeled the entire population of the Peloponnese (perhaps with the exception of Sparta proper) at the beginning of the Peloponnesian War as *autourgoi*, farmers who did their own labor, no doubt loosely in contrast with his own Athens, which had a sizable minority divorced from the soil. The honorable farmers of Euripides' *Electra* and *Orestes*, who own their own plots and houses, and do their own work, are simply known to the audience as the *autourgoi*.[8]

A much different word, *klêros* ("share," "lot," "part") is also used commonly of one's inheritance. More specifically the term often means one's farm or landed property, ground that was allotted to a person at the creation of the *polis* community (e.g., Hes. *Op.* 37, 341), when in many areas the land was traditionally believed to have been divided, or at least redivided, by lot into equal shares.[9] In Homer's *Odyssey*, Nausithoös supposedly allotted equal farms to the original settlers of Scheria (6.9–10; cf. *Il.* 15.495, 6.243). Later in Greek literature, there is the implication that most Greeks felt that the *klêros* or "home" place originally was a small plot of agricultural land roughly *equal* to that of all the other citizens of the *polis*, a farm that was somehow crucial to the continued existence of the family and even the agrarian community at large. It is clear—in an economic, emotional, and spatial sense—that although there are few, if any, words in Greece during the *polis* period to denote "big/wealthy" or "small/poor" independent farmers, there *are* terms such as the more specialized *autourgos* and *klêros*. They reemphasize that the general rubric *geôrgos* at this time referred in most cases to a man who owned and worked his own inherited piece of ground.

Hoi mesoi ("the middle ones," see Chapter 3), *hoi hoplitai* ("the hoplites," see Chapter 6), and, at Athens, *hoi zeugitai* ("the yoked ones," see Chapter 3) are often used in association with the *geôrgoi*, and likewise suggest yeomanry. The notion, linguistically at least, is that the farmers were originally "middle" people, who fought as "hoplites" in the phalanx—at Athens and perhaps elsewhere being drawn from the so-called "yoked" class.

In this country, the noun "agrarianism" is now infrequently used. It is also unfortunately confused with the more nondescript adjective "agrarian" in its most simplistic sense (i.e., "related to land or farming"). Most people, I have discovered, now believe the term "agrarianism" is roughly equivalent to "farming" or "agriculture." But "agrarianism" ("the principle of a *uniform* division of lands," *OED*) has *always* had political connotations. Thus good standard English definitions usually concentrate on the egalitarian aspect of land holding, defining the idea of agrarianism as "the theory of equal or equitable distribution of lands," "the agitation for the redistribution of lands," or "the calls for the equalization of farm income, especially by government control."

The problems, however, in all these definitions are their *subjective* political and social context. "Redistribution of lands" can be voiced by the landless poor, who demand either land confiscations or collectivized agriculture, or by the middle-class yeoman farmer, who either fears encroachment on his small plot by utopian bureaucracies or wishes to break up corporate conglomerates, or finally by wealthy estate holders, who feel they are losing political influence to mercantile and commercial interests. A much better English definition of agrarianism for our purposes in this book is simply to emphasize the importance to society of agriculture and the people who farm. Here, I do not mean that farmers are merely important. Agrarianism instead refers to the idea that farmers are the *most* important element in a culture, important in both the sense of the general perception by the community at large, and by the actual fact of their contribution to the life of the society as a whole. James Montmarquet (viii) has written similarly and, I think, described the concept of agrarianism in a fashion nearly identical to the manner in which it is used in this present study:

> Agrarianism, as I conceive it, is committed to that very basic value judgment about the worth of agriculture and those who are involved in this activity. Of course, like most value judgments, this one is imprecise. The bare idea of agrarianism does not carry any specific implication about just how valuable agriculture is or whether it is necessarily more valuable than this or that other occupation. But it carries at least the strong suggestion that agriculture is more valuable than most other activities—in particular that it is more valuable than ordinary commercial and legal ones. An agrarian will not typically hazard a judgment about the relative worth of farmers and doctors, but an agrarian will typically be quite definite about the relative value of farmers versus lawyers, bankers, stock traders, and grain shippers!

Agrarianism, and its accompanying culture of independent small communities—the Greek city-states, for example—are notions, it seems to me, impossible when there are either sizable majorities of impoverished subsistence "peasants" or, on the other hand, enormous estates comprising the majority of the community's farmland, controlled and owned by the few and worked exclusively by the unfree or propertyless many.

In the ancient Greek world during our *polis* period, agriculture and the families employed in it were perceived by Greek society in general as its most important constituency simply because farmers *were* in a factual sense the most valuable members of the community. The *geôrgoi* usually composed the largest segment of the free citizen population of the early *polis*. They employed the greatest number of workers. They set the political, economic, and political agenda of most of the city-states of Greece. Until the fifth century B.C. they supplied nearly all the food of their surrounding communities and fought nearly all the wars.

This book argues that the ancient idea of agrarianism—that farmers were the most important members of the ancient Greek community—emerged at the end of the eighth century B.C. in Greece and endured to the end of the fourth century B.C., corresponding to, and responsible for, the life of the Greek city-state. For most of this time there was *no word at all in their language for agrarianism*. After all, for the Greeks agrarian life was an accepted daily reality, not a sought-after ideal. Under our definition of agrarianism, the Greeks *were* agrarian. We, for example, are not.[10]

NOTES

Introduction

1. For the extensive modern discussion of the origin and nature of the city state, see, Weber 1968: 1,282–1300; Finley 1973a: 123–25; 1981b: 3–21; Sallares 161–64; Starr 1986: 43–51; 1977: 29–34; Fustel de Coulanges 109–215; Sculley 4–5; Ehrenberg 1937: 152–59; Murray and Price 2–5; and cf. M. H. Hansen 55–64. See also ancient views at Paus. 10.4.1; Arist. *Pol.* 1.1252b28ff.; [Arist.] *Oec.* 1.1343a10–11. I cannot be concerned here with an account of early urban culture. Nor is there much here concerning early Greek trade routes (cf. O. Murray 38–39). The origins of literacy, East–West contacts (Jeffery 1976: 24–29), Panhellenism, the spread of coinage, monumental architecture, or population growth and the development of metalworking (cf. Grant 1–34; Starr 1977: 21–97) are only discussed in passing. Those phenomena are the standard subjects of controversy when scholars now seek, as they must, motive forces for the "rise of the city-state," the central moment in Greek and, indeed, Western civilization.

2. Some scholars argue for a more static history of agriculture. They see a Greek countryside without much change or innovation from Mycenean times down to the Hellenistic era. But that belief raises problems. If it is agreed that (1) the vast *majority* of the ancient Greeks were always rural people and drew their living from the soil and (2) the eighth-century rise of the *polis* was essentially a *new* social and political phenomenon in the Greek-speaking world unseen in either Mycenean or Dark-Age times, then (3) city-states must be reflections of fundamental *changes* in the way the Greeks grew food and held

445

property. Otherwise neither (1) nor (2) can be an accurate generalization, and are we then to confess either that the Greeks were not a rural people or that their *polis* was not novel?

3. There have been a few classicists, historians, and archaeologists who have always realized in passing that ancient Greece was primarily an agrarian society. See Finley 1973a: 97; Richter 5–6; Osborne 1987: 16, 26; Salmon 1984: 155, 158; Detienne 1963: 54; Francis 277; Alcock 12; *pace* Isager and Skydsgaard 114. Nor had much changed until recently in Greece. In 1821, still only six percent of the Greeks lived in an urban environment (Walcott 1970: 25). Modern ethnographers found that as late as 1960 well over seventy percent of the Greek population was still agricultural (e.g McDonald and Rapp 178; cf. Bintliff and Snodgrass 154).

4. Recently, for example, the revisionist James Whitley (Whitley 41; cf. van Effenterre 20–21), in a book on Dark-Age Greece (1100–700 B.C.), summarized nine agreed-on "symptoms" of early Greek state formation, the innovations that most scholars feel marked the novel appearance of the *polis*:

1. a dramatic increase in the number of visible burials
2. an increase in metal artifacts at Greek sanctuaries
3. colonization
4. the adoption of alphabetic scripts
5. the development of figurative art
6. the introduction of hoplite armor and tactics
7. the creation of national and international sanctuaries
8. an interest in epic and the cult of heroes
9. the appropriation of a heroic past to create new cults and temples, as part of a reordering of the eighth-century present.

Whitley's critique of the present status of modern scholarship omits agriculture entirely (and ubiquitous chattel slavery as well). *No* suggestion is made that the restructuring of Greek rural life (i.e., improved agricultural production and incorporation of permanent crops and marginal lands, creation of private farm properties, dispersion of land among a wide body of citizens) resulted in the creation of city-states, in increased capital and productivity that allowed for greater trade, commerce, and a larger minority freed from work.

Nor, to speak of effects rather than causes, is agrarian change mentioned as evidence for these new Greek communities—even though new *polis* ideas of broad-based oligarchy, hoplite protocol, and citizenship itself were all concepts based exclusively on novel ideas about the possession and role of farmland in society. So whether scholars now ask "what were the manifestations, the characteristics of a Greek *polis*?" or "what caused a Greek *polis*?," agriculture and agrarian change continue to be left completely outside the discussion.

5. There have always been problems with such parallel lives. Stobaeus

records the ancient story of a Stoic philosopher watching an inexperienced intellectual farm disastrously: "If you do not destroy the farm," he says, "it will destroy *you*" (Stob. *Flor.* 15.31). The two professions, farming and academic contemplation, I have belatedly understood, are entirely antithetical, irreconcilable in every respect. That gulf was, I think, felt even in antiquity (cf. the Corinthian farmer, who, Aristotle apparently heard, had abandoned his vines and plot for philosophy [Arist. fr. 64 Rose³]; and see also the fragment of Diogenes of Oenoanda (fr. 21) about utopian Epicureans who "shall plough and dig and mind flocks and divert rivers. And such activities will *interrupt* the continuous study of philosophy for needful purposes; for farming operations will provide us with the things our nature wants"; emphasis added). Plutarch, at any rate, thought that the teacher of philosophy could learn from the no-nonsense character of the agrarian, in adopting both the rough and nurturing side of a farmer, who possessed the rare ability to tear out weeds violently but also to prune vines carefully (Plut. *Mor.* 529B).

I turn then often to my own experience as a fifth-generation tree- and vine-farmer on a 120-year-old small family farm near Selma, California, some thirty miles southwest of Fresno, roughly in the center of the San Joaquin Valley of California. Although the family farms of Selma are very different institutions from those surrounding the ancient Greek *polis,* their crops, climate, weather, and latitude are roughly identical. It is my view that they can provide some empathetic comparative perspective on the practice of Mediterranean viticulture and arboriculture.

6. Do not forget that much of Greek agricultural technique survives in Latin literature. Whereas the later Roman agricultural writers Cato, Varro, Columella, Pliny, and Palladius ostensibly confine themselves to Italian farming and emphasize the larger estates of their time (e.g., Spurr 1986: x–xiii; Frayn 54–55), nearly *all* their research either derives from lost Greek writers (Varro alone mentions fifty authors [*Rust.* 1.1.7–9]) or is drawn from experience roughly analogous to Greek agrarian practice. That is understandable. Nearly all Roman cultivated species and agricultural techniques were known earlier to the Greeks (Andre xiii–liv; Sallares 330–31; White 1970: 15–34; de Ste. Croix 1981: 508–509; Meiggs 260–61). Roman observations, even though they may be written by and for the estate holders of the leisured class, may also be relevant for some aspects of agricultural technique characteristic of homestead farming centuries earlier in the Greek countryside (but cf. Isager and Skydsgaard 6–7). The degree to which these Roman writers borrow from an earlier (and mostly lost) Greek agronomic tradition suggests an agricultural sophistication unlikely to have originated from a purely peasant society.

Chapter 1. The Liberation of Agriculture

1. More recent accounts of the social and cultural changes from Mycenean to Dark-Age society are found in Finley 1981a: 69–86; Donlan 1985:

293–308; Austin and Vidal-Naquet 36–49. Most note the catastrophic loss of population and political organization, but do not emphasize the opportunities that arose out of the destruction of such a rigid and collectivized regime. The chaos of post-Soviet Russia, replete with petty fiefdoms and rival gangs, nevertheless still offers more hope of eventual viable family-run enterprises than did the former communist bureaucracy.

2. On supposed Dark-Age kingship, see Drews 1983: 129–131. Donlan (1985: 305), notes that "by the middle of the end of the eighth century the fragile hierarchy of ranked chiefs had given way to a system of collegial rule by a landowning nobility."

3. For serfs and indentured servants in the *Odyssey*, see Hom. *Od.* 14.14–28; 17.212–14. Snodgrass (1980: 35–39) emphasizes the Dark-Age concern with pastoralism. Throughout the *Politics* Aristotle emphasizes the transformation from monarchy to aristocracy, and is aware of its connections with horses and cavalry (*Pol.* 4.1289b31–9; 4.1290b10ff.; 4.1297b16). See Shipley 30–41 for early conditions on Samos.

4. For a brief sketch of Mycenean agriculture and land use, see Finley 1981b 209–213; Chadwick 102–133. On the general economic limitations of palatial bureaucracies, see Tainter 10–11; 201–204.

5. The Mycenean lords no doubt sanctioned the "siphoning of resources upwards to the elite" (Halstead 1992: 114–15) "The economic base of Mycenean states," Robert Sallares (15) also reminds us, "was impoverished in the sense that it rested on a small range of what on the whole were rather primitive crops." This is understandable when we remember that there is not much evidence to suggest that individual farmers ever owned title to their own plots (cf. Vernant 1982: 31–35).

6. Even the ancients had some notion that horse raising was connected to small populations, cavalry, and less-intensive land use (Arist. *Pol.* 4.1297b12–25; 4.1289b35–4.1289b36; 6.1321a11). Since horses were not eaten, and only rarely employed in farming—lacking the slow, steady power of the ox—the justification for devoting valuable time and extensive land to their upkeep during the Dark Ages was primarily social. They were an accouterment of the wealthy to be used for showmanship, transportation, and war making. (Isager and Skydsgaard 85; McDonald and Rapp 57). Once they were largely done away with, areas could become densely settled with considerable food surpluses. See Hodkinson and Hodkinson 278, for the radical transformation of Mantineia.

7. Drews 1983: 112–15. Donlan has given a nice summary: "Given the conditions of life at this time—a sparse population of pastoral and farming families, huddled in unfortified hamlets, with no centralized authority or corporate kin-groups—the establishment of numerous small, independent bands, centered around local 'big men' (*basileis*), seems assured" (1985: 303).

8. Viticulture, arboriculture, and improved species were believed to be later, civilizing activities associated with the *polis* (Thuc. 1.2.2; Theopompus *FGrH* 115 fr. 276; Hes. *Op.* 146–7; Pl. *Tim.* 77B; cf. *Polit.*272A). The inferiority of both the quality and quantity of the harvests of feral species is striking and was recognized throughout Greek history (Pl. *Resp.* 9.589B; *Polit.* 272A). See McDonald and Rapp 181, 194, 249; cf. 49–50; J. Hansen 1988: 44–46; 47–48; Runnels and Hansen 1986: 302–306; Sallares 15–16; 301–8; Sarpaki 70; Hehn 65–68; 103–7, for the relative absence of intensive farming of domesticated trees and vines before the *polis.* For a more conservative, static view, see Boardman 1977: 188–200; Burford 1993: 8–10; 12; 137; Isager and Skydsgaard 20.

9. For the difficulty of propagating domesticated species in the wild, see Theophr. *HP* 2.2.4; cf. *CP* 1.9.1, and Plut. *Mor.* 86E; Amouretti 1992: 80–83; Gavrielides 153a. Sarpaki makes the fascinating observation that grafting and budding may have been deliberately restricted by the palaces: "The agricultural secret of how to tend and propagate both the olive and the grape, could have been well guarded, one could suppose, just as the production of silk was for the Chinese. This could explain their rather limited distribution in Neolithic Greece and even in the Bronze Age except for the Late Bronze Age when their distribution becomes far more extensive" Sarpaki 70; see also Runnels and Hansen 1986: 303–4; cf. Isager and Skydsgaard 33–43; White 1970a: 248. In short, "The technique of grafting only became known in the eastern Mediterranean in the first millennium B.C." (Sallares 29)

10. On wild species of trees and vines before the *polis*, see Renfrew 125–34; but cf. Sallares 306–8. They took on less and less importance as domesticated agriculture spread (Amouretti 1986: 43–45).

11. These trees and vines species were not widely known or at least cultivated extensively during most of the Mycenean period (Sallares 30, 33, 305–7; Amouretti 1986: 41–46), but they were ideally suited to the natural environment of eighth-century Greece, where increased population called for new agricultural approaches. Imagine that for the first time in the agricultural history of Greece, its unique climate and relief were properly utilized.

12. McDonald and Rapp 144; Renfrew and Wagstaff 46–7; 143; Cartledge 1979: 68, 70, 92; van Andel and Runnels 1987: 98–101; Bintliff 1977: 259–61; Garnsey 1988: 90; cf. Sallares 67–68. For increase and variety in local pottery, see Desborough 19–20. The Greeks themselves felt that there had been marked growth in the countryside at the beginning of their *polis* history (e.g., Thuc. 1.13–15; Plut. *Sol.* 23–24). For motifs on coins, see Andrews 317–18.

13. For the importance of population expansion in driving the intensified use of land, see Boserup 38–43, Grigg 1982: 21–36; but cf. Tainter 110–11. Gallant 1982: 115; O. Murray 47, 65–66, 107–8; Donlan 1989: 144; all discuss Greek political and cultural responses to population growth. Runciman summarizes the trend best, "As nomadism and pastoralism declined, which they evi-

dently did, there was a progressive shift to agriculture; and if population was si-multaneously increasing, intensification of land use is the natural concomitant as well" (Runciman 1982: 367). For the general phenomenon elsewhere, see Netting (21): "Why do some groups rely largely on slash-and-burn while others systematically terrace, irrigate, fertilize, and rotate crops and in other ways seek to ensure permanent production from a piece of land? There is now consider-able agreement that, other things being equal, the agricultural system is func-tionally related to the density of local population and the resulting pressure on land resources."

14. For the idea that age-class systems retarded population growth in Greece, see Sallares 160–192.

15. For an absence of early famines, see Garnsey 1988: 17–39. On colo-nization, see Thuc. 1.15; Pl. *Leg.* 4.708B, 740E; Hdt. 4.153–159. Cf. Gwynn's summation (91–92): "The constant pressure of a population outgrowing the productive capacity of land at home, and chafing too at the restraints of a social system wholly founded on the hereditary tenure of land." In the chauvinistic Greek mind of this age colonization was also seen as the unstoppable march of Hellenic culture, the inevitable expression of a preexisting and dynamic local farming, an agrarianism which was spreading its civilizing agriculture from its home base in Greece proper to more backward indigenous peoples across the sea (see Vanbremeersch 85–87). On nonagricultural factors involved in over-seas settlement, see Graham 1971: 40–47.

16. On farming marginal land, see Starr 1986: 38–39; Donlan 1989: 136–38. Netting has remarked on a similar trend in modern pre-industrial soci-eties. "As population pressure introduces land scarcity and makes intensive methods increasingly desirable, group control of property encounters difficul-ties. . . . There may not be enough good land to go around, and people grumble about their shares. More important, those who improve their land are unwilling to see it revert to some community pool. If a farm has been brought into annual production by the investment of labor in planting trees, manuring the soil, or digging irrigation channels, in effect the rights of usufruct become permanent" (23). Xenophon, centuries after the establishment of agrarianism, reflected the standard Greek view of the *polis*, similarly contrasting tenancy with farm owner-ship: unlike the renter who "milked" the land, the owner of a farm was "like an established friend, not a passing lover" (*Symp.* 8.25–26), one interested in the long-term view of working the land.

17. See *Jeremiah* 35.6–10; *I Kings* 4.25; *Isaiah* 36.16; *II Chronicles* 2.10.15, cf. Boardman 1977: 194. At the end of the Dark Ages the Greeks, through trade, mercenary service, travel, and colonization, began to adopt and then greatly improve a number of Eastern discoveries, ranging from the alphabetic script to body armor and new crop species.

18. Cole 38; cf. 4, 7, 17, 45; Thuc.1.2.2.

Chapter 2. Laertes' Farm: The Rise of Intensive Greek Agriculture

1. The realistic and commonplace character of the Laertes scene, an episode quite apart from the feasting, fighting, and raiding more typical elsewhere in the Homeric poems, is also further emphasized by the traditional controversy over the authenticity of the end of the *Odyssey* (from Book Twenty-three, line 297, to the end of Book Twenty-four). The question of authorship of Book Twenty-four (whether Homer or a later oral bard), is not fundamental to an understanding of the nature of early Greek agriculture. But it is significant that skeptics of Book Twenty-four's authenticity, besides noting inconsistencies in Homeric diction within these last lines, have also remarked on the peculiarly "unheroic" nature of Laertes' farm and his isolated lifestyle in comparison with the rest of the poem. In this view, Laertes in rags and on his knees is irreconcilable with his apparent perceived status as the *rex emeritus* of Ithaca (see Postlethwaite 187; Finley 1978: 90; cf. Wender, 45–62). The force of these arguments, whether we agree that Homer or some clever and subsequent imitator composed the scene, is to situate Laertes' farm not in Mycenean times nor in the early Greek Dark Ages, but rather *late* in the oral tradition. That is to say: in the late eighth century, or even in the first quarter of the seventh century, roughly during the period when the Greek *polis* emerged from the obscurity of the Dark Ages.

2. In Books Six and Seven of the *Odyssey*, the estate of Alkinoös of Phaiacia has a variety of diverse crops: a "flowering orchard" (6.293), one "four measures (*guai*; i.e., about four acres) in size" (7.113), planted in "pear trees and pomegranate trees and apple trees with their shining fruit, and the sweet fig trees and the flourishing olive" (7.115–116). In addition to a "vineyard planted which gives abundant produce" (7.122), Alkinoös' farm (it is no mere garden) also has, like Laertes' estate, irrigated vegetables (7.127) and grain (7.104). His fruit trees are of widely diverse species, spreading the harvests throughout the year, and thereby providing a constant supply of fresh fruit. Alkinoös does not commute to his fields but seems to live on the estate. Although the land is near the town center, as befitting his role as king (land near city walls may have traditionally been the most prized [see Audring 1989: 17–32; Lewis 1990: 253–55]), it is clearly an *isolated* residence "near the road, and a spring runs there, and there is a meadow about it, and there is . . . the estate and the flowering orchard, as far from the city as the shout of a man will carry" (6.292–94). Alkinoös' produce is similarly processed right on the premises. Servants are busy milling the grain into flour (7.104), straining processed olive oil over their woolwork (7.107), trampling grapes into wine (7.124–25), and laying others out to dry into raisins (7.123– 34). We are not told precisely that some of his fields encompass *eschatia*. But there is indication that Alkinoös' farm extends into rough terrain. At one point, Homer says that one part of the vineyard is on "level" ground (7.123), implying also a part that is not. The idea that a hillside

vineyard is meant is clear from Homer's following description of the nearby garden which, he says, is "below" or "in front of" the vineyard. Finally, the farm of Alkinoös has a rudimentary irrigation system that provides water to his garden: "Two springs distribute the water, one through all the garden space and on the other side jets out by the courtyard door" (7.129–31).

Homer goes to great lengths to portray the wealth, prestige, and abundant resources at Alkinoös' disposal. All are assets that Odysseus can draw on during his sojourn and relaxation. His farm, then, is part and parcel of a general image of serenity and affluence. It should appear on a more lavish scale than Laertes' property. After all, the poet's literary aims here are entirely different: Homer seeks now to emphasize the luxuriousness and bounty of Alkinoös' land (e.g., "a Greek land of happiness," Isager and Skydsgaard 26), rather than, as in the case of Laertes, to remind us of the hard work and isolation involved in farming.

Under close examination, however, the two farms seem nearly identical (e.g., Ferriolo 89–90; 92 n. 43). Both plots contained fine orchards, no doubt producing bountiful harvests after the investment of considerable labor. Naturally, Homer describes Laertes' farm merely as "well-worked" (24.226), whereas Alkinoös' land instead is exaggerated, described as "flowering" with "shining" fruit" (6.293; 7.115). Alkinoös' estate must appear the more lavish: Laertes' vines ripen one right after another, while Alkinoös' fruit "never gives out, neither in winter time nor summer, but always the West Wind blowing on the fruit brings some to ripeness while he starts others" (7.117–19). So Homer has deliberately emphasized the *realism* of Laertes' diversified farm, but in the case of Alkinoös, he has taken it to an *excessive idealism,* a near fantasy (cf. Isager and Skydsgaard 41). That does suggest once again that when Homer turns to the Greek countryside for various scenes in his epic he knows of a standard type of agricultural property, at times encompassing permanent residence on the property, servile help, diversified crops, food processing, and rough terrain—one that could have served well enough as a general model for the poet's rural scenarios, whether the *work* or, in contrast, the *wealth* of the land was to be emphasized, depending on the poet's own precise literary needs in the particular context.

Elsewhere in the Homer's *Iliad* and the *Odyssey* there are recurring references to what can be legitimately understood as diversified crops, intensification of technique, servile agricultural labor, irrigation, marginal land, and on-the-farm food processing (e.g., Hom. *Il.* 5.87–91; 6.194–96; 9.578–79; 10.351–52; 12.314; 14.121–24; 18.541–86; 20.185; 20.495–98; 21.36; 21.257–62; *Od.* 16.139–45; 18.365–75; 19.110–14; 9.131–35; 13.242–47; 15.405–6). Even the antithesis of the homestead farmer, the lazy, cruel Cyclopes portrayed in the Ninth Book of the *Odyssey,* monsters who live apart from both law and religion, *by negative example* suggest that the poet once more has an image of what successful agriculture should be like (e.g., Sculley 3–4;

Ferriolo 90–91). The land of the Cyclopes, Homer tells us, was "never held by farmers, never ploughed up and never planted." Nonetheless, the poet emphasizes that "it is not a bad place at all, it *could* bear all crops in season, and there are meadow lands near the shores of the gray sea, well-watered and soft; there *could* be grapes grown there endlessly, and there is smooth land for plowing, men *could* reap a full harvest always in season, since there is very rich subsoil" (*Od.* 9. 122–35; emphases added). No wonder that there was a tradition that these anti-farming, bloodthirsty, and shiftless Cyclopes had driven out the agriculturally skilled Phaiacians from their original homes (Hom. *Od.* 6.4–10). In the Greek mind, without clear title to a parcel of agricultural property, without ploughed or planted farmland (cf. *Od.* 9.123), how could such brutes ever develop the culture of a *polis?*

3. See *Odyssey* 24.208, 358, 361–362.

4. Wood sums up the standard opinion best: "The evidence overwhelmingly testifies to the rarity of isolated farmsteads worked by farmers residing away from a nucleated settlement" (Wood 102). Cf. Bradford 180; Bolkestein 19–21; Finley 1952: 62–63; Kirsten 91–92; Michell 4–5; Semple 1932: 539; Osborne 1985a: 17–19; Morris 1987: 5; and cf. Burford 1993: 58–59; Chisholm 113.

5. On the excavations and sitings, see e.g., J. E. Jones 1974: 303–12; 1975: 63–140; Jones, Sackett, and Eliot 152–89; Jones, Sackett, and Graham 355–452; Young 1956a: 122–46; Pritchett 1956: 266–68. Subsequent skeptics of Athenian rural residence (e.g., Osborne 1985a: 32–35; cf. 1992b: 376), who believed that there was neither the water, the desire, nor the need to live in country residences, have sought to explain away the structures as rural cult centers, small villages, or temporary harvest barracks. Their efforts have, I think, found little acceptance. See Pritchett *War* 5.352–54; Langdon 1991: 209–13; Roy 1988: 55–59. A great many more isolated ancient farmhouses have been identified and explored, but not excavated systematically. See Langdon and Watrous 162–77; Hanson 1983: 38–39; Lohmann 1983: 98–117; 1985: 71–96; 1992: 29–60; Watrous 193–197.

6. Arist. *Ath. Pol.* 16.2–5; *Pol.* 5.1305a19–21; cf. Dio. Chrys. 1.75.3. Thucydides also (2.14–16) says that the Athenians from very early times had lived on their farms (*en tous agrous*), an observation hard to reconcile with the image of commuting peasants who predominantly lived in towns outside of Athens (cf. Cooper 1993: 59). That notion of numerous homestead farms in the countryside is also confirmed elsewhere throughout the ancient Greek-speaking world. Investigation—both through excavation, topographical reconnaissance, random salvage operations, and more systematic surface survey in Euboea, the Greek islands, the Crimea, the Argolid, Boeotia, and other places—continues to turn up isolated residences in a rural, agricultural context; see Kent 243–335; Keller and Wallace 1988: 151–57; Pecírka 1973: 113–47;

1970: 459–77; Pecírka and Dufkova 1970: 123–74; Boardman 1956: 41–54; Lambrinoudakis 295–304; Bintliff and Snodgrass 123–61; Cherry, Davis, and Mantzourani 294–297. As scholars gather additional archaeological evidence, the appearance of houses and towers in an agricultural setting in the ancient Greek countryside seems to have been commonplace. It reflects the good sense of Young's initial identification of these towers as the ancient equivalents of "farmhouses" (see especially Pritchett *War* 5.352–54; 5.355 n. 510).

7. Passages in the Athenian orators: Isocr. 4.17; Dem. 18.38; 29.3.3; 30.1.29; 57.65; [Dem.] 47.62; 53. 4–6; 55.23; cf. Roy 1988: 57–59. Passages in ancient historians: Aen. Tact. 7.1; 10.1; Thuc. 2.5.4; 2.5.5; 2.5.7; 4.84; 4.103.5; 4.104.1; Hdt. 1.17; Polyb. 4.3.10; Xen. *Hell.* 6.2.6; 7.5.14; 8.5.15; cf. Snodgrass 1990: 127–29. When Thucydides writes that the Athenians ransacked the houses around the isolated sanctuary at Delium, he must be referring to local homesteads (4.90.2). The Roman agronomist Columella (*Rust.* 12. *praef.* 10) recalled that the ancient custom of antiquity had been to live on the farm.

8. Men. *Dys.* 5–6,23; *Georg.* 77; Eur. *Elec.* 78–79; 208–10; cf. Arist. *Pol.* 6.1319a36) ([Arist.] *Oec.* 1.1345a25–33.

9. See Bintliff and Snodgrass 136, 143. There is a *vast* literature on the nature of the ancient farmhouses, some still arguing that these remains signify only temporary harvest shacks. On the controversy, see Lambrinoudakis 303; Lauter 1980: 284–85; Osborne 1992a: 22–23; van Andel and Runnels 158–59; Snodgrass 1987: 116–19; 1990: 121–25; 128–29; Cherry, Davis, and Mantzourani 294–95; Langdon 1991: 212; Hanson 1983: 40–41; J. Carter 1990: 412; Lohmann 1992: 35; 30–33; Salmon 1984: 156; Isager and Skydsgaard 69. There are frequent references in Greek literature and inscriptions to rural walls, fences, farm buildings, wells, and storage facilities which suggest a settled countryside, cf. [Dem.] 55.11, 23; SIG³ 963; Men. *Dys.* 376; Kent 297–99; Plut. *Sol.* 23.4; Osborne 1985c: 124–27; Richter 23–26; cf. Hanson 1983: 38–39; Burford 1993: 116; Ferriolo 87–88, and especially Lohmann 1992: 59. And the Greeks sometimes referred to family tombs on their property. Often the graves were part of a long rural tradition spanning many generations, places where several generations might be interred. see, e.g., Aeschin. 1.99; Arist. *Ath. Pol.* 55.2–3; Plut. *Arist.* 1. 27; [Dem.] 55.13; FGrH 228: 43, 45; Humphreys 1978: 97–98; 105–112; Wickens 96–98; and especially J. Carter 1990: 408–9; J. Carter *et al.*: 305–9. This pattern of residence is especially true if the ancient Greek farm was not as widely fragmented as is usually believed, inasmuch as farm residence is usually associated with a generalized concentration of holdings (cf. Osborne 1987: 70; Chisholm 62–64; 113). Ancestral tombs on farms do not mean that every plot was unfragmented and equipped with a permanent residence, but it is one more piece of evidence that suggests that scenario was at least commonplace in the Greek countryside.

10. On the problems of the commute, Chisholm 45–49; 52–55; Engels

28–31; Weaver 217. Scholars in remarking on this contemporary practice at Melos (it is still common throughout the modern Greek and indeed the entire Mediterranean countryside) have concluded that "the consequent inefficiencies of daily travel must be offset by benefits which are almost certainly social in character." (Renfrew and Wagstaff 110–11; 165–66; cf. Chisholm 51–59; 113). I can attest that after farming a parcel over ten miles distant from my home, any advantages accruing from "dispersed" ownership are overshadowed by the bothersome and wasteful commute.

11. On extensive farming in Greece after antiquity, see Halstead 1987: 83. On ancient farm buildings, see Osborne 1987: 70–71; 1988: 296. Problems with intruders and animals: [Dem.] 47.52; Hom. *Il.* 9.540; Ar. *Vesp.* 952. See Richter (97–98) for fencing. For the evacuation of Plataea, cf. Thuc. 2.5.4–7; and on the general Greek practice in time of war, see Hanson 1983: 87–101.

12. *Odyssey* 24.227–31. See Langdon 1991: 213; L.B. Carter 76–78, for the distinct culture of those who lived outside the walls.

13. See Osborne 1985a: 185. In this view there is no radical distinction between city and country, since almost all lived in town and commuted to work, see Humphreys 1978: 130–35; but cf. Ehrenberg 1951: 86–87.

14. Arist. *Poet.* 1448a36-b1; see Figueira 1985: 141; cf. Gernet 1981: 320 n. 24.

15. For avoidance of public service, Ar. fr. 100 Kock; for the expression "Back to the farm": (*eis agron*), see Ar. *Pax* 552, 569; fr. 107 Kock; cf. fr. 387; unfair preference for city residents: Ar. *Pax* 1179–85; on farm work preventing frequent and needless trips to town: Arist. *Pol.* 6. 1292b25–29; 1318b9–14; cf. again 1319a30–36.

16. On the complete unfamiliarity of rural residents with Athens, cf. Arist. *Ath. Pol.* 16.5; Dion. Hal. *Rom. Ant.* 10.8.4–5; Isoc. 7.48–55; cf. Hodkinson and Hodkinson 285.

17. Polyb. 4.73.5–10; Isocr. 7.52; Pl. *Leg.* 745B; Arist. *Pol.* 6.1330a14–16; cf. Pl. *Phaedr.* 230D.

18. Plutarch *Mor.* 518F; 519E. On rural speech, see Ar. fr. 685 Kock; and cf. Eur. frs. 185, 188 Nauck; on wary, leather-clothed farmers: Alciphr. 1.25; Ael. *Ep.* 18; Ar. *Nub.* 268.

19. On the differences between Dark-Age residence and rural inhabitation during the *polis*, see Snodgrass 1991: 13; cf. van Andel and Runnels 165; Coldstream 1977: 312–13; Gallant 1982: 118–19; Donlan 1985: 301.

20. For watering small gardens and plots, see Hodkinson and Hodkinson 283; *Anth. Pal.* 6.42; Theoprh. *HP* 7.1.3; 7.5.1; Pl. *Euthrph.* 2D, and Theophr. *CP* 3.4.3 for watering during vine planting. The Greeks and early Romans saw that their own agrarian communities were far different from the collective, irrigated regimes of Asia and the Near East; see Hdt. 1.193; Pliny *NH* 18.161; Strabo 16.1.9–10. For the critical relationship in modern Greece between

homestead residence and irrigation, see Thompson 39. Absentee ownership is often associated either with dry farming or vast, public water projects. The Federal Reclamation Act of 1902 ("and no such water shall be delivered unless the farmer is a bona fide resident on land or a neighboring resident thereof," see Scheuring 369; cf. Goldschmidt xxv) was justifiably concerned that dams and huge canals not lead to farm consolidation and an absence of homesteads.

21. Laertes' garden: Hom. *Od.* 24.247; the Phaecaian irrigation system: Hom. *Od.* 7.112–30; the irrigation simile in the *Iliad*: 21.257–62; 346–47; see too 5.87–92; 16.384.

22. Strabo 1.2.15; Dem. 50.61; cf. too Eur. *Med.* 824–42. On dams and ditches, see Jones, Sackett, and Graham 81–82; IG I³ 422.187–90; Murray 1984: 195–203. The remains of small dams and retaining basins have also been uncovered near ancient farmhouses of the fifth and fourth centuries in southern Attica (e.g., Lohmann 1992: 48, 51). Near Metapontum in southern Italy, a fifth-century Greek farmhouse was excavated, revealing a large sophisticated spring reservoir for its own use (J. Carter 1990: 410; Carter et al. 287).

23. *CP* 2.2.1–4; 3.8.3: "streams and irrigation ditches"; *HP* 2.7.1; 7.5.1–2. In other instances in Greek literature water ditches are also explicitly mentioned: "I dug furrows and deep trenches and so was able to plant my young olive trees and to bring them spring water from a nearby gully" (Alciphr. 3.13). Similarly in another later source (which also must draw on earlier accounts dating back to Aristotle and the literature of the fourth century B.C.), Aelian remarked that falcons did not drink from irrigation ditches if single farmers were there directing water, but did land "when many men were irrigating" (NA 2.42; cf. too *Ant. Pal.* 7.321). Plato says in his *Laws* that his rural patrols will make dams, along with walls and channels, "in order that by storing up and collecting the rains from heaven, and by forming pools or springs in the low-lying fields and rural districts, even the driest places can be supplied with plentiful amounts of good water" (Pl. *Leg.* 6.761B–C). Here Plato seems to envision much more than small, private gardens. He must refer instead to more substantial irrigated farm plots that lie downhill from streams and lakes. No wonder he sees the need for "agricultural laws" (*nomoi geôrgikoi*) to administer the considerable infrastructure in the countryside (e.g., *Leg.* 8.842E; 843D–846B; 847–850A). These laws were a part of nearly every Greek *polis* and colony (Guiraud 184–191), statutes that gave ample attention to disputes over both irrigation and drinking water in the countryside (Klingenberg 62–123). To read Plato's agrarian legislation is *not* to envision commuting peasants, who devote minimal labor and capital to a static agricultural regimen in a relatively empty countryside. Instead, farmland in the *Laws* seems to be the domain of busy, squabbling residents, like-minded agrarians who compete for precious land and water for their trees and vines, who thus warrant the constant attention from the legislative arm of the *polis*. Other Greek authors generally refer to legislation governing the use of

rural water supplies, wells, and streams (Plut. *Sol.* 23; Arist. *Meteor.* 349b30–34; 350a7–9; Men. *Dys.* 190–91; Xen. *An.* 2.4.13.), what Plato knew as the "excellent old laws concerning water established for farmers" (Pl. *Leg.* 8.844A). They also make random, almost incidental reference to "watered fields" (Ar. *Nub.* 282; *Anth. Pal.* 7.321).

24. Arist. *Part. An.* 668a14–15. For rural roads, canals, and paths, see Dem. 55.10; Arist. *Ath. Pol.* 50.2; 54.1; *Pol.* 6.1321b20–21; Soph. *Oed. Col.* 10; Pl. *Leg.* 844A; *Euthrph.* 4C; IC IV 43B, 73A.

25. See Guiraud 70–77, for the presence of slaves before the *polis*. Garlan (1988: 25–29) and Howe (53) remark on the enormous growth of chattels at the end of the Dark Ages. Ancient views that slaves were a late phenomenon in Greek history: Pherecrates 10.1 (Kock); Hdt. 6.137; Theopom. *FGrH* 115 fr.122 (for the tradition that the Chians were the first of the Greeks to practice viticulture and enter into the slave trade); Timaeus *FGrH* 566 fr.11 (for the idea that the early Greeks were not served by purchased slaves). The need for slaves, not a prior, plentiful pool of servile workers, explains their growing presence in Greek agriculture, and in large part "made it possible for the Greeks gradually to acquire a position of hegemony vis-à-vis a barbarian world overflowing with human livestock" (Garlan 1988: 25–29, 40). In Mycenean and Dark-Age times, our scanty evidence suggests that adult male field workers were relatively uncommon. "The pre-Greek world," M. I. Finley has written, "the world of the Sumerians, Babylonians, Egyptians, and Assyrians, and I cannot refrain from adding the Myceneans, was in a very profound sense, a world without free men, in the sense in which the West has come to understand that concept. It was equally a world in which chattel slavery played no role of any consequence" (1981b: 114–15; cf. 1973a: 70–71; cf. van Effenterre 220–22). Agricultural slavery, even more than homestead residence, made intensive agriculture possible. It prevented the spread of helotage. It sharply defined the independence and freedom of the rising Greek yeoman in a way not found elsewhere.

26. The slaves are called *dmôes* at 24.210. They apparently live in a *klision* 24.208; cf. Kent 298. For the Sicilian slave woman, cf. 24.211. Laertes almost appears as a proto-hoplite of sorts, standing firm along side his slave attendant (e.g., 24.208–211; 223–27; 387–90; 400–409; 495–500).

27. For passages concerning Laertes and his slaves, see *Odyssey* 24.224–25; 363–65; *Od.* 16.140–41; 11.188–91.

28. See M. I. Finley on the modern political implications involved in the debate over ancient Greek slavery, 1981b: 111; 1980: 11–66. De Ste. Croix 1981: 505–7, and Garlan 1988: 63–65, give a good account of the importance of slaves in the city-state, approaching the question from a largely Marxist viewpoint of exploitation. In contrast, most others discount the importance of slaves in the rural Greek economy in general and at Athens in particular. See

Wood 42–80; Ober 1985: 22–3; 1989: 24–27; Starr 1977: 90–92; Glotz 1927: 202–3. Cf. Sallares 56; Gallant 1991: 30–33; Osborne 1985a: 144–45.

29. See Jameson 1992: 140–46; 1978: 122–45; de Ste. Croix 1981: 506ff; Garlan 1988: 63–65; Hodkinson and Hodkinson 279; Amouretti 1986: 212–14; Ehrenberg 1951: 182–83; Guiraud 452–53; Hanson 1992b: 21–25; and cf. Morrow 148–152. After Homer, Greek comedy, tragedy, oratory, philosophy, and history all record their presence in a variety of special circumstances: calls to a slave out in the field in a play of Aristophanes: "Let Syra call in Manes from the fields" (e.g., *Pax* 1146–1148, 1249), a remark by a historian about families who ate their meals side-by-side with their servile agricultural workers (e.g., Philochorus *FGrH* 328 fr. 97), an inscription at Mantineia associating land ownership with slaves (e.g., Hodkinson and Hodkinson 279), and Plato's tacit assumption in his *Laws* that slaves are ubiquitous in the countryside (*tois oiketais tois en tô topô hekastô*, 6.761A).

30. For the idea that literary references to agricultural slaves are distortions, exaggerations, or a result of confused interpretations, see Wood 51, 173–77; but cf. Hanson 1992b: 222–23. Passages that assume that slaves are at work in the countryside: e.g., Alciphr. 3.24, 25, 26; Aen. Tact. 10.1; Ar. *Ach.* 243, 259; *Vesp.* 243–59; 433–47; *Pax* 1127, 1139, 1247; *Ecc.* 591–93; *Plut.* 26–29; 43ff; 254; 510–21; 1105; Men. *Dys.* 23–27; 208–210; 328–331; 414ff; *Georg.* 18ff, 33, 56; Theophr. *Char.* 4. 4–5; Dem. 18.21; 42.20; 53.5, 55.31, 35; [Dem.] 47.52, 56; [Arist.] *Oec.* 1252b; Pl. *Leg.* 6.761A; 6.763A; Hes. *Op.* 470, 573, 597, 766; Eur. *Rh.* 74–75; 176–77; Athen. 272d; Thuc. 3.73; 8.40.2; Xen. *Hell.* 3.2.26; 4.6.6; 6.2.6; 7.5.14; Plut. *Mor.* 519A; Lys. 7.18–19; *IG* V 2.262.

31. Terraces: Hanson 1983: 37–38; Men. *Dys.* 376. Pruning: Colum. *Rust.* 5.9.15; Plut. *Per.* 33.4; Theophr. *HP* 2.7.2; *CP* 3.10.4; 14.1–15.5. Fertilizing: Hom. *Od.* 17.297–99; 24.225; Theophr. *CP* 3.6.1; 3.9.3; 3.17.5; 3.20.6; *HP* 8.2.9; 8.7.2, 8.9.1; Xen. *Oec.* 17.10; 18.2; 20.11; Varro *Rust.* 1.29; Pliny *HN* 18.43,670. Dense plantings: Xen. *Oec.* 16.9–15, 17.13–15; Plut. *Sol.* 23. Theophrastus sums up the key to intensive Greek viticulture and arboriculture as "digging, watering, manuring, and pruning" (*CP* 2.7.1; cf. 3.20.6, 4.13.3), strikingly familiar to the modern viticulturist's dictum that summer's work was mostly "water and weeds."

32. For the harvesting of fruit, see Cato *Rust.* 144; Colum. *Rust.* 12.52.3; Varro *Rust.* 1.55.5; Pliny *HN* 15.13.4; cf. Brumfield 27–8; Amouretti 1986: 73–74; and Hurwit 289 on the Antimenes painter. For vine stakes, see Men. *Dys.* 113. The old idea that half the ancient farm always lay fallow (and unworked) each year is simply not supported by the evidence. See Gallant 1991: 54; Halstead 1987: 83–85; Hodkinson 1988: 39–40, 41–50; 1992: 55. The sophisticated state of Greek agronomy and its awareness of plant deviancy (e.g., Theophr. *CP* 5.3.1–6.9), the knowledge of grafting technique, and the improvement of crop species all argue for an intensive routine, one of manured and

cover-cropped fields beside (or intermingled within) established vineyards and orchards, *not* the static monocropped world of the "peasant." When Theophrastus (CP 3.20.3) advises that farmers mix light and heavy, red and white soils to remedy its infertility, he was referring to the most intensive of agricultural practices, requiring shoveling and transportation of earth (see Brumfield 156–70). As in the case of manuring (e.g., Semple 1928: 130–38), soil improvement was accomplished not with the modern tractor-drawn scraper (a formidable task in itself, as I can attest), but rather with a small spade, a wicker basket, an ox or donkey, muscular arms and a strong back.

33. On the practicality of ancient small farms for a family and a slave or two, see Jameson 1992: 145; Amouretti 1986: 204–8. The work needed for farmland development only increased if the terrain was rugged, the soil poor, and there was a garden or orchard irrigated. Terraced land, of course, was less often ploughed, more often intensively dug by hand (Halstead 1987: 85; Halstead and Jones 49–50). On following, see, Gallant 1991: 113–14; Halstead 1987: 81–83; Garnsey 1988: 93–94; labor needed for particular crops: Jameson 1978: 122–45; Halstead 1987: 77–87; White 1970a: 336–37. In our sources few women are found working in agriculture (see Brown 71–74). Their absence should not indicate that Greek farming required low labor inputs (e.g., despite Sallares 83). As the households of Laertes and Hesiod attest, the growing presence of adult male servants out in the fields *relieves* women of that obligation, and explains why, unlike the situation during Mycenean times, male slaves in the literature of the *polis* now appear in equal or greater numbers than female servants.

34. Xenophon on the diversified farm: *Oec.* 11.15–16; the *Oeconomica* on diversification: 1. 1344b29–31. For the constant labor demands of diverse crops, see McDonald and Rapp 50–52; Halstead and Jones 44–50. References to harvest laborers: Hom. *Il.* 18.357–60, 550–59; Hes. *Op.* 370, 602–3; Ar. *Vesp.* 712; Theoc. 10.45; Dem. 18.51; Xen. *Hier.* 6.10; *Hell.* 6.2.37, 2.1.1. Such hired work was considered undignified for the free man, see Ste. Croix 1981: 179–88; Burford 1993: 186–91.

35. On the agricultural status of the slaves that fled to Decelea, see Hanson 1992: 218–19. Lazy slaves: Alciphr. 3.24; cf. the harvesters known as "figwood fellows" at Theoc. 10.45.

36. See Pritchett 1956: 255–58, 276–79; Ober 1985: 22–23; Jameson 1978: 139; de Ste. Croix 1981: 508; Markle 153 n. 11, and cf. Meiggs and Lewis 247 who point out the mean price of slaves in general on the Attic Stelae is 154 drachmas. It is not known whether each classical farm family owned body armor, livestock (e.g., Ar. *Ach.* 1022–36; *Av.* 582–85; frs. 82; 109; 387 Kock; cf. Thuc. 2.14), *and* a slave or two. It is surely possible. In any case for the yeomen who somehow purchased or inherited arms, it seems no greater difficulty to acquire or inherit a slave in place of, or in addition to, oxen—especially if recent

studies are correct in seeing draft animals as somewhat rarer than once thought on Greek farms (e.g., Halstead 1987: 84). Scholars previously have seen that the so-called *zeugitai* class of hoplite farmers at Athens had enough capital to afford slaves for their plots (e.g., Kinkel 56–58; Jameson 1978: 122–45).

37. On hoplite attendants, see Thuc. 3.17.4; Ar. *Ach.* 1123–96; Hdt. 9.29; Polyaen. *Strat.* 3.52; Theophr. *Char.* 21.8; cf. Welwei 57–65. Hired hands or relatives at work on farms were probably rare in peacetime (de Ste. Croix 1981: 182–84). For the servile status of hoplite attendants, see Sargent 205–7; Pritchett *War* 1.49–51; Garlan 1988: 64–65; Hanson 1992b: 222–23; Kinkel 52–54. See Jameson 1992: 141 on the apparent exceptions at Isaeus 5.11 and cf. the curious instance at Plut. *Mor.* 194F21. Cf. the opprobrium of a free man serving as a laborer in the army at Xen. *An.* 5.8.5.

38. On the importance of slaves to the rural *polis* economy, see Garlan 1988: 38–39. Aristotle remarks on the free man owning property and not working under compulsion to another, Arist. *Pol.* 6.1317b11–13; *Rhet.* 1367a28–33. Goldschmidt (379–80) has described the cultural ramification of an agrarian economy with few owners and many wage laborers. Kreibig contrasts Greek slave-owning yeomen with Eastern peasantry: "If individual ownership of land (the typical Classical ownership) brings forth slavery as the most essential factor within the conditions of production, the typical producer in Oriental society is the dependent peasant. The town is here, above all, the seat of government institutions (the court, the satrapy, and others) and all those producers whose work serves the court or the cult" (Kreibig 6).

39. On Laertes' crops and livestock, see *Od.* 23.139; 24.215, 246–47, 340, 341, 364; cf. 14.5. It is odd that Laertes' diversified scheme—appearing here at the beginning of Greek literature—has been unappreciated by scholars, who have usually seen early Greek agriculture as one of livestock and cereal specialization (Finley 1978: 57). Even when the later and more plentiful literary evidence of the fifth and fourth centuries made it clear that diversified crops were frequent phenomena on Greek farms, this trend was thought to be a "new" development of "garden-farming" or "cash-cropping" for large, urban markets (Ehrenberg 1951: 73–75; Mossé 1969: 54–55). It was not seen as part of a long tradition in Greek agriculture going all the way back to Homer and the emergence of small independent farmers around the eighth century.

40. See *Il.* 9.578–80; 6.194–95; 14.122–25. Much later the trend only continued. The chorus of Aristophanes' *Peace* sings: "May the gods give wealth to the Greeks, allow us to harvest much barley, and plentiful wine, with figs to eat too" (1321–24). In Aristophanes' earlier comedy the *Acharnians* (425 B.C.), the chorus of farmers had promised "first to lay out a long row of small vines, next alongside them small cuttings of young figs, and then a third row of domesticated stock, and—even though I'm an old man—olive trees all in a circle around the field" (994–99). In fact, a diversified farm is just the strategy the

fourth-century writer Theophrastus later advised concerning the interplanting of various crops (*CP.* 3.10.3–11).

41. See Hes. *Scut.* 291–301; Xen. *An.* 5.3.8–13. And the diverse evidence found in leases and sales: *SIG³*963; Osborne 1987: 42–43; Andreyev 15; Kent 288–89; 299–300; ephebeic oath: *SEG* 16.140; handbooks: Theophr. *HP* 8.1.2; cf. Plut. *Mor.* fr. 19. On crop diversity in general: Theophr. *HP* 7.4.1–7.5.4; *CP* 4.3.1–4.4.1; *IG* I³ 422. 81–89.

42. See Alciphr. 3.20; Ar. *Eccl.* 817; Pl. *Polit.* 289E; cf. Zenob. 1.74. Aëthlius of Samos wrote that the Samians had developed a wide variety of cultivars that allowed them twice-yearly crops of figs, grapes, apples, roses, and a fruit called *homomêlis* (some type of apple or pear?), spreading the harvest season throughout the year (Aëthlius *FGrH* 536 fr.1; cf. Shipley 18).

43. See Theophr. *HP* 4.14.6,13; Ar. *Vesp.* 264; Ar. *Av.* 578, 587, 709; Plut. *Sol.* 23.5; Hom. *Il.* 18.579–82; [Dem.] 47.52; Theophr. *HP* 8.7.1–8.8.4; McDonald and Rapp 53; cf. Colum. *Rust.* 5.9.11–12; Pind. *Nem.* 11.39–42; Xen. *Vect.* 4.1–17; Arist. *Pol.* 1.1259 a10–39.

44. On the advantages of modern-day crop diversity in Greece, see Forbes 1976c: 236–50. On orchards as windbreaks, see Pecírka and Dufkova 1970: 153–57. Pliny on the barberry: *NH* 18.45.161; cf. Sallares 293.

45. For manuring on post-harvest stubble, and the role of livestock in crop diversity, see Hodkinson 1988: 45–50; Gavrielides 1976a: 155; Brumfield 25–27; cf. Xen. *Oec.* 5.3: "the art of raising animals is closely connected with farming"; Hodkinson and Hodkinson 37–39. Columella later wrote of a certain "alliance and concord" (*quaedam societas atque coniunctio*) between farming and livestock (*Rust.* 6. *praef.* 2). For sheep browsing in vineyards: Weaver 213. Aelian knew of a tradition at Keos where farmers had little open pasture, but instead fed their livestock fig and olive leaves, husks, and weeds (*HA* 16.32). In turn, they supplied manure piles for systematic, heavy—and labor intensive—manuring, rather than random incidental fertilization (e.g., Halstead 1987: 83; Halstead and Jones 47–48.

46. Alternate bearing and problems of scarcity and surfeit: Theophr. *CP* 1.20.3; Pind. *Nem.* 11.39–42; Colum. *Rust.* 5.8.1–2; 5.9.11–12; Boardman 1977: 189; and cf. Xen. *Vect.* 4.6.

47. See Gallant 1991: 36, for reliability at the expense of output; cf. Semple 1928: 155–56. On the different type of labor requirements for a diversified farm, see Theophr. *HP* 8.1.2; Jameson 1978: 128–31; Halstead 1987: 83–85; Osborne 1987: 46–48. There survive various laws from antiquity prohibiting the early harvesting of wine grapes. Thus on the island of Thasos, a preserved inscription from the late fifth century warns: "No one is allowed to purchase grape juice or wine from the current crop still on the vines before the first day of the month Plynterion" (*IG* XII, suppl. 347; cf. Alc. fr. 119). These measures, which are designed to protect the reputation of the local wine industry, proba-

bly do not guard against a farmer's desire to "beat" the market, since the grapes are to be sold as wine (requiring time for crushing and fermentation), not as fresh fruit. Instead, this legislation must be an acknowledgment that growers tended to harvest too early in fear that some of their crop might become over-ripe or (more likely) be caught by unseasonable weather during the protracted harvest (cf. Pl. *Leg.* 8.844D-845C).

48. Theophrastus on micro-climates and the suitability of specific crops for particular soils: *CP* 3.6.2–9; cf. *HP* 2.5.7, 3.6.7–8; *CP* 1.18.1–2. Deviations in agricultural conditions within small areas: Forbes 1976c: 244; Renfrew and Wagstaff 101–5; Osborne 1987: 38–40. Olives and vines as a means of utilizing otherwise worthless soils, cf. Amouretti 1986: 51–77; Richter 134–140. "They represent, in other words, a way of extracting a cultivated crop from soils un-suited for crops such as cereals, and which would otherwise have been given over to rough grazing" (Sarpaki 1992: 70).

49. For *autarkeia,* see Sallares 297–300; Campell and Sherrard 323–24; Osborne 1987: 17–18. For more specific examples of self-sufficiency in Greece, see Foxhall and Forbes 66; Boardman 1977: 192; Amouretti 1986: 177–196; McDonald and Rapp 54–57. "A farm," the comic playwright Philemon makes his rustic say, "supplies every human want, wheat, oil, wine, figs, and honey" (fr. 105 Kock). Such bounty, Timocles says, is not a farm, "but a crown" (Timocles fr. 36 Kock).

50. Ancient views that arboriculture and viticulture were more recent devel-opments of the *polis:* Pl. *Leg.* 6.782B; *FGrH* 115 fr. 276; Thuc.1.2.2; Plut. *Sol.* 23–24; Dio. Chrys. 1.75.3. See also Sallares 305–307; Amouretti 1986: 44–45; J. Hansen 44–46; Runnels and Hansen 1986: 302–6; Amouretti 1986: 43–46. On the relative rarity of early wheat species, see Howe 44–45; Amouretti 1986: 36–46.

51. "Distant from the city: 24.212; cf. 4.757: "the far-off fields"; "Much hard work": 24.205–7; an "outer estate": 18.357–65; Clearing stones and build-ing terraces: 24.223–25; "the high ground of his vineyard": *Od.* 1.194; cf. 11.187–93; 24.149. For Plato's belief of early hillside reclamation: Pl. *Leg.* 3.680E. There is a vast literature on *eschatia:* see Audring 1989: 100–113; Lewis 1973: 210–12; Donlan 1989: 135–37; Richter 12–13; Jardé 42–43; Bisinger 31; Guiraud 65–68; 134–35; cf., too, Frayn 98–101.

52. See Xenophon's statement that "nothing has greater profit than land that is transformed from the wild into a productive farm" (Xen. *Oec.* 20.19; cf. Plut. *Mor.* 552C; Is. 9.28). For terraces and stone removal: Hom. *Il.* 18.564; *Od.* 24.224; 18.359; *SIG*³ 963 17–20; cf. Rackman and Moody 128; Bradford 1956: 172–80. Various problems in cultivating hillsides: (erosion) Dem. 55; Pliny HN 18.49; (less fertility) Colum. *Rust.* 2.51; 2.10.6; Theophr. *HP* 2.5.7; 2.8.1). In addition, elevation results in earlier and later frosts and difficulty in transport-ing harvests. See also Osborne 1992b: 375; Audring 1989: 93–94; Halstead and Jones 49.

53. Theophrastus: "Use rich soil for grains, thin soil for trees. . . . Trees, with long and strong roots, draw their nutrients from the depths. In rich soils trees develop their wood and foliage, but yield little if any fruit" (CP 2.4.2–3, 3.6.6–8; *HP* 3.2.5; Virg. *Georg.* 2.179–83; and cf. Colum. *Arbor.* 17.1: "The olive tree thrives best in the hills which are dry and have clay soil; but in the damp, rich plains it produces lush foliage without fruit"). Xenophon: "Even land that lies waste reveals its potential. If the wild flora growing on the land are hardy, then by good farming that ground is also capable of producing excellent cultivated crops" (*Oec.* 16.4–6). On early Italian arboriculture, see Cato *Rust.* 1.2–6: "Grafting on wild trees makes it possible to include land that would otherwise not be arable"; Colum. *Arbor.* 18.2: "Land that is ideal for vines is also suitable for fruit trees" (cf. Colum. *Rust.* 2.1.4–6). "Fruit trees," Theophrastus again reminds us, "as a class do fine in the foothills" (CP 3.6.7). Cf. Homer on the hillsides of Thrace as a fine wine district (*Od.* 9.208). See also Isager and Skydsgaard 38, and Langdon and Watrous 175 (on the ancient cliff farm of Timesios in southern Attica).

54. Eurymachos challenges Odysseus to plant "tall trees" and build walls on his *eschatia* (*Od.* 18.357–59). If this section of the *Odyssey* reflects practice contemporary with Homer's own life (as I think Homer's knowledge of agricultural technique must suggest), trees now seem to allow high ground to become quite farmable. The "higher-ups" there will be sturdy yeoman, not nomadic herdsmen nor vagrant woodcutters. Because Laertes himself apparently had carved out the land for his farm, and since he was to pass on to his son Odysseus the fruit trees that he had planted, the reclamation of his land *and* the creation of orchards and vineyards, as in the case also of Eurymachos' farm, were *simultaneous* phenomena. In the *Iliad*, we hear on occasion of *temenê*, land "cut out" from surrounding plains and given to prominent men of the local agrarian community as rewards for past heroic service. (Notice that such lands are "cut out" from the largely private landowning domain, rather than vice versa.) In most of these cases, the bestowed farmland was *not* previously worked, but instead required considerable effort to draw off excess water in order to plant vineyards and orchards (see Donlan 1989: 140, 141–45; cf. later practice, Theophr. CP 5.14.2–3). In other words, a great deal of *eschatia* land came into production earlier than is usually supposed, well before the fifth and fourth centuries. On the elastic nature of marginal land in relation to population growth and decline, see Audring 1989: 83; Osborne 1988: 287; Rackman 1990: 104.

55. Eurymachos' farm: 18.357–59; Hesiod's Ascra: Hes. *Op.* 640; Solon's legislation: Plut. *Sol.* 23.7; cf. Phot. *Bibl. s.v. sykophantein*; the rock farmer on Mt. Hymettus: *Ath. Pol* 16.6 ff.; Diod. 9.37.2; remains of ancient farms at Chios: Lambrinoudakis 303–4. Similarly, a later source tells us that under Peisistratus the country residents turned their attention to planting the slopes of Attica with olive trees (Dio Chrys. 1.75.3; cf. Guiraud 199), hillsides that were apparently assumed

to have been previously unplanted. Understandably at Athens in the early sixth century, there were farmers labeled either *huperakrioi* or *diakrioi*, the so-called higher-ups, early cultivators who probably farmed land that incorporated some hillsides and felt their interests were in opposition to more established men of "the Plain" (see Hopper 1961: 193ns. 41, 42, 45). Aristotle, at any rate, believed that early factions at Athens—"Plain, Shore, and Hill"—"derived their names from the places *where they farmed*" (Arist. *Ath. Pol.* 13.3–5; Hdt. 1.59; Dion. Hal. *Ant. Rom.* 1.13). In the southern Argolid, there were also efforts to work poor ground and plant olives in the face of population growth and greater economic opportunity for disposal of food surpluses. "Adjacent markets, methods of intensified production, and a shift from farming for subsistence to farming for cash crops brought a relative measure of prosperity even to a place like the southern Argolid" (van Andel and Runnels 104–5). And the well-known ancient reputation for the shallowness of Attic soil (e.g., Thuc. 1.2.5; Plut. *Sol.* 22.3; Plut. *Crit.* 111B–C; Alciphr. [3.35]: "We who live on the thin soil of Attica") may reflect the widespread fruit-tree farming of rugged terrain there. Surely such a pejorative generalization does *not* capture well the rich farming plains found surrounding Athens, Eleusis, and Marathon, and in the hinterland of southern Attica. Instead the appellation "thin" suggests the efforts of the more numerous Attic hill farmers.

56. On California, see Scheuring 385. Perhaps *half* of Attica's total land area by the fifth century was used for agricultural activities (e.g., Foxhall 156), possible only through the use of widespread terracing of upland ground, as intensive farming creeped onto even steeper terrain.

57. Isocr. 8.117; cf. Theophr. *CP* 3.20.4. The *Palatine Anthology* records the dedicatory epigram of one old Euphron, who "farmed not the furrowed plain, but shallow-soil just able to be scraped by the plough" (*Anth. Pal.* 6.238). In a famous fragment of Attic comedy (fr. 380 Kock) farmers are reminded that "it is better for those who have bad neighbors to farm rocks than to cultivate plains." A similar fragment of Menander's advises that even if a farmer works rocks during peace, he will do better than the rich on the plain during war (Men. fr. 719 Kock). Another (anonymous) fragment of Attic comedy decries the amount of usable land on a farm; it is less than a laconic letter of the legendary terse Spartans (fr. 417–19 Kock). On preserved confiscation inventories of the late fifth century nearly one fourth of all the plots sold at Athens were marginal lands (*eschatiai*) (Andreyev 16). "Aches and pains," "farming rocks," "hill-men," "bad in winter, bothersome in summer" are the disparaging, though understandable, descriptions of marginal lands that required a great deal of hand labor from their small-farmer owners. Outside of allusions to Thessaly and Messenia and other non-*polis* territory, rarely, if ever, are there references in Greek literature to the bounty of plentiful flat and accessible grain land.

58. Pl. *Leg.* 4.704E–705B. Most Greeks felt that rich plains created an entirely different type of culture, cf. Plut. *Mor.* 181B; Isoc. 8.117–18; Hdt. 9.122.

59. See Plato on the grower and processor, Pl. *Theaet.* 178D; *Theag.* 124A; and cf. his disdain for the middle man peddler, e.g. Pl. *Resp.* 2.371C; *Polit.* 289E. Laertes' finished products: Hom. *Od.* 1.375–77; 2.56–78; 2.123–27; 17.212–14; 17.532–40. So the strictly economic advice of the later Roman agriculturalist Varro that "the threshing floor should be on the farmland" (*Rust.* 1.51.1; cf. Colum. *Rust.*1.6.23) was generally followed earlier by Greek farmers; the science of on-the-farm food storage was an integral element in the Hellenic agronomic tradition (see Brumfield 42–43). Despite the occasional presence of communal storage centers and threshing floors (e.g., Starr 1977: 151–52; cf. Plut. *Mor.* 114E), in the *polis* period yeomen normally did not hand over their production to some centralized collection center, manor, or palace to be milled, pressed, and stored by others who themselves were not farmers (cf. Hes. *Op.* 618–45). We hear occasionally of slaves engaged on the farm's threshing floor, winnowing the grain (e.g., Alciphr. 3.26). Pressing and milling right at the farm rather than shipping produce to village or palace centers also tended to reduce losses from spoilage and rot (Cato *Rust.* 96–144; Varro *Rust.*1.55; Colum. *Rust.*12.4–52). Worry about insect damage and spoilage on the farm abounds in descriptions of Greek farms (e.g., Theophr. *CP* 4.3.17; 4.15.3–16.4; *HP* 8.11.7; Plut. *Mor.* 676B). And at any given time, there may have been more food stored out in the countryside than inside the walls of the Greek *polis* (e.g., [Arist.] *Oec.* 1348b17ff.).

60. Threshing floors and presses in the archaeological record: Pecírka and Dufkova: 125–29; Pecírka 1970: 471–73; van Andel and Runnels 106–7; Cherry, Davis, and Mantzourani 193–95; Halstead and Jones 79; Morris 1991: 32; and cf. Burford 1993:141–43. On the Aegean island of Chios, "fragments of olive-presses and millstones bear witness to the existence of a self sufficient, well-equipped farmhouse in the complex" (Lambrinoudakis 303; cf. Boardman 1956: 49–51). In Attica, threshing floors were found near farmhouses (Young 1956a: 122–23, 124–26; cf. Lohmann 1992: 42–43; Langdon and Watrous 173), and storage annexes apparently were a part of rural homesteads (Jones, Sackett, and Graham 419). Greek land-leases inscribed on stone often refer to hundreds of permanent storage jars and vats that are to come with the property (e.g., Osborne 1985c: 124–25; IG I3 426. 4–56). Unlike mention of metal or wood fabrication, during the polis-period we rarely hear in Greek literature of food processing operations (*ergasteria*) in town, where raw agricultural products might be transported to be milled and pressed (Heichelheim 2.102–103). Presses in villages and cities seem more a Hellenistic phenomenon, when a densely populated Greek countryside was disappearing (see Isager and Skydsgaard 68).

61. That is what Philodemus meant when he reported that the poor, who did not have storerooms (unlike the intensive agriculturalist), were at a disadvantage because they had to sell all their produce at once cheaply (Philod. *Peri*

Oik. 7.26–27). Hesiod advised his middling farmers: "It will not always be summer; build yourself granaries" (*Op.* 503). As we have seen, every diversified farm must have taken careful precaution to have grain bins, plenty of wine amphorae or vats, and other storage facilities for food right on the farm (e.g., Alciphr. 3.14). This picture is quite understandable within the framework of homestead residence. But is it not difficult to imagine vats, bins, and presses on the land in an exclusively commuting peasantry? In the Aristotelian *Oeconomica*, there are anecdotes in which *poleis* in times of crisis pass decrees asking the populace to empty their private stores of grain and oil for public consumption (*Oec.* 2.1348b17–23; 1348b34–1349a3). In an extant boundary description from Sicily, a threshing floor appears as part of a rich rural infrastructure; mention is made in the inscription of roads, a threshing floor, orchards, ditches, streams, and a farm tower (*IG* XIV 353). The contexts are usually understood to be rural. The storage vessels found in the vicinity of ancient farms suggest that rarely would a Greek intensive agriculturalist have left valuable food out on his land, and then commuted into town. Even historians who envision a primitive state of Greek agriculture during the *polis*, distinguished by town living and relatively unsophisticated farming technique, note the potential advantages of the opposite regime, see, e.g., Isager and Skydsgaard 70.

62. Early slavery and viticulture: Theopompus *FGrH* 115 fr.122; fr. 276; hillside farmhouses on Chios: Lambrinoudakis 295–304; Boardman 1956: 49–51. For the inscription from Chios, see Meiggs and Lewis 8; cf. Finley 1981b 114; Ehrenberg 1937: 152; Garlan 1988: 38–39; Koerner 444–45.

Chapter 3. Hesiod's Works and Days: *The Privilege of the Struggle*

1. For the view that Greece was largely a society of peasants, see Millet 1984: 103–6; Walcot 1970: 12–17; but cf. Burford 1993: 85–86.

2. Although the *Works and Days* is, like the Homeric epics, composed in dactylic hexameter and exhibits the repetitive formulae characteristic of oral composition, there are fewer problems in Hesiod's work caused by multiple layers of historicity. Although Hesiod drew on a long tradition of Near Eastern and local Boeotian epic, little in his *Works and Days* can be intended to represent the life of the Greek Dark Ages (1150–800 B.C.). Even less are his images distant echoes from the Mycenean palaces (1600–1250 B.C.). Hesiod's world is vintage early seventh-century, a community of small farmers in central Greece. The value of the *Works and Days* as "a historical document," Paul Millet has written, "has been persistently underrated. This is a striking omission, as by general consent we have in the *Works and Days* a written source, giving detailed information about life in the early archaic period, for which virtually no other documentary evidence exists" (Millet 1984: 84).

3. Controversy among scholars rages over the precise class and status of Hesiod. Central to this are the poet's own ideas about work. Redfield has sug-

gested that for peasants "agriculture is a livelihood and a way of life, not a business for profit" (J. M. Redfield 27). Other scholars, despite vast differences in locales and chronology, have added all kinds of criteria to this sweeping definition of "peasant"—baffling, contradictory, and unworkable concepts reflective of the historic difficulty of distinguishing the various classes who work the soil. Chief among the usual economic qualifications of "peasantry" are the subsistence level of the peasant's production, his manipulation by a nonfarming class of overlords and city folk (e.g., de Ste. Croix 210–11), his resistance to new techniques and crops, his chronic underemployment, his skepticism that success or failure are in his own hands, his disbelief that increased labor can create new wealth and thus improve his status—in short, the complete absence of an economic ideology associated with agriculture.

Hesiod, like Laertes himself, is something altogether different than a peasant. Like most later small farmers, he sees agriculture *both* as a way of life *and* as a means to obtain profit (cf. Pl. *Leg.* 5.743D). Of this balance between market-oriented profit and the need for self-reliance, Peter Garnsey has written: "The pull of the market was never powerful enough to engender a thoroughly entrepreneurial mentality. Profit was looked for, but not profit maximization, the 'productivity ratio' was understood partially, not in its totality" (Garnsey 1992: 152; cf. Detienne 1963: 56–57).

4. See Hodkinson and Hodkinson 276, Table III, for estimates of the numbers of hoplite yeomen. Ruschenbusch (1985: 258, 263) discusses the "typical" *polis* of twenty-five to a hundred square kilometers of territory and an average population of adult males numbering between 130 and 800. Problems also arise in assessing whether a majority of Greek *geôrgoi* failed and fell into the ranks of the abject poor, or found unusual bounty and became part of the landed elite. In the case of Hesiod, one is at least able to differentiate him from *both* the very wealthy and the very poor: "Hesiod is often called a peasant, but he totally fails to fit the modern anthropological definition of a peasant as a rural producer dependent on a secondary group which uses the surpluses extorted from the peasant class for itself and other non-farming groups. Hesiod did not belong to the top level of society, but economically he occupied an independent position and addressed the bulk of his poem to farmers capable of finding capital for the purchase of a team of oxen and female and male slaves or the maritime trips to dispose of surpluses on their own account" (Starr 1986: 93; cf. Burford 1993: 85–86; Detienne 1963: 26–28).

5. On modern Italy, see Galt 210; Walcot 1970: 97–106, for peasant resistance to traditional authority.

6. Of the creation of this early hoplite farming stratum in the Greek *polis*, Max Weber observed: "It was of decisive importance for the development of the characteristic features of Hellenic civilization, including its art, that members of this order did not lead the life of grand seigniors. Rather, they were compelled

to live in a simple, unpretentious manner, and this precisely in the period when they were developing self-consciousness as a class" (Weber 1976: 184–85).

7. For the idea that Hesiod resembles the modern peasant, see Walcot 1970: 12–18; Millet 1984: 85–88; cf. Wood 54–56; Francis 294–95. On the need to redefine the range encompassed by "peasant," cf. Millet 1984: 89: "Historically, there have often been significant groups of better off peasants set apart from the mass of poor peasantry." We should not forget the accurate, but currently unfashionable, note of Western chauvinism in Chester Starr's observation: "One final point, however, cannot be emphasized too strongly. Culturally the modern connotations of the word 'peasants' are seriously misleading when applied to the chorus of the Acharnians in Aristophanes or to any other Greek rural elements. Those Greeks who visited the Persian empire or the Nile valley met abjectly ignorant, downtrodden masses very different from the small farmers they knew at home, who were citizens in the *polis*" (1977: 167; cf. Forbes 1989: 88).

8. See Osborne 1985: 142. The dynamic nature of the early Greek agrarianism must explain why in G. E. M. de Ste. Croix's monumental *Class Struggle in the Ancient Greek World,* no more than a few pages are devoted to the Greek city-state of the seventh, sixth, and fifth centuries. Despite the sweeping title, the preponderance of de Ste. Croix's examples of rural exploitation, and of conflict between landed and landless, by necessity must derive from the latter fourth century, and even more frequently from either Hellenistic and Roman Greece or outside the culture of the *polis* altogether.

9. Howe 60. Implications of limiting rural families: de Ste. Croix 1981: 278–79; Starr 1977: 119–46. This "manual" of Hesiod is, in fact, the forerunner to a rich agronomic tradition, to a whole host of later Greek technical writing, which like the *Works and Days* always reflected a pragmatic, not solely a theoretical, approach to agriculture. "There is some evidence," wrote the circumspect Albert Trever of the *Works and Days* (159), "of a growing interest in the details of successful agriculture. This knowledge of cultivation is, of course, to be expected in a poem by a farmer. The very fact that an epic should be written, at this early age, with such a primary emphasis on the agricultural life, is significant in itself. Though the theme of the *Works and Days* is not agriculture, it is the pioneer of a long line of Greek and Roman works on the subject."

10. "The dependent *kakoi* of 1050–750 B.C. became the citizens of Late Geometric times" (Morris 1987: 175; cf. Starr 1977: 126–28).

11. At this time a general *topos* in Greek philosophy thought that the middle course was best. "It was this center that was now valued; the welfare of the *polis* rested on those who were known as *hoi mesoi,* because, being equidistant from the extremes, they constituted a fixed point on which the city was balanced" (Vernant 1982: 125; cf. Busolt and Swoboda 212; Ehrenberg 1951: 250–52). This fixation with the "mean" was not mere theory, but a precise soci-

ological term used to distinguish groups present among the citizenry (e.g., Rhodes 72). There is no reason to suppose that a middle group of farmers did not, in fact, exist. Their presence and success during the early years of the polis (i.e., the eighth and seventh centuries) *gave rise to* the later philosophical fascination with citizens neither rich nor poor (Bisinger 4–7). Even though all political factions in the early *polis* were still fairly undeveloped, and even though hoplite wars were at this time small and exclusively over minor border disputes, there was enough common ground, enough common experience to forge shared principles in the agrarian middle.

12. Gernet 1981: 305. See Osborne 1989: 319–22, on political recognition of the emerging hoplite farmers. Cf. Rhodes 72–73, 182–83; Whitehead 1981: 282–86.

13. On the early notion of "Plain, Shore, and Hill," see Hopper 1961:196–208; and cf. Rhodes 184–85.

14. On the early strife between aristocratic livestock men and yeomen, see Gernet 1981: 282–83. Hodkinson (1988: 36–37; 1992: 53–59) discusses the complex and evolving relationship between livestock and intensive agriculture. Even in the fifth and fourth centuries, livestock raising was dominated by and for the rich.

15. Starr 1986: 46–47. For the new disdain for horses and cavalry, see Sallares 311; cf. Hodkinson 1988: 37.

16. Most standard histories of early Greece until very recently have glossed over agriculture and farmers. Similarly, theorists (not always simply poststructuralists, and Marxists) sometimes associate anything in the middle with their own antibourgeois sentiments, and so, I believe, have been traditionally reluctant to acknowledge the presence of a sizable, stable middle citizenry in the Greek *polis*, of the *mesoi* themselves, e.g., Lintott 1992: 126–28: "The domination of the *mesoi* is a pipe-dream or a might-have-been for Aristotle"; Ober 1990: 119–121; Burford 1993: 80: "There is really no middle group that has just about enough." Much less do scholars employ the romantic term "yeomanry" to describe Greek farmers.

It is therefore surprising just how often both ancient literary sources and occasional modern historians have remarked in passing on this middle agrarian presence. M. I. Finley, himself always one to caution us about the naive usage of modern rubrics when describing the sociology of the ancient Greek *polis*, quite clearly labeled these new landowners of the seventh century "a middle-class of relatively prosperous, but non-aristocratic farmers," including "the hoplite soldiers who held sufficient land" and "who were given a role in government for the first time" (1981a: 98–99).

By "class" Finley did *not*, of course, mean the modern idea of *bourgeoisie*, not the contemporary notion of a manufacturing or commercial stratum, but simply middling farmers neither wealthy nor poor (see Patterson 183–85). The gifted Russian scholar V. N. Andreyev similarly wrote of Attica: "On the contrary, Athens maintained a large 'middle group' of owners and this imbued it with a surprising degree of internal stability" (23), a group that W.S. Ferguson had seen as crucial: "The presence of a middle class in the background, made up largely of agriculturalists, could never be ignored by extremists. It was a steadying influence in everyday politics and an arbiter in the event of a crisis" (Ferguson 4). Peter Spahn devoted an entire study to the role of middleness in the formation of the Greek city-state, demonstrating that the presence of the *mesoi* was an early development, not a later manifestation of mere political infighting (*Mittelschicht und Polisbildung*; cf. especially 7–15; 174–82). See also the sober discussion of de Ste. Croix 1981: 69–89.

17. On Aristotle and the middle group, see the various, sometimes conflicting, views of de Ste. Croix 1981: 71–72; Ober 1990: 120–21; Mossé 1962: 247–52.

18. Paul Rahe has rightly concluded that this political idea of moderation, sprung as it was from the broad-based group who created the city-state, was eventually extended to become the entire sociopolitical foundation upon which the later Greek *polis* was based:

"This is why *to meson* comes to be identified with the political community itself, and it accounts for the fact that the middle ground was thought to be the proper sphere in which to weigh and determine what is measured, fitting, timely, needful, and the like. It also helps to explain much that would otherwise be puzzling about ancient life—why, for example, rightful authority was thought to emanate from *to meson,* why the middle position was deemed the seat of honor, why a Greek proverb associated occupation of the middle or common ground with the assumption of risk and the rolling of the dice, why departure from the middle ground (*ek mesou*) was synonymous with withdrawal from the contest for rule, and why neutrals who distanced themselves from the debate taking place in the common council were described as sitting or standing *ek mesou.* If the Greek *polis* of the archaic and classical periods was peculiar, it was because it offered its citizens more than mere protection. It provided them, in addition, with middle ground in which to display those qualities which distinguished them from animals" (Rahe 42; cf. Starr 1986: 96–97; Morrow 534–43).

19. Rhodes 91; cf., N. Lewis 150–51; Woodhouse 18–19; but cf. Busolt and Swoboda 779–80. See Rihll 102, who notes that the nobles could not have owned all of Attica. Information about Solon's legislation derives largely from his own poetry, a cursory account in Herodotus's history (e.g., 1.23–33, 86; 2.177; 5.113), Aristotle's *Constitution of Athens* (5–12), Plutarch's biography (*Sol.* 13), and scattered anecdotes concerning his legislation in later compendia.

20. In short: "Hoplites might reasonably be expected to oppose violent revolution whilst maintaining sympathy with any reasonable complaints of the

poor" (Holladay 1977: 51). This Solonian package ensured that Athens would never turn to serfdom, helotage, and the culture of oppressed peasantry found in the atypical *polis* societies of Crete, Thessaly, and Sparta (see Woodhouse 196–98; N. Lewis 156), where those who owned the land outright and those who worked it were often separate peoples "in an everlasting state of war" (Isager and Skydsgaard 152). On land that reverted to the wild on the exit of their owners, see Rihll 118; for Solonian protection of the family plot, cf. Asheri 1963: 8–12.

21. For later hoplite pride in the Solonian timocracy, see Asheri 1966: 106; Ostwald 337–411; and especially Morrow 521–43; cf. 79. Elsewhere even more dramatic solutions codified the economic contributions of the *mesoi* in the growing city-state. It is perhaps incorrect to speak of an "Age of Tyrants" in the history of the Greek city-states, since only between twenty and thirty of more than a thousand *poleis* experienced anything that could be formally called "tyranny" (Snodgrass 1980: 111–13; but cf. Thuc. 1.13.1). Most communities instead made the transition well enough from Dark-Age aristocracy to landed timocracy without recourse to extreme measures. But between the eighth and sixth centuries we do hear of some of the major Greek city-states—Argos, Corinth, Sicyon, Mytilene, Megara, Athens, and others—experiencing a radical, though temporary, change from aristocratic government to personal despotism (the Lydian word "tyrant" implies nothing much more in its original sense than an unlawful seizure of power). Even in city-states like Corinth, Mytilene, Samos, and Athens—traditional centers of trade and maritime commerce—there was often an agrarian connection with tyranny, an association between a strong man and hoplite-landowners, as well as the destitute landless. This tyrannical affinity for the *mesoi* suggests that in some instances the changeover from aristocracy to representative government, typical of most of Greece by the fifth century, was simply too slow. "The tyranny," writes M. I. Finley of this agrarian support for usurpers, "was the period when the class of small and medium-sized farmers became firmly entrenched" (1981a: 124; cf. Spahn 158–60). Of the Corinthian tyrant Cypselus, John Salmon observes: "The strength behind the political upheavals in the mid-seventh century was provided by hoplites: Cypselus was successful because he enjoyed their support" (1984: 191). On the Aegean island of Samos in the early sixth century Syloson, followed by his successors Aiakes and the famous Polycrates, ended the dominance of aristocratic estate-holding *geômoroi*. Samian tyranny (about 590–522 B.C.) encouraged the arts and craftsmanship, but also achieved increased economic prosperity through growing exportation of foodstuffs and the construction of rural bridges and roads (e.g., Shipley 48–99; 240–42), measures indicative of the activity of small landowners.

So in some areas of Greece, the gradual ebb and flow of agrarianism had been interrupted, and cultivators turned to the more radical solution of tyranny (e.g., Arist. *Pol.* 5.1310b25–1311a23). Perhaps that is what Aristotle means in a controversial passage in his *Politics,* where in a general discussion of the end of aristocracy he remarks that "as the city-states grew and those who wore hoplite armor became more influential, then more people began to take a part in government" (*Pol.* 4.1297b23–25). Earlier the philosopher had pointed out that the tyrants Theagenes of Megara and Peisistratus of Athens had both taken up the cause of small agriculturalists "who lived on their farms busily engaged in agriculture" (*Pol.* 5.1305a19–21).

That statement seems believable, for Peisistratus especially was associated with a distinctive program of visiting rural districts and encouraging olive production, homestead residence, and accessible capital (e.g., Arist. *Ath. Pol.* 16.3; Dio. Chrys. 7.107–8; 1.75.3; cf. J. Holladay 1977: 48–50). His supposed tax on the wealthier estates of aristocrats perhaps even provided the grubstake for some tree and vine farmers (J. Holladay 1977: 50–52). Of these general practices, Anthony Andrewes observes: "In classical times the hoplites are a sort of middle class, including the more substantial of the small farmers, for the equipment of Greek armies was not provided by the state, and the hoplites were just that income-group which could afford hoplite armour. Thus we might expect, as a political effect of the change to hoplite tactics, that the middle class would start to claim its share of power in the state, breaking into the monopoly held by the aristocrats" (Andrewes 1963: 34; cf. Nilsson 1929: 240).

Another often associated with the connection between tyranny and the hoplite-landowner is the usurper Pheidon of Argos (about 700 B.C.), a tyrant who led his Argives—"the goads of war"—on to victory against the Spartans at Hysiae in 669 B.C., perhaps with the aid of small farmers also equipped with hoplite armor (*Anth. Pal.* 14.73). In his aftermath, the epigraphic and archaeological record at Argos suggests the growth of a landed hoplite timocracy. For example, of the surface evidence from the landscape of the southern Argolid, modern archaeologists observe: "The evolution of the rural economy is, we think, what lay behind the origin and growth of the small Argolid towns we know from Classical sources" (van Andel and Runnels 107). Rural infrastructure and small farms apparently went hand in hand at Argos with the destruction of hereditary aristocracy. Already by the early and middle sixth century, well after the end of the tyranny, a few Argive inscriptions (SEG XI 314; SEG XI 302; SEG XI 336; SEG XVIII 147) suggest that constitutional government, a broad-based oligarchy or timocracy of farmers, was well established at Argos, replete with a board of annual magistrates and law courts.

Chapter 4. The Ways of Farmers

1. Burford 1993: 31. On land as the key to all social and political privilege in the Greek *polis,* see Guiraud 143–45. Ironically, it was in an atypical *polis,* Sparta—where the equation between hoplite fighter and yeoman farmer was

perverted by the presence of the indentured helots—that women may have been granted an exceptional voice in landholding. Aristotle, in his general critique of inegalitarian property ownership, cites the example of Sparta. There, because of the peculiarities of a professional army, an enslaved helot population, a dwindling population of elite "Peers" and traditions of inheritance, "women own nearly two-fifths of the entire country," a region that Aristotle believed could have supported thirty times more hoplite infantry than it fielded in the late fourth century (*Pol.* 6.1270a17–32).

2. Urban residents of the *polis* could also have their belongings stolen or might quarrel with an irksome family nearby. The difference is that all such disputes were more social, and not exclusively economic. Bothersome and sometimes expensive as theft or assault might be to the town dweller, those losses, nevertheless, usually did not threaten a family's entire way of life. But the attack on the homestead farmer, subtle or direct, ultimately was seen by every grower as *both* a social and an economic challenge, something that would not merely disturb his peace, but end his existence as well. Xenophon reasoned that a farmer who saw his own land attacked—being in superb mental and physical shape, and knowledgeable about the gravity of the situation—could just as well go on the offensive to plunder the farms of his adversaries (*Oec.* 5.13).

Was it not a fundamental difference in urban and rural outlook that Aristophanes played on so successfully in his *Acharnians* (425 B.C.)? In that comedy, the rustics of the deme Acharnae saw the Peloponnesian occupation of their farms in a far different light from their kindred urban citizens at Athens. For them the sight of ravagers on their soil was an economic, social, and psychological challenge to their existence, not a mere chapter in the grand strategy of the Peloponnesian War (Ar. *Ach.* 204–37; Thuc. 2.21; cf. Hanson 1983: 148–51). In response to this tension between farmers and city residents that arose during the Peloponnesian War and continued in its aftermath, both Plato and Aristotle thought the ideal state should mandate dual ownership on the part of each of its citizens. "Of the land that belongs to private persons," Aristotle wrote, "one portion should be in the outlying districts, while the other should be near the *polis*. This way two plots might be assigned to every citizen, and everyone then would have a stake in both districts. Consequently, there is both equity and justice, and also there is a general overall consensus in regard to border wars. When this system is not followed, one group of the citizenry is too ready to struggle with neighboring states, while the other group is too cautious and overlooks provocation" (Arist. *Pol.* 7.1330a14–18; cf. Pl. *Leg.* 5.745C).

3. Another defense was probably the sheer stoutness of the farmers' enclaves. The stone towers discussed in Chapter 2, which appear so ubiquitously in the archaeological record, could provide some defense if the farmer brought his family, livestock, and slaves inside his fortification and rode out the attack

(see Hanson 1983: 62–63, 88–101). The image of a farm "besieged" is reminiscent of the Rhodesian civil wars of the late 1960s and mid 1970s, when men drove armored tractors and irrigated carrying sidearms. That is too dramatic a picture for ancient Greece. Nevertheless, even in the relatively tranquil times of the *polis* there must have been some anxiety that during general unrest attack could come suddenly and from unexpected quarters to anyone toiling in the countryside. Of those stout farm towers in southern Attica, Hans Lohmann (1992: 39) remarked: "Although the towers—even the stronger ones—could have not withstood an organized siege, they provided adequate protection against attack by robbers or pillaging soldiers."

4. Aristotle in his *Politics* records a statute at Thebes that regulated the procreation of children, designed "to preserve the original number of land allotments" (2.1274b3). Plato in his *Laws* has a lengthy, ingenious discussion about how the ideal state might limit the number of children to prevent the disintegration of the family plot (5.740B–D; cf. *Resp.* 5.460A). Later (*Leg.* 11.923C–D); he went further, and raised the possibility that in his utopia the property owner might simply name one son as the principal heir who would inherit the family plot: "the owner of the *klêros* shall always leave behind [as heir] one son, whichever one he wishes." Aristotle, in his criticism of Plato, also addresses maintaining the family estate: either fertility had to be limited or some offspring left without inheritance, *if* the original number of plots in the community were to remain constant—the keystone to the entire agrarian regime of the early Greek *polis*. He suggests that birth control be carefully monitored to prevent fragmentation of farm properties (*Pol.* 2.1265.b1–28).

The historian Polybius later believed (wrongly?) that by his own time (the second century after the end of the agrarian *polis*) Greece had become depopulated in many areas because that old fear of diluted inheritance had led to the opposite extreme, farmers apparently limiting severely the size of their families to ensure integrity of the ancestral plot (36.17.5–8). Rivalries among offspring and disputes over inheritance were a constant worry for the farmer, who had managed to solidify his own position on the farm, and thus had pragmatic experience with siblings to chart the best course for the next generation of owners (cf. Burford 1993: 36–46).

Nevertheless, assume that in most cases farmers triumphed, carried on, and prevented farms from becoming fractionalized. David Asheri, in a review of constitutional practice among the Greek city-states, detects ubiquitous concern over divisive inheritance. In response to the problem, early Greek agrarian communities often drafted precise preventive legislation. "We may conclude," Asheri wrote (1963: 6), "that moderate constitutions were generally inclined to preserve the integral lots by allowing their succession only as undivided units to a single male heir, being interested in preserving, as much as possible, the original distribution of land property and the original composition of the citizen body."

In Greece today land fragmentation is a perennial problem (Campbell and Sherrard 329–33; K. Thompson 213–52), because of the absence of primogeniture, the dowering of daughters, and the prestige of land ownership. In modern villages envy can discourage the concentration of even small plots (Slaughter and Kasimis 130–31). The average farm in many areas of Greece today is no larger than two or three acres, with widely distant component plots of even smaller dimensions. Modern ethnographers and anthropologists who have studied this system and interviewed local farm owners suggest that fragmentation *does have advantages* in spreading risks from natural disaster and crop failure (Gallant 1991: 41–5; Osborne 1987: 37–39; Forbes 1982: 324; 1989: 91ff.). To some extent this is true (as I can attest from farming two widely distant parcels), even though micro-climates do not vary widely among small dispersed plots in the same general area.

But hedging against disaster cannot hide the intrinsically *uneconomical* nature of working tiny plots widely dispersed (as I can also confirm: many farmers defend their farming of unconnected land *until* they finally can consolidate their farm; no one would pass up such an opportunity merely in order to "spread risks"). Time is lost in commuting to various scattered plots. Numerous pathways and borders gobble up arable land; confusion and argumentation with scores of neighbors over multifarious boundaries raise havoc (e.g., K. Thompson 10–12; Chisholm 46–64).

Nor must we imagine, as is often assumed, that land fragmentation was the norm in *ancient* Greece. ("It may be concluded," concluded Kenneth Thompson, "that, generally speaking, farm fragmentation in Greece, at least in its present form, is a *modern* development" [21; emphasis added]) Besides the attention in utopian literature of the *polis* to limiting offspring, we also hear that lessees of farm land attempted to consolidate by renting parcels adjoining their own (Osborne 1987: 71–72; 1988: 316–17; cf. Chisholm 64–65), or through trading and other special arrangements (e.g., Lane-Fox 1983: 210, 219–20; Hodkinson 1988: 40–41). There seems to be little evidence that the ancient Greek farmer was ever forced to farm a number of minuscule, widely separated plots, or even to dower all daughters with land. The few scattered bits of evidence that do suggest multiple parcels are nearly all from Attica in the late fifth and fourth centuries—and all, I think, refer to the estates of the most wealthy (e.g., Davies 1971: 52–54; Pritchett 1956: 275–76; Osborne 1985: 48–52; 1987: 38–40). I can find nowhere in ancient literature mention that the five to fifteen acre farms of the hoplite farmers were *routinely* broken up into smaller and widely separated plots. On every occasion when scholars assert that the Greeks worked fragmented farms, the chief evidence cited is simply the custom in modern, not ancient, Greece.

The Greek farmer, given time and patience, resolved the issue of inheritance in a manner that preserved the integrity of his farm. Sometimes a man could deliberately limit offspring or would prove infertile (e.g., Arist. *Pol.* 2.1265b5–12; Plut. *Sol.*21.3). More radically, farmers might disown heirs (cf. Ael. *Ep.* 19), or acquire land from (childless?) others (e.g., Pl. *Resp.* 1.330B–C). Untimely death—from disease, accident, or war—could reduce the potential number of inheritors. Constant peril is a fact somewhat ignored; many recent studies show that in antiquity only two of six children might outlive their parents, indicating there was often a likelihood that only one *male* child was in a position to take over the farm. It has been argued that sixty-seven percent of Athenian families numbered only between two and four persons (e.g., Gallant 1991: 23–24). Robert Sallares, quoting more precise figures, argues that an average completed family size of 5.5 children was no guarantee that male children would survive the father. In fact, in over fifty percent of such cases either *no* children at all, or only a *single* male heir, would outlive the father. There were mechanisms—trading, marriages, special bequests—by which heirless landowners were able to transfer their holdings to those who had inherited either small properties or none at all (see Sallares 214–16; Osborne 1988: 309), in order that land intactness could continue (see, e.g., Galt 182–91; Forbes 1982: 151).

Some children who had no wish to farm or even to own property (e.g., Is. 2.28; Dem. 44.10) could receive payment in cash or other property *in lieu* of land (e.g., Halstead and Jones 1989: 42). Perhaps the question of land division might be put off for a generation, two siblings agreeing to share the land. That way, if one proved childless, the other's offspring could inherit the grandfather's farm. In short, no uniform picture is possible for agricultural inheritance in ancient Greece. Farms, if all else failed, might be partitioned, later recombined, and then partitioned again, generation after generation. An endless cycle of diminution and then aggregation is far more likely than inevitable fragmentation, which logically would have no end. The ancient Greek family farm plot may not always have remained pristine within its exact ancestral borders, but farms would tend to remain largely in the same area, expanding and contracting depending on the changing success or failure of each ensuing generation.

5. See Forbes 1976c: 7, for soil pulverization; Semple 1928: 96, for straw mulches. On the reverence for gardens and groves, see Ferriolo 89–91; Osborne 1992b: 377–82, 39.

6. In general, the ancients were well aware of a wide spectrum of tree and vine pests, and knew various substances (e.g., minerals, plants, animals) that could be placed in orchards and vineyards as repellents (see Burford 1993: 138–9). Their rich agronomic tradition is surely a sign that ancient Greek farmers continually experimented with various methods of improving crop production (e.g., Theophr. *CP* 5.8.2–5.18.4; cf. especially Amouretti 1986: 223–238). Simplistic and mistaken is the old idea that "agricultural techniques were stabilized at a rather primitive level and thereafter did not develop" (Weber 1976: 147; cf. Isager and Skydsgaard 199).

7. Most anecdotes in literature revolve around agrarians traveling into the *polis* to peddle their harvests (e.g., Aen. Tact. 28.5). The image of Chremes in Aristophanes' *Ecclesiazusae* (815–22; cf. Pl. *Polit.* 289E; Plut. *Arat.* 8) selling his grapes in town to buy barley was not a new phenomenon of fifth- or fourth-century Athens, a time when considerable profits and losses on the local level were constantly taking place (Osborne 1988: 290–91). Nor is Theophrastus's "loud mouth" simply a fourth-century "character," when he babbles on about the falling price of wheat and his uncertainty of what to plant the next year on his farm (Theophr. *Char.* 3.3–4). The picture of the Attic farmer packing food for the local market is also confirmed in a play of the comedian Philemon (e.g., fr. 89 Kock). Herodotus believed that the ubiquity and accessibility of open markets (like the Hellenic brand of hoplite fighting) made the Greeks quite unlike their Persian and Egyptian neighbors (1.153; 2.35, 39; 9.7.2; cf. Pritchett *War* 1.42). Hesiod's early seventh-century farmer likewise was advised to travel off the farm to unload surpluses (*Op.* 617–40; cf. Hahn 1983: 30–31).

8. Theophrastus warns of strong manure: "But even things that help the tree and give it aid will destroy it if accumulated in too much quantity or potency or at the wrong time, as for example, manure that is put on either without interruption all at once or in too much quantity or having too much power, as for example tanner's manure. For this manure when put on undiluted is believed to kill just about every kind of tree. And so do all manures that are too hot and dry and in short too strong, and that are not the right type for the particular tree. For as we have said, there are certain manures that are suited for different trees" (CP 5.15.3).

9. On the complexity and greater labor and skill required by viticulture, see Amouretti 1988: 5–6; Brumfield 28–37. The Greek notion that civilization could be gauged by the degree of intensive, stable agriculture is explored by Vanbremeersch 79–82.

Chapter 5: Before Democracy: Agricultural Egalitarianism and the Ideology Behind Greek Constitutional Government

1. Modern political science has rediscovered that egalitarian thinking and shared economic enterprise lead, not follow, political reform: "Where norms and networks of civic engagement are lacking, the outlook for collective action appears bleak. . . . The civic community has deep historical roots. This is a depressing observation for those who view institutional reform as a strategy for political change" (Putnam 183).

2. E.g., Plut. *Mor.* 226B2; cf. Aristotle's comparison of Greek municipal layout to the planting of a vineyard (*Pol.* 7.1330b29–30) or Thrasyboulos' identification of those citizens with excessive ambition with the tall ears that tower over the others in a grainfield (Hdt. 5.92; cf. Arist. *Pol.* 3.1284a30–1). This ideology of agrarian egalitarianism and uniformity was definitely not communistic

(Arist. *Pol.* 2.1263b2–1264b25). The notion of common property ownership is discussed (and more or less rejected) in the utopia of Plato's *Republic,* in the fantasy of Aristophanes' *Ecclesiazusae* (revealingly, both works derive from the fourth century when agrarianism gradually came under assault) and found in a few atypical communities on the fringes of the Greek world (Dawson 37–43; Figueira 1984b:204–6; Guiraud 638–639). Everywhere else equality in property ownership was to be accomplished through social pressure, constitutional government, military arms—and ethical, moral, and religious stricture.

3. Davis 1991: 131 (emphasis added); cf. Starr 1977:159, 246. Other rural sociologists bear out these observations that small farms are more efficient economically and thus have a greater propensity to foster rural development: "Quality of social conditions is associated with scale of operation . . . and it is reasonable to believe that farm size is the most important cause of these differences" (Goldschmidt 423).

4. Evidence of larger farms: Ar. *Eccl.* 592; [Dem.] 13.30; Dem. 23.208. On the estate of Phainippos: [Dem.] 42. 5, 7, 9, 20, 24, 28; de Ste. Croix 1966: 112; Burford 1993: 69–70. On the holdings of Alcibiades, Aristophanes, and Lysimachos: Pl. *Alc.* 123C; Lys. 19.29, 42; cf. de Ste. Croix 1966: 111; Davies 1971: 19–21; 202; Isager and Skydsgaard 78; Dem. 20.115; Plut. *Arist.* 27.1; Is. 5.22; see Finley 1981b: 64–65. On Plato's "myriad plethra," see Pl. *Tht.*174E2; Lucian *Icar.* 18.5; on the occasional exaggeration and inexactness of the Greek "myriad" cf. Hanson 1992: 210–15.

5. Finley 1981b: 65; on moderate farm size as the Greek standard, see Hodkinson and Hodkinson 274–76; Weber 1976: 197–99; Bolkestein 26–27; Finley 1952: 58, 63; Guiraud 391–434; Jardé 120–22; Michell 43; Pritchett 1956: 275–6. For the "big farms," cf. Lohmann 1992: 51; Osborne 1992a: 23–25; Foxhall 1992: 156–57. For the Cliff House, see Langdon and Watrous 175; southern Attica: Lohmann 1992: 49–51; farms on Euboea: Keller and Wallace 1988: 154.

6. Andreyev 14–15; see also Finley 1952: 58–60; Lewis 1973: 187–212; Cooper 1978: 168–72; Burford 1993: 67–72. On the viability of small farms in antiquity, see Bintliff and Snodgrass 142; Gallant 1991: 82–86; Osborne 1987: 46; Cooper 1978: 168–72; Hanson 1983: 37–38; Isager and Skydsgaard 78–79; Burford 1993: 27–28. The ten-acre size of farm seems to have been fairly common in Attica in the fifth century. If the cultivable area of ancient Attica surrounding Athens was a little larger than 200,000 acres (Cooper 1978: 171; see Jardé 49–50; 78–79; Garnsey 1988: 90–91; Osborne 1985a: 225 n.82) and *if* there were about 20,000 landholding citizens (cf. Hanson 1992: 225–28), then there may have been about 20,000 farms of the typical eight- to ten-acre-size, perhaps including 1,000–2,000 larger plots, together with a few very small farms of the poor. That there was an average size plot of about ten acres, that there was a total of about 20,000 landowning citizens in fifth-century Athens, and

that the available land in Attica was somewhat greater than 200,000 acres are all compatible, rather than incompatible, figures. Later, at Athens in the fourth century there may have been a census qualification of about 2,000 drachmas demarcating infantry service, a cash qualification used in place of the old Solonian classification of 200–300 annual measures of produce. (A. H. M. Jones 1957: 142 n.50; Ferguson 25–26; but cf. Patterson 176–78). We also have seen that Athens could sell farm property for a uniform price of about fifty drachmas per *plethron* (.221 acres, Lewis 1973: 196–97; Andreyev 14–15; cf. Boeckh 89). If we translate *plethra* into drachmas (i.e., farm size into cash equivalents), the 2,000-drachma qualification would be about the same as owning forty *plethra* (8.9 acres). This equation might suggest that in the fourth century Athens for official purposes may have based its net cash worth for the hoplite census on the old notion of a typical yeoman plot. Michael Jameson has correctly rejected the idea of a subsistence "peasantry" at Athens: "If all of these hoplites owned land and we use the largest current estimate for the cultivable land of Attica (96,000 hectares = 237,120 acres) and suppose that their properties averaged 50 *plethra* (4.5 hectares = 11.115 acres) in size they would have held 90,000 hectares (222,3000 acres), leaving some 6,000 hectares (14,820 acres) for the richest and poorest. . . . In any case, the notion of a mass of self-sufficient, independent subsistence farmers as the backbone of Athenian society becomes very questionable. It seems much more likely that the bulk of Classical Athenian farmers were in the hoplite class, had at least one male slave and generally lived above the subsistence level, as in most of the more populous and prosperous parts of Greece" (Jameson 1992: 144). Critics on the other extreme, who argue not for a "mass" of minuscule plots owned by a horde of subsistence peasants, but an "elite" in the Attic countryside composed of a few aristocrats, can prove much less than they think. They have suggested that the Athenian liturgical class (about 1,000 to 2,000 male citizens) held nearly twenty to thirty percent of all land in Attica (e.g., Osborne 1992a: 24–26; Foxhall 1992: 156–57). Even if that were true (and there is *no* evidence that it is), it still would suggest that these more elite farms were of only about fifty acres or so in size (i.e., 1,500 wealthy estate holders owning fifty-acre farms = 75,000 acres or .316 percent of the 237,120 total acres in Attica), and that *nearly two-thirds of the arable land of Attica was in the hands of the hoplite, landowning class*, which perhaps numbered half of the citizen population. This pattern was a remarkably *egalitarian* system of property ownership!

  7. Hellenistic and Roman farm size: Pl. *HN* 13.92; 18.35–37, 33.135; *Ep.* 3.19; Sen. *Ep.* 87.7; Col. *Rust.* 1.3.12; cf. Day 230–51; Rostovtzeff 1979: 75; Green 368; Duncan-Jones 127–42; Jones 1974: 120–24.

  8. For Melos, see Thuc. 5.116; cf. Jameson 1977: 125; for later Roman and Hellenistic farms, see Finley 1973a: 111–13.

  9. The agrarianism in Plato's *Laws* is clear (indeed an entire set of agrari-

an legislation [*nomoi geôrgikoi*] is found in his *Laws* at 8.842E6–846C8; see Klingenberg 29–139). Every citizen by law is to retain a plot of land, his *klêros*. This ground cannot be reduced beyond a necessary minimum (*Leg.* 5.744D–E; 9.855B, 8.850A). Such farm property is sufficient to support a citizen's family. It is to be forever unchangeable, indivisible, and incapable of being sold, donated, mortgaged, or confiscated by the state (*Leg.* 5.740A–741E, 740B, 741B, 9.855A, 11.928E–929A; Klingenberg 5–20). Plato desires a reactionary return to the agrarian property-holding scheme of the *early polis* of at least a century past. In his ideal countryside "the *klêros* remains forever tied to a single individual, passed on to a single natural or adopted heir" (Fuks 148–49; 153; Guiraud 582–88). "The egalitarian logic of this development," Paul Rahe points out, "Plato carried to its conclusion. In constructing his imaginary Cretan city, he proposed a comprehensive body of legislation aimed at stabilizing the division of wealth. To foster concord, he made the original allotments of farmland roughly equal in product and decreed them inalienable" (Rahe 71; cf. Lauffer 233–39; Bisinger 12–55).

   10. Even at Sparta, which was in many ways an atypical city-state, there was a long tradition that the privileged Spartiates held land on an equitable basis. Much of Spartan land-tenure remains obscure (see Hodkinson 1986: 404–6; cf. Isager and Skydsgaard 129–32; Spahn 88–111), but it seems that the mythical lawgiver Lycurgus supposedly had parceled out the land of Laconia, dividing it up afresh as a basis of uniformity among the citizens (e.g., Plut. *Lyc.* 8.3.6). The difference at Sparta was her conquest of neighboring Messenia and the ensuing need for constant subjugation of that larger land and its subservient population. Annexation of foreign territory had arrested the usual evolution of Greek agrarianism: serfdom in place of chattel slavery; a much smaller landowning citizenry than the other Greek city-states of comparable size in both relative and absolute numbers; a huge cultivable area under the control of a single *polis*; a farm-owning, but not farmworking, citizenry; a professional, rather than an amateur, hoplite army; public rather than private ownership of arms. True, we see a veneer of agrarianism among the few Spartiates (cf. Plut. *Mor.* 226B2)—hoplite infantry, equal plots, restrictions against the wealthy, the idea of shared ordeal (e.g., Plut. *Mor.* 228E27). But the majority outside the agrarian net was *so large* that the population of the surrounding region as a whole was never able to create agricultural *poleis* along more typical Greek lines. The nature of Spartan society in general reflects a *non*agrarian direction for the vast majority of the population.

   11. For agrarian egalitarianism in colonies, see Asheri 1963: 20–21; Runciman 1982: 366; Isager and Skydsgaard 123; Boyd and Jameson: 332–37. For the Crimea, see, Pecírka and Dufkova 123–74; for Halieis: Boyd and Jameson 332–37; for southern Italy: J. Carter 1981: 167–78; for Thurii: Dawson 23–26. So-called foundation decrees, surviving formal public documents on

stone and metals that outline precise procedures to be followed in creating Greek colonies, confirm the evidence of archaeology. The inscribed laws concerning the foundation of the Greek cities Cyrene (630 B.C.?) and Naupactus (500–475 B.C.?) list provisions concerning the systematic division of land along egalitarian lines and strict laws governing inheritance (e.g., *SEG* IX.3. 31–37; Meiggs and Lewis 20.17–19, 22–29, 35–38; cf. Koerner 445–48). Similarly, statutes governing new settlements in West Locris and at "Black" Corcyra (an island in the northern Adriatic) stipulated penalties for any who advocated redistribution of the original egalitarian land division (see Graham 1983: 58–60; Métraux 75–78). The epigraphic evidence also confirms the archaeological picture that colonies started out with an equitable division of farmland, a product of careful land division and statutes outlining inheritance and land acquisition procedures (Graham 1983: 59–62). In short, in colonies "subdivision, inalienability and fixed allotments of land are basic principles" (Métraux 87; Isager and Skydsgaard 124–25).

12. Michael Jameson has written that these remarkably uniform colonial grids, "like new constitutions, have the great virtue for the historian of making explicit the principles espoused by community. Initially the principle of equality prevailed" (1990: 175; cf. especially Guiraud 81–89). If we examine carefully some additional formally organized colonies, land divison there inevitably proceeds from the assumption that existing territory should be divided into equal shares, *not* simply sold to the highest bidder. There may have been a few colonists who, for some meritorious service, were granted parcels two or three times larger than the ideal size. But this was rare and apparently something decided by the community as a whole. Even as late as the third century, during the twilight of Greek agrarianism, many colonists apparently maintained the old creed that property divisions should be small and roughly of equal size. At Pharsalos in northern Greece in the third century sixty *plethra* (13.3 acres) was the standard-sized farm, a stereotypical figure also appearing at Larissa in Thessaly, where a redistribution scheme resulted in an average-sized plot of about thirteen acres (see Gallant 1991: 86; cf. Burford 1993: 67). On the Crimean Chersonesos a vast complex of about 25,000 acres of rectangular agricultural plots has been uncovered. The land was at some date (the fourth century) parceled out according to a *uniform* grid, resulting in roughly equal farms (usually with an accompanying farmhouse) of about eleven or twelve acres (Pecírka and Dufkova 129–31, 134).

13. On the concern of the wealthy for the poor, see Gallant 1991: 148–49; 194–95; Isocr. 7. 20, 31, cf. Fuks 57–59; Métraux 64–65; Woodhouse 143 n.42.

14. Rarity of Greek property tax during the *polis* period: Padgug 101; Alcock 26. *Eisphora* at Athens falling largely on the more wealthy: Hodkinson 1992: 54; Thomsen 140–41; Isager and Skydsgaard 141–42. On Dionysius's looting and taxing, see Polyaen. *Str.* 5.2.19, 21; Arist. *Pol.* 5. 1313b25–30. For

the general increase in taxes during Hellenistic times, see Kreibig 11–12. For deleterious effects of taxation on the countryside, see Arist. *Pol.* 5.1313b25–29; cf. Pl. *Leg.* 8.850A–B.

15. Even at Athens by the fifth and fourth centuries—a city-state hardly the most devoted of the Greek *poleis* to local farmers—E. M. Wood believed that the would-be exploitive wealthy man and his apparatus of government "were restricted by the configuration of social and political power represented by the democracy, which limited opportunities for concentrating property and afforded protection to small producers against certain forms of dependency" (Wood 56). J. K. Davies has pointed out that "of fifth and fourth century Athens fewer than 1,000 men out of a total population which may have reached 250,000 could be called 'rich' in normal Greek parlance" (1981: 35).

16. Small percentage of public land at Athens: Lewis 1973: 198–99; 1990: 259; Andreyev 43; cf. Thuc. 3.50.2; cheap rents of temple estates: Osborne 1988 284–85; temple lands rented to the less well-off: Métraux 63–66. Taxes for unproductive Hellenistic monarchs and Christian dignitaries: Kreibig 20–25; de Ste. Croix 1981: 495–96. In fact, most of Greek religion was agrarian centered and without large bureaucracies. The goddess Athena's blessing in Aeschylus' *Eumenides* was largely agrarian and called for sunlight, breezes, and enough harvests to keep the *polis* strong (*Eum.* 905–9; cf. 938–45). At Athens, a city where the myth of the gift of the olive tree by Athena (Hdt. 8.55) was the foundation of Athenian public religion itself, all olive stumps and "sacred" olive trees were protected by religious strictures, and often bypassed during enemy invasions (e g., Dem. 43.71; Lys. 7.7; 7.25; Androtion *FGrH* 324 fr.39; Philochorus *FGrH* 328 fr.125; Istros *FGrH* 334 fr.30). Some fig trees, like olives, were also given religious protection (see Boeckh 62–63). Recent arguments have suggested that the birth of the *polis* in its formal sense is not to be marked by the construction of the infrastructure in the city-state proper, but rather by the prior appearance of *rural* sanctuaries and cults, which reflected the immediate needs of the incipient farming population (e.g., de Polignac 49–66; cf. 23–34), which arose *before* a resident municipal citizenry. City-state religion, in short, was originally of an agrarian nature, and continued to cherish rural cults and festivities, which were based on precise tasks of the agricultural year (Brumfield 1–10; 54–117; 223–40; Isager and Skydsgaard 165–68; Burford 1993: 104–5). At Athens, the festival of the "holy sowing" was a ritualistic public enactment of cereal planting with imprecations and offerings given up to ensure continual supply of food for the *polis* (Ashmole 9–10). We hear of a variety of local and minor deities who had a hand in the agricultural success of farmers (cf. Jameson 1951: 54–56). In addition to communal religious observance, individual *geôrgoi* often, like modern farmers today, prayed privately and constantly for agricultural success. A man offered a lamb to Demeter so that "every year she should make his field rich in barley and wheat" (*Anth. Pal.* 6.28). Xenophon's Socrates

observes: "The gods are in control of farming operations no less than they are in war." He adds: "The prudent offer prayers to them for their fruits, cereals, cattle, horses, sheep, and for everything they possess" (*Oec.* 5.19–20; Plut. *Mor.* fr. 67; cf. Plut. *Mor.* fr. 67; Xen. *Oec.* 5.19–20). Quite unmistakably, the impression we receive from Greek literature is that whether a farmer sowed, reaped, planted, or dug, he prayed, sang, and cursed to the gods who inhabited the superstitious world out on his farm (e.g., Hes. *Op.* 780–2; 391–3; and cf. 764–821).

17. Asheri 1963: 2; 20–21; see Pecírka 1968: 192–95; Métraux 86–88; cf. Isager and Skydsgaard: "Everything indicates that there was no major difference in the size of farms in Classical Athens. It was a direct consequence of a consistent legislation with regard to citizenship and inheritance." Asheri posits an agrarian exemplar between the two extremes of rich estate holders and landless poor, between rightist aristocracies and left-leaning landless democracies: "The freedom of selling family lots happened to be frequent in radical democracies and narrow oligarchies, while the moderate constitutions abated or limited this power in order to prevent land concentration" (Asheri 1963: 4). The impression in our ancient sources is that the moderate agrarian constitution with a low property qualification was the model of Greek constitutional government among the Greek city-states of the entire *polis* period, the benchmark from which those few "deviant" communities both on the left and the right either expanded or restricted the franchise as they saw fit. No wonder that one scholar, despairing of the inadequacy of Greek constitutional rubrics to identify these agrarian governments, recently concluded that "the differences between the ideal middle constitution, the moderate democracy, and the moderate oligarchy do not seem that significant anyway" (Dawson 109 n.45).

18. Early Greek vocabulary for equality: *Carm. Convival.* 893, 896 [Page]; Alcmaeon 4; Anaximander 12B1[DK]; Theogn. 678; cf. Hdt. 5.92.a1. Aristotle's agrarian democracy not the same as radical Athenian democracy: M. H. Hansen 68–69. Aristotle at least "clearly recognized that democracy normally meant the absence of a property qualification for citizenship, or the participation of all freeborn and native-born males in government" (Dawson 48 n. 35; cf. Larsen 3).

19. Displeasure over influence of urban poor at Athens: [Xen.] *Ath. Pol.* 1.2, 2.14; Xen. *Hell.* 2.3.48–49; Pl. *Leg.* 4.706B–C. On the numbers present in the Athenian *ekklesia*, see M. H. Hansen 130–32. For the idea that those in the assembly and law courts more often were urban and poor, see Ar. *Eccl.* 300; cf. M. H. Hansen 127; A. M. Jones 1957: 109–11.

20. In that same tradition, much later the agricultural grandee Cicero could write in Roman times: "Nothing is better than agriculture; nothing more fruitful, nothing sweeter, nothing more suitable for a free man" (*Off.* 1.150–51). Throughout the Roman Republic most agronomists and philosophers echoed the advantages of the legacy of Greek agrarianism—just as the Italian yeoman

was giving way to the absentee owner and the much larger estate. Columella believed that a well-ploughed small farm produced more profit than a (typically) poorly managed estate (*Rust.* 1.3.8–13), a truism that soon became a hackneyed theme in Latin literature in general: "Praise large estates but cultivate a small one" (Virg. *Georg.* 2.412); "It is wiser to sow less and plough more" (Pliny *HN* 18.7); and in general, cf. White 1970a 346–47; Wolf 67–74.

Chapter 6 The Ways of Fighters

1. Exaggeration of phalanx innovation in the fourth century: Hanson 1988: 204–7; tactics of Spartan phalanxes: Lazenby 1991: 103–5; use of cavalry during the *polis* period: Greenhalgh 96–145; Bugh 36–38; reluctance for sieges, missile troops, and integration of heavy and light infantry before the fifth century: Hanson 1989: 27–39; Anderson 1970:111–40. Traditional interest in the improved military science of the Hellenistic era: Delbrück 175–252.

2. See Salmon 1977: 90. On this presence of less formal massed attack in the eighth century, see Wheeler 1991: 126–50; Anderson 1991: 15. Mass fighting without the hoplite panoply: Xen. *An.* 1.8.9; 7.8.15; *Cyr.* 6.2.10; 6.3.23; 7.1.33; various weapons employed in the mass: Tyrt. 10.21–25; 11. 23–24; 35–38; complex construction and difficult usage of the panoply, see Blyth 14; Cartledge 1977: 20 n. 71.

3. Cavalry were often irrelevant in battle between phalanxes (Bugh 36–37; Adcock 47–53; Nilsson 246), but became of real value in rugged terrain against non-hoplite troops, cf. Bugh 39–78; Delbrück 55. The idea that wealthy knights would play no important role in the defense of their community was a peculiarity of classical culture, not to be embraced by any society in the West until modern times.

4. On our knowledge of hoplite warfare before the fifth century, see Hanson 1989: 43–44; Connor 3–24; cf. Wheeler 1991: 125–26; Frost 183–86; Lonis 28–30. For the connection between farming and hoplite service, see Starr 1977: 177–87; Finley 1981a 120–52; Andrewes 1956: 31–42; Busolt and Swoboda 823–24. For the unusual idea that farmers should not be the infantry of the community, cf. *Pol.* 7.1329a40-1330b43; Pl. *Resp.* 2. 369E; 374E; cf. Isager and Skydsgaard 149–52.

5. Ironically, hoplite fighting originated over poorer soil distant in highlands and foothills; see Jameson 1991: 210; Connor 9; Pritchett 1956: 256; Métraux 50–52. We *do* hear occasionally of men killed, ambushed, and lost in rough terrain. But at least before the fifth century, these occurrences either happened under special circumstances or were not decisive resolutions to major campaigns. Instead, they involved rout and escape, the presence of foreign troops, or the frequent plundering raid, rather than formal pitched battle between like-minded equals of warring *poleis*.

6. For the wings of phalanxes, see Pritchett *War* 1.134–54; *War*

2.190–207. For the usual neglect of trickery, see Pritchett *War* 2.156; cf. Wheeler 1988: 25–49. On occasional collapse before battle, see Hanson 1989: 96–104. Some examples of rudimentary tactics of the phalanx are the following: the strengthening of wings at Marathon (490 B.C.), the exchange of Spartans and Athenians at Plataea (479 B.C.), the outflanking attempts of the Spartans at Mantineia (418 B.C.), Coroneia (394 B.C.), Nemea (394 B.C.), and Leuctra (371 B.C.), the Theban tendency to stack deep at Delium (424 B.C.), Coroneia (394 B.C.), Nemea (394 B.C.), Leuctra (371 B.C.), and Mantineia (362 B.C.. Lack of opportunity for battlefield command: Hanson 1988: 200–206; Hanson 1989: 107–16; cf. Delbrück 286. Agrarian distrust of those in authority: Walcot 1970: 97–106.

7. See Pl. *Ion* 540C–542B; cf. Ar. *Ran.* 1034–5; Pl. *Lach.* 191A–B; Xen. *Symp.* 4.6. Hoplite initiative and insubordination in decision making: Hdt. 9.53.2; Plut. *Phoc.* 25.1; Xen. *Hell.* 6.4.4–5; *An.* 3.4.4–46; Thuc. 5.6.2, 5.7.2, 5. 65.6, 8.78.1; Theophr. *Char.* 13.7. A soldier's general: Hanson 1989: 106–16; questioned by Wheeler 1991: 152–154; but see Pritchett *Topography* 8.62. n. 67.

8. For the old and poorly fit in the phalanx, see Hanson 1989: 89–95; Andoc. fr. 3.1; Hdt. 1.30; Eur. *Heracl.* 723–25; Plut. *Mor.* 192C–D; Pl. *Resp.* 8.556D. Examples of idealized youth on vases: Ducrey 51, 56, 136. Even today in the final decades of American agrarianism to see an exclusive array of farmers is an arresting enough sight, far from the sanitized photo on the farm magazine cover. Visit a farm auction or an end-of-the-year cooperative meeting. The visual and acoustical imagery is striking: deeply tanned and wrinkled folk of few words and weathered hands and faces, overwhelming middle-aged. They present with the incongruous combination of muscular arms and ample guts, their more formal attire in worse taste than their everyday work clothes; they are men whose word for "yes" is inevitably "you bettcha," "sure can," or "why not?" (cf. Ar. fr. 685 Kock: "rugged speech with a rural flavor").

9. On the hoplite war cry, see Xen. *An.* 1.8.18; Ar. *Av.* 364; Aesch. *Sept.* 270; Plut. *Thes.* 22.4; Pind. fr. 78. For hoplite activity and relaxation in the hours before battle, see Lonis 126; Hanson 1989: 126–31; Ducrey pl. 39; Hdt. 1.63; Pritchett *War* 2.155.

10. Loss of morale when losses were tallied: Aen. Tact. 26.7–8; the use of wagons after battle: Aen. Tact. 16.5–6; occasional rotting and bloated corpses: Men. *Asp.* 69–72, 109–10; Pl. *Resp.* 10.614b; Thuc. 4.97–101; decaying bodies improve the soil: Archil. fr. 148; cf. Plut. *Mor.* 669A; Strabo 16.4.26; Plato's protestation against stripping bodies: *Resp.* 5. 469C–D; problems in identification of remains: Men. *Asp.* 76–77; cf. Polyaen. *Strat.* 1.17; Diod. 8.27.2.

11. Occasional Spartan victories abroad at the battles of Amphipolis (422 B.C.) and Nemea River (394 B.C.); cf. Thuc. 5.6–11; Xen. *Hell.* 4.2.9–23. More numerous defeats outside Laconia: Cartledge 1979: 126 (Hysiae); Hdt. 1.66–68; 7.212–19; Xen. *Hell.* 3.5.22–24; 4.5.11ff.; 6.4.16–26; Plut. *Pel.* 16.1–17.3.

12. Twenty-one major battles involving hoplites on at least one side: Hysiae, Tegea, Sepeia, Marathon, Plataea, Dipaea, Tanagra, Oinophyta, first and second Coroneia, Delium, Amphipolis, first and second Mantineia, Syracuse, Assinarus River, Haliartos, Nemea, Tegyra, Leuctra, Crimesus. Sixteen of the twenty-one battles where there were clearly hoplite defensive troops fighting on their native soil: Hysiae, Tegea, Sepeia, Marathon, Plataea, Dipaea, Tanagra, Oinophyta, first Coroneia, Delium, Syracuse, Assinarus River, Haliartos, Tegyra, Leuctra, Crimesus. Twelve of these sixteen battles where the defenders were victorious: Hysiae, Tegea, Marathon, Plataea, Tanagra, first Coroneia, Delium, Assinarus River, Haliartos, Tegyra, Leuctra, Crimesus.

Chapter 7. The Economy of Agrarian Warfare

1. On the laws of the Greeks, see Wheeler 1987: 180; Pritchett *War* 2.251–52; Karavites 13–26; Arnould 138–53; de Romilly 1968: 207–20; Garlan 1975: 23–77; Busolt and Swoboda 1260–62. Fourth-century views of the prior economy of hoplite warfare: Polyb. 18.3.3; Aeschin 2.115; Plut. *Phil.* 13.6; Thuc. 5.41; Isoc. 8.48–54; Pl. *Resp.* 5.469B-71B; *Menex* 242D.

2. For defense expenditure during the Peloponnesian War, see Kagan 36–42; Meiggs and Lewis 61, 78, 84; Michell 361–63; Gomme *Comm.* 2.16–47; Kinkel 84–87; and cf. especially Boeckh 345–400. Fourth-century awareness of the cost of fighting: Arist. *Rhet.* 1.1359a–1360a; Xen. *Vect.* 1.1–2.

3. Plundering and raiding as sources of financial gain in warfare: Finley 1978: 49–50; 99–100; 125–128; Pritchett *War* 5.568–504.

4. On Spartan military practice, see Lazenby 1985: 3–7; Anderson 1970: 225–50; Cartledge 1987: 43–46. Her military infrastructure (i.e., training, finance, organization, control of arms) is unlike any found in the other Greek city-states. After all, few other agrarian *poleis* chose to solve their growing problems of population and food supply in the eighth and seventh centuries by simply annexing and enslaving their neighbors. Incidentally, the same ambiguity is nearly true of Sparta's agrarian infrastructure. Her nightmarish system of helotage—the ancient equivalent of *apartheid*—was reproduced only sporadically in a few kindred atypical *poleis*. Nevertheless, the crops grown and the agricultural technique practiced on her farms by helot workers may not have been dissimilar to farms elsewhere surrounding other Greek city-states. Among the small elite of Spartiates themselves, most farm properties until the fourth century were probably of about equal size.

5. Distrust of seafaring: Theog.1200–1202; Hes. *Op.* 630, 641–42; Plut. *Mor.* 239E42. For the absence of early navies, see Thuc. 1.13–14; Hdt. 7.144; cf. Amit 19–20; Morrison and Williams 128–29; de Ste Croix 1972: 393–95. The trireme—the backbone of the later fifth-century Athenian navy—may not even have been invented until 550 B.C. (see Davison 18–24). That was a full century and a half *after* the appearance of hoplite arms and armor and the emergence of diversified, intensive agriculture.

6. For unusual conditions when hoplites might not supply their own arms, see Xen. *Lac. Pol.* 11.2; *Ages.* 1.26; Nep. *Ages.* 42.4; Pl. *Men.* 249A; Arist. *Ath. Pol.* 42.4. For the later practice of state-supplied armies or individual donations, see Diod. 12.68.5, 14.43.2–3, 15.13.2; Polyaen. *Str.* 3.8; Dem. 18.116; cf. Thuc. 6.72.4, 8.25.6.

7. For the cost of arms, see Connor 10–11 n. 30; cf. Jackson 1991: 229; McKechnie 94 n.12. On the wage of a day worker, see Busolt and Swoboda 195–210.

8. To take a better illustration of the affordability of the hoplite panoply in the fifth century, 75 to 100 drachmas might represent only a moderate cost to the owner of an average forty to sixty *plethra* hoplite farm (about nine to thirteen acres). At that time it was worth in a cash equivalent perhaps 2,000–3,000 drachmas (i.e., 50 drachmas/per *plethron*; Lewis 1973: 196–97). By the fourth century, many Greek farms were mortgaged out at an average of 1,000 drachmas—*ten times* more than the cost of a panoply alone—for private expenditure on dowries and gifts (e.g., Finley 1982: 66). The equipment of a larger city-state's armed force of (say) five thousand men (cf. Delbrück 63–66) represented the local agrarian community's total investment of about sixty to eighty talents (five thousand panoplies at 75–100 drachmas one talent = 6,000 drachmas). Sixty to eighty talents is a small fraction (i.e., three to four percent) of our token city-state's collective worth in land alone of between 1,660 and 2,500 talents (five thousand hoplites owning farms each worth 2,000–3,000 drachmas would have a total value roughly between 1,660 and 2,500 talents). At Athens in the later fourth century, 2,000 drachmas of net worth may have officially signaled the landowner's eligibility to purchase armor and so to enter the hoplite phalanx. (In actuality, these rubrics were by this time often ignored.) The farmer's outlay on military equipment (about 100 out of 2,000 drachmas) represented about five percent of his assessed landed capital. We must thus change our notion of the cost of hoplite arms and its relationship to service in the Greek phalanx: hoplite-farmers were not an elite bunch. Too often scholars have assumed that early census figures, such as the various classes of annual agricultural produce established by Solon at Athens (about 600 B.C.), were based solely on the individual's ability to purchase or to fabricate arms. These qualifying requirements were more likely predicated on more general economic and political criteria (e.g., Bugh 26–28).

9. Weapons dedicated, stockpiled, and stored: Hdt. 8.27; Polyb. 5.8.9; Xen. *Hell.* 5.4.8; Plut *Mor.* 598B; cf. Pritchett *Topography* 8: 73–74; see too Snodgrass 1980: 131 for the hypothetical estimate of 100,000 helmets dedicated at Olympia alone between 700 and 500 B.C.; Pritchett *War* 3.258–59, for the hundreds of shields stored on the Athenian acropolis. Duplicate sets of arms and armies outfitted in mass: Aen. Tact. 10.7, Thuc. 6.72.4; 8.25.6; Xen. *Hell.* 4.4.10; Diod. l2.68.5; 15.73.2; 14.43.23 (140,00 shields, 14,000 helmets); for

mass gifts of arms: Dem. 18.116; Diod. 17.85; Strabo. 10.4.16; Plut. *Mor.* 761B; *Demetr.* 17.

10. Enemy's weapons are "no good": Men. *Sent.* 239; Soph. *Ajax* 664–65; Spartans' reluctance to collect weapons of the defeated: Jackson 1991: 231; Pritchett *War* 3 292–93; utopian objections to stripping fallen Greeks: Pl. *Resp.* 5.469C–470A; Polyb. 10.17.1–5. Reemployment of enemy weaponry: Archil. 5; Diod. 16.80.6; Polyaen. *Str.* 3.8; Xen. *Ages* 12.6; cf. Plut. *Pel.* 12; Xen. *Hell.* 5.4.8; sale of defeated's arms: Xen. *An.* 5.3; adoption of enemy's weapons: Diod. 16.80.6; Polyb. 5.8.9; cf. Archil. 5; sale of weapons on the open market: Diod. 16.80.6; Dem. 45.65.

11. Mass production of weapons in workshops: Lys. 12.19; Diod. 14.43; Pl. *Polit.* 280D; Plut. *Mor.* 835B–C; Ar. *Aves* 491 *Pax* 1210ff; Dem. 36.11; and Ducrey pl. 135. Suggestions that a community's arms might be sold to rivals: Pl. *Leg.* 8.847D; Dem. 19.286; cf. Aen. Tact. 29–30.

12. Evidence that hoplite weapons might last for extended periods of time: Paus. 4.16.7; 8.21.1; 9.39.14; Arrian *An.* 1.11.7; Diod. 17.18; cf. Weiss 195–207. Breakage of wooden shields and spears: Plut. *Mor.* 219C; Xen *An.* 4.1.18; *Ages.* 2.14; Men. *Asp.* 75; Diod. 15.86.2; Hdt. 7.22.5; *Anth. Pal.* 6.84; and cf. the epitaph of Pythion of Megara (446 B.C.): who "broke seven spears (*hepta logchas*) in their bodies" (Meiggs and Lewis 51.2–3) and the ceramic evidence of at least seven broken spears portrayed about 570 B.C. on an unguent vase (Hackett 75).

13. For the literal pushing of phalanx battle, see Thuc. 4.96.2; 4.35.3; 6.70.2; Xen. *Hell.* 2.4.34, 6.4.14; Ar. *Vesp.* 1081–85; cf. A. J. Holladay 1982: 94–104; Pritchett *War* 4.65–67; Hanson 1989: 171–84. For many inside the phalanx in the center and at the rear, the shield must have been their chief mechanism for affecting the outcome of the battle.

14. For the rarity of major infantry campaigns before the fifth century, see Connor 5–6; Adcock 10; Wheeler 1991: 156n.19. Border hot spots that became the focus of repeated hoplite clashes: the high upland plateau of Thyreatis between Argos and Laconia (Hdt. 1.82; cf. Thuc. 5.83.2; *Anth. Pal.* 7.244; 7.431–2); the Mantinean-Tegean border (Thuc. 5.41.2); the Phocian-Locrian disputes over Parnassus (*Hell. Oxy.* 13.3); the battle in 461–460 between Megara and Corinth over boundary land (Thuc. 1.163.4); the Megarian-Athenian territorial squabbles over the *hiera orgas* (Thuc. 3.70.4–6; Dem. 23.212); the *methoria* at Panakton between Attica and Boeotia (Thuc. 5.42.1); the Oropos between Boeotia and Attica (Xen. *Hell.* 7.41; Diod. 15.76.1; see, too Thuc. 1.15.2, 4.134), and squabbles between members of the Boeotian confederacy (Hdt. 5.79.2).

15. Hoplite training in weapon handling and tactical maneuver was minimal for most of the life of the *polis*, see Xen. *Mem.* 3.12.5; *Lac. Pol.* 13.5; Thuc. 2.38–39; Arist. *Pol.* 8.1338b25–40; and see Pritchett *War* 2.208–31; 4.61–65; Anderson 1970: 84–110; Parke 54; Lazenby 1985: 3–5.

16. For the relationship between campaigning and the agricultural year, see Thuc. 1.141.3, 5; 1.142.7; 3.15.2; cf. 4.84.1–2; 4.88.1–2; Plut. *Agis* 15.2, Hdt. l.82; 7.9.2; Thuc. 5.41.2–3; Strabo l0.1.l2. Hoplite warfare not intended for extended mobilization and conquest: Arist. *Pol.* 7.1338b24–29; Thuc. 1.141.3–5; 2.39; 3.15.2; Plut. *Ages.* 26; *Mor.* 190A.

17. That is a scenario like German submarine or Allied bomber crews during the Second World War, who took no solace in the mathematics of a five percent "acceptable" loss ratio on any given mission, in light of their thirty-mission requirement and the slow, steady slaughter of kindred in their midst. When losses began to reach ten to eleven percent per mission, the rates immediately prompted "reappraisal" by strategic planners (e.g., Keegan 1989: 429).

18. Passages suggesting that casualties may have been light in hoplite fighting before the late fifth century: Lelantine War: Strabo l0.1.l2; cf. Wheeler 1987: 157–82; *monomachia:* Eur. *Phoen.* l227; Apollodorus 3.68; Hdt. 9.26.4; 9.75; cf. 5.1.2–3; battle of the three hundred: Hdt. l.82; battle of fetters: Hdt. 1.66–68; Persian War battles: Hdt. 6.ll7; 7.228–29; cf. Pritchett *War* 4.166–73; Hdt. 9.70.5; but cf. Plut. *Arist.* 19.5; Lazenby 1993: 246. Fatalities in fifth- and fourth-century hoplite battles at Delium, Mantineia, Coroneia, and Leuctra were never more than four thousand combined dead: Thuc. 4.101; 5.74; Xen. *Hell.* 4.3.1; 6.4.15; *Ages.* 7.5; Diod. 14.83.1; 14.84; Plut. *Ages.* 28.5; Paus. 9.13.12.

19. Generals at the head of their troops: Xen. *Hell.* 4.7.38, 6.4.13; Plut. *Per.* l0.l; *Mor.* 231F4; and see Adcock 82–91; Anderson 1970: 67–83; Hanson 1989: 107–116; Delbrück 133–71. Few battle victories can be attributed to superior tactics or generalship (cf. Lazenby 1993: 257–58).

20. Brief tenure of hoplite commanders: Polyaen *Str.* l.l8; Diod. 8.37; Paus. 4.l5.6; Arist. *Ath. Pol.* 26.l; little supporting command staff: Anderson 1970: 39–40; killed or wounded hoplite generals: Thuc. 1.63.3, 4 .44.l, 4.l0l.2, 5.10.9; and especially 3.l09.l, 4.38.l, 5.74.3, 2.79.7, cf. Hanson 1989: 107–8; 1988: 201–2.

21. The idea that anything other than stand-up fighting between hoplites was unheroic is frequent in all genres of Greek literature, see, e.g., Thuc. 4.40.2; Eur. *HF* 157–63; Plut. *Mor.* 191E; 234E; Hdt. 9.72.2; cf. Thuc. 3.98.4; Polyb. 18.3.3; Diod. 30.18.2.

Chapter 8. Hoplites as Dinosaurs

1. The topographer Pausanias preserves a tradition that at Marathon even Athenian hoplites had not been enough. Instead the *polis* had enfranchised slaves to join the ranks against this most unusual challenge (Paus. 1.29.7; 1.32.3; 7.15.7; cf. Sargent 209–11; Loraux 35–36; Welwei 22–36). The French historian Henri van Effenterre ended his history of the Greek city-state with the "defeat of Marathon," correctly seeing that the Athenians' victory on the

battlefield in 490 B.C. was a harbinger of the end of the traditional *polis*. Marathon was proof in the battle's aftermath that the Greek city-state was now to be reintegrated with larger economic, military, and political challenges far beyond its control (268–84).

2. See Polybius for the natural limitations of the later phalanx (Polyb. 18.30–32). On the Athenians' belief in their superior courage at Marathon, see Pl. *Leg.* 4.707A–D; Meiggs and Lewis 26. See Hdt. 7.9.2, for the famous carica-ture of hoplite battle.

3. On the size of Xerxes force, see Hignett 1963: 40, 94–95; 355; cf. Del-brück 35–36; 118–20.

4. Consider also the Theban turncoats who joined forces with the Per-sians at the battle of Plataea. As we have seen in Chapter 5, no region better typified the agrarian infantry ideal than the rural Boeotians. But now most no-toriously (they later blamed their treachery on a narrow cabal of aristocratic el-ements) they fought to enslave other Greeks (Hdt. 9.2–3; 9.15–17; 9.31; 9.67; 9.77–78). Boeotian duplicity was in sharp contrast to the patriotism of the land-less sailors of the other Greek city-states (Hdt. 9.8.1–2). The treachery of Thebes further brought into question (and disrepute?) the two-century exclu-sivity of war by hoplite phalanx. While much has been written about the effects of the Greeks' naval victories on the old *polis*, it is too readily forgotten that the disgraceful conduct of Thebes, the agrarian city-state *par excellence*, during the Persian Wars also irrevocably harmed the reputation of hoplite agrarianism.

5. On the problems of agricultural states in the new war, see Thuc. 1.141; cf. 3.15.1, 3.16.1–2. For the thousands of Athenians not involved in farming, see Ar. *Vesp.* 709; Arist. *Ath. Pol.* 24.3; cf. Plut. *Per.* 9.1. On the importance of capital, see again Thucydides 1.41.2–1.42.1. Hans Delbrück (341) once re-marked of the unusual strain on Roman manpower during the second Punic wars that only fifth-century Athens had a larger percentage of its population under arms, something only supportable from the tribute of subject *poleis*. Simi-larly, in lieu of cash contributions, the Spartan army and its entire culture of a permanent, mobilized military rested on the agricultural labor of some 170,000–200,000 indentured helots (cf. Cartledge 1987: 174–75).

6. E.g., Xen. [*Ath. Pol.*] 1.1–2; Pl. *Leg.* 4.706B–C; 707C; Arist. *Ath. Pol.* 27.1; *Pol.* 7.1327b5–17; Isocr. 8.48, 64, 69, 75, 101; Plut. *Them.* 2.3, 4.3, 7.9, cf. Hdt. 7.144.4; Thuc. 1.93.3. On the changes in battle practice during the Pelo-ponnesian war years, cf. Busolt and Swoboda 1194–98; Cartledge 1987: 45: "Set-piece battles, however, were thin on the ground in the Athenian War"; Adcock 17: "Before the first summer of that war was over, it had become plain that it would not be decided by a great pitched battle on land." On the unrivaled escala-tion of fighting between Athens and Sparta, see Thuc. 1.1; 1.23.1–3.

7. Arist. *Pol.* 7.1327b5–18. For noncitizen rowers, cf. Thuc. 1.121.3; 1.143.1; 7.13.2; 7.63.3–4; Xen. *Hell.* 1.6.24; cf. scholiast to Ar. *Ran.* 694.

8. On Sparta's use of non-hoplite warfare, see Thuc. 2.19–28, 8.5–44; Xen. *Hell.* 1.1.1–6.37; 2.1.1–2.2.23, and for the composition of her crews, cf. Gomme *Comm.* 4.35; Welwei 195–97; Garlan 1988: 165–69. For the various locales where non-hoplite battles took place in the Peloponnesian War, see Thuc. 2.2.12, 2.71–8; 3.2–4; 3.27–8; 3.36; 3.52–68; 3.98.4; 4.8–23; 5.114–116; 6.99–7.54. For sieges in the war, see Pritchett *Topography* 8.127–28, and on the various non-hoplite contingents, Parke 15–17.

9. For Brasidas, see Thuc. 2.93–94; 3.76–81, 4.11–12, 4.78–89, 4.102–16; 4.120–22; 4.123; 5.6–11; Demosthenes: Thuc. 3.94–98; 3.102; 3.105–14; 4.2–5; 4.8–14; 4.28–40; 4.66–74; 4.76–77; 7.16–17; Gyllipus, Lysander, and later commanders: Thuc. 5.93, 5.104; 7.1–2; 7.3–7; 7.59–85; Cartledge 1987: 90–98; Xen. *Hell.* 2.4.2; 2.4.28; 4.8.32; 7.1.12; cf. *Lac. Pol.* 14.4; Alcibiades: Thuc. 6.15; 6.90–91; 6.61; 6.88–93; 8.11–12; 8.14–17; 8.81.

10. For the fourth-century changes in warfare, see Garlan 1974: 106–47; 1975: 127–33; Hanson 1983: 68–69; Ober 1985: 32–50; Kromayer and Veith 87–88; McKechnie 26, 79–107; Wheeler 1988: 24–49; Lazenby 1985: 38–40; Lonis 16–19; Karavites 77–90. On the oath of Athenian ephebes, see Tod 2.204; *Poll.* 8.105. Stob. *Flor.* 4.1.8.

11. On confiscation of arms, see Diod. 14.10.4; 16.10.1; Aen. Tact. 10.7, 17.2–4, 29.4–30.1; enormous armories: Diod. 14.41.3–4; Xen. *Hell.* 3.4.17; ad hoc arming of infantry: Thuc. 8.25.6; Xen. *Hell.* 4.4.10; Diod. 12.68.5; 15.73.2; 14.43.23; use of non-hoplites as hoplites, cf. McKechnie 80–85.

12. On Socrates' purported poverty, see Pl. *Ap.* 36D, 37C, 38B, and on his military service: Pl. *Lach.* 181B; *Symp.* 221B; Plut. *Mor.* 581D; Plut. *Alc.* 7.3. See Jameson 1980: 213–235; cf. *IG* I³ 138; *IG* IV 42–43, for the gulf between citizen status and military service; Thuc. 2.13.6–7 records Athenian forces by battle, rather than citizen, status. There was growing chaos in the mustering of infantry troops, the increasing acceptance that neither agricultural produce nor middle-agrarian status was the sole determinant of Greek war service, or even of duty in the phalanx. At Athens now it was almost certain that many residents (small craftsmen, day laborers, urban property owners) could qualify for hoplite service on strictly a cash basis (perhaps 2,000 drachmas of *net worth*, rather than annual income) *without* either meeting the old annual food production requirements (300–200 *medimnoi* of liquid or dry harvests) or even possessing an appropriate net worth in landed property. Cf. Busolt and Swoboda 839–40.

13. On public or private arming of armies: Thuc. 6.72.4, 8.25.6; Diod. 12.68.5, 14.43.2–3, 15.13.2; Xen. *Hell.* 4.4.10; Polyaen. *Str.* 3.8; Dem. 18. 114–16; Aen. Tact. 10.7, 13.1–2; cf. Lys. 16.14, 31.15. On middling citizens and non-thetes used as rowers: Thuc. 3.16.1, 3.18.3–4; [Dem.] 50, 6, 16, 47; cf. Arist. *Pol.* 7.1327b13–15; see Rosivach 53–54. On metics and foreigners as hoplite infantry: Thuc. 2.13.6, 2.31.2; cf. 4.28.4, 5.8.2, 7.57.2; Xen. *Vect.* 2.2–5.

On absence of class considerations in the ephebes: Arist. *Ath. Pol.* 42.3–5; Lycur. *Leocr.* 1.176; cf. Arist. *Ath. Pol.* 42.4. Slaves on land and sea: Xen. *Hell.* 1.6.24; Dem. 4.36; Paus. 1.32.3, 7.15.7. Wealthy knights as hoplites, rowers, and skirmishes: Lys. 14.7, 10–11, 14–5, 22; Xen. *Hell.* 1.6.24. Specialized contingents: Plut. *Phoc.* 13.2–3; cf. Aeschin. 2.169.

Chapter 9. The Erosion of the Agrarian Polis

1. On grain imports into Athens and the significance of importing food, see Thuc. 6.20.4; Isoc. 17.57; [Xen.] *Ath. Pol.* 2.2–3; IG I³ 61.32–41; Arist. *Pol.* 7.1326b29–30. See also Garnsey 1988: 131–133, 150–164; but cf. Pritchett *War* 5.465–472; Ehrenberg 1951: 93.

2. See Gomme 1933: 24–26; Garnsey 1988: 90–91; A. M. Jones 1957: 165; M. H. Hansen 92–93; Guiraud 156–59. These modern estimates of metic and slave numbers at Athens can only be approximate guesses, but they do show enormous numbers of adults without access to political participation in democracy.

3. Quite a few scholars have seen the integration of the Greek *polis* into the Mediterranean as a crisis for its traditional agrarian exclusivity and chauvinism, See Fuks 17; de Ste. Croix 1981: 295–300; Runciman 1990: 365–67; McKechnie 16–29; Pecírka 1976: 19–21; Padgug 92–104.

4. A few examples of such tension can be found at Xen. *Hell.* 5.1.33–34; 5.236; 7.1.44; Diod. 15.57.3–58.3; 70.3; *FGrH* 434 fr. 1; Just. *Epit.* 16.4.20ff.

5. Hoplite infantry used outside of phalanx battle: Thuc. 1.98.2–4; 1.100.1; 1.100.2; 1.102.1–2; 1.104. 2; 1.105.1–2; 1.106; 1.114; 1.115–117; Plut. *Per.* 23.4.

6. Most authors take a dim view of the rise of the landless, maritime "mob," see [Xen.] *Ath. Pol.* 1.1–2; Hdt. 7.144.4; Thuc. 1.93.3; Plut. *Them.* 7.19; Nep. *Them.* 2.3; Pl. *Leg.* 4.706 B–C; 707C; Arist. *Ath. Pol.* 27.1; cf. Isoc.8.48, 64, 69, 75, 79, 101.

7. For playwrights' preference for Athenian democracy see Eur. *Andr.* 445–53; 595–601; 724–26; *Suppl.* 187; Aesch. *PV* 1069–70; cf. Eur. *Suppl.* 352–53; *Ion* 670–75; *Phoen.* 535–45.f; for acknowledgment of the role played by landless rowers: Aesch. *Pers.* 373–81; Ar. *Ach.* 162–63; *Ran.* 1072–73; *Vesp.* 909; *Eq.* 1065–66; 1186; 1366–67; *Aves* 108; praise for hoplite landowners: Aesch. *Pers.* 85–86, 147–49, 238–45; Ar. *Ach.* 179, 625, *Eq.* 1334; *Nub.* 986; *Pax* 353–56; *Vesp.* 711; Eur. *Andr.* 681; *Vita* Aesch; cf. Eur. *Orest.* 920; Ar. *Pax* 603, 511.

8. Role of hoplite marines in sea battles: Hdt. 8.90.2; Diod. 13.40, 45–46, 77–80; Thuc. 7.70; 8.104–5; cf. especially Plut. *Cim.* 12.2. For hoplites recruited onto ship as rowers, see Rosivach 54–56.

9. For late fifth-and fourth-century investment in the protection of the Attic countryside, see Garlan 1974: 19–86; Hanson 1983: 78–83; Ober 1985: 69–86.

10. See, for example, Diod. 12.44.3; 12.76.3; Thuc. 1.98.1–2; 2.26, 32, 69.1; 3.51, 96; 4.41, 45.2; 5.56.3, 116.2; 6.105.2; 7.18.3; 8.35.1–2.

11. Reduction in power of the Areopagus: Arist. *Ath. Pol.* 25.1; 28.2; 41.2; rise of the assembly, council, and law courts: Arist. *Ath. Pol.* 25.2; Athenian aid in Spartan suppression of helot revolt: Thuc. 1.102; Ar. *Lys.* 1138–44; Plut. *Cim.* 15.2; 16.8–17.3 ; Arist. *Ath. Pol.* 26.1; Pay for public service: Arist. *Ath. Pol.* 27.3; Pl. *Gorg.* 515E; Plut. *Per.* 9; Ar. *Ach.* 66, 90; Thuc. 8.67.3; [Xen.] *Ath. Pol.* 1.3; building program: Plut. *Per.* 13–14; manning of permanent fleet: Thuc. 2.13.

12. Arist. *Ath. Pol.* 7.3–4; 26.2; 47.1; see also M. H. Hansen 106–7; A. M. Jones 1957: 79–81.

13. Dem. 23.199. For Thessaly in general, see Arist. *Pol.* 2.1269a34ff; cf. Weber 1976: 219, "the second largest area which remained largely untouched by *polis* organization." It was the rich plains (in a purely agricultural sense) of Sparta and Thessaly that fostered agrarian stasis. The more rugged and marginal ground (as we saw in Chapter 2) elsewhere in Greece actually enhanced the emergence of hard-working *geôrgoi*. "The Greek concepts of freedom and autonomy, then," E. M. Wood rightly observed of the differences between *all* Greek city-states and Spartan/Thessalian/Cretan serfdom, "may have their roots in the experience of a free peasantry, a distinctive phenomenon which existed not only in the democracy, where the last vestiges of peasant dependence disappeared with the abolition of debt-bondage and clientship in the reforms of Solon, but perhaps even before those reforms and in any *polis* in which peasants were not serfs or helots, permanently subjected to an alien ruling community" (Wood 135; cf. Burford 1993: 193–207). "Before those reforms" and "in any *polis* in which peasants were not serfs or helots" refer to the creation of agrarianism and the culture of yeomanry throughout the Greek-speaking world in the eighth and seventh centuries.

14. "In the late-classical and the Hellenistic Age, from the seventies of the fourth century to the middle of the second century, I count about seventy cases of social-economic conflict and social-economic revolution, as compared with six such cases in the classical period, from the Persian Wars to the end of the Peloponnesian War." So wrote Alexander Fuks (17) in a sweeping generalization, the truth of which has never been refuted. The value of Fuks' observation, besides the notion that the viability of small farmers seems to have been a natural check on social chaos and disequilibrium, is that it shows that the decline of agrarianism was felt throughout the Greek-speaking world.

15. Susan Alcock has systematically collated the recent evidence from some twelve of these regional field surveys of various Greek landscapes. While there are local differences and occasional incongruities that can nuance generalizations, the rough picture for Greece after the last century of the *polis* period as a whole is clear. "All the regions for which detailed information is available

experienced a drop, often severe in the number and area, of inhabited settlements. There is some variation in the phenomenon from region to region; the starting point for this development seems to come in the middle to end of the third century in some areas, slightly later in others. If survey performs best in revealing activity at the lower end of the settlement hierarchy, then settlement patterns are a prime index of the intensity of land use. With the large-scale evacuation of the countryside, witnessed in the loss of most loci of rural activity, it seems an inescapable conclusion that land earlier pressed into service was either allowed to revert to wild or was less intensively cultivated" (Alcock 66, 67).

16. Modern scholars have generally been impressed by this archaeological, epigraphic, and literary evidence of rural depopulation, farm abandonment, and the creation of enormous landed estates in Hellenistic and Roman Greece. "There is little doubt," Robin Osborne has remarked in this regard, "that the move away from isolated residence and back to town life led to a reduction in the continuity of agricultural activity, even perhaps to a reduction in the area farmed" (1987: 135). John Day summarized the epigraphic evidence of land ownership in Hellenistic and Roman Attica: "The formation of comparatively large holdings in landed properties took place at a rapid rate" (Day 235). Of the evidence from land records in the Roman Empire, Richard Duncan-Jones concluded that "almost all the registers point unequivocally to heavy aggregation of property in the hands of the rich. Although the registers vary so much, the proportion occupied by the largest single estate is almost always significant" (Duncan-Jones 140).

17. Tainter 145–46. A. M. Jones earlier comes to the same conclusion: "The evidence does suggest that over-taxation played a significant role in the decline of the empire. . . . It can be plausibly argued that the high rate of tax was the main reason for the abandonment of marginal land and the consequent impoverishment of the empire" (1974: 88; 166–185). On the Aegean island of Keos nearly the same process had already occurred by Hellenistic times. "Neither depopulation nor brigandage can explain the remarkable transformation of the archaeological landscape of northwest Keos; there is on the other hand no evidence of the kinds of impact on the archaeological record that likely resulted from small-scale diversified farming in earlier times. The most likely explanation seems to be that expansive tracts of land had been redirected to other purposes; if so, such a change implies at the very least a restructuring of rights of land use and perhaps suggests the formation of large estates" (Cherry, Davis, and Mantzourani 343). "Restructuring of rights of land use" is a euphemism for the destruction of hoplite agrarianism. "A marked redirection in rural settlement," and "an overall decrease in the intensity of cultivation" (Cherry, Davis, and Mantzourani 340) are synonyms for the end of Greek yeomanry.

18. Alcock 44. Of the vulnerability of complex systems in general, Joseph

Tainter (e.g., 115–16; cf. A. M. Jones 1974 129–39; 166–85) adds that this bureaucratic interference from above finally wears away the agrarian productivity of the countryside, by creating specialization that does not provide a commensurate return in investment. He notes: "The reasons why investment in complexity yields a declining marginal return are: (a) increasing size of bureaucracies; (b) increasing specialization of bureaucracies; (c) the cumulative nature of organizational solutions; (d) increasing taxation; (e) increasing costs of legitimizing activities; and (f) increasing costs of internal control and external defense." All such phenomena are characteristic of the Hellenistic kingdoms, and to a greater extent Roman control in Greece, but *not at all applicable to conditions during the earlier* polis period, when the countryside was under the protection of Greek yeomanry.

19. "In the all important agrarian base of the economy, *disintensification* in agricultural production on the regional level is signaled by the observed changes in settlement and land use patterns" (Alcock 176; emphasis added; cf. A.M. Jones 1974: 82–89; 120–23; 135: "Taxation rose so high as to discourage the cultivation of marginal land and the cultivated area, and with it agricultural production, sank.")

20. "In the late Archaic and the Classical Periods," Michael Jameson once remarked, "private wealth was exploited for political purposes and then harnessed by the city in the form of liturgies. As it reappears in the Hellenistic period it is more an instrument for the social advancement of the rich than a reliable resource for the community" (Jameson 1983: 13; cf. Garnsey and Morris 104–5).

Appendix: Farming Words

1. The meaning of "agriculture" is clear enough in English. It reflects its Latin etymology *ager* ("field") plus *cultura* ("cultivation"). Thus agriculture means "cultivation of the land." The only ambiguity in its usage may arise over the inclusion of animal husbandry and livestock. Both activities are more an indirect, rather than a direct, result of the cultivation of the soil. The ancients might at times assume stock was included within definitions of "farming" (e.g., Pl. *Leg.* 2.674 C; Arist. *Pol.* 1.1256a35–b20), although the more precise ancient agricultural writers often point out that, strictly speaking, agriculture should denote land, not animals (e.g., Cato *Rust.* 8–9; Colum. *Rust.* 2.16–17).

In this book, I therefore use the English "farming" interchangeably with "agriculture," although properly there should be a slightly different emphasis in its meaning. One can, for example, "farm" fish (i.e., aquaculture), or "farm" out particular tasks, in contexts quite unconnected with the working of the soil. These nuances in the meaning of the English "farming," then, do not only reflect general metaphorical language. They can also include more specific aspects of land use beyond the strict cultivation of the soil, such as rents, payments, leases and other elements of property ownership (thus "farm" derives from Latin *firma:* "firm," "a fixed payment"). In general, no real ambiguity arises over the interchangeable use of "farmers" and the more formal "agricultural-ists." Both words in modern American parlance identify those who grow crops or raise livestock on plots of ground.

2. There is no comprehensive discussion of the Greek vocabulary of agri-culture. But helpful analyses of particular words are found randomly in Richter 6; Rhodes 72; Pritchett 1956: 262, 268–69; Guiraud 446–51; Osborne 1985: 143; Isager and Skydsgaard 153–54; Burford 1993: 15; Audring 1974: 447; Jameson 1992: 145; de Ste. Croix 1981: 13.

3. Xen. *Mem.* 3.11.4: "Have you an *agros?*"; see also Is. 6.33; [Dem.] 53.6. From this root word *agros* (cf. Latin *ager*), we also find *agroikoi* (*agros* + *oikoi* "field dwellers") a rough equivalent to *geôrgoi* "farmers" (as are the earlier and more poetic words for farmers, *agroitai* and *agrotai*, and a host of other related terms, such as *agronomoi* "country magistrates," *agroponoi* "field workers," and so on.

4. There is yet a third and even larger family of words used by the Greeks to describe farming. This group is connected to the more general term *chôra*, and the nearly identical *chôros*, "space" or "room," which, by extension, often (even more than *agros*) denotes the open space or roominess of the countryside. Typically, this particular root supplies an array of related Greek agricultural vo-cabulary. Good examples are *chôrion* ("plot" or even "farm") and *chôrikos* ("rural"). *Chôritês* properly means "rural dweller," but like *agrotês* occasionally implies patronization along the lines of "boor" or "rustic" (e.g., Xen. *Hell.* 3.2.31). Because *chôra* is a more expansive term, including space as well as land proper, it is usually used in a broad context in reference to agriculture. The *chôra* is all the land surrounding the Greek *polis* (whether farmed or not). It is the general idea of "rural" when used in opposition to "urban": *chôra* versus *polis*.

5. For example, land measurement: *plethron, guês, akaina, ouron, schoinos;* types of land: *haloê* (developed ground), *aroura* and *arotos* (plowable or arable cereal land), *pedion* (fertile land in the plain), *kêpos* (irrigated or garden ground), *gêpedon* (land within the city, gardens), *eschatia* (marginal, rugged, or distant land), *psilê* (open or unplanted land), *phutalia* or *orchatos* (vineyard or orchard ground), and *skiros* (wild or forested land). On the vast vocabulary of land and its measurement, see Ridgeway 325–27; Richter 5–7; 13–14; 90–91; 96–7 Cooper 1978: 169–71; Audring 1989: 5–14; Osborne 1985:19–20; Don-lan 1989: 130, 138–39; Pritchett 1956: 261–69; Hennig 45–46; Brumfield 156–57; Burford 1993: 113–15; Glotz 1927: 38–39; Hehn 124–26; and espe-cially Guiraud 64–66.

6. The odd adjective "most-acred" (*poluplethrotatos*) is a rare and late Greek word (e.g. Lucian *Icar.* 18.5). Instead, when an ancient Greek author

wishes to contrast the poor against the middling farmers and the very rich, he usually speaks of these wealthier two groups as *distinct* entities: the *plousioi* and the *geôrgoi* (e.g., [Xen.] *Ath. Pol.* 2.14; Ar. *Eccl.* 197). That makes it clear that these two classes, "farmers" and the "rich," were *not* usually seen as one and the same group (Arist. *Pol.* 4.1296b37–1297a13). When those rare wealthy landowners of the *polis* period appear in literature (often in an archaic or quasi-*polis* context), specialized and localized vocabulary that never becomes widespread is used. For example, occasionally we see *geômoroi* ("land sharers" or "landed gentry," Hdt. 7.155.2; Thuc. 8.21) or *basileis* ("barons" or "princes," Hes. *Op.* 37–39; cf. 248–73). Outside of the non-*polis* systems of Sparta, Crete, and Thessaly, where we do see rubrics denoting specific types of farm size and wealth, labels of tenancy and lordship nearly always are associated with archaic Attic practice in general, and the Solonian class structure in particular (i.e., *hektêmoroi*, "sixth-partners"), a vestigial language of an early age (about 600 B.C.) during the establishment and emergence of small Athenian farmers.

7. Similarly, even today in Greece one can argue there are no distinct social classes among Greek farmers: "all citizens own property and resources. There are no extreme variations in wealth or property-holding" (Gavrielides 1976b: 271). Robin Osborne rightly rejected the term "peasant" for the Athenian small landowner, partly because "there was no sharp dividing line between small and large landowners" (1985: 142; Audring 1974: 447; Jameson 1992: 145). Even the Marxist historian G. E. M. de Ste. Croix wrote that until the end of the free Greek *polis* "although the cultured gentleman living in or near the city could be a very different kind of person from the boorish peasant, who might not often leave his farm, except to sell his produce in the city market, they spoke the same language and felt that they were to some extent akin" (1981: 13). That affinity was possible only because there was not wide divergence in farm size, agricultural technique, or agrarian outlook during the era of the Greek *polis*.

8. "*Autourgos* may be as close as we get to the concept of citizen farmer or yeoman farmer in the Greek world" Burford 1993:172. On Pericles, see Thuc. 1.141.3; scholiast on Thuc. 1.141.3; for farmers in Euripides, Eur. *Or.* 920; *Elect.* 37ff; see also Plut. *Per.* 9; Men. *Dys.* 326; Arist. *Rhet.* 1381a23. The word *autourgos* is also discussed in Heitland 12–13, 123; L. B. Carter 76–79; de Ste. Croix 1981: 263; Burford 1993: 168–172.

9. See, e.g., Bisinger 15–17; Richter 14–17; Ridgeway 330–31; Guiraud 100–105. The ideal of dividing the land up equally among the citizenry reflects an agrarianism far removed from large tracts and concession run by lords, worked by serfs.

10. Only sporadically in our period do we hear of an ancient expression somewhat equivalent to agrarian agitation, *gês anadasmos,* the "redistribution of land" (see Bisinger 14–16; Asheri 1966: 21–25; Busolt and Swoboda 214 n. 1).

Quite revealingly, that phrase is usually heard during the first and last centuries of the *polis* period (i.e., 700–600 B.C. and 400–300 B.C.), at a time contemporaneous with the original establishment and later erosion of the *geôrgoi* as the backbone of the city-state. "Redistribution of the land" is an expression, in other words, largely out of place in Greek history during much of the *polis* period.

ABBREVIATIONS OF ANCIENT AUTHORS AND WORKS

Ael.	Aelian	
	NH	*De Natura Animalium* (The Nature of Animals)
	VH	*Varia Historia* (Assorted History)
	Ep.	*Epistlulae* (Letters)
	Tact. Praef.	Preface to *Tactics*
Aen. Tact.	Aeneas Tacticus	
Aesch.	Aeschylus	
	Ag.	*Agamemnon*
	Eum.	*Eumenides*
	Pers.	*Persae* (Persians)
	PV	*Prometheus Vinctus* (Prometheus Bound)
	Sept.	*Septem contra Thebes* (Seven Against Thebes)
	Supp.	*Suppliants*
Aeschin.	Aeschines	
	In Ctes.	*Against Ctesias*
Aëthlius		
Alc.	Alcaeus	
Alciphr.	Alciphron	
Alcmaeon		
Alexius		

Ameipsias
Amphis
Anaxilas
Anaximander

Andoc.   Andocides
Androtion
Anon. fr.   Anonymous fragment
Anth. Pal.   *Anthologia Palantina (Palantine Anthology)*
Antiphanes
Antiphon
Apollodorus

Ar.   Aristophanes
Ach.   *Acharnians*
Av.   *Aves* (Birds)
Eccl.   *Ecclesizusae* (Women at the Ecclesia)
Eq.   *Equites* (Knights)
Lys.   *Lysistrata*
Nub.   *Nubes* (Clouds)
Pax   *Pax* (Peace)
Plut.   *Plutus* (Wealth)
Ran.   *Ranae* (Frogs)
Thesm.   *Thesmorphoriazusae* (Women at the Thesmorphoria)
Vesp.   *Vespae* (Wasps)

Archil.   Archilochus
Arist.   Aristotle
Ath. Pol.   *Athenaion Politeia* (Constitution of the Athenians)
Eth. Nic.   *Ethica Nicomachea* (Nichomachean Ethics)
HA   *Historia Animalium* (History of Animals)
Meteor.   *Meteorologica*
[Oec.]   *Oeconomica* (Economics)
Part. An.   *De Partibus Animalium* (Parts of Animals)
Poet.   *Poetica* (Poetics)
Pol.   *Politica* (Politics)
Rhet.   *Rhetorica* (Rhetoric)

Arr.   Arrian
An.   *Anabasis*
Tact.   *Tactica* (Tactics)

Athen.	Athenaeus
Aul. Gell.	Aulus Gellius
NA	Noctes Atticae (*Attic Nights*)
Caes.	Caesar
Bell. Afr.	*Bellum Africanum* (African War)
Cato	
Rust.	*De Re Rustica* (Country Matters)
Cic.	Cicero
Off.	*De Officiis* (Duties)
Colum.	Columella
Arb.	*De Arboribus* (Trees)
Rust.	*De Re Rustica* (Country Matters)
Deinarchus	
Democr.	Democritus
Dem.	Demosthenes
Dio. Chrys.	Dio Chrysostomus
Diod.	Diodorus Siculus
Diog. Laert.	Diogenes Laertes
Dion. Hal.	Dionysius Halicarnassensis
Ant. Rom.	*Antiquitates Romanae* (Roman Antiquities)
Edmonds	J. M. Edmonds, *Fragments of Attic Comedy*, 1957–1961
Eupolis	
Eur.	Euripides
Andr.	*Andromache*
Bacch.	*Bacchae*
Cyc.	*Cyclops*
El.	*Electra*
HF	*Hercules Furens*
Ion	
Or.	*Orestes*
Phoen.	*Phoenissae*
Supp.	*Supplices*
FGrH	F. Jacoby, *Fragmente der griechischen Historiker*, 1954–1962
Fr.	Fragment
Front.	Frontinus
Str.	*Strategemata*
Harp.	Harpocration

Heracl.	Heracleitus
Hdt.	Herodotus
Hell. Oxy.	Hellenica Oxyrhynchia
Hes.	Hesiod
Op.	*Opera et Dies* (Works and Days)
Scut.	*Scutum* (Shield)
Theog.	*Theogony*
Hipponax	
Hom.	Homer
Il.	*Iliad*
Od.	*Odyssey*
Hymn. Hom. Merc.	Hymnus Homericus ad Mercuriam (*Homeric Hymn to Hermes*)
Hyper.	Hyperides
IC	Inscriptiones Creticae, 1935–1950, (*Cretan Inscriptions*)
IG	Inscriptiones Graecae, 1873–1981 (*Greek inscriptions*)
Is.	Isaeus
Isoc.	Isocrates
Areop.	Areopagus
Paneg.	Panegyricus
Istros	
Just.	Justinus
Epit.	*Epitome*
Kock	T. Kock, *Comicorum Atticorum Fragmenta* (1880–88)
Lucian	
Anach.	*Anacharsis*
Icar.	*Icaromenippus*
Lycurg.	Lycurgus
Leocr.	*Against Leocratus*
Lys.	Lysias
Men.	Menander
Asp.	*Aspis*
Dys.	*Dyscolus*
Georg.	*Georgos*
Sent.	*Sententiae*
Nep.	Nepos
Ages.	*Agesilaus*

Milt.	*Miltiades*
Them.	*Themistocles*
Ov.	Ovid
Met.	*Metamorphoses*
Paus.	Pausanias
Pherecrates	
Philemon	
Philochorus	
Philodemus	
Phocylides	
Phot.	Photius
Bibl.	*Bibliotheca* (Library)
Pind.	Pindar
Nem.	*Nemean Odes*
Olymp.	*Olympian Odes*
Pl.	Plato
Amat.	*Amatores* (Lovers)
Alc.	*Alcibiades*
Ap.	*Apology*
Clit.	*Clitopho*
Criti.	*Critias*
Ep.	*Epistulae* (Letters)
Euthyphr.	*Euthyphro*
Gor.	*Gorgias*
Hipp.	*Hipparchus*
Ion	
Lach.	*Laches*
Leg.	*Leges* (Laws)
Menex.	*Menexenus*
Min.	*Minos*
Phaedr.	*Phaedrus*
Polit.	*Politicus* (Statesman)
Prot.	*Protagoras*
Resp.	*Respublica* (Republic)
Soph.	*Sophista*
Symp.	*Symposium*
Theag.	*Theages*

Theaet.	Theaetetus
Tim.	Timaeus
Pliny	
Ep.	Epistuale (Letters)
HN	Naturalis Historia (Natural History)
Plut.	Plutarch
Ages.	Agesilaus
Agis	
Alc.	Alcibiades
Arat.	Aratus
Arist.	Aristides
Cim.	Cimon
Comp. Lyc et Num	Comparison of Lycurgus and Numa
Demetr.	Demetrius
Flamin.	Flamininus
Lyc.	Lycurgus
Lys.	Lysander
Mor.	Moralia
Nic.	Nicias
Pel.	Pelopidas
Per.	Pericles
Phil.	Philopoemen
Phoc.	Phocian
Pyrrh.	Pyrrhus
Sol.	Solon
Them.	Themistocles
Thes.	Theseus
Poll.	Pollux
On.	Onomasticon
Polyaen.	Polyaenus
Str.	Strategemata
Polyb.	Polybius
Praef.	Praefatio (Preface)
Ps. Her. Att.	Pseudo-Herodes Atticus
Peri Pol.	Peri Politeias (About Constitutions)
Sappho	

Schol.	Scholiast
SEG	Supplementum Epigraphicum Graecum, 1923–
Sen.	Seneca
Ep.	*Epistulae* (Letters)
SIG	W. Dittenberg, *Sylloge Inscriptionum Graecum*, 1915–24
Soph.	Sophocles
Ajax	
Ant.	*Antigone*
Oed. Col.	*Oedipus Coloneus*
Stob.	Stobaeus
Flor.	(Anthology)
Strabo	
Strato	
Timaeus	
Timocles	
Theocr.	Theocritus
Id.	*Idylls*
Theog.	Theognis
Theophr.	Theophrastus
Char.	*Characters*
CP	*De Causis Plantarum* (The Aetiology of Plants)
HP	*Historia Plantarum* (Researches of Plants)
Theopomp.	Theopompus
Thuc.	Thucydides
Val. Max.	Valerius Maximus
Varro	
Rust.	*De Re Rustica* (Country Matters)
Virg.	Virgil
Ec.	*Eclogues*
Georg.	*Georgics*
Vit. Aesch.	Vita Aeschyli (Life of Aeschylus)
Vit. Aesop.	Vita Aesopi (Life of Aesop)
Xenocr.	Xenocrates
Xenophanes	
Xen.	Xenophon
Ages.	*Agesilaus*
An.	*Anabasis*

Cyn.	*Cynegeticus* (On Hunting)
Cyr.	*Cyropaedia* (Education of Cyrus)
Hier.	*Hiero*
Hell.	*Hellenica*
Hipp.	*Hipparchus* (The Cavalary Commander)
Lac. Pol.	*Lacedaimonion Politeia* (Spartan Constitution)
Mem.	*Memorabilia*
Oec.	*Oeconomicus*
Symp.	*Symposium*
Vect.	*De Vectigalibus* (Ways and Means)
[Xen.]	Pseudo-Xenophon
Ath. Pol.	*Athenaion Politeia* (Constitution of the Athenians)
Zen.	Zenobius

BIBLIOGRAPHY OF
WORKS CITED

The following books and articles are those that appear in the text by the author's last name and, when necessary, by date of publication as well.

Abbreviations of Titles of Periodicals

ABSA	*Annual of the British School at Athens*
AC	*Antiquité classique*
AHR	*American Historical Review*
AJA	*American Journal of Archaeology*
AJP	*American Journal of Philology*
BCH	*Bulletin de correspondance héllenique*
CJ	*Classical Journal*
CP	*Classical Philology*
CQ	*Classical Quarterly*
CR	*Classical Review*
CW	*Classical Weekly*
JFA	*Journal of Field Archaeology*
JHS	*Journal of Hellenic Studies*
PCPS	*Proceedings of the Cambridge Philological Society*
REA	*Revue des études anciennes*
REG	*Revue des études grecques*
TAPA	*Transactions of the American Philological Society*
ZPE	*Zeitschrift für Papyrologie und Epigraphik*

Adcock, F. E. *The Greek and Macedonian Art of War* (Berkeley 1956).

Adkins, A. W. H. *Moral Values and Political Behaviour in Ancient Greece* (London 1972).

Ahlberg, G. *Fighting on Land and Sea in Greek Geometric Art* (Stockholm 1957).

Alcock, S. *Greek Society and the Transition to Roman Rule: Archaeological and Historical Approaches* (doctoral dissertation, University of Cambridge, Cambridge, UK, 1992).

Amit, A. *Athens and the Sea* (Brussels 1965).

Amouretti, M. C. "Les instruments aratoires dans la Grèce archaïque," in *Dialogues d'Histoire ancienne* (Besançon 1976), 26–52.

_____. "Les céréals dans l'antiqué: Espéces, mouture et conservation, liaison et interferénces dans la Grèce classique," in M. Gast and F. Sigaut (eds.), *Les techniques de conservation des graines à long terme* (Paris 1979), 57–69.

_____. *Le pain et l'huile dans la Grèce* (Paris 1986).

_____. "La viticulture antique, contraites et choix techniques," *REA* 90 (1988), 5–16.

_____. "Oléiculture et viticulture dans la Grèce antique," in Wells 1992, 77–86.

Amyard, A. *Études d'histoire ancienne* (Paris 1967).

_____. "L'Idée du travail et autarche individuelle," *Revue d'histoire de la philosophie* in *Études d'histoire ancienne* (Paris 1968), 461–73.

Anderson, J.K. *Ancient Greek Horsemanship* (Berkeley 1961).

_____. *Military Theory and Practice in the Age of Xenophon* (Berkeley 1970).

_____. "Hoplite Weapons and Offensive Arms," in Hanson 1991a, 15–37.

André, J. *Notes de lexicographie botanique grecque* (Paris 1958).

Andrewes, A. *The Greek Tyrants* (New York 1956).

_____. *Greek Society* (New York 1971).

_____. "The Hoplite *Katalogos*," in G. S. Shrimpton and D. J. McCargar (eds.), *Classical Contributions: Studies in Honor of M. F. McGregor* (New York 1981), 1–3.

Andrews, A. C. "Plant Symbolism on Greek Coins," *Economic Botany* 17 (1963) 317–18.

Andreyev, V. N. "Some Aspects of Agrarian Conditions in Attica in the Fifth to Third Century," *Eirene* 12 (1974), 5–46.

Arnould, D. *Guerre et paix dans la poésie grecque* (New York 1981).

Ashburner, W. "The Farmer Law," *JHS* 30 (1910), 97–108.

Asheri, D. "Laws of Inheritance, Distribution of Land, and Political Constitutions in Ancient Greece," *Historia* 12 (1963), 1–21.

_____. *Distribuzioni di terre nell'antica Grecia* (Memorie dell'Academia dell scienze di Torino, classe di scienze morali, storiche e filologiche 4. ser. 10 [1966]).

Ashmole, B. "Kalligenia and *Hiera arotos*," *JHS* 66 (1946), 8–11.

Audring, G. "Über Grundeigentum und Landwirtschaft in der Krise der Athenischen *polis*," in Wekiskopf (ed.), *Hellenische Poleis. Krise—Wandlung—Wirkung*, 4 vols. (Berlin 1974a), 108–31.

_____. "Grenzen der Konzentration von Grundeigentum im Attika wahrend des 4 Jh. v.u.Z.," *Klio* 56 (1974b) 445–96.

_____. *Zur wirtschaftlichen und sozialen Lage der attischen Bauern im ausgehend 5. und im 4. Jahrhundert v.u.Z.* (*Studien zur athenischen Sozialstruktur und römischen Wirtschaftspolitik in Kleinasien, Sonderband des Jahrbuchs für Wirtschaftgeschichte*, Berlin 1977).

_____. *Zur Struktur des Territoriums griechischer Poleis in archaischer Zeit (Nach den schriftlichen Quellen)* (Berlin 1989).

Austin, M. "Hellenistic Kings, War and the Economy," *CQ* 36 (1986), 450–66.

Austin, M., and P. Vidal-Naquet. *Economic and Social History of Ancient Greece* (London 1977).

Badian, E. (ed.). *Ancient Society and Institutions. Studies Presented to Victor Ehrenberg* (Oxford 1966).

Balkhuizen, S. C. "Social Ecology of the Ancient Greek World," *Antiquité classique* 44 (1975), 211–18.

Barlett, P. F. "Adaptive Strategies in Peasant Agricultural Production," *Annual Review of Anthropology* 9 (1980), 545–5.

Beloch, K. J. "Die Landwirtshaft Athens, I" *Opus* 4 (1985, ed. C. Ampolo) 7–28.

Bennett, E. L., Jr. *The Olive-oil Tablets of Pylos* (Salamanca 1955).

_____. "The Landholders of Pylos," *AJA* 60 (1956) 103–33.

Berdan, F. "The Reconstruction of Ancient Economies: Perspectives from Archaeology and Ethnohistory," in S. Ortiz (ed.), *Economic Anthropology: Topics and Theories* (New York 1983), 83–98.

Bergquist, B. *The Archaic Greek Temenos. A Study of Structure and Function* (Lund 1967).

Berry, W. *A Continuous Harmony. Essays Cultural and Agricultural* (New York 1972).

Billiard, R. *La vigne dans l'antiquité* (Lyon 1913).

Bintliff, J. L. "Pedology and Land Use," *ABSA* (1971), 24–30.

_____. *Natural Environment and Human Settlement in Prehistoric Greece* (BAR Supp. 28, Oxford 1977).

Bintliff, J. L., and A. M. Snodgrass. "The Cambridge/Bradford Boeotian Expedition: The First Four Years," *JFA* 12 (1985), 123–161.

_____. "Mediterranean Survey and the City," *Antiquity* 62 (1988), 57–71.

Bisinger, J. *Der Agrarstaat in Platons Gesetzen* (*Klio* Supp. 17 Leipzig 1925; reprinted 1963).

Blyth, H. "The Structure of a Hoplite Shield in the Museo Gregoriano Etrusco," *Bullentino Dei Musei E. Galleri Pontifice* 3 (1982), 5–21.

Boardman, J. M. "Delphinion in Chios," *ABSA* 51 (1956), 41–54.

_____. "The Olive in the Mediterranean: Its Culture and Use," in Hutchinson, J. *The Early History of Agriculture* (Oxford 1977), 187–96.

_____. *The Greeks Overseas* (2nd ed., London 1980).

Boardman, J. M., and C. E. Vaphopoulou-Richardson (eds.). *Chios. A Conference at the Homerion in Chios 1984* (Oxford 1986).

Boeckh, A. *The Public Economy of the Athenians* (trans. A. Lamb, Boston 1857).

Bolkestein, H. *Economic Life in Greece's Golden Age* (Leiden 1958).

Bommeljé, S., and P. K. Doorn. *Aetolia and Aetolians: Towards the Interdisciplinary Study of a Greek Region* (Utrecht 1987).

Boserup, E. *The Conditions of Agricultural Growth* (London 1981).

Boucher, A. "La tactique grecque à l'origine de l'histoire militaire," *REG* 25 (1912), 300–312.

Boyd, T., and J. Carpenter. "Dragon Houses: Euboia, Attika, Karia," *AJA* 81 (1977), 189–215.

Boyd, T., and M. H. Jameson. "Urban and Rural Land Division in Ancient Greece," *Hesperia* 50.4 (1981), 327–42.

Bradford, J. "Fieldwork on Aerial Discoveries in Attica and Rhodes," *Antiquaries Journal* 36 (1956), 172–80.

Braudel, F. *The Mediterranean and the Mediterranean World in the Age of Philip II* (vols. 1–2, trans. S. Reynolds, New York 1978).

Bravo, B. "Remarques sur les assises sociales, les formes d'organization et de terminologie du commerce maritime grec à l' époque archaïque," *Dialogues d'histoire ancienne* 3 (1977), 1–59.

_____. "Le commerce des céréals chez les grecques de l' époque archaïque," in Garnsey and Whittaker 1983, 17–29.

Brelich, A. *Guerre, agoni e culti nella Grecia arcaia* (Antiquitas 1.7 Bonn 1961).

Brothwell, D., and P. Brothwell. *Food in Antiquity* (London 1969).

Brown, A. D. Fitton. "The Contribution of Women to Ancient Greek Agriculture," *Liverpool Classical Monthly* 9.5 (1984), 71–74.

Brumfield, A. C. *The Attic Festivals of Demeter and Their Relation to the Agricultural Year* (New York 1981).

Buck, R. J. *A History of Boeotia* (Alberta 1979).

Bugh, G. *The Horsemen of Athens* (Princeton 1988).

Burford, A. (see under Cooper, A.B.).

Burkert, W. *Greek Religion: Archaic and Classical* (Oxford 1985).

Burn, A. R. *The World of Hesiod* (London 1936).

Busolt, G., and H. Swoboda. *Griechische Staatskunde* (2 vols., Munich 1920–26).

Campbell, J. K., and P. Sherrard. *Modern Greece* (New York 1968).

Camp, J. "A Drought in the Late Eighth Century," *Hesperia* 48 (1979) 397–411.

Carpenter, R. *Discontinuity in Greek Civilization* (Cambridge 1966).

Carter, F. W. *An Historical Geography of the Balkans* (London 1977).

Carter, J. "Rural Settlement in Metaponto," in G. Barker and R. Hodges (eds.), *Archaeology and Italian society* (BAR Int. Ser. 102, Oxford 1981) 167–77.

_____. "Metapontum—Land, Wealth, and Population," in Descoeudres 1990, 405–41.

Carter, J. C., *et al.* "Population and Agriculture: Magna Graecia in the Fourth Century B.C.," in C. Malone. and S. Stoddart (eds.), *Papers in Italian Archaeology IV The Cambridge Conference: Part I, The Human Landscape* (BAR Int. Ser. 243, Oxford 1985), 281–312.

Carter, L. B. *The Quiet Athenian* (Oxford 1986).

Cartledge, P. "Hoplites and Heroes: Sparta's Contribution to the Technique of Ancient Warfare" *JHS* 97 (1977), 11–28.

_____. *Sparta and Lakonia* (London 1979).

_____. "'Trade and Politics' Revisited: Archaic Greece," in Garnsey, Hopkins, and Whittaker 1983, 1–15.

_____. *Agesilaos and the Crisis of Sparta* (Baltimore 1987).

Cartledge, P. A., and F. D. Harvey (eds.), *Crux: Essays Presented to G. E. M. de Ste. Croix on his 75th Birthday* (Exeter 1985).

Cary, M. *The Geographic Background of Greek and Roman History* (Oxford 1949).

Cavanagh, W. G. "Surveys, Cities, and Synoecism" in Rich and Wallace-Hadrill, 97–118.

Chadwick, J. *The Mycenean World* (Cambridge 1976).

Chamoux, F. *The Civilization of Greece* (London 1965).

Chantraine, P. *Dictionnaire étymologique de la langue grecque* (Paris 1968).

Cherry, J. F. L. "Frogs Round the Pond: Perspectives on Current Archaeological Survey Projects in the Mediterranean Region," in and Rupp 1983, 375–416.

"Pastoralism and the Role of Animals in the Pre- and Protohistoric Economies of the Aegean," in Whittaker 1988, 6–34.

Cherry, J. F. L., and J. L. Davis. "The Nemea Valley Survey," *AJA* 89 (1985), 327; 90 (1986) 204–5; 91 (1987) 327.

Cherry, J. F., J. L. Davis, and E. Mantzourani. *The Archaeological Landscape of Northern Keos* (Los Angeles 1991).

Chevalier, A. "L'origine de l'olivier cultivé et de ses variations," *Revue de botanique appliquée et d'agriculture tropicale* 28 (1948), 1–25.

Chisholm, M. *Rural Settlement and Land Use* (London 1962).

Chrimes, K. *Ancient Sparta* (Manchester 1949).

Clark, C., and M. Haswell. *The Economics of Subsistence Agriculture* (4th ed., London 1977).

Cohen, E. E. *Athenian Economy and Society. A Banking Perspective* (Princeton 1992).

Coldstream, J. N. *The Formation of the Greek Polis: Aristotle and Archaeology* (Rheinisch-Westfälische Akademie der Wissenschaft, Vorträge G 272 [Opladen 1974]).

_____. Geometric Greece (New York 1977).

Cole, T. Democritus and the Source of Greek Anthropology (Cleveland 1967).

Colinvaux, P. A. The Fates of Nations. A Biological Theory of History (Harmandsworth 1980).

Comstock, G. (ed.). Is There a Moral Obligation to Save the Family Farm? (Ames, IA 1987).

Connor, W. R. "Early Greek Warfare as Symbolic Expression," Past and Present 119 (1988) 3–29.

Cooper, A. B. Burford, "The Family Farm in Ancient Greece," CJ 73 (1977/78), 162–75.

_____. Land and Labor in Ancient Greece (Baltimore 1993).

Currie, J. M. The Economic Theory of Agricultural Land Tenure (Cambridge 1981).

d'Agostino, B. "Military Organization and Social Structure in Archaic Etruria," in Murray and Price 1990, 59–84.

Damaskenides, A. N. "Problems of the Greek Rural Economy," Balkan Studies 6 (1965) 21–34.

Davidson, O. G. Broken Heartland. The Rise of America's Rural Ghetto (New York 1990).

Davies, J. K. Athenian Propertied Families 600–300 B.C. (Oxford 1971).

_____. Democracy and Classical Greece (New York 1978).

_____. Wealth and the Power of Wealth in Classical Athens (New York 1981).

Davis, J. "Contributions to a Mediterranean Rural Archaeology: Historical Case Studies from the Ottoman Cyclades," Journal of Mediterranean Archaeology 4.2 (1991), 131–215.

Davison, J. "The First Greek Triremes," CQ 41 (1947), 18–24.

Dawson, D. Cities of the Gods. Communist Utopias in Greek Thought (New York 1992).

Day, J. An Economic History of Athens Under Roman Domination (reprint, New York 1973).

Delbrück, H. History of the Art of War, Vol. I (English trans. of Geschichte der Kriegskunst im Rahmen der politischen Geschichte [Berlin 1920], Westport, CT. 1975).

De Light, L., and P. W. de Neeve. "Ancient Periodic Markets: Festivals and Fairs" Athenaeum 3–4 (1988), 391–416.

Desborough, V. R. d'A. The Greek Dark Ages (London 1972).

Descoeudres, J. P. (ed.). Greek Colonists and Native Populations (Oxford 1990).

Detienne, M. Crise agraire et attitude religeuse chez Hésiode (Paris 1963).

_____. "La phalange: Problèmes et controverses," in Vernant 1968, 119–42.

_____. Les jardins d'Adonis (Paris 1972).

_____. "L'olivier: Un mythe politico-religieux," in Finley 1973b, 293–306.

Dimen, M., and E. Friedl (eds.). Regional Variation in Modern Greece and Cyprus:

Toward a Perspective on the Ethnography of Greece (Annals of the New York Academy of Sciences, 268, New York 1976).

Donlan, W. "Changes and Shifts in the Meaning of *Demos* in the Literature of the Archaic Period," *La Parola del Passato* 135 (1970), 381–95.

_____. "The Tradition of Anti-Aristocratic Thought in Early Greek Poetry," *Historia* 2.2. (1973), 145–154.

_____. *The Aristocratic Ideal in Ancient Greece: Attitudes of Superiority from Homer to the End of the Fifth Century B.C.* (Lawrence, KS 1980).

_____. "The Social Groups of Dark Age Greece," *CP* 80 (1985) 293–308.

_____. "Homeric Temenos and the Land Economy of the Dark Age," *Museum Helveticum* 46 (1989), 130–45.

Drews, R. L. "The First Tyrants in Greece," *Historia* 21 (1972), 129–44.

_____. *Basileus. The Evidence for Kingship in Geometric Greece* (New Haven 1983).

Drachmann, A. G. *Ancient Oil Mills and Presses* (Copenhagen 1932).

Ducrey, P. *Warfare in Ancient Greece* (New York 1989).

Duncan-Jones, R. *Structure and Scale in the Roman Economy* (Cambridge 1990).

Easterling, P. E. and J. V. Muir (eds.). *Greek Religion and Society* (Cambridge 1985).

van Effenterre, H. *La cité grecque. Des origines à la défaite de Marathon* (Paris 1985).

Ehrenberg, V. "When Did the Polis Rise," *JHS* 57 (1937), 147–59.

_____. *The People of Aristophanes* (Oxford 1951).

Eliot, C. W. J. *Coastal Demes of Attica* (Toronto 1962).

Engels, D. *Roman Corinth: An Alternative Model for the Classical City* (Chicago 1990).

Ferguson, W. S. *Hellenistic Athens* (London 1911, reprinted Chicago 1974).

Ferriolo, M. V. "Homer's Garden," *Journal of Garden History* 9.2 (1989), 86–94.

Figueira, T. J. "Mess Contributions and Subsistence at Sparta," *TAPA* 114 (1984a) 87–109.

_____. "The Lipari Islanders and their System of Communal Property," *Classical Antiquity* 3 (1984b), 179–206.

_____. "The Theognidea and Megarian Society," in Figueira and Nagy 1985, 112–58.

_____. "*Sitopolai* and *Sitophylakes* in Lysias' *Against the Graindealers*: Governmental Intervention in the Athenian Economy," *Phoenix* 40 (1986), 149–71.

Figueira, T. J., and G. Nagy. *Theognis of Megara. Poetry and the Polis* (Baltimore 1985).

Fine, J. V. A. *Horoi: Studies in Mortgage, Real Security and Land. Tenure in Ancient Athens* (Hesperia Supplement 9, Princeton 1951).

Finley, M. I. *Studies in Land and Credit in Ancient Athens 500–200 B.C.: The Horos Inscriptions* (New Brunswick 1952).

_____. *The Ancient Economy* (Berkeley 1973a).

_____. (ed.). *Problèmes de la terre en Grèce ancienne* (Paris 1973b).

_____. *The Use and Abuse of History. From the Myths of the Greeks to Lévi-Strauss, the Past Alive and the Present Illuminated* (New York 1975).

_____. *Aspects of Antiquity: Discoveries and Controversies* (2nd ed., Harmondsworth 1977).

_____. *The World of Odysseus* (2nd. ed., Harmondsworth 1978).

_____. *Ancient Slavery and Modern Ideology* (London 1980).

_____. *Early Greece. The Bronze and Archaic Ages* (New York 1981a).

_____. *Economy and Society in Ancient Greece* (London 1981b).

Fisher, N. R. E. *Social Values in Classical Athens* (London 1976).

Foley, A. *The Argolid 800–600 B.C.: An Archaeological Survey Together with an Index of Sites from the Neolithic to the Roman Period* (Göteborg 1988).

Forbes, H. A. "The Thrice-Ploughed Field" *Expedition* 18 (1976a), 5–11.

_____. "Fire, Axe and Plough: Human Influence on Local Plant Communities in the Southern Argolid," in Dimen and Friedle (New York 1976b), 109–26.

_____. "'We Have a Little of Everything': The Ecological Basis of Some Agricultural Practices in Methana, Trizinia," in Deimen and Friedl 1976c, 236–50.

_____. *Strategies and Soils: Technology, Production and Environment in the Peninsula of Methana Greece* (University of Pennsylvania Ph.D. dissertation, 1982).

_____. "Of Grandfathers and Grand Theories: The Hierarchised Ordering of Responses to Hazard in a Greek Rural Community," in Halstead and O'Shea 1989, 87–97.

_____. "The Ethnoarchaeological Approach to Ancient Greek Agriculture," in Wells 1992, 87–101.

Forbes, R. J. *Studies in Ancient Technology, Vol. 2* (Leiden 1955).

Fornara, C. W., "The Hoplite Achievement at Psyttaleia" *JHS* 86 (1966) 51–54.

Fowden, G. "City and Mountain in Late Roman Attica," *JHS* 108 (1988), 48–59.

Foxhall, L. "The Control of the Attic Landscape," in Wells 1992, 155–161.

Foxhall, L., and H. A. Forbes. "SITOMETREIA: The Role of Grain as a Staple Food in Classical Antiquity," *Chiron* 12 (1982), 41–89.

Francis, E. K. L., "The Personality Type of the Peasant According to Hesiod's *Works and Days*, a Culture Case Study," *Rural Sociology* 10 (1945), 275–95.

Frayn, J. M. *Subsistence Farming in Roman Italy* (Fontwell, UK 1986).

French, A. "The Economic Background to Solon's Reforms," *CQ* 50 (1956), 11–25.

_____. *The Growth of the Athenian Economy* (London 1964).

Frost, F. "The Athenian Military Before Cleisthenes," *Historia* 33 (1984), 283–99.

Fuks, A. *Social Conflicts in Ancient Greece* (Leiden 1984).

Fustel de Coulanges, N. D. *The Ancient City. A Study on the Religion, Laws, and Institutions of Greece and Rome* (reprinted with a new forward by A. Momliagno and S. Humphreys, Baltimore 1980).

Gabriel R., and K. Metz. *From Sumer to Rome. The Military Capability of Ancient Armies* (Westport, CT 1991).

Gallant, T.W. "Agricultural Systems, Land Tenure and the Reforms of Solon," *ABSA* 77 (1982), 111–24.

_____. *Risk and Survival in Ancient Greece. Reconstructing the Rural Domestic Economy* (Stanford 1991).

Gallo, L."Alimentazione e clasi sociali: una nota su orzo e frumento in Grecia," *Opus* 2 (1983) 449–72.

Galt, A. H. *Far From the Church Bells. Settlement and Society in an Apulian Town* (Cambridge 1991).

Garlan, Y. *Recherches de poliorcétique grecque* (Athens 1974).

_____. *War in the Ancient World: A Social History* (trans. J. Lloyd, New York 1975).

_____. "Le travail libre en Gréce ancienne" in Garnsey 1980, 6–22.

_____. *Slavery in Ancient Greece* (trans. J. Lloyd, Ithaca, NY 1988).

_____. *Guerre et économie en Grèce ancienne* (Paris 1989).

Garnsey, P. D. A (ed.). *Non-slave Labor in the Greco-Roman World* (Cambridge 1980).

_____. "Grain for Athens," in Cartledge and Harvey 1985, 62–75.

_____. *Famine and Food Supply in the Graeco-Roman World: Responses to Risk and Crisis* (Cambridge 1988).

_____. "Yield of the Land," in Wells 1992, 147–54.

Garnsey, P. D. A. and C. R. Whittaker (eds.). *Trade and Famine in Classical Antiquity* (PCPS, Supp. 8, Cambridge 1983).

Garnsey, P. D. A., K. Hopkins, and C. R. Whittaker. *Trade in the Ancient Economy* (Berkeley 1983).

Garnsey, P. D. A., and I. Morris. "Risk and the Polis: The Evolution of Institutionalised Responses to Food Supply Problems in the Ancient Greek State," in Halstead and O'Shea 1989, 98–105.

Gavan, T. P. "Agrarian and Agrarianism. A Study in the Use and Abuse of Words," *Journal of Southern History* 30 (1964), 35–47.

Gavrielides, N. "The Impact of Olive-growing on the Landscape in the Fourni Valley," in Dimen and Friedl 1976a, 143–57.

_____. "The Cultural Ecology of Olive Growing in the Fourni Valley," in Dimen and Friedl 1976b, 265–274.

Gernet, L. "L'approvisionment d'Athènes en blé aux Ve et IVe siècles," in G. Bloch (ed.), *Mélanges d'histoire ancienne* (Paris 1909), 269–391.

_____. *The Anthropology of Ancient Greece* (English trans. of *Anthropologie de la grèce antique*, Baltimore 1981).

Glotz, G. *Ancient Greece at Work* (English trans. of *Le Travail dans la Grèce ancienne*, London 1927).

_____. *The Greek City and Its Institutions* (London 1929).

Goldschmidt, W. *As You Sow* (New York 1947).

Gomme, A. W. *The Population of Athens in the Fifth and Fourth Centuries* (Oxford 1933).

_____. *Historical Commentary on Thucydides*, Vols. *i–v* (vols. iv–v with A. Andrewes and K. Dover, Oxford 1945–1970).

Goodman, D., and M. Redclift. *From Peasant to Proletarian: Capitalist Development and Agrarian Transitions* (Oxford 1981).

Graham. A.J. "Patterns in Early Greek Colonization," *JHS* 91 (1971) 35–47.

_____. *Colony and Mother City in Ancient Greece* (2nd ed., Chicago 1983).

Grand, R. *L'histoire de l'agriculture dans l'antiquité* (Paris 1935).

Grant, M. *The Rise of the Greeks* (New York 1987).

Green, P. *Alexander to Actium. The Historical Evolution of the Hellenistic Age* (Berkeley 1990).

Greenhalgh, P. A. L. *Early Greek Warfare: Horsemen and Chariots in the Homeric and Archaic Ages* (Cambridge 1973).

Griffith, G. T. *The Mercenaries of the Hellenistic World* (Cambridge 1935).

Grigg, D. B. *Population Growth and Agrarian Change: An Historical Perspective* (Cambridge 1980).

_____. *The Dynamics of Agricultural Change: The Historical Experience* (London 1982).

Griswold, A. W. *Farming and Democracy* (New York 1948).

Groningen van, B. A. *Hésiod et Persès* (Amerstdam 1957).

Grundy, G. B. *Thucydides and the History of his Age* (London 1948).

Gudeman, S. *The Demise of a Rural Economy* (London 1978).

Guiraud, P. *La propriété foncière en Grèce jusqu' à la conquête romaine* (Paris 1893).

Gwynn, A. "The Character of Greek Colonization," *JHS* 38 (1918), 88–123.

Hackett, J. (ed.). *Warfare in the Ancient World* (London 1989).

Hägg, R. (ed.), *The Greek Renaissance of the Eighth Century* B.C. (Stockholm 1983).

Hahn, I. "Temenos and Service Land in the Homeric Epic," *A. Ant. Hung.* 25 (1977), 300–316.

_____. "Foreign Trade and Foreign Policy in Archaic Greece," in Garnsey and Whittaker 1983, 30–36.

Halstead, P. L. J. "From Determinism to Uncertainty: Social Storage and the Rise of the Minoan Palace," in A. Sheridan and G. Bailey (eds.), *Economic Archaeology* (BAR. Int. Ser. 96, Oxford 1981), 187–213.

_____. "Traditional and Ancient Rural Economy in Mediterranean Europe: Plus Ça Change?" *JHS* 107 (1987), 77–87.

_____. "Agriculture in the Bronze Age. Towards a Model of Palatial Economy," in Wells 1992, 105–19.

Halstead, P. L. J. and G. E. M. Jones. "Agrarian Ecology in the Greek Islands: Time Stress, Scale and Risk," *JHS* 109 (1989), 41–55.

Halstead, P. and J. O'Shea (eds.). *Bad Year Economics: Cultural Responses to Risk and Uncertainty* (Cambridge 1989).

Hannah, P. and R. Hannah. "Athens—Sicily—Campania: Warriors and Painters," in Descoeudres 1990, 267–76.

Hansen, J. M. "Agriculture in the Prehistoric Aegean: Data Versus Speculation," *AJA* 92 (1988), 39–52.

Hansen, M. H. *The Athenian Democracy in the Age of Demosthenes* (Oxford 1991).

Hanson, V. D. *Warfare and Agriculture in Classical Greece* (Pisa 1983).

_____. "Epameinondas, the Battle of Leuktra, and the 'Revolution' in Greek Battle Tactics," *Classical Antiquity* 7.2 (1988), 190–207.

_____. *The Western Way of War. Infantry Battle in Classical Greece* (New York 1989).

_____. (ed.). *Hoplites: The Classical Greek Battle Experience* (London 1991a).

_____. "Hoplite Technology in Phalanx Battle," in Hanson 1991b, 63–83.

_____. "Practical Aspects of Grape-growing and the Ideology of Greek Viticulture," in Wells 1992a, 161–167.

_____. "Thucydides and the Desertion of Attic Slaves During the Decelean War," *Classical Antiquity* 11.2 (1992b), 210–228.

Harmand, J. *La guerre antique, de Sumer à Rome* (Vendome 1973).

Harrison, A. R. W. *The Law of Athens: The Family and Property* (Oxford 1968).

Hasebroek, J. *Trade and Politics in Ancient Greece* (1928; reprint of English trans. from German, London 1965).

Hehn, V., with O. Schräder. *Kulturpflanzen und Haustiere in ihrem Übergang aus Asien nach Griechenland und Italien sowie in das übrige Europa* (Berlin 1911).

Heichelheim, F. M. *An Ancient Economic History, Vols. I–II* (Leiden 1958–1964).

Heitland, W. E. *Agricola. A Study on Agriculture and Rustic Life in the Graeco-Roman World from the Point of View of Labour* (Cambridge 1921).

Hennig, D. "Grundbesitz bei Homer und Hesiod," *Chiron* 10 (1980) 35–52.

Hignett, C. *Xerxes' Invasion of Greece* (Oxford 1963).

Hodkinson, S. J. "Land Tenure and Inheritance in Classical Sparta," *CQ* 36 (1986), 378–406.

_____. "Animal Husbandry in the Greek Polis," in Whittaker 1988, 35–74.

_____. "Imperialist Democracy and Market-Oriented Pastoral Production in Classical Athens," *Anthropolozoologica* 16 (1992), 53–61.

Hodkinson, S. J., and H. Hodkinson. "Mantineia and the Mantinike: Settlement and Society in a Greek Polis," *ABSA* 76 (1981), 239–96.

Holladay, A. J. "Hoplites and Heresies," *JHS* 102 (1982) 94–104.

Holladay, J. "Followers of Peisistratus," *Greece and Rome* 24 (1977), 40–56.

Hopper, R. J. "'Plain,' 'Shore,' and 'Hill' in Early Athens," *ABSA* 56 (1961), 189–219.

_____. *Trade and Industry in Classical Greece* (London 1979).

Howe, T. P., "Linear B and Hesiod's Breadwinners," *TAPA* 89 (1958), 44–65.

Hughes, J. D, "Ecology in Ancient Greece," *Inquiry* 18 (1975), 115–125.

Humphreys, S. C. *Anthropology and the Greeks* (London 1978).

_____. *The Family, Women, and Death* (London 1983).

Hurwit, J. M. *The Art and Culture of Early Greece, 1100–480 B.C.* (Ithaca, NY 1985).

Isager, S., and J. E. Skydsgaard. *Ancient Greek Agriculture. An Introduction* (London 1993).

Jackson, A. J. "Hoplites and the Gods: Dedication of Captured Arms and Armor," in Hanson 1991a, 198–228.

Jameson, M. H. "The Hero Echetlaeus," *TAPA* 57 (1951), 49–61.

_____. "The Southern Argolid: The Setting for Historical and Cultural Studies," in Dimen and Friedl 1976, 74–91.

_____. "Agriculture and Slavery in Classical Athens" *CJ* 73 (1977/8), 122–41.

_____. "Apollo Lykeios in Athens," *Archaiognosia* 1.2 (1980) 213–35.

_____. "The Leasing of Land in Rhamnous," *Hesperia Supplement* 19 (1982), 60–74.

_____. "Famine in the Greek World," in Garnsey and Whittaker 1983, 6–16.

_____. "Private Space and the Greek City," in Murray and Price 1990, 171–98.

_____. "Sacrifice Before Battle," in Hanson 1991a, 197–221.

_____. "Agricultural Labor in Ancient Greece," in Wells 1992, 135–46.

Jardé, A. *Les céréals dans l'antiquité grecque I. La production* (Paris 1925).

Jasny, N. "Competition Among Grains in Classical Antiquity," *AHR* 47 (1942), 747–64.

_____. *The Wheats of Classical Antiquity* (Baltimore 1944).

_____. "The Daily Bread of the Ancient Greeks and Romans," *Osiris* 9 (1950), 121–50.

Jeffery, L. H. *The Local Scripts of Archaic Greece* (Oxford 1961).

_____. *Archaic Greece: The City-States c. 700–500 B.C.* (London 1976).

Jones, A. M. *Athenian Democracy* (Oxford 1957).

_____. "The Roman Economy," in P. A. Brunt (ed.), *Studies in Ancient Economic and Administrative History* (Totowa, NJ 1974).

Jones, J. E. "Two Attic Country Houses," *Athens Annals of Archaeology* 7 (1974), 303–12.

_____. "Town and Country Houses of Attica in Classical Times," in *Miscellanea Graeca: Thorikos and Laurion in Archaic and Classical Times 1*, (Brussels 1975), 63–140.

Jones, J. E., L. H. Sackett, and C. Eliot. "The Dema House in Attica," *ABSA* 57 (1962), 75–114.

Jones, J. E., L. H. Sackett, and A. J. Graham, "An Attic Country House Below the Cave of Pan at Vari," *ABSA* 68 (1973), 355–452.

Jongman, W. *The Economy and Society of Pompeii* (Amsterdam 1988).

Jordan, B. *The Athenian Navy in the Classical Period. A Study of Athenian Naval Administration and Military Organization in the Fifth and Fourth Centuries B.C.* (Berkeley 1972).

Kagan, D. *The Archidamian War* (Ithaca, NY, 1974).

Karavites, P. *Capitulations and Greek Interstate Relationships* (Göttingen 1982).

Kayser, B., and K. Thompson. *Economic and Social Atlas of Greece* (Athens 1964).

Keegan, J. *The Second World War* (New York 1989).

Keller, D., and D. W. Rupp (eds.). *Archaeological Survey in the Mediterranean* (*BAR* Int. Ser. 155, Oxford 1983).

Keller, D., and M. Wallace. "The Canadian Karystia Project: How to Catch a Cleruch," *Canadian Mediterranean Institute Bulletin* 8 (1987), 6–7.

———. "The Canadian Karystia Project: Two Classical Farmsteads," *Classical Views* 7 (1988). 151–57.

Kent, J. H., "The Temple Estates of Delos, Rhenia, and Mykonos," *Hesperia* 17 (1948), 243–335.

Kern, P. "Military Technology and Ethical Values in Ancient Greek Warfare: the Siege of Plataea," *War and Society* 6.2 (1988), 1–20.

Kerridge, E. *The Agricultural Revolution* (New York 1967).

Kerschensteiner, J. "Zu Aufbau und Gedankenführung von Hesiods Erga," *Hermes* 79 (1944), 149–91.

Kinkel, J. *Die sozialökonomischen Grundlagen der Staats- und Wirtschaftslehren von Aristoteles* (Leipzig 1911).

Kirsten, E. *Die griechische Polis als historisch-geographisches Problem des Mittelmeeraumes* (Bonn 1956).

Klingenberg, E. *Platons NOMOI GEORGIKOI und das positive griechische Recht* (Münchener Univeritätsschriften, Juristiche Fakultät. Abhandlungen zur rechtswissenschaftlichen Grundlagenforschung, (Berlin 1976).

Knapp, C. H. "Irrigation Among the Greeks and Romans," *CW* 12 (1919), 73–74, 81–82.

Koerner, R. "Zur Landaufteilung in griechischen Poleis in älterer Zeit," *Klio* 69.2 (1987), 443–49.

Kreibig, H. "Landed Property in the 'Hellenistic' Orient," *Eirene* 15 (1977) 5–26.

Krentz, P. "Casualties in Hoplite Battles," *Classical Antiquity* 4 (1985) 50–61.

Krochmal, A. "Olive Growing in Greece," *Economic Botany* (1955), 228–32.

Kromayer, J., and G. Veith. *Heerwesen und Kriegführung der Greichen und Römer* (Munich 1928).

Lacey, W. K. *The Family in Classical Greece* (London 1968).

Laiou-Thomadakis, A. *Peasant Society in the Late Byzantine Empire* (Princeton 1978).

Lambrinoudakis, V. "Ancient Farmhouses on Mount Aipos," in Boardman and Vasphopoulou-Richardson 1986, 295–304.

Lane-Fox, R. "Aspects of Inheritance in the Greek World," in P. Cartledge and H. D. Harvey (eds.), 208–32.

Langdon, M. K. *A Sanctuary of Zeus on Mount Hymettos* (*Hesperia supp.* 16, Princeton 1976).

––––––. "An Attic Decree Concerning Oropos," *Hesperia* 56 (1987), 47–58.

––––––. "On the Farm," *CJ* 86 (1991), 209–13.

Langdon, M., and L.V. Watrous. "The Farm of Timesios: Rock-cut Inscriptions in South Attica," *Hesperia* 46 (1977), 162–77.

Larsen, J. A. O. *Representative Government in Greek and Roman History* (Berkeley 1966).

Latacz, J. *Kampfparänese, Kampfdarstellung, und Kampfwirtlichkeit in der Ilias, bei Kallinos und Tyrtaios* (Munich 1977).

Lauffer, S. "Die platonische Agrarwirtschaft," *Vierteljahrschrift für Sozial-und Wirtschafts-Geschichte* 19.3 (1936), 233–69.

Lauter, H. "Zum Heimstätten und Gutshausern im klassischen Attika," in F. Krinzinger et al., *Forschungen und Funde, Festschrift Bernard Neutsch* (Innsbruck 1980), 279–86.

––––––. "Klassisches Landleben in Attika" *RUB-Aktuel* 76 (Oct. 19, 1981).

Lazenby, J. F.,*The Spartan Army* (Warminister 1985).

––––––. "The Killing Zone," in Hanson 1991, 87–109.

––––––. *The Defense of Greece, 490–479 B.C.* (Warminister 1993).

Lekas, P. *Marx on Classical Antiquity: Problems of Historical Methodology* (New York 1988).

Lewis, D. M. "After the Profanation of the Mysteries," in Badian 1966, 177–92.

––––––. "The Athenian Rationes Centesimarum," in Finley 1973b, 187–212.

––––––. "Public Property in the City," in Murray and Price 1990, 245–64.

Lewis, N. "Solon's Agrarian Legislation," *AJP* 62 (1941), 149–56.

Levy, H. L. "Property Distribution by Lot in Present-day Greece," *TAPA* 87 (1956), 42–46.

Linforth, I. M. *Solon the Athenian* (Berkeley 1919).

Lintott, A. *Violence and Civil Strife in the Classical City* (London 1982).

––––––. "Aristotle and Democracy," *CQ* 42 (1992), 114–28.

Lloyd, C. "Greek Urbanity and the Polis," in R. T. Marchese (ed.), *Aspects of Graeco-Roman Urbanism: Essays on the Classical City* (Oxford, BAR Int. Ser. 188, 1983), 11–41.

Lohmann, H. "Atene, eine attische Landgemeinde klassischer Zeit," *Hellenika Jahrbuch* (1983), 98–117.

_____. "Landleben im klassischen Attika, Ergebnisse und Probleme einer archäologischen Landesaufnahme des Demos Atene," *Jahrbuch der Ruhr-Univerität* 1985, 71–96.

_____."Agriculture and Country Life in Classical Attica," in Wells 1992, 29–60.

Lonis, R. *Guerre et religion en Grèce à l'époque classique* (Paris 1979).

Loraux, N. *The Invention of Athens. The Funeral Oration in the Classical City* (trans. A. Sheridan, Cambridge, Mass. 1986).

Lorimer, H. L. "The Hoplite Phalanx, with Special Reference to the Poems of Archilochus and Tyrtaeus," *ABSA* 42 (1947) 76–138.

Loussert, R., and G. Brousse. *L'olivier* (Paris 1978).

MacDowell, D. M. "The *Oikos* in Athenian Law," *CQ* 39 (1989), 10–21.

Malkin, J. *Religion and Colonization in Ancient Greece* (Leiden 1987).

Manville, B. "Solon's Law of Stasis and Atimia in Classical Athens," *TAPA* 110 (1980), 213–21.

Markle, M. M. "Participation of Farmers on Athenian Juries and Assemblies," *Ancient Society* 21 (1990), 149–65.

Martin, R. *L'urbanism dans Grèce antique* (Paris 1956).

Mazon, P. *Hésiode, Les Travaux et les Jours* (Paris 1914).

McDonald, W. A., and G. Rapp. *The Minnesota Messenia Expedition. Reconstructing a Bronze Age Regional Environment* (Minnesota 1972).

McGrew, W. W. *Land and Revolution in Modern Greece* (Kent, OH 1985).

McKechnie, P. *Outsiders in the Greek Cities in the Fourth Century* B.C. (London 1989).

McNeill, W. H. *The Metamorphosis of Greece Since World War II* (Oxford 1978).

Meier, C. "Die Role des Krieges im klassischen Athen," *Historische Zeitschrift* 251 (1990), 555–605.

Meiggs, R. *Trees and Timber in the Ancient Mediterranean World* (Oxford 1982).

Meiggs, R., and D. M. Lewis. *A Selection of Greek Historical Inscriptions to the End of the Fifth Century* B.C. (Oxford 1969).

Meikle, S. "Aristotle and the Political Economy of the Polis," *JHS* 99 (1979) 57–73.

Mele, A. *Il commercio greco arcaio. Praxis ed emporie* (Naples 1979).

Métraux, G. *Western Greek Land-Use and City Planning in the Archaic Period* (New York and London 1978).

Michell, H. *The Economics of Ancient Greece* (Cambridge 1957).

Mickwitz, H. "Economic Rationalism in Graeco-Roman Agriculture," *English Historical Review* 52 (1937), 577–89.

Miler, H.F. "The Practical and Economic Background to the Greek Mercenary Explosion" *Greece and Rome* 31 (1984) 153–59.

Millet, P. "The Attic Horoi Reconsidered in the Light of Recent Discoveries," *OPUS* 1.2. (1982), 219–40.

_____. "Hesiod and his World," *PCPS* 210 (1984), 84–115.

Momigliano, A. "Sea-Power in Greek Thought" *CR* 58 (1949), 1–7.

Montmarquet, J. A. *The Idea of Agrarianism. From Hunter-Gatherer to Agrarian Radical in Western Culture* (Moscow, ID 1989).

Moore, J. M. *Aristotle and Xenophon on Democracy and Oligarchy* (Berkeley 1975).

Morgan, C. A. *Settlement and Exploitation in the Region of the Corinthian Gulf,* c. 1000–700 B.C. (Cambridge University PhD thesis, 1986).

Morrison, J. S., and R. T. Williams. *Greek Oared Ships 900–322 B.C.* (Cambridge 1968).

Moritz, L. A. "ALPHITA: A Note" *CQ* 43 (1949) 113–17.

_____. "Husked and 'Naked' Grain," *CQ* 49 (1955a), 129–34.

_____. "Corn," *CQ* 49 (1955b) 135–41.

_____. *Grain-Mills and Flour in Classical Antiquity* (Oxford 1958).

Morris, I. "The Use and Abuse of Homer," *Classical Antiquity* 5 (1986), 81–138.

_____. *Burial and Ancient Society: The Rise of the Greek City-State* (Cambridge 1987).

_____. "The Early Polis as City and State," in Rich and Wallace-Hadrill 1991, 25–58.

Morrow, G. R. *Plato's Cretan City. A Historical Interpretation of the Laws* (Princeton 1960).

Mossé, C. *The Ancient World at Work* (trans. by J. Lloyd of *Le Travail en Grèce et à Rome,* New York 1969).

_____. "Le statut des paysans en Attique au IVe Siècle," in Finley 1973b, 179–86.

_____. *Athens in Decline* (trans. of *La fin de la démocratie athénienne* Paris 1973b).

Murray, W. M. "The Ancient Dam of the Myktikas Valley" *AJA* 88 (1984), 195–203.

Murray, O. *Early Greece* (London 1980).

Murray, O., and S. Price (eds.). *The Greek City. From Homer to Alexander* (Oxford 1990).

Myres, J. L. "The Causes of Rise and Fall in the Population of the Ancient World," *Eugenics Review* 7 (1915/16), 15–45.

Netting, R. M. "The Ecological Approach in Cultural Study," *McCaleb Module in Anthropology* 6 (1971) 1–30.

Nieto, F. *Los acuerdos bélicos en la antiqua Grecia II* (Santiago 1975).

Nilsson, M. P. "Die Hoplitentaktik und das Staatswesen," *Klio* 22 (1929) 240–49.

Nowicka, M. *Les maisons de tour dans le monde grec* (Warsaw 1965).

Nuttonson, M. Y. *Ecological Crop Geography of Greece* (Washington 1947).

Ober, J. "Rock-cut Inscriptions from Mount Hymettos," *Hesperia* 50 (1981) 68–77.

_____. *Fortress Attica: Defense of the Athenian Land Frontier* (Leiden 1985).

_____. *Mass and Elite in Democratic Athens: Rhetoric, Ideology, and the Power of the People* (Princeton 1989).

_____. "Aristotle's Political Sociology: Class, Status and Order in the *Politics*," in C. Lord and D. K. O'Connor (eds.), *Essays on the Foundations of Aristotelian Political Science* (Berkeley 1990), 112–35.

_____. "Hoplites and Obstacles," in Hanson 1991, 173–96.

Osborne, M. J. *Naturalization in Athens* (4 vols. Brussels 1981–83).

Osborne, R. G. *Demos: the Discovery of Classical Attika* (Cambridge 1985a).

_____. "The Land Leases from Hellenistic Thespiai: A Reexamination," in G. Arngould and P. Roesch (eds.), *La Boéotia antique* (Paris 1985b), 317–21.

_____. "Buildings and Residence on the Land in Classical and Hellenistic Greece: The Contribution of Epigraphy," ABSA 80 (1985c), 119–28.

_____. *Classical Landscape with Figures: The Ancient City and Its Countryside* (London 1987).

_____. "Social and Economic Implications of the Leasing of Land and Property in Classical and Hellenistic Athens," *Chiron* 18 (1988), 279–323.

_____. "A Crisis in Archaeological History? The Seventh Century B.C. in Attica,"ABSA 84 (1989), 297–322.

_____. "Pride and Prejudice, Sense and Substance: Exchange and Society in the Greek City," in Rich and Wallace-Hadrill 1991, 119–47.

_____. "'Is It a Farm?' The Definition of Agricultural Sites and Settlements in Ancient Greece," in Wells 1992a, 21–28.

_____. "Classical Greek Gardens: Between Farm and Paradise," in J. D Hunt (ed.), *Dumbarton Oaks Colloquium on the History of Landscape Architecture XIII* (Washington DC, 1992b), 373–91.

Ostwald, M. *From Popular Sovereignty to the Sovereignty of Law. Law, Society, and Politics in Fifth-Century Athens* (Berkeley 1986).

Owens, E. J. "The *Koprologoi* at Athens in the Fifth and Fourth Centuries B.C." CQ 33 (1983), 44–50.

Padgug, R. A. "Classes and Society in Classical Greece," *Arethusa* 8 (1975), 85–118.

Parke, H. W. *Greek Mercenary Soldiers from the Earliest Times to the Battle of Ipsos* (Oxford 1933).

Patterson, C. *Pericles' Citizenship Law 451–450 B.C.* (New York 1981).

Pecírka, J. "Land Tenure and the Development of the Athenian Polis," in Vard and Willets 1968, 183–201.

_____. "Country Estates of the Polis of Chersonesos in the Crimea," in *Richerche Storiche ed Economiche in Memoria di Corrado Bargallo, Vol. I* (Rome 1970), 459–477.

_____. "Homestead Farms in Classical and Hellenistic Hellas," in Finley 1973b, 113–47.

_____. "The Crisis of the Athenian Polis in the Fourth Century B.C." *Eirene* 14 (1976), 5–29.

Pecírka, J., and M. Dufkova. "Excavations of Farms and Farmhouses in the Chora of the Chersonesos in the Crimea," *Eirene* 8 (1970), 123–74.

Perisynakis, I. "Hesiod's Treatment of Wealth," *Metis* 1 (1986), 97–119.

Philippson, A. *Die griechischen Landschaften, Vols. I–IV* (Frankfurt 1950–59).

Pippidi, D. M. "Le problème de la main-d'oeuvre agricole dans les colonies grecques de la mer Noire," in Finley 1973b, 63–82.

Pöhlman, R. V. *Geschichte der sozialen Frage und des Sozialismus in der antiken Welt* (Berlin 1925).

Polignac, F. de. *La Naissance de la cité grecque* (Paris 1984).

Postlethwaite, N. "The Continuation of the Odyssey: Some Formulaic Evidence," *CP* 76 (1981), 177–87.

Pouilloux, J. *Recherches sur l'histoire et les cultes de Thasos I (Paris 1954).*

Pritchett, W. K. "The Attic Stelai, Part II," Hesperia 25 (1956) 178–328.

_____. *The Greek State at War, Parts I–V* (Berkeley 1971–1991).

_____. *Studies in Ancient Greek Topography, Parts I–VIII* (Berkeley 1965–1993).

Putnam, R. *Making Democracy Work. Civic Traditions in Modern Italy* (Princeton 1993).

Qviller, B. "The Dynamics of the Homeric Society," *Symbolae Osloenses* 56 (1981), 109–55.

Rackman, O. "Land-Use and the Native Vegetation of Greece," in M. Bell and S. Limbrey (eds.), *Archaeological Aspects of Woodland Ecology* (BAR Int. Ser. 146, Oxford 1982) 177–198.

_____. "Observations on the Historical Ecology of Boiotia" *ABSA* 78 (1983), 291–351.

_____. "Ancient Landscapes," in Murray and Price 1990, 85–112.

Rackman, O. and J. Moody. "Terraces," in Wells 1992, 123–30.

Rahe, P. *Republics, Ancient and Modern* (Chapel Hill, NC 1993).

Raven, P. H. "The Evolution of Mediterranean Floras," in F. di Castri and H. A. Mooney (eds.), *Mediterranean Type Ecosystems: Origins and Structure* (London 1973), 213–24.

Redfield, J. M. *Peasant Society and Culture* (Chicago 1953).

Redfield, R. M. "The Growth of Markets in Early Greece," in B. L. Anderson and A. J. H. Latham (eds.), *The Market in History* (London 1986), 29–58.

Renfrew, J., *Palaeoethnobotany* (New York 1973).

Renfrew, C., and J. M. Wagstaff (eds.). *An Island Polity: The Archaeology of Exploitation on Melos* (Cambridge 1982).

Rheinmuth, O. W. *The Ephebic Inscriptions of the Fourth Century B.C.* (Leiden 1971).

Rhodes, P. J. *Commentary on the Aristotelian Athenaion Politeia* (Oxford 1981).

Rich, J., and A. Wallace-Hadrill (eds.). *City and Country in the Ancient World* (London 1991).

Richter, W. *Die Landwirtschaft im homerischen Zeitalter* (*Archaeologia Homerica II*, H (Gottingen 1968).

Ridgeway, W. "The Homeric Land System," *JHS* 6 (1885), 319–339.

Ridley, R. T. "The Economic Activity of the Perioikoi," *Mnemosyne* 27.3 (1974) 281–292.

_____. "Hoplite as Citizen: Athenian Military Institutions in their Social Context" *AC* 48 (1979), 508–48.

Rihll, T. E. "*HEKTEMOROI*: Partners in Crime?" *JHS* 111 (1991), 101–27.

Rihll, T. E., and A. G. Wilson. "Modelling Settlement Structures in Ancient Greece: New Approaches to the Polis" in Rich and Wallace-Hadrill 1991, 59–96.

Robertson, N. "Solon's Axones and Krybeis and the Sixth-century Background," *Historia* 35 (1986), 147–176.

Rodman, J. "The Other Side of Ecology in Ancient Greece: Comments on Hughes," *Inquiry* 19 (1976), 108–12.

Roebuck, C. "Some Aspects of Urbanisation at Corinth," *Hesperia* 41 (1972) 96–127.

de Romilly, J. "*Guerre et paix entre cités,*" in Vernant 1968, 215–225.

_____. *The Rise and Fall of Greek States According to Greek Authors* (Ann Arbor 1977).

Rosivach, V. J. "Manning the Athenian Fleet, 433–426 B.C.," *American Journal of Ancient History* 10.1 (1992), 41–66.

Rossiter, J. J. "Wine and Oil Processing at Roman Farms in Italy," *Phoenix* (1981) 345–361.

Rostovtzeff, M. *A Large Estate in Egypt in the Third Century* B.C. (1922; reprinted New York 1979).

_____. *The Social and Economic History of the Hellenistic World, vols. i-iii* (Oxford 1941).

Roussel, D. *Tribu et cité* (Paris 1976).

Roy, J. "Tribalism in Southwest Arcadia in the Classical Period," *Acta Antiqua Academiae Scientiarum Hungaricae* 20 (1972), 43–51.

_____. "Demosthenes 55 as Evidence for Isolated Farmsteads in Classical Attica," *Liverpool Classical Monthly* 13 (1988), 57–59.

Runciman, W. G. "Origins of States: The Case of Archaic Greece," *Comparative Studies in Society and History* 24 (1982), 351–77.

_____. "Doomed to Extinction: The *Polis* as an Evolutionary Dead-end," in Murray and Price 1990, 348–367.

Runnels, C., and J. M. Hansen. "The Olive in the Prehistorical Aegean: The Evidence for Domestication in the Early Bronze Age," *Oxford Journal of Archaeology* 5 (1986), 299–308.

Runnels, C. N. and van Andel, T. H., "The Evolution of Settlement in the Southern Argolid Greece: An Economic Explanation," *Hesperia* 56 (1987) 303–34.

Ruschenbusch, E. "IG XII 5 609. Eine Bürgerliste von Iulis und Koresia auf Keos" *ZPE* 48 (1982), 175–88.

_____. "Die Zahl der griechischen Staaten und Areagrösse und Bürgerzahl der Normalpolis," *ZPE* 59 (1985), 253–63.

Sallares, R. *The Ecology of the Ancient Greek World* (Ithaca 1991).

de Ste. Croix, G. E. M. "The Estate of Phainippos (Ps. Demosthenes XLII)," in Badian 1966, 109–14.

_____. *The Origins of the Peloponnesian War* (Ithaca, NY 1972).

_____. *The Class Struggle in the Ancient Greek World* (Ithaca, NY 1981).

Salmon, J. "Political Hoplites?" *JHS* 97 (1977), 84–101.

_____. *Wealthy Corinth* (Oxford 1984).

Sargent, R. "The Use of Slaves by Athenians in Warfare. Part I" *CP* 22 (1927), 199–212.

Sarpaki, A. "The Palaeoethnobotanical Approach. The Mediterranean Triad or Is It a Quartet?" in Wells 1992, 61–76.

Saviat, F. "Le vin de Thasos, amphores, vin, and sources écrites," in *Recherches sur les amphores grecques,* supp. 13 BCH (1986) 145–96.

Saviat, F., and C. Vatin. "Le Cadastre de Larissa," *BCH* 87 (1974), 247–62.

Scheuring, A. F., *A Guidebook to California Agriculture* (Berkeley 1983).

Sculley, S. "The Polis in Homer," *Ramus* 10 (1981), 1–34.

Semple, E. C. "Ancient Mediterranean Agriculture," *Agricultural History* 2 (1928), 61–98, 129–156.

_____. *The Geography of the Mediterranean Region: Its Relation to Ancient History* (Cambridge 1932).

Shaw, D. "The Problem of Land Fragmentation in the Mediterranean," *Geography Journal* 53 (1963), 40–51.

Sherwin-White, S. *Ancient Cos: An Historical Study from the Dorian Settlement to the Imperial Period* (Gottingen 1978).

Shipley, D. G. J. *A History of Samos 800–188 B.C.* (Oxford 1987).

Skafte Jensen, M. "Tradition and Individuality in Hesiod's *Works and Days,*" *Classica et Mediaevalia* 27 (1966), 1–27.

Skydsgaard, J. E. "Transhumance in Ancient Greece," in Whittaker (Cambridge 1988), 75–86.

_____. "Agriculture in Ancient Greece. On the nature of the Sources and the Problems of their Interpretation," in Wells 1992, 9–13.

Slaughter, C., and C. Kasimis. "Some Social-Anthropological Aspects of Boeotian Rural Society: A Field Report," *Byzantine and Modern Greek Studies* 10 (1986), 103–60.

Slicher van Bath, B. H. *The Agrarian History of Western Europe A.D. 500–1850* (London 1963).

Snodgrass, A. M. "Carian Armourers: The Growth of a Tradition," *JHS* 84 (1964a), 107–18.

_____. *Early Greek Armor and Weapons* (Edinburgh 1964b).

_____. "The Hoplite Reform and History," *JHS* 85 (1965), 110–22.

_____. *Arms and Armor of the Greeks* (Ithaca, NY 1967).

_____. *The Dark Age of Greece. An Archaeological Survey of the Eleventh to the Eighth Century* B.C. (Edinburgh 1971a).

_____. "The First European Body-armor" *Studies in Honor of C. F. C. Hawkes* (London 1971b), 33–50.

_____. "An Historical Homeric Society?" *JHS* 94 (1974), 114–125.

_____. *Archaeology and the Rise of the Greek State* (Cambridge 1977).

_____. *Archaic Greece: The Age of Experiment* (London 1980).

_____. "Two Demographic Notes" in R. Hägg 1983, 167–71.

_____. "The Site of Ascra," in P. Roesch and G. Argoud (eds.), *La Béotie antique* (Lyon 1985), 87–96.

_____. *An Archaeology of Greece: The Present and Future Scope of a Discipline* (Berkeley 1987).

_____. "Survey Archaeology and the Rural Landscape of the Greek City," in Murray and Price 1990, 113–36.

_____. "Archaeology and the Study of the Greek City," in Rich and Wallace Hadrill 1991, 1–24.

Solmsen, F. *Hesiod and Aeschylus* (Ithaca 1949).

Spahn, P. *Mittelschicht und Polisbildung* (Frankfurt 1978).

Spurr, M. S. *Arable Cultivation in Roman Italy, ca. 200* B.C.—*ca.* A.D. *100* (London 1986).

Standish, R. *The First of All Trees. A Study of the Olive* (London 1961).

Starr, C. G. *Economic and Social Growth of Early Greece, 800–500* B.C. (Oxford 1977).

_____. *Individual and Community. The Rise of the Polis 800–500* B.C. (New York 1986).

Staten, J., *The Embattled Farmer* (Golden, CO, 1987).

Strange, M. *Family Farming. A New Economic Vision* (San Francisco 1988).

Strauss, B. *Athens after the Peloponnesian War: Class, Faction, and Policy 403–386* B.C. (Ithaca 1986).

Strauss, J. "The Theory and Comparative Statics of Agricultural Household Models," in I. Singh, I. Squire, and J. Strauss, (eds.), *Agricultural Household Models: Extensions, Applications, and Policy* (Baltimore 1986), 71–94.

Symeonoglou, S., *The Topography of Thebes from the Bronze Age to Modern Times* (Princeton 1985).

Tainter, J. *The Collapse of Complex Societies* (Cambridge 1991).

Taillardat, J. *Les images d'Aristophane, études de langue et de style* (Paris 1965).

Thiel, J. H. "On Solon's System of Property-Classes" *Mnemosyne* 4.3 (1950) 1–11.

Thompson, K. *Farm Fragmentation in Greece: The Problem and Its Setting* (Athens 1963).

Thomsen, R. "War Taxes in Classical Athens," in *Armées et fiscalité dans le monde antique* (Paris 1977), 135–48.

Tod, M. N. *A Selection of Greek Historical Inscriptions, Vol. II* (Oxford 1948).

Todd, S. "Lady Chatterley's Lover and the Attic Orators," *JHS* 110 (1990), 146–73.

Trever, A. A. "The Age of Hesiod: A Study in Economic History," *CP* 19 (1924), 157–68.

van Andel, T.H., and C. N. Runnels. *Beyond the Acropolis: A Rural Greek Past* (Stanford 1987).

van Andel, T. H., C. N. Runnels and K. O. Pope. "Five Thousand Years of Land Use and Abuse in the Southern Argolid, Greece," *Hesperia* 55 (1986), 103–28.

Vanbremeersch, N. "Représentation de la terre et du travail agricole chez Pindare," *Quaderni di Storia* 13 (1987), 73–95.

Vanderpool, E. "Roads and Forts in Northwest Attica," *California Studies in Classical Antiquity* 11 (1978), 227–45.

van Wees, H. "Leaders of Men? Military Organizations in the *Iliad*," *CQ* 36 (1986), 285–303.

Vard, I., and R. F. Willets (eds.), *Geras: Studies Presented to George Thomson* (Prague 1968).

Vernant, J. P. (ed.). *Problèmes de la guerre en Grèce ancienne* (Paris 1968).

_____. *The Origins of Greek Thought* (Ithaca 1982).

Volkman, J. "Die Waffentechnik in ihrem Einfluss auf das soziale Lebe der Antike," in L. Wise (ed.), *Die Entwicklung der Kriegswaffe und ihr Zusammenhang mit der Sozialordnung* (Berlin 1953).

_____. *Myth and Society in ancient Greece* (Brighton 1980).

Wagstaff, M. "Greek Rural Settlements: A Review of the Literature," *Erdkunde* 23 (1965), 306–17.

_____. "A Note on Settlement Numbers in Ancient Greece," *JHS* 115 (1975), 163–68.

_____. *The Development of Rural Settlements. A Study of the Helos Plain in Southern Greece* (Amersham 1982).

_____. *Landscape and Culture* (Oxford 1987).

Walbank, M. B. "Leases of Sacred Property in Attica," *Hesperia* 52 (1983),. 100–135.

Walcot, P. *Hesiod and the Near East* (Cardiff 1966).

_____. *Greek Peasants, Ancient and Modern* (New York 1970).

Wardman, J. "Tactics and Tradition of the Persian Wars," *Historia* 8 (1959), 49–60.

Wasson, M. O. *Class Struggle in Ancient Greece* (reissue of 1947 ed., New York 1973).

Watrous, V. "An Attic Farm near Laurion," *Hesperia Supp.* 19 (1982), 193–97.

Weaver, J. "Grape Growing in Greece," *Economic Botany* 14 (1960), 207–24.

Weber, M. *Economy and Society* (2 vols., English trans., New York 1968).

_____. *The Agrarian Sociology of Ancient Civilizations* (Engl. trans., London 1976).

Weiss, C. "An Unusual Corinthian Helmet," *California Studies in Classical Antiquity* 10 (1977), 195–207.

Wells, B. (ed.). *Agriculture in Ancient Greece.* Proceedings of the Seventh International Symposium at the Swedish Institute at Athens, 16–17 May 1990 (Stockholm 1992).

Welwei, K.-L. *Unfreie im antiken Kriesdienst. Erster Teil: Athen und Sparta* (Wiesbaden 1974).

Wender, D. *The Last Scenes of the "Odyssey"* (Leyden 1978).

West, M. L. *Hesiod, Works and Days* (Oxford 1978).

Wheeler, E. "The Legion as Phalanx," *Chiron* 9 (1979), 303–18.

_____. "Ephorus and the Prohibition of Missiles," *TAPA* 117 (1987), 157–82.

_____. *Stratagem and the Vocabulary of Military Trickery* (Leiden 1988).

_____. "The General as Hoplite," in Hanson 1991a, 121–72.

Whibley, L. *Greek Oligarchies. Their Character and Organization* (London 1896).

White, K. D. *Agricultural Implements of the Roman World* (Cambridge 1967).

_____. *Roman Farming* (London 1970a).

_____. "Fallowing, Rotation, and Crop Yields," *Agricultural History* 44 (1970b), 281–90.

_____. *Farm Equipment of the Roman World* (Cambridge 1975).

_____. *Greek and Roman Technology* (London 1984).

Whitehead, D. *The Ideology of the Athenian Metic* (PCPS, Supp. 4, Cambridge 1977).

_____. "The Archaic Athenian Zeugitai," *CQ* 31 (1981), 282–86.

_____. *The Demes of Attica 508/7-ca. 250 B.C.: A Political and Social Study* (Princeton 1986).

Whitley, J. *Style and Society in Dark Age Greece. The Changing Face of a Pre-literate Society 100–700 B.C.* (Cambridge 1991).

Whittaker, C. R. (ed.). *Pastoral Economies in Classical Antiquity* (PCPS, Supp. 14, Cambridge 1988).

Wickens, J. M. "Deinas' Grave at Timesius' Farm," *Hesperia* 52 (1983) 96–99.

Wilkinson, T. J. "The Definition of Ancient Manured Zones by Means of Extensive Sherd-sampling Techniques," *Journal of Field Archaeology* 9 (1982), 322–33.

Will, Ed. "Aux origines de la régime foncier grec" *Revue des études anciennes* 59 (1957), 5–50.

Will, Ernst. "Hésiode, crise agraire ou recul de l'aristocratie," *REG* (1965), 542–56.

Willets, R. F. *Aristocratic Society in Ancient Crete* (London 1955).

———. "The Servile System of Ancient Crete: A Reappraisal of the Evidence," in Vard and Willets 1963, 257–71.

Winkler, A. J. et al, *General Viticulture* (Berkeley 1962).

Wolf, A., "Saving the Small Farm: Agriculture in Roman Literature," *Agriculture and Human Values* 4.2–3 (1987) 65–75.

Wood, E. M. *Peasant-citizen and Slave: The Foundations of Athenian Democracy* (London 1988).

Woodhouse, W. J. *Solon the Liberator* (Oxford 1938).

Yalouris, E. "Notes on the Topography of Chios," in Boardman and Vaphopoulou-Richardson 1986, 141–68.

Yoffee, N. and G. Cowgill (eds.). *The Collapse of Ancient States and Civilizations* (Tuscan 1988).

Yoshiyuki, S. "Isolated Farms in Classical Attica," *Kodai* 4 (1993), 1–19.

Young, J.H. "Studies in South Attica, Country Estates at Sounion," *Hesperia* 25 (1956a), 122–46.

———. "Greek Roads in South Attica", *Antiquity* 30 (1956b), 94–97.

Zadawadski, T. "L'agriculture de la Grèce antique," *Archaeology* 11/12 ([in Polish] 1960/61), 104–27, 19–47.

Zangger, E. "Prehistoric and Historic Soils in Greece: Assessing the Natural Resources for Agriculture," in Wells 1992, 13–20.

Ziebarth, E. *Beiträge zur Geschichte des Seeraubs und Seehandels in alten Griechenland* (Hamburg 1929).

Zimmermann, H. D. "Die freie Arbeit in Griechenland wahrend des 5. und 4. jahrhunderts v.u.Z." *Klio* 56 (1974), 337–52.

Zimmern. A., *The Greek Commonwealth* (5th ed., Oxford 1931).

INDEX